BALANCING WEALTH AND HEALTH

LAW AND GLOBAL GOVERNANCE SERIES

Editors:
Andrew Hurrell, Benedict Kingsbury, and Richard B. Stewart

Global governance involves the exercise of power, beyond a single state, to influence behaviour, to generate resources, or to allocate authority. Regulatory structures, and law of all kinds, increasingly shape the nature, use, and effects of such power. These dynamic processes of ordering and governance blend the extra-national with the national, the public with the private, the political and economic with the social and cultural. Issues of effectiveness, justice, voice, and inequality in these processes are growing in importance. This series features exceptional works of original research and theory—both sector-specific and conceptual—that carry forward the serious understanding and evaluation of these processes of global governance and the role of law and institutions within them. Contributions from all disciplines are welcomed. The series aims especially to deepen scholarship and thinking in international law, international politics, comparative law and politics, and public and private global regulation. A major goal is to study governance globally, and to enrich the literature on law and the nature and effects of global governance beyond the North Atlantic region.

ALSO AVAILABLE IN THE SERIES

Governance by Indicators
Global Power through Quantification and Rankings
Edited by Kevin E. Davis, Angelina Fisher, Benedict Kingsbury, and Sally Engle Merry

The Design of Competition Law Institutions
Global Norms, Local Choices
Edited by Eleanor M. Fox and Michael J. Trebilcock

The Rise of the Regulatory State of the South
Infrastructure and Development in Emerging Economies
Edited by Navroz K. Dubash and Bronwen Morgan

Balancing Wealth and Health

The Battle over Intellectual Property and Access to Medicines in Latin America

Edited by
ROCHELLE C. DREYFUSS
and
CÉSAR RODRÍGUEZ-GARAVITO

OXFORD
UNIVERSITY PRESS

OXFORD
UNIVERSITY PRESS

Great Clarendon Street, Oxford, OX2 6DP,
United Kingdom

Oxford University Press is a department of the University of Oxford.
It furthers the University's objective of excellence in research, scholarship,
and education by publishing worldwide. Oxford is a registered trade mark of
Oxford University Press in the UK and in certain other countries

First Edition published in 2014

Published in the United States of America by Oxford University Press
198 Madison Avenue, New York, NY 10016, United States of America

British Library Cataloguing in Publication Data
Data available

Library of Congress Control Number: 2013956285

ISBN 978–0–19–967674–3

Foreword

In most critical iconographies of iniquities of contemporary global regulatory governance, a prominent place is accorded to the complex regime of intellectual property law and its effects on universal affordable access to, and development of, essential medicines. The rules and supervisory institutions of the Trade-Related aspects of Intellectual Property Agreement of 1994 (TRIPS), and the various "TRIPS plus" rules in a congeries of different bilateral and regional or plurilateral agreements including the Central American Free Trade Agreement (CAFTA), the Anti-Counterfeiting Trade Agreement (ACTA) and the draft Trans-Pacific Partnership agreement (TPP), are explained in a familiar political account. In that narrative, the powerful governments of the North, themselves highly responsive to their major innovation creative industries including pharmaceutical companies, have by dividing and dragooning brought developing country governments to make agreements which increase local prices of pharmaceutical products without incentivizing local production capacity or investment in combatting major diseases other than those occurring in rich countries. The case studies and analysis in this highly original and indeed pathbreaking book do not so much challenge as look behind this overarching narrative to document, within a common conceptual framework, a highly variegated experience among eleven Latin American democracies with similar overall trajectories of movement from essentially no patent protection of pharmaceutical products in the 1980s to becoming, over the next two decades, compliant with TRIPS or TRIPS plus. These countries have varied not only in what they have sought and been able to achieve in relevant international negotiations and institutions, but also in very specific but significant features of the implementation and application of international rules in their national law and institutions (such as patent offices) allowing for greater or lesser access to medicines. As the country studies show, pro-access national intellectual property practices do not necessarily correlate with lower prices, let alone better health outcomes—much more is involved in achieving health improvements—but the variations and the explanatory factors presented in the rich and fine-grained studies by the contributors are of great interest and importance.

The study of Global Administrative Law (GAL) is the investigation of quotidian governance—how power works in practice on a daily basis—and in particular of how specific legal-procedural features channel, magnify and check that power. Necessarily it must be concerned with all elements of global regulatory governance: the constitutive rules and design features of international and national institutions, their substantive output, the procedural rules and practices and mechanisms by which they operate, the intricate relations between (formal and informal) institutions, and the resulting dynamics of winner and losers, justice and injustice over time within the global administrative space. Adherence to GAL norms of good process can help secure support for global and domestic governance regimes in ways which differ from legitimation based on state delegation, human rights considerations, or quality of outputs. The reasons for adoption of GAL norms are diverse. For instance, "baptist and bootlegger" coalitions of business and NGO interests may in some cases unite on the importance of transparency while diverging sharply on fundamental goals and policies. This is one element of an explanation for the rapidity of uptake of GAL procedures in diverse fields of global governance. GAL procedures and mechanisms may often align with the overall interests of the powerful within a neo-liberal agenda. Yet democratic governments have sought to evade some such controls in pursuing that agenda, for example in choosing to conduct ACTA and TPP negotiations in almost complete secrecy from wider publics. Overall, the relations between procedural arrangements—for transparency, notice and comment, participation, reason-giving, review, and overall accountability—and substantive justice in global regulatory governance are underresearched, undertheorized, and poorly understood. Illuminating these relations, in the specific context of intellectual property and pharmaceuticals in Latin America, is one of the major general contributions of this volume.

Taking as its criterion of substantive justice the achievement of affordable access to medicines, against a stipulated background of continuing large-scale poverty and intensive pressure from the North Atlantic governments for adoption of very strong intellectual property protection for pharmaceuticals, the book views the pursuit of substantive justice largely in terms of counter-power: resistance and contestation. This counter-power is evaluated by the case studies in relation to two domains which we suggest may usefully be distinguished. The first domain is that of standard law-making: international treaty negotiation or making of ensuing national legislation. In this domain contestation and resistance vary (subject to basic structural constraints including degrees of power asymmetry or dependence) with levels of access-related expertise available, involvement of national and extra-national civil society advocacy organizations, and dynamics in the political economy of the particular developing country (e.g. a strong generics industry). The key links posited between the political economy of decision-making in these domains and GAL procedural elements is through the organizing variables of international and national political opportunity structures; further examination of the link between GAL processes and the openness of opportunity structures is a promising area for further research. The second domain is the sub-treaty and sub-legislative operationalization of the legal regime of intellectual property and access to medicines. Within each developing country, national pharmaceutical regulatory or procurement and oversight agencies, patent offices, courts, and constitutional litigation institutions play notable roles in different case studies, as do regional juridical bodies such as the Andean Court of Justice and (potentially) the Inter-American Commission and Court of Human Rights, and global entities such as the World Trade Organization's Dispute Settlement Body, along with the conceptual and interpretive resources provided by rival regimes such as that of the constitutional or international law right to health. In this second, administrative domain the insights on process-substance-justice relations in the case studies in this volume interlock with other work of the Global Administrative Network, including the immediately preceding volumes in the Law and Global Governance series to which the present book is a welcome addition. The research strategy, concepts, and methodologies developed in this book repay careful consideration not only for fruitful deployment to examine dynamics of health and intellectual property in other regions, but also for generating innovative insights in other fields of global regulatory governance.

Benedict Kingsbury
Richard B. Stewart

Acknowledgements

We are grateful to the International Development Research Centre (IDRC) for providing financial support to this research project and to NYU's Global Administrative Law Project and the University of los Andes' Program on Global Justice for encouraging our efforts. We thank the Engelberg Center on Innovation Law and Policy for sponsoring a workshop that allowed the individual research groups to exchange ideas and present their findings to commentators. That event contributed significantly to the quality of the final product. We also thank the Center for Law, Justice and Society (Dejusticia) and the Ford Foundation for sponsoring exchanges among the country case study authors. Jose Acosta (NYU JD Class of 2014), Maria Etchegorry (NYU LLM Class of 2011), Anthony R. Enriquez (NYU JD Class of 2013), and Celeste Kauffman (Dejusticia) provided invaluable legal and linguistic assistance compiling information and editing texts. We appreciate the efforts of Shayon Ghosh and Andrew Moore (NYU Class of 2015), who did all the thankless, last-minute tasks of nailing down citations and factual information. The Filomen D'Agostino and Max E. Greenberg Research Fund provided financial support for Rochelle Dreyfuss's contributions. The Ford Foundation provided financial support for César Rodríguez-Garavito's contributions.

Without the superb organizational capabilities of Nicole Arzt (NYU) and Camila Soto (University of los Andes), this volume would not have been possible.

Rochelle Cooper Dreyfuss
César Rodríguez-Garavito

Table of Contents

PART II COMMENTARIES

List of Contributors

Karen Alter

Karen J. Alter is Professor of Political Science and Law at Northwestern University, and a permanent visiting professor at the iCourts Center for Excellence, University of Copenhagen Faculty of Law. Alter is author of *The New Terrain of International Law: Courts, Politics, Rights* (Princeton University Press, 2013); *The European Court's Political Power* (Oxford University Press, 2009); *Establishing the Supremacy of European Law* (Oxford University Press, 2001) and more than forty articles and book chapters. She is also co-editor of the *Oxford Handbook on International Adjudication* (Oxford University Press, 2013). Fluent in Italian, French, and German, Alter's research has been supported by the John Simon Guggenheim Foundation, the American Academy of Berlin, the Howard Foundation, the German Marshall Fund, the DAAD, and the Bourse Chateaubriand Scientifique. Alter is a member of the New York Council on Foreign Relations, and serves on the editorial board of *International Organization*, and (previously) *Law and Social Inquiry* and *European Union Politics*.

Tatiana Andia

Tatiana is a PhD candidate in Sociology at Brown University. Her research interests include the global political economy of development; health regulation; trade, industrial policy, and development; and transnational social movements. Tatiana holds an MSc degree in Development Studies from the London School of Economics and Political Science and a BA in Economics and one in History from Los Andes University in Bogotá, Colombia. She has worked as managing editor of *Studies in Comparative International Development* (*SCID*) and as a researcher and director of graduate studies at the Cider, an Interdisciplinary Development Studies Center at Los Andes University in Bogotá. Tatiana has also worked in consultancy projects for the Pan American Health Organization, the World Bank, and the Colombian government on intellectual property rights and access to medicines, and on health systems and health litigation. Her most recent publications include "The State of States in International Organizations: From the Who to the Global Fund," *Review* 34/3 (2011) (with Nitsan Chorev); and "The Invisible Threat: Trade, Intellectual Property, and Pharmaceutical Regulations in Colombia," pp. 77–109 in *Intellectual Property, Pharmaceuticals, and Public Health: Access to Drugs in Developing Countries*, edited by Ken Shadlen, Samira Gueniff, and Alenka Guzman (Edward Elgar Press).

Paola Bergallo

Paola Bergallo is a law professor at Universidad de Palermo in Buenos Aires, Argentina. She holds an LLB with honors from the Universidad de Buenos Aires, an LLM from Columbia University, a JSM and a JSD from Stanford University. Prof. Bergallo was a Fellow at Hewlett Foundation, Stanford University, and the Norwegian Research Counsel. In Argentina, she has been a Professor of Law at Universidad de San Andrés and Universidad de Buenos Aires. Prof. Bergallo has held several visiting positions at Universidad Pompeu Fabra, Barcelona, at Universidad de Puerto Rico, and at Instituto Tecnológico Autónomo de México (ITAM). She has worked as researcher and consultant in projects of the Centro de Estudios de Estado y Sociedad (CEDES), the Center for Reproductive Rights, the UN Fund for Population (UNFPA), the Pan-American Health Organization (PAHO), and the

Nordic Trust Fund at the World Bank. She has advised the National Ministry of Health and participates in several human rights organizations in her country. Her areas of work and research include sexual rights, health law, and socio-legal studies.

Rochelle Dreyfuss
Rochelle Cooper Dreyfuss is Pauline Newman Professor of Law at New York University School of Law and Co-director of the Engelberg Center on Innovation Law and Policy. Her teaching and scholarship largely focus on national and international patent law and civil procedure. She currently serves on the National Academies of Science's Committee on Science, Technology. She was a member of the National Academies Committee on Intellectual Property in Genomic and Protein Research and Innovation as well as the Committee on Intellectual Property Rights in the Knowledge-Based Economy. She was a consultant to the Federal Courts Study Committee, to the Presidential Commission on Catastrophic Nuclear Accidents, and to the Federal Trade Commission and has served on the Secretary of Health and Human Services' Advisory Committee on Genetics, Health, and Society. She is the author of numerous articles and books, most recently, *A Neofederalist Vision of Trips: Building a Resilient International Intellectual Property System* (Oxford University Press, 2012) (with Graeme Dinwoodie).

Sean Flynn
Sean Flynn is Associate Director of the American University Washington College of Law (AUWCL) Program on Information Justice and Intellectual Property (PIJIP). He received his law degree *magna cum laude* from Harvard Law School in 1999. Prior to joining AUWCL, Flynn clerked for Chief Justice Arthur Chaskalson on the South African Constitutional Court and for Raymond Fisher on the US Court of Appeals for the Ninth Circuit and served as a Staff Attorney for the Consumer Project on Technology and Associate at Spiegel & McDiarmid.

Angelina Godoy
Angelina Snodgrass Godoy is the Helen H. Jackson Chair in Human Rights at the University of Washington. At UW, she teaches courses on human rights in two interdisciplinary programs (Law, Societies, and Justice, and International Studies), and directs the UW Center for Human Rights. Her research focuses on human rights in Central America, a region she has studied since the 1990s. She is the author of two books, *Popular Injustice: Violence, Community, and Law in Latin America* (Stanford University Press, 2006) and *Of Medicines and Markets: Intellectual Property and Human Rights in the Free Trade Era* (Stanford University Press, 2013). She holds degrees in Sociology from Harvard University (1994) and the University of California, Berkeley (1997, 2001).

Laurence Helfer
Laurence R. Helfer is Harry R. Chadwick, Sr. Professor of Law and co-director of the Center for International and Comparative Law at Duke University. Professor Helfer has authored more than sixty publications relating to his diverse research interests, which include international human rights, and international intellectual property law, treaty design, international adjudication, and interdisciplinary analysis of international law and institutions. He is a member of the Board of Editors of the *American Journal of International Law* and the *Journal of World Intellectual Property*.

Amy Kapczynski
Amy Kapczynski is an Associate Professor of Law at Yale Law School and faculty director of the Global Health Justice Partnership. Her areas of research including information policy,

intellectual property law, international law, and global health. Prior to coming to Yale, she taught at the University of California, Berkeley, School of Law. She also served as a law clerk to Justices Sandra Day O'Connor and Stephen G. Breyer at the US Supreme Court, and to Judge Guido Calabresi on the US Court of Appeals for the Second Circuit. She received her AB from Princeton University, M. Phil. from Cambridge University, MA from Queen Mary and Westfield College at University of London, and JD from Yale Law School.

Molly Land
Molly Land is Professor of Law at the University of Connecticut School of Law and holds a joint appointment with the University's Human Rights Institute. Her scholarship focuses on the effect of new technologies on human rights fact-finding, advocacy, and enforcement, as well as the role of human rights norms and framing strategies in organizing around human rights issues. She was a Fulbright Scholar at the University of Bonn and earned her JD at Yale Law School. She clerked for Judge Denise Cote of the US District Court for the Southern District of New York.

Agustina Ramón Michel
Agustina Ramón Michel holds an LLB (with the silver medal) from the Universidad de Tucumán and is a PhD student (currently on leave) in the School of Law at Universidad de Palermo. She has received a doctoral fellowship from the National Research Council CONICET and during 2013–14 she will be a Fulbright scholar and an LLM student at the University of Texas at Austin. Mrs Ramón Michel pursued postgraduate studies in international relations and negotiations at Universidad de San Andrés/FLACSO. Since August 2007, Mrs Ramón Michel has been a member of the research team at the Department on Health, Economy and Society of CEDES and has worked in projects funded by the World Health Organization, the UNFPA, the University of Bergen and Harvard University. Mrs Ramón Michel has received several fellowships and has participated in the Universidad de Palermo-Yale Law School linkage program. She has taught courses at Universidad de Palermo and Universidad de San Andrés and has written on abortion, health rights, and pharmaceutical patents. Her areas of work include public health and reproductive rights.

Salvador Millaleo H.
Salvador Millaleo, Chilean lawyer and PhD in Sociology (University of Bielefeld, Germany), is a researcher and an assistant professor at the University of Chile. He works on and teaches about topics at the intersection of law and technology. He has published books on the sociology of law and internet activism. He has been Fellow at the University of Bielefeld and the Max Planck Institute for Foreign and International Criminal Law in Freiburg, Germany.

Smita Narula
Smita Narula is Associate Professor of Clinical Law and Faculty Director of the Center for Human Rights and Global Justice at NYU School of Law. Both her scholarship and clinical work focus on key human rights issues, including the impact of economic globalization and counter-terrorism policies on human rights, and the accountability of corporations and international financial institutions for human rights abuses. She has authored numerous articles, book chapters, and human rights studies and reports on these subjects. In 2008 she was appointed legal advisor to the UN Special Rapporteur on the right to food. Before joining NYU, Narula spent six years at Human Rights Watch, first as the organization's India researcher and later as Senior Researcher for South Asia. A world-renowned expert on caste discrimination, Narula helped form India's National Campaign for Dalit Human Rights and co-founded the International Dalit Solidarity Network.

Adelina de Oliveira Novaes

Adelina Novaes holds a PhD in Psychology of Education from Pontifícia Universidade Católica de São Paulo and her thesis was based upon the analysis of social representations on Bralizian law teaching. Adelina is a Professor of Research Methodology at Fundação Armando Alvares Penteado Law School. She is also a Permanent Researcher at the International Center of Social Representations and Subjectivity–Education (CIERS-ed) and at UNESCO Chair on Professional Development of Teachers. Both belong to the Research Educational Department of Fundação Carlos Chagas.

Ruth Okediji

Ruth L. Okediji is the William L. Prosser Professor of Law at the University of Minnesota Law School where she teaches and writes in the areas of intellectual property, law and development, and international trade. Her widely cited scholarship focuses on the integration of developing countries in the multilateral economic system, international copyright regulation, comparative intellectual property law, and knowledge governance. Professor Okediji has served as a policy advisor to many intergovernmental organizations, regional economic communities, and national governments on the formulation of copyright and patent policies, and on the relationship between intellectual property protection and development goals. She is a member of the Board of Editors of the *Journal of World Intellectual Property* and IP-Watch.

César Rodríguez-Garavito

César Rodríguez-Garavito is Associate Professor of Law and founding Director of the Program on Global Justice and Human Rights at the University of the Andes (Colombia). He is a founding member of the Center for Law, Justice, and Society (Dejusticia). He has been a visiting professor at Stanford University, Brown University, the University of Pretoria (South Africa), the Getulio Vargas Foundation (Brazil), the Åbo Academy of Human Rights (Finland), the Central European University, and the Andean University of Quito. He serves in the Editorial Board of the *Annual Review of Law and Social Science*.

Mônica Steffen Guise Rosina

Mônica Steffen Guise Rosina is a Professor of Law at Fundação Getulio Vargas Law School in São Paulo (DIREITO GV), where she coordinates the Research Group on Law and Innovation and teaches Intellectual Property, International Law, and Legal Research. Mônica holds a PhD in International and Comparative Law from the University of São Paulo (USP) and an LLM from the Federal University of Santa Catarina. Mônica is also a visiting professor at the Brazilian Bar Association's School for Advanced Legal Studies (Escola Superior de Advocacia – ESA OAB/SP).

Chapter 1

The Battle over Intellectual Property Laws and Access to Medicines in Latin America

A Primer on Global Administrative Law, Intellectual Property, and Political Contestation

Rochelle Cooper Dreyfuss and César Rodríguez-Garavito

The emergence of a global "knowledge economy" heavily dependent on innovation has brought the regulation of intellectual property to the center of academic and policy debates. From the perspective of international relations and trade, the importance of the topic is evident in the recent spate of multilateral and bilateral trade negotiations, where the contours of protection are invariably hotly contested (Stiglitz 2007). From a legal standpoint, knowledge governance constitutes one of the few fields in which a multinational system has been firmly established. The World Intellectual Property Organization (WIPO) Conventions—the Paris Convention, covering patents and trademarks, and the Berne Convention, on copyright—have existed since the late nineteenth century.[1] And in 1995 the World Trade Organization (WTO) added the Agreement on Trade Related Aspects of Intellectual Property Rights (TRIPS) to its list of obligatory instruments. TRIPS significantly raised the standards of protection, imposed enforcement obligations,[2] and established an international compliance mechanism, the Dispute Settlement Understanding (DSU).[3]

In terms of the global administrative law (GAL) framework articulated by Benedict Kingsbury, Nico Krisch, and Richard Stewart (2005), intellectual

[1] Berne Convention for the Protection of Literary and Artistic Works, July 24, 1971, 1161 U.N.T.S. 31 [hereinafter Berne Convention]; Paris Convention for the Protection of Industrial Property, July 14, 1967, 21 U.S.T. 1583, 828 U.N.T.S. 305 [hereinafter Paris Convention]. The Paris Convention also addressed the protection of other forms of industrial property, such as designs, utility models, and geographical indications. *See* Paris Convention, art. 1.2. See generally Ricketson and Ginsburg (2006); Ladas (1975).

[2] Agreement on Trade-Related Aspects of Intellectual Property Rights (TRIPS), April 15, 1994, Marrakesh Agreement Establishing the World Trade Organization, Annex 1C, Legal Instruments—Results of the Uruguay Round, Vol. 31, 33 I.L.M. 81 (1994) [hereinafter TRIPS Agreement].

[3] Understanding on Rules and Procedures Governing the Settlement of Disputes, April 15, 1994, Marrakesh Agreement Establishing the World Trade Organization, Annex 2, Legal Instruments—Results of the Uruguay Round, 33 I.L.M. 1125 (1994).

property is, like climate control, monetary policy, and national security, an area where the activity in one country has significant spillover effects in others. Thus, as with these other areas, it too has become subject to a highly complex transnational regulatory framework. As the shift from WIPO to the WTO suggests, the creative industries, along with the governments in the global North where this sector is largely based, have mounted increasing pressure for regulatory convergence on high standards (Sell 2003) and have used a variety of national, international, and private forums in their efforts to ratchet up protection. The regulatory regime now emanates from diverse sources, ranging from the hard law adopted by WIPO and the WTO, to soft law and enforcement initiatives undertaken by such public institutions as the World Health Organization (WHO), the World Customs Organization (WCO), and Interpol (Robinson 1999; Sandhu 1999). Further, it includes reactive counter-norms articulated for the benefit of the South by pro-development organizations such as the United Nations Conference on Trade and Development (UNCTAD) and WHO (Dinwoodie and Dreyfuss 2012); measures promulgated by private bodies, such as ICANN, which administers the internet, and standard-setting organizations, which determine the technical specifications for new products; as well as distributed administration carried out by national governments and dispute resolution panels, such as the DSU's Dispute Settlement Body (DSB) and the arbitral panels created by free trade agreements (FTAs), bilateral investment treaties (BITs), and the like (Grosse Ruse-Khan 2011). In the final analysis, the intellectual property system represents a prime example of a "global administrative space," in which "states, individuals, firms, NGOs [(non-governmental organizations)], and other groups or representatives of domestic and global social and economic interests who are affected by, or otherwise have a stake in, global regulatory governance, interact in complex ways" (Kingsbury et al. 2005: 26).

But notwithstanding this multilayered regulatory environment, intellectual property law remains quintessentially territorial law. For many reasons this is not surprising: intellectual property is intimately tied to culturally constructed notions of authorship and inventorship. The law must take into account national views on the value of innovation, local intellectual capabilities and propensities, as well as the population's capacity to pay for, and the government's commitment to supply, knowledge products. The TRIPS Agreement is, therefore, a minimum standards regime. It establishes a global network of rights through requirements for national treatment and most favoured nation privileges. However, it is not a fully harmonized system. Nations retain considerable sovereign authority to tailor the law to their own interests. TRIPS, for example, allows governments to define terms (such as "inventive step") in a fashion that reflects local interests, to use flexibilities (such as compulsory licenses and rules permitting importation from low-price providers) to meet local demand, and to make exceptions (such as defenses based on national health needs and *ordre public* imperatives) to respond to local circumstances. In short, the global framework leaves considerable space for national variation.

This book focuses on how the variation in legal norms and practices occurs; how the complex interactions among actors in this regulatory field—national governments, international institutions, public and private regulators, courts, transnational corporations (TNCs), national producers, corporate lawyers, and NGO activists—shape (and are shaped by) local and international law. Specifically, we examine the debates concerning those aspects of intellectual property law that bear on access to medicine; that is, the measures that regulate the acquisition, recognition, and use of patent rights on pharmaceuticals and trade secrets in data concerning them, along with the conditions under which these rights give way to the interest in public access to cheaper generic drugs.

One of a series of studies commissioned as part of a larger project on global administrative law, the volume has three goals. First, we aim to document cross-country variation in this critical area, where the need to offer monetary incentives to research aimed at curing disease is as uncontestable as the public benefit in providing wide access to the fruits of that intellectual labor. To this end, the volume presents the results of a comparative study on intellectual property and access to medicines in eleven Latin American countries: five from South America (Argentina, Brazil, Chile, Colombia, and Ecuador), and six from Central American (Costa Rica, Dominican Republic, El Salvador, Guatemala, Honduras, and Nicaragua). Through detailed socio-legal studies of this region using a standardized analytical framework and methodology, the book delves into the legal, political, and economic processes that explain the commonalities and differences among laws and practices adopted from the early 1990s until the early 2010s, during a period when each country was undergoing massive institutional and legal transformation.

Second, we theorize as to how the differentials among countries occur and why they endure within a common transnational regulatory framework. Here, our analytical and methodological approach draws on theories of political opportunity structures articulated by international relations scholars and political sociologists, as well as on the socio-legal literature that has documented the role of transnational networks of lawyers and consultants, government officials, activists, and NGOs in constructing and contesting legal rules in the context of globalization.

Third, we examine the core thesis of the global administrative law movement, which equates the problem of legitimating national administrative action with the challenge to legitimate the complex regulatory environment developing at the international level. To commentators such as Kingsbury, Krisch, and Stewart (2005), procedural principles—such as rights to notice, access to documents, transparency, and participation; a requirement for reasoned decisions and a right to review—which were developed in national settings to constrain administrative action and make it accountable to the people, can serve equivalent aims internationally. By comparing the outcomes for access to medicine in these eleven countries, all with similar commitments to democracy and comparable opportunities for contestation, we consider the force of this thesis. In the process, we identify conditions that permit administrative norms to empower constituencies that might otherwise be disregarded and that thus enable procedural approaches to provide a functional approximation of democratic governance.

Because this volume draws on diverse disciplines, we begin with an introduction to the discourse of global administrative law, to the theories of political contestation that underlie the analysis, to the concepts of intellectual property law relevant to the medicines debate, and to a history of the region. We end the chapter with an overview of the remainder of the book, including a description of the methodology employed and a summary of the studies (set out in Chapters 2–7) and the accompanying commentary (found in Chapters 8–13). In Chapter 14, we return with a discussion of the findings that emerge from the case studies.

I. Global Administrative Law: Potential and Challenges

Noting the explosive growth of international instruments, Benedict Kingsbury, Nico Krisch, and Richard Stewart (2005) launched the global administrative law research project to study an accompanying phenomenon, the upsurge in transnational regulatory activity. In their view, the rise in transnational regulation is a response to the cross-border movement of people, knowledge, and goods; to concerns such as pollution and climate change, which are indifferent to national boundaries; to actions, such as conspiracies to restrain trade, where activity in one country has spillover consequences in others; and to problems, such as labor standards, monetary policy, and national security, which nations best address cooperatively. Whereas international treaties and conventions provide the broad strokes for dealing with such issues, Kingsbury, Krisch, and Stewart (2005) focus on a range of regulatory approaches which have been developing to implement these instruments and to address more granular concerns.

In the case of formal multilateral agreements, the principal actors are international representatives of national governments or officers operating under the auspices of an international agreement or within the framework of an international institution (such as the WTO or the World Bank). However, much of the current regulatory activity is more informal and less hierarchical: decentralized administration by national actors or national administrators (for example, patent offices and antitrust agencies), private-public partnerships (including ICANN and the Codex Alimentarius Commission), or private parties (e.g. anti-doping sports organizations and standard-setting bodies). In some instances the parties' actions are localized; in other cases, the actors form transnational networks that operate in concert. Under a variety of auspices and configurations, these international organizations, national governments, national regulators, courts, private organizations, TNCs, and NGOs are engaged in activities with an impact—often a direct impact—on states and individuals.

In part, the GAL project is intended to be descriptive: to develop a taxonomy of regulatory regimes, to learn more about the allocation of regulatory responsibility among the various systems, and to examine how they function. In large part, however, the goals are normative and prescriptive. These transnational systems developed organically and can be quite effective. But those that operate autonomously—independent of both states and international institutions—or outside traditional hierarchies can lack legitimacy and accountability. To be sure, a normative critique of administrative action is hardly new; many nations delegate substantial power to domestic regulatory agencies in ways that raise similar concerns. But as Kingsbury, Krisch, and Stewart (2005) point out, within national systems, a body of administrative law had developed to constrain regulators and render them accountable. Procedural principles, such as rights to notice, access to documents, transparency, and participation; a requirement for reasoned decisions; and a right to review, set significant limits on what administrators can do and on how they may proceed. These norms give voice to those affected by the regulatory regime and alter the political economy, empowering constituencies that might otherwise be excluded or underrepresented. Kingsbury, Krisch, and Stewart (2005) suggest that similar mechanisms could operate effectively in the realm of global regulation.

At the heart of the GAL project (and this book) lies the question of whether—or more accurately, when—they are right. There are many reasons to be concerned that national approaches cannot be effectively transposed to the international context. First, the global administrative norms thus far identified represent the values of a specific set of countries, largely in the global North. They do not derive from international instruments, nor can they be considered general principles on which all nations have converged. Thus, these norms have a legitimacy problem of their own. Other countries may not accept them. Indeed, the administrative law of the North may be viewed elsewhere as simply another form of imperialism: as a system of accountability *to* the North, as empowering the North at the expense of the South; as disruptive of other approaches to social ordering or as undermining other, equally valid, concepts of legitimate governance.

Second, in many transnational administrative settings there is no judiciary to review decisions or impose procedural mandates. Informal regulations may not be framed as binding rules suitable for review. Private actors do not ordinarily owe cognizable duties to a higher (national or international) authority. Thus, as Eyal Benvenisti (2005) suggested, administrative values may be driven mainly by a desire by administrative bodies to appear legitimate. But that requires administrators to see their reputations as on the line and to believe that the advantages of a good reputation outweigh the benefits that can be obtained by responding to political pressure, by self-dealing, or through more active forms of corruption. In some cases, the problem may be deeper: since the actions of networks cannot always be attributed to any single actor, there may be no one shouldering the responsibility to act in accordance with procedural norms.

As Martin Shapiro (2005) pointed out, administrative law is also something of a cat-and-mouse game. An agency bent on adopting its own approach will find ways around administrative constraints. The law might catch up, but only for a time. The more technical the issues, the worse the potential outcome. Expert decisions on technologically complicated matters can be difficult for lay reviewers to consider. When the technocrats' solutions are so complex they are not as a practical matter reviewable, regulators can readily displace the public interest with their own. At the same time, if a field is technologically complex and the regulators or those reviewing their actions have too little expertise, or the wrong kind of expertise, they can equally easily (but perhaps less intentionally) undermine important social values (Büthe and Mattli 2011).

Further, capacity deficits or asymmetries may make the availability of procedural opportunities ineffective, no matter how well fortified by GAL norms. It is expensive to field international delegations of negotiators. Legal and economic advisors may not be positioned to fully discern the consequences of a proposed rule; diplomats new to the international stage may be unable to build alliances to press their nation's interests. Furthermore, richer countries have bargaining chips that permit them to isolate effective negotiators and split potential allies (Drahos 1995; Sell 2003). And for the rich, no loss is permanent. They can impose new costs by shifting their demands to a different regime (Helfer 2004). Worn down by repeated negotiations in far flung locations, poorer states ultimately succumb. These countries then face political, informational, and logistical obstacles as they are forced to compromise local interests in order to meet obligations poorly tailored to their circumstances.

Some transnational governance systems include international tribunals that are themselves cabined by GAL norms. But even here, a state with limited capacity may be disadvantaged. Defending its actions (let alone mounting a challenge) is costly and requires skilled lawyering. A country unwilling to risk the possibility of dispute resolution may be forced to enact laws that are beyond reproach—but which have local consequences that are far more severe than the international instrument, in fact, requires. If countries with equivalent concerns are similarly hampered, the international tribunal may be unable to generate sufficient law to provide adequate guidance on compliance matters (Dinwoodie and Dreyfuss 2012).

Admittedly, administrative law also includes a set of substantive standards—Kingsbury, Krisch, and Stewart (2005) mention requirements of proportionality, preservation of legitimate expectations, use of the least (or less) restrictive-means, along with testing for means-end rationality. But these doctrines beg the question: which expectations are legitimate? Against what metric are means and ends tested? Deeper substantive content—such as conceptions of fairness, of distributive justice, of human rights, of finality and repose—would appear to be required, but they are not, strictly speaking, a part of the administrative law enterprise.

These concerns make the descriptive exercise all the more important. While no one study can consider all these issues, an examination of global administration in diverse substantive areas and across a spectrum of countries, can reveal the problems with relying on global administrative values to achieve legitimacy. With a contextual approach, it is possible to illuminate the social and legal conditions necessary for operationalizing global administrative norms. As shown by the subsequent chapters in this volume, case studies can provide clues for adjusting the principles to particularized needs and suggest other stratagems for legitimating the imposition of transnational regulation on individuals and states.

In the final analysis, however, the power of administrative norms is heavily dependent on political opportunities for contestation and the capacity of those affected by regulation to contest effectively. Thus, the analytical framework and empirical evidence presented in the chapters of this book foreground the role and effects of contestation in transnational regulation. This task calls for additional conceptual and methodological tools, to which we now turn.

II. Contesting Transnational Regulation: The Political Field

According to Lustig and Kingsbury (2006: 413), "[p]rocedural approaches drawing on administrative law principles can act as an instrument of resistance and change." As Lustig and Kingsbury's work illustrates, the Global Administrative Law framework has tended to focus on whether the *use of existing rules* can give leverage to subaltern actors resisting injustices and seeking social change.[4] But as suggested above, these rules may not be sufficient to confer legitimacy everywhere. Accordingly, in this book, we supplement the GAL focus with an analysis of the *production of new rules*. By inquiring into this genealogical moment, we show that the very content of procedural rules results from contestation among national and transnational actors advancing contrasting political and legal agendas. For instance, while some central actors in the transnational regulation of intellectual property—for example, the WTO, TNCs in the pharmaceutical sector, OECD governments (at times in conjunction with some governments in the global South), lawyers, and other technical and legal experts—have advocated greater protection of intellectual property rights in the global economy, other key actors—WHO, national and transnational human rights NGOs, some Southern governments (notably India, South Africa, and Brazil), firms producing generic drugs, also accompanied by lawyers and experts—have advanced an agenda that seeks to limit intellectual property rights in order to facilitate access to essential medicines (Kapczynski 2008; Klug 2005).

Procedural rules, therefore, embody provisional equilibria within legal regimes and reveal the correlation of forces among contending actors promoting alternative conceptions and standards of procedural fairness. Further, both in theory and in practice, the application of procedural questions cannot be entirely separated from substantive and distributional questions as to who benefits from a particular rule (Chimni 2005; Lustig and Kingsbury 2006). We argue that the political nature and substantive connotations of procedural rules can be seen with particular clarity at critical historical junctures when such rules are produced or transformed, for the new rules draw the line between competing claims of procedural and substantive justice and choose from alternative legal standards.

To this end, the studies in this volume draw on theories and methods from two lines of social science and socio-legal research on global governance. First is the growing literature on transnationalism and transnational networks, which complements the structural analysis that accompanies theories of political opportunities.

4 Indeed, Lustig and Kingsbury themselves engage the issue of resistance within GAL in analyzing the impact of existing national and international legal rules on policies and debates regarding conservation-induced displacement and relocation of rural communities in India.

The focus of this literature is on formal and informal networks of global and local experts, advisors, scholars, and activists through which rules are circulated (and contested), at both official negotiations (for instance, negotiations within the context of FTAs) and in unofficial venues (such as at WIPO workshops, and professional meetings) (Slaughter 2004). Taking a cue from the literature on epistemic communities (Hall 1993) and the globalization of legal cultures and expertise (Dezalay and Garth 2002a), particular attention is given to the diffusion of ideas and normative frameworks through networks of patent and trade lawyers, public-health experts, human rights advocates, and other transnational actors (Halliday 2009). Borrowing from socio-legal studies on bottom-up construction and contestation of legal rules (Santos and Rodríguez-Garavito 2005), contributors also consider activist networks, which have proliferated in the last decade to advocate for more relaxed standards of protection in the name of promoting access to essential medicines.

Second, is the international relations and transnational social movement literature, which considers what political scientists and political sociologists have termed "political opportunity structures," that is, "consistent—but not necessarily formal or permanent—dimensions of the political environment that provide incentives [and constraints] for collective action by affecting people's expectations of success and failure" (Tarrow 1998: 77). Importantly, international relations scholars have expanded this concept to include not only domestic political opportunities, but also those associated with international institutions and actors. Drawing to various degrees on the tradition of two-level game theories of the interaction of international and domestic political structures (Evans, Jacobson and Putnam 1993; Putnam 1988), international relations scholars have sought to develop interactive explanatory models of a wide range of political processes, from the development of trade policy to the use of force in conflict resolution (Milner and Rosendorff 1997).

Loosening the game-theoretical assumptions of the original model, social movement scholars within the subfield of international relations have theorized and documented the ways in which two-level governance structures shape and are shaped by cross-border activist networks and coalitions (Khagram, Riker, and Sikkink 2002; Keck and Sikkink 1998). They have shown that opportunities for contestation at the local level are profoundly influenced by transnational institutions (for instance, the WTO, the International Monetary Fund (IMF), and the World Bank), as well as by national institutions in other countries (for instance, trade-promotion agencies in the North, such as the office of the United States Trade Representative (USTR)). In their view, the incentives for contestation stemming from national institutions may point in the opposite direction from those emanating from supra-national institutions. In the concluding chapter and the case study on Colombia, we specifically draw on Kathryn Sikkink's "dynamic multilevel governance" approach, which offers an interactive theory of transnational mobilization (Sikkink 2005a, 2005b).

In sum, while the analysis of political opportunities allows us to study structural constraints, the literatures on transnationalism and bottom-up transnational mobilization gives us leverage on the role of actors and networks in exploiting and shaping those constraints. The detailed accounts in the case studies specify the mechanisms through which structures shape (and are shaped by) actors' strategies. Further, it shows how they develop institutions and norms appropriate to their own circumstances.

III. Intellectual Property as a Site of Transnational Regulation and Contestation

A. The Regulation and Administration of Global Intellectual Property

For many reasons, intellectual property furnishes an excellent context in which to analyze the dynamics of transnational regulation. To begin, this is an area in which the need for global governance is acute. As noted at the outset, exclusive rights in knowledge goods are quintessentially territorial: the right to exclude others from using an invention, a writing, or a mark, depends solely on the law of the country where the information is used. Without multilateral agreements, creators in one country would not be eligible for protection in foreign markets. In those territories, innovators would be unable to maintain the value of their marks or the reputation of their products or secure a return on their investments. Furthermore, each country could undermine the innovation policy of all others. Especially with the advent of the internet and digitization, cheap reproductions and imitations (or knowledge about making them) can easily spread, undercutting prices worldwide, including in the creator's own market, and thus reduce incentives to innovate.

This is also a good place to consider global governance because experience with it is extensive and varied. The Berne and Paris Conventions are over a century old (although their administration by WIPO is relatively recent, dating from 1970[5]). At their inception, both instruments relied primarily on a requirement of national treatment (the guarantee that members will extend to the nationals of other members the same protection they offer to their own citizens),[6] along with provisions that facilitated the acquisition of protection.[7] Over time, however, each instrument was renegotiated to include (and eventually, raise) substantive standards of protection (more in Berne than in Paris; and more in Paris for trademarks than for patents). In addition, new instruments were negotiated. WIPO now administers over twenty intellectual property agreements, including a set of instruments that further facilitates the acquisition of rights; treaties on the protection of other kinds of creative works; and two conventions largely directed at internet distributions.[8]

[5] Convention Establishing the World Intellectual Property Organization, July 14, 1967, 21 U.S.T. 1749, 848 U.N.T.S. 3.

[6] Berne Convention, art. 5; Paris Convention, art. 2.

[7] Paris Convention, art. 4 (requiring Union members to give priority to applications based on the first filing date in a Paris member; Ricketson and Ginsburg (2006: 341–56) (noting that Berne eventually made copyright automatic).

[8] For a full list of the instruments administered by WIPO, see <http://www.wipo.int/treaties/en/>. The recent agreements were concluded in 1996, see WIPO Copyright Treaty (WCT), December 20,

Despite WIPO's efforts to keep international intellectual property law responsive to new needs, developed countries were long dissatisfied with the substantive standards for protection (especially for patents) and the absence of requirements for enforcing the rights established. At a time when negotiations within WIPO were at an impasse, these nations—with considerable prodding from representatives and coalitions of the creative industries (Sell 2003)—brought intellectual property into the Uruguay Round of trade negotiations. The outcome was the TRIPS Agreement. TRIPS, which came into force in 1995 (and is described more fully in subsection B), raised the level of protection for patents, copyrights, and trademarks, and also included requirements to protect and enforce rights over geographical indications, industrial designs, topographies, and trade secrets, including rights of exclusivity over data generated to prove the safety and efficacy of new drugs. In addition to establishing the DSU to assure compliance, the Agreement created an administrative arm, the Council for TRIPS, which reviews implementation, considers issues left open at the conclusion of the Uruguay Round, and takes up new problems.[9]

To some extent, WTO and WIPO work together. TRIPS specifically contemplated cooperation with WIPO and, in a separate agreement, the two organizations undertook to "establish a mutually supportive relationship."[10] Most significantly, TRIPS included promises to give developing nations technical assistance in meeting their obligations,[11] and WIPO agreed that its International Bureau would make such assistance available. In a similar vein, WIPO also agreed to furnish the WTO's Secretariat with help.[12] But since WIPO also continues with its own work, shifts back to WIPO are possible. For example, TRIPS entered into force before the internet became popular; negotiations to protect distribution in this new medium were conducted in WIPO. Especially relevant for our study, by 2001, it was clear that the TRIPS Agreement had created particularly difficult medical problems in countries that were not able to manufacture their own pharmaceuticals. In the Doha Round of WTO negotiations, the Ministerial Conference issued a statement (the Doha Declaration) acknowledging the access to medicines issue and pledging modifications.[13] At around the same time, Argentina and Brazil persuaded WIPO to take on an ambitious Development Agenda and look more generally at the impact of intellectual property protection on development and on disadvantaged

1996, 36 I.L.M. 76, 2186 U.N.T.S. 121; WIPO Performances and Phonograms Treaty (WPPT), December 20, 1996, 36 I.L.M. 76, 2186 U.N.T.S. 203.

[9] TRIPS, arts. 1.3, 3.1, 4(d), 63.2, 68, 71.

[10] Arts. 63 and 68 of TRIPS; Agreement between the World Intellectual Property Organization and the World Trade Organization, Preamble (22 December 1995), available at <http://www.wipo.int/treaties/en/agreement/pdf/trtdocs_wo030.pdf>.

[11] TRIPS, art. 67.

[12] WTO/WIPO Agreement, arts. 4(1) and (3).

[13] See World Trade Organization, Ministerial Declaration of November 14, 2001, WT/MIN(01)/DEC/1, 41 I.L.M. 746 (2002) [hereinafter Doha Declaration]; Declaration on the TRIPS agreement and public health, WT/MIN(01)/DEC/2 (November 14, 2001)[hereinafter Declaration on Public Health].

populations.[14] As part of that effort, WIPO hosted the successful effort, based on a proposal of Brazil, Ecuador, and Paraguay, to conclude a treaty to improve access to copyrighted works for the blind.[15]

But as global administrative law theorists posit, the ubiquity of intellectual property has brought other institutions into the regulatory process. Countries in the North had understood TRIPS to impose significant obligations regarding enforcement. When efforts to improve protection and enforcement through WTO negotiations stalled and dispute resolution in the WTO failed to fully achieve enforcement objectives,[16] they moved negotiations to bilateral and plurilateral settings—FTAs, BITs, the Anticounterfeiting Trade Agreement (ACTA), and the Transpacific Partnership Agreement (TPP).[17] These agreements (or draft agreements) include chapters requiring the ratification of various WIPO-administered agreements and recommendations, clarify disputed provisions within TRIPS, and add "TRIPS-plus" requirements (Lopert and Gleeson 2013).[18] In addition, some countries interested in strong protection engage in unilateral actions. For example, under its so-called Special 301 procedure,[19] the USTR conducts annual reviews of intellectual property protection in foreign countries and files a yearly Report, putting those nations that are deemed to accord insufficient protection on graduated "watch lists." Unless these countries increase protection, they are in danger of sanction, for instance by the loss of tariff preferences. The EU's Trade Barrier Regulation and partnership agreements adopt similar strategies (Santa Cruz 2007).[20]

[14] See, e.g., Proposal by Argentina and Brazil for the Establishment of a Development Agenda for WIPO, WO/GA/31/11 (August 27, 2004) (supported by, among other countries, Bolivia, Ecuador, and Venezuela). Documents on the Development Agenda are available at <http://www.wipo.int/ip-development/en/agenda/>.

[15] World Intellectual Property Organization, Diplomatic Conference to Conclude a Treaty to Facilitate Access to Published Works by Visually Impaired Persons and Persons with Print Disabilities, VIP/DC, 8 (June 27, 2013).

[16] *China—Measures Affecting the Protection and Enforcement of Intellectual Property Rights*, WT/DS362/R (January 26, 2009).

[17] Anti-Counterfeiting Trade Agreement, May 2011 Text, available at <http://www.ustr.gov/acta>; the draft text of the Trans-Pacific Partnership Trade Agreement remain confidential, however information on negotiations through 2013 is available at <http://www.ustr.gov/tpp>; text of all free trade agreements involving the United States are available at <http://www.ustr.gov/trade-agreements/free-trade-agreements>.

[18] An example is the Dominican Republic—Central America—United States Free Trade Agreement (August 5, 2004) (CAFTA), available at <http://www.ustr.gov/trade-agreements/free-trade-agreements/cafta-dr-dominican-republic-central-america-fta/final-text>.

[19] 61 Omnibus Trade and Competitiveness Act of 1989, Pub. L. 100-418, 102 Stat. 1176–9 (1989); 19 U.S.C. § 2242. For examples of these Reports, see Office of the United States Trade Representative, Special 301 Reports, available at <http://search.usa.gov/search?sc=0&query=special+301+reports&affiliate=ustrgov&locale=en&m=>. The Special 301 procedure is examined in detail in Sean Flynn's contribution to this volume, see Chapter 8.

[20] Council Regulation (EC) of December 22, 1994 No. 3286/94 Laying Down Community Procedures in the Field of the Common Commercial Policy in Order to Ensure the Exercise of the Community's Rights under International Trade Rules, in Particular those Established under the Auspices of the World Trade Organization, 1994 O.J. (L 349) 71, as amended by Council Regulation (EC) No. 356/95 of February 20, 1995, 1995 O.J. (L 41) 3.

Other international organizations, many with little prior experience with intellectual property, have also become involved in the regulatory framework. The World Bank and the IMF have written a variety of reports on the impact of intellectual property on health, commerce, and promoting innovation and foreign investment (Sonderholm 2010; Watt 2007; Scandizzo 2001); Interpol, the World Customs Organization (WCO), and the International Chamber of Commerce are now focusing on transnational distribution of counterfeit products (Yu 2011). And despite its efforts to define intellectual property norms to improve access to medicines, WHO is also working on measures to fight counterfeiting.[21]

The regulatory environment is further complexified by efforts, such as the Development Agenda, to combat enhanced protection through the articulation of counternorms. Concerned about the impact of patents and data exclusivity on drug prices, WHO has created guidelines to help developing countries deal with their intellectual property obligations and has focused the attention of the North on the problem of neglected diseases.[22] Similarly, UNCTAD has issued reports on intellectual property, technology transfer, and direct investment, as well as a Resource Book on TRIPS and Development which is intended to provide guidance to developing nations (Dinwoodie and Dreyfuss 2012; Rangnekar 2005).[23]

In the human rights arena, similar developments are unfolding. While both the Universal Declaration of Human Rights and the International Covenant on Economic, Social and Cultural Rights protect interests "in scientific, literary or artistic production,"[24] these provisions have been interpreted to support procedural norms, such as the right to have applications for intellectual property protection duly considered (Helfer 2008). Crucially, both instruments also recognize substantive rights to health and education.[25] The 1966 International Covenant on Economic, Social and Cultural Rights, in particular, has gained considerable legal and political traction over the last two decades. Furthermore, as constitutions and constitutional courts around the world have incorporated international norms on socio-economic rights into domestic law, an increasing number of NGOs have become interested in the intersection between intellectual property, human rights, and access to knowledge. Examples include Knowledge Ecology International (KEI, formerly CP Tech), Oxfam, Médecins Sans Frontières (Doctors Without Borders), and Public Citizen (PC). Similarly, court cases on the right to health—including access to

[21] World Health Organization, Department of Essential Drugs and Other Medicines, Counterfeit Drugs, Guidelines for the development of measures to combat counterfeit drugs, WHO/EDM/QSM/99.1 (1999).

[22] World Health Organization, Trade, Intellectual Property Rights and Access to Medicines (2010), available at <http://apps.who.int/medicinedocs/en/m/abstract/Js17521en/>. See also WHO, Report of the Commission on Intellectual Property Rights, Innovation and Public Health (2006), available at <http://www.who.int/intellectualproperty/documents/thereport/ENPublicHealthReport.pdf>.

[23] See, e.g., WHO Agenda, available at <http://www.who.int/about/agenda/en/index.html>.

[24] Universal Declaration of Human Rights, December 8, 1948, GA Res. 217A(III), UN Doc. A/810, at 71, art. 27(2); International Covenant on Economic, Social and Cultural Rights, adopted December 16, 1966, art. 15(1)(c), S. Exec. Doc. D, 95–2, at 13 (1997), 993 U.N.T.S. 3, 5 (entered into force January 3, 1976).

[25] UDHR, arts. 25 and 26; ICESCR arts. 10 and 12.

medicines—have proliferated apace (Yamin and Gloppen 2011). The work of the UN Committee on Economic, Social and Cultural Rights (UNCESCR) and the human rights rapporteurs appointed by the UN Human Rights Council, especially the Special Rapporteur on the Right of Everyone to the Enjoyment of the Highest Attainable Standard of Physical and Mental Health, have provided essential details on the content of state obligations regarding these rights (Helfer and Austin 2011). Key documents include the UNCESCR's General Comment No. 14 on the right to health,[26] and the Special Rapporteur's Human Rights Guidelines for Pharmaceutical Companies in relation to Access to Medicines.[27]

In addition to a complicated environment, in which regulatory competition could play either a positive role in the evolution of legal norms or lead to inconsistency, conflict, and illegitimacy (Cassese 2005a), the intellectual property regime has several other features that make it an interesting arena in which to study transnational governance and global administrative law. The stakes are extremely high. International regulation of knowledge products can have a significant impact on individuals. Trademark protection, especially the requirement for protecting well-known marks, gives out-of-state competitors a leg up on exploiting new markets (Leaffer 1998). Copyright protection raises the costs of educational materials, making it harder for people to acquire the training necessary to compete in a knowledge-based economy where sophisticated skill sets are often required (Chon 2006). Most pertinent for this study, patents, trade secrecy, and data exclusivity laws can raise the cost of medicine, medical procedures, and medical devices. Ironically for the global South, they do so without creating incentives to invent products that treat conditions, such as dengue fever, river blindness, or malaria, that uniquely afflict those who live in nonmarket economies (Wong and Dutfield 2011).

Intellectual property is also technically abstruse and applies to products that can be technologically complex. Thus, it is an area where Shapiro's concerns about technocratic administration are at their zenith (Shapiro 2005). For example, disputes over intellectual property and access to medicines can require specialized knowledge about chemical components and products, cost-benefit analysis, financial risk assessment, and the economics of generic competition. The values that traditionally undergird information law can easily be lost in the analysis (Sell 2003; Keating 2005; Dinwoodie and Dreyfuss 2012). Technical complexity can also accentuate capacity and resource problems. Many of the issues in intellectual property law are empirical in nature: without data on the effect of patents on the price and profitability of pharmaceuticals, and without medical information on the interchangeability of the drugs on the market, it is difficult to know when intellectual property protection is necessary to promote innovation and when it

[26] UN Economic and Social Council, The Right to the Highest Attainable Standard of Health, E/C 12/2000/4 (August 11, 2000).

[27] UN General Assembly, *Report of the Special Rapporteur on the Right of Everyone to the Enjoyment of the Highest Attainable Standard of Physical and Mental Health*, A/63/263 (August 11, 2008).

will mainly impede access to medication or impair health. Much of the law is also extremely arcane. Countries that previously lacked patent protection for pharmaceuticals may, for instance, have great difficulty understanding the choices available in fulfilling their duties to protect undisclosed data or lack a nuanced grasp of the ways in which the inventive-step requirement in patent law can be implemented.

Finally, intellectual property is a fruitful area in which to investigate transnational legal production and administration because it furnishes an occasion to conduct a natural experiment. Even with all the recent regulatory activity, the international regime sets only baseline protection. Accordingly, control over the exploitation of knowledge products in a particular place depends, at the end of the day, on both the quality of the contestation opportunities presented (including the degree to which each adheres to global administrative norms) and the capacity of each country to fully utilize them and generate norms of their own. As the case studies show, these opportunities can be divided into three stages.

The first, the *creation* of substantive intellectual property rules, arises at the international level, most prominently within WIPO and the WTO. Both organizations are the situs of formal rule making and also, importantly, interpretation. WIPO, through its working groups and Standing Committees monitors the creative environment and issues Reports on a variety of technical matters.[28] The WTO's Council for TRIPS provides a forum for discussions about compliance, and the DSB resolves disputes on what TRIPS requires. The output of these activities may begin as "soft" law, but (in the words of William Cornish) they have strong "Genevan bootstraps" (Cornish 1997) and harden over time through incorporation into bilateral agreements,[29] subsequent citation in DSB Reports, and adoption by the WTO's Ministerial Conference (Heald 1996; Abbott and Reichman 2007).[30]

Formally, both organizations offer procedural safeguards. WIPO, for example, holds itself out as open to the participation of industry groups, NGOs, the WTO, as well as other international organizations and stakeholders (Okediji 2008). WTO negotiations are somewhat more opaque (Esty 2006), but the Council is open to all members and permits observers (Dreyfuss 2009). The DSB follows the quasi-judicial procedures set out in the DSU and has added more procedural principles through interpretation (Cassese 2005b).[31] Indeed, both organizations have been responsive to the South. For instance, they have clarified the scope of exceptions

[28] See, e.g, WIPO Model Provisions on Protection Against Unfair Competition, WIPO Publication No. 832 (Geneva, 1996), which defines the term "unfair competition" in art. 10bis of the Paris Convention.

[29] See, e.g., WIPO, Memorandum of the Director on the Joint Recommendation, WIPO Doc. A/34/13 para. 8 (August 4, 1999), available at <http://www.wipo.int/meetings/en/doc_details.jsp?doc_id=1101>, which is referenced in various FTAs.

[30] See, e.g., World Trade Organization, Ministerial Declaration of November 14, 2001, WT/MIN (01)/DEC/1, 41 I.L.M. 746 (2002).

[31] An example is the decision to accept amicus briefs, see European Communities—Measures Affecting Asbestos and Asbestos-Containing Products, WT/DS135/AB/R, paras. 50–7 (March 12, 2001); cf. United States—Import Prohibition of Certain Shrimp and Shrimp Products, WT/DS58/AB/R, para. 110 (October 12, 1998).

and limitations[32] and modified the compulsory license provision.[33] However, a comparative study of the success of individual nations provides an opportunity to gauge the extent to which local capacity problems can diminish the ability of countries to fully utilize these openings to craft international law responsive to their needs and values.

The second opportunity for contestation comes at the *implementation* stage. Parts of the Paris and Berne Conventions may be self-executing, at least in some countries (Ladas 1975). For the most part, however, international intellectual property instruments contemplate implementation by each member state into domestic law. To be sure, there is less flexibility at this stage: one reason that participation at the international level is important is because the agreements cabin the choices states can make. But the TRIPS Agreement—even when augmented by bilaterals—still leaves room to maneuver. Here, a comparative study can identify the factors that affect the ability of nations to use these flexibilities to shape law that balances access needs against the interest in using intellectual property law to promote innovation.

For patents and trade secrets, the third opportunity for contestation arises at the *application* stage, in connection with the examination of patents and the administration of data exclusivity laws by regulatory agencies (and later, by courts). In terms of impact on individuals this is where the rubber meets the road. For example, it is ultimately the patent office that determines whether a particular medicine will be sold at a supracompetitive price or whether generic competition will improve availability. Once again, what happened at the international level penetrates the local, but it is the capacity, resources, and procedural opportunities at these agencies that ultimately operationalize the balance the regulatory regime has struck (Kapczynski 2009; Drahos 2009).

B. The TRIPS Agreement: Overview and Terminology

A short overview of the parts of the TRIPS Agreement relevant to a discussion of medicines illustrates these points (and provides a glossary of technical terms[34]). TRIPS, like its predecessor instruments, relies heavily on **national treatment** to insure that members treat creators in foreign countries the same as they treat their own citizens regarding the enjoyment of intellectual property rights; it also contains a **most favoured nation** guarantee which requires members to treat all foreigners equivalently.[35] At the same time, however, TRIPS imposes higher standards of protection than earlier agreements, particularly in the pharmaceuticals arena. For

[32] See, e.g., Standing Committee on Exclusions from Patentable Subject Matter and Exceptions and Limitations to the Rights, SCP/15/3 Annex I (September 2, 2010) (prepared by Lionel Bently, Brad Sherman, et al.).

[33] See, e.g., TRIPS, art. 31bis.

[34] This section includes terms which may be used somewhat differently in each of the countries covered by this study. This background is meant to serve as a general glossary; when a term is defined differently in a particular study, the authors will highlight the difference.

[35] TRIPS, arts. 3 and 4.

the patent rights that are the focus of this study, the Agreement requires WTO members to protect all "new" inventions, provided that they are "capable of industrial application" and include an "inventive step." It also imposes a **nondiscrimination** requirement. Members must make patents "available and patent rights enjoyable without discrimination as to the place of invention, the field of technology and whether products are imported or locally produced."[36] As to **scope**, every country must prevent unauthorized manufacture, sale, offers to sell, use, and importation of patented products (with analogous provisions on unauthorized exploitation of patented processes).[37] The **term** of protection must be at least twenty years, measured from the date of application.[38] TRIPS granted developing nations a period of five years (later extended) to **transition** their laws into compliance,[39] but countries taking advantage of that period were required to create a **pipeline** to safeguard the protectability of pharmaceutical products discovered after TRIPS came into force.[40] For trade secrets (undisclosed information), the Agreement requires protection against "unfair competition."[41] More particularly, when a country requires the submission of data to secure marketing, it must accord **data exclusivity** to the information.[42]

But despite the apparent stringency of these requirements, TRIPS furnishes nations with several dimensions on which they can adjust the balance between promoting innovation through intellectual property protection and securing access to medicines. First, there are a number of **exclusions** and **exceptions.** Countries can exclude from patentability inventions that are necessary to protect *ordre public*, morality, and health, as well as "diagnostic, therapeutic and surgical methods for the treatment of humans."[43] There is also a **general exceptions provision** which permits limited exceptions so long as they do not unreasonably conflict with normal exploitation and do not unreasonably prejudice the patent owner's interests, taking into account the legitimate interests of third parties.[44] In addition, the Agreement permits countries to issue **compulsory licenses** to local manufacturers or to the government in cases where local supply is inadequate.[45] These licenses are issued without the authorization of the patent holder, but they require the payment of "adequate remuneration"[46] and are subject to other requirements, such as efforts to obtain the patent holder's authorization, case-by-case adjudication, and judicial review. The original version of the Agreement also limited authorization to use "predominantly for the supply of the domestic market."[47] However, the **Doha Declaration** and the **Declaration on TRIPS and Public Health** eliminated that constraint, permitting countries with the ability to produce active ingredients or medications to sell to countries that lack manufacturing capacity.[48] Compulsory licenses can also be used when the patentee has engaged in abuse; historically, this has included its refusal, after a period of years, to work the patent locally. The Paris

[36] TRIPS, art. 27.1. [37] TRIPS, art. 28. [38] TRIPS, art. 33.
[39] TRIPS, art. 65.1 and 2. [40] TRIPS, art. 70.8. [41] TRIPS, art. 39.1.
[42] TRIPS, art. 39.3. [43] TRIPS, art. 27.2 and 3(a). [44] TRIPS, art. 30.
[45] TRIPS, arts. 31 and 40. [46] TRIPS, art. 31(h). [47] TRIPS, art. 31(f).
[48] Ministerial Declaration and Declaration on the TRIPS Agreement and Public Health (n. 43); TRIPS, art. 31bis.

Convention specifically provided for **local working requirements** as a way to create jobs and insure technology transfer.[49] While arguments have been made that this flexibility was *sub silentio* eliminated by TRIPS's nondiscrimination provision, the United States abandoned a challenge to a Brazilian compulsory license issued for nonworking.[50]

Most important, TRIPS does not define key terms. For medicines, the absence of definitions for **new** and **inventive step** provides a great deal of leeway. Thus, while many countries award patents for new uses of known compounds (that is, patents on the process for using a known compound to treat a new disease), some countries regard such **second-use patents** as invalid on the ground that they attempt to protect inventions that are not sufficiently novel (new) or inventive. By the same token, there are national differences as to whether patents will be granted on minor variations of known chemicals (for example, a new salt of a known active ingredient). TRIPS's requirement for **pipeline** protection is similarly flexible. At one time, the United States claimed that countries in transition must immediately grant patents on inventions patented elsewhere, but the Appellate Body rejected that contention.[51] As a result, countries in transition must register patent applications during the transition period, but they can delay protection until after the transition period has elapsed. More important, they may apply their own law to these patents. Thus, a country that does not recognize second-use patents can reject a patent on a new use even though another country (such as the United States) awarded a patent on that advance.

Other flexibilities are also available. The TRIPS Agreement takes no position on **parallel importation** (other than to require national and most favoured nation treatment).[52] Thus, a country may consider the authorized sale of a patented product in another country to "internationally exhaust" the patent holder's interest, allowing the product to be imported and sold locally without permission. These **international exhaustion rules** permit countries where the price of medicine is high to obtain supplies from countries where the prices are lower.

Prior to the TRIPS Agreement, several countries refused to award patents to pharmaceutical products (although some awarded them to processes for manufacturing pharmaceuticals). As a result, many established strong **generic drug industries**, which developed considerable expertise in methods for manufacturing unpatented pharmaceutical products cheaply. Some generic companies compete solely on price; others—**branded generics**—develop strong reputations for quality and valuable trademarks.[53] They can sell these branded drugs at higher prices, but the cost is usually below the price that could be demanded by a proprietary firm for

[49] Paris Convention, art. 5.

[50] Brazil—Measures Affecting Patent Protection, WTO Doc. WT/DS199/1G/L/385/IP/D/23 (June 8, 2000).

[51] India—Patent Protection for Pharmaceutical and Agricultural Chemical Products, WT/DS50/AB/R (5 September, 1997).

[52] TRIPS, art. 6.

[53] Terms associated with generic drugs are particularly likely to be utilized differently in the countries surveyed, see Homedes and Ugalde (2005).

a patented product. Furthermore, some countries require that generic manufacturers prove that each generic product is as biologically available in the body as the stated equivalent proprietary drug. In some countries, however, such proof of **bioequivalence** is not required, or required only of high-risk medicines. When it is not, copies may be called by another name (**similars**, for example).

While product patents are now required by reason of the non-discrimination provision, several of the flexibilities in TRIPS protect the viability of this important industry. There is no requirement that existing process patents be converted into product patents. Further, as a Panel of the WTO Dispute Resolution Body recognized, the general exceptions provision permits countries to adopt a so-called **Bolar (regulatory review) exception.**[54] The Bolar exception allows generic drug companies to use the patent period to compare their drugs to the patented product, prove bioequivalence, and thus prepare to enter the market as soon as the patent expires.

The generics industry is also affected by the **data exclusivity** provision of the TRIPS Agreement, which protects information generated (often at high cost) in order to obtain pre-market clearance from agencies that monitor safety and efficacy.[55] The provision refers to protection against "**unfair commercial use**" and applies to data on "**new chemical entities**" obtained with "**considerable effort**," but (as with the patent provisions) none of these terms is defined. Countries are thus free to decide whether the right to invoke this protection requires the invention of a new *active ingredient* or simply adaptation of a known ingredient to create a new *product* (for example, by tableting the active ingredient differently). Each nation can also determine the *period* of data exclusivity for itself, and decide whether the period begins when the data is submitted for the first time anywhere in the world or when it is submitted locally. Arguably, TRIPS would also permit countries to refuse to accord exclusivity to data that was initially generated for review in another country and thus requires no additional local effort.

Finally, even though TRIPS contemplates that pharmaceutical products will be scrutinized for safety and efficacy, it does not require **term extension** to compensate for delays in this process (or, for that matter for delays in patent examination), even when countries adopt a Bolar exemption that permits use of the patented invention by generics during the patent term. Nor does TRIPS require **linkage** between patenting and market clearance determinations by the agencies that protect safety and efficacy. Some linkage between the efforts of a patent office and the agency regulating drugs may be desirable. For example, in the United States, a generic company must notify the Food and Drug Administration when it is seeking to market a patented drug and the law deems the expression of that intention to constitute a technical infringement. This creates a justiciable controversy and allows the generic manufacturer to test patent validity and thus determine its freedom to

[54] Canada—Patent Protection of Pharmaceutical Products, WT/DS114/R (17 March 2000). The provision takes its name from *Roche Products v. Bolar Pharmaceutical*, 733 F.2d 858 (Fed. Cir. 1984), which led the US Congress to enact a regulatory review exception.

[55] TRIPS, art. 39.3.

operate prior to investing in efforts to copy and commercialize the drug. The US scheme also provides patent holders with a degree of protection and the generic with an incentive to challenge the patent.[56] However, nothing in TRIPS mandates this regime, nor does the Agreement require the regulatory agency that determines safety, efficacy, and bioequivalence to enforce patents or to refuse to clear generic drugs for marketing because they would be infringing if sold.

Because the standards established by TRIPS are minimal, WTO members also enjoy flexibility to "implement in their law more extensive protection than is required by [the] Agreement."[57] As noted earlier, there are regional and bilateral agreements, as well as unilateral actions, which demand revision upwards. Our studies turn on the fact that some nations have withstood these pressures better than others.

IV. Historical Background of the Region: Neoliberalism, Neoconstitutionalism, and Institutional Reform (1990–2010)

Because we start from the premise that the impact of procedural rules can be observed with particular clarity at critical historical junctures—at times when new lines are drawn between claims and choices must be made among alternative legal standards—we take the early 1990s as the starting point for our study of Latin America. The onset of global neoliberalism and the knowledge economy, which undergirded the rise of the transnational regulation of intellectual property at that time, had an important echo within Latin America. In the mid-twentieth century, the Economic Commission for Latin America and the Caribbean (ECLAC) and other governments throughout the region had embraced an import substitution industrialization (ISI) model of development. Centered on a proactive state entrusted with the task of promoting national industry, the ISI approach restricted imports and established mechanisms to promote the growth of domestic industries. For intellectual property, the ISI model aimed to foster local pharmaceutical production. Most important for pharmaceutical TNCs, the Andean Community's Decision 85 of 1974 prohibited patents on certain products, including medicaments and therapeutically active substances. With these products unprotected, a local generic industry could flourish.

But this approach was not to endure. A few years after Decision 85 was adopted and as the so-called "debt crisis" hit Mexico in 1982 and spread throughout the region, the ISI model became discredited in both academic and policy circles. Unable to sustain the budget deficits accumulated during the ISI years and prompted by the IMF and the World Bank, the countries of the region liberalized their economies and adopted the set of policies that would become known as the "Washington Consensus." According to Williamson's canonical formulation

[56] 21 U.S.C. § 355 (known as the Hatch–Waxman Act); Rius Sanjuan (2006).
[57] TRIPS, art. 1.1.

(1990), the Washington Consensus programs promoted by the World Bank and the IMF typically included ten key policy reforms: fiscal discipline, public expenditure reduction and reorientation, tax reform to broaden the tax base, financial liberalization, competitive exchange rates, tariff reduction, elimination of barriers to foreign direct investment, privatization of state-owned enterprises, promotion of market competition, and provision of secure property rights (including intellectual property rights).

The transformation of intellectual property law was an integral part of these market-oriented, neoliberal reforms. The reforms in this area were most visible in those countries that adopted the "shock therapy" version of the Consensus. The iconic case was that of Chile, which established patents over pharmaceutical products through Law 18.935 of 1989, during the last year of the Augusto Pinochet dictatorship. A similarly orthodox attempt at neoliberal reform was undertaken by the governments of Carlos Menem in Argentina. It included repeated (and ultimately unsuccessful) efforts to convince Congress to pass aggressively pro-intellectual property legislation between 1989 and 1995.

Growing evidence of the failure of structural adjustment led neoliberal advocates (including Williamson himself) to call for a second wave of structural reforms, this time centered on institution building (Naím 1994; Williamson 2003). The global turning point was the Asian crisis of 1997, which proved that critics who had warned against the perils of rapid and unconditional deregulation of the economies of the global South were correct. In response and to avert further crises, promoters of the Washington Consensus advocated the establishment of a regulatory regime capable of overseeing the operation of liberalized markets. The outcome was an even broader reform agenda. To the original ten-point list, a wide range of loosely connected and vaguely formulated reforms were added. Among them were the "flexibilization" of labor laws, the establishment of financial regulations and standards, the revamping of market oversight agencies, and the implementation of targeted social policies (Navia and Velasco 2003). Importantly for our purposes, the institutions targeted for reform included national patent offices. Throughout Latin America, national governments came under heavy and increasing international pressure—mainly through the periodic reports and threats of unilateral sanctions by the USTR's Special 301 mechanism—to streamline patent-granting procedures and agencies, so as to swiftly and efficiently protect the rights of patent applicants and holders.

A considerable number of Latin American countries have also gone through a third phase of neoliberal reforms. These were required to implement the provisions of multilateral FTAs (CAFTA and the North American Free Trade Agreement, NAFTA) or bilateral FTAs (such as those signed by Colombia, Peru, and Chile with the United States, Canada, and the European Union). As the case studies on Central America, Colombia, and Chile show, the FTAs have often been the conduit through which TRIPS-plus standards have been incorporated into national legislation. Illustrations include FTA clauses requiring states to further streamline patent-granting procedures for pharmaceuticals by establishing an administrative linkage between the national agency responsible for reviewing applications for patents and the agency in charge of reviewing the drug's safety and effectiveness. Important exceptions to this ongoing wave of reforms are those countries in which left-leaning governments have shied away from FTAs and strengthened the role of the state in the regulation of the economy. To varying degrees and with different connotations, Brazil, Argentina, and Ecuador illustrate this trajectory in our sample.

However, neoliberalism has not been the only influential project of institutional reform in the region at the turn of the century. Overlapping in time with the Washington Consensus—but defending a markedly different vision of regulation and human rights—new constitutions and constitutional reforms throughout the region incorporated generous bills of rights and judicial review mechanisms (Rodríguez-Garavito 2011a). The 1988 Brazilian constitution inaugurated a regional wave which many others joined, including Colombia (1991), Peru (1993), Argentina (1994), Mexico (1994), Venezuela (1998), and, more recently, Ecuador (2008) and Bolivia (2009). Importantly, constitutions, institutional reforms, and activist courts embodying this type of "neoconstitutionalism" are centrally concerned with socio-economic rights, including the right to health (Rodríguez-Garavito 2011b). By explicitly incorporating the international law on socio-economic rights into national constitutions and court decisions, the neoconstitutional project has provided human rights advocates with enforceable legal tools to contest regulations, including patent laws and patent rights, that limit access to affordable healthcare. The result has been a veritable explosion of court cases on the right to health, which have become by far the most litigated issue in constitutional jurisdictions across the region (Yamin and Gloppen 2011).

For our purposes, the relevant element of the clash between neoliberal and neoconstitutional reforms in Latin America is the resulting tension between intellectual property protection (which figures prominently in the former) and the judicial enforcement of the right to health (which is central to the latter). The tension came to life in multiple court cases over the regulation or enforcement of both TRIPS and TRIPS-plus provisions. The question of pipeline protection is a case in point. In Argentina, pharmaceutical TNCs brought court challenges of the national patent office's refusal to provide automatic protection for patents granted in other countries (*patentes de reválida*). The case reached the Supreme Court in 2000. In *Unilever NV v. INPI*,[58] the Court ruled for the government, stating that the national legislation did not recognize such patents. In Brazil, the same issue has given rise to a highly visible case, brought to the Supreme Court by the National Pharmaceutical Association, in alliance with a country-wide human rights access coalition (the Brazilian Network for the Integration of the Peoples). The case reached the Court in 2007; an exceptional hearing was granted in 2009. However, the Court has yet to rule in the matter, thus attesting to the intensity with which this issue is contested.

[58] Corte Suprema de Justicia de la Nación (Supreme Court of Argentina), JA-2001-I-413, October 24, 2000.

V. Overview of the Book: Studying Intellectual Property and Access to Medicines in Latin America. Background and Methods

The tangible consequences of the global intellectual property regime on access to medicines are felt at the domestic level. In order to capture the operation and variation of rules on the ground, these case studies focus on Latin America during the period when the profound political, economic, and legal transformation described above occurred. This section begins with a description of the methodology employed in the studies. It then provides an overview of the studies as well as a series of comments solicited from other students of the region and human rights scholars.

A. Research Design: Case Studies, Goals, and Methodology

This volume encompasses individual case studies of five South American countries, Argentina, Brazil, Chile, Colombia, and Ecuador, and a composite examination of six countries in Central America, Costa Rica, Dominican Republic, El Salvador, Guatemala, Honduras, and Nicaragua. The studies were conducted by scholars at institutions affiliated with the Global Administrative Law network and coordinated through the University of the Andes. Given that the project's overall objective was to tease out the reasons behind national differences, we selected countries that were hypothesized to vary on the dependent variable of interest: the strength of intellectual property rights implicated in accessing medicine. The countries all had similar commitments to democratic governance. However, we chose nations that differ on a host of explanatory variables associated with our analytical point of departure: national, regional, and international institutional structures; participation in relevant national and international networks of experts and activists; size of the local generic industry; participation in FTAs; economic and geopolitical clout; strength and impact of civil society mobilization; and recognition of human rights, including the right to health.

Drawing on a common research protocol, the case studies have three objectives. First, they offer an analysis of the general trajectory of the law and politics of balancing intellectual property interests and access to medicines in their respective country from the early 1990s until the early 2010s. Second, they empirically document the actual operation of institutions involved in the enforcement of intellectual property rights and access-to-medicines legal standards. Thus, while the first goal relates the evolution of "law on the books," the second considers the trajectory of "law in action." Third, the case studies present detailed accounts of key episodes in that trajectory, including activists' campaigns, legislative battles, national litigation, and international negotiations and legal disputes.

To attain those goals, participants in the project used a combination of socio-legal research methods. The starting point consisted of a thorough examination of the relevant national laws and international treaties for each country, as well as the rulings and proceedings from pertinent court cases. The second phase entailed systematic archival research, which included both physical archives (at relevant government agencies, industry associations, and NGOs) and online archives (e.g., of transnational civil society organizations involved in campaigns and fact-finding missions in the countries under study). Finally, the researchers conducted semi-structured interviews with government officials, NGO activists, intellectual property lawyers, human rights lawyers, representatives of transnational pharmaceutical companies and local generics producers, leaders of patients' associations, agents of intergovernmental organizations (e.g., WHO), and local academics. Contributors carried out an average of thirty interviews in each country.

B. Summary of the Case Studies

Organized in alphabetical order in Part I of this volume, the national studies present the following cases:

Argentina (Chapter 2). Paola Bergallo and Agustina Ramón's study shows that the Argentine story has been one of a protracted, intense, and highly visible struggle over the regulation of patents on pharmaceutical products. The authors examine the twists and turns of this story during two periods. The first one, from 1989 to 1995, overlapped with the "shock-therapy" version of the Menem government's neoliberal economic policies, which included an aggressive, sustained effort by the Ministry of the Economy to please the United States (and the USTR) by enacting a new intellectual property law that incorporated strong pharmaceutical patents. The reform drive encountered fierce resistance from the powerful national pharmaceutical industry, in alliance with influential sectors of Argentina's Congress and certain agencies within the Executive branch, who managed to defeat Menem's repeated attempts at legal reform.

The second period, from 1996 to 2010, revolved around the national implementation of TRIPS, as the United States and the international pharmaceutical industries increased pressure on the Argentine government, legislature, and courts to adopt a maximalist interpretation of intellectual property obligations under TRIPS. However, the same actors who successfully fended off efforts to ratchet up patent protection during the heyday of neoliberalism in the early 1990s largely succeeded in preserving and exploiting the flexibilities of TRIPS. The pro-access position received decisive political backing as the Menem legacy ended in the country's economic collapse in 2001. New governments instead promoted regulations that created economic incentives for the use of generic drugs and adopted a proactive, pro-access stance in global forums such as WIPO and the WTO. Importantly, the authors conclude by showing that this outcome has not translated itself into lower drug prices, as national producers have profited from regulatory loopholes that allow them to set prices that are above those in similar countries, while passing on the additional charge to the healthcare system and—to some extent—to patients.

In sum, from a comparative perspective, the Argentine case is the clearest illustration in our sample of a relatively even and thus highly contentious and protracted dispute over patent regulations. As evident in Table 1.1, the result has been a legal framework that, although compliant with the global TRIPS regime, makes allowance for virtually all of the flexibilities and exceptions that signal a pro-health commitment, while resisting TRIPS-plus standards. As we discuss in the concluding chapter, this outcome appears rooted in the political alliance between the domestic pharmaceutical sector and the long nationalist tradition of the Peronist party, which benefited from a wealth of local expertise. In a sense, Argentina achieved the best of both worlds: it complied with TRIPS, and it also assured access by funding medication for all Argentinians. At the same time, however, state support uses resources that could be deployed elsewhere. Furthermore, new relationships among local and foreign pharmaceutical companies and between pharmaceutical companies and insurance companies open opportunities for drug companies to charge outrageous prices and to receive kickbacks.

Brazil (Chapter 3). Mônica Rosina and Adelina de Oliveira Novaes's chapter reconstructs the regulatory path Brazil followed as it transitioned from the "lost decade" of the 1980s into years of spectacular growth and effected the political transformation that launched the country into the status of emerging world power.

The Brazilian story is punctuated by the country's incorporation of TRIPS obligations through Law No. 9279, which introduced patent protection and sacrificed several of the flexibilities allowed by TRIPS, among them the ten-year transition period. Tellingly, the law went beyond TRIPS by incorporating pipeline protection. The authors attribute the pro-intellectual property bent of this foundational legislation to the successful lobbying of transnational pharmaceutical corporations, in alliance with a sympathetic sector of the Brazilian Congress.

In reaction to this early trend, the 1990s saw the development of a vibrant coalition of civil society organizations at the national level, and the Brazilian left-leaning government, advocating at the international level for a more pro-health approach. Domestically, organizations such as ABIA, Conectas, and Doctors Without Borders, in alliance with the national industry, challenged pipeline protection before the courts and actively promoted the use of flexibilities such as the right of parallel importation. Although the law did not change, activists found a sympathetic ear in key sectors of the Cardoso and Lula governments—notably the ministries of health and international relations, which have been behind Brazil's leading role in such pro-access initiatives as the Doha Round and the WIPO Development Agenda.

Although currently in flux due to ongoing legal challenges before domestic courts, the Brazilian story is paradoxical (the authors call it schizophrenic) in comparative perspective, for it combines strong patent protection at the legislative level with a decidedly pro-access stance at the implementation level, as shown by the government's use of compulsory licensing and the Bolar exception. In part, the result can be explained by Brazil's strong institutions—locally, a proactive health agency (ANVISA) and, internationally, negotiators able to create common cause with other emerging economies (including India, China, and South Africa) to bring development interests to the fore. In larger part, however, the outcome appears attributable to a strong government commitment to pay for healthcare.

Central America (Chapter 4). Angelina Snodgrass Godoy's chapter offers a comparative analysis of Costa Rica, Dominican Republic, El Salvador, Guatemala, Honduras, and Nicaragua, which highlights both the commonalities and the differences among these countries. On the one hand, they all went through the decisive regulatory change associated with the signing of CAFTA, which was ratified by the United States in 2005. Since the intellectual property standards in CAFTA are more demanding than those included in the FTAs that preceded it and in those that followed it, CAFTA is widely seen as the high-water mark of intellectual property protection. On the other hand, contrary to the customary treatment of Central American countries as a whole, the author shows how there have been important differences among them in the implementation and application of the CAFTA standards. These are reflected in Table 1.1.

The Central America story is the clearest illustration of a path of low resistance vis-à-vis proprietary interests. This path stems from both structural factors—especially the small size of domestic markets and the lack of geopolitical influence of countries in the region—and strategic factors—especially the fact that civil society organizations, weakened by the legacy of civil wars, were incapable of mounting a sustained counter-movement in defense of access to medicines. Indeed, the limited resistance that did occur was led and controlled by international NGOs. Snodgrass argues that the Central America trajectory offers a cautionary tale with regards to the more visible and hopeful stories of South American countries like Brazil and Argentina, whose size and geopolitical clout contrast with the realities of most countries in the global South.

Chile (Chapter 5). Salvador Millaleo's account of the evolution of Chilean regulation of patents reveals the most linear, ostensibly pro-intellectual property story in our sample. Remarkably, its official stance favoring proprietary interests has remained steady since the failed attempt of the Pinochet dictatorship at regulating the issue before the transition to democracy in 1989. Indeed, the centrist coalition that ruled the country since the return of democracy in 1990 until 2010 (the *Concertación*) maintained the country's commitment to global economic integration, and accepted increasingly strong intellectual property rules as part of the process, through three legislative steps.

First, Law No. 19.039 of 1991 introduced patents over pharmaceutical products. Second, No. 19.996 of 1996 (which entered into force belatedly, in 2005) increased standards of patent protection in compliance with TRIPS, which Chile had ratified in 1995. Finally, the signing of an FTA with the United States in 2003 entailed further obligations for Chile to expand patent protection (for instance, through the extension of patents beyond the twenty-year period to compensate for administrative delays), which the country honored through Law No. 20.160 of 2007.

But despite its apparent staunch pro-intellectual property stance, Chile engaged in "back door opposition," and through that route has preserved the health of its national pharmaceutical industry, which still accounts for around 80 percent of sales in the country. Unlike in other countries under study, the low density and relative weakness of pro-health coalitions in Chile thwarted political coalitions with national industrial associations. However, the domestic industry's expertise significantly influenced the tenor of negotiations. Although Chile accepted the broad demands of the United States, it found subtle ways to shape the law to its particular needs.[59]

Colombia (Chapter 6). César Rodríguez-Garavito's study traces the Colombian regulatory path, from regional regulation at the Andean scale, to national legislation in response to pressure from the United States, to bilateral regulation as a result of the Colombia–US FTA. Due to Colombia's commitment to Andean integration up to the 1990s, the introduction of patent protection and post-TRIPS expansion were the result of regulations at the Andean level (Decision 311 of 1991 and Decision 486 of 2000, respectively). However, Colombia gradually parted ways with its Andean neighbors and moved through a series of three political and legal processes toward a decidedly pro-patent orientation. First, its role as the key ally of the United States in the so-called "war on drugs" in the region and its position as the second-largest recipient of US military aid entailed a high exposure to unilateral pressures as embodied in Special 301 Reports. This led, for instance, to the government's decision to yield to US demands to incorporate data protection into national legislation, which it did through Decree 2085 of 2002.

Second, Colombia stands out in our sample as the country with the most visible and protracted negotiation of intellectual property clauses in an FTA. Although negotiations of the FTA with the United States were inaugurated in May 2004 and scheduled to end with the ratification of the treaty in 2005, the FTA was eventually signed in 2006, but entered into force only in 2012. Although the general orientation of intellectual property clauses in the FTA is similar to that of the Chile FTA and CAFTA, the Colombia story is significant because the duration of the process allowed for the rise of a dynamic coalition of national and transnational pro-health organizations. In alliance with the domestic generic industry, this coalition effectively exploited international political opportunities (notably changes in the political majority in the US Congress in 2006) to prompt a renegotiation of the intellectual property provisions to avoid some of the most extreme concessions made by Chile and the CAFTA countries.

Third, as Colombia embarked on a wave of FTAs with the European Union, Canada, and countries around the world in the 2000s and 2010s, it consolidated its commitment to a pro-patent regulatory framework. This helps explain why, unlike other countries in our sample, it has largely skipped the use of TRIPS flexibilities and patent-related mechanisms to promote access to medicines. In the face of skyrocketing medicine prices, it has resorted instead to timid price-control measures. However, evidence of the negative impact of rigid patent protection and other regulatory failures has led the government to be more open to flexibilities in the implementation phase of the FTAs. High costs have also prompted activists and human rights lawyers to resort to courts to advance the pro-access cause.

[59] In this way, Chile is not dissimilar from the United States. The United States' demands for strong protection abroad stand in contrast to its domestic laws, which often balance proprietary and access interests in subtle but effective ways. The US version of linkage, recounted above, is an example.

Ecuador (Chapter 7). Tatiana Andia's chapter documents the zigzagging trajectory of this Andean country, which, like Colombia, followed the Andean turn towards a pro-intellectual property framework in the 1990s through the above-mentioned Decisions 311 and 486. In fact, Ecuador went beyond the Andean regulations by prematurely introducing pipeline protection through a bilateral agreement with the United States in 1993, which was incorporated into national legislation by Decree 1344-A. Like Brazil, its interests in access were ultimately defeated. But unlike Brazil, which has considerable clout of its own, Ecuador was saved by a strong regional institution—the Andean Tribunal of Justice.

Two factors make the Ecuadorean case unique within our sample. First, it joined TRIPS voluntarily in order to participate in a trade dispute over the importation of bananas into the EU. The challenge ended well for Ecuador when it threatened to retaliate against the EU by suspending obligations under the TRIPS Agreement.[60] Its success created familiarity with both the WTO and intellectual property law. Second is Ecuador's sharp turn in 2006 towards a pro-access, nationalist strategy under the Rafael Correa government. With political backing from a strong indigenous movement, along with a diverse coalition of human rights NGOs, and social justice organizations, the government sought to "insure universal access to essential medicines and consolidate the authority and sovereignty of the State in the use of medicine and phytotherapeutic resources," as established by the Decree 118 of 2009. The Ecuadorean story thus offers rare evidence of the potential and the consequences of a small country's decision to challenge the global intellectual property regime by maximizing the use of flexibilities and exceptions.

To facilitate a comparison among the case studies, Table 1.1 summarizes the results of the debates over intellectual property and access to medicines in the countries in our sample as of the end date of the studies. It thus offers a synthesized view of the outcome that concerns us: the degree to which national regulations protect proprietary and access interests. It lists eleven variables which affect access interest, framed so that YES designates a provision that is pro-access, while NO signifies a measure promoting proprietary interests. The variables include the availability of a diagnostic exception, a Bolar provision, or other health-related exemptions; the freedom to engage in parallel importation from countries with lower costs; the existence of compulsory licensing laws that can be used to compel working, to protect public health, or in favor of government use; whether the country has agreed to extend the patent term for delays in examination or market clearance; whether linkage is required; whether the country excludes the broadest possible protection for data (which is to say, protection for data on new products, as opposed to molecules) and second-use patents (which is to say, patents for second uses that represent only incremental change).

Although the Table includes the variables that have been the key objects of contention in the countries under study, it should be construed as an approximation

[60] Decision by the Arbitrators, European Communities—Regime for the Importation, Sale and Distribution of Bananas—Recourse to Arbitration by the European Communities Under Article 22.6 of the DSU, para. 152, WT/DS27/ARB/ECU (March 24, 2000).

Table 1.1 The Effects of International Obligations on Intellectual Property Protection

Does the country make an allowance for the following issues in its patent laws? Yes (Y) or No (N) or Not explicit (—)	Allowance for diagnostic and therapeutic exception	Allowance for a Bolar-type exception	Other health-related exceptions to patent rights	Allowance for parallel importation	Working requirement imposed	Public health grounds for compulsory licenses	Grounds for government use	No patent extensions available	No linkage required	Data protection exclusively for new chemical entities (not products)	Second-use patents are invalid
ARGENTINA	Y	Y	Y	Y	Y	Y	Y	N	Y	Y	—
BRAZIL	Y	Y	Y	N	Y	Y	Y	N	—	—	—
CAFTA Costa Rica	Y	N[a]	N[a]	N	Y	Y	Y	N	N	?	—
Dominican Republic	Y	Y	N	N	Y	Y	Y	N	—	?	—
El Salvador	Y	Y	N	N	—	Y	—	N	N	?	—
Guatemala	Y	N[a]	Y	N	—	Y	Y	N	N	?	Y
Honduras	Y	N[a]	N	N	Y	Y	Y	—	N	?	—
Nicaragua	Y	N[a]	N	N	—	Y	Y	N	N	?	—
CHILE	Y	Y	Y	Y	N	Y	—	N	Y[b]	Y[c]	Y
COLOMBIA	Y	Y	Y	Y	N	Y	Y	N[d]	N[d]	N	Y
ECUADOR	Y	Y	Y	Y	Y	Y	Y	Y[e]	Y	Y	Y

[a] General exception; not geared specifically to health issue.
[b] Agreed in FTA, but not implemented in domestic law.
[c] Limited protection.
[d] Agreed in FTA signed with the US (pending ratification in US Congress).
[e] Extension law does not apply to pharmaceuticals.

rather than as a definitive assessment of the outcomes. Because the Table uses a binary (Yes/No) format for clarity purposes, it omits subtle but relevant differences in these laws.[61] Furthermore, the Table does not reflect commitments made in FTAs that have not been implemented in domestic law or which were rejected at the time of the study; nor does it consider how the laws which had been implemented into domestic law are applied by patent offices, public health agencies, courts, lawyers, activists, and other actors shape the outcomes of the laws. We leave for the Discussion section and the case studies a more nuanced treatment of intellectual property "law in action."

Part II of this volume supplements the case studies with comments by scholars versed in the underlying theoretical framework. Laurence Helfer, Karen Alter, and Amy Kapczynski have all conducted country studies using similar methodologies to our authors. Helfer and Alter (Chapter 9) contribute their perspective on the role of regional capacities—Andean law and the Andean Tribunal of Justice—in the balance that members of the Andean Community strike between health and innovation concerns. Kapczynski (Chapter 10) considers the next phase of the international intellectual property story: the impact of locally developed law on international norms, and the ways that one country's experience can shape the contestation opportunities elsewhere.

Sean Flynn and Ruth Okediji take closer looks at how pressures build and are diffused at the international level. Our case studies show that the USTR's Special 301 procedure plays an outsize role in implementation and application decisions; Sean Flynn (Chapter 8) considers how the Special 301 Reports have changed as contestation opportunities within the USTR have improved. The case studies also suggest that despite WIPO's agreement to provide technical assistance on implementing TRIPS, the Organization is not perceived as helping countries strike the appropriate balance between proprietary interests and access to medicine. In her contribution, Ruth Okediji (Chapter 13) examines the role of WIPO. She explains why WIPO has, historically, not had a significant impact on the health debate. Starting from the proposition that greater linkage among the relevant international organizations would be desirable, she proposes an "action plan" for improving WIPO's responsiveness to health concerns.

For many countries, success in adapting international obligations to local needs has turned heavily on national commitments to human rights and on the presence of human rights advocates, both foreign and domestic. Smita Narula (Chapter 12)

[61] For instance, outcomes such as administrative linkage and patent extensions to compensate for delays are mandatory for Central American countries under CAFTA (which are thus assigned a "No" in the Table), but have been rejected by other countries like Argentina and Ecuador (a "Yes" in the Table). However, a third regulatory option has obtained under other FTAs (such as the one signed by Colombia and the United States), which include provisions on linkage and patent extensions but make their enforcement optional (rather than mandatory), and thus leaves open these questions for further rounds of engagement between the parties as the implementation of the treaty unfolds. Since it is probable that the United States will exert heavy pressure to enforce those provisions during the implementation phase, we assign a "No" to Colombia under these two variables, while being aware that the binary format of the answer misses the fact that this intermediate alternative is not identical to the CAFTA requirements.

provides an overview of the rights-based approach to access to medicines, focusing on the work of international human rights bodies, mechanisms, and procedures. Molly Land (Chapter 11) takes a hard look at places where the human rights frame was unsuccessful, asking why it had so little traction in many of these countries and explores whether the developing A2K (access-to-medicines) frame will act as a stronger or weaker safeguard of access interests.

In the final chapter (Chapter 14), the authors suggest conclusions that can be drawn from the case studies and related commentary.

References

Abbott, Frederick, and Jerome Reichman. 2007. "The Doha Round's Public Health Legacy: Strategies for the Production and Diffusion of Patented Medicines under the Amended TRIPS Provisions." *J. Int'l Econ. L.* 10: 921–87.

Benvenisti, Eyal. 2005. "Public Choice and Global Administrative Law: Who's Afraid of Executive Discretion?" *Law & Contemp. Probs.* 68: 319–39.

Büthe, Tim, and Walter Mattli. 2011. *New Global Rulers: The Privatization of Regulation in the World Economy*. Princeton, NJ: Princeton University Press.

Cassese, Sabino. 2005a. "Administrative Law without the States? The Challenge of Global Regulation." *NYU J. Int'l L. & Pol.* 37: 663–94.

——. 2005b. "Global Standards for National Administrative Procedure." *Law & Contemp. Probs.* 68: 109–26.

Chimni, B. S. 2005. "Co-Option and Resistance: Two Faces of Global Administrative Law." *J. Int'l L. & Pol.* 37: 799–837.

Chon, Margaret. 2006. "Intellectual Property and the Development Divide." *Cardozo L. Rev.* 27: 2821–912.

Cornish, William. 1997. "Genevan Bootstraps." *Eur. Intell. Prop. Rev.* 19: 336–8.

Dezalay, Yves, and Bryant Garth. 2002. *Global Prescriptions: The Production, Exportation, and Importation of a New Legal Orthodoxy*. Ann Arbor: University of Michigan Press.

Dinwoodie, Graeme, and Rochelle Dreyfuss. 2012. *A Neofederalist Vision of TRIPS: Building a Resilient International Intellectual Property System*. New York: Oxford University Press.

Drahos, Peter. 1995. "Global Rights in Information: The Story of TRIPS at the GATT." *Prometheus* 13: 6–19.

——. 2009. "The Jewel in the Crown: India's Patent Office and Patent-Based Innovation." Pp. 80–100 in *Intellectual Property Policy Reform: Fostering Innovation and Development*, edited by C. Arup and W. van Caenegern. Cheltenham: Edward Elgar Publishing.

Dreyfuss, Rochelle. 2009. "Fostering Dynamic Innovation, Development and Trade: Intellectual Property as a Case Study in Global Administrative Law." *Acta Juridica*: 237–82.

Esty, Daniel. 2006. "Good Governance at the Supranational Scale: Globalizing Administrative Law." *Yale LJ* 115: 1490–562.

Evans, Peter, Harold Jacobson, and Robert Putnam, eds. 1993. *Double-Edged Diplomacy: Bargaining and Domestic Politics*. Berkeley: University of California Press.

Grosse Ruse-Khan, Henning. 2011. "Protecting Intellectual Property Under BITs, FTAs, and TRIPS: Conflicting Regimes or Mutual Coherence." Pp. 485–515 in *Evolution in*

Investment Treaty Law and Arbitration, edited by K. Miles, C. Brown. Cambridge: Cambridge University Press.

Hall, Peter. 1993. "Policy Paradigms, Social Learning, and the State: The Case of Economic Policymaking in Britain." *Comparative Politics* 26(3): 275, 296.

Halliday, Terence C. 2009. "Recursivity of Global Normmaking: A Sociolegal Agenda." *Ann. Rev. L. & Soc. Sci.* 5: 263–89.

Heald, Paul. 1996. "Trademarks and Geographic Indications: Exploring the Contours of the TRIPS Agreement." *Vand. J. Transnat'l L.* 29: 635–60.

Helfer, Laurence. 2004. "Regime Shifting: The TRIPS Agreement and New Dynamics of International Intellectual Property Lawmaking." *Yale J. Int'l L.* 29: 1–83.

——. 2008. "The New Innovation Frontier? Intellectual Property and the European Court of Human Rights." *Harv. Int'l L. J.* 49: 1–52.

Helfer, Laurence, and Graeme Austin. 2011. *Human Rights and Intellectual Property: Mapping the Global Interface*. Cambridge: Cambridge University Press.

Homedes, Núria, and Antonio Ugalde. 2005. "Multisource Drug Policies in Latin America—A Survey of 10 Countries." *Int'l J. Public Health* 83(1): 64–70.

Kapczynski, Amy. 2008. "The Access to Knowledge Mobilization and the New Politics of Intellectual Property." *Yale LJ* 117: 804–85.

——. 2009. "Harmonization and its Discontents: A Case Study of TRIPS Implementation in India's Pharmaceutical Sector." *Calif. L. Rev.* 97: 1571–649.

Khagram, Sanjeev, James Riker, and Kathryn Sikkink, eds. 2002. *Restructuring World Politics: Transnational Social Movements, Networks and Norms*. Minneapolis: University of Minnesota Press.

Keating, Dominic. 2005. "Access to Genetic Resources and Equitable Benefit Sharing through a New Disclosure Requirement in the Patent System: An Issue in Search of a Forum." *J. Pat. & Trademark Off. Soc'y* 87: 525–41.

Keck, Margaret, and Kathryn Sikkink. 1998. *Activists beyond Borders: Advocacy Networks in International Politics*. Ithaca, NY: Cornell University Press.

Kingsbury, Benedict, Nico Krisch, and Richard B. Stewart. 2005. "The Emergence of Global Administrative Law." *Law and Contemp. Probs.* 68: 15–61.

Klug, Heinz. 2005. "Campaigning for Life: Building a New Transnational Solidarity in the Face of HIV/AIDS and TRIPS." Pp. 118–39 in *Law and Globalization from Below: Toward a Cosmopolitan Legality*, edited by B. de Sousa Santos and C. Rodríguez-Garavito. Cambridge: Cambridge University Press.

Ladas, Stephen. 1975. *Patents, Trademarks, and Related Rights: National and International Protection*. Cambridge, MA: Harvard University Press.

Leaffer, Marshall. 1998. "The New World of International Trademark Law." *Marq. Intell. Prop. L. Rev.* 2: 1–32.

Lopert, Ruth, and Deborah Gleeson. 2013. "The High Price of 'Free' Trade: U.S. Trade Agreements and Access to Medicines." *JL Med. & Ethics* 41: 199–218.

Lustig, Doreen, and Benedict Kingsbury. 2006. "Displacement and Relocation from Protected Areas: International Law Perspectives on Rights, Risks and Resistance." *Conservation & Soc.* 4(3): 404–18. Retrieved July 2, 2013 (<http://www.iilj.org/research/documents/LustigKingsbury.RightsRisksandResistance2006.pdf>).

Milner, H. V., and B. P. Rosendorff. 1997. "Democratic Politics and International Trade Negotiations: Elections and Divided Government as Constraints on Trade Liberalization." *Journal of Conflict Resolution* 41: 117–46.

Naím, Moisés. 1994. *Latin America's Journey to the Market: From Economic Shocks to Institutional Therapy*. Budapest: International Center for Economic Growth.

Navia, Patricio, and Andrés Velasco. 2003. "The Politics of Second-Generation Reforms." Pp. 265–303 in *After the Washington Consensus: Restarting Growth and Reform in Latin America*, edited by J. Williamson. Washington, DC: Institute for International Economics.

Okediji, Ruth. 2008. "WIPO-WTO Relations and the Future of Global Intellectual Property Norms." *Neth. YB Int'l L.* 39: 69–125.

Putnam, Robert. 1988. "Diplomacy and Domestic Politics: The Logic of Two-Level Games." *Int'l Org.* 42(3): 427–60.

Rangnekar, Dwijen. 2005. *Resource Book on TRIPS and Development: An Authoritative and Practical Guide to the TRIPS Agreement.* Geneva: UNCTAD-ICTSD Capacity Building Project. Retrieved October 30, 2013 (<http://www.iprsonline.org/unctadictsd/ResourceBookIndex.htm>).

Ricketson, Sam, and Jane C. Ginsburg. 2006. *International Copyright and Neighboring Rights: The Berne Convention and Beyond.* Oxford: Oxford University Press.

Rius Sanjuan, Judit. 2006. "US and EU Protection of Pharmaceutical Test Data". CP Tech Discussion Paper. Retrieved October 30, 2013, (<http://www.cptech.org/publications/CPTechDPNo1TestData.pdf>).

Robinson, Will. 1999. "The World Customs Organization." *Int'l Crim. Police Rev.* 476–7: 81–6.

Rodríguez-Garavito, César. 2011a. "Toward a Sociology of the Global Rule of Law Field: Neoliberalism, Neoconstitutionalism, and the Struggle over Judicial Reform in Latin America." Pp. 156–82 in *Lawyers and the Rule of Law in an Era of Globalization*, edited by B. Garth and Y. Dezalay. New York: Routledge.

——. 2011b. "Beyond the Courtroom: The Impact of Judicial Activism on Socioeconomic Rights in Latin America." *Tex. L. Rev.* 89: 1669–98.

Sandhu, Harjit. 1999. "Product Counterfeiting and Interpol." *Int'l Crim. Police Rev.* 476–7: 98–101.

Santa Cruz, Maximiliano. 2007. *Intellectual Property Provisions in European Union Trade Agreements: Implications for Developing Countries.* Geneva: ICTSD Programme on IPRs and Sustainable Development. Retrieved October 30, 2013 (<http://www.iprsonline.org/resources/docs/Santa-Cruz%20Blue20.pdf>).

Santos, Boaventura de Sousa, and César Rodríguez-Garavito. 2005. "Law, Politics, and the Subaltern in Counter-Hegemonic Globalization." Pp. 1–26 in *Law and Globalization from Below: Toward a Cosmopolitan Legality*, edited by B. de Sousa Santos and C. Rodríguez-Garavito. Cambridge: Cambridge University Press.

Scandizzo, Stefania. 2001. "Intellectual Property Rights and International R&D." Working Paper QP/01/81, International Monetary Fund, Washington, DC. Retrieved October 30, 2013 (<http://www.imf.org/external/pubs/ft/wp/2001/wp0181.pdf>).

Sell, Susan K. 2003. *Private Power, Public Law: The Globalization of Intellectual Property Rights.* Cambridge: Cambridge University Press.

Shapiro, Martin. 2005. "'Deliberative,' 'Independent' Technocracy v. Democratic Politics: Will the Globe Echo the E.U.?" *Law & Contemp. Probs.* 68: 341–56.

Sikkink, Kathryn. 2005a. "Patterns of Dynamic Multilevel Governance and the Insider-Outsider Coalition." Pp. 151–74 in *Transnational Protest & Global Activism*, edited by D. Della Porta and S. Tarrow. New York: Rowman & Littlefield.

——. 2005b. "The Transnational Dimension of the Judicialization of Politics in Latin America." Pp. 263–92 in *The Judicialization of Politics in Latin America*, edited by R. Sieder, L. Schjolden, and A. Angell. London: Palgrave.

Slaughter, Ann-Marie. 2004. *A New World Order.* Princeton: Princeton University Press.

Sonderholm, Jorn. 2010. "Intellectual Property Rights and the TRIPS Agreement: An Overview of Ethical Problems and Some Proposed Solutions." Policy Research Working Paper 5228, World Bank Development Research Group, Washington, DC.

Stiglitz, Joseph. 2007. "Multinational Corporations: Balancing Rights and Responsibilities." *Am. Soc. Int'l L. Proc.* 101: 3–63.

Tarrow, Sidney. 1998. *Power in Movement: Social Movements and Contentious Politics*. Cambridge: Cambridge University Press.

Watt, Stanley. 2007. "Firm Heterogeneity and Weak Intellectual Property Rights." Working Paper WP/07/161, International Monetary Fund, Washington, DC.

Williamson, John. 1990. "What Washington Means by Policy Reform." Pp. 7–38 in *Latin American Adjustment: How Much Has Happened?*, edited by J. Williamson. Washington, DC: Institute for International Economics.

——. 2003. "Summing Up." Pp. 305–21 in *After the Washington Consensus: Restarting Growth and Reform in Latin America*, edited by J. Williamson and P. Kuczynski. Washington, DC: Institute for International Economics.

Yamin, Alicia, and Siri Gloppen. 2011. *Litigating Health Rights: Can Courts Bring More Justice to Health?* Cambridge: Cambridge University Press.

Wong, Tzen, and Graham Dutfield, eds. 2011. *Intellectual Property and Human Development: Current Trends and Future Scenarios*. Cambridge: Cambridge University Press.

Yu, Peter. 2011. "Six Secret (and Now Open) Fears of ACTA." *SMU L. Rev.* 64: 975–1094.

PART I

COUNTRY STUDIES

Chapter 2

The Recursivity of Global Lawmaking in the Struggle for an Argentine Policy on Pharmaceutical Patents

*Paola Bergallo and Agustina Ramón Michel**

In the last decade, a new generation of socio-legal studies has begun to inquire into the dynamics of norm making in the era of globalization. New studies show that national and transnational actors are involved in cyclical disputes with results dependent on circumstance, personalities, and political happenstance. Studies in areas such as bankruptcy law, telecommunications regulation, and control over gender violence, reveal fluid processes taking place in international, regional, and national forums (Braithwaite and Drahos 2000; Halliday and Carruthers 2007; Merry 2006).

As described by Halliday, such processes are characterized by their recursivity (2009). Recursivity results from the intersection of cycles with stages of global and domestic norm making, and the interaction between them. Within such cycles, phases of enactment are followed by phases of rule implementation. Throughout these cycles, contending actors compete to shape new norms and to profit from the gaps and opportunities generated by such mechanisms as the actors' mismatch; the diagnostic struggles to frame the issues; and the indeterminacy of, and the contradictions ubiquitous in, the law. Ultimately, the cyclicality of such reform processes endures until distributive lawmaking struggles reach a settlement, in which new regulations and agreements are produced.

The transformations of intellectual property (IP) regimes, and especially, the regulation of pharmaceutical patents, provide a fertile field to explore the recursivity of global norm making and its counter-hegemonic mobilizations. Such changes also offer an opportunity to examine the results of the inescapable tension between IP

* The authors are grateful to Sonia Ariza and Sabrina Cartabia for research assistance and their comments on an earlier version of this chapter. We also want to thank Marcelo Alegre, Roberto Gargarellaand Diana Osorio, as well as participants of the workshop "Balancing Wealth and Health" (May 2011) at New York University School of Law. We owe special thanks to Cesar Rodríguez-Garavito, Rochelle Dreyfuss, and Laurence Helfer for their helpful suggestions and observations. We are also thankful for María Alejandra Etchegorry for her help editing a prior English draft.

rights and the right to health as regards access to medicines (Almeida do Reis, Bermudez, and Oliveira 2006).[1]

In the last twenty years we have witnessed the emergence and codification of new global IP norms through the adoption of the Agreement on Trade-Related Aspects of Intellectual Property Rights (TRIPS) and the Doha Declaration as well as the passage of hundreds of domestic legislative reforms around the world. Furthermore, the dispute settlement mechanism of the World Trade Organization (WTO), which includes disputes under the TRIPS Agreement, offers an interface to forge the relationship between international norms and domestic law. In its international dimension, this upheaval in IP regulation has gone through at least two cycles distinguishable by their discursive framing. While the first cycle was marked by the expansion of patent protection, redefined as a matter of international trade law (Drahos 1997), the second cycle has been characterized by the definition of pharmaceutical patents as an issue on the health agenda (Sell 2008). Each of these two key moments—partially overlapping in practice—encompassed, in turn, phases of enactment and implementation in which the promoters of an expansive IP regime (hereinafter, pro-IP actors) and their opponents struggled to define, first, the text of the TRIPS Agreement, and then the scope of its interpretation. As suggested in Figure 2.1, these cycles have in turn had a transnational stage, a national (domestic) stage, and instances of global-domestic interface.

Several studies have explored the international dimensions of the attempt to redefine the transnational IP regime. Works by Susan Sell (2003, 2008, 2009) and John Braithwaite and Peter Drahos (2000), among others, have demonstrated how pro-IP actors as well as their challengers, including nongovernmental organizations (NGOs), the domestic pharmaceutical sector, governments of the global South, technical professionals, and international organizations such as the World Health Organization (WHO), have engaged in forum shifting and subsequent reframing of the international IP agenda. However, the relationship between the international cycle and domestic experiences of IP legal reform, and events taking place at their interface, remain relatively unexplored (but see Kapczynski 2009; Klug 2007).

Against this backdrop, our chapter offers a case study with a twofold purpose. In the first place, we seek to contribute to the study of the recursivity of global norm making from a bottom-up perspective (Sousa Santos and Rodríguez Garavito 2007) by examining the Argentine experience in the reception of the new international IP

[1] Under Argentine law, this is a right protected by several references scattered throughout the federal and provincial Constitutions, human rights treaties, statutes, and legal precedents of the Supreme Court. The Argentine Constitution as amended in 1994 protects the collective right to "a healthy and balanced environment fit for human development" (art. 41) and consumers' rights "to the protection of their health, safety, and economic interests" (art. 43). In addition, art. 75 establishes Congress's mandate to legislate in keeping with a social justice agenda and to provide certain specific health protections on the basis of equality. The human rights treaties included under art. 75.22 also contain several provisions regarding the right to health. At the federal level this regulatory framework is supplemented by a number of statutes. At the provincial level, constitutions and provincial statutes further expand the content of the right within provincial health systems. Finally, a number of Supreme Court precedents defining aspects of the right to health have also helped to shape the interpretation of the right. For a review of the main precedents, see Bazán (2012).

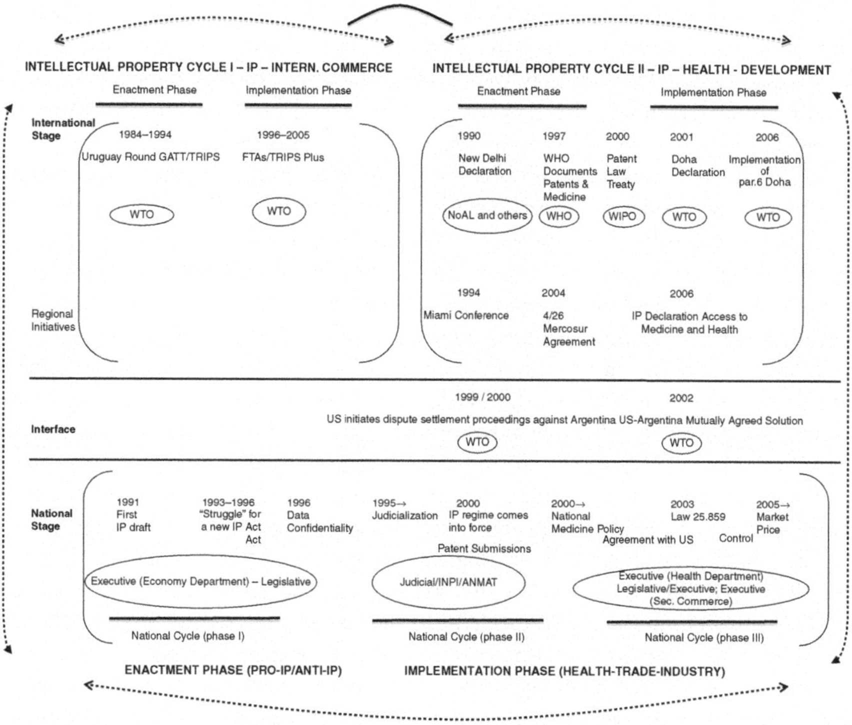

Fig. 2.1 The recursivity in the legal change of the IP regime

norms for the regulation of pharmaceutical patents. As explained in the following sections, our observations show the coexistence of three stages of debate, interrelated in the recursive process that is typical of the era of globalization. The chapter reveals how, through the enactment and implementation phases of the process of renovating the national IP regime, prominent domestic actors repeatedly managed to frustrate attempts by the US government and the multinational pharmaceutical industry to expand patent rights over medicines. Our chapter highlights how, throughout the decade of more confrontation over a new IP regime, the four mechanisms referred to by Halliday (2009) were used by the local pharmaceutical industry and its government allies to their advantage. Moreover, the chapter shows how, after this decade, the roles and alliances of the pharmaceutical industry and the government were later reconfigured until they reached their current form.

Secondly, our chapter analyzes how the patent regime and the protection of the right to health were balanced throughout the different moments in which new international IP norms were received domestically. We question those who tend to equate the interests of the national pharmaceutical industry with those of the general public regarding access to medicines. Our chapter shows that the tensions present in the struggle for an IP regime during the 1990s have been overcome and replaced by new cooperative mechanisms that today bring together multinational and local pharmaceutical companies. We argue that, together with other transformations, these close ties may well have contributed to marginalizing the role of patents in determining the cost of medicines and to reducing the impact of patenting decisions on fair and efficient access to healthcare.

Our study is based on archival data, documents, and in-depth semi-structured interviews. We reviewed legislative files, laws, administrative documents, court precedents, and other relevant legal materials;[2] the press news published between 1990 and 2010 in the three most heavily circulated national newspapers;[3] and reports and other documents regarding the healthcare system, and the pharmaceutical industry and market. Additionally, we conducted thirty-two interviews with representatives of the national and the multinational pharmaceutical sector; current and former public officials of the National Ministry of Health (including former ministers of health) and other government agencies; former legislators and congressional advisors; lawyers and other experts in the pharmaceutical industry, in IP, international trade, and healthcare; trade unionists; and representatives of NGOs working in the areas of human rights, health, and science and technology.[4]

The chapter is organized as follows. In section I, we present a summary description of the recursivity of the struggle for the renovation of the IP legal regime, with its international, local, and interface stages. Section II then offers an overview of the Argentine pharmaceutical industry and health system—that is, the context in which the balancing between pharmaceutical patents and the right to health was struck. In section III, we describe the intricate process that was initiated in 1980 and culminated in the adoption of a new IP regulatory framework in the mid-1990s. Section IV describes the actors and mechanisms involved in that process. In section V, we illustrate the implementation phase of the new patent regulations that ensued, stressing the confrontation between pro-IP actors and their opponents. In this section, we review the continuity of congressional negotiations over the passage of a new data exclusivity law (section V.A), the impact of the Instituto Nacional de Propiedad Industrial (INPI), and the emergence of courts as settings for contestation (section V.B). Section VI, which looks at Argentina's negotiations before the dispute settlement mechanisms of the WTO, demonstrates the reconnection of the domestic stage with the global arena in the interface provided by the WTO forum. In section VII, we proceed to study the changes that followed Argentina's 2002 economic crisis, with special emphasis on the new national medicines policy and the participation of the country in a host of international IP initiatives. Finally, section VIII critically assesses the potential effects of the recursivity of the debate over the right to health.

[2] The review of court decisions is limited to those related to disputes over pharmaceutical patents that were available in the database of the Federal Court of Appeals in Civil and Commercial Matters located in the City of Buenos Aires, and in the databases of two of the most important local legal reporters: *La Ley* and *Jurisprudencia Argentina*.

[3] Press articles were reviewed for the three main national newspapers: *La Nación*, *Clarín*, and *Página 12*.

[4] The interviews were conducted between November 2010 and January 2011.

I. Recursivity in the Reform of the Argentine IP Regime

Our study of the domestic experience in the development of a contemporary IP regime begins in late 1989, when the US government intensified its pressures on Argentina to adopt a new regulatory framework, and concludes twenty years later, when the controversy over pharmaceutical patents had been significantly tamed. Based on our empirical findings, we reconstruct the path of domestic IP reform and its interface with the global IP regime (see Figure 2.1). As mentioned above, following other researchers we assume that the international struggles over pharmaceutical IP rules have undergone two different cycles defined by their framing of pharmaceutical patents: first, in terms of international trade, and, second, as a public health matter. In observing the domestic experience, we argue that these two international cycles have overlapped with one large cycle at the national stage. From the perspective of the local IP regime, the domestic cycle can itself be divided into three different phases. The initial phase, from 1989 to 1995, led to the enactment of a new IP law. This phase was characterized by the participation of a powerful domestic pharmaceutical sector that, together with its local allies in the Argentine Congress, faced the demands of the US government, the multinational pharmaceutical industry, and their domestic partners in the Ministry of Finance, in what has been described as the "battle on patents."[5] During that phase, in a clear deployment of available mechanisms (Halliday 2009), domestic players managed to first delay, and then frustrate, a large part of the pro-IP agenda. In the following years, this process also led to a reconfiguration of both the local IP regime and the local pharmaceutical market and to more effective resistance to the harmonization of local laws with international IP standards.

The second phase of the domestic cycle began in 1995/6 and was dedicated to the implementation of the TRIPS commitments reached during the Uruguay Round of the General Agreement on Tariffs and Trade (GATT). In this period, our study identifies two salient confrontations. In the first, which took place from 1995 to 2002, the conflict over implementation of the new legislation extended to other forums, including Executive branch agencies and courts. Once again, actors in conflict over pharmaceutical patents went head to head without sparing resources. In that period, the multinational industry attempted to apply the new legislative framework broadly and to close off spaces that might offer the national industry room to maneuver. In a series of administrative proceedings in the INPI, Argentina's patent office, and cases taken to the federal courts, large international companies promoted a strict interpretation of IP rules.

Meanwhile, the US government continued its coercive strategies to impose its views of TRIPS and to impose TRIPS-plus standards. Additionally, toward the end of the 1990s, American pressure was exerted through the WTO dispute settlement

[5] The press frequently used the expression "battle" to refer to the dispute over patents and legal change (*Página 12* 1990a, 1990b).

mechanism.[6] The United States pressured the Argentine government to harmonize its legislation to TRIPS and, later, to adopt "TRIPS plus" demands. Once again, both in domestic settings as well as in the WTO, negotiations provided opportunities for resistance, in which the Argentine government and pharmaceutical industry had the chance to foil various demands of the supporters of strong protection.

In the last months of 2001 and during 2002, Argentina faced a deep social, economic, and political crisis. The rapid succession of events in the first months of the crisis and its effects on the structure of the healthcare system offered an unprecedented window of opportunity to promote change. The National Ministry of Health used this opening to establish an equally unprecedented national policy on medicines (Spanish: *políticanacional de medicamentos*, PNM) (De La Puente and Tobar 2007). The inclusion of medicines in a health agenda in which they had previously been practically absent, together with the transformations in the domestic pharmaceutical market that had been partially motivated by the struggle over the IP regime, led to a redrawing of the map of domestic disputes. In this new regime, the issue of patents became significantly less salient, and created a space in which old opponents forged new alliances (Vasallo and Falbo 2007). We identify the years that run from the 2002 crisis to the end of 2011, when the research for this chapter was completed, as the third phase in the domestic cycle for a new IP regime. This period marked a different implementation experience from the one typical of the second half of the 1990s.

Starting in 2002, the newly adopted measures of a PNM provoked multiple tensions, which caused the national and multinational pharmaceutical laboratories to reach an agreement on key issues on which to confront the new initiatives. As a result, the two sectors joined efforts to oppose a congressional policy, established in August of that year, to require doctors to prescribe medicines by international nonproprietary names (the INN policy). At around the same time, the intensity of American demands for pharmaceutical patents abated: a dispute focused on patent protection was resolved in the context of the WTO settlement procedures and both countries submitted a mutually agreed solution to the Dispute Settlement Board of the WTO.[7] The results of the agreement were immediately implemented by the new domestic legislation passed in 2003.

[6] American pressure was also exerted through the WTO dispute settlement mechanism, where the United States contended that Argentina failed to provide exclusive rights to commercialize pharmaceutical products and that it offered ineffective protection for pharmaceutical test data. Argentina—Patent Protection for Pharmaceuticals and Test Data Protection for Agricultural Chemicals—Request for Consultations by the United States, WT/DS171/1 (October 5, 1999). One year later, the American government requested further consultations with the government of Argentina, referring to article 4 of the Understanding on Rules and Procedures Governing the Settlement of Disputes and article 64 of the TRIPS Agreement, which related to different aspects of Law 24,481 (as amended by Law 24,572), which was implemented by Decree 260/96, and also concerned data protection. WT/DS196/1, IP/D/22 (June 6, 2000).

[7] Argentina—Patent Protection for Pharmaceuticals and Test Data Protection for Agricultural Chemicals and Argentina—Certain Measures on the Protection of Patents and Test Data. WT/DS196, WT/DS171/3l, WT/DS196/4 (June 20, 2002).

Since then, although the conflict over the pharmaceutical patents endures, it has lost the vigor it had in the nineties. Likely explanations for the marginalization of the subject in recent years include the radical transformation of the Argentine strategic position on the global map, as well as the migration of international disputes toward other IP matters; changes in the position of the national and multinational industry in the medicines market; and the limited use of patents on medicines sold within Argentina. As a result, the battle has been lately relegated to isolated episodes that include the intermittent participation of Argentina in global initiatives such as the Development Agenda in the World Intellectual Property Organization (WIPO), and regional initiatives like the Declaration on Intellectual Property, Access to Medicines, and Public Health, which was signed by ten Latin American countries. However, new tensions have emerged. The Argentine pharmaceutical industry has become a potential beneficiary of the TRIPS compulsory licensing provisions: countries that lack the capacity to manufacture medicines on their own can now make Argentina a potential source for safe and inexpensive products, to the arguable detriment of foreign manufacturers.

From a distributive point of view, the domestic cycle of the IP global episode that began in the late 1990s still poses questions from the perspective of the right to health. Our findings suggest that in the course of the last two decades, the public's interest in access to medicines has remained largely unprotected, in spite of its alleged vindication. Even though some important measures were adopted in the last decade in order to regulate aspects of the pharmaceutical market, throughout the twenty years studied in this chapter, government oversight of the pharmaceutical market has been sparse. What is more, from a comparative perspective, during this period, the cost of medicines remained high, and the proportion of spending on medicines held steadily at an average of 30 percent of the total health expenditure (Tobar 2008). This relatively high spending on drugs has been criticized as irrational. It has taken place against the backdrop of an unfair and inefficient health system—a system that has undergone only piecemeal reforms to tackle some of its serious deficits (McGuire 2010)—and in the absence of strong actors capable of mobilizing in defense of the right to health.

II. Background: The Argentine Pharmaceutical Industry and Market

When the domestic IP norm-making phase began in the late 1980s, the 1864 Patents for Inventions Law No. 111, which excluded patents for pharmaceutical products, was in effect.[8] Together with longstanding industrial policies, this

[8] Despite the fact that Argentina had ratified the Paris Convention for the Protection of Industrial Property in 1966, Law No. 111 was never adapted to the requirements of this treaty. Argentina, as did most of the countries in Latin America, remained in a position of "absolute reserve" regarding the territorial expansion of IP regulation through both the Berne Convention and the Paris Convention (Roffe 2007: 53).

regulatory framework had provided rules that facilitated the emergence of a wide and powerful domestic pharmaceutical sector. However, in the early 1990s, the expected results of the Uruguay Round and the liberalization reform policies threatened to destabilize this historic protection of local laboratories (Vasallo 1999).

Between 1950 and 1980, Argentina applied an Import Substitution Industrialization (ISI) policy. Through high tariffs on imported pharmaco-chemical raw materials, and the prioritization of national companies in the registration of medicines for marketing (Katz et al. 1997: 86), the ISI policy led to the expansion of the local pharmaceutical industry. As in Brazil and Mexico, the ISI period contributed to the emergence of an industrial sector of national "medium-sized family [companies] that achieved relative importance and certain technical soundness" (*our translation*) (Katz et al. 1997: 20).[9] Since then, one of the most stable traits of this "peculiar and idiosyncratic model of industrial organization" (Katz et al. 1997: 20) has been the local production of "copies"[10] with active principles (ingredients) acquired abroad by Argentine firms.

In Argentina, "copies" or "similar drugs" differ from originals and also from generics with respect to the type of studies that are required for approval by the health authorities. As part of the cycle of research, the manufacturers of original drugs (generally covered by patents) must produce pre-clinical studies and clinical trials showing bioavailability (the concentration of the drug in the body), safety, and therapeutic effect. In the Argentine market, the segment of non-original drugs (secondary source off-patent) includes generic drugs and copies. These are distinguishable, as the generics are required to certify bioequivalence studies in the health registry; the similar drugs do not need to meet this requirement (Homedes and Ugalde 2005). While pharmaceutical products must be sold under their international nonproprietary names (INN), drug companies generally make efforts to distinguish their products through the use of trademarks. Thus, not only do the manufacturers of original patented drugs use branding as a key resource, so do the producers of generics and similar drugs. For this reason, the industry has been embroiled in considerable and ongoing litigation over rights to prestigious brand names.

Equally important, the local production of "copies" has historically been complemented by the importation of finished drugs, carried out by both the subsidiaries

[9] From the 1950s until the late 1970s, three models of organization for pharmaceutical manufacturers prevailed in the country (Katz et al. 1997: 85). The first model included the group of national laboratories importing active principles (ingredients) and other supplies from "non-patent markets" such as those in Italy and Spain (Katz et al. 1997: 70). A second type of firm was part of a vertically integrated industry along with fine chemistry (principally starting materials), which enabled the production, in small and multipurpose manufacturing plants, of pharmaceutical primary materials, especially antibiotics. Finally, a third group of companies were the subsidiaries of multinational pharmaceutical companies that received supplies at transfer prices in a tariff protection context (Katz et al. 1997: 87–8). The politics of economic liberalization implemented by the military government in 1976, and later reintroduced in the 1990s, frustrated the development of the second type of firms—that is, the national pharmaceutical sector that had tried to achieve vertical integration with pharmacochemistry.

[10] Exceptions include drugs that use high-risk molecules (e.g. some antiretroviral drugs), for which bioequivalence studies are required.

of multinational pharmaceutical companies as well as by domestic firms (Katz et al. 1997). Over the past four decades, the presence of these multinational companies in the local market has varied significantly. In the late seventies, as a result of the domestic economic crisis, several major multinational pharmaceuticals transferred some of their products to Argentine firms and then left the country (Katz et al. 1997: 89). After the withdrawal of the foreign companies, local laboratories seized the opportunity and managed to accumulate experience and knowledge of the internal market. As a result, they progressed to the point where they could add value to products by tailoring them to domestic conditions and to the needs of the local healthcare system. These firms also built strong ties with governmental authorities, and developed lobbying power with government and financing agents (Vasallo 1999). Their political and market capital would bear fruit during the IP reform process that is studied in the following sections.

Among other things, the comparative advantages on which the national pharmaceutical sector was built include the production of similar drugs. This feature of industrial behavior developed because of the exclusion in the patent laws for pharmaceuticals. In that competitive environment, national firms were able to base their business strategy on the introduction of new molecules simultaneously with the patent holder (Katz et al. 1997: 72). The copies of products launched into some Asian and Latin America markets, accompanied by strong local brand differentiation, generated brand loyalty to domestic firms (e.g. the Roemmers' Enalapril, marketed as Lotrial).[11] This practice even allowed for a small number of prestigious local pharmaceuticals to impose prices equivalent to those of their multinational counterparts.[12]

During the nineties and in the context of the battle for a new IP regime, this pharmaceutical market made up of "brand copies" produced by national laboratories was strengthened through the takeover of distribution and marketing chains and through a fierce marketing strategy in which the industry invested nearly 50 percent of its earnings (Tobar 2008: 15). The strategy, directed towards health professionals through so-called detail men (Vasallo 1999), was complemented by a high rate of product launches and by a broad portfolio of medicines that provided other comparative advantages favoring the expansion of domestic pharmaceutical firms (Katz et al. 1997).

This model prompted "the rapid relative expansion [of the national industry] vis-à-vis the subsidiaries of international companies and the achievement of high profitability rates" (Katz et al. 1997: 87). Thus, except for brief periods of time, Argentine pharmaceuticals have maintained a share accounting for more than 50 percent of the total sales in the local market (González García, De la Puente, and Tarragona 2005: 106). In 2010, national companies controlled 56.1 percent of the market and 61.3 percent of units sold (IMS Health 2010). The predominance of national pharmaceuticals in the local market is a special feature of the Argentine

[11] It is estimated that branded drugs are approximately 1,200 percent more expensive than non-branded medicines prescribed by INN (Szuba 2003 cited by De la Puente et al. 2009: 10).

[12] See Manual Farmacéutico Kairos, available at <http://www.alfabeta.net/mf/>.

context that differentiates it from other local industries in the developing world. Indeed, at the global level, this is a characteristic shared only by US, Japanese, and German markets (De la Puente et al. 2009: 15).

Another important feature of the local pharmaceutical industry is that it has been highly concentrated in the hands of a small group of domestic and foreign firms, among which Argentine companies have a high market share.[13] In 1992, eight of the top fifteen pharmaceuticals were local manufacturers (González García 1994: 41), and, in 2010, nine Argentine firms were among the fifteen leading companies (IMS Health 2010). Today, Bagó and Roemmers, the main national pharmaceutical holdings, are positioned in the first and the second place of this ranking (Vincent, Suárez, and Franciosi 2007; IMS Health 2010). This characteristic, which endures with minor fluctuations, is, once again, shared only by the United States, Japan, and Germany. Although the market is in the hands of a small group of companies, both national and foreign, the main Argentine companies were among those with the strongest sales. By 1992, for instance, eight out of the fifteen laboratories with the highest market share were Argentine, and the first three among them were Roemmers, Bagó, and Sidus, longstanding companies in the sector (González García 1994: 41).

Finally, this pharmaceutical market functions against the backdrop of an overtly fragmented healthcare system: divided into national, provincial, and municipal levels, there is a public and a contributory healthcare subsector at each level (McGuire 2010).[14] In this system, expenditures in medicines account for 30 percent of the total health spending. Moreover, until 2002 such expenditures accounted for almost 50 percent of out-of-pocket expenses (Perticara 2008). Significantly, however, in the last decade and as a result of the national pharmaceutical policies implemented in 2002, various institutions within the different subsectors of the health system finance most drug expenditures.[15]

III. The First Phase of the Domestic Cycle, 1989–1995

The triggering moment for the global norm making struggles that are the background of our domestic case study can be traced to a series of transformations generated in the United States in the mid-1980s which reinforced the relationship between IP and international trade (Drahos 1997). This link was foreshadowed by the United States Trade Act of 1974. It was strengthened through the efforts of the

[13] Ten percent of the firms are responsible for 77 percent of the total sales of the sector (González García, De La Puente, and Tarragona 2005: 113). Data from 2010 show that the largest ten companies own 42.8 percent of the pharmaceutical market (IMS Health 2010).

[14] The contributory healthcare system comprises in turn a number of private insurers and social funds, known as *Obras Sociales*, run by unions. For a comprehensive description of the Argentine healthcare system and all its subsectors, see Programa Naciones Unidaspara el Desarrollo (2011).

[15] Several of our interviewees pointed to the rules that allocate most of the expenditures in medicine to financing institutions and the public health system as an explanation for civil society demobilization in the fight for better prices.

Advisory Committee on Trade Negotiations (ACTN), a consortium of research-intensive industries (including the pharmaceutical sector), along with their lobbyists, consultants, and lawyers, to devise international policies aimed at increasing protection for intellectual property protection abroad (Sell 2003, 2008; Braithwaite and Drahos 2000: 61).

The episode began when the United States, encouraged by the ACTN leaders, initiated two global forum shifts (Drahos 2004a; Helfer 2007, 2009; Sell 2009).[16] In the first, a horizontal forum shift, IP norm making was moved from its traditional home in WIPO to negotiations over the General Agreement on Tariffs and Trade (the GATT, later the WTO). Then, in a second, vertical, forum shift, the United States used trade promises, threats of commercial retaliation, and pressure through the mechanism of Special 301 Reports and Watch Lists to negotiate bilateral and regional agreements for the protection of patents.[17] These transformations set off a global norm-making process that culminated internationally in the adoption of the TRIPS Agreement. At the domestic level, the changes inaugurated the cycle that led to the creation of a new IP regime for Argentina.

This globalization process, launched by the United States in the mid-eighties, arrived in Argentina around 1989, when direct pressures for a new patent law intensified.[18] That year, facing the threat of commercial retaliations and a demand for compensation in the amount of $100 million, Domingo Cavallo, then Ministry of Foreign Affairs, committed to the US government to enact a new IP regime within two years (Jauregui 2003). At the time, Argentina was facing a complex economic crisis that culminated in the replacement of Raúl Alfonsín by Carlos Menem as President of Argentina. The changes also precipitated a decision by the United States to place the country on the Special 301 Watch List, where it was threatened with trade sanctions similar to those imposed earlier on Brazil (*Clarín* 1990).

During the following years, Menem implemented a combination of market liberalization and state reform programs, both of which were strengthened in March 1991 by Domingo Cavallo, who had by then switched jobs and was put in charge of the Ministry of Finance. At that point, the new Minister quickly

[16] The dynamic of forum shifting includes moving an agenda from one international forum to another, pursuing agendas simultaneously in different forums, or the abandonment of a certain forum by a country or other global actors (Drahos 2004a).

[17] Special Section 301 Reports and Watch Lists, Omnibus Trade and Competitiveness Act of 1989, Pub. L. No. 100-418, 102 Stat. 1176–9; 19 U.S.C. § 2242, are used when the US government finds that a country is affecting US exports through unfair trade practices. Persistent behavior (and presence on a Watch List) can lead to commercial retaliation, which can include restrictions on imports into the United States. As restrictions are not necessarily directed at the sector that infringed the relevant rule, they generate internal pressures (from the sector affected by the retaliation) within the country being sanctioned. For other examples of regional negotiations, see Chapters 7 and 4 (on Ecuador and Central America) in this volume.

[18] Pressures had already appeared in the mid-1970s (interview with Ezequiel Holmberg), and they increased through the following decade. At the time, Alfonsín's government tried to stop US and EU demands, winning "as much time as possible" (interview with Roberto Lugones). International experiences such as those of Spain and Italy provided a warning about the potential consequences of reforming the IP regime in line with US demands (interview with Aldo Neri).

achieved what his predecessors could not: the decrease of high inflation rates through his Convertibility Plan. By the early months of 1992, Argentina had entered the Brady Plan, which the United States instituted to deal with the debt crisis. As part of the arrangement, Argentina implemented several deregulatory initiatives, privatized various state companies, and decentralized public utilities. In a short period of time, the country had converted itself into a "model student" of the Washington Consensus[19] (Torre 1997).

In those years, American pressure for a new IP regulatory framework did not cease. According to contemporary press accounts, United States Ambassador Terence Todman was the principal domestic spokesperson for the pro-IP demands. Each of the Ambassador's public appearances, each visit from United States government representatives (*Clarín* 1991a; *Clarín* 1991b), and Menem and his delegations' trips to the North, provided opportunities for further pressures in favor of a new framework. The United States also used every available inducement mechanism to pursue the adoption of a new IP statute (Braithwaite and Drahos 2000).[20] Beginning in 1990, the United States' threat to retaliate against Argentine exports and its claims for compensation were further supplemented by a system of rewards that included promises of new investments in business as well as the relaxation of the conditions for loans from the International Monetary Fund (IMF) and the World Bank.[21] As the Menem administration confirmed its alignment with the United States, the pressure increased. At the same time, however, the United States' plans for the fast enactment of a patent law had become part of what was now a more ambitious bilateral relationship for both partners.

The fall of the Berlin Wall and the dismantling of the Soviet bloc had convinced Menem of the overwhelming triumph of capitalism. By 1991, it was clear that the country needed to secure global integration through alignment with the United States and Europe. The abandonment of the Non-Aligned Movement (NAL), the freeze of sovereignty claims over the Malvinas (the Falkland) Islands, and the release of Argentine troops to the Persian Gulf War were three of the principal signs that the government spent that year in its efforts to attract attention and capital. Those initiatives heralded the "carnal relations" Argentina would enjoy with the United States throughout the decade (Novaro 2009).

Meanwhile the demands of the United States for a new patent regime continued.[22] Yet, foreseeing Congress's resistance, even within his party,[23] Menem sought to reduce the pressures for a new law. Finally, in September 1991, right at

[19] See Dreyfuss and Rodriguez, Chapter 1 in this volume.

[20] According to Drahos (2004b: 210), the enforcement pyramid, used by powerful actors, is a sequential system that links punishment and persuasion—a pyramid that begins with persuasion as the tool in the base of the pyramid and ends with punishment at the apex of the pyramid.

[21] As Braithwaite and Drahos indicate (2000: 62), the ACTN had proposed that the US Executive Directors examine background information on donors' compliance with IP protection rules while voting at the IMF, the World Bank, and regional banks.

[22] Although the EU has promoted a pro-IP agenda outside its bloc, in this paper we focus mostly on the initiatives driven by the United States due to its strong presence in the fight for an Argentine IP framework during the enactment phase of the patent legislation.

[23] Interview with Mirta Levis.

the expiration of Cavallo's promised two-year period, the Executive branch presented its first draft bill, elaborated in the Ministry of Finance. The bill, which was to enter into force immediately, provided for the recognition of exclusive patents rights on pharmaceutical products for a term of twenty years. While it recognized compulsory licensing, it allowed it only in exceptional circumstances. The text, in short, reflected the main demands of the United States and multinational companies; it was justified locally as a tool to penetrate international markets and to develop domestic competitive conditions that would reduce the price of medicines (*Clarín* 1991a).[24]

However, when the bill was introduced into the House of Deputies in September 1991, it soon became clear that the experience of Chile, where adoption of a new law proceeded rapidly, would not be repeated in Argentina.[25] Rather, the politics of enactment of a new IP law would demand considerably more time, effort, and pressures than had been predicted in 1989 when Cavallo had made his commitment for a new law. The process of putting the new patent regime on "the books" was to be marked by resistance from a group of domestic actors. In the "battle" for the law, these actors would manage to redefine the scope of the 1991 Executive's draft bill and to delay its final approval until 1995.[26] The domestic pharmaceutical industry, represented by the Cámara Industrial de Laboratorios Farmacéuticos Argentinos (CILFA), legislators from the Peronist Party (Partido Justicialista, PJ)[27] and its factions, along with the opposition, led then by the Radical Party (Unión Cívica Radical, UCR), mounted the counterattack.

Although the same political party (the PJ) controlled both the Presidency and the majority in Congress, the fight between the executive and legislative branches to shape the new patent law took five years and exposed significant divisions among the different factions of the ruling party. Furthermore, the negotiations illustrated the maneuvering room that Menem had available to interact with an increasingly powerful Minister of Finance and with the opposing factions of the Peronist Party in Congress.[28] As recalled by prominent actors,[29] throughout the struggle for a new

[24] Towards 1991, this last concern appeared especially important due to the exceptional increase in the price of medicines after the economic deregulation of the sector (*Página 12* 1992).

[25] See Millaleo's chapter in this volume for further details regarding the process of legal reforms of the Chilean IP regime.

[26] Before or during 1996, and together with Brazil, Barbados, Panamá, and Trinidad and Tobago, Argentina was one of the first countries to enact a new IP framework. Neither Honduras, México, Panamá, nor Uruguay made use of the transitional deadline of five years granted by the TRIPS Agreement to developing countries, as they reformed their legislation in 1999 (Oliveira and Costa Chavés 2010: 395). Furthermore, most of the countries that delayed the reform of their legal regimes also chose to postpone their entrance into the WTO (Oliveira and Costa Chavés 2010: 401).

[27] Partido Justicialista (PJ) is another name for Partido Peronista or the Peronist Party as we refer to it in this chapter.

[28] During these years, the country witnessed the reorganization of the different factions of the ruling party and the establishment of a volatile relationship between Menem and his Minister of Finance.

[29] Several interviewees referred to the complexity of the enactment process. In particular, they made reference to the succession of events between 1994 and 1996. The complexity was also evidenced by the broad coverage the subject received in the local media.

IP regime, the country witnessed one of the most complex lawmaking processes in its history (Quintana and Piani 2009: 23).[30]

The first victory for the domestic resistance to a new IP regulation was the delay in the consideration of the 1991 Executive's bill, which lost parliamentary status by the end of 1992. While the negotiations of the Uruguay Round of the GATT were still open, and the country had other issues under negotiation with the United States, the option of playing for time figured highly among the strategies of domestic resistance.[31] The impasse ostensibly concluded in March 1993, when the Executive branch reintroduced its bill in the Senate. But even at its submission, both Peronist Party and Radical Party legislators made clear that the process for assessing the bill would take time (*Clarín* 1993b). Statements in this regard were grounded in appeals to nationalists' arguments. Congressional speakers announced their intention to examine the bill and to take all the time they needed to understand the technical issues, listen to interested parties and experts, and deliberate on the advisability of adopting a regulatory framework of the sort proposed in the bill. Legislators were not alone; a powerful parliamentary lobby led by CILFA (domestic pharmaceutical companies) offered support and technical expertise to oppose pro-IP demands. These demands, they argued, would lead to the end of the development of a high-tech national industry, which in turn would send a negative signal regarding investment in science and technology (Novaro 2009: 445).

Against the backdrop of GATT multilateral negotiations and renewed United States pressure on the country, Congress began, in June 1993, an unusual set of public hearings to consider the bill.[32] During eighteen sessions led by José Genoud, a member of the Radical Party in the Senate, and by other members of the five parliament commissions, Congress heard the opinions of the Ministers of Finance and Health, representatives of business chambers—the Cámara Argentina de Especialidades Medicinales (CAEME) and CILFA—along with experts, and academic institutions. The meetings helped to highlight the decisive importance of patent rights over pharmaceutical products in the struggle for a new IP regime.

In the course of the hearings, United States pressure mounted. James Cheek, who became the United States Ambassador to Argentina in 1993, began a series of media appearances, which continued throughout his entire term, where he insistently urged the reform of the IP regime (*Pagina 12* 1995d). Simultaneously, another sector of the United States government tried to seduce Menem with promises to let Argentina join the North American Free Trade Agreement (NAFTA) (*Página 12* 1994b). However, Menem did not press Congress; he simply sent a new bill to the legislators.[33] Throughout 1994, American pressure reached such intensity that the press of the time reported monthly negotiations held by

[30] One of the characteristics of this complex process was the resort to questionable legislative practices, such as the use of decrees and vetoes by the National Executive branch.

[31] Some interviewees suggested that this aspect of the local strategy was developed by the government and the pharmaceutical industry.

[32] In 1993, under the Clinton administration, the United States once again placed Argentina on the Priority Watch List of Special 301 (*Clarín* 1993a).

[33] Interview with Mirta Levis.

Menem and the Minister of Finance with high-level US officials, including Vice President Al Gore.[34] Nonetheless, despite American efforts, Congress—already on the side of resistance to patents—announced that it would not be intimidated.

Spectators of, and players in, the confrontation observed that at the time knowledge about IP was scarce, both locally and around the developing world.[35] However, even if the political momentum and the technical capacities of the anti-IP contingent were mostly of local origin, many of the technical tools for moderating patent rights used throughout the struggle for a new IP regime were nurtured in international and regional exchanges (e.g. *Página 12* 1993a). The Third World Patent Convention, held in New Delhi on March 1990, represented a milestone as it gathered experts, politicians, and Argentine businessmen. Advocating a new instrument on intellectual property rights for the developing world as well as several proposals for the modification of the draft agreement for the Uruguay Round of GATT, the gathering resulted in the "New Delhi Declaration towards a Third World Convention on Intellectual Property and Obligations" (*Página12* 1993b).

Meanwhile, in line with his counterparts from India and Brazil, the Argentine ambassador to the Uruguay Round of the GATT, Nestor Stancanelli, undertook arduous negotiations over what would later be formalized as part of the TRIPS Agreement.[36] Concomitantly, the Asociación Latinoamericana de Industrias Farmacéuticas (ALIFAR),[37] a group of national pharmaceutical firms from Latin America, constantly warned about the potential dangers involved in the adoption of a universal IP regime.[38] In small forums, there were already signs of what would later become a counter-hegemonic position in the global fight for harmonization of IP regimes.[39] Throughout the IP norm-making cycle going on in the region and within Argentina, this resistance would involve political interventions including lobbying, public statements, and other legal advocacy initiatives (Sousa Santos 2007: 32).

As repeatedly asserted by Cheek, the US government considered the Uruguay Round agreements as "a floor and not a ceiling" (*Pagina 12* 1994b). In contrast, anti-IP actors referred to the TRIPS Agreement as a set of minimum standards that allowed each country to modulate and adapt their domestic IP laws and policies to local conditions. This was the view of the Argentine Congress, which by 1994 was already considering a bill with substantial differences from the bill originally drafted

[34] In February 1995, Menem met with Michael Kantor, the United States Trade Representative; in March the American Vice President Al Gore visited the country; in May, Ron Brown, the Secretary of Commerce, traveled to Argentina, and after his visit the country was given two months to enact a new IP regime, after which sanctions were to be imposed (*Página 12* 1994).

[35] Interviews with Mirta Levis, Roberto Lugones, and Roberto Bisang.

[36] Interview with Mirta Levis.

[37] For further information regarding the role of ALIFAR in Latin America see Andía's chapter in this volume.

[38] During the parliamentary debate, ALIFAR rejected the pressure of the Unites States government (*Página 12* 1993c).

[39] The description of the reactions of the national industry, its experts, public officials, and local politicians as counter-hegemonic praxis does not necessarily imply identification with a progressive perspective (Rajagopal 2005: 275).

by the Executive Branch. By then, the dispute over patents had also become part of a larger conflict within the Peronist Party, with different factions questioning Menem's reforms to liberalize the economy, as well as his strategies for integrating the country into the first world.

After the conclusion of the constitutional reform process, which occupied the country's attention between August and September 1994, the Senate unanimously voted in favor of the patent bill on November 16. The approved bill was far from satisfying US desires, however. The American government immediately communicated its discontent and tried to pressure the House to adopt modifications (*Página 12* 1994c). Nonetheless, on March 23, 1995, the House passed the bill without changes. With the enactment of the Patent and Utility Models Law No. 24,481,[40] once again the Peronist members of the House showed their discipline, a discipline exercised also to defy the President.[41]

A few months earlier, through Law No. 24,425, Congress had ratified the Final Act of the Uruguay Round of GATT containing the WTO Agreements, and the ministerial decisions and declarations, including the TRIPS Agreement. With regard to pharmaceutical patents, however, Argentina's new IP regime represented an important concession to the anti-IP demands. As in the original Executive bill, the new law extended patent protection to pharmaceutical products. However, the law also included: (a) an eight-year transitional period, (b) only two years of retroactive protection (basically, a refusal to grant protection to all inventions in the patent pipeline as had been demanded), (c) a fifteen-year term of protection, counted from the grant date, and (d) expiration of the patent in the event the invention was not practiced in Argentina. The law also incorporated wider criteria for parallel imports, which was based on the principle of international exhaustion of rights, and it permitted compulsory licensing. Finally, though very vaguely, the law put the burden of proof on the plaintiff in civil proceedings involving the infringement of process patent rights.

Domestic actors had transformed the central structure of the Executive branch's proposal, straying too far from US demands. Immediately, the United States renewed pressure on the Executive branch to veto the law. In addition to calls from the White House, in April 1995, former President George H. W. Bush visited Argentina. After a lunch with Menem, Bush declared to the local media that the IP law issue "would be solved" (*Página 12* 1995a). The United States spared no efforts, and with the constant visits of high-level officials, it resumed the use of coercion and conditioning mechanisms, to which it added the threat of challenging Argentina under the Dispute Settlement Understanding established as part of the WTO system. Meanwhile, domestic supporters of a strong pro-IP regime in the

[40] In March 1995, just before the enactment of the new law, Menem met Vice President Al Gore and requested him to avoid interfering in the House of Deputies, for this would contribute nothing to the IP reforms (*La Nación* 1995).

[41] This was a typical trait of the Peronist legislative behavior at the time, as described extensively by Jones and Hwang (2005).

Ministry of Finance and CAEMe ignited a heated conflict that would only abate in 1996, after the resignation of Cavallo.

Enactment of the law in March 1995 inaugurated a striking succession of exchanges between the Congress and the Executive. The first reaction occurred days after the law was passed, when Menem partially objected to it by vetoing sixteen articles through Decree No. 548/95. A month later, while Congress was in the process of overriding the veto, Cavallo tried to impose an alternative regulatory framework through Decree No. 621/95. The decree repealed old Law No. 111 and declared the TRIPS Agreement to be self-executing. Congress then announced, by unanimity, its insistence on ten of the vetoed articles, rejecting only the domestic manufacturing requirement. Thus modified, and with a unanimous vote in the Senate, Law No. 24,481 was formally enacted.

Without other legal tools, the Ministry of Finance tried to win time and to negotiate a new norm. In doing so, it delayed for several months the publication of the law in the Official Gazette. In its clear role as *intermediary* between foreign and domestic interests, as per the categories proposed by Carruthers and Halliday (2006), the Ministry of Finance resisted and negotiated throughout the year—a year that was also marked by the presidential election that led to Menem's second term. Confronted with the escalation of the conflict, the President summoned his ministers, the speakers of both houses of Congress, and the leaders of the majority in Congress. Despite Cavallo's objection to the Law No. 24,481, which adjusted Argentine law to the TRIPS Agreement, he and the rest of the people convened by Menem reached a reform agreement reflected in the First Corrective Law No. 24,572, which was passed in September 1995.[42] The law reduced the transitional period from eight years to five and the retroactive recognition of patents granted in foreign countries (known as *patentes de reválida*) from two years to one.[43] Argentina had had a broad view of parallel imports and the new rule also imposed constraints on its application in accordance with the discussions surrounding the TRIPS Agreement. Further, the law clarified the circumstances for the reversion of the burden of proof in infringement cases (Murphy 1997). That is, it limited the authority of the judiciary to shift the burden of proof in "process of exclusion" proceedings.[44]

Disagreeing with the provisions on parallel imports and compulsory licensing, the US government and the Minister of Finance once more demanded a veto (Murphy 1997: 30). Failing in this attempt, Cavallo convinced Menem to issue Decree No. 590/95,[45] which was meant to regulate these two items by

[42] Simultaneously, upon request of the Ministry of Finance, the tax authorities investigated the assets of some legislators (*Página 12* 1995b).

[43] Despite this reduction in the transition period, Argentina was, together with Paraguay and Uruguay, one of the few countries that made use of the regulatory margins left open by TRIPS (Levis 2010: 289).

[44] "Process of exclusion" is the name given to the judicial proceedings by means of which the alleged owner of a patent demands the suppression of use by a third party that is infringing its IP right.

[45] There were multiple irregularities in the approval process of this Decree. For example, there were two Decrees regulating patents that were both registered with the number 590/95s. Due to the progress of numeration through the year, one of the Decrees should have borne a higher number.

appealing to the self-executing nature of the TRIPS Agreement. Interpreting this measure as an undue interference, Congress reacted by passing the Second Corrective Law No. 24,603 on December 7, 1995. In its third patent law in less than a year, Congress insisted on its legislative priority in the determination of the IP regime in force, which was then considered as emerging from a harmonious interpretation of Laws No. 24,481 and No. 24,572 (the First Corrective Law).[46]

Still, the conflict was not settled. In the struggle for the last word regarding the valid text, and as a result of the interventions of the Minister of Finance, one month later the President vetoed the Second Corrective Law through Decree No. 3 of January 1996. In March 1996, however, the complex legislative process finally came to its conclusion. Congress and Menem reached an agreement to issue Decree No. 260/96, which approved the final valid text of the law.[47] This approval marked the end of the first phase of the domestic cycle over the fight for a new patent law.

In spite of the pressures exercised by the United States and CAEMe (*Página 12* 1995e), the intense confrontations for a new IP regime brought favorable results to the domestic industry. Argentina obtained a more flexible patent regime than those adopted by countries such as Chile, Mexico, or Brazil (Oliveira and Costa Chavés 2010: 397). The new regulatory framework "on the books" recognized patent holders' rights for pharmaceutical processes and products, but it also adopted the principle of international exhaustion, recognized ample exceptions to exclusive rights, and provided for other unauthorized uses, including an array of compulsory licenses. Furthermore, it was the Second Corrective Law No. 24,603 that created INPI, the patent office, as a new administrative agency.[48] As regards time limits, Argentine norms provided for a patent term of twenty years from the date of filing and a five-year transitional period for application of the TRIPS Agreement. As shown in Table 2.1, the enactment phase of the cycle resulted in the passage of four national laws, several vetoes, and decrees. It was also a process marked by mutual accusations of bribery between Congress and the Executive branch (*La Nación* 2001; *Página 12* 1995c), conflicts between factions of the Peronist Party, and multiple complaints from Senators and members of the House about Ambassador Cheek (*Página 12* 1993c, 1995d), and even a demand for the impeachment of President Menem for his overuse of vetoes and regulatory decrees (*Página 12* 1995f).

[46] Therefore, the new norm revoked Decree No. 590/95, replacing it by a second text that organized Laws No. 24,481 and No. 24,572.

[47] Later that same year, Congress approved a new law implementing article 39 of TRIPS (regarding data exclusivity). We discuss this episode in section V.A while considering the first stage of the implementation of the new patent regime.

[48] It was created as an independent agency, part of the National Finance Ministry.

Table 2.1 Evolution of IP laws and executive decrees, 1989–1996.

Date	Congress	National Executive Branch (Spanish: *Poder Ejecutivo Nacional*, PEN)
September 1989		The Ministry of Foreign Affairs concludes an agreement with United States promising the enactment of a new patent law within two years.
September 1991		PEN drafts bill and submits it to Congress.
November 1991	Senate Industrial Commission issues report on PEN bill.	
December 1993	1991 bill loses parliamentary status.	
March 1993		New bill drafted.
March 1993	Senators endorse PEN bill.	
	3 alternative bills are submitted in the Senate.	
April 1993	5 Senate Commissions, coordinated by Senator Genoud (UCR), begin public hearings with experts and interested parties.	
April 1993–4	18 public hearings.	
September 1994	Constitutional Convention.	1994 Constitutional Reform.
November 1994	Bill approved by Senate Commissions.	
	Senate unanimously passes bill	
December 1994	Enactment of Law No. 24,425, which approves the Final Act of the GATT Uruguay Round.	
March 1995	House of Deputies passes the Patent and Utility Models Law No. 24,481.	
April 1995		Decree No. 548/95 vetoes 16 articles of the law (partial veto)

(*Continued*)

Table 2.1 *Continued*

Date	Congress	National Executive Branch (Spanish: *Poder Ejecutivo Nacional*, PEN)
April 1995		Issuance of Decree No. 621/95, which regulates Law No. 111 and the TRIPS Agreement.
May 1995	Congress insists on approval of 10 vetoed articles of the law.	
September 1995	Congress passes Law No. 24572 (First Corrective Law).	
October 1995		By promulgating the First Corrective Law No. 24,572 through Decree No. 590/95, PEN regulates the law and alters its content.
December 1995	Congress passes Law No. 24,603 (Second Corrective Law) to indicate Law No. 24,572 takes precedence over Decree No. 590/95.	
January 1996		PEN vetoes Law No. 24,603 through Decree No. 3/96.
March 1996		Issuance of Decree No. 260/96.
December 1996	Congress passes the Confidentiality of Registered and Patented Data Law No. 24,766.	

IV. The Politics of Domestic Enactment: Actors and Mechanisms

A. Actors

The participants in the process of enactment of the new IP regulatory framework included an assortment of international and domestic actors that fought for the translation of global norms into Argentine law "on the books." A constant feature of this process was the continuous presence of representatives of the pharmaceutical industry, which served as the dynamic force driving the "battle" for the new law. Public officers, lobbyists, and representatives of the US government were also directly involved in the norm-making process. Together with the multinational pharmaceutical companies' lobby, CAEMe,[49] American ambassadors and high-profile US officials—supported later by representatives from European countries—mounted pressure on the Argentine government and deployed several mechanisms to press local authorities within the Executive and Congress.

Throughout this process, pro-IP actors benefited from the advice of experts and prestigious law firms. The Centro de Estudios para el Desarrollo de la Industria Químico-Farmacéutica Argentina (CEDIQUIFA) and the Asociación Argentina para el Desarrollo Tecnológico (ADEST) also provided information and acted in association with CAEMe. The Fundación de Investigaciones Económicas Latinoamericanas (FIEL), a local think tank formed by economists to support the views of the pro-IP groups, provided one of the pioneering research studies regarding the effects of patents on the local pharmaceutical industry (*Página 12* 1990a).[50]

In the domestic realm, the principal pro-IP intermediary during the enactment process was Domingo Cavallo and his team, first in the Ministry of Foreign Affairs, and later in the Ministry of Finance. In the different phases of debate for the enactment of a new law, the Minister confronted every sector of the Peronist Party, whose members resisted his agenda from both within the Executive Branch and Congress.

On the other side of the dispute was a powerful alliance set up by the domestic pharmaceutical industry, supported by the Peronist Party, the Radical Party (UCR), and the minority parties in Congress. Moreover, this alliance was represented by CILFA, which produced data and analyses regarding the impact of patents on the price of medicines. CILFA's reports competed in turn with the documents generated by FIEL.[51] Unlike the group on the other side of the struggle, and perhaps due to the precarious stage of the international anti-IP alliance, during

[49] Generally multinationals, represented by CAEMe, did not play a leading role. Instead, their interests were aligned with the actions carried out by the US authorities. Interview with Mirta Levis.

[50] See e.g. the document "Protection of the intellectual property rights" (1991).

[51] Interview with Mirta Levis.

the enactment process there were no global or regional players resisting passage of the new IP legislation.[52]

Throughout the process, Menem played an ambiguous and fluctuating role in his apparent tendency to favor "foreign" demands. His oscillating moods, especially in the last phase of the process for the enactment of a new regime, were probably among the reasons why Congress disfavored the bills put forward by the Ministry of Finance, although it had acted (essentially) as the speaker for US interests.

Among the local industry, the Cooperativa de Laboratorios Argentinos de Especialidades Medicinales (COOPERALA), the Unión Industrial Argentina (UIA), and the Confederación General Industrial (CGI) joined CILFA. Business associations concurred in the defense of one of the most powerful sectors of the domestic industry. But the challenge to the pro-IP model was also supported by prestigious professionals, including Professors Carlos Correa and Darío Bergel, and other members of the Centro de Estudios Interdisciplinarios de Derecho Industrialy Económico (CEIDIE) of the School of Law of the University of Buenos Aires. By the time of the Argentine debate over patents, these groups had already coalesced into an epistemic community with solid knowhow about patents and their economic impact. In the public hearings held in the Senate, they were joined by experts from the Instituto Nacional de Tecnología Agropecuaria (INTA), the Foro Argentino de Biotecnología (FAB), and other scholars, including members of the School of Pharmacy and Biochemistry of the University of Buenos Aires.

A relatively small group of civil society actors accompanied the "big players" in the struggle. According to the records of congressional hearings, the Asociación Argentina de Inventores (AAI) and the Asociación de Derechos Intelectuales (ASDIN) were among those that supported CAEMe, albeit moderately. On the other hand, the group resisting the expansion of patent protections included the Confederación Médica de la República Argentina (COMRA), the Confederación Farmacéutica Argentina (COFA), the Asociación de Farmacias Mutuales y Sindicales de la República Argentina (AFMSRA), and the Liga de Amas de Casa, Consumidores y Usuarios de la República Argentina (LAC) (*Secretaría Parlamentaria* 1995).

Despite the magnitude of the conflict, other actors linked to the health field did not participate in a substantive way. Neither the Ministry of Health, nor the unions in charge of social healthcare insurance, nor private health insurers (which were eventually the ones in charge of covering part of the price of medicines) took an active part in driving the dispute. Even though prior to 1993, the former heads of the Ministry of Health had tried to balance pro-IP initiatives, Alberto Mazza, Minister of Health at the time of the debate over the IP law, endorsed Cavallo's allegations about the importance of patents for economic development and the promotion of research.[53]

[52] As we have mentioned earlier, at this point certain experts had relationships in the global arena and were supported by regional and business organizations such as ALIFAR.

[53] In that vein, in his statement before the Senate, Minister Mazza stated: "Health is a resultant of all other factors that relate to the economic development of the country" (*Secretaría Parlamentaria* 1995: ii. 108–9).

In a similar vein, neither the media of the time nor the records of the Senate public hearings reflect participation by representatives from the most popular professional associations or university authorities from the medical or public health fields. In this regard, it is significant that the Asociación Argentina de Medicina (AAM)—the institution that brings together the Argentine medical associations—sent a brief two-page memo to the Senate expressing its interest that the new framework "address all aspects of the issue and safeguard intellectual property rights" (our translation).[54] Only in its fifth point did the AAM suggest that the regime "identify efficient mechanisms to ensure access to safe, effective and affordable medicines for everyone (cost, benefit, risk)" (our translation) (*Secretaría Parlamentaria* 1995: ii. 110–11).

The debate received widespread media coverage. The media of the time closely followed the different stages of the process. A review of the articles published by the three principal national newspapers at that time between 1990 and 1996 reveals that at least 391 commentaries were published on patent regime reform.

B. Mechanisms

The domestic IP norm-making process was driven by the tension between the global and national disputes and operated through the four mechanisms identified by Halliday and Carruthers (2007) in the struggle for shaping insolvency regimes in Asia.

1. *Actors' mismatch.*[55] The enactment of the IP law provides a good example of how the exclusion of the actors responsible for the domestic implementation of a global agreement can frustrate the goals of the transnational negotiations. As our study suggests, the agreement struck between the Ministry of Foreign Affairs and the United States in 1989 for the enactment of a new patent law illustrates one of the dimensions of this mismatch. Actors participating in the bilateral negotiations clearly ignored the interests of the national industry and brushed aside direct dialogue with high-level officials in the Executive Branch and Congress. Another instance of actors' mismatch occurred during the GATT negotiations. There, the multinational pharmaceutical industry played an important role. But other players were either entirely absent or substantially marginalized. The latter included the Argentine pharmaceutical industry, which was as powerful as the multinational actors within the domestic sphere. In the first phase of IP enactments, the Ministry of Health was also excluded; only after 2002 did the Ministry of Health appear to build pro-health alliances both in regional and international forums.

[54] Expressed as a reaction to the invitation to participate in the public hearings (*Secretaría Parlamentaria* 1995: ii. 108–9).

[55] Halliday and Carruthers (2007) explain that "almost always a mismatch occurs between parties in practice and actors in lawmaking" (1152) and add that "the mechanisms that produce or mitigate 'mismatch' are critically important in the recursivity of law for they set in play numbers of subsidiary adjustments" (1152).

The Argentine enactment phase also demonstrates the extent to which the presence of a powerful local actor with the ability to influence the whole political spectrum could create room to maneuver and reduce the domestic effectiveness of the bilateral agreement with the United States and the global TRIPS Agreement. The mismatch between the interests represented in the Uruguay Round of GATT and the interests of the Argentine pharmaceutical industry—a true anomaly in the developing world in terms of its relative power—surprised the United States and its partners, who were forced to expend more resources than anticipated in the struggle for a new law.

The mismatch between the actors who participated in the global negotiations and those involved in the domestic ones brought important consequences through the process to harmonize the local IP laws to the international demands, for it was in that phase where unforeseen important political considerations and public policy issues appeared (Sell 2009: 29–30). Such considerations included concern about the fate of the national pharmaceutical industry. This mismatch worked as a contestation mechanism, which was taken over by the local actors who had been excluded from the international negotiations. In addition, the ambiguous position adopted by Menem in several moments of the enactment phase of a new IP regime also suggests that even those who had participated in the global negotiations, once back in the country and facing the tension produced by the conflict between the international and the local interests, would be inclined to favor the latter, given their assessment of the political costs at stake (Sell 2009: 30).

2. *Diagnostic struggles.*[56] The debate over the IP regime enabled the national industry and its political allies to defeat part of the maximalist demands of the United States and CAEMe. The local pro-IP sector framed the debate to parallel the discussion at the global stage, as based on a link between trade and IP and on the significance of research and development (R&D) activities and the country's need to integrate into the international community as a precondition for development (Sell 2003). In the domestic diagnostic struggle, however, the Argentine industry succeeded in reframing the argument. The national industry successfully set aside the claims about R&D and trade, countering them with appeals to more central domestic interests. It warned, first and foremost, about the impact of patents on the price of medicines.

Despite the appeals to the cost of medicines, the right to health did not arise in domestic debates. At the time, the international counter-hegemonic discourse had not yet been framed in terms of such a right. The domestic industry did occasionally refer to the rights of consumers, who—they alleged—would be directly affected by price increases. Appeals to "national dignity" in the protection of a domestic industry that created jobs and wealth for the Argentine people were also repeated.

[56] As described by Halliday and Carruthers (2007) the "diagnosis involves the identification of a problem, the application to that problem of various rules of relevance for a given reform (e.g., how broadly construed will be the depiction of the problem), and relating the problem so construed to a way of classifying problems for purposes of law reform" (1150).

On the other hand, both CAEMe and CILFA, along with private research centers closely associated with one or the other chamber (FIEL, CEDIQUIFA, and CEIDIE, et al.), emphasized the need for global and market integration, but from different perspectives. References to other nations' experiences were also widely used by each sector in defining its diagnosis of the situation. While Chile, Italy, and Canada were lauded as model nations in the adoption of new patent regimes that had, according to CAEMe, benefited the consumers of medicines, the same countries were used by CILFA to point to the collapse of national industries and an increase in the price of medicines (*Secretaría Parlamentaria* 1995, vols. ii and iii). Additionally, CILFA representatives framed the dilemma posed by a new patent regulation as a question of sovereignty, demanding a choice between "imposition and self-adoption" of a regulatory framework (*Secretaría Parlamentaria* 1995, vol. ii). For CAEMe, on the other hand, the choice was between "isolation and harmonization" (*Secretaría Parlamentaria*1995, vol. ii).

In this battle, and especially on the side of the anti-IP group, experts played a significant role, participating in the hearings during the legislative debate in the Senate (Carlos Correa is an example) or influencing the process as part of larger epistemic communities. Finally, the parties offered empirical studies supporting their own diagnoses. Research by FIEL, CEDIQUIFA, and CILFA provided support for their framing of the struggle. Both the press and the submissions made at the public hearings in the Senate made reference to those studies as a basis for their assertions on the future effects of IP norms.

3. *Contradictions.*[57] Advances in norm-making and implementation phases in the cycles are partially driven by contradictions that the law internalizes with different degrees of stability (Halliday and Carruthers 2007). Contradictions occur on two levels: the institutional and the ideological. According to Halliday (2009: 280), institutional contradictions occur when competing logics (e.g., of markets, politics) or institutions articulate norms in tension with each other. Ideological contradictions, by contrast, may occur between different global institutions that may appear to forge agreements, but in fact allow nations implementing those agreements to follow divergent courses of action (Halliday 2009).

The United States' success during the 1980s at shifting the IP agenda to the GATT negotiations and away from the agencies of the United Nations had the effect of displacing WIPO and marginalizing the Conference on Trade and Development (UNCTAD).[58] The WHO was also sidelined; it first incorporated patents and public health into its agenda in 1996. As a result, during a significant part of the 1990s, GATT negotiators, and later the WTO, lacked a serious capacity to generate institutional contradictions such as those identified by Halliday (2009).

[57] Halliday and Carruthers (2007) state that "cycles of lawmaking and implementation frequently are driven by contradictions that are internalized within the law. When lawmakers cannot definitively resolve underlying economic, political or ideological contradictions, they settle for partial or temporary solutions" (1149).

[58] Some years later, WIPO partially recovered its role when it had to design and promote the Patent Law Treaty and the Substantive Patent Law Treaty as well as provide technical assistance to developing countries.

Nonetheless, ideological contradictions were present in the theory underlying the forum shift. In fact, the United States' proposed model to regulate patents in GATT was based on a structural contradiction, which was discursively exploited more than once in the Argentine media and the Senate. GATT negotiations sought to promote trade liberalization and to eliminate trade barriers in order to facilitate competition among nations. Thus, it was contradictory to include in those negotiations the debate over a property protection model favoring an extreme monopoly of certain rights that were detrimental to free competition (and, indeed, to trade) (Roffe 2008).[59]

In spite of this contradiction, during the first years, the dominance of the argument linking trade and IP was such that it was not easy to identify areas of ideological contradiction or to identify spaces for counter-hegemonic reactions. Only after the New Delhi Declaration in March 1990 did the global campaign to counteract the trade approach begin. The campaign, which had an impact on the final TRIPS text, ultimately led to a redefinition of the agendas of WHO and WIPO (Sell 2008). In the domestic context, the local industry exploited the contradictions built into the Argentine discourse that had associated patent protection with global integration, economic liberalization, and development, demonstrating the inadequacy of the project to further other national goals. Moreover, the industry resorted to a nationalist discourse, which was still ingrained in the domestic political class.

4. *Indeterminacies.*[60] As with all norms, indeterminacies in agreements formalized in treaties also offer opportunities for interpretation and resistance through the assignment of divergent meanings. In the case of TRIPS, two levels of indeterminacy became evident as soon as the Agreement was concluded. The first affected the global script into which the treaty fit. In terms of the script categories proposed by Carruthers and Halliday (2006: 540), the United States argued that the treaty was a directly operative norm, a set of specific standards—a code—applicable to domestic law as a directive for developing the IP protection framework. By contrast, the opposing sectors, led by CILFA, interpreted the treaty as a set of minimum standards that left room for adaptation by WTO members during the incorporation process (Correa 2006b: 49).[61]

Secondly, indeterminacy can be viewed as a characteristic of the TRIPS text. The normative gaps in the standards and principles were arguably made to be exploited—and, indeed, were exploited—by the Argentine Congress to tilt

[59] For a theoretical discussion of IP and antitrust laws in Argentina, see Cabanellas de las Cuevas (2005: 263).

[60] Halliday and Carruthers (2007) assert that "all statutes, court opinions, and regulations contain ambiguities and gaps that create uncertainty and lead to unanticipated consequences" (1149) and that "the occurrence of indeterminacy and unintended consequences regularly drives a turn of the reform cycle, as original crafters of law seek to remedy its deficiencies in order to achieve their original purposes, or subjects of the law react to unwanted outcomes, or courts seek to settle meanings. And more contentious lawmaking is likely to result in vague, ambiguous law that will produce inconsistency in application and provide ample opportunity for creative compliance" (1149).

[61] Sell refers to the same dissonance regarding TRIPS. While developed countries viewed TRIPS as "a platform, as a line of base for the protection of the intellectual property," developing nations thought of the treaty as "a roof, as a maximum standard of protection beyond which they were not disposed to go or/and would not be willing to go" (2008: 194).

the treaty implementation process in favor of CILFA's demands. Examples of the interpretive room within TRIPS used by Argentine legislation include the flexibility to define the patentability criteria and exceptions to IP rights, the space to determine applicable transition times, and the conditions for the use of compulsory licensing and toleration of parallel imports. In addition, Argentina did not specifically protect pharmaceutical data generated to meet regulatory requirements (Correa 2009). In relation to each of these items, representatives of CILFA's interests maneuvered during the elaboration of the domestic norm, playing with divergent interpretations. The outcome was a more favorable result for the national industry.[62]

V. The Politics of Implementation, 1996–2002

The ink on the TRIPS Agreement was barely dry when a new round of negotiations began. Two agendas coexisted in that phase: the counter-hegemonic mobilization of a development-oriented agenda and the health umbrella on the one hand, and on the other, the United States' agenda. The United States tried to obtain local laws based on restrictive interpretations of TRIPS, with the purpose of reducing the room for flexibility and the exit options granted in the negotiation of the Uruguay Round. At the same time, it sought to introduce higher—TRIPS-plus—standards through bilateral free trade agreements (FTAs) or bilateral investment treaties (BITs) with less developed nations.

On both sides of the conflict, state actors, civil society, and the pharmaceutical industry sought to redefine and to renegotiate the content of the TRIPS Agreement. While global influences on the domestic norm-making process continued, after the conclusion of the treaty developing countries began using more complex resistance strategies. National norm-making at this stage interrelated in a more balanced manner and did so in a more globalized setting, with a greater number of players fighting in a greater number of forums.

A. Intervention by Congress: Interpreting TRIPS and TRIPS-plus Initiatives

In 1996, those who thought that the United States would moderate its demands once a new patent regime was enacted discovered they were wrong. The patent regulation model established in the approved statute was far from satisfactory to the United States. As soon as TRIPS was concluded, the United States began to promote a strict interpretation that would reduce the margins of flexibility and loopholes left by the GATT negotiations. Those more exacting standards, known as TRIPS-plus,[63] were negotiated in bilateral and regional free trade agreements

[62] See, the chapters in this volume about Central America, Chile, Colombia, and Ecuador regarding these strategies.

[63] The TRIPS-plus standards include: (1) data confidentiality and exclusivity; (2) linkage between the sanitary agency that is in charge of registering medicines and the agency responsible for awarding

and enforced through strategies such as the WTO Dispute Settlement mechanism. For Argentina, TRIPS-plus demands were channeled into the frustrated negotiations for an FTA with the Mercado Comúndel Sur (Mercosur), and through bilateral promises to include Argentina in the Group of Twenty (G-20), and as an associate member of the North Atlantic Treaty Organization (NATO).

In the case of Argentina, the global strategy for a reconfiguration of national IP regimes launched by the United States in the 1980s coincided with the development of the intense bilateral relations that both countries maintained in the first half of the 1990s. That relationship, captured by the metaphor "carnal relations," provided room for President George H. W. Bush, and later for President Bill Clinton, to urge the adoption of a new IP legal framework. After the approval of the final text of the IP regime in early 1996, a new struggle began. The fight was now centered on the demands by the United States for the reform of the new patent regime and for the implementation of a new regulatory framework.

The US government continued pressuring Menem[64] by demanding immediate enactment of a new law that would adopt TRIPS-plus standards.[65] The domestic situation was not, however, conducive to meeting those demands.[66] The Peronist factions in Congress had weakened Menem's leadership during the fight over the earlier Patent Law and he no longer had sufficient political capital to weather another attack. In 1996, Menem made an effort to persuade Congress to avoid US sanctions by enacting a data protection law, but his efforts were relatively moderate (*La Nación* 1996a). The bill sent by the Executive Branch to Congress suffered changes that, once again, fell short of US demands. On December 19, 1996, Congress enacted Law No. 24,766, which dealt a further blow to American interests.

One of the issues that provoked considerable anxiety at the time was the protection of the data presented in order to register pharmaceutical products and clear them for marketing, and their direct or indirect use for the subsequent registration of copies and generic drugs (*La Nación* 1996b).[67] If data from clinical studies on pharmaceutical drugs were protected, then local manufacturers of generics and copies would be unable to rely on the studies produced and filed for the approval of the original drugs; instead, they would have to conduct their own

patents; (3) restrictions on the conditions for the granting of compulsory licenses; (4) prohibition of parallel importations; (5) patent-term extension; and (6) expanding the criteria of patentability.

64 During 1996, imminent threats of commercial retaliation and the return of the country to the Priority Watch List of Special 301 concerned the Executive branch.

65 In the following years, the press took account of several initiatives related to the IP regime. These actions included meetings between officers and representatives of the United States and the Argentine government and negotiations between CAEMe and CILFA (*Página 12* 1997).

66 By mid-1996, the United States had lost its unconditional advocate and spokesperson. Cavallo left the Ministry of Finance in July 1996. Moreover, since 1995, the success of trade exchanges at the Mercosur level had faltered because Brazil had replaced the United States as the largest buyer of Argentinean exports.

67 The requirements of the sanitary agency for the registration of pharmaceutical products include the filing of data about quality, efficacy, and security of drugs (called testing data) and additional information about their chemical characteristics and physical composition.

clinical tests in order to obtain authorization for marketing or wait until the period of exclusivity ended (Sell 2008: 195–6). Arguably required by the TRIPS Agreement, data exclusivity, together with the linkage requirement,[68] were the legal tools conceived to widen the protection of patent owners (Correa 2002; Sell 2008: 195). For the national industry, however, what was at stake was the survival of its business model for producing and marketing drugs; the industry did not consider these demands a part of what had been agreed in the Uruguay Round.

On November 19, 1996, Congress passed Law No. 24,766 on data exclusivity. Even though the law prohibited the diffusion of data provided by the drug companies during the procedures for the registration of the medicines with the Administración Nacional de Medicamentos, Alimentos y Tecnología Médica (ANMAT), the legislation limited the law's reach. The new legislation reproduced article 39.3 of the TRIPS Agreement and granted protection only against "unfair uses" of clinical data (Najurieta 2006). Moreover, Law No. 24,766 limited the application of the provision to drugs that "used new active principles that were not previously registered in Argentina or any other country" (Section 4, Law No. 24,766). At the same time, article 5 granted ANMAT the power to authorize the marketing of copies of drugs previously approved in Argentina or in any of the countries listed in an Annex to the legislation. ANMAT was permitted to grant such approval without requiring the production of data on clinical trials provided the data had already been filed by the first pharmaceutical company.[69] In other words, since the law permitted copies to obtain regulatory approval without extensive testing (Najurieta 2006),[70] Congress perpetuated the conditions under which the domestic pharmaceutical industry had developed its comparative advantages.

Another important issue in the context of this legislative resistance cycle concerned the approval of the so-called Bolar Exception.[71] In the version promoted by the developing countries—which was the version adopted by article 8 of Law No. 24,766—the Bolar Exception allowed for the initiation of the experimentation required for the registration of pharmaceutical products before the patent on the original drug expired. Once approved by the health authorities, generics and copies could then be rapidly launched onto the market, where they would induce a

[68] See Sell (2008) and Dreyfuss and Rodriguez, Chapter 1 in this volume, for a technical definition of *linkage* and other IP terms used in this chapter.

[69] Law No. 24,766 was supplemented by Decree No. 150/92 about procedures for prior authorization for the marketing of specialty medicines and pharmaceutical products.

[70] The concept of similarity had been specified in Resolution No. 5755/96 of the ANMAT, which served as precedent for Law No. 24,766 (Azpiazu 1997: 35). Pursuant to art. 5 of the new law: "The approval of registration or the authorization of commercialization granted, by means of the local administrative authority, under the procedures of approval for similar products established in this article does not imply permission for the use of confidential information protected by this section."

[71] This exception authorizes the production of the data necessary to approve a drug before the expiration of the exclusive rights of the pharmaceutical patent owner, with the purpose of shortening the period of time between when the patent expires and when generics or copies can be marketed. For the transnational industry, the suppression of the Bolar Exception was a way of extending the protection recognized by the patent, since competitors would be required to start their testing only after expiration of the patent.

reduction in price (De la Puente et al. 2009: 41). The pro-IP faction did not object to this provision, but they did ask that it be accompanied by an extension in the term of patent protection to compensate right holders for delays caused by registration. The new law did not, however, provide for such extensions.[72] What was more, the new law did not include a linkage requirement between ANMAT and the patent agency, INPI. Congress thus used the complexity of the IP regime and the opportunities it created to resist the strategy of employing regulatory requirements as a tool for protecting patent rights (Lustig and Kingsbury 2006).

The United States government immediately made its objections to the new law known. It brought a complaint against Argentina to the WTO Dispute Settlement Board, claiming the country had breached the provisions of the TRIPS Agreement. Furthermore, in 1996, Argentina was placed back on the Special 301 Priority Watch List and threats were made to withdraw the country from the Generalized System of Preferences (GSP). One year later, the United States withdrew $260 million in tariff privileges (*La Nación* 1997), to which the Argentine Congress responded by threatening to raise internal taxes on soft drinks (*Página 12* 1997) and to reform the Patent Law to extend the transitional period from five to ten years (*Página 12* 1997). The latter proposal was destined to remain on the agenda as a negotiating card until well into 1999 (*Página 12* 1999). However, US pressure for more legislative reform never let up. Until the end of the Menem administration, and even after Fernando De La Rúa succeeded him in December 1999, the United States insisted on a new norm on data, while local actors were repeatedly warning about the prospective increase in the prices of medicines once the Patent Law went into force in 2000 (*Clarín* 2000a, 2000b; *Página 12* 2000).[73] Despite Argentina's rebellion regarding several issues of the IP agenda, its position on the Watch List, and the challenge before WTO, the United States granted Argentina benefits that signaled approval of the larger market and institutional reforms adopted by the country throughout the Menem administration. As a result, Menem ended his second term in 1999 leaving Argentina as an associate member of NATO and a member of the G-20.

B. The Fight over Implementation Moves to the Courts and INPI

While US pressure continued, multinational companies expanded the battle ground by shifting their focus to INPI (which was then a new agency) and to the federal civil and commercial courts. In both forums, the struggle to capitalize on the indeterminacies of the domestic laws and the TRIPS provisions was renewed. In 2000, after the new pharmaceutical patent regime had entered into force, multinational companies tried other strategies, such as intervening in public auctions for

[72] This kind of compensation had been adopted by the United States, Italy, and other countries that enacted a Bolar Exception. Instead, the Argentine Congress followed the example of Canada, which had incorporated the exception to benefit its generic industry without providing any compensatory term extensions.

[73] Under the IP laws, it was permissible to apply for patents on drugs as soon as January 1, 1995, but patent grants would begin only on October 24, 2000.

the purchase of medicines, where they objected to the acquisition of generics and copies (*Clarín* 2005).

Even in 1995, during the tangled process of enacting the new IP law, multinational companies had begun to mobilize and demand the implementation of TRIPS norms. They sought to play with the room available for interpretation, profiting from the confusion generated by the exchanges between the Executive and the Legislative branches, and the terms of application that attempted to reconcile the old Law No. 111 regime with the TRIPS Agreement. According to Rodríguez, between 1990 and 2004, 54,444 patent requests were filed with INPI, 12,890 of which were granted by the agency (2006). Close to 40 percent of those requests pertained to pharmaceutical patents (Correa 2009: 7). Requests included diverse types of patents. Notably, some sought to extend the terms and criteria for awarding patents on inventions claimed in applications pending in INPI.

During the period between 1996 and 2000, with the aim of maximizing patent rights, multinational companies requested—either from INPI or from courts—the rights to: (1) revalidation patents (*patentes de reválida*) provided for in Law No. 111, (2) "divisional" patents, which, in Argentina, are used to convert process patents granted under the old regime into product patents, (3) the extension of the term of patents granted under the regime set forth by Law No. 111, (4) biotechnology patents, and (5) transitional patents, which would provide compensation for local production.[74] The INPI rejected such demands in resolutions issued starting in 1996. The consequent transfer of these demands to the courts set up an adjudicative conflict that persisted into the next decade.[75] In that setting, both the transnational and national industries would find new room to practice their offensive and resistance strategies.

The first group of law suits that reached the courts concerned *revalidation patents*. Although neither Law No. 24,481 nor its amendments provided for revalidation patents, the confusion generated by the succession of partial vetoes and corrective laws left room for multinational companies to allege that such patents had been available between Decrees No. 625/95 and No. 590/95, and the enactment of the First Corrective Law—that is, during the period when Cavallo had withheld publication of Law No. 24,481. Multinational corporations were thus demanding that INPI recognize exclusive rights to inventions simply because they were patented in foreign countries. INPI consistently denied requests for such

[74] Transitional patents allowed those who had made investments for using a patented invention before January 1, 1995 to continue to use the patented invention if they offered reasonable compensation to the owner of the patent (Kors 2004: 7).

[75] According to Kors (2004), from 1995 to 2005, the Federal Court of Appeals in Civil and Commercial Matters decided approximately 250 IP cases. The main legal reporters of the country published 180 decisions, of which 77 percent concerned claims regarding patents on pharmaceutical or agrochemical products. Among the latter, 64 percent of the cases referred to revalidation patents, 87 percent of these concerned disputes over the application of the deferral of the validity period of the patents and 100 percent of this last group of cases requested application of article 70.7, one of the transitional provisions of the TRIPS Agreement (Kors 2004: 7). Moreover, 74 percent of the court decisions related to the disputes generated over the validity of Law No. 111 and its relationship to the new regulatory framework.

patents. Dissatisfied, the industry brought claims before the federal courts. After a few years of relatively favorable decisions in the lower courts (Moncayo Von Hase 2004), the Supreme Court finally considered the issue in October 2000. In *Unilever NV v. INPI*[76] the Court found for the defendants, rejecting the claims of the multinational industry. The Court held that although Law No. 111 envisioned revalidation patents, it had been repealed by the inventive step requirement for patentable subject matter provided for in the TRIPS Agreement. According to the Court, those standards were immediately operative, and thus revalidation patents no longer qualified as patentable subject matter (Moncayo Von Hase 2004: 19).

A second set of lawsuits challenging INPI denials focused on *divisional patents.* Under article 100 of the Patent Law, and in accordance with the transitional provision in article 70.7 of the TRIPS Agreement, multinational companies demanded that INPI recognize divisional patents. Multinational companies had parent patents registered under Law No. 111, and demanded the extension of these process patents to pharmaceutical products. In those suits, the three panels of the Federal Court of Appeals in Civil and Commercial Matters ruled in favor of the multinational industry, reversing INPI's decisions to the contrary (Kors 2004b: 103).[77] Once again, the Supreme Court settled the dispute. In *Pfizer v. INPI,*[78] the Court tested the compatibility of Argentine laws with articles 70.7 and 70.8 of the TRIPS Agreement. The Court found article 100 was constitutional and compatible with the treaty. Because the date of application of the treaty for Argentina was October 23, 2000, INPI's denials were permissible, as this agency did not have to issue product patents before that date.

A third set of the demands filed with INPI by international companies involved the *extension of the term of patents granted under Law No. 111* (for five, ten, or fifteen years) to provide for the same patent term established in the TRIPS Agreement, i.e. twenty years. That dispute gave rise to two types of controversies: those concerning requests for extensions regarding patents granted under Law No. 111, and those relating to requests for the extension of patents applied for under the old regime but not yet granted. In both cases, the transitional provisions on patent terms in both the old and new regimes lent themselves to conflicting interpretations that could either favor or restrict patent holder rights. Consequently, multinationals could choose between the interpretation that favored the terms applicable under Law No. 111, or the one that favored the terms applicable under the new law, whichever yielded a longer patent term in the particular case (Genovesi 2004: 51). Capitalizing on the complex web of norms generated by the convoluted enactment process of the new law and the TRIPS Agreement, in 1995 companies began to demand the extension of patent terms under article 33 of the TRIPS Agreement, article 35

[76] Supreme Court, *Unilever NV v. Instituto Nacional de la Propiedad Industrial s/denegatoria de patente.* October 24, 2000.

[77] For a critique of some of the arguments offered by the Chamber, see Correa (2008a: 410–11).

[78] Supreme Court, *Pfizer Inc. v. Instituto Nacional de la Propiedad Industrial s/denegatoria de patente.* May 21, 2002.

of Law No. 24,481, or article 71 of Decree No. 590/95, whichever was more advantageous. Those requests were also denied by INPI. However, while their cases were pending before the agency, companies whose patents were near expiration requested court injunctions in order to extend patent terms.

Once again, such claims were resolved in favor of the patent holders by the majority of the panels of the Federal Court of Appeals in Civil and Commercial Matters, which first granted the injunctions, and later accepted the claims on the merits. Yet after several injunctions and decisions on the subject, the Supreme Court once again turned the tables. In its decision in *Karl Thomae*,[79] on February 13, 2001, the Court explained the difference between the date of *entry into force* of the Agreement, which was January 1, 1995, and its date of *application*, which depended on the length of the transition periods. In accordance with that distinction, the Court concluded that it was possible to delay the effective date of article 33's term of protection until 2000, thus ending the multinational industry's manipulation of patent term extensions.

In the early years of the new IP legal framework, these three types of cases occupied most of the work of multinational firms organized in CAEMe in the fight to define the scope of the new law and to profit from the indeterminacies of both the law and the TRIPS Agreement. Subsequently, the same companies would return to the courts, this time in order to stop national pharmaceutical firms from infringing.[80] In this round, they adopted an even more aggressive strategy. To that end, two procedural options were available. The first was a proceeding called *incidente de explotación*[81] under article 87 of Law No. 24,481, which gave alleged infringers the choice between providing a security to continue exploitation, or suspending it in exchange for a security from the patent holder. The second (more efficient) alternative consisted of the use of preliminary injunctions (known as autonomous injunctions) available under article 50 of the TRIPS Agreement and the National Code of Civil and Commercial Procedures (Genovesi and Kors 2004). As these injunctions could be obtained quickly and ex parte, multinational players relied on them in various cases brought against national firms selling copies of patented products. Their use was limited, however, after the United States and Argentina terminated the WTO case in a mutually agreed solution, which settled, among other things, the conditions for awarding preliminary relief. As reflected in section VI, US demands during the negotiations at the WTO paradoxically frustrated the availability of this pro-IP tool.[82] After the procedures before the

[79] Federal Court of Appeals in Civil and Commercial Matters, *Dr. Karl Thomae Gesellschaft mit beschränkter Haftung v. Instituto Nacional de la Propiedad Industrial y otro s/denegatoria de patente.* February 13, 2001.

[80] Some of the drugs that were involved in this litigation were antiretroviral drugs, Atorvstatin (for high cholesterol), Amlodipine (for hypertension), and Orlistat (for obesity), among others (Levis 2010: 378).

[81] "Incidentes de explotación" (a type of injunctive relief) granted priority to the defendant for the unjustified use of a patented invention, as it allowed him to continue the exploitation until the final decision if he offered a sufficient guarantee that he could pay the judgment in the event the case was decided in favor of the plaintiff.

[82] For further details, see Najurieta (2006) and Genovesi and Kors (2004).

WTO's Dispute Settlement Board (DSB) concluded in 2005, the Federal Court of Appeals in Civil and Commercial Matters had a new opportunity to address the issue. In *Eli Lilly v. Viocrom*[83] it concluded that both the *incidente de explotación* and preliminary injunctions were compatible with the TRIPS Agreement, but that to obtain the latter, claimants had to demonstrate the alleged patent infringement.

VI. The New IP Legislation at the Dispute Settlement Body Interface

Upon the 1996 defeat of US demands regarding data exclusivity, the US offensive moved to the new interface created by the WTO Agreements. In the late 1990s, the United States began to bring complaints against Argentina before the WTO, alleging the country had breached its duties to protect patent rights over pharmaceuticals and chemical products. These consultations and negotiations at the WTO remained open for almost three years.[84] In May 2002, the parties reached a mutually agreed solution whereby the United States recognized that four out of its nine original complaints had been incorporated into Argentine law and were consistent with the TRIPS Agreement. These included compulsory licensing, exclusive marketing rights for inventions covered by patents in the pipeline, and import restrictions.[85] Argentina agreed to modify its legislation regarding four other issues (De la Puente et al. 2009):[86] the extension of protection for process inventions to cover products, the shift of the burden of proof in proceedings involving patent infringement, the conditions for awarding injunctions, and the recognition of patents on microorganisms and other living matter. The microorganisms issue was addressed by INPI,[87] and in December 2003, Congress amended the Patent Law by enacting Law No. 25,859 to incorporate the agreements concerning the exclusive rights conferred under process patents, the reversal

[83] Federal Court of Appeals in Civil and Commercial Matters, Sala I. *Eli Lilly and Company v. InstitutoNacional de la Propiedad Industria.* December 22, 2005.

[84] During these negotiations, the Argentine Ambassador at Ginebra, Roberto Lavagna, worked with the Oficina de Solución de Controversias of the Ministry of Foreign Affairs. At the same time, his Office received cooperation from the Secretaría de Industria and CILFA (interview with Mirta Levis).

[85] WT/DS171/1 (October 5, 1999); WT/DS196/1, IP/D/22 (June 6, 2002). This can be read as a victory for the local industry. Consider, for example, that, because it keeps the provisions on compulsory licenses, if a national firm decides to produce a drug patented by another firm, it can demand a license. If the license is denied, and the firm can establish that the patentee's practices are anti-competitive, it may request a license from the local agency. The agency may compulsorily confer the license and set the royalties the laboratory should pay to the patent owner. The governments also agreed that Argentinean licensees of a patent may use those licenses to import products from abroad, if the patentee has authorized the foreign sale (Isalud 2009: 89–90).

[86] On December 2003 Congress passed Law No. 25,859 amending the Patent Law, and thus accepting the points of the Mutually Agreed Solution reached at the WTO by Argentina and the United States.

[87] A guide, which clarified the terms of the law as required by the TRIPS Agreement, was adopted (Isalud 2009: 89–90).

of the burden of proof in civil cases of infringement of process patents, and the issue related to injunctive relief.

The only issue left outside the mutually agreed solution was the dispute over rights related to the protection of undisclosed test data. Given the failure to reach an agreement on the subject, the parties agreed to continue consultations. Furthermore, Argentina stated it would modify its legislation in the event that the WTO clarified the meaning of article 39.3 of the TRIPS Agreement.

Although initiated to put pressure on Argentina, consultations at the WTO were relatively favorable to the interests opposed to patents. The result of the mutually agreed solution had a direct impact on the judicial harassment strategy that multinational companies had developed in Argentine courts to stop national companies from using patented processes or marketing patented products.[88] As noted above, until the solution was agreed to, members of CAEMe had used the *incidente de explotación* and, later, the precautionary injunctions to fight alleged patent infringements. In particular, companies had used TRIPS article 50 and Argentine procedural rules to obtain ex parte precautionary injunctions that suspended the use of the patented inventions by local manufacturers whenever the breach of a patent was argued. Foreign pharmaceutical companies had preferred these fast procedures over the *incidentes de explotación.*

The legal reform negotiated at the close of 2003 to end the WTO dispute between the United States and Argentina incorporated the precautionary injunctions into the IP regime. However, it made the conditions for obtaining them equivalent to the standards used in the United States to award preliminary relief. Since these standards were stricter than those applied by Argentine courts in IP cases, the negotiation ended up curtailing access to a simplified method for obtaining preliminary relief. It thus effectively undermined a key legal strategy deployed by the multinational industries to press the local industry.

VII. Implementation Continues: Global Reframing and the Domestic Crisis, 2002–2010

Towards the end of the 1990s, the transnational demand for a balance between IP rights and the right to health had gained strength. Starting with the struggle to introduce health concerns into the IP agenda, various global initiatives managed to diminish the force of the pro-IP lobby (De Beer 2009). These initiatives included revisions in the positions and global scripts of existing actors and the arrival of new transnationally mobilized actors.[89] High-impact episodes linked to the expansion of HIV/AIDS and malaria also contributed to the change. Most significantly, in

[88] Interviews with Bernardo Kors and Interviewee A.

[89] At this point, it had become clear that important transnational pharmaceutical firms had lost the monopoly on global mobilization. Towards the late 1990s, transnational social movements, international nongovernmental organizations, and UN agencies combined to challenge the framework of the TRIPS Agreement, based on the right to health and access to medicine.

November 2001 the WTO Ministerial Conference held in Doha adopted the Declaration on the TRIPS Agreement and Public Health. The Doha Declaration became a turning point in the global struggle against stricter IP rules, for it underscored the importance of applying and interpreting the TRIPS Agreement consistently with the protection of public health (Correa 2008b).[90]

At the national stage, the new implementation phase coincided with the severe economic crisis that hit Argentina during 2001 and 2002 and with the gradual recovery process initiated in 2004. Public health and access to medicines became an important issue in the political discourse. However, the most important policies adopted in the context of the new PNM (the national policy on medicines) were not concerned with the dispute over pharmaceutical patents. In fact, in the following years the conflict over IP became marginal. As the Ministries of Health and Foreign Affairs began a series of public health-oriented efforts on behalf of the country, patent initiatives lost momentum within domestic circles.

A. The Crisis and the Rise of a National Policy on Medicines (PNM)

In December 2001, Argentina experienced some of the worse moments of a severe economic, political, and social crisis. During that period, unemployment and poverty rates skyrocketed, the currency board system, which pegged the Argentine peso to the US dollar, was abandoned; economic activity stagnated; social conflict intensified; and political leadership faced a deep legitimacy crisis. The health system was one of the areas hit particularly hard by these changes, and healthcare services suffered a deep decay.

In March 2002, Decree No. 486/02 declared a public health emergency and Ginés González García, the newly appointed Minister of Health, began to implement policies that would later become known as part of an innovative national policy on medicines. The initial measures of the new PNM sought to address the most pressing needs of the most impoverished sectors of the population. However, the high price of essential medicines created a serious limitation on access. The new measures included three key features: a change in the content and coverage standards of the Programa Médico Obligatorio de Emergencia (PMOE), the minimum mandatory package of services and medicines covered by the contributory health systems; a requirement to prescribe drugs by international nonproprietary names (INN), commonly known as prescription by generic names; and free public supply of essential medicines for primary care through the Plan Remediar. In addition, certain public health programs like the Plan Nacional de Lucha contra el VIH/SIDA were strengthened, the price of antiretroviral drugs was negotiated internationally, and imports of basic supplies for drug production were granted tax-exempt status (Godoy Garraza 2004).

The new policy marked a change in the style of public health interventions, which had previously been characterized by a weak or absent national policy

[90] It also demonstrated how developing countries could work with organized groups and use their experiences and domestic processes to generate change.

regarding medicines.[91] The window opened by the crisis provided an opportunity to make changes.[92] Certain sectors, historically successful in defeating similar proposals, could not manage to frustrate the new measures.[93] By Resolution No. 201/02, the PMOE established a suite of essential benefits to be guaranteed by health insurance agents. Moreover, the new PMOE mandated the coverage of 40 percent of the cost of outpatient medicines[94] and 100 percent of special medicines (oncologic and antiretroviral drugs, contraceptives, etc.). In an effort to promote the rational use of medicines, the measure was accompanied by the National Therapeutic Handbook,[95] which included more than 200 active ingredients and covered approximately 95 percent of health problems (González García, De la Puente, and Tarragona 2005: 215).[96] Together with the PMOE, the second important revision of the PNM was adopted in the first months of 2002. By Resolution No. 326/02, and later by decree, the Ministry of Health ordered that international nonproprietary names should be used for all medical and dental prescriptions. Congress ratified the proposal in August of that year through the passage of Law No. 25,649 for the Promotion of Use of Medicines by Generic Name (Abrutzky, Bramuglia, and Godio 2008: 7–8).[97]

Those involved in the manufacturing and marketing of medicines questioned the adoption of the National Therapeutic Handbook and the rules mandating prescriptions by INN. The new policies were also opposed by other actors including the Argentine Medicare Institute, Instituto Nacional de Servicios Socialespara

[91] This cannot be completely explained by the federal design of the health system. As in other realms, the national government shared jurisdiction with the provinces. However, this structure had not affected other federal government policies.

[92] The political context in which the new public health policies were introduced included changes in the ruling party, the political shift started by President Eduardo Duhalde and deepened by President Néstor Kirchner, the reconfiguration of Congress, and the political support given to the ruling party. In the second stage, the administration, especially Ginés González García, head of the National Health Department, was a key factor.

[93] At the same time, González García's agenda was supported by several sectors of the "Mesa del diálogo argentine." More than fifty organizations were involved in calling for a debate and a proposal for a National Health Emergency Plan.

[94] Later, Resolution No. 310/04 mandated coverage of 70 percent of the medicines needed for chronic illnesses.

[95] Resolution No. 201/02 MSN.

[96] Experts and groups working on health matters, such as the Comisión de Medicamentos (COMRA) in the 1980s, the Grupo Argentino para el Uso Racional de Medicamentos (GAPURMED), Médicos sin Fronteras, and the Foro Social de Salud had demanded a rational policy on medicines (interviews with Horacio Barri, Gonzalo Basile, Héctor Buschiazzo and Perla Mordujovich).

[97] During the parliamentary debate regarding the law, several other bills introduced by members of the House were considered. The debates encompassed several aspects of the law, including prescription by INN, the production of generics, price regulation for pharmaceuticals, the role of the ANMAT, expenditures on health, the "independent" practices of the Argentine Medicare Institute (PAMI), the rational use of drugs, and the public production of medicines. Despite the broad scope of the issues discussed by Congress, the final version of the law was limited to the issue of compulsory prescription by INN. The debate and its results were followed by greater recognition of the administration and of the Health Minister and support of the national policy on medicines from many different sectors of society. Moreover, at the time, approximately eleven of Argentina's twenty-three provinces adopted similar rules.

Jubilados y Pensionados, known as PAMI.[98] Mandatory prescriptions by INN especially troubled multinational and domestic pharmaceutical companies. Yet, the Plan Remediar was well received by the provinces and civil society organizations working on health matters.[99] Moreover, smaller local producers of essential medicines were particularly enthusiastic about the prospects of becoming suppliers under the program.[100]

Most of these policies gave birth to a strong resistance in the pharmaceutical industry.[101] Important changes in the pharmaceutical market during the 1990s had led to a rearrangement of the industry's interests. Faced with the prospect of a patent regime stronger than the one multinationals ultimately obtained, the Argentine pharmaceutical industry had adopted significant production reforms. Anticipating the enforcement of patents on medicines, national laboratories had turned from manufacturing medicines to their assembly, marketing, and distribution. In addition to becoming stronger players in the marketing chain, these laboratories had also tried to protect their local comparative advantages via strategies for the protection of locally recognized brand names, the expansion of their lobbying power, and the supply of rapid market access (Godoy Garraza 2004).

Additionally, in the late 1990s and throughout the years of the judicial fight over patents, the multinational and national laboratories had struck several important marketing deals. One of the most important was the Master Agreement with PAMI, whereby the national and the multinational industry negotiated the terms and conditions for the supply of medicines to the largest institutional customer in the country. As part of the deal, the principal domestic and foreign companies agreed to self-regulate in order to allocate their individual supply of pharmaceutical products to PAMI.[102] By 2002, this rearrangement facilitated the birth of an alliance among old enemies (Vasallo 1999), which now united to resist PNM initiatives and other new policies. The emergence of the alliance was especially apparent at the launch of the National Therapeutic Handbook and the passage of Law No. 25,649.

[98] At first, PAMI refused to enforce the PMOE and instead put forward its own list of branded medicines. Later, it frustrated the INN prescription law.

[99] Some civil society groups, many of which were later part of the Foro Social de Salud, criticized some aspects of the Plan Remediar, especially those regarding the government's decision to finance the program through credits from multilateral financial entities (such as the International Development Bank and the World Bank), as well as the reluctance of the Ministry of Health to foster the public production of drugs (interview with Gonzalo Basile, Gonzalo Moyano, and Claudio Capuano). For more on the public production of drugs and the Plan Remediar, see Cátedra Libre de Salud y Derechos Humanos (2004).

[100] The program aimed to reach 15 million people, which was the estimated population receiving healthcare services from the primary care centers, known in Spanish as Centros de Atención Primaria (Abrutzky, Bramuglia, and Godio 2008: 7).

[101] As time passed, and given the lack of impact of the INN prescription policies, the pharmaceutical industry did not continue to challenge the initiative (interview with Fabio Rozenek).

[102] The Agreement has been characterized as one creating "two clubs within PAMI: the club of special medicines run by Roche and Novartis (transnational firms), and the club of the ambulatories, Roemmers and Bagó (local laboratories). This is Argentina today" (Touloupas 2010: 71).

B. Argentina's Role in New Transnational IP Ventures

Once the most pressing public health problems of the crisis stabilized, the Ministry of Health set out to address the problem of pharmaceutical patents. As part of the new foreign policy agenda, Minister of Foreign Affairs Ginés González García engaged in various efforts to resist pro-IP interests at the global level. To begin with, the Ministry of Health was concerned about the INPI, and the relationships that officers of the agency had developed with the US patent office and with WIPO. As part of the global patent agenda, WIPO had begun to train examiners—including INPI's personnel—in national patent offices, teaching them to apply the patenting criteria used in the United States and the European Union.[103] This training had become part of the "procedural" strategy adopted by the United States and other developed countries to strengthen IP protection. The strategy became apparent in June 2000, with the adoption of the Patent Law Treaty harmonizing national and regional patent application procedures (Roffe 2007: 84).

Attempts to accelerate substantive and procedural IP harmonization were viewed with consternation in Argentina. In 2004, the Ministry of Health joined neighboring countries and African states to promote the WIPO Development Agenda. During the process, Argentina and Brazil played a leading role (Yu 2009). Simultaneously, the country joined several Latin American initiatives to review the impact of patent protection on public health and access to medicines. In 2004, the Mercosur countries signed Agreement 26/4, which included several recommendations regarding patent protection and access to medicines. Two years later, in May 2006, ten countries of the region signed the *Declaración de Ministras y Ministros de América del Sur sobre Propiedad Intelectual, Acceso a los Medicamentos y Salud Pública*. The new statement, grounded in the Doha Declaration and its redefinition of the global IP agenda, rejected attempts to impose TRIPS-plus requirements and defended the right to use TRIPS flexibilities (Sell 2008: 202–3); it was also instrumental in strengthening the determination of the signatories to withstand the escalating demands made by pro-IP players in international settings.

During 2003, Argentina also implemented another of the PNM measures by negotiating, together with nine South American countries, the support of civil society organizations, and international agencies, the acquisition of antiretrovirals (Herrera Parra 2003). In doing so, these countries were able to set maximum reference prices acceptable to the manufacturers of generics and to the international patent holder, Abbott Laboratories (Bumbak and Stanley 2006). Although some of the drugs were under patent protection in certain of these countries, the deal allowed the governments to save $120 million a year (Bumbak and Stanley 2006: 9). Argentina coordinated the negotiations, revealing, on the one hand, González García's political decision to make the defense of public health a key feature of his agenda. On the other hand, the initiative showed that the foreign policies of several of these countries had shifted. The center-left governments that had gained power

[103] Interview with Mirta Levis.

during the decade were now interested in building a regional consensus (Palermo 2010). Although pharmaceutical companies continued to bring patent infringement actions, the Ministry of Health decided to use the litigation to resolve open issues regarding TRIPS implementation (Madies 2010) and to answer questions concerning institutional purchases of copies (Levis 2010: 378).[104]

C. Actors and Mechanisms in the Implementation of the New IP Regime

In the first phase of the implementation of the new patent regime—running from 1996 to 2001—the actors involved did not differ significantly from those involved in the prior enactment phase of 1995–6. Despite changes in the transnational scene, during those years no new actors joined the conflict in the domestic realm. At the time, local players both within and outside government dominated the conflict over the implementation of the new IP norms. Their victories were won within the margins of indeterminacy and contradiction remaining in the IP laws adopted in the mid-1990s. As expected, actors closer to the centers of domestic power found mechanisms to influence the results of the implementation process, frustrating the internalization of the global game in a typical exercise of the routines of resistance to globalization (Gillespie and Peerenboom 2009).

After the enactment of the IP Law and up to the negotiation of the mutually agreed solution before the WTO Dispute Settlement Body, the US government and the multinational industry continued to exert pressure and to expend resources in both the international and the domestic contexts. The implementation of the IP regime was sought not only through economic threats but also through legal reforms that would adjust the procedures before ANMAT and INPI. After the frustration ignited by the data exclusivity law and the failure to obtain other reforms in the Argentine IP regime, the United States shifted the dispute to the WTO.

At that point—during the second part of the implementation phase that began around 2001—changes in the configuration of actors involved in both global and local confrontations over patents could be observed. In Argentina, the 2001 crisis had made the issue of medicines a central concern of the government's emergency agenda. The Ministry of Health became a proponent of a new PNM, participating in the ongoing disputes in domestic forums. The courts and the INPI also became important actors. The cases initiated by the multinational companies gave the

[104] Some of these episodes highlighted important questions concerning the availability of antiretroviral drugs. For example, Bristol Myers requested a judicial injunction to stop Richmond, a local pharmaceutical company, from offering antiretroviral drugs in a public bid arranged by the Ministry of Health (*Página 12* 2007). In one of these encounters, the Ministry of Health declared: "the patents system for many drugs is coming to an end, because the patents are expiring. Then, some laboratories, as has happened in this case, come up with a small innovation to say they have a new drug in order to achieve a new patent. These are maneuvers that allow laboratories to artificially extend their exclusive rights by several years more and to fix high prices." The Minister also alluded to a "strategy of the pharmaceutical multinationals that, working with law firms, attempted through this means to dodge the law and to ensure their monopolistic position in the market."

agency and the courts an opportunity to mediate the struggle to define the scope of the IP regime. Ultimately, INPI rejected almost all attempts to expand patent protection, and the judiciary, in piecemeal fashion, finally did the same by means of decisions issued by the Supreme Court after 2000.

In the global arena, the Ministry of Health began to play a role different from that of prior heads of the department. Developing countries set up new channels of influence, using forums such as the WTO, WIPO, and the WHO to foster reforms in transnational IP rules. The countries that were more proactive in resisting IP regulations were now accompanied by international NGOs who helped fight pro-IP proposals and establish the Development Agenda (Yu 2009). At this point, along with peer health authorities in developing counties, the Argentine Minister of Health took part in the negotiations of the WTO Conference that produced the Doha Declaration and in other efforts that led to reframing the global debate as a public health matter. Moreover, González García was also involved in challenging the work of WIPO and opposing conservative interpretations of the existing rules fostered by proponents of orthodox pro-IP initiatives.

VIII. Balancing Patent and Health Rights

Insofar as IP rights have the potential to influence the prices of medicines, they also have the capacity to affect the population's access to their health rights. As we have seen, however, this concern was not a unifying thread in the successive struggles over the country's pharmaceutical patent regime. In the early 1990s, during the conflict over the domestic patent regime, the dispute was centered on a clash between the economic interests of multinational and domestic pharmaceutical firms. The congressional enactments that began in 1995 were driven by appeals to nationalism and to the defense of an industry considered of strategic importance to the development of the country. Nonetheless, the economic interests of the domestic pharmaceutical industry were not the exclusive focus of the discussion in Congress. In fact, as evidenced by the content of the hearings and discussions held in Congress, the industrial/business framework sought to legitimize itself through references to other concerns, including the impact patents would have on the price of medicines. As CILFA pointed out, the increase in the price of medicines had been the result of the new rules adopted in the United States.

In spite of the national industry's claim that patents were to blame for higher prices, data from the time indicate that the rate of increase in the price of medicine, including the prices of locally produced copies, in the 1990–5 period (that is, *before* the enactment of the Patent Law) increased by 51.5 percent. In comparison, during that same period, the wholesale price index for non-agricultural goods increased only 19.5 percent (Azpiazu 1997: 38). Furthermore, during the following years, in the period of transition from the old patent regime to the new law (1995–2000), the price of medicines continued to increase without interruption. In 1999, one year before the entry into force of the Patent Law, Argentina had the highest average price of medicines in Latin America (Isalud 1999: 74). In other words, before the entry into force of the new IP regime, prices were rising faster than their cost, while consumption of medicines was sharply dropping. Towards 2000, the entry into force of the patent legislation coincided with the economic recession that culminated in the crisis previously described. Even during the early months of the 2002 crisis, the price of medicines registered several increases: in part, this was due to the increase in the cost of imports and in part, to the contemporaneous termination of Cavallo's Convertibility Plan, which prompted various speculative moves by the market (Godoy Garraza 2004).

As of 2004, when the country had resumed its climb towards economic growth, prices continued their upward trend. This time, however, the Secretary of Trade had instituted an informal price control policy (Tobar 2008: 21–2). Furthermore, new rules required insurers to cover medicines. For consumers, payments were thus no longer entirely out-of-pocket expenses; in the case of the contributory healthcare sector, the new rules mandated that coverage of up to 70 percent of the cost shifted to the insurer. The result was that the issue of patents, which was of limited interest in 2000, began to affect only a small proportion of medicines sold in the country, including mostly low-incidence and high-cost drugs.

However, the overall outcome of the dispute over the patent regime and the effect of patents on the right to health and access to medicines continue to command attention. The prices of medicines in Argentina are still among the most expensive in the region (Tobar 2008). As noted, they were considerably above cost before the new IP regime was enacted and they have remained so (Godoy Garraza 2004). At the same time, the new IP legislation acted as a catalyst for transformations in the pharmaceutical sector and in its business organization. These had redistributive effects on the healthcare system; the defense of consumers' rights was marginal and consumers lost out (even if they did not fully feel it in their pocketbooks) (Vasallo 1999).

For decades, national companies had copied pharmaceutical formulas from foreign laboratories, producing and selling those copies in the country at regulated prices. This allowed them to expand and permanently capture close to 50 percent of sales in the domestic market (González García, De la Puente, and Tarragona 2005: 106). The entry of the IP law into the legal and institutional framework, together with the market liberalization reforms and the deregulation of the sector in the early 1990s (Katz et al. 1997), contributed to the destabilization of this industrial pattern.

National laboratories reacted by making the distribution chain more complex,[105] which resulted in an increase in the price of medicines,[106] while the weak position of individual consumers—then typically charged 50 percent of expenses—went

[105] New actors appeared in the commercialization chain: distributors of medicines (intermediaries between the laboratories and pharmacies or institutional buyers) and managing agents (Farmalink and Preservar) that absorbed the agreements with the largest health insurance institutions in the country (Vasallo 1999). Along the way, a small group of owners of the strongest pharmaceutical companies in Argentina "had the contracts that decided who was going to buy medicines and in whose name" (Touloupas 2010: 70).

[106] Under some estimates the price of medicines rose 75 percent due to the markups applied by drugstores, distributors, and pharmacies in the chain of commercialization.

unnoticed (Vasallo 1999). Furthermore, pharmaceutical firms and insurers (especially mandatory health insurance providers, *obrassociales* in Spanish) negotiated contracts[107] and adopted closed handbooks of brand name medicines. In exchange for limiting the medicines that would be prescribed, the pharmaceutical firms granted insurers discounts. The insurers did not, however, pass these discounts on to patients, even though the patients were responsible for paying a percentage of the cost. In other words, "the strategy of the suppliers consisted of foregoing profits from insurers in order to keep profits from patients, from whom they obtained extraordinary revenues" (Vasallo and Falbo 2007: 64). Thus the brand name market (made up of both national and foreign brands) was strengthened, and pockets of monopolistic medicines were created within each insurance agency, negatively impacting the prices paid by consumers.

This set of defensive strategies over the marketing chains adopted by national pharmaceuticals in the medicines market (Bisang 2010: 368) was developed side by side with the offensive transnational companies carried out in courts, where they sought to modify the scope of IP protection. Even so, in 2002 the confrontational tenor of the patent dispute began to abate. The Argentine Supreme Court's precedent, together with the legal modifications resulting from the WTO's Doha Declaration, defused the part of the battle waged by foreign companies in courts. Just as important, it became evident that only a small number of patents would be granted under the post-2000 laws (Vasallo and Falbo 2007: 80). As one of our interviewees stated, "We believed that we were going to be overrun by patent requests but this was not the case; there is nothing truly important that makes us feel threatened. Today there are many medicines with valid patents across the World that have not been registered in Argentina and that we have copied."[108]

The lack of retroactivity of the new IP regime, that is, the decision not to recognize pipeline protection for pharmaceuticals patented elsewhere, also contributed to the low impact of patent reform on the local pharmaceutical market (De la Puente et al. 2009: 75). Moreover, in relation to patented medicines, national laboratories that could leverage the market strength of their brand names and control of the marketing chain were able to obtain non-mandatory licenses (Vasallo and Falbo 2007: 80). Furthermore, multinational companies voluntarily licensed some of their patents, thus transferring certain lines of production for marketing in Argentina to local companies (IMS Health 2010). This further diluted the conflict over patents.

Nevertheless, while the number of patented essential medicines is low, several important drugs—monoclonal antibodies, antiretrovirals, new-generation antibiotics, and immune response modifiers—are patented. These medicines have a high impact on insurers and on government budgets. They account for approximately 9.24 percent of the total Argentine expenditure on medicines and they are the basis

[107] The pharmaceutical companies (holders of well-known brands) had managed to counterbalance the incentives of financing agents to reduce their expenditures in providing insurance coverage for medicines by offering price discounts on them in exchange for fidelity to branded medicines.

[108] Interview with Interviewee B (from the national pharmaceutical sector).

for the majority of monopolistic marketing practices and other entrance barriers. Yet there is no state regulation (Tobar 2008: 13); apparently, the institutional design of the healthcare system, in particular its financing and the rules regarding the supply of medicines,[109] has removed all political-legal tension between patent protection and access to medicines.[110]

An additional reason for the diffusion of the conflict over patents lies in the high concentration of firms in the pharmaceutical sector. Encouraged by the market liberalization of the 1990s, the subsequent increase in foreign direct investment, and the return of some foreign pharmaceutical companies to Argentina (Isalud 1999: 165), an elite sector comprised of leading national laboratories and a group of transnational firms formed. This elite group has agreed on "modes of competition" and market share, and negotiated certain critical issues in their relationship, including patents. In this sense, Vasallo and Falbo explain that the domestic pharmaceutical sector has tended to "negotiate with multinational laboratories market shares and 'compliance' with the patent law in exchange for silence on medicines with expired patents (and which have copies)" (2007: 81).

Regulatory delay has also reduced the impact of the patent system. In order to be commercialized, a patented drug must have the authorization of the sanitary agency. As has been extensively documented in other countries, this can take eight to twelve years; by that time, the patents have almost lapsed and the period of effective protection has been substantially reduced (Seuba Hernández 2008: 53).

A further factor that appears to contribute to defusing the dispute is related to the growing international expansion of large national pharmaceutical companies (Bisang 2010: 368). The new government policy supporting industrial production prompted by Kirchner's administration in the late 2000s, together with a favorable exchange rate, led to the expansion of large Argentine pharmaceutical companies and the internationalization of their production beyond the neighboring countries that were the traditional buyers of Argentine medicines (Vincent, Suárez, and Franciosi 2007; IMS Health 2010). Pursuant to 2010 data offered by CILFA, exports of pharmaceutical products have doubled in the last five years, reaching a record amount of $659 million (Maito 2010). The increase in the relevance of

109 Civil society organizations working on HIV/AIDS, multiple sclerosis, and oncologic diseases have demanded that private health insurers and the state provide recognized branded medicines, many of them from transnational laboratories under patent protection.

110 This tension was reduced, in part, as a result of (a) the multiple institutional purchases of medicines conducted by the HIV/AIDS and Cancer Governmental Programs run by the National Ministry of Health and (b) the compensation for certain high-cost medicines provided by the Administración de Programas Especiales (Administration of Special Programs, APE) to the contributory healthcare insurers. Until recently, the APE (dissolved in 2012 amidst serious allegations of corruption) has operated a compensatory mechanism whereby national social funds and private health insurance companies received a reimbursement for the expenses incurred as a result of certain high-cost diseases or prolonged treatments. For this purpose, the APE managed the Fondo Soliciario de Redistribución, a fund for the redistribution of resources among rich and poor social health insurers that had been established in 1970.

exported pharmaceutical products has brought about a change in the concerns of these national elites.

It is also probable that the progressive dissolution of the patent dispute is closely linked to the inertial dynamic of the healthcare system, in which internal conflicts between national and transnational groups are dealt with and negotiated behind closed doors. The PNM, implemented in response to the 2001 Argentine crisis, is the most recent example of this phenomenon. This policy was the cornerstone of the struggle for the right to health. The administration enjoyed a great symbolic victory when it raised the PNM as a banner of its public health initiatives. However, an assessment of the PNM must be tempered by its weak or temporary implementation, especially with regard to the INN policy, and its more permanent contributions to public policy, such as the Plan Remediar. In a way, the PNM laid bare the reluctance of even the most motivated or audacious actors to introduce reforms that could destabilize the structure and operation of the healthcare system. The indefinite postponement of the discussion on a generics policy, the ambiguity in the approach to public production of pharmaceuticals,[111] the lack of regulation of PAMI's purchasing policies, the poor oversight of the rules regarding prescription by INN, and the maintenance of the financing and medicines supply mechanisms are signs that the government was not ready to make more structural reforms, even during a crisis, when several windows of opportunity offered the possibility for significant change.

During this period—which coincided with the entry into force of the Patent Law—the Ministry of Health remained on the alert for pharmaceutical patents on the domestic stage, and participated in global forums where the issue was on the agenda.[112] However, one cannot clearly speak of a consistent and deliberate attempt to strike the appropriate balance between the right to health and IP protection or an intentional effort to restructure the pharmaceutical industry. Rather, one must consider both to be circumstantial, linked to the person who happened to head the Ministry of Health at each juncture, and inspired by changes in Argentine foreign policy centered on vindicating the interests of the developing world. Other contributory factors included the deceleration of the rate of drug innovation, the reduced number of new molecular entities introduced into the market, and the expiration of a great number of patents.

This is not to imply that all discussions on pharmaceutical patents have disappeared. Developed countries have maintained the issue on the agenda of global institutions and continue to engage in forum shifting.[113] Transnational

[111] Interviews with Claudio Capuano, Martín Isturiz, and Gonzalo Moyano.

[112] In fact, the National Health Department, which administers the healthcare economy, is in charge of the surveillance of patents at the global stage, especially under the forum shifting strategy carried on by the US and EU (interview with Tomás Pippo).

[113] The World Customs Organization (WCO) has among its functions the duty to regulate the importation of infringing products, and to monitor for criminal activity; it has become a key terrain for strengthening IP protection.

pharmaceutical companies continue to use various strategies that would increase the term of protection and to demand increasingly strong protection[114] (Correa 2008b: 78–9). The commercial agreements between Mercosur and the European Union,[115] health crises such as the H1N1 outbreak,[116] and infringement actions based on public bids for the purchase of medicines (*Página 12* 2007) suggest that while the discussion has calmed, it remains open and could readily resume.

In sum, the capture of the medicines chain by a closed group of actors, changes in the mechanisms for purchasing drugs and financing medicines, the appearance of new actors (including domestic laboratories in India, NGOs, and alliances between multinational and national companies), and the high prices of pharmaceutical products have given rise to a new corporate pact, more complex and opaque than the one in force in prior decades. In the iron triangle formed by trade unions, the State, and corporate businesses, national and transnational pharmaceutical firms act together in defense of their interests. This framework of mutual dependencies has led to an abatement of the patent dispute, yet it does not seem to have generated more and deeper access to medicines. During 2007, Argentine expenditure on medicines reached USD16,115 million, amounting to almost 30 percent of the total health expenditures of the public and the contributory sectors (Tobar 2008). The resources devoted to medicine purchased in Argentina differ sharply from the costs expended by other countries with similar per capita incomes. This high expenditure rate is taking place in a country with health indicators that demonstrate a high degree of inequality in care. These problems are generated by an overly fragmented health system, with significant governance deficits, where public and private health expenditure is both inefficient and regressive (McGuire 2010).

We, therefore, believe that it is necessary to continue to question the way in which the reform cycle Argentina experienced in the last two decades balanced the right to health against protection for intellectual property.

[114] Some of the issues that are continually contested include the fight over patenting of second indications, attempts to nullify the use of the Bolar Exception, and claims about the role of data exclusivity in delaying the entrance of similar medicines.

[115] We refer to the Free Trade Association (EFTA) Agreements that the EU has been concluding with other countries outside the bloc. Negotiations with Mercosur were initiated by the late 1990s and were suspended in 2004. In 2010, negotiations recommenced. One of the strongest points of conflict in the section regarding IP regulations is the issue of geographical indications and the pressure by the European group to adopt TRIPS-plus standards. In relation to geographical indications, the alignment of the different interests is not divided on a "North–South" line. Instead, countries are now grouping themselves in a more complex form (Roffe 2007: 126). Thus, Argentina has a different position from Brazil (its main ally at the Mercosur level). Furthermore, Brazil and the EU differ, especially about wines.

[116] In 2009, during the H1N1 influenza in Argentina, President Cristina Kirchner asked international laboratories to relinquish patents on their vaccines against this disease. She stated that "due to the admission of the laboratories about their incapacity to produce vaccines to deal with influenza A for everyone, it was appropriate to suspend economic rights in order to protect everybody's health" (*La Nación* 2009).

References

Abrutzky, Rosana, Cristina Bramuglia, and Cristina Godio. 2008. "Aspectos de la Política Nacional de Medicamentos Ley de Prescripción de Medicamentos por su nombre genérico y Plan Remediar." Working Paper No. 51, Instituto de Investigaciones Gino Germani, Universidad Nación de Buenos Aires, Buenos Aires.

Almeida do Reis, André Luis, Jorge A. Z. Bermúdez, and María Auxiliadora Oliveira. 2006. "Efectos del Acuerdo sobre los ADPIC en el acceso a los medicamentos: consideraciones para la vigilancia de los precios de los medicamentos." Pp. 107–26 in *La propiedad intelectual en el contexto del acuerdo de la OMC sobre los ADPIC: desafíos para la salud pública*, edited by J. A. Z. Bermudez and M. A. Oliveira. Río de Janeiro: ENSP.

Azpiazu, Daniel. 1997. *Cuadernos de Economía*. 28, *La industria farmacéutica argentina ante el nuevo contexto macroeconómico, 1991–1996*. Buenos Aires: Ministerio de Economía de la Provincia de Buenos Aires.

Bazán, Víctor. 2012. "El derecho a la salud en el escenario jurídico argentino y algunas líneas jurisprudenciales de la Corte Suprema de Justicia en la materia." *Revista Jurisprudencia Argentina* 2012(2): 3–68.

Bisang, Roberto. 2010. "Perfil actual y evolución reciente de la industria argentina de medicamentos." Pp. 365–74 in *Propiedad intelectual y medicamentos*, edited by C. Correa, S. C. Negro, and M. Basso. Montevideo: B de F.

Braithwaite, John, and Peter Drahos. 2000. *Global Business Regulation*. Cambridge: Cambridge University Press.

Bumbak, Sonia, and Leonardo Stanley. 2006. "Propiedad intelectual y salud: del multilateralismo al bilateralismo." *Nuevos Documentos CEDES* 21: 1–27.

Cabanellas de las Cuevas, Guillermo. 2005. *Derecho antimonopólico y de defensa de la competencia*. Vol. ii. Buenos Aires: Heliasta.

Carruthers, Bruce G., and Terence C. Halliday. 2006. "Negotiating Globalization: Global Templates and the Construction of Insolvency Regimes in East Asia." *Law and Social Inquiry* 31: 521–84.

Cátedra Libre De Salud y Derechos Humanos. 2004. "*Política actual de medicamentos en nuestro país: un análisis del Programa Remediar.*" Buenos Aires: Cátedra Libre De Salud y Derechos Humanos, Facultad de Medicina, Universidad Nacional de Buenos Aires.

Correa, Carlos. 2002. *Protección de los datos presentados para el registro de productos farmacéuticos, implementación de las normas del Acuerdo TRIPS*. Geneva: South Centre.

——. 2006a. Economía de las patentes, el Acuerdo TRIPS y la salud pública. En Remiche, Bernard y Kors, Jorge. 2006. *Propiedad Intelectual y Tecnología: El Acuerdo ADPIC diez años después, visiones europeas y latinoamericanas*.

——. 2006b. *Propiedad intelectual y salud pública*. Buenos Aires: Facultad de Derecho UBA and La Ley.

——. 2008a. "Retroactividad del acuerdo sobre los ADPIC a la luz de la protección de la salud pública." Pp. 389–418 in *Salud pública y patentes farmacéuticas: cuestiones de economía, política y derecho*, edited by X. Seuba Hernández. Barcelona: Bosch.

——. 2008b. "Abuso de derechos de patentes y efectos sobre la salud pública." Pp. 71–98 in *Salud pública y patentes farmacéuticas: cuestiones de economía, política y derecho*, edited by X. Seuba Hernández. Barcelona: Bosch.

——. 2009. "Access to Medicines in Argentina: Implementing and Defending TRIPS Flexibilities." Available at <http://www.yaleisp.org/access-knowledge/research-series>.

De Beer, Jeremy. 2009. *Implementing the World Intellectual Property Organization's Development Agenda.* Waterloo, Canada: Wilfred Laurier University Press.

De La Puente, Carolina, Sonia Tarragona, Carola Musetti, Marcelo D'Amore, Diego Slucki, and Nicolás Rosenfeld. 2009. *Propiedad intelectual y medicamentos: el caso de la República Argentina.* Buenos Aires: Isalud.

De la Puente, Catalina, and Federico Tobar. 2007. *Políticas y estrategias de adquisición de medicamentos esenciales: Un análisis sistematizado de modelos y experiencias clave en América Latina.* Buenos Aires: Ediciones Isalud. Serie de Estudios No 2.

Drahos, Peter. 1997. "Thinking Strategically about Intellectual Property Rights." *Telecommunications Policy* 21(3): 201–11.

——. 2004a. "Securing the Future of Intellectual Property: Intellectual Property Owners and the Nodally Coordinated Enforcement Pyramid." *Case Western Reserve Journal of International Law* 36(1): 53–77.

——. 2004b. "Intellectual Property and Pharmaceutical Markets: A Nodal Governance Approach." *Temple Law Review* 77(2): 401–24.

Genovesi, Luis M. 2004. "El plazo de duración de las patentes: Prórroga de la protección a veinte años." Pp. 49–98 in *Patentes de invención: Diez años de jurisprudencia,* edited by J. Kors. Buenos Aires: Facultad de Derecho UBA and La Ley.

—— and Jorge Kors. 2004. "Medidas cautelares." Pp. 153–82 in *Patentes de invención: diez años de jurisprudencia,* edited by J. Kors. Buenos Aires: Facultad de Derecho UBA and La Ley.

Gillespie, John, and Randall Peerenboom. 2009. "Pushing back on Globalization: An Introduction to Regulation in Asia." Pp. 1–23 in *Regulation in Asia: Pushing back on Globalization,* edited by J. Gillespie and R. Peerenboom. London: Routledge.

Godoy Garraza, Lucas. 2004. "El acceso a los medicamentos esenciales y las políticas para garantizarlo: notas desde el caso argentino." Pp. 263–72 in *Acceso a medicamentos: derecho fundamental, papel del Estado,* edited by J. Bermudez, M. A. Oliveira, and A. Esher. Río de Janeiro: ENSP.

González García, Ginés. 1994. *Remedios políticos para los medicamentos.* Buenos Aires: Ediciones Isalud.

—— Catalina De la Puente, and Sonia Tarragona. 2005. *Medicamentos: salud, política y economía.* Buenos Aires: Ediciones Isalud.

Halliday, Terence C. 2009. "Recursivity of Global Normmaking: A Sociolegal Agenda." *The Annual Review of Law and Social Science* 5: 263–89.

—— and Bruce G. Carruthers. 2007. "The Recursivity of Law: Global Norm Making and National Lawmaking in the Globalization of Corporate Insolvency Regimes." *The American Journal of Sociology* 112(4): 1135–202.

Helfer, Laurence. 2007. "Navigating Institutional Density in Intellectual Property Regimes: The Strategy of Regime Shifting." Presented at the Politics of International Regime Complexity workshop. March 1, Northwestern University, Chicago.

——. 2009. "Regime Shifting in the International Intellectual Property System." *Perspectives on Politics* 7(1): 39–44.

Herrera Parra, Nelly. 2003. Proceso de negociación conjunta de precios para medicamentos antiretrovirales en la subregión andina, Argentina, México, Paraguay y Uruguay. Lima: Panamerican Health Organization (PAHO). Available at <http://www.bvsde.paho.org/texcom/sct/045996.pdf>.

Homedes, Nuria, and Antonio Ugalde. 2005. "Multisource Drug Policies in Latin America: Survey of 10 Countries." *Bulletin of the World Health Organization* 83(1): 64–70.

IMS Health. 2010. "Perspectiva mundial del mercado farmacéutico." IMS Health, PMA, MAT December 2010. Unpublished.

Isalud. 1999. *Estudios de Economía Real. Vol. xiii: El mercado de medicamentos en la Argentina.* Buenos Aires: Centro de estudios para la producción.

Jauregui, Lisandro L. 2003. "La Constitución Nacional y la participación del poder legislativo en la formulación de la política exterior Argentina." Retrieved July 12, 2013 <http://www.senado.gov.ar/bundles/senadomicrositios/pdf/TercerPremio.pdf>.

Jones, Mark P. and Wonjae Hwang. 2005. "Provincial Party Bosses: Keystone of the Argentine Congress." Pp. 115–38 in *Argentine Democracy: The Politics of Institutional Weakness*, edited by S. Levitsky and M. V. Murillo. University Park, PA: Pennsylvania State University Press.

Kapczynski, Amy. 2009. "Harmonization and Its Discontents: A Case Study of TRIPS Implementation in India's Pharmaceutical Sector." *California Law Review* 97 (6): 1571–649.

Katz, Jorge M., Gustavo Burachik, Joan Brodovsky, and Sérgio Queiroz. 1997. *Apertura económica y desregulación en el mercado de medicamentos: la industria farmacéutica y farmoquímica de Argentina, Brasil y México en los años 90.* Buenos Aires: Alianza Editorial.

Klug, Heinz. 2007. "Una campaña por la vida: la construcción de una nueva solidaridad trasnacional frente al VIH/SIDA y al ADPIC." Pp. 109–27 in *El derecho y la globalización desde abajo: hacia una legalidad cosmopolita*, edited by B. Sousa Santos and C. Rodríguez Garavito. Barcelona: Anthropos Editorial and Universidad Autónoma Metropolitana.

Kors, Jorge (ed.). 2004a. *Patentes de invención: diez años de jurisprudencia.* Buenos Aires: Facultad de Derecho UBA and La Ley.

——. 2004b. "La mayor protección bajo el acuerdo sobre los ADPIC." Pp. 99–122 in *Patentes de invención: diez años de jurisprudencia*, edited by J. Kors. Buenos Aires: Facultad de Derecho UBA and La Ley.

——. 2005. "Medidas cautelares en juicios de patentes." Presented at I Congreso Internacional de Derecho Comercial y de los Negocios, Facultad de Derecho de la Universidad Nacional de Buenos Aires, May 30, Buenos Aires.

Levis, Marta. 2010. "La visión de la propiedad intelectual por la industria farmacéutica nacional latinoamericana." Pp. 375–92 in *Propiedad intelectual y medicamentos*, edited by C. Correa, S. C. Negro, and M. Basso. Montevideo: B de F.

Lustig, Doreen, and Benedict Kingsbury. 2006. "Displacement and Relocation from Protected Areas: International Law Perspectives on Rights, Risks and Resistance." *Conservation & Soc.* 4(3): 404–18.

Maito, Miguel. 2010. "La industria farmacéutica argentina: su carácter estratégico y perspectivas." Buenos Aires: CILFA.

McGuire, J. W. 2010. *Wealth, Health, and Democracy in East Asia and Latin America.* New York: Cambridge University Press.

Madies, Claudia. 2010. "Protección de datos de prueba. Regulación y situación actual." Pp. 323–36 in *Propiedad intelectual y medicamentos*, edited by C. Correa, S. C. Negro, and M. Basso. Montevideo: B de F.

Merry, Sally. 2006. *Human Rights and Gender Violence: Translating International Law into Local Justice.* Chicago: University of Chicago Press.

Moncayo Von Hase, Andrés. 2004. "Patentes de reválida." Pp. 9–39 in *Patentes de invención: diez años de jurisprudencia*, edited by J. Kors. Buenos Aires: Facultad de Derecho UBA and La Ley.

Murphy, Tomás E. 1997. "Un análisis económico del proceso de formación de leyes: el caso Argentino de la ley de patentes." Graduation paper, Universidad de San Andrés, Buenos Aires.

Najurieta, María S. 2006. "Reflexiones sobre casos jurisprudenciales en materia de patentes resueltos por tribunales argentinos." Presented at the OMPI-OEPM-OEP Fifth Regional Seminar on Intellectual Property for judges and prosecutors of Latin America, November 17, Cartagena de Indias, Colombia.

Novaro, Marcos. 2009. *Argentina en el fin de siglo: democracia, mercado y nación (1983–2001).* Buenos Aires: Paidós.

Oliveira, María A., and Gabriela Costa Chavés. 2010. "Implementación del acuerdo sobre la ADPIC dela OMC." Pp. 393–404 in *Propiedad intelectual y medicamentos,* edited by C. Correa, S. C. Negro, and M. Basso. Montevideo: B de F.

Palermo, Vicente. 2010. "De Néstor Kirchner a Cristina Fernández de Kirchner. La política de la contra posición." Observatório Político Sul-Americano Análise de Conjuntura (n.9, set. 2010). Río de Janeiro: Instituto de Estudos Sociais e Políticos Universidade do Estado do Rio de Janeiro IESP/UER.

Perticara, Marcela. 2008. *Incidencia de los gastos de bolsillo en salud en siete países latinoamericanos.* Santiago, Chile: CEPAL, División de Desarrollo Social.

Programa Naciones Unidas para el Desarrollo. 2011. El sistema de salud argentino y su trayectoria de largo plazo: logros alcanzados y desafíos futuros/1a ed.—Buenos Aires: Programa Naciones Unidas para el Desarrollo—PNUD.

Quintana, Brenda L. and Liliana Piani. 2009. "El Mercado de medicamentos en Argentina: un componente excluyente en el diseño del sistema de salud." Manuscript developed for a Congress debate in Argentina. Unpublished. Available at <http://www.buenastareas.com/ensayos/Laboratorios-Argentinos/4128298.html>.

Rajagopal, Balakrishnan. 2005. *El derecho internacional desde abajo: el desarrollo, los movimientos sociales y la resistencia del Tercer Mundo.* Bogotá: ILSA.

Rodríguez, Hugo M. 2006. "Innovación tecnológica en Argentina: uso del sistema de patentes." *Revista Espacios* 27(3): 1–36.

Roffe, Pedro. 2007. *América Latina y la nueva arquitectura internacional de la propiedad intelectual: de los Adpic-Trips a los nuevos tratados de libre comercio.* Buenos Aires: Facultad de Derecho UBA.

——. 2008. "La cuestión de la 'materia existente' y los productos farmacéuticos: una interpretación del artículo 70 del ADPIC a la luz de su contexto, objeto, fin y circunstancias." Pp. 335–87 in *Salud pública y patentes farmacéuticas: cuestiones de economía, política y derecho,* edited by X. Seuba Hernández. Barcelona: Bosch.

Secretaría Parlamentaria. 1995. *Investigación a cargo de la Comisión de Industria.* Vols. ii and iii. Buenos Aires: Secretaría Parlamentaria.

Sell, Susan K. 2003. *Private Power, Public Law: The Globalization of Intellectual Property Rights.* Cambridge: Cambridge University Press.

——. 2008. "Acuerdos de Libre Comercio con Disposiciones ADPIC PLUS y acceso a los medicamentos." Pp. 169–215 in *Salud pública y patentes farmacéuticas: cuestiones de economía, política y derecho,* edited by X. Seuba Hernández. Barcelona: Bosch.

——. 2009. "Cat and Mouse: Forum-Shifting in the Battle over Intellectual Property Enforcement." Presented at the American Political Science Association Meeting, September 3–6, 2009, Toronto.

Seuba Hernández, Xavier (ed.). 2008. *Salud pública y patentes farmacéuticas: cuestiones de economía, política y derecho.* Barcelona: Bosch.

Sousa Santos, Boaventura. 2007. "Más allá de la gobernanza neoliberal: el Foro Social Mundial como legalidad y política cosmopolitas subalternas." Pp. 31–60 in *El derecho y la globalización desde abajo: hacia una legalidad cosmopolita*, edited by B. Sousa Santos and C. Rodríguez Garavito. Barcelona: Anthropos Editorial and Universidad Autónoma Metropolitana.

—— and César Rodríguez Garavito (eds.). 2007. *El derecho y la globalización desde abajo: hacia una legalidad cosmopolita*. Barcelona: Anthropos Editorial y Universidad Autónoma Metropolitana.

Tobar, Federico. 2002. *Acceso a los medicamentos en la Argentina: diagnóstico y alternativas*. Buenos Aires: Centro de Estudios de Estado y Sociedad.

——. 2008. "Precio de los medicamentos en Argentina y su regulación." Unpublished manuscript on file with authors.

Torre, Juan C. 1997. *Las dimensiones políticas e institucionales de las reformas estructurales en América Latina*. Santiago: Naciones Unidas.

Touloupas, Constantino. 2010. Intervention in the blog "Foro de Salud en carta Abierta." November 28, 2010. Available at <http://forodesaludencartaabierta.blogspot.com.ar/2010/11/politicas-de-medicamentos-desde-la_28.html>.

Vasallo, Carlos. 1999. "Los cambios en la producción y comercialización de medicamentos." Presented at the Asociación de Economía de la Salud, Buenos Aires.

—— and Rodrigo Falbo. 2007. "Estructura de la oferta y política de medicamentos." Pp. 49–82 in *Política de medicamentos en la Argentina*, edited by G. Ventura and L. Godoy Garraza. Buenos Aires: Comisión Nacional Salud Investiga–Ministerio de Salud de la Nación.

Vincent, Rodolfo, Clara Suárez, and Eduardo Franciosi. 2007. "Actores y agenda en el sistema de salud argentino. Sector farmacéutico." Presented as Seminar VII of the Seminar Series on Public Health, Centro de Estudios de Estado y Sociedad (CEDES), December 17, Buenos Aires.

Yu, Peter. 2009. "Building Intellectual Property Coalitions for Development." Pp. 79–99 in *Implementing the World Intellectual Property Organization's Development Agenda*, edited by J. de Beer. Waterloo, Canada: Wilfred Laurier University Press.

NEWSPAPER ARTICLES

Clarín, Una píldora amarga, August 14, 1990, página 8. Unknown author, page 8 (*Clarín* 1990)

Clarín, Sin ley de medicamentos habrá represalias de EEUU, August 28, 1991. Osvaldo Demaría, page 18 (*Clarín* 1991a)

Clarín, La ley de patentes, según Economía, September 28, 1991. Omar Báez, page 14 (*Clarín* 1991b)

Clarín, Patentes: Brasil y Argentina en la mira de EEUU, May 2, 1993. Washington unidentified reporter, page 29 (*Clarín* 1993a)

Clarín, La ley de patentes va para largo, June 18, 1993. Unknown author (*Clarín* 1993b)

Clarín, Fernández Meijide salió a defender a los laboratorios, February 16, 2000. Digital edition (no page), Unknown author (*Clarín* 2000a)

Clarín, Medicamentos: regirá en 10 días la polémica Ley de Patentes, October 15, 2010. Marcelo Canto, Digital edition (no page) (*Clarín* 2000b)

Clarín, Procedimiento para otorgar licencias para la fabricación nacional: Un fallo judicial vuelve a enfrentar a laboratorios locales y extranjeros, June 25, 2005. Section El país. Unknown author (*Clarín* 2005)

La Nación, Estados Unidos: No dará marcha atrás con los subsidios. March 3, 1995. Ovidio Bellando (*La Nación* 1995)

La Nación, Menem quiere modificar otra vez la ley de patentes, May 3, 1996. Jorge Elías, politics (section), digital edition (no page) (*La Nación* 1996a)

La Nación, Vuelve el fantasma de la ley de patentes, November 20, 1996. Graciela Guadalupe, politics (section), digital edition (no page) (*La Nación* 1996b)

La Nación, Más restricciones a las ventas externas, April 16, 1997 (*La Nación* 1997)

La Nación, Sebastiani negó las acusaciones; presunto sobornos a cambio de la ley, August 31, 2001. Laura Zommer, Politics (section), digital edition (no page) (*La Nación* 2001)

La Nación, Otro reclamo para liberar las patentes de las vacunas, August 19, 2009. Alerta sanitaria, general information (section), digital edition (no page) (*La Nación* 2009)

Página 12, La batalla recién comienza, September 21, 1990. Daniel Sosa, page 6 (*Página 12* 1990a)

Página 12, Laboratorios en pie de guerra, November 22, 1990. Daniel Sosa (*Página 12* 1990b)

Página 12, Medicamentos en mira, January 10, 1992. Unknown author (*Página 12* 1992)

Página 12, Rechazo del Sur a las presiones, September 11th, 1993. Alejandra Folgarait (*Página 12* 1993a)

Página 12, Patentes farmacéuticas: las penas son de nosotros, los remedios son ajenos, Suplemento de Salud, September 10, 1993. Alejandra Folgarait (*Página 12* 1993b)

Página 12, Respuesta a Cheek, June 6, 1993, Sección El País. Unknown author, page 2 (*Página 12* 1993c)

Página 12, Diputados se toma su tiempo, October 17th, 1994. Unknown author, page 6 (*Página 12* 1994a)

Página 12, Cheek no tiene remedio, March 20, 1994. Unknown author (*Página 12* 1994b)

Página 12, Los diputados buscan remedio para la herida por el Pampa, Sección El País, December 7, 1994. Alberto Dearriba, page 12 (*Página 12* 1994c)

Página 12, Se va a solucionar, April 4, 1995. Unknown author (*Página 12* 1995a)

Página 12, Un esperado ajuste de cuentas, May 24, 1995. Unknown author, page 3 (*Página 12* 1995b)

Página 12, Cavallo desbocado, June 10, 1995. Román Leijman y Ernesto Tenembaum, page 3 (*Página 12* 1995c)

Página 12, Menem lo critica a Cheek pero a dará una manito. Denuncia, March 31, 1995. Unknown author, page 2 (*Página 12* 1995d)

Página 12, Los diputados no quieren entregar, May 21, 1995. Unknown author, page 3. (*Página 12* 1995e)

Página 12, Ira por la ley Cheek, April 28, 1995. Unknown author, page 9 (*Página 12* 1995f)

Página 12, Presión de EEUU, December 15, 1997. (*Página 12* 1997)

Página 12, Patentes: prometen mantener la ley, June 17, 1999. Unknown author (*Página 12* 1999)

Página 12, Riesgo de aumento de precios: entrada en vigencia de la ley de patentes medicinales, November 6, 2000. (*Página 12* 2000)

Pagina 12, Un límite para los monopolios, November 7, 2007. Pedro Lipcovich. El Pais section. (*Página 12 2007*)

Chapter 3

Brazil and the Case of Patents and Access to Medicines: A Medical Condition?

Mônica Steffen Guise Rosina and Adelina de Oliveira Novaes

Introduction

The debate surrounding intellectual property (IP) rights and their relation to access to health has been a central feature in the contemporary agendas of states engaged in promoting development and enhancing social welfare.[1] As nations gradually cease to understand the concept of development as pure and simple economic growth, the tension between patents and access to medicines has become more evident.[2] And as IP has become a target of both domestic and international debate, the study of development increasingly requires an understanding of the workings and regulation of "global administrative spaces." These are characterized by Kingsbury, Krisch, and Stewart (2005) as follows:

> Instead of neatly separated levels of regulation, a congeries of different actors and different layers together form a variegated "global administrative space" that includes international institutions and transnational networks involving both governmental and non-governmental actors, as well as domestic administrative bodies that operate within international regimes or cause transboundary regulatory effects.

Within these global administrative spaces, Dreyfuss and Rodríguez-Garavito (this volume) identify the regulation of intellectual property rights—which has a long international history,[3] but with a profound domestic impact—as one of the most interesting spheres for analysis. The rules, along with the institutions administering IP, have diverse origins (multilateral agreements coexist with regional and bilateral agreements) and allow different actors (including states, businesses,

[1] The conception of development utilized here is part of a more comprehensive model suggested by Amartya Sen (1999) and embodied, in terms of global indicators, in the Human Development Index. The main focus of such a developmental approach is to consider the subject in its social context, whether as a generator of economic wealth or as an interested party in public policies that increase freedom.

[2] Tension exists when a private interest (the pursuit of profit) juxtaposes with public interest (feasibility of access to knowledge products, for instance).

[3] On the history of international regulation of intellectual property, see Maristela Basso (2000), Daniel Gervais (1998), and Merges and Ginsburg (2004).

nongovernmental organizations (NGOs), and international organizations) to interact in multiple ways. In this sense, the term "legal kaleidoscope," coined by Rodríguez-Garavito (2005), seems appropriate to describe the dynamics that govern such a legal framework.

With a population of 190,732,694 people and a total area of 8,514,876.599 km^2 (3,287,612 sq mi), Brazil is the largest country in Latin America (IBGE 2011). If we look solely at the Gross Domestic Product (GDP), Brazil is definitely the richest country in both South and Latin America, followed by Mexico and Argentina. A more comprehensive approach, however, takes into account other important wealth and development indicators. The United Nations' 2012 State of the World's Cities Report, for instance, ranks Brazil as the fourth most unequal country in the Latin America and Caribbean regions when it comes to distribution of wealth, losing only to Guatemala, Honduras, and Colombia. According to the same report, despite all progress achieved over the past ten years, 124 million people still live in poverty in the region, of which 37 million are Brazilians.[4] Furthermore, the United Nations' Human Development Index has been featuring Brazil in the 84th position for the last couple of years, lagging behind much smaller and less industrialized economies.[5]

Despite its wealth inequalities, however, Brazil is widely viewed as a strong actor in the effort to promote public health and development interests in the international sphere. Along with Argentina, Brazil has put forward the Development Agenda at the World Intellectual Property Organization (WIPO), an effort that resulted in the adoption of 45 recommendations, and several active projects.[6] At the World Trade Organization (WTO), Brazil has been a key player in the negotiation process, leading, for instance, the G21 group of developing countries that advocated for a social agenda and for more development-oriented trade discussions. At the World Health Organization (WHO), among other initiatives, Brazil has had a leading role in discussing a global binding treaty on Research and Development, aimed at addressing diseases that disproportionately affect developing countries.[7] Brazil's success in treating HIV patients through a national program that is built upon free distribution of antiretroviral (ARV) drugs to all infected citizens is an international statement of the country's stance on public health matters. The 2007 issuance of a compulsory license for the ARV drug Efavirenz made that statement even stronger.

When it comes to the regulation of IP rights, however, the image of Brazil as a supporter and strong guardian of public health becomes blurred, for the country's eagerness to integrate into the world economy has required it to embrace other—often conflicting—interests. From at least the time of the early Uruguay Round leading to the creation of the WTO, intellectual property has become increasingly

[4] <http://www.onuhabitat.org/index.php?option=com_docman&task=cat_view&gid=362&Itemid=18>.

[5] <http://hdr.undp.org/en/media/HDR_2011_EN_Tables.pdf>.

[6] See WIPO, The 45 Adopted Recommendations under the WIPO Development Agenda (2007), available at <http://www.wipo.int/ip-development/en/agenda/recommendations.html>.

[7] <http://www.who.int/phi/CEWG_Report_5_April_2012.pdf>.

connected to free trade, as opposed to development and health concerns. And as will be seen in greater detail, trade-oriented intellectual property rules do not always work for the benefit of public health interests. Indeed, that has been Brazil's experience, particularly in connection with access to medicines.

As the main and most comprehensive international agreement on intellectual property rights, the WTO's Agreement on Trade Related Aspects of Intellectual Property Rights (TRIPS) is a milestone in the history of intellectual property protection. It binds the entire WTO membership (currently, over 150 countries) to the same rules and it relies on the WTO's dispute settlement mechanism for enforcement purposes. Most notably, the TRIPS Agreement establishes a set of minimum standards for intellectual property protection. For many developing and least developed countries, joining TRIPS thus meant that their domestic patent regime—in many cases incipient, and in some, nonexistent—now had to comply with new rules and patterns of protection quite similar to those of most developed and industrialized nations.

The debate over whether these high levels of protection are in the best interest of developing countries remains unsettled. The international discourse[8] that dominated the Uruguay Round was based on the argument that high levels of intellectual property protection would naturally generate more technology transfer and economic development, and thus be of extreme value to Southern nations. However, many scholars disagree.[9] Boyle (2004), for instance, points out that some of the countries that now advocate for strong IP rules took advantage of low (or no) IP protection in their own process of industrial and economic development. In addition, when viewing intellectual property protection through a development-oriented lens, it is important to look beyond the economic benefits the international system promised developing nations. Granting property rights to knowledge and knowledge products generates an access issue. And health is perhaps the field where friction between public and private interests is the most evident: by generating economic incentives, patents are supposed to spur drug innovation and, thus, make more drugs available. But because patents, as exclusive rights, can lead to higher prices and lower output, they also constitute a significant obstacle to access.

With this backdrop in mind, Brazil is quite an interesting case to consider, for its government—uniquely among nations in the world—bears full responsibility for access to health. As will be seen in greater detail later in this chapter, since the 1988 establishment of the constitutional right to health, federal, state, and municipal governments have taken action aimed at providing access to health services and products (including essential medicines) to the entire Brazilian population. The Brazilian government is, accordingly, a very interested party. It must make sure drug costs are low because the efficacy of its public health system depends, to a large extent, on medicines reaching its population free of charge. Not surprisingly,

[8] On the history of the negotiations that led to TRIPS, see Gervais (1998) and UNCTAD and ICTSD (2005).

[9] See Abbot and Reichman (2007).

therefore, its pre-TRIPS patent law did not provide protection to chemical-pharmaceutical products and processes.[10]

The patent landscape, however, changed radically in 1995, when Brazil chose to join the WTO at the earliest possible moment and to forgo use of the transitional period included in the TRIPS Agreement to help developing countries adjust to their new obligations. The 1996 patent law, now WTO and TRIPS compliant, established, among other things, that patents for pharmaceuticals and pharmaceutical products would now be available. In practice, the move from no patent protection to full patent protection had a profound impact on the availability of medicines at low cost. Drugs became more expensive not only to individuals purchasing over-the-counter or through prescription, but also to the government.

Additionally, the new patent provisions have created substantial confusion regarding the patent examination procedure, as it applies to medical innovations. As will be seen in greater detail, the Brazilian National Health Surveillance Agency (Agência Nacional de Vigilância Sanitária—ANVISA, in Portuguese) could play an important role in making sure that pharmaceutical patents are not unduly granted in the country. Controversy, uncertainty, and lack of transparency, however, surround the Agency's mandate, undermining its ability to defend public health interests.

Thus, if we confront the new patent rules with the government's increasing need to make sure that public health needs are met, metaphorically speaking, it might just be that Brazil is suffering from a case of schizophrenia.

As defined by Laplanche and Pontalis (2001), schizophrenia is a term originally created in 1911 by Eugen Bleuler to designate a group of psychoses. By introducing the term schizophrenia (from the Greek, to split, cleave, and spirit), Bleuler highlighted what, in his view, constitutes its main symptom: *spaltung* ("dissociation"). The term is currently used in psychiatry and psychoanalysis, in spite of disagreements over what exactly gives schizophrenia its specificity. Clinically, there are several types of schizophrenia, but the following characteristics are common to them all: incoherence of thoughts, actions, and affectivity; a separation of oneself from reality; an inner life where phantasmatic productions are predominant (autism); and delusional activity that is more or less accentuated and nonsystematic.

Our study of Brazil's regulation of patents and access to medicines shows that schizophrenia characterizes much of Brazil's approach, especially in regard to "incoherence of actions." National legislative and political choices do not coherently reflect the country's stance on the promotion of access to health and medicines. On the contrary, many of the decisions taken seem to be dissociated from reality and from one another. This, then, is, the background that contextualizes our study. The chapter seeks to tell the story of patent protection and access to medicines in Brazil by describing the legal and political framework—as well as highlighting the main facts and actors—that over the last two decades or so, have shaped the country's stance on the patent/access issue.

[10] Law No. 5.772, 1971. Chapter II, article 9 (c) stating that "chemical-pharmaceutical products shall not be subject to patent protection."

Much has been written about how Brazil has handled these problems and we have relied on the most updated literature and case law. We did, however, supplement a study of these sources with a series of reflexive interviews, as we believe the perceptions of our respondents broaden our understanding of Brazil's behavior and cast extra light on some of the dynamics described by most of the authors whose texts appear in this chapter as references.[11] We worked with a group of seventeen respondents and the data collected were grouped according to the number of times they appeared in the answers (frequency).[12]

We start the chapter by describing the importance of the right to health for the construction of the current Brazilian public health system and how the issue of access to medicines fits into that frame. We then describe the main actors and events that have, in our view, played essential roles in defining health and patent rules and policies. Throughout the text, we highlight the incoherence that characterizes several legislative and political decisions regarding patents and public health and creates the overall schizophrenic effect. We close with a list of recommendations that, from a global administrative perspective, may be helpful in dealing with the country's "psychiatric" condition.

I. Fulfilling the Constitutional Right to Health: The Case of Access to Medicines

Understanding access to medicines in Brazil demands consideration of a broader perspective—that of the legal structure governing the national right to health. The 1988 Constitution of Brazil establishes:

> Art. 196 Health care is a universal right and obligation of the state, guaranteed through social and economic policies aimed at reduction of the risk of disease and other losses and universal and equal access to efforts and services intended for their promotion, protection, and reclamation.

Before 1988, healthcare in Brazil was only available to those formally employed who contributed to the public insurance system or one of the many private ones. As described by Ferraz (2009), the system divided the population into those who were insured and those who were not. The 1998 Constitution changed this scenario as—in theory—it created the right of every Brazilian citizen to seek healthcare through public health facilities, regardless of his or her contribution to an insurance system.

By ranking health as a fundamental right, the Constitution thus generated substantial obligations in terms of fulfilling health needs for the Brazilian state

[11] The reflexive interview (Szymanski 2008) differs from the conventional interview in that it seeks to understand, by means of reflexivity, the meaning of the interviewee's speech. In general terms, reflexivity may be characterized by the expression of understanding from the interviewer of the interviewee's story. By expressing this understanding to the interviewee, the latter may legitimate his own speech, thus improving the trustworthiness of results.

[12] The respondents were chosen according to our own perception of them as relevant actors in the public and academic debate surrounding patents and access to medicines in Brazil.

(Silva 2005).[13] Unlike many other jurisdictions, in Brazil, the right to health is not an abstract goal to be eventually achieved, but rather a highly concrete undertaking.

But for such a large country bearing the weight of great wealth inequality, turning the Constitutional mandate into reality was and still is a huge task. Several laws were subsequently passed in order to allow for the establishment and proper functioning of a Unified System of Healthcare (Sistema Único de Saúde—SUS, in Portuguese).[14] These laws also lay down the principles upon which the Brazilian public health system ought to be governed: (i) universal access; (ii) equal access; and (iii) comprehensiveness of the health services provided.[15]

Twenty-five years later and there remains much to be done. Laws and policies continue to be enacted in order to further develop the efficacy of the system and broaden the scope of coverage. Hospitals still lack doctors and beds, and people still lack treatment. However, one cannot deny the profound impact of the 1988 provision on the lives of those who were previously excluded from any kind of care whatsoever.

The National Policy on Medicines mandates the government to keep a National List of Essential Medicines (Relação Nacional de Medicamentos Essenciais—RENAME, in Portuguese). Periodically updated by the Ministry of Health, RENAME lists the drugs needed for treatment and control of the main diseases in the country. Furthermore, several specific laws mandate the free distribution of drugs for diseases not covered by RENAME. These include Ordinance 2.577 of 2006 (National Program for Exceptional Medicines), Law 9.313 of 1996 (HIV/AIDS), and Law 11.347 of 2006 (Diabetes), among others. Because these obligations are quite extensive, they make the Ministry of Health by far the main (although not the sole) purchaser of medicines in the Brazilian market.[16]

When drugs are not available through regular channels, the judiciary plays an important role. Through litigation, state and municipal governments are increasingly required, on an individual basis, to provide drugs to plaintiffs.[17] Such suits are

[13] See Art. 6 (Title II, of Fundamental Rights and Guarantees, Chapter II, of Social Rights): "Education, health care, work, housing, leisure, safety, welfare, protection of maternity and infancy, and assistance to the less fortunate are social rights under this Constitution."

[14] Federal Laws 8.080 and 8.142 (both enacted in 1990) provide the legal bases and guidelines for the establishment of SUS, for instance.

Art. 6(I)(d) of Law 8.080/90 provides that SUS is responsible for the "execution of efforts of integral therapeutic, even *pharmaceutical* assistance" (emphasis added); Administrative Law 3.916 establishes that the main objective of the National Policy on Medicines is "to guarantee affordable, effective, and good quality *access to medicines*" (emphasis added); Administrative Law 2.577 provides medical strategies for the treatment of determined diseases, including the provision of medicines to patients; Law 9.313/96 mandates SUS to provide free medicines to all citizens infected with the HIV/AIDS virus; Law 11.347/06 determines the supply of free medicines to diabetics.

[15] For a more in-depth analysis of the three principles governing public healthcare in Brazil, see Ferraz and Vieira (2008). The authors argue, for instance, that the ideal of universal care has concretized the notion of citizenship as a central feature of the system.

[16] One might ask why people would buy drugs if the government is mandated to provide them for free. Several hypotheses can be offered: bureaucratic distributions channels; long waiting lists; lack of drugs, the absence of a particular medicine on the list of government-approved pharmaceuticals.

[17] Not all decisions, of course, take this stance, but most of them do. For a detailed study on the judicial enforcement of access to medicines, see Guise et al. (2010).

filed when the drugs that are supposed to be available are not, or when the patient suffers from a medical condition that requires a pharmaceutical not supplied by the system. Studies conducted by Guise et al. (2010) and Silva and Terrazas (2008) demonstrate that the large majority of Brazilian court decisions favor the claimants, interpreting access to medicine as a constitutional right of every citizen.[18] Thus, whether through direct supply via SUS, or by means of judicial decisions, the Brazilian state has accepted the constitutional obligation to provide access to a large array of drugs.

The state's ability to supply medicines for free depends, however, on a number of factors, of which its budget ranks quite high. Government resources are limited. Guise et al. (2010) and Ferraz and Vieira (2008) point out that federal, state, and municipal expenditures on public healthcare have grown significantly in recent years, in a globally recognizable trend. Between 2003 and 2004, the costs of the National STD/AIDS Program alone rose 97.6 percent, going from R$689 million to R$1.36 billion (Programa Nacional DST e AIDS 2008). The cost of drugs accounts for a significant portion of these expenses. Vieira et al. (2007: 10–11) conclude that, between 2002 and 2006, the increase in the cost of medicines (123.9 percent) overtook the increase of total healthcare costs (9.6 percent) in Brazil.[19] Taking into account medicines granted to patients via judicial decisions,[20] government expenses have increased by 5,000 percent over the last six years (O Estado de São Paulo 2011).[21]

The granting of patents to pharmaceutical products, introduced in Brazil in 1996, is among the main factors that explain why medicines have come to weigh heavily upon the Brazilian public health budget. As suggested earlier, in the 1940s, patent legislation did not cover chemical-pharmaceutical products. In 1971, the scope of this exception was expanded with the passage of Law No. 5.772 (Industrial Property Statute), which extended the area of non-patentability to certain chemical-pharmaceutical processes.[22] Thus, the earlier Brazilian legislation led to the production and

[18] The same study shows, however, that the most recent decisions of the Federal Supreme Court may point to a different direction, as concerns such as allocation of scarce financial resources are beginning to be considered in some decisions.

[19] The same study also points out that, in order to guarantee access to progressively more expensive medicines, the Ministry of Health must reallocate its budget, or significantly reduce investment in other areas.

[20] Over 3,400 lawsuits were adjudicated in 2010. Twenty-five thousand lawsuits are currently awaiting decision in the state of São Paulo alone (O Estado de São Paulo 2011).

[21] For further figures, see the study of Ferraz and Vieira (2008), as it provides a thorough analysis of the increase in health expenditures in Brazil.

[22] The 1971 Code established the non-patentability of (among other things): "substances, materials or products obtained through chemical processes, except, however, respective processes for obtaining or modifying... food, chemical-pharmaceutical, and medicinal substances, materials, mixtures, or products, of any variety, as well as the respective processes for their obtaining and modification." Process patents protect processes of obtaining determined products and may be used to introduce competitive advantages even after the expiration date of a product's patent, because it makes the cost of production for similar companies (in this case, the makers of generics and similar) relatively higher.

sale of two types of medicine: (i) those originally released and produced by global industrial leaders, with widely known brand names (called reference or innovator drugs); and (ii) similar drugs,[23] copies that contained the same active ingredients, in the same concentration and pharmaceutical form (but not necessarily the same bioavailability) as the innovator ones, normally released by medium-sized or small national pharmaceutical companies (Quental et al. 2008).

The absence of pharmaceutical patents allowed the Ministry of Health to purchase similar version of branded drugs royalty free and assure free access to Brazilian patients through SUS supply (Oliveira et al. 2006; Gadelha 2003; Quental et al. 2008). As studies show, a national pharmaceutical industry grew to meet this demand (Costa et al. 2005; Hasenclever 2002). At the same time, national public laboratories also played a central role in drug production and distribution, for they made versions of the drug available at marginal cost.

The advent of the WTO and Brazil's immediate entry changed this scenario, in which copying was largely responsible for the success of a public healthcare policy regarding access to medicines. In 1996, Brazil adopted a new Industrial Property Law, which complied with the patent provisions of the TRIPS Agreement.[24] Among key provisions of the new statute was the obligation to patent both chemical-pharmaceutical products and processes. For a national industry that based its business solely on copying existing branded drugs, the new patent rules posed an insurmountable obstacle: by granting exclusive rights to patent holders for twenty years, copying and subsequent marketing of now patent-protected inventions by unauthorized third parties (the similar industry and national public laboratories) became illegal.

Even though all drugs created prior to 1995 remained in the public domain and, thus, could still be lawfully copied, innovative drugs, new to the market, had their prices fixed by the patent holders. Costs naturally rose and, gradually, patented drugs started to account for larger shares of the Ministry of Health's budget. The impact of the change was exacerbated by the fact that Brazil chose not to make use of certain flexibilities allowed by TRIPS. Indeed, as will be seen in greater detail, the country in fact surpassed, on several fronts, the minimum WTO standards of intellectual property protection.

[23] The National Health Agency (ANVISA) defines a similar medicine as one that uses the same active ingredient, in the same concentration, in the same pharmaceutical form, and requires the means of administration, dosage, and therapeutic, preventative, or diagnostic indication as the reference medicine registered with the responsible federal body of health maintenance. Similar drugs differ in characteristics related to the size and shape of the product, its effectiveness period, labeling, packaging, excipients, and carriers. Similar medicines are different from generic medicines in that they are not interchangeable with the innovative product, because they do not show bioequivalence, and must be identified by a commercial name. As described more fully herein, generics were introduced in Brazil in 1999, and Law 9.787 regulates their production and sale. For further information on similar and generics regulation in Brazil, see Hasenclever (2004) and Quental et al. (2008).

[24] Law No. 9.279, which entered into force one year later, in 1997.

II. Main Actors and Events Contributing to the Current Legal Approach to Patents and Access to Medicines in Brazil

The second half of this chapter aims at highlighting the main actors and events that have contributed to shaping the current legal framework on patents and access to medicines in Brazil. Figure 3.1 illustrates the result of the reflexive interviews we conducted.

The analysis of the data allows us to learn facts *perceived* by our respondents as the most important in determining the current Brazilian approach towards patents and access to medicines. Interestingly, however, not all the events we describe in this chapter and consider relevant in the legal and political development of Brazil's

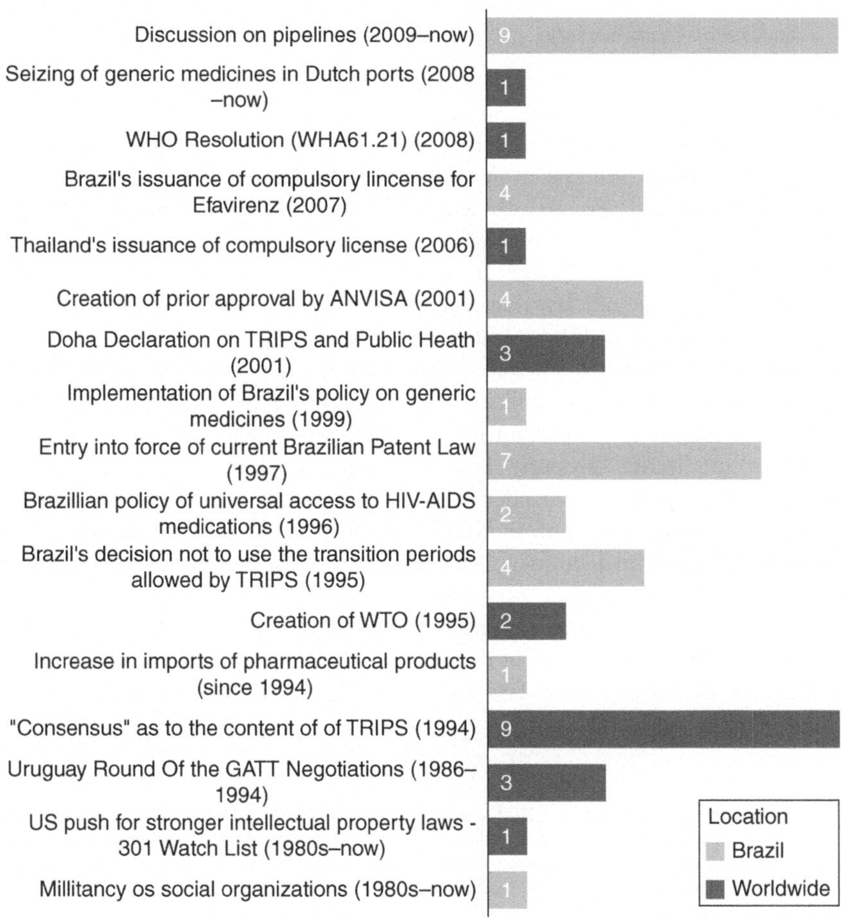

Fig. 3.1 Factors contributing to the current patent and access to medicines legal framework in Brazil, by frequency of appearance in respondents' speech.

position appeared in the respondents' answers. Learning, however, that certain—and, in fact, crucial—facts have not been perceived as relevant raises the possibility that technical issues are poorly understood, even by the principal actors. This, in turn, suggests that it is necessary to promote the dissemination of knowledge about intellectual property beyond a restrictive group of lawyers and patent examiners. Furthermore, it may be that greater transparency is required on the part of governmental bodies and agencies.

A. Actors

Because the circle of actors with knowledge of IP is small, we can identify the groups that have played key roles in developing Brazil's policies regarding the impact of IP on health and access to medicines.

1. The Role of Civil Society

In regard to turning the concept of access to health into concrete action, the militancy of civil society stands out as highly important.[25] In a previous study, Guise et al. (2010) argued that Brazil's current success in treating HIV/AIDS owes a great deal to efforts undertaken by civil society throughout the 1980s and 1990s. Many NGOs worked very actively with HIV/AIDS-infected individuals, helping them file hundreds of suits that sought access to ARV medicines (at the time very expensive and unavailable through the public health system). The outcome of such efforts was the passage of a law that specifically mandates that ARV drugs are to be supplied at no cost to all HIV-infected citizens in Brazil.[26]

Civil society's efforts, which were key to adopting laws guaranteeing free access to ARVs drugs, had positive spillovers to other diseases as well. And civil society continues to play a very important role in protecting public health interests in the context of intellectual property law. To mention two concrete and current examples, the initiative to consider the validity of pipeline patents as a constitutional issue was put forward by an NGO, and an NGO has challenged at least two patents (on Kaletra and Tenofovir, both ARVs) in pre-grant oppositions before the Patent Office.[27]

Three NGOs most frequently appeared in our respondents' answers, most likely because of their very active role in the defense of access to medicines. They are: (i) the Brazilian Interdisciplinary Association for AIDS (ABIA, Associação Brasileira

[25] It is interesting to note that the 1988 constitutional text, which guaranteed access to health and made feasible the creation of a national unified system of healthcare, did not appear in respondents' answers. This is most probably due to the fact that the state's duty to provide and guarantee healthcare to all Brazilians is, by now, regarded by the respondents as a natural fact.

[26] Law No. 9.313 of 1996.

[27] The oppositions were put forward by ABIA through its Working Group on Intellectual Property issues (Grupo de Trabalho sobre Propriedade Intelectual—GTPI), a joint effort with REBRIP in 2006. For further details on the oppositions, see Chaves et al. (2008).

Interdisciplinar de AIDS in Portuguese);[28] (ii) CONECTAS Human Rights;[29] and (iii) the Brazilian Network for Integration of the People (REBRIP, in Portuguese).[30]

Transnational advocacy groups, such as Doctors Without Borders and Oxfam, also played and continue playing an important role in the access to medicines movement in Brazil.[31] They did not, however, appear in our respondents' interviews, probably because much of their efforts are conducted jointly with Brazilian NGOs.[32]

2. *The Role of Government*

According to many of our respondents, actors operating within the Brazilian government played crucial roles. The Ministries of Health, of Science and Technology, of Development, Industry, and Foreign Commerce, and of Foreign Relations were specifically mentioned, with the Ministry of Health the most frequently cited. Respondents' answers were normally accompanied by the name of José Serra, the Minister of Health from 1998–2002. José Serra is regarded as mainly responsible for expanding the Brazilian population's access to medicine, as during his tenure he worked diligently for the promulgation of a new law to promote the introduction of generic medicines in the Brazilian market. He was also the one who initiated the public debate in favor of compulsory licensing in Brazil. Furthermore, in the very competitive presidential election of 2010, in which José Serra ran against Dilma Rousseff, he made access to medicines a significant element in his campaign platform.

The legislative branch also appeared frequently in the respondents' answers. As with references to the Ministry of Health, these references were normally accompanied by the names of specific representatives. These were notable because they worked for more flexible patent laws in order to promote wider access to medicines (proposing, for instance, laws that would allow for parallel imports).[33] The Parliamentary Front for Health—a nonprofit, nonideological, nonpartisan political entity active in the Chamber of Deputies—too appeared in respondents' answers regarding legislative activity.

3. *Academia*

Academia appeared to play an important part in the processes that shaped the regulatory environment in Brazil as it performs several roles. First, scholars can

[28] Information available at: <http://www.abiaids.org.br>. Last visited: February 12, 2011.

[29] Information available at: <http://www.conectas.org>. Last visited: February 12, 2011.

[30] Information available at: <http://www.rebrip.org.br>. Last visited: February 12, 2011.

[31] See, for instance, <http://www.msf.org.br/conteudo/38/campanha-de-acesso-a-medicamentos-essenciais/>.

[32] For further information on the role of civil society groups in Brazil, see Chaves et al. (2008).

[33] Federal Deputy Paulo Teixeira, for instance, was one of the names that stood out. At the time the interviews were conducted, he was leading an agenda for legislative reforms that advocated for more flexibilities in intellectual property.

develop and disseminate knowledge about the issues at stake, providing information, for example, regarding the impact of patents on price or challenging the efficacy of specific regulations. Second, academia can be helpful in promoting and facilitating debate as it provides neutral space for discussions that otherwise would not exist. And it brings together people with diametrically opposed positions, allowing government, civil society, and industry to confront each other. Their discussions can promote consensus and may positively influence the lawmaking processes and help shape public policy.

4. The Pharmaceutical Industry

In regards to the pharmaceutical industry as an actor, our respondents drew a clear distinction between the multinational and national firms. The perception is that the national industry does not innovate; it merely copies. Thus, it is recognized mainly as a producer of generic and similar medicines. Brazilian production patterns of manufacturing drugs is likely responsible for this view. However, there also appears to be skepticism as to the Brazilian capacity for innovation. Industrial policies that recognize and foment national production of innovative knowledge in the pharmaceutical sector are relatively recent.[34] As a result, the national pharmaceutical industry is perceived as weak and dependent on government partnerships for development.

As the same time, however, respondents identified the national industry as aligned with national public health interests and the promotion of access to medicines, converging, in this sense and in its activities, with civil society's efforts. Among national laboratories, Fundação Oswaldo Cruz (Oswaldo Cruz Foundation) (FIOCRUZ, in Portuguese) stands out as highly significant. FIOCRUZ is an institution dedicated to biological research, especially in the sphere of human health. Known for its scientific rigor, as well as its historical contribution to the development of vaccines, the laboratory is named after Oswaldo Cruz, who was responsible for the most important hygiene projects of the early twentieth century, and later influenced other national public health policies. To Brazilians, then, FIOCRUZ serves as a brand of integrity. In addition, of course, national public laboratories are perceived as playing an important role because they provide the vaccines and generic drugs that largely supply the Ministry of Health's access programs.

5. International Organizations

International organizations constitute another set of actors that play an important role in shaping the legal framework of patents and access to medicines in Brazil. Indeed, when specifically questioned about them, respondents seemed to have a strong opinion, promptly identifying them as positive, negative, and/or neutral.

[34] The Brazilian Innovation Act, for instance, which regulates incentives to innovation and R&D efforts, was not enacted until 2004 (Law No. 10.973).

The WHO has issued a global strategic plan on the relationship between intellectual property and global health and has also offered guidance on the meaning of TRIPS.[35] Not surprisingly, it stood out in our interviews. WHO was identified as "*an important forum for international debate*;" "*a counterweight to WTO decisions on health and access to medicines*;" and "*an important mediator in trade and public health debates.*" The only negative comment on WHO's role regards its relevance: "*it does less than it could*" (thus recognizing it has the potential to play a far more ambitious role).

A second organization that appeared frequently in respondents' answers is the WTO. Perceptions related to the role it plays ranged from negative ("*it favors the multinational pharmaceutical industry*;" "*it provides little voice for developing countries;*" "*it is pro-intellectual property*") to neutral ("*it administers an international treaty*;" "*it was responsible for the 1996 Brazilian legislative alteration*").

WIPO was also mentioned, but uniformly perceived by respondents as having a negative influence on the patent/access issue: "*It was absent in the international discussions leading to the adoption of TRIPS*;" "*it is controlled by the WTO*;" "*it plays a negative role in developing countries by proposing the adoption of laws that expand the scope of intellectual property protection*;" "*it plays a small role in the international scene.*"

It is interesting to note that WIPO, a forum for discussions that has been historically more favorable to developing countries' interests, is, in the current international context, perceived more negatively than the WTO, a forum that traditionally privileges trade interests. It is possible that a more positive perception of the WTO is a result of Brazil's active participation in its Dispute Settlement Body: although defeated in many resolutions in the trade context, Brazil also enjoyed a series of victories, including the withdrawal of a US challenge concerning intellectual property protection.[36] Whenever the country emerges victorious in a commercial dispute, the matter dominates headlines,[37] which may influence perceptions and might have led our respondents to see the WTO as a forum aligned with national interests.

B. Government Policies

As important as actors is the availability of opportunities for contestation; several policy debates were critical to setting the balance between patent rights and access interests in Brazil. In this section, we explore the main policies that have accentuated the country's role as the custodian of public health, but we also highlight the

[35] See, e.g., World Health Organization, Public Health, Innovation, and Intellectual Property, available at <http://www.who.int/phi/en/>.

[36] Brazil—Measures Affecting Patent Protection, WTO Doc. WT/DS199/1G/L/385/IP/D/23 (June 8, 2000) (concerning a local working requirement).

[37] See, e.g., "Brazil Wins in Dispute with the US at the WTO over Subsidies for Cotton Farmers" (O Globo 2008); "Brazil Wins in Suit at WTO against US on Orange Juice" (UOL Economia and Folha Online 2010).

steps that were taken in the opposite direction, thus shaping the overall schizophrenia effect.

1. HIV/AIDS Universal Access Policy

The Brazilian policy of universal access to HIV/AIDS drugs was crucial to concretizing the promise of access to medicines in Brazil. As mentioned before, Law 9.313 (passed in 1996) mandated SUS to provide free ARV drugs to all HIV/AIDS-infected citizens.

Currently, the National Sexually Transmitted Diseases and AIDS Program supplies eighteen ARV drugs—as well as other medicines that fight opportunistic infections—to more than 220,000 patients. Guise et al. (2010) point out that the life expectancy for patients infected with HIV/AIDS has increased significantly since the program's inception: the average life expectancy of an AIDS-infected individual had been six months; currently, it exceeds five years. The program has also contributed to a significant reduction in the cost of treating opportunistic infections: between 1997 and 2002, close to 358,000 stays in public hospitals were avoided as a result of the program (Programa Nacional DST e AIDS 2008).

The paradox we see in 1996 is that it marks the passing of two laws that, from an access to medicines perspective, are not coherent with each other. The promulgation of the new Industrial Property Law (which, under TRIPS's transition provisions, could have been delayed for at least four years) created exclusive rights that made drugs more expensive. Law 9.313, on the other hand, obliged the state to make significant purchases of medicines to treat HIV-infected patients from patent holders, at high prices.

This sense of legislative incoherence stood out in the interviews we conducted: "*The laws are ambiguous;*" "*Our patent law is not balanced with public health interests;*" "*The government does not seem to make coherent decisions when it comes to patents and health.*" When questioned about why they thought this happened, the answers ranged from "*Different interest groups in the government* [trade v. health] *are just not talking to each other*" to "*Trade concerns were more relevant at the time of the passing of the laws than health.*"

2. Policies Regarding Generic Drugs

Starting in 1999, with the adoption of the National Generic Medicines Policy, the government implemented several measures to lower the cost of medicine, improve access to treatment, and assure the sustainability of Brazil's public health system.

In 1999, Law No. 9.787 established the legal foundations for the production and sale of generic medicines in Brazil. Among its most important provisions is the obligation it imposes on the Ministry of Health to prioritize generics when purchasing all drugs. The same obligation applies to doctors who work at SUS: when prescribing medicines to any patient, they must indicate the generic alternative when it exists. Furthermore, Law No. 9.787 eliminates the need of the generic producer to repeat the clinical trials that were already performed by the patent holder of the original medicine. This has a substantial impact on the final price of the medicine, allowing generic drugs to enter the market at more affordable prices.

The introduction of generics thus has improved access to medicines considerably: the drugs are less costly to introduce to the market and the increase in supply naturally lowers prices. When the government spends less to obtain the same drugs it had previously acquired at significantly higher prices, it is able to buy in greater quantities, and, as a result, negotiate even lower prices with the drug companies.

Generic entry has also been accelerated by another legal mechanism, which was introduced into the Brazilian Industrial Property Law in 2001 (art. 43, VII): the so-called Bolar Exception authorizes generic industries to request health registration for the marketing of a medicine before the patent on the drug has expired. This measure is important because health registration applications can take a long time to process. In practice, the registration obligation would thus extend the period in which the patent holder enjoys exclusivity. Indeed, this problem was considered so critical, Guise et al. (2010) report that judicial precedents had, prior to the enactment of the new provision, achieved much the same result through a liberal interpretation of article 3 of the Industrial Property Law. The Bolar Exception also allows for both early production and stockpiling of soon-to-be-generics. As with the National Generic Medicines Policy, it shows a clear intent on the part of both the legislative and the judicial branches to make drugs more easily available through actions that favor price reduction.

In furtherance of the same goals, Brazil also chose to exploit the right under the TRIPS Agreement to issue compulsory licenses. Frequently mentioned by respondents as a very positive influence on access to medicines and public health, the use of compulsory licenses represents an important flexibility that Brazil chose to embrace. The process is typified by the country's treatment of Efavirenz, an antiretroviral that Merck & Co. had patented. Issued in 2007, the compulsory licensing was the result of a long trajectory of negotiations led by the Ministry of Health. After no longer being able to reduce prices through a bargaining strategy (mostly founded on the *threat* of a compulsory license), the government finally decided to go forward with the decision to award a compulsory license. Local production began over a year later. In the meantime, a generic version was purchased from India.

The compulsory licensing saga demonstrates an interesting point. According to our respondents, Brazil's actions were influenced by Thailand, which had previously issued such a license. If true, this episode suggests the power of global administrative space. Even when governments act within their domestic spheres, they influence others and thus contribute to the development of global norms and, in the case of compulsory licensing, improve the transnational bargaining leverage of developing countries.

3. *Prior Approval Mechanism*

The 2001 creation of a Prior Approval mechanism—which frequently appeared in our respondents' answers—was also an important step towards safeguarding access and public health interests (although it too has a schizophrenic element).

The National Institute of Industrial Property (INPI) is the sole autonomous federal body responsible for the examination of patents in Brazil. In 2001, however, Law 10.196 established that ANVISA's prior approval was required before INPI could grant a pharmaceutical patent. As a result, when a drug patent application is filed, INPI analyzes the formal patent requirements, but applications are then sent to ANVISA for a second analysis, for the purpose of guaranteeing that the patent examination in question has been performed rigorously. The process thus aims at deterring awards of inappropriate patents, such as patents on chemicals that were already known in the art. In other words, the 2001 law provides that ANVISA may deny a patent on an invention that has already survived examination before the INPI.[38]

At the time of its creation, the prior approval mechanism sparked an intense debate in Brazil. According to Barbosa (2004), granting ANVISA power to deny or award patents on the basis of the Administration's discretion would be incompatible with the Constitution, which can be read to create a constitutional right to a patent based on legal principles. Public health and access to medicines advocates, however, praised the decision to include ANVISA in the process of analyzing pharmaceutical patent applications. They viewed the mechanism as a very concrete way of making sure patent requirements would be strictly observed and that it would result in fewer patent grants. Excerpts from the interviews we conducted corroborate this perception: "*ANVISA has the technical skills needed to analyze pharmaceutical patent requests, while INPI doesn't*;" "*ANVISA follows more rigorous standards when analyzing patent requests for pharmaceuticals, which is good for public health interests*;" "*ANVISA is highly more qualified than INPI to analyze these requests.*"

Because it generated such controversy and put two autonomous government agencies in conflict, the issue was assessed by the country's Federal Counsel-General (AGU, Advocacia Geral da União in Portuguese). In a 2009 decision (AGU 2009), later validated by a 2010 document (AGU 2010), the Federal Counsel-General decided that ANVISA is not *legally* equipped to examine the technical criteria of patentability through the Prior Approval mechanism. Even though the decision recognized that ANVISA's technical arm was superior to INPI's with regard to applying the patent requirements to pharmaceutical products, the issue at stake was the legality of the process. ANVISA's advice would thus fall outside its institutional mandate. As a consequence, the provision for Prior Approval must undergo the long process of being eliminated from the Industrial Property Law.

We have not, however, seen any steps given in this direction. While the law is still in place, the matter remains unsettled and further regulations are emerging. Just recently, on April 10, 2013, ANVISA issued a Resolution (Resolução RDC

[38] For more detailed information of administrative problems regarding ANVISA's prior approval process, see Barbosa (Guise et al. 2010).

No. 21[39]) that aims at clarifying its role in the prior approval mechanism. According to the current rule, which binds the Agency, all examinations shall be done in light and in favor of public health. The text further provides that the only pharmaceutical patent requests that shall be subject to ANVISA's scrutiny are the following: (i) those related to molecules that have at some point been forbidden in the country, as they may pose health risks; (ii) patent requests deemed strategic to public health interests and which do not comply with the legal patent requirements.

In practice, the scenario as a whole shows that when it comes to prior approval in Brazil, there is little lucidity regarding who should do what and how: on the one hand, the federal law that creates the mechanism is challenged and found inconsistent by the Federal Counsel-General, but it is still in place as no legal reforms have been made to revoke ANVISA's mandate; on the other hand, the Agency itself has not much clarity as regards to its role, thus finding the need—twelve years after the original mandate was laid down—to issue a regulation that finally defines the scope of its examination procedure.

4. Pipeline Patents

Brazil's actions regarding pipeline patents created yet another constitutional debate. These patents are not fully addressed by the TRIPS Agreement and our respondents viewed the debate over the 1998 Industrial Property Statute, which recognized them, as shedding light on the dynamics established among the diverse set of actors involved in the normative process of reconciling patent rights with access to medicines in Brazil.

The TRIPS Agreement contemplates a system—often referred to as "pipeline protection"—that is intended to preserve the patentability of pharmaceuticals invented after TRIPS went into effect, but before a country implements its requirements.[40] This provision does not, however, require countries to forgo domestic examination. Articles 230 and 231 of the 1996 Industrial Property Law solve the *vacatio legis* problem in Brazil but add a twist to it, as according to the law, as long as a patent has been granted in another country, INPI will not conduct a domestic analysis of whether the invention meets patentability requirements in Brazil. Instead, it will simply confirm the patent. Thus, Brazil's version of the pipeline mechanism is best considered "TRIPS-plus."

Its major problem is that by subjecting patent requests to a merely formal analysis of whether a patent had been previously granted on the invention, the requirement of novelty is no longer analyzed by the competent Brazilian body. In its analysis of the pipeline mechanism, Guise et al. (2010) argue that:

> [T]he pipeline mechanism . . . allows for retrospective patents of medicines already invented. The traditional argument for patent protection—that high prices must be assured to provide

[39] Officially available at: <http://www.in.gov.br/visualiza/index.jsp?data=15/04/2013&jornal=1&pagina=68&totalArquivos=148>.

[40] TRIPS, art. 70.8.

incentives for innovation—does not carry weight when considering innovations that have already been brought to market. Companies benefiting from pipeline patents received an additional reward—at great public cost—without having to invest in any additional innovation. In practice, the pipeline patents granted in Brazil had a strong impact on the public health budgets as they inhibited the production and purchase of generic medicines. Important drugs used in the treatment of HIV/AIDS (lopinavir/ritonavir, abacavir, nelfinavir, amprenavir) and leukemia (glivec) were patented in Brazil via the pipeline mechanism.

The pipeline mechanism was brought to the fore when, in November 2007, the National Federation of Pharmacists (FENAFAR, Federação Nacional de Farmacêuticos in Portuguese), on behalf of the Brazilian Network for Integration of the People (REBRIP), brought a case to the Federal Supreme Court (STF, in Portuguese), alleging the unconstitutionality of patents granted in Brazil via the pipeline mechanism.[41] The issue received greater attention during April and May of 2009, when the STF held a public hearing on patents and access to health. Such hearings are held when the Supreme Court feels that ministers need more information on key subjects in order to make more informed decisions.[42]

As of this writing, the decision on the constitutionality of pipeline patents has yet to be issued. But it is interesting to note that the constitutional discussion of pipeline patents ranks second in our respondents' answers as to the events that were most relevant in shaping the landscape regarding patents and access to medicines in Brazil. We believe that such high frequency may be attributable to the respondents' interest in the SFT's then-pending decision.

5. Parallel Importation (International Exhaustion)

Curiously, the issue of parallel importation did not appear in our respondents' answers. It is nonetheless an important tool for fulfilling the obligations regarding the right to health and access to medicines. The TRIPS Agreement leaves every WTO member free to decide whether a patented product lawfully sold outside its jurisdiction can be imported without the authorization of the patentee (or further payment of royalties).[43] This is an important flexibility favoring health interests. When the foreign price is lower than the domestic price, parallel importation represents an alternative means of improving access to medicines.

But although TRIPS does not restrict this practice, art. 43, IV of the Brazilian Industrial Property Law establishes a rule on the exhaustion of rights for patents that forbids parallel importation. The only exception to this clause is found in the regulation of Compulsory Licenses, when they are issued on account of the abuse of

[41] For Barbosa (2006), art. 230 [of the Brazilian industrial property law], by making possible the granting of patents already granted outside of Brazil, fails to apply the basic principle of novelty, "the constitutional basis of patents."

[42] The transcription of the public hearing, which includes documents submitted to the Supreme Court by civil society, can be found, in Portuguese, at: <http://www.stf.jus.br/portal/cms/verTexto.asp?servico=processoAudienciaPublicaSaude> Last visited: February 12, 2011.

[43] TRIPS, art. 6.

economic power.[44] Attempts to expand the scope of parallel importation for drugs have been made in recent years by members of Congress, but so far no concrete results have been achieved.[45]

III. Conclusion

Taking Brazil's decisions as a whole, it is difficult to escape the conclusion that it has been behaving schizophrenically. It accepted the constitutional mandate to supply medicines to its population, but then adopted TRIPS (and its adverse effect on prices) before that was necessary; it issued a compulsory license, but refuses to use the far less controversial mechanism of parallel importation; it found an excellent check on INPI, but then invalidated ANVISA's involvement. Interestingly, however, when our respondents were questioned about the future, they appeared optimistic. Some believe, for example, that the deepening of the debates currently in play at the STF on the unconstitutionality of pipeline patents will have positive spillovers for health and access to medicines. Others envision a doctrine that would reconceptualize patent rights as a tool for social development; in this regard, they anticipate greater appreciation for, and use of, the flexibilities provided under the TRIPS Agreement. In this view of the future, universities appear as knowledge generators—actors of growing importance in resolving the health and social issues the country faces.

Our respondents also held great expectations about INPI's future role. INPI is clearly perceived as the most relevant institution for the application and enforcement of patent rights, followed by ANVISA. In general, INPI is viewed as a problematic institution, mainly due to its flawed infrastructure: it has an insufficient number of examiners, who are not fully qualified to conduct examinations and that leads to, among other things, enormous delays in patent grants. Respondents recognize, however, the recent efforts for improvements, which have started to result in better analyses of patent applications.

Nonetheless, there are misgivings. Institutionally, INPI is viewed as autonomous in relation to government pressures, but "*aligned with private sector interests.*" These private sector interests draw negative perceptions. Multinational pharmaceutical industry strategies are seen as prejudicial to national public healthcare interests. There is also a noticeable apprehension of a global trajectory that would strengthen patent rights through new international obligations. TRIPS-plus standards, such as an obligation to award patents on second uses of known chemicals, for instance, would make Brazil's situation even more complicated.

44 On the exhaustion of rights and parallel importation in Brazil, see Barbosa (2002) and Basso (2011).

45 See, for instance, Bill of Law 199, which has been stuck in the process of debates and voting since 1999. <http://www.camara.gov.br/proposicoesWeb/fichadetramitacao?idProposicao=15088>. Also, bills 3.562 of 2000 and 7.066, of 2002.

But given the proper medicine and proper care, the country's schizophrenia can be managed. Our diagnosis and recommended treatment are as follows:

(i) The decision to bring Brazilian IP into early compliance with the TRIPS Agreement had negative consequences for public health national interests.

(ii) National initiatives that seek to promote greater access to medicines via flexible measures (such as ANVISA's prior approval, the Bolar Exception, and compulsory licensing) should be expanded, and not abandoned.

(iii) More effort should be devoted to questioning the IP regime and proposing legislative change that would improve access to medicines; the current debate over pipeline patents is a good example of where contestation opportunities lie.

(iv) Civil society plays a fundamental role in the promotion of human rights and access to healthcare in Brazil, and its participation in the patent field is essential to the achievement of public health interests.

(v) International forums are important spaces for normative production regarding patents, but notably privilege commercial over social aspects. Thus, it is important to pursue a more development-oriented approach to trade.

(vi) Further knowledge of IP is needed. In other words, discussions must leave closed rooms and reach a broader audience. Law schools around the country should be more prepared to teach intellectual property and more courses should be made available in order to build IP capacity for those who do not have a legal background but who are dealing with issues related to it.

(vii) Finally, more transparency as a whole is needed. Especially when it comes to the terms of international negotiations that will result in direct domestic consequences for the patent/access debate.

We hope that the results presented here will contribute to the current debate on patents and access to medicines in a way that will influence the political and normative agendas not only of Brazil, but of every country engaged in the promotion of development. Building global administrative spaces that enable a more balanced interaction between interests of the developed and developing world seems to us a possible way forward.

References

Abbot, Frederic M., and Jerome H. Reichman. 2007. "The Doha Round's Public Health Legacy: Strategies for the Production and Diffusion of Patented Medicines under the Amended TRIPS Provisions." *Journal of International Economic Law* 10(4): 921–87.

AGU—Advocacia Geral Da União. Procuradoria Geral Federal. 2009. Parecer n. 210/PGFI AE/2009, Processo 00407.005325/2008-71. Conflito positivo de atribuições. INPI e ANVISA. Finalidade institucional. Patente. Anuência prévia. Poderes administrativos implícitos. Inexistência. Princípios da legalidade, especialidade e autotutela. Alcance e aplicação dos artigos 229-C e 230, introduzidos na Lei n. 9.279, de 14.5.1996, pela Lei

No. 10.196, de 2001. Manifestação conclusiva da Consultoria-Geral da União. Ação anulatória.

———. 2010. Parecer n. 337/PGFI AE/2010, Processo 00407.005325/200871. Pedido de reconsideração. Parecer n. 210/PGFI AE/2009. Conflito positivo de atribuições. INPI e ANVISA. Finalidade institucional. Patente. Anuência prévia. Alcance e aplicação dos artigos 229-C e 230, introduzidos na Lei No. 9.279, de 14.5.1996, pela Lei No. 10.196, de 2001. Manutenção do entendimento.

Barbosa, Denis Borges. 2004. *A inconstitucionalidade da anuência da ANVISA no procedimento de concessão de patentes como manifestação discricionária da administração federal.* <http://denisbarbosa.addr.com/anuência.doc>. Date of access: January 10, 2011.

———. 2002. *Inconstitucionalidade das Patentes Pipeline.* <http://denisbarbosa.addr.com/pipeline.doc>. Date of access: January 10, 2011.

Basso, Maristela. 2000. *O direito internacional da propriedade intelectual.* Porto Alegre: Livraria do Advogado.

———. 2011. *Propriedade intelectual e importação paralela.* São Paulo: Atlas.

Boyle, James. 2004. "A Manifesto on WIPO and the Future of Intellectual Property." *Duke Law and Technology Review* 9: 1–12.

Chaves, Gabriel Costa, Marcela Fogaça Vieira, and Renata Reis. 2008. "Access to Medicines and Intellectual Property in Brazil: Reflections and Strategies of Civil Society." *SUR—International Journal on Human Rights.* Year 5, issue 8. Available at: <http://www.surjournal.org/eng/conteudos/pdf/8/completo.pdf>.

Costa, Ediná Alves, Tania Maria Fernandes, and Tânia Salgado Pimenta. 2005. *Novas tecnologias, novos riscos: a vigilância de medicamentos no Brasil—décadas 1940 a 1990.* <http://www.necso.ufrj.br/esocite2008/trabalhos/36324.doc>. Date of access: February 4, 2008.

Ferraz, Octavio Luiz Motta. 2009. "Right to Health Litigation in Brazil: An Overview of the Research." Available at: SSRN <http://ssrn.com/abstract=1426011> or <http://dx.doi.org/10.2139/ssrn.1426011>.

——— and Fabiola Sulpino Vieira. 2008. "The Right to Health, Public Policies and Inequalities in Brazil: Equity as the Fundamental Principle" (Direito à Saúde, Políticas Públicas e Desigualdades Sociais no Brasil: Eqüidade como Princípio Fundamental). Available at: SSRN <http://www.ssrn.com/abstract=1137872> or <http://dx.doi.org/10.2139/ssrn.1137872>.

Gadelha, Carlos Augusto. 2003. "O complexo industrial da saúde e a necessidade de um enfoque dinâmico na economia da saúde." *Ciência e Saúde Coletiva* 8(2): 521–35.

Gervais, Daniel J. 1998. *The TRIPs Agreement: Drafting History and Analysis.* London: Sweet and Maxwell.

Guise, Mônica, Daniel Wei Li Wang, and Thana Cristina de Campos. 2010. "Access to Medicines: Pharmaceutical Patents and the Right to Health." Pp. 103–43 in *Access to Knowledge in Brazil: New Research on Intellectual Property, Innovation and Development,* edited by L. Shaver. London: Bloomsbury.

Hasenclever, Lea. 2002. *Diagnóstico da indústria farmacêutica brasileira.* Rio de Janeiro: UFRJ.

Hasenclever, Lia. 2004. *O mercado de medicamentos genéricos no Brasil.* Texto preparado para o simpósio Franco-Brasileiro "O Novo Direito da Propriedade Intelectual no Domínio da Saúde e dos Seres Vivos (implicações para o acesso aos tratamentos anti-retrovirais), Brasília, June 23–4.

IBGE—Instituto Brasileiro de Geografia e Estatística. 2011. *Censo 2010.* <http://www.ibge.gov.br/home/presidencia/noticias/noticia_visualiza.php?id_noticia=1766>.

Kingsbury, Benedict, Nico Krisch, and Richard B. Stewart. 2005. "Foreword: Global Governance as Administration—National and Transnational Approaches to Global Administrative Law." *Law and Contemporary Problems* 68(15) 1–14.

Laplanche, Jean, and Jean-Bertrand Pontalis. 2001. *Vocabulário da Psicanálise.* São Paulo: Martins Fontes.

Merges, Robert P., and Jane C. Ginsburg. 2004. *Foundations of Intellectual Property.* New York: Foundation Press.

O Estado de São Paulo. 2011. Gasto do Governo com Remédios Via Ação Judicial Cresce 5.000% em 6 Anos. <http://www.estadao.com.br/estadaodehoje/20110428/not_imp711740,0.php>. Date of access: April 28, 2011.

Oliveira, Egléubia Andrade de, Maria Eliana Labra, and Jorge Bermudez. 2006. "A Produção Pública de Medicamentos no Brasil: Uma Visão Geral. *Cadernos de Saúde Pública* 22 (1): 2379–89.

Programa Nacional DST e AIDS. 2008. *Targets and Commitments Made by the Member-States at the United Nation General Assembly Special Session on HIV/AIDS.* UNGASS—HIV/AIDS. <http://data.unaids.org/pub/Report/2008/brazil_2008_country_progress_report_en.pdf>. Date of access: May 12, 2010.

Quental, Cristiane et al. 2008. "Medicamentos genéricos no Brasil: impactos das políticas, públicas sobre a indústria nacional." *Ciência e Saúde Coletiva* 13: 619–28.

Rodríguez-Garavito, César. 2005. "Nike's Law: The Anti-Sweatshop Movement, Transnational Corporations, and the Struggle over International Labor Rights in the Americas." Pp. 64–91 in *Law and Globalization from Below: Toward a Cosmopolitan Legality,* edited by Boaventura Santos and César Rodríguez-Garavito. Cambridge: Cambridge University Press.

Sen, Amartya. 1999. *Development as Freedom.* New York: Anchor Books.

Silva, José Afonso da. 2005.*Comentário contextual à constituição.* São Paulo: Malheiros.

Silva, Virgilio Afonso da, and Fernanda Vargas Terrazas. 2008. "Claiming the Right to Health in Brazilian Courts: The Exclusion of the Already Excluded." Available at SSRN: <http://ssrn.com/abstract=1133620 or http://dx.doi.org/10.2139/ssrn.1133620>.

Szymanski, Heloisa. 2008. *A Entrevista na Pesquisa em Educação: A Prática Reflexiva.* 2nd edn. Brasília: Iber Livros.

UNCTAD; ICTSD. 2005. *Resource Book on TRIPs and Development.* Cambridge: Cambridge University Press.

VIEIRA, Fabiola Sulpino et al. 2007. *Evolução dos gastos do Ministério da Saúde com medicamentos.* <http://portal.saude.gov.br/portal/arquivos/pdf/estudo_gasto_medicamentos.pdf>. Date of access: May 12, 2010.

Chapter 4

CAFTA, Intellectual Property, and the Right to Health in Central America

Angelina Snodgrass Godoy

In recent years, the application of intellectual property (IP) to pharmaceutical products has generated increasing controversy in many contexts around the world. Like other parts of Latin America, Central American countries were required to introduce reforms to their IP laws under the terms of the World Trade Organization's Trade Related Aspects of Intellectual Property Agreement (the WTO's TRIPS Agreement), and later by the ratification of their regional trade agreement with the United States, which required yet stricter provisions. In the context of discussions generated by the US-Dominican Republic-Central America Trade Agreement (CAFTA[1]), which was finalized in 2004, health advocates argued that the new IP rules threatened developing countries' ability to protect public health. While campaigns against CAFTA were ultimately unsuccessful in stopping the agreement, I argue here that they did achieve some gains, and furthermore that these experiences offer important insights into the strengths and limitations of transnational advocacy for health rights in the context of IP reforms.

In this chapter, I focus first on describing the content of CAFTA, the multi-sited activism it inspired, and some of the results of that activity in specific points of law. I argue that this case shows why these kinds of transnational struggles require a rethinking of "success." Although in the big picture, the battle against the trade agreement was lost, in at least some ways Central American legislation became more public health sensitive as a result of the mobilization engendered by the agreement. And furthermore, Central American efforts helped contribute to later gains in various South American contexts. In some ways, this is the "good news" I offer readers.

In the latter part of the chapter, however, I also use this case to reflect on some of the limitations of this type of transnational activism—the "bad news" for those of

[1] Although it is not a part of Central America, the Dominican Republic was added to the agreement following its negotiation; for this reason, the agreement is sometimes referred to as DR-CAFTA, but I use the less unwieldy acronym CAFTA here. Although I include data on Dominican legislation in Table 4.1, my research focuses on Central America and I have not tracked the agreement's implementation in the Dominican Republic.

us committed to placing public health before private profits. In this context, I argue that although the existence of the trade agreement opened a transnational opportunity structure, making possible the aforementioned gains, there were also significant disjunctures between the frames used by international and domestic activists for discussing the right to health, and the objectives of their activism. Empirically, these limited the long-term impact of mobilization, and theoretically, they suggest the need for more attention to power differences between differently situated activists in the transnational networks we study.

I. Methodology

This chapter draws on research conducted as part of a multi-year study of IP in Central America, which I am currently developing into a book manuscript. From 2004 to 2010, I conducted a comprehensive review of IP implementation legislation in five Central American countries, and dozens of in-depth interviews with policymakers, activists, and pharmaceutical industry representatives in Costa Rica, El Salvador, and Guatemala. My thinking is also informed by my own participation as an opponent of CAFTA's IP provisions in many discussions in the United States—and some in Central America—during this period, and my experience directing a network of Central American researchers monitoring the impacts of new IP rules in their countries, the Red CEPIAM (Red Centroamericana para el Estudio de la Propiedad Intelectual y el Acceso a Medicamentos) from 2007 to 2009.

Central America as a Case Study. The Central American isthmus, home to some 30 million people organized into five small nations, is not often considered pivotal in global geopolitical debates. Even among scholars who specialize in Latin America, the region is often overlooked, assumed to be a less developed version of Mexico or its South American neighbors. And yet, for those concerned about IP and health, I argue that the Central American experience offers particularly important lessons of broad relevance.

First, in some regards, CAFTA's standards represent a global high-water mark in IP protection. The IP standards in CAFTA are, on balance, more demanding than those contained in agreements that preceded it *and* in agreements that followed it.[2] At the time of CAFTA's drafting in 2003, the agreement was widely hailed by both supporters and opponents as heralding the dawn of a new era in IP protection.[3] Thanks in part to the activism generated around CAFTA, trade politics in the

[2] "On balance" is an important qualifier here: there are so many fine points of IP law contained in any one agreement that it would be unlikely that any one agreement would be more demanding than all others on every single element. I am aware of selected points of IP law on which CAFTA is less demanding, for example, than the US–Singapore agreement which preceded it (for instance, CAFTA allows a longer transition period for implementation). There may also be similarly selected points on which other agreements that followed CAFTA were more demanding.

[3] As one industry advisory committee wrote, "CAFTA takes into account the significant legal and technological developments that have taken place since the TRIPS and NAFTA agreements . . . to establish clear precedents in most key areas of IP protection for future FTA negotiations" (IFAC-3 2004: 4).

United States[4] and South America subsequently shifted, and later agreements with more powerful countries contained slightly softer IP demands. For this reason alone, then, it is important to study IP and health in Central America.

But beyond that, I argue, what happened—and is happening—in Central America might be a useful indicator of what may happen in many poor countries, a counterpoint of sorts to the more frequently invoked cases of Brazil or India. In those cases, formidable local actors teamed up with the generic drug industry to challenge global IP dictates in powerfully counterhegemonic ways. Their stories are inspiring and important, but in how many countries should we expect them to take root?

The Central American story reflects a fundamentally different reality. Ultimately, Central American countries put up relatively little resistance to the onslaught of newly aggressive IP policies, for at least three reasons. First, although there are important differences from country to country, as a general rule civil society faces deep and well-documented challenges in Central America (Guzmán León and Solís Rivera 2005). As a whole, the region is still reeling from the prolonged armed conflicts of the 1970s and 1980s; with the exception of Costa Rica—an outlier in many regards—the isthmus is plagued by deep poverty and low educational levels, as well as alarmingly high levels of contemporary criminal violence. Civil society groups, many of which were decimated by the repression of recent decades, are struggling to grapple with the legacies of war while adapting to the shifting political and economic terrain of recent years. While the ratification of CAFTA generated some of the largest public protests seen in the region in decades, it was extremely difficult to mount a coherent resistance strategy across diverse nations whose governments negotiated the agreement as a bloc without any involvement of civil society groups. The sheer breadth of issues addressed in the agreement, coupled with the highly technical nature of the IP changes mandated, led to a lack of sustained civil society engagement with the agreement's specific effects on health. As a result, as discussed in this chapter, most mobilization on this issue was driven by transnational groups rather than local leaders.

Secondly, Central American countries face further tactical disadvantages in contesting IP dictates. Their ability to resist through the invocation of TRIPS safeguards is deeply constrained. Not only are the states in question small, highly dependent on the United States, and possessed of tiny health budgets, but they also lack the capacity to manufacture generic versions of most recently developed drugs. This means that, for example, the widespread use of compulsory licensing—or at least the invocation of the threat to do so—may seem unrealistic from a Central American viewpoint. Although the Doha Declaration (2001) allows for the possibility of one country's use of compulsory licensing to manufacture medicines in another country, the complexities of such arrangements and the political consequences that seem likely to flow from them are daunting. Indeed, my interviews

[4] This is because the 2006 US congressional elections swept in a new Democratic majority which issued, in its May 2007 New Trade Policy for America, a more public health-friendly set of expectations on IP.

with trade officials and health policymakers underscore the fact that such bold steps are largely viewed as off the table for poor Central American countries who rely on maintaining positive relationships, not only with the United States but with the pharmaceutical companies with whom they must regularly negotiate prices on their institutional purchases. Many of the exhortations of transnational health rights groups revolved around the need to protect the ability to invoke such mechanisms, in ways that simply did not resonate with local activists whose assessment of the possible did not include such measures.

Thirdly, and more fundamentally, Central American countries lack the capacity to effectively monitor the safety of their drug supply. This has a number of important effects, for both generic and originator[5] drugs, with implications for IP. First, it leads to low levels of consumer acceptance of drugs with unfamiliar brand names; both originator companies and generic producers therefore invest heavily in trademarking strategies. In the Central American context, typically more than 90 percent of the drugs on the market are branded—either originator drugs, or branded generics. This leaves less than 10 percent of the market to drugs sold by the name of the active ingredient rather than a distinctive brand name (Martínez and Castro Bonilla 2008), and limits the price reductions that should be expected with generic entry. Furthermore, some local generics producers have engaged in ethically questionable practices, of which leading public health advocates and civil society groups have been vocal critics.[6] In this context, during the campaign against CAFTA, transnational advocates' underlying assumption that IP was important because it threatened generics' access to market—and that generics producers were natural allies in this struggle—did not reflect many local health advocates' perceptions of the industry.

In short, the Central American case speaks to the pitfalls of unquestioned assumptions about why IP matters, and what should be done about it. If we are truly interested in the counterhegemonic potential of mobilization around health rights in the context of trade talks, we should examine the conditions under which tools such as compulsory licensing become realistic and meaningful options for policymakers in poor countries, and indeed the conditions under which the generic industry acts as an ally in movements for access. Otherwise, we risk proposing

[5] I have used the term "originator" here to indicate the largest transnational pharmaceutical laboratories, many of whom are commonly referred to as "Big Pharma" in the United States: Abbott Labs, Eli Lilly, AstraZeneca, Novartis, etc. I use the term "originator" in reference to the fact that these companies typically bring new drugs to market, whereas other transnational pharmaceutical giants (Ranbaxy, Cipla, etc.) are primarily involved in the production of generics. However, these terms are tricky. Originator companies typically describe their segment of the industry as "research-based," in purported contrast to generic production, but this terminology obscures the fact that generic companies also engage in considerable research, and indeed that originator companies often do not conduct early-stage research themselves, relying on universities or biotech firms to do so. Other common designations include "brand-name" versus "generic," but many generics are in fact branded, an important but frequently overlooked point. In Central America, some favor the terms "transnational" versus "local" but even these distinctions can be misleading, given the growing reach of transnational generic producers like Cipla. For lack of a better term, then, I will here use "originator" and "generic."

[6] See, for example, ConSuAcción 2007; Espinoza and Guevara 2007; Defensoría del Consumido 2007; Consejo Centroamericano de Protección al. Consumidor 2008.

"one size fits all" resistance strategies, draped thinly over unquestioned assumptions about the salutary nature of market competition, that simply may not bear out in all national contexts.

II. Pharmaceutical IP Comes to Central America: The IP Ratchet in Action

Peter Drahos (2003) has referred to a "global intellectual property ratchet" whereby the United States and the EU have used a combination of multilateral and bilateral strategies to push in concerted fashion for ever higher IP standards. Central America provides a perfect illustration of this trend.

Prior to the 1994 passage of TRIPS, many countries simply did not consider it appropriate to patent medicines. In Central America, only Costa Rica and El Salvador had patent laws on the books, though their short patent terms, small markets, and lax enforcement meant that few companies bothered to seek patents in the region. TRIPS granted Central American countries a five-year transition period to become IP compliant or face WTO sanctions; most countries of the region introduced legislation in late 1999 and early 2000. With some exceptions[7] the bulk of the 2000-era reforms were limited to introducing the twenty-year patent term and test data exclusivity (although in three countries, consistent with the text of TRIPS, no set term was established for test data protection). For the most part, these laws generated little discussion in Central America at the time of their passage.[8]

A second round of IP legislation was passed following the ratification of CAFTA, which occurred in 2005 in Guatemala, Honduras, Nicaragua, and El Salvador, and in 2007, following a national referendum, in Costa Rica. These reforms sought to harmonize existing legislation with new, more stringent "TRIPS-plus" standards contained in the trade agreement. CAFTA's IP rules are very complex; limited space precludes a full explanation here. Yet in very general terms, they might be grouped into two categories: monopoly-expanding and responsibility-shifting. I discuss each of these, briefly.

First, CAFTA *extends the monopoly provisions* contained in TRIPS. CAFTA mandates the extension of patent protection beyond the twenty-year term established in TRIPS, to compensate for "unreasonable" procedural delays (either in granting patents, per art. 15.9(6)(a), or in securing marketing approval for pharmaceuticals, per art. 15.9(6)(b)). And CAFTA establishes a minimum of five years

[7] In Guatemala, for example, legislation was passed in 2000 that mandated fifteen years of test data exclusivity, a standard well beyond that required by TRIPS and indeed far exceeding the US or European standards.

[8] Guatemala is a notable exception to this rule: after its legislature passed the world's most aggressive law to protect pharmaceutical test data (see below), considerable outcry and popular mobilization followed, eventually provoking several reforms to the law.

for test data protection,[9] where TRIPS leaves the protection period open to interpretation. While not a patent, test data exclusivity is effectively "patent-like" in that it grants a market monopoly. Furthermore, where TRIPS mandates the application of test data protection to new chemical entities, CAFTA requires the application of test data exclusivity to new products—a broader category, thus casting the monopoly net wider.

And second, in a departure from TRIPS, CAFTA *tasks states with enforcing private rights*. This is achieved through the introduction of mechanisms such as "linkage," whereby drug regulatory offices are mandated to ensure that products they license are in full compliance with IP law. This saddles drug regulatory authorities with a task they are neither trained nor funded to do; under previous patent systems, and indeed under US law, it falls to private IP holders to detect any infringement of their patent. Under CAFTA, this responsibility falls to the state.

III. Resistance to CAFTA

Resistance to CAFTA was vibrant and transnational. Across Central America, and in the United States, activists organized forums and marches, conducted media campaigns, lobbied elected officials, and engaged in civil disobedience. New transnational coalitions emerged, with a number of differently situated participants. The most salient of these, based in the United States but established in partnership with Central American organizations, was the Stop CAFTA Coalition. Participants in this coalition hailed from a diverse list of organizations of at least four types. These comprised, first of all, groups first formed during the civil wars of the 1980s, including the Committee in Solidarity with the People of El Salvador (CISPES), as well as faith-based groups such as the Maryknoll Office for Global Concerns which had been active in Central America throughout the wars. Although many activists in these groups had remained committed to their cause over the years, the salience of Central American issues in US politics had faded; CAFTA revived interest, albeit temporarily, in this world region and revitalized solidarity groups whose influence had waned. The groups, while typically lacking sizeable financial resources, offered historic connections to specific Central American countries and communities, along with a small but highly motivated membership base which was re-energized by participation in the anti CAFTA campaign. Second, large transnational humanitarian groups like Oxfam and Doctors Without Borders joined in these efforts, bringing significant resources, both financial and reputational. Third, although

[9] Furthermore, as Carlos Correa notes, CAFTA expands the concept of test data protection from its use in TRIPS. TRIPS article 39.1 introduces "protection against unfair competition" but does not mandate exclusivity; a state could choose to interpret this mandate in ways that still allow generic competition by recognizing it as fair. Argentina, in fact, has followed such a path. CAFTA, on the other hand, tightens this restriction by mandating test data *exclusivity* (Correa 2006a). A similar analysis would apply to the mandate to protect data under art. 39.3, which refers to "unfair commercial use."

there were efforts to build coalitions in opposition to CAFTA within Central America, the grassroots organizations active in these coalitions were, for the most part, issue specific: indigenous rights groups in Guatemala, vendors of pirated CDs in El Salvador, peasant organizations, unions, and environmentalists. And lastly, the inclusion of IP brought a novel sector to the table: in some countries, representatives of local generic drug companies participated in the lobbying effort against CAFTA.

Yet among the issues involved in CAFTA, IP received very little attention relative to concerns about agricultural sustainability, labor rights, or the environment. While these latter issues drew on the concerns and expertise of long-established civil society groups in Central America, IP was a relative newcomer. Few organizations in the region were equipped to understand its implications in detail—a formidable challenge, given the general inscrutability of CAFTA's IP chapter. Moreover, IP intersected only peripherally with the central concerns of longstanding health rights advocates in Central America. Indeed, the region has a history of significant mobilization around health rights; the best-known example is probably the early 1990s mass protests against privatization of the Salvadoran health system, called "white marches" because they were led by doctors and healthcare workers wearing their white lab coats. While access to medicines has been a key concern of many in the region, the issue has historically been framed in terms of the ill-functioning of state institutions in charge of purchasing and administering drugs, rather than the impact of international market forces on prices. The promotion of generic drugs by progressive activists battling the trade agreement was an awkward match given longstanding local perceptions that generic producers also charge inflated prices and offer products of often questionable quality (ConSuAcción 2007; Espinoza and Guevara 2007).

This relative lack of local engagement with, and expertise about, IP is reflected in the membership lists of coalition groups, where the names of unions, faith groups, solidarity organizations, and environmental groups are numerous but no IP-specific grassroots organizations are listed. It is also apparent in the Stop CAFTA Coalition's later efforts to monitor the agreement's impacts over time. While detailed reports feature chapters on IP among those on agriculture, labor, and the environment, the research contained in the IP chapters reveals an ongoing lack of familiarity with the specific technicalities of IP law. The lack of IP-based expertise also represents a key difference between the Central American case and that of many South American countries. In Colombia, for example, key civil society groups like Misión Salud and Fundación IFARMA made IP a central focus prior to and after the negotiation of the US-Colombia FTA. Although there are numerous civil society organizations focused on health rights in Central America, IP never figured among their priorities, and they played only very limited roles in the debates over CAFTA. Similarly, Central American health ministries did not take public stances against CAFTA on IP grounds.

During the campaign, therefore, most of the general information about IP was provided by the transnational humanitarian groups (especially Oxfam and Doctors Without Borders), with country-specific IP information filled in by local generics producers in some countries.[10] While grassroots advocacy groups embraced these analyses and used them to mobilize in the context of agreement contestation, they did not develop an IP focus of their own.

In the end, legislatures across the region ratified the agreement despite mass protests. In El Salvador, anti-CAFTA activists occupied the legislative chambers in an effort to forestall the vote on December 16, 2004; security flushed them out and legislators, locked inside overnight, brought CAFTA to the floor at 3 a.m. As Rose Spalding writes, "In an overnight process that truncated public hearings, violated institutional procedures, and precluded meaningful legislative debate, El Salvador became the first country to ratify CAFTA" (Spalding 2007: 101). In Guatemala, on March 8, 2005, with thousands of protestors converging on Congress, deputies moved to hastily approve the agreement without subjecting it to the standard procedure of three readings normally required for the ratification of international treaties. In Costa Rica, a country with deeper democratic traditions, the agreement was put to a popular referendum in October 2007; after months of unprecedented mobilization on both sides, it passed by a narrow margin amid allegations of illegal campaigning by the US Ambassador.

In addition to mass mobilization aimed at stopping ratification, activists took the agreement to their national courts or Human Rights Ombudspeople, arguing that some elements—among them the IP chapter—violated their Constitutions. Costa Rica's Constitution is the only one in Central America that does not explicitly recognize the right to health, though it grants many associated rights, and subsequent jurisprudence has constructed the right to health from the right to life. Despite this, courts upheld the agreement as constitutional, although some Ombudspeople issued strongly worded declarations expressing concerns about its human rights implications. These challenges, ultimately, failed to stop the onset of the agreement.

IV. The Agreement Goes Forward: Implementation

By standard definitions of success, then, the movement to stop CAFTA failed to achieve its stated objective. Yet in important ways, legal mobilization around this issue had significant spillover effects. In the United States, for example, by contributing to a growing sense that the prevailing trade model was harmful to human rights, these activists helped put pressure on the Democratic Party to reconsider core tenets of US trade policy, including the IP provisions that had reached their maximum expression in CAFTA. When the Democrats regained control of Congress in 2006 and announced A New Trade Policy for America, it included

[10] Here an important variation emerges among the countries: in Costa Rica and Guatemala, generic producers were active participants in anti-CAFTA efforts, with Costa Rican generic agrochemicals advocate Ramón Macaya in particular serving as a frequent participant in transnational discussions of the issue; in El Salvador, by contrast, the generics industry did not participate publicly in debates over the agreement, and even issued limited statements expressing tepid support for the agreement.

significantly less demanding IP provisions.[11] As a result, subsequent trade deals with Colombia, Peru, and other nations contained IP standards that were less demanding on several specific points.

In Central America, too, the mobilization around IP and human rights made a difference that is measurable in concrete policy outcomes. To assess how IP policy has changed in Central America, then, we must look beyond the ratification or rejection of the agreement to the actual implementation policies and practices in each country. A systematic review of legislation, regulations, and practices around IP and medicines in the six CAFTA countries (excluding the United States) permits some observations that challenge prevailing assumptions about trade agreements. These findings are summarized in Table 4.1, which presents an analysis of the multiple public health concerns raised by IP and their presence or absence in Central American legislation before and after CAFTA, using an "opportunities" and "threats" framework first proposed by Chaves and Oliveira (2007) and first applied to the Central American context in Cerón and Godoy (2009). Opportunities denote important flexibilities in the TRIPS regime, such as the ability to grant compulsory licenses. Countries that have incorporated such provisions into national laws are in a better position to later invoke them in defense of public health. Threats, on the other hand, are IP tools that introduce TRIPS-plus provisions such as the right to claim data exclusivity. The shifting content of these countries' IP laws through the CAFTA negotiation, ratification, and implementation process permits some observations, discussed below.

A. Variation among Countries

First, substantial variation is found among the countries in question, despite the fact that all were responding to the same general dictates in the agreement. For law and society scholars this may be ultimately unsurprising, since it is well known that policies do not spring intact from the letter of international law, but require substantial processes of local interpretation, negotiation, and implementation. Yet these examples provide the perfect illustration of Drahos's "IP ratchet" in action: if TRIPS established for the first time a universal standard for IP protection, and CAFTA exceeded this standard by mandating "TRIPS-plus" provisions, the laws that some individual countries passed to implement CAFTA raise the bar yet higher, to a level that might be termed "CAFTA-plus." Although space precludes a full discussion of all the elements in Table 4.1, I offer an illustration of two: the extension of patents and the definition of new products.

Thus, TRIPS established, for the first time, a twenty-year patent term, but did not contemplate the *extension of patents* beyond this duration. As noted above, CAFTA went a step further, mandating the extension of patents beyond the twenty-year term in circumstances where "unreasonable" delays were incurred in the process of prosecuting the patent or granting marketing approval (CAFTA

[11] For more on the New Trade Policy for America, see <http://waysandmeans.house.gov/media/enewsletter/5-11-07/07%2005%2010%20New%20Trade%20Policy%20Outline.pdf>.

Table 4.1 Public health sensitivity in intellectual property legislation in CAFTA Countries

		Opportunities						Threats					
	Before/after CAFTA?	Patentability exemptions	Bolar-type exception	Other exceptions to patent rights	Parallel importation	Grounds for compulsory license	Grounds for gov't use	Patent extension	Linkage	Data protection	"New product" definition	Grace period	"New uses" protection
Costa Rica	before	+	+	+	0	+	+	0	0	+	0	0	0
	after	+	0	0	0	+	+	–	–	–	–	0	0
Dominican Republic	before	+	+	–	0	+	+	0	0	+	0	0	0
	after	+	+	–	0	+	+	–	0	–	–	–	0
El Salvador	before	+	0	–	0	+	0	0	0	+	0	0	0
	after	+	+	–	0	+	0	–	–	–	–	–	0
Guatemala	before	+	0	+	0	+	+	0	0	–	0	0	0
	after	+	+	+	0	+	+	–	–	–	–	–	+
Honduras	before	–	0	–	0	+	+	0	0	0	0	0	0
	after	–	+	–	0	+	+	0	–	–	–	–	0
Nicaragua	before	+	0	–	0	+	+	0	0	+	–	0	0
	after	+	+	–	0	+	+	0	–	–	–	–	0

+ TRIPS flexibility or the TRIPS Plus provision allows an interpretation that privileges breaking the IP protection for public health needs.
0 TRIPS flexibility or TRIPS Plus provision is not explicitly included in the legislation.
– TRIPS flexibility or the TRIPS Plus provision privileges the intellectual property protection even if it confronts public health needs.

Source: First published in Cerón and Godoy, "Intellectual Property and Access to Medicines: An Analysis of Legislation in Central America," *Bull. World Health Organ.* 87 (2009): 787–93.

art. 15.9(6)). Yet the affected countries have chosen to interpret this mandate differently: Costa Rica, Nicaragua, and El Salvador stipulate a maximum extension of eighteen months; the Dominican Republic stipulates a maximum of three years, and Guatemala included no such limit whatsoever on the duration of the extension. Honduras, meanwhile, apparently did not pass legislation to implement this provision of CAFTA.

As noted, article 39.3 of TRIPS mandates test data protection for "*new chemical entities*," whereas CAFTA mandates protection for "*new products.*" The difference is significant; the meaning of "new chemical entities" has been hotly debated in a number of contexts, including most notably the discussions surrounding the 2005 reforms to India's patent law. Yet CAFTA introduces an entirely new category—that of new products, defined as follows: "A new product is one that does not contain a chemical entity that has been previously approved" in the country (art. 15.10(1)(c)).

Yet several Central American countries go a step further, in a textual change that is easy to miss. In Guatemala, for example, a new product is defined as a product "which contains a chemical entity not previously approved in the country" (Congreso de la República de Guatemala 2005, translation by author). Nicaragua's and El Salvador's definitions are identical to Guatemala's. In Spanish, the distinction between the two definitions is merely the placement of the word "no" at different points in the same sentence. But this apparently trivial difference is significant, as a number of new drugs on the market are compounds involving previously marketed substances; this is particularly the case with second-line antiretroviral treatments for HIV/AIDS. Under the definition of a "new product" applied by CAFTA, a drug—such as Abbott Lab's Kaletra, recognized as an Essential Medicine by the WHO—which combines a previously recognized substance and a new one would not be eligible for test data exclusivity (and thus, essentially, a market monopoly). Under the definition in force in Guatemala and Nicaragua, however, such a product would be granted exclusivity. Because Central American markets are small and registering patents is costly—and because many products new to the market may not be eligible for patents—in many cases, test data protection (rather than a patent) provides the sole mechanism by which generic competition is forestalled. The differences in language thus make a real difference in the lives of patients.

What's more, the variation reflected in the text of domestic legislation is most likely augmented further as different national and local institutions develop practices for implementation. While we lack systematic studies of how health ministries and patent offices are working to carry out the new tasks mandated them by law, some indicators suggest dramatically different impacts on drug markets from one Central American country to the next. For example, as Godoy and Cerón (2011) document, in December 2009/January 2010 test data exclusivity was applied to ninety-eight molecules in Guatemala, versus nineteen in El Salvador and only five in Nicaragua. Not only do the sheer numbers of affected products vary widely, but there is surprisingly little overlap between the actual drugs. In other words, the drugs enjoying exclusivity in El Salvador and Nicaragua were not simply a subset of the larger Guatemalan list, but included different products not protected in Guatemala. Further research is required to understand the extent to which this reflects differences in institutional purchases, IP interpretations, or other factors.

Other studies, such as Shaffer and Brenner (2009), report what would appear to be highly capricious—and capacious—interpretations of the applicable scope of IP protection by the Guatemalan authorities, resulting even in the removal of some drugs from the market. Another article based on the same research (Shaffer, Brenner, and Lewis 2009) further suggests that government purchasing choices may reflect a shift in power to originator companies even when not required by IP law. This type of in-depth impact analysis, extending beyond the letter of the law to the way it is actually being applied in practice, should be conducted in other countries—and where possible, its data corroborated by sources other than the generics industry—to enable a deeper understanding of how the agreement is being implemented across the region.

B. Improved Policies through Agreement Contestation

Table 4.1 also permits a second observation, relating to the unanticipated (and still quite limited) positive impacts of CAFTA. In six of the twelve points of law examined, Central American countries saw a net worsening of their ability to protect public health. In four of the twelve, the situation was unchanged. But in two of the twelve, legislation became *more* public health-friendly as a result of the CAFTA process: four countries incorporated early-working exceptions into their patent laws, and one country rejected the application of patents to new uses for existing drugs. How did this happen?

The outcome can only be understood by bearing in mind the multiplicity of venues through which IP norms have been instituted across the globe. While trade agreements—particularly those with the United States—generate the most public reaction in Latin America, many IP laws were crafted before CAFTA's arrival. In fact, while IP opponents tend to decry the IP agenda as a sort of South-bound steamroller in the form of free trade agreements (first crushing resistance in Mexico, then Central America, then Colombia . . .) we might better understand IP's introduction like a cloud or fog which gradually enveloped Central America.

In many ways, of course, such gradual seepage is difficult to contest, particularly after the fact: in the ratification debates, defenders of the agreement typically argued that the bulk of its IP provisions were already law anyway, and for the most part they were right. Most of the IP laws already in force had been passed with virtually no engagement, and often times with little awareness, from civil society. But the arrival of the trade agreement opened a new opportunity for mobilization, and with it, the interest of transnational organizations with greater access to resources. The gains achieved were not, therefore, the result of CAFTA itself, as agreement proponents might like to argue, but rather the result of the opportunity created by its negotiation and ratification. In creating a high-visibility political opening for attention to this issue, CAFTA helped enable the engagement of critical actors whose involvement led to a relaxation of some of the most harmful IP policies already in place. To explore these dynamics in greater depth, I turn now to the particular experience of Guatemala, the country that saw the most significant mobilization around these issues—and, notably, experienced an improvement in public health sensitivity on two of the twelve points of law examined in Table 4.1.

V. The Example of Guatemala: Transnational Alliances for IP Advocacy

In order to implement TRIPS and to demonstrate the country's readiness for the much-anticipated CAFTA, Guatemala passed legislation in 2000 that mandated fifteen years of test data exclusivity, a standard well beyond that required by TRIPS and indeed far exceeding the US or European standards. At the time, it made the country the world's most aggressive protector of pharmaceutical test data (Chase and Lueck 2004). This provision was, however, repealed in 2002 by Decree 76–2002 (Congreso de la República de Guatemala 2002), leaving the country without any test data protection and prompting Guatemala's assignation to the Special 301 Watch List maintained by the Office of the United States Trade Representative.[12] In response to these pressures, heightened by the then-ongoing negotiations of CAFTA, the Guatemalan Congress passed Decree 9-2003 the following year, reestablishing test data protection, now for a period of five years (Congreso 2003). This action prompted the formation of a civil society coalition, the Alianza Civil por el Acceso a Medicamentos (ACAM). The group enjoyed diverse participation from HIV/AIDS patients, public health advocates, academics, health sector unions, and other groups, and benefited from the expertise, energy, and material resources contributed by Doctors Without Borders, then operating in the country; its efforts also intersected with those of transnational coalitions opposing the IP rules that, by this time, had been written into the draft of the CAFTA agreement.

Thanks in large part to these efforts, in November 2004 an overwhelming majority of Guatemala's Congress repealed the five years' protection (Decree 34-2004) (Congreso 2004). Again, the United States reacted by exerting considerable pressure on Guatemala to change its laws, the most visible manifestations of which were public declarations by then-US Ambassador John Hamilton that Guatemala's perceived failure to "take its obligations seriously" might imperil the country's inclusion in CAFTA (Hamilton 2005). CAFTA was ratified in March 2005, and within days, protection was reinstituted for a period of five years (Decree 30-2005) (Congreso 2005).

The ACAM coalition was successful—temporarily—at reversing a law that was vocally supported by the United States and its powerful supporters in Guatemala, including the American Chamber of Commerce and FEDEFARMA, a private group comprising the major pharmaceutical corporations. Although ACAM did challenge Decree 9-2003 in the courts, their effort was unsuccessful: what worked,

[12] For more on the Special 301 Watch List, see Dreyfuss and Rodriguez, Chapter 1 in this volume.

instead, were public protests, press conferences, the repeated lobbying of legislators, and other forms of rights mobilization both in public and private venues.

In the view of at least some participants in the effort (Miranda n/d), the controversies surrounding CAFTA created an opening in which protest groups were able to invoke the participation of powerful transnational actors. These included Doctors Without Borders, Oxfam, Health GAP, and many other public health and human rights advocates based in the United States and Europe. Their participation helped elevate the issue from something of only limited interest to a broad, public issue, of which many Guatemalan citizens became aware. Although public opinion data to estimate the extent of this awareness is unavailable, widespread coverage of the issue in the major newspapers of the country reflects the groups' success in positioning the issue on the national agenda.[13] Some protestors who took to the streets following Guatemala's ratification of CAFTA in March 2005 wore jerseys emblazoned with the slogan "My life is not for sale," invoking concerns about the impact of the agreement on the right to life.

At the same time, this mobilization focused on the agreement's negotiation and ratification rather than its implementation. Thus, it was ultimately short-lived. Once the ratification battle was lost, the more powerful transnational organizations turned their attention to other trade battles emerging in the Andean region. In Guatemala, this turning-away of transnational attention was felt particularly acutely after CAFTA because the period coincided with Doctors Without Borders' departure from the country for reasons unrelated to CAFTA. While smaller grassroots groups remained concerned with the access issue, without the active accompaniment and resources of transnational allies, they lacked the capacity to track or influence implementation legislation. Ultimately, this meant that laws were drafted with virtually no public scrutiny; the widespread perception was that since CAFTA had passed, few (if any) options remained. Indeed, CAFTA's passage mandated many changes; but others, such as the indefinite granting of patent extensions or the application of test data protection to the widest possible set of products, were imposed despite being unnecessary under the terms of the agreement.

VI. Conclusion

The Central American case speaks to both the promises and pitfalls of transnational efforts to promote access to medicines in the face of unduly restrictive IP reforms.

Most important, the promises are real. Alliances with powerful transnational advocates like Oxfam and Doctors Without Borders enabled Central American activists to improve the public health sensitivity of their IP legislation through the process of contestation that CAFTA's negotiation unleashed. Although these gains

[13] A review of media coverage of the issue in the four or five largest newspapers of the five Central American CAFTA countries suggests more systematic attention to the topic in Guatemala. Although CAFTA in general generated more attention in Costa Rica, it appears that in Guatemala more attention was paid to the specific topic of medications.

are small and scattered, against a backdrop of overwhelmingly more demanding IP practices, they are nevertheless significant, especially when one takes into account the magnitude of the challenge faced by health advocates in the Central American case.

This suggests some possible avenues for improving access, even without renegotiating the terms of CAFTA or invoking TRIPS safeguards. Central American countries could significantly improve their policies by striking down the CAFTA-plus provisions which exceed the requirements of the agreement itself. Furthermore, because the prevailing standards for IP protection today are on some specific points less demanding than those required by CAFTA, Central American countries could seek to modify their IP rules in line with those contained in other South American agreements as a way of capitalizing upon this opportunity.

And yet, the Central American story also speaks powerfully to the pitfalls of transnational mobilization. With some important exceptions, the struggle against IP's encroachment on health rights was mostly the result of the perceptions and preoccupations of activists from North and South America. Health advocates from groups like Oxfam and Doctors Without Borders worked hard to build alliances with, and to transfer capacity to, local leaders. But ultimately campaigns conceived abroad touched down in Central American countries in only very limited ways. By way of conclusion, I offer some reflections on three dimensions of those limitations.

First, campaigns to challenge restrictive IP laws in Central America were severely limited by their time horizons. The involvement of international actors in the negotiation and ratification period helped spur attention to the issue, but was ultimately short-lived. The attention to ratification votes does create an important opening for mobilization, but the real human rights impact of the agreements is determined later, typically after public attention to this issue has subsided. Legislators draft laws, committees formulate regulations that seal the fate of thousands, yet the issue has slipped from the headlines, international experts have turned their attention elsewhere, and activists are often off recovering from a battle they think they lost. In fact, to achieve more lasting gains for human rights, campaigns need to influence not only ratification votes but also the much lower profile work of elaborating local norms and regulations. This is easy to say, but very difficult to do, particularly given the resource drain that such work would represent in a region where other health and human rights concerns also cry out for immediate action.

The emphasis on the ratification rather than implementation phase also relates to questions about targets for action. It is clear that these policies are imposed by the United States government, at the behest of US pharmaceutical companies, so humanitarian organizations' emphasis on pushing for change within the US Congress is appropriate and has shown itself to be (moderately) effective. Yet this may surrender or supplant an important space for human rights work within poor countries where, as this research shows, steps can be taken to ensure less disastrous human rights impacts. Ultimately, there is a clear need to develop lasting expertise *in*, not just "on," poor countries. Transnational mobilization and partnership, and the involvement of US- or European-based NGOs (or, for that matter, academics) may always be necessary. But without the ongoing, informed advocacy of actors familiar with local conditions and able to engage in a sustained way with local politics, significant battles are surrendered. To ensure the protection of the human right to health from the incursion of excessive intellectual property protection in the long term, therefore, greater attention must be paid to capacity building among those leaders who will be in place to monitor and shape implementation one, two, ten years after the high-profile battle against trade agreement ratification has subsided.

A second set of limitations relates to the politics of resistance. In Central America, progressive health activism has long focused on promoting access to primary health care as a human right. Major battles have been fought around efforts to privatize health services, and much public attention is focused on the need to improve the quality of health services delivered by state agencies. Within such a framework, access to affordable medicines is undeniably important, but not necessarily perceived as the central issue by those most involved in longstanding struggles. Furthermore, in many cases leading health advocates have been deeply critical of the role played by generic companies; in the largely unregulated Central American market, some generics can even be more expensive than brand-name drugs, and fears about generic drug quality are not only fanned by the machinations of originator companies, but also sometimes fed by the research and advocacy of local scholars and consumer rights organizations. In this context, absent more effective state regulation of the drug supply, an argument for access that sidesteps safety concerns is destined to have limited public resonance. What's more, given preexisting political alignments in some Central American countries, transnational activists' efforts to ally with local generics producers to challenge IP can create a situation of odd bedfellows. Ultimately, in the battle over IP in CAFTA, decisions about which health issues mattered most, and which partnerships were strategic and beneficial, appear to have been made based on assumptions that meshed imperfectly with Central American realities.

And lastly, a third set of limitations involves the substantive content of advice offered by transnational organizations to local health activists. In the context of battles over CAFTA, for example, Central American legislators were urged to hold the line on using TRIPS flexibilities. Argentine expert Carlos Correa drafted a "Model Law" for Central American countries, outlining ways that local legislation could be brought into compliance with CAFTA's demands while still preserving as many flexibilities as possible. The "successes" documented in Table 4.1—areas in which some Central American countries were able to take advantage of the scrutiny afforded by the agreement ratification process to insert legislation allowing grounds for things like government production of drugs or compulsory licensing—are assumed to be successes based on the example of other countries that have successfully invoked such provisions. In urging the adoption of legislation that in other contexts has provided openings, advocates may be projecting Northern—or Southern—fantasies on Central America. Is it truly meaningful that Honduran law contemplates the government manufacture of pharmaceuticals, given the extremely limited capacity in-country? Does it matter that El Salvador permits exemptions to patentability, if local patent officers are trained to exercise their duties in a framework that favors exclusion over access?

Of course, it is a tall order indeed to expect transnational organizations to adopt country-specific frameworks for fighting IP battles, or even to decide which battles are worth fighting; the nature of the work requires activists to shift attention rapidly from one trade agreement to another. My comments here are not intended as an indictment of their efforts, which clearly and unambiguously created an important site of valuable struggle over IP and health, with spillover effects beyond the Central American region. Indeed, I count myself as a supporter of such work, and contributed directly to it in the context of the campaign against CAFTA. But the limitations discussed above invite reflection on how such transnational advocacy campaigns are conceived and conducted.

As Mark Goodale writes, discussing the importance of understanding transnational efforts as mutually constitutive,

> [i]n moving away from the global/local dichotomy... we must be cautious not to over-privilege the role of cosmopolitan elites, those 'activists without borders' whose very movements across both cultural and territorial boundaries seem to symbolize the normative transnationalism they advocate.... Many of the most important actors whose encounters with human rights discourse contribute to its transnationalism never physically leave their villages, or towns, or countries. (2007: 21–2)

Indeed, IP's arrival in Central America was undeniably a top-down story, whereby policies originating in the global North were foisted upon weaker countries with little effective capacity to resist them. But IP resistance, too, has largely been a top-down story, conceived, funded, and led by globally oriented activists concerned about the health impacts of this new wave of legislation. We still need an understanding of IP politics and practices more rooted in Central American realities, not only to enable us to draw better conclusions about the real impact of these policies on public health, but also to point the way to more sustainable strategies for contestation and resistance.

References

Cerón, Alejandro, and Angelina Snodgrass Godoy. 2009. "Intellectual Property and Access to Medicines: An Analysis of Legislation in Central America." *Bulletin of the World Health Organization* 87(1): 787.

Chase, Marilyn, and Sarah Lueck. 2004. "In New Trade Pacts, US Seeks to Limit Reach of Generic Drugs." *Wall Street Journal*, July 6. A1.

Chaves, Gabriela Costa, and Maria Auxiliadora Oliveira. 2007. "A Proposal for Measuring the Degree of Public Health-Sensitivity of Patent Legislation in the Context of the WTO TRIPS Agreement." *Bulletin of the World Health Organization* 85(1): 49.

Congreso de la República de Guatemala. Decreto 76-2002, published as Acuerdo 6-2003 in the *Diario Oficial*, January 28, 2003.

——. April 15, 2003. "Decreto 9-2003." Available online as <http://www.sgp.gob.gt/PaginaWeb/Decretos%202003/DG9-2003.pdf>.

——. November 2004. "Decreto 34-2004. Reformas a La Ley De Propiedad Industrial, Decreto no. 57-2000."

——. March 9, 2005. "Decreto 30-2005."

Consejo Centroamericano de Protección al Consumidor, CONCADECO. 2008. "Sondeo de precios de medicamentos centroamericano." <http://www.meic.go.cr/esp2/noticias/estudios/2009/medicamentos/medicamentos_ca_2008.pdf>

ConSuAcción (Consumidores en Acción de Centroamérica). 2007. "Promoción etica y precio justo en los medicamentos? Una mirada desde las organizaciones de consumidores en Centroamérica." Available at <http://www.cdc.org.sv/noticias/piden-reducir-margenes-de-ganancias-a-farmacias>.

Correa, Carlos. 2006. "Implementación de la protección de datos de prueba de productos farmacéuticos y agroquímicos en DR-CAFTA-Ley Modelo." Geneva: International Centre for Trade and Sustainable Development (ICTSD).

Defensoría del Consumidor. 2007. Dirección de Estudios, verificación y vigilancia. Estudio de Precios de Medicamentos. Available at <http://www.defensoria.gob.sv/descargas/estudio_precios_medicamentos_07.pdf>.

Drahos, Peter. 2003. "The Global Intellectual Property Ratchet: Why it Fails as Policy and What Should Be Done about it." Paper for the Open Society Institute. <http://cgkd.anu.edu.au/menus/PDFs/IPRatchet_Drahos.pdf>, accessed July 19, 2011.

Espinoza Fiallos, Eduardo, and Giovanni Guevara. 2007. "Disponibilidad y precio de los medicamentos en El Salvador durante el segundo semestre de 2006." Universidad de El Salvador. <http://www.haiweb.org/medicineprices/surveys/00611SV/sdocs/survey_report.pdf>

Godoy, Angelina Snodgrass, and Alejandro Cerón. 2011. "Changing Drug Markets under New Intellectual Property Regimes: The View from Central America." *American Journal of Public Health* 101(7): 1186.

Goodale, Mark. 2007. "Locating Rights: Envisioning Law between the Global and the Local." Pp. 1–38 in *The Practice of Human Rights: Tracking Law between the Global and the Local*, edited by M. Goodale and S. E. Merry. Cambridge: Cambridge University Press.

Guzmán León, Juany, and Luis Guillermo Solís Rivera. 2005. "New Actors, Democracy, and Challenges Face Central America on the Threshold of the Twenty-First Century." *Social Forces* 84(1).

Hamilton, John. 2005. "TLC y genéricos sí coexisten." *Siglo Veintiuno*, January 9.

Industry Functional Advisory Committee on Intellectual Property Rights for Trade Policy Matters (IFAC-3). 2004. "The U.S.-Central American Free Trade Agreement (FTA) the Intellectual Property Provisions: Advisory Committee Report to the President, the Congress and the United States Trade Representative on the U.S.-Central American Free Trade Agreement."

Martínez, Gerson Elí, and Alejandra Castro Bonilla. 2008. *Propiedad intelectual y acceso a medicamentos esenciales de calidad en Centroamérica.* San Salvador: FUNDE.

Miranda, José. n/d. "Una experiencia de acción colectiva en torno al acceso a medicamentos esenciales en Guatemala." Unpublished ms.

Shaffer, Ellen, and Joseph Brenner. 2009. "A Trade Agreement's Impact on Access to Generic Drugs." *Health Affairs* 28(5): 957–68.

Shaffer, Ellen, Joseph Brenner, and Shayna Lewis. 2009. "Cafta: Barriers to Access in Medicines in Guatemala." Health and Human Rights Open Forum. <http://www.hhropenforum.org/2009/11/cafta-barriers-to-access-to-medicines-in-guatemala/>, accessed July 19, 2011.

Spalding, Rose. 2007. "Civil Society Engagement in Trade Negotiations: CAFTA Opposition Movements in El Salvador." *Latin American Politics & Society* 49(4): 85.

Chapter 5

Chile: The Case of IP Opposition from Predominantly Private Interests

Salvador Millaleo H.

In this chapter, I describe the political field on which the tensions between intellectual property laws and access to medicine play out in Chile. This description includes the political opportunities that have arisen during the period of the study (roughly, 1990–2011) and the positions of the actors that participated in those opportunity structures. The most important feature of this field is that its contours are largely determined by the legal norms imposed by international trade agreements. Because these have changed over time, the implementation game is a dynamic one. However, the field is highly circumscribed. The intellectual property laws propounded in international trade agreements are inescapable starting points. Thus, the conflicts and tensions occur within a narrowly delineated area of action. And given that these agreements allow for the realization of international economic policies defined by a political elite promoting private interests, and that these state policies are largely unquestioned by the population at large, the conflicts involve the government and private economic agents; they rarely include actors from civil society.

Nonetheless, the introduction of the global framework of intellectual property norms followed the adoption of a liberal economic policy and it opened an implementation game where the starting points could be—if not superseded—then relativized in their later administrative and legal application. Subsequent political efforts effectively limited the impact of the international norms on the Chilean population. But here too, private interests dominated. The political processes did not lead to the formulation of public-regarding policies favoring access to medicine. Rather, they involved "back-door opposition" on the part of representatives of the national pharmaceutical industry and government employees who were interested, for private reasons, in opposing barriers to entry into the pharmaceutical market. As a result, questions of distributive justice have remained underrepresented in the implementation game and also in the legal cases addressing access issues.

So far, the cost of medicines has remained low. Accordingly, this strategy, which limits intellectual property rights without considering the public interest, has not led to any significant conflict. However, as the United States increases pressure to raise Chile's compliance levels with international obligations, tensions are growing. Additionally, problems related to the quality of the generic medicines that dominate the domestic market remain unresolved.

This chapter focuses on patent rights and the protection of non-disseminated information concerning the safety and efficacy of pharmaceutical products. It is structured as follows: section I presents the conceptual framework for the globalization of intellectual property and its local opposition. Section II describes the Chilean pharmaceutical market, showing how it is that it gave rise to a dispute involving largely private interests. Section III provides a chronological and systematic examination of the political opportunities Chile experienced in developing and implementing its international obligations. Section IV concludes. The appendix looks at confrontation in the judicial arena and summarizes the most important legal cases on the issues of debate in Chile. For the purposes of this study, I have reviewed public documents elaborating the policies of governmental agencies, reports from private institutions, press releases, and legal documents (laws and regulations and legal and administrative decisions). I also undertook a series of interviews with diverse actors involved in the relevant political processes.

I. The Conceptual Framework: The Globalization of the Rules of Intellectual Property and Back Door Opposition

The field of medicine is subject to the rules of international trade within the normative framework of the World Trade Organization (WTO) and is governed, in particular, by the TRIPS Agreement, which binds all WTO members. Within these rules, all innovative technology is subject to protection through patent rights. As regards medicines, WTO member states must provide patent protection for pharmaceutical inventions. Additionally, they must protect trade secrets, including information generated for the authorities responsible for clearing pharmaceutical products as effective and safe for marketing. The rights to patents and trade secrets must be enforceable in court and they are subject to a formal multilateral monitoring system through the TRIPS Council (Zangl and Zürn 2004). In addition, they are the target of a permanent system of both formal and informal unilateral monitoring and reporting, including through the public-private operations of the Office of the United States Trade Representative (USTR), acting under its Special 301 procedure (Sell 2003).[1]

The TRIPS rules constitute a minimum global framework, but TRIPS has been merely one step in the upward trajectory of intellectual property rights. Within the last few decades, protection has increased with respect to aims, time limits, methods of protection, and the efficiency of enforcement. For example, the Chile–US Free Trade Agreement imposes more detailed ("TRIPS-plus") standards; similar free

[1] See the description of Special 301 actions in Chapter 1 and Sean Flynn's comment in Chapter 8 in this volume.

trade agreements (FTAs) have been signed with many other nations. Together, TRIPS and these FTAs create a true international legal regime and form one of the most recognizable structures of global governance institutions. This regime has, however, mainly responded to the interests of large global technology companies, among which the pharmaceutical consortium holds a prominent position. Thus, the intellectual property rights imposed tend to reduce public access to medicines and make the provision of healthcare more difficult. For Tansey,

> Health is but one of the areas affected by the struggles regarding who will control and benefit from scientific and technological changes that are occurring. They could bring larger changes in the distribution of wealth and power in the world, and the big players that now have power know it, and want to determine the rules in such a way that lets them maintain their positions. And for this to occur, as some key industries recognized 30 years ago, they need global patent, copyright, trademark and other laws that have been called "intellectual property rights". (Tansey 2006: 2)

TRIPS is a public-private normative regime, in that through the agreement, public actors (governments) protect the interests of the large multinational companies that develop and make intensive use of technology. The pharmaceutical sector is a prime example. The regime builds both through the incorporation of the multinational companies' interests into the normative framework, as well as through the monitoring of compliance with these norms, especially in those countries that are not knowledge producers but rather recipients. Because of the indeterminate reach of exclusive rights and the technical complexity involved in determining compliance, public agents depend heavily on private actors that possess the infrastructure to undertake the monitoring task; these actors are then well positioned to strengthen their interests (Brousseau and Bessy 2006). As Susan Sell states, "in general, TRIPS reflects and promotes the interests of global corporations that seek to increase their control over their intellectual property. These companies, acting through the government of the United States (and with the support of Europe and Japan), dominate the WTO processes and managed to create international public rules in accordance with their particular needs" (Sell 2004: 372).

Chile, by joining the WTO, entered into the TRIPS system and assumed international obligations that demand compliance. But the decision to join does not mean that compliance was free from controversy. The implementation process does not necessarily flow directly from the political process that led to the adoption of TRIPS. Rather, the obligation to implement creates new conflicts and opens new political opportunities. The opportunity structures developed in these domestic spaces can be very different from the structures that surrounded the adoption of the international agreement. The concept of "back door opposition" pertains to this context. "Back door opposition" describes the attitudes of the actors in the political process as they attempt to compensate for, or limit the reach of, the previously adopted obligations. Examining its operation exposes the differences in the options facing policymakers and implementers and shows the conditions under which the goals of the implementers can be fulfilled (Thomson 2010).

The concept of back door opposition was originated in studies of the European Union (EU) (Falkner et al. 2004). There, it was shown that the transposition of EU laws into practice was affected by the preferences and opportunities of political actors in the implementation sphere. That is, in the two spheres (national and international), the capacity of states to propose norms differ, as do the structures of political opportunities that arise in the internal political process of implementation. Because global political processes do not predetermine domestic political opportunities, the results in the implementation process can be partially or completely contradictory to the global processes of rule formation (Meyer 2004). This occurs both because of the separation of opportunity structures at the policymaking and implementation stage (Mazmanian and Sabatier 1983; McLaughlin 1987; Hill and Hupe 2006) and because of differences in the characteristics of global policy arenas when compared with domestic policy arenas (Grande 2001). Following Meyer and Minkoff (2004), it is also important to consider the effect of differences between the general aspects of the global expansion of intellectual property laws and the specifics of developing policy and law related to drugs.

In the final analysis, the structure of the pharmaceutical market, the actors, the lack of important civil society intervention, and the role of governmental intermediation can have immense explanatory power with respect to outcomes. This is certainly true in the case of Chile. Chile adopted a strong intellectual property regime, without limitations or flexibility in the health sphere.[2] However, when it confronted the implementation process, back door opposition found variations in the permissible rules and chose laws that improved the position of the domestic pharmaceutical industry without openly breaking with the policies that had led to the adoption of the strict regime. These variations have not resulted in serious public litigation concerning the right of access to health or even in private litigation over patents rights. Rather, there is relatively light enforcement activity, both by the administrative branch and the legislating power.

II. The Pharmaceutical Sector in Chile: Concentration and Low Prices

To comprehend the political processes that we describe, it is necessary to understand the structure of the national drug market in Chile. It is here where the hegemonic actors predominating at the implementation phase appear.

In Chile, the pharmaceutical market operates under imperfect conditions. On the side of suppliers, there are two subsectors: domestic and international laboratories. The demand side is highly concentrated among pharmaceutical chains and institutional acquisitions. As a result, laboratories tend to lose negotiating power to the pharmaceutical chains (Latinpharma 2006: 12). The domestic pharmaceutical

[2] Indeed, its law may soon be strengthened by the Trans-Pacific Partnership (TPP) Agreement which was under negotiation at the time of this writing. For more information, see <http://www.ustr.gov/tpp>.

industry is composed of more than 159 companies, domestic and international, that together produce and/or import finished product (Vassallo 2010: 13).

In the last decade the structure of the Chilean pharmaceutical market has changed, mainly through mergers among pharmacy chains and between chains and department stores. A critical point in these mergers was the union between the Salco and Brand pharmacy chains, which formed S and B Pharmaceutical (S y B Farmaceutica) in 2000, thus gaining 32.1 percent of the distribution market. According to Vassallo, this situation developed from a price war among chains that, together with the strong presence of generic drugs, let to a large reduction in the price of pharmaceuticals. Thus, drug prices in Chile were the lowest in Latin America, with an average of USD 3.33 (Vassallo 2010: 6).

Four types of drugs coexist in the Chilean pharmaceutical market. In the first category are "originator" or "brand name" drugs, usually produced by international laboratories. Developing the products in this category requires a great deal of effort, including between twelve and fifteen years of research. Normally, these drugs are protected by pharmaceutical patents. Their average price is estimated to be around USD 8.50 per box. The market percentage of brand name sales is slightly more than 20 percent.[3]

"Brand name generics" form the second category, and account for 44 percent of the market. They have an average price of USD 4.8 per box. They are copies of the original product and are brought to market after the patent has expired. The laboratories distributing these drugs will usually invest in marketing and product improvement, such as making coated tablets or developing slow-release formulations. These do not fit the definition of generics used by the US Food and Drug Administration (FDA) or the World Health Organization (WHO). For example, the FDA provides that "a generic drug is the same as a brand name drug in dosage, safety, strength, how it is taken, quality, performance, and intended use."[4] Because these drugs differ from the original formulation, they cannot obtain a certification of bioequivalence. Therefore, the only guarantee of quality, safety, and effectiveness of the "brand name generic" drug in Chile is trust in the laboratory that produces it. To identify themselves, brand name generics frequently adopt trade names for their commercialization.

The third category of drugs is referred to as "Chilean generics" or simple "similars." These are commercialized under the name of the medical ingredient. They represent around 40 percent of drug sales in Chile, with average prices of USD 1.10 per box. They are generally manufactured by domestic laboratories and do not include a certification of bioequivalence. The only difference between these and brand name generics is that the brand name generics add unique names to their marketing materials, while the Chilean generics rely only on generic names.

[3] Valeria Ibarra, "Pharmaceutical Market in Chile" (in Spanish, "Mercado farmacéutico en Chile facturó más de US$1.300 millones"), June 11, 2011. Retrieved January 15, 2011 at: <http://chile-hoy.blogspot.com/2011/06/mercado-farmaceutico-en-chile-facturo.html>.

[4] US Food and Drug Administration, Glossary of Terms, <http://www.fda.gov/drugs/informationondrugs/ucm079436.htm>.

The designation of "generics" in Chile is thus very confusing from an international perspective and is not even well understood by experts. Chileans use the designation "generic," but the designation corresponds to the concept of "International Common Denomination (ICD)" or "International Nonproprietary Name (INN)." These describe terms granted by an international committee in order to enhance communication among medical, pharmaceutical, and regulatory personnel. The terms precisely identify a medicine (or an active ingredient) and they do so more conveniently than the chemical name. They are not protectable as trademarks. In sum, for Chileans, a "generic" is simply a drug sold under a common international denomination. These medicines are authorized for public sale without scientific tests or technical evidence of safety and effectiveness, although in some cases, the brand name generics rely on scientific information generated by the originators (Saavedra 2010: 13).

The fourth category of medicines is "WHO generics." These are authentic generic drugs and correspond to international definitions of generic products. They are copies of brand name (originator) drugs and appear in the market once the inventor's patent has expired. They are registered under an ICD generic name, and are approved and registered by drug authorities on the basis of therapeutic bioequivalence studies. These may be *in vivo* or *in vitro* bioequivalence, or clinical studies, undertaken in laboratories approved and certified by the drug authority (Saavedra 2010: 13). The studies are intended to show that the drugs have the same active ingredients, pharmaceutical form, kinetic, dynamic, and technical characteristics as a medicine used as a technical legal reference (Saavedra, Saldaña, and Ruminot 2006: 206). These drugs thus have a certification of bioequivalence in accordance with international standards.

There are, however, very few WHO generics available on the Chilean market (Saavedra, Saldaña, and Ruminot 2006: 207). Decisions to undertake bioequivalence studies are purely voluntary and are made for marketing reasons—fundamentally, because the drugs are to be commercialized internationally.[5] Until 2010, in Chile there was only one laboratory that could undertake bioequivalence studies, the Pharmacokinetics and Bioavailability Laboratory Program of Molecular and Clinical Pharmacology, Faculty of Medicine, University of Chile. In 2011, two more labs opened: the Bioequivalence Laboratory of the University of Development and the Bioequivalence Unit of the Clinical Research Center of the Catholic University. Furthermore, laboratories enjoy a higher profit margin on similar drugs than on true bioequivalent generics. Accordingly, the labs tend to increase the supply of these. Vertical integration of chains has also had an effect on the composition of the market. One conglomeration can be the owner of a chain of pharmacies, the business that distributes the drugs, and a laboratory (León and Martínez 2011: 12). Since the process of integration began with the labs, their products tend to dominate the market. Chains also have considerable marketing power because they interact directly with patients.

[5] Interview with Ivan Saavedra.

Table 5.1 Map of Chilean pharmaceutical market suppliers

Map of Supplier Players	DESCRIPTION
Laboratories	Domestic (control 50% of pharmacy sales) and foreign.
Pharmaceutical Wholesalers	Undertake the commercialization and distribution as wholesale operators. There are currently two important private wholesalers: Socofar (controls 20% of the market) and Droguería Nuñoa.
	The Ahumada and Salcobrand pharmacy chains have pharmaceutical wholesalers but do not sell to independent pharmacies.
Pharmacy chains	Farmacias Ahumada, Salco- Brand, and Cruz Verde Pharmacies are the 3 most important.
	Farmalíder is smaller, but boasts important growth and is tied to the most important supermarket chain in the country.
Pharmacies	1,800 private pharmacies, of which 1,300 belong to chains and 500 are small pharmacies located in sparsely populated areas.

Source: Vassallo 2010: 16.

The structure of the industry demonstrates that the pharmacies form the main distribution network (Vassallo 2010: 12). The landscape of drug suppliers in Chile is shown in Table 5.1.

With respect to demand, there is a public institution with considerable buying power. This player is CENABAST, or the National Drug Supply Center, created in 1920 and whose legal mandate is to centralize public purchases of drugs for Ministry of Health programs, hospitals, municipal offices, and other public health programs. CENABAST purchases amounted to $210,654,000 pesos (around USD 460,000,000) in 2010. The CENABAST model is one of economies of scale, through large volume purchases, mostly of generics without certifications of bioequivalence, from emerging economies, such as India, China, Malaysia, and the Ukraine. To make these purchases, the Chilean health system has incurred a heavy debt. By April 30, 2011, the public sector owed drug providers, in particular foreign labs, $79,069 million pesos (around USD 173,000,000) (CENABAST 2011). This debt poses a difficult political problem because it reinforces the influence of foreign laboratories over the Chilean state.

Despite spending by the public sector, private expenditures also remain high. Figures from 2007 suggest that 47 percent of all spending is private and of this, 55 percent is out-of-pocket spending. More than half of this is spent on originators or brand-name drugs. (Cid and Prieto 2010). These expenditures are not the result of high prices—drugs in Chile are lower than in the rest of Latin America. However, that is not because the country has articulated a policy protecting access to medicines (see Table 5.2).[6]

[6] Interview with Marianela Castillo (health economist).

Table 5.2 Average price of medicines in Latin America

Average prices of medicines in Latin America 2006–2008 (in USD and percentages)	Average Price in USD			Percent of Annual Variation	
Country	2006	2007	2008	Al 07/06	Al 08/07
Argentina	5.93	6.36	7.30	7.4	14.7
Bolivia	4.73	4.90	5.98	3.6	22.0
Brazil	6.86	8.03	8.97	17.1	11.7
Chile	4.15	4.12	4.73	−0.6	14.8
Colombia	4.40	5.41	5.93	23.1	9.5
Ecuador	4.35	4.57	4.77	5.2	4.3
Paraguay	3.65	4.17	4.73	14.2	13.4
Peru	5.81	6.34	7.22	9.0	14.0
Uruguay	3.30	3.47	4.05	5.0	16.8
Venezuela	6.14	7.40	9.42	20.5	27.4

Source: Vassallo 2010: 40, Cuadro 2.3.

Rather, in the Chilean case, the containment of drug prices is due to a combination of factors: a domestic industry dominated by generics; "de facto" substitution of more expensive medications for similar, less expensive, medications by pharmacies; prescription of generics by doctors, and an efficient system of aggregate purchases by CENABAST for the public sector (Godoy 2001). Nonetheless, the market remains relatively small. In 2008, sales amounted to around USD 1,060,000, which makes up 2.6 percent of the total Latin American market, according to figures from IMS Health Chile (Vassallo 2010: 5). According to that institution, between March 2010 and March 2011 the sales volume of the pharmaceutical industry reached USD 1,344,000.

Geographically, the pharmaceutical market is composed of international businesses, small drug importers, and local businesses (Escobar 2006: 50). More than 80 percent of medicines consumed in Chile are produced by domestic labs. Among these, various laboratories stand out. For example, the conglomerate RECALCINE boasts increased growth and presence within the Latin American market. Among foreign labs, Laboratorio Chile (TEVA) is dominant, followed by North American labs such as Abbott, Pfizer, Bristol Myers Squibb, and Merck Sharp & Dhome (MSD) and European labs, in particular German firms, such as Grunenthal, Bayer, Merck, and Swiss firms, including Roche and Novartis. With the exception of Grunenthal, these labs rely on production facilities outside the country, and final products are imported into Chile.

Structurally, laboratories in Chile are organized into large associations. These include the Pharmaceutical Industry Association (CIF) and the Industrial Association of Pharmaceutical Laboratories (ASILFA), which represent foreign and domestic labs, respectively. Along with these, there are various smaller associations of laboratories (see Table 5.3).

Table 5.3 Main pharmaceutical lab associations in Chile

Main Pharmaceutical Lab Associations	Associated Businesses	Characteristics
Pharmaceutical Industry Association (CIF)	20	Multinational Laboratories
Industrial Association of Pharmaceutical Laboratories (ASILFA)	10	Domestic: Bago, Biosano, Labomed, Chile, Pharma Invest, Saval, Sanderson, Sanitas, Tecnofarma, Royal Pharma.
National Association of Laboratories (1999) CANALAB	14	Pasteur, Prater, Knop, Ximena Polanco, Garden House, and others
Association of Over the Counter Medications (CAVEMED)	—	Laboratories that produce over the counter medications

Source: Vassallo 2010: 19.

As suggested earlier, these characteristics of the pharmaceutical market are key to understanding the fundamental players and political processes that are involved in determining the balance between intellectual property protection and access to medications in Chile. The history of domestic implementation of intellectual property rights related to medicine is marked by the confrontation of private interests among local and foreign pharmaceutical companies. As we shall see in section III, in this confrontation, the government has acted mainly as an intermediary between local and global pressures. At the same time, Chilean civil society actors have not consistently articulated the public interests at stake nor have they raised questions of distributive justice. Accordingly, the effect of intellectual property laws on access to medications has largely gone unexamined. This state of affairs, can be attributed, at least in part, to the lack of robust constitutional support for the right to health (Zúñiga 2011; Jordán 2013) in Chile and to its pro-market policies. Moreover, until at least until 2011, there was little debate over access to medicines, relative to other South American countries.

III. Political Opportunities: Developing and Implementing Intellectual Property Policy

In this section we shall analyze, in chronological order, four sets of controversies, describing the actors and the political opportunities they faced.

A. The Patentability of Medications

The first set of controversies that appeared in Chile regarding the relationship between intellectual property and medications revolved around the patentability of medications. Until the middle of the twentieth country, medications were not considered patentable in Chile. Decree No. 958 of the Ministry of Economy, July

27, 1931 regulated patents and inventions. Under Article 5(a), "all types of medications, medicinal pharmaceutical preparations, and chemical, reaction and mixed preparations" were excluded from patentability. This followed the 1844 French model of patent law and did not violate the international norms that existed at the time.

The patentability of medications and pharmaceutical products was first considered in 1984, during the dictatorship of Augusto Pinochet. The military government wanted to accede to the demands of the international pharmaceutical sector to make medications patentable as a way to improve foreign relations, in particular relations with the United States. Thus, in 1989, during his last year as dictator, Pinochet instituted Law No. 18.935, published in the Official Journal on February 24, 1990, which modified Decree No. 958 in various aspects. It not only provided for patents on the excluded subject matter, it also made the protection retroactive to inventions in the so-called "pipeline." Article 10 of the new law allowed for the patenting of medications whenever a request for a patent had been filed in the country of origin prior to December 31, 1984. Article 12 granted legal protection for a period of fifteen years.

At that time, the new patent law, and in particular its application to medications, led to strong criticism from the domestic laboratory industry and society in general. Deliberation on the matter continued until the end of the dictatorship (National Library of Congress 1991: 174–5). Later, the first democratically elected government withdrew the executive regulation of the law, effectively preventing it from entering into force. The same government later presented a new proposal and that measure, Law No. 19.037, became law in 1991. It too covered medications and granted protection for fifteen-year periods. However, this law specified that inventions would be patentable only if they were new—produced and distributed after the law's publication (and, of course possessed an innovative aspect and an industrial application). Thus, this law was not retroactive: it did not allow for the patenting of medications in Chile on the basis of prior-filed applications. The law also excluded surgical, therapeutic, and diagnostic methods for humans and animals, with the exception of products designed to put those methods into practice (art. 37). Finally, the new law contemplated the possibility of compulsory licensing, but only in the case of monopoly abuse (art. 59) and declared all patents to be of "public utility," thereby permitting their expropriation. During the congressional debate, an idea to mitigate the effect of pharmaceutical patents on medication prices was also contemplated. However, that approach was not included in the final text (National Library of Congress 1991: 88).

Even with these limitations, the introduction of Law No. 19.039 provoked resistance and criticism from domestic laboratories. They did not consider that patents were needed as an incentive for pharmaceutical research, arguing that pharmaceutical innovation largely occurred outside Chile and thus incentives to innovation were already guaranteed by patents granted in the companies' home countries (Huenchuñir and Escudero 2002). On the other hand, the CIF, acting on behalf of foreign firms, insisted that the pharmaceutical patents law would stimulate local marketing of foreign products and improve quality. Further, CIF maintained that patenting would not necessarily increase the cost of medications (National Library of Congress 1991: 160). Various political sectors supported the local industry and intimated that the legislation responded primarily to pressure from the United States Department of Commerce (National Library of Congress 1991: 172). Nonetheless, as reflected in the report of the Senate Economic Commission, members of Congress were convinced that the introduction of drug patentability was a global trend, from which Chile had little possibility of escaping (National Library of Congress 1991: 260–2).

Congress's position on patenting was consistent with another larger trend. At the beginning of the transition to democracy, one of the underlying ideas of the political elite was that the power to legislate was escaping the sphere of national sovereignty and that the country had to focus instead on adapting to the challenges of global systems. Former methods for regulating strictly domestic issues were, in short, no longer options. This view did not, however, eliminate disputes among private interests involved in pharmaceutical patents. As a result, political institutions and the government became reactive. Laws were geared toward the execution of global policies, with the government assuming the role of mediator rather than regulator.

B. Adapting to TRIPS

From its return to democracy at the beginning of the 1990s, the Chilean government made international political integration a main objective of its foreign policy. Towards the end of the 1990s, the specific goal was economic integration at the regional and international level. This objective set the context for the negotiation of free trade and other commercial agreements. Thus, even after a democracy was established, foreign policy was continuous with that of the Pinochet dictatorship. Like Pinochet, the new government pursued an economic policy of trade liberalization; it treated foreign trade relations as untouchable in relation to other policies. The practice of keeping these objectives distinct from other spheres of government was not modified by later democratic governments and remained in the organizational culture of the actors that molded Chilean foreign policy (Giacaman and Faundez 2003: 7). This strategy was based on a viewpoint shared by the elites concerning the relevance of medicines for health in Chile. Because the health system is predominantly private and based on the concept of freedom of choice, the right to health is not guaranteed to the entire population (Goyenechea and Sinclair 2013). Thus, medicines have been considered goods of private consumption rather then goods of common necessity (Goyenechea 2013).

Because Chile's international strategy moved toward incorporation into global markets, entry in the WTO became a priority. In order for a country to join the WTO, it is required to accept a series of multilateral agreements that impose robust legal obligations related to tariffs, intellectual property rights, and a variety of other matters (Kottow 2009: 2). In 1995, Chile accepted these conditions when it ratified the WTO Agreements, including TRIPS, and published its accession in the Official Journal on May 17. The government's behavior with respect to TRIPS set a pattern that was repeated subsequently. Its actions marked the starting point for a tendency to adopt rules and accept participation in global trading frameworks as something inevitable, while later assuming a pragmatic role of mediator when addressing controversies between private actors during the implementation phase. In effect, the government commits to rules of trade without regard to questions of distributive justice and then attempts to ameliorate friction between private interests during the implementation process.

In a way, the situation was inevitable. The adoption of TRIPS (as well as the later chapter regarding intellectual property included in the FTA with the United States) was seen as necessary for the success of Chile's economic policy. As a result, the negotiations were characterized by asymmetric power positions, as one of the parties, Chile, was willing to accept any and all conditions in order to obtain access to other parties' markets. In addition, there was a very obvious asymmetry of knowledge regarding the effects of intellectual property rules. Thus, in the words of the ex-director of the Department of Industrial Property (DPI), Chile was willing to exchange gold for trinkets.[7]

But there was a saving grace. The TRIPS Agreement contains the obligation to grant patents in all areas of technology and to give patent owners a minimum of twenty years of exclusive rights. It also requires states to protect clinical studies and other undisclosed information from dissemination and unfair competition. Nonetheless, it also includes flexibilities that allow states to adopt necessary measures for the protection of public health or the life of individuals. Article 39.3, on undisclosed information, does not establish a right of exclusivity and it does not explicitly determine the scope of its applicability. The Agreement does not impose obligations regarding parallel importation. It permits compulsory licensing, subject to a series of conditions. And it includes both general and specific exceptions to patentability. On the whole, TRIPS (along with the later FTAs) reduces legislative competence, but as subsequent events have demonstrated, it left an important sphere for government action.

To implement the TRIPS Agreement, Law No. 19.039 was replaced by a new law, Law 19.996, which modified its predecessor in various ways. The new measure was proposed in 1999, reevaluated in 2001, and a revised version was presented in August 2001. It was finally published as a law six years after its initial proposal, on March 11, 2005, significantly later than the January 2000 deadline that TRIPS established for the adaptation of internal legislation.

The new law established a non-renewable period of patent protection of twenty years (art. 39). Second-use patents in all technological fields are permitted only if the new use resolves a previously unsolvable technical problem, possesses an inventive aspect, and is adaptable to industrial application (art. 37.e). In legal proceedings regarding patent infringement, the law allows the judge to place the burden of proof on the defendant, forcing it to prove that its procedure is novel and different from that described in the patent. Undisclosed information that concerns

[7] Interview with José Pablo Monsalve, Director of the DPI at the time that the FTA with the US was negotiated.

new chemical formulas for pharmaceutical products is protected for five years from the first health registry. Such information refers to test data or other undisclosed information related to the safety and effectiveness of a pharmaceutical product that uses a new chemical makeup not previously approved by the relevant authority (art. 89). The new law also includes a clause that permits third parties to market the protected product if they obtained access to it after it was introduced into the market, and such access was granted by the right-holder or with his consent (art. 49).

The debates surrounding the adoption of Law No. 19.996 provide an excellent opportunity to view and analyze the aforementioned back door opposition, as key players drew out the legal implementation of the Agreement. They presented competing views on various topics, rival interpretations regarding the content of the instrument, and debated the best strategy for fashioning intellectual property law protective of access to medications.

1. *Domestic Laboratories Lobby to Limit Implementation of Intellectual Property Rights*

When the reform proposal for Law No. 19.039 was first debated, the majority of the domestic pharmaceutical industry, grouped under ASILFA, strongly criticized the original proposal that was sent to the Executive, considering it an obstacle to the growth of the domestic industry.[8] ASILFA's fundamental strategy was to defend the domestic pharmaceutical industry, which was oriented mainly toward the production of generics, and to refute the position of foreign labs and representatives of the United States government. To that end, ASILFA engaged in systematic lobbying with governmental authorities and members of Congress and appealed to the media to attract public attention. In addition, it gathered facts, commissioned expert economic reports, and offered its own experts and attorneys. ASILFA benefited from uncertainty in various sectors, including successive governments and their opposition, regarding the effect of the new order and how the rules would affect or inhibit the government's ability to provide public goods and protect access to health. Although ASILFA consistently advocated for the need to balance the intellectual property norms that Chile had assumed with public interest concerns, in particular public health, its discourse was clearly characterized by the promotion of the particular interests of the domestic industry.

Even before the proposal was put to debate in the National Congress, national laboratories denounced the pressure foreign labs were exerting on the government to interpret existing international laws in ways that provided for strong protection and to accept new international intellectual property obligations. In some cases, these forces were successful. For example, ASILFA opposed second-use patents, arguing that they were not required by TRIPS and were an underhanded method of prolonging patents that were about to expire. While Congress would have

[8] Interview with María Angélica Sánchez.

effectively adopted ASILFA's position, second-use patents were nonetheless incorporated into the final text of the law on the theory that their recognition was an obligation of the WTO framework, and therefore could not be rejected.

But in some instances, the generic industry won. ASILFA also opposed laws on protecting clinical data and linking premarket approval to the protection of patent rights. María Angélica Sánchez of ASILFA argued that "if our already robust present legislation is expanded to establish so-called linkage, and is modified to include the protection of clinical trial data, we must be prepared as a country for prices of medications to increase considerably. In accordance with the last study undertaken by the School of Economics at the University of Chile, prices will increase by 75 percent, which will have a considerable influence on the treatment of illnesses under the AUGE [Chile's Universal Access Plan] and other common illnesses in the country."[9] This view was strengthened by the disparity in price between domestic and foreign manufactured drugs. In 2001, the average price of medications in Chile was calculated to be USD 3.30, while foreign medications cost an average of USD 6.30, in the context of a pharmaceutical market valued around USD 552,000,000. Additionally, ASILFA referenced a study by the Center for Applied Studies for Business of the University of Chile (CIADE), which in 1991 indicated a possible increase in costs if intellectual property rights were strengthened. This study was commissioned by ASILFA and appeared during the initial debates regarding the adaptation of Chilean law to TRIPS.

The then-director of CIADE, David Geller, supported the need for strong intellectual property laws, but indicated that public access to medications also needed to be ensured.[10] He was supported by the North American economist Stephen Schondelmeyer—a pharmacology professor at University of Minnesota—who also maintained that if patent protection in Chile was extended or reinforced, the price of medications would increase. While the then-president of CIF, Jorge Véliz, countered that the price of medications would not increase more than 3.5 percent, considering that very few (37) medications in Chile had patent protection, in comparison to the 4,000 that did not, CIADE's study had an impressive impact on public opinion and members of Congress. They trusted in the credibility of the University of Chile's economists and kept the study in mind during the debate over adapting Chilean intellectual property law to the requirements of TRIPS. As a result, Congress failed to accede to all the demands presented by multinational pharmaceutical companies.

RECALCINE was another player critical of elevating intellectual property norms. Its position was especially interesting. RECALCINE is a network composed of various national laboratories that produce generics. But unlike other generic labs, its partners also put significant resources into research and development. In the debate, RECALCINE was particularly aggressive in questioning the strategies of foreign labs, proposing and defending a process for adapting to international

[9] *El Mercurio*, February 19, 2010, Section A, page 2, Letters.

[10] *El Mercurio*, November 20, 2001. Retrieved February 20, 2011 at: <http://diario.elmercurio.com/detalle/index.asp?id=%7B426ca169-e9d8-4688-9a0d-23f12cbd5542%7D>.

frameworks to promote national public health. Thus, the director of RECALCINE argued that one of the major objections of national laboratories was the extension of the period of patent protection from fifteen to twenty years, given that the lifetime of a medication is not greater than approximately five years. RECALCINE also accused foreign labs of inflating the amount of money invested in new medications, claiming that they actually invest a mere one-fifth of their stated numbers.[11] But despite these arguments, the discursive strategy of RECALCINE was not entirely public regarding. In fact, it was driven by the private interests of its partners, which it saw as impaired by the actions of foreign laboratories. This positioning can also be seen in a case, described in the Appendix, that RECALCINE filed against Novartis in the Free Competition Court for actions designed to impede its partners' access to markets.

2. *Chilean-American Chamber of Commerce and CIF Support for Strengthening Intellectual Property Laws*

The group holding views closest to the position of the United States was represented by the Chilean-North American Chamber of Commerce, AmCham. AmCham attacked the government's initial proposals on the ground that the legislation would not sufficiently safeguard the three non-discrimination principles included in the TRIPS patent provisions: non-discrimination based on the country of origin of the invention, its field of technology, and whether the products embodying the invention were imported or produced domestically.[12] AmCham also claimed that the proposals did not fully protect undisclosed information and offered too little in the way of enforcement. In particular, the proposed laws did not provide for appropriate civil legal proceedings in respect to the presentation of evidence; nor did it provide for adequate provisional measures. Finally, AmCham argued that the legislation failed to provide for extensions in the time of patent protection to compensate for delays in patent prosecution.[13]

In addition to AmCham, the most active supporters of intellectual property laws and multinational pharmaceutical interests were the national subsidiaries of such multinationals, grouped under the CIF. CIF mainly employed discourses used by international public policy networks to support the formation of a robust and strict intellectual property regime. Principally, it sought to reward innovation and support businesses that invent medications and bring them to Chile. It held itself out as an intermediary between the market and the forces favoring trade liberalization. It unreservedly supported the proposal sent by the Ministry of the Economy to Congress, arguing that it strictly followed WTO norms and that streamlining the law was necessary. As evidence, it pointed to the fact that in the absence of linkage between the organization authorizing the commercialization of a medication (the Institute of Public Health (ISP)) and the patent office (then the DPI), 6 of 57

[11] *El Metropolitano*, September 10, 2001, p. 13.

[12] TRIPS, art. 27.1.

[13] *El Diario*, June 29, 2001, p. 29.

patented medications had been copied. Furthermore, CIF offered evidence that enhancing patent protection would not lead to an increase in the price of medications. It compared countries where pharmaceutical patents were and were not available, showing that in countries where pharmaceuticals were protected, the cost of medications was reduced by 50 percent after patent expiration and generic entry into the market. In contrast, in countries without patent protection, generics had prices close to those of patented medications, and these prices did not decrease once the patents expired.[14]

Throughout the extended period of debate regarding the law, CIF also argued that limitations on patent protection should be as narrow as possible and that the availability of compulsory licenses should be highly restricted. It demanded that undisclosed information shared with health authorities should not be used for a reasonable amount of time when the health authorities are considering marketing requests for similar products (National Library of Congress 2005: 717). ASILFA responded to this position, arguing that the protection of undisclosed information should be limited to cases of pharmaceutical products that used new chemical combinations, because only novelty justified protection; information on other products was not of a confidential nature (National Library of Congress 2005: 723).

3. Chilean Government and its Internal Disagreements

Within governmental sectors, high-level officials were also in disagreement regarding the proposed law. The ex-director of the ISP, Gonzalo Navarrete, directly criticized the proposal and argued that it was written from a purely economic point of view, failing to consider the interests and opinions of the health sector, even those views coming from within the government. This criticism may have been warranted, given that the project had been mainly developed by specialists from the Ministry of the Economy, without considering the opinion of the ISP.[15]

A former legal advisor of the ISP suggested that the position of the Coalition of Parties for Democracy, then in power, was fundamentally ambiguous.[16] On the one hand, it wanted to keep foreign economic policies intact by agreeing to elevate normative standards of intellectual property. On the other hand, it wished to limit the reach of these provisions by imposing obstacles to their implementation. Again, the criticism was warranted. There were various sectors of the government ideologically opposed to increasing patent rights and to providing further protection for information, as well as groups within the government that supported these changes. In short, two contradictory discursive governmental strategies could be identified: First, the supporters of following Chile's trade agreements (TRIPS—and later on, the FTAs), who thought the state could conform to higher standards and address possible price increases by subsidizing the cost of medication. Second, those who believed that despite international obligations and demands, the effect on price was

[14] *El Mercurio*, October 16, 2001, Section B, p. 9.
[15] *La Nación*, November 22, 2001, p. 9.
[16] Max Fuenzalida, in an interview with the author.

so problematic, Chile should refuse to extend further protection to pharmaceuticals. These divergent viewpoints within governmental policies allowed interested players, in particular ASILFA, RECALCINE, and CIF, to intervene through lobbying. The government's susceptibility to different arguments partly explains the delay in adaptation to international norms. But the cause can also be attributed to the lack of an integral medications policy on the part of the four governments of the Coalition, as well as to the government's lack of necessary experience.

Ambivalence within the government did more than cause delay. Alliances between factions of the government and various industrial sectors, and disagreements among government coalitions on the advisability of implementing international intellectual obligations, once again put the emphasis on private interests. No one articulated a coherent public health policy. Indeed, no player was capable of establishing definitions or developing discursive tools to use in the debate that went beyond a discussion of private interests. This situation was only worsened by the fact that civil society failed to mobilize around a right to health in Chile.

4. The Absence of Civil Society

In the majority of discussions regarding medications in Chile, civil society actors have failed to intervene to address questions of distributive justice. As a result, the government has largely played the role of intermediary among private interests. While professional associations and consumer organizations have made pronouncements on topics such as the advisability of selling drugs in supermarkets and whether doctors should be required to prescribe drugs by generic name, they have not intervened on questions related to intellectual property protection.

General characteristics of civil society in Chile help to explain this weakness. Social research has shown that Chilean society has long experienced great difficulties in undertaking collective action (PNUD 2000). The privatization of social services and the deterioration of trust in social ties affect the possibility of cooperation and social mobilization. In Chile, there is a clear trend toward individualism, accompanied by privatization. People obtain more autonomy by retracting from social ties, thus creating an impasse with respect to the possibilities for collective action (Rojas 2012). Although the advent of the student movement may have weakened the trend in recent years, Chilean civil society still lacks more durable actors.

The centralist, hierarchical, and non-participative tendencies of the Chilean political system also contribute to the problem. Only since 2000 have there been discussions regarding participation in governmental activities. In that year, via Presidential Instruction, President Ricardo Lagos established a series of ministerial duties for civic participation and the Ministry of Foreign Relations committed to undertake an annual consultative conference with civil society representatives in which the government's foreign policy would be discussed. But even this initiative is weak. It reflects a conception of participation in the formulation of public policy that is, first, unilateral and, second, subordinate to state power. It is of a merely consultative, informative, and sporadic nature. Essentially, such participation is a post-facto validation of decisions that have already been made. This hierarchical concept of social participation means that NGOs and other civil society organizations still have negligible influence.

The price of drugs constitutes another factor. Although the pharmaceutical market in Chile is partly based on the proliferation of generic drugs that lack bioequivalence certification, prices through 2012 were low and that has led to certain complacency. Despite the volume of private spending on medications, medicines are available. Since the public has not felt the effect of intellectual property laws, it has had little reason to debate the effect of these laws on access. Groups that traditionally represent the public interest in health in Chile, such as health professionals and pharmaceutical unions, could have focused the public's attention and made it see the connection between price and intellectual property protection, but they have been marginal players in the debates. To be sure, this does not mean that the market solved the problem of access to medication in Chile: there is a significant difference in the quantities spent on medication between different socio-economic groups. For example, a study in 2007 established that the quintile with the smallest income spent around 57.2 percent of their total income on medication, while the quintile with largest income only spent around 39 percent (MINSAL 2007). Politically, however, the issue has not achieved any degree of salience.

In addition, civil society actors that have attempted to defend public interests in health have not been capable of establishing lasting coalitions, as we will see later with respect to the debate on FTAs. Instead, the arguments, posturing, and framing of those who support contradictory positions have crystallized the debate as about private business. With one exception, the result is that there has been little effort to develop information and evidence that would support public-regarding arguments. The one exception has been the School of Public Health of the University of Chile, through its Medical-Social Journals. The rest of the debate has been dominated by private lawyers, with economists as ad-hoc allies to support particular positions.

5. *The Courts Evolve a Jurisprudence on the Right to Health in Chile and Push the Government into Action*

Perhaps because of the lack of activism with respect to medications, judicial recognition of the right to health as a fundamental right was initially quite weak. The 1980 Constitution incorporates the right to health protection in article 19.9, but it is based on an economic market approach. This constitutional text has thus been understood not as a judicially enforceable right, but rather as a pragmatic norm to guide state action (Diego Portales University 2008: 208; Zúñiga 2011; Jordán 2013). Since 1980, more than 100 modifications have been made in the constitutional text. But article 19.9 has remained untouched and the right to health has not been otherwise addressed (Couso and Reyes 2009).

Two subsystems, one public and the other private, address the provision of healthcare. The most important in terms of coverage, is the public system, as two-thirds of the population depends upon it. The system is administered by the National Health Fund (FONASA), a service within the Ministry of Health, which coordinates the health needs of its affiliates and is responsible for funding healthcare providers. FONASA collects contributions from its affiliates as well as fiscal support from the state. The second subsystem is composed of private health companies (ISAPRES). These institutions offer private health insurance to more than 2.7 million beneficiaries. The system was constituted principally during Pinochet's regime through a series of reforms to the universal system of healthcare that has existed since 1951. Because these changes were attempts to create a new private market for health services, it is not surprising that the only justiciable constitutional guarantee with respect to the right to health is the constitutional right to choose one's health system: public or private. Otherwise, the constitutional guarantee has no direct effect.

Nonetheless, there is an important jurisprudence that has conferred a justiciable right to health based on the protection of the right to life included in article 10.1 of the Constitution. On September 24, 2001, the Court of Appeals of Santiago resolved an appeal for legal protection filed by the Chilean Association for the Defense of People with Catastrophic and Terminal Illnesses. Although the case was brought as a class action and the court rejected that procedure, the decision established that the state has the obligation to grant free, preferential, and integral medical and pharmaceutical attention to individuals affected by certain illnesses, as a derivation of their right to life (Diego Portales University 2008).

In later cases, courts have considered the reach of the decision. For example, in a 2006 case, *Segura et al v. Isapre Consalud S.A.*, the Court of Appeals of Concepción affirmed ISAPRE's refusal to cover ENBREL medication and specialist visits for a patient suffering from systemic juvenile idiopathic arthritis on the theory that the claim was based not on the right to life, but rather the right to health, which was not protected.[17] The Supreme Court confirmed the decision. On the other hand, in the case of *Carlos Fuentes v. Isapre Consalud*, the Supreme Court held that Isapre Consalud had to cover the home treatment of a patient suffering from various illnesses and epilepsy.[18] The decision held that the suspension of coverage was illegal because it breached a contract and threatened the constitutional right to life and integrity of the patient (Henríquez 2010).

HIV/AIDS patients have not been so successful, at least not in court. Between 2000 and 2001, claims were made for triple drug therapy on behalf of patients who could not afford them. On one occasion, the Court of Appeals of Santiago admitted an appeal, indicating that the state allegations of lack of resources for the provision of triple drug therapy were unacceptable because the right to life was absolute, and the combination of drugs in the three-drug therapy was necessary to prolong the lives of the patients.[19] The Supreme Court, however, overturned the decision. But

[17] Court of Appeals of Concepción, Case of Maritza Lilian Segura Figueroa; *Helen Nicole Lagos Segura v. Isapre Consalud Sociedad Anónima*, Ruling of July 19, 2006.

[18] Supreme Court, Case of *Carlos Fuentes Rivas v. Isapre Consalud SA.*, Ruling of July 18, 2007.

[19] Court of Appeals of Santiago, Ruling of August 26, 2001, Rol No. 3.025.

despite failing to obtain definitively favorable results, these cases have had an impact on public policy. Toward the end of 2001, they led the government to approve a law regarding HIV/AIDS (Contesse and Lovera 2005). This law, Law No. 19.779, establishes Norms Relative to the Human Immunodeficiency Virus and creates a Fiscal Supplement for Catastrophic Illnesses. It also imposes the duty to safeguard medical care for people with HIV/AIDS and to develop adequate public policies (art. 6). Later, HIV/AIDS treatment was incorporated into the AUGE plan (described below), and thus it became financed by the state. The provision of medications for fulfillment of this state duty was possible thanks to an agreement between the government of Chile and foreign labs that held patents on such drugs. The agreement led to a large price reduction in the necessary drugs, allowing the state to cover the needs of HIV/AIDS patients in the public health system.[20]

Starting in 2005, a constitutional reform led to further judicial recognition of the right to health. The Constitutional Tribunal began to hear new claims of unconstitutional deprivation of healthcare. Thus, the Tribunal upheld an action against ISAPRE for gender discrimination in their health plans. In that decision, the Constitutional Tribunal began to treat the right to health as something more than a programmatic right (Couso and Reyes 2009). Rather, it declared that health was a social right, not a simple declaration or mere expectation "whose effective materialization remains suspended until budgetary availabilities of the State can put it into practice."[21]

As noted with regard to AIDS, judicial activism had an effect on the government. During the Ricardo Lagos administration (2000–6), a large health reform known as Plan AUGE was undertaken. With respect to medications, Plan AUGE required the development of a National Policy of Medications (Exempt Resolution No. 515 of April 2, 2004). The reform was codified by Law No. 19.966 of March 11, 2005. The objective of this legislation was to guarantee the population access to essential medications. It created specific guarantees for the actions of promotion, protection, and maintenance of health, with respect to sixty-nine pathologies. The specific guarantees include guarantees of access, attention, quality, and financial protection. Each pathology covered by the AUGE, which is the basic healthcare plan, covers different treatments, and in some cases coverage includes medications. In Supreme Decree No. 44 of 2007, the Health and Housing Ministries began to clarify the scope of this coverage.

In spite of the strengthening of the right to health through its (rather precarious) recognition in the Constitution, judicial activism for catastrophic illnesses, and attempts to protect the right to health via its close relationship to the right to life, much remains to be accomplished. Because of the extensive private interests at play and the lack of knowledge regarding technological products among civil society, the operative contents of this right are not clearly defined with respect to medications. Furthermore, the Exempt Resolution failed to address intellectual property issues:

[20] Interview with José Manuel Cousiño.

[21] Ruling Rol 976-07, of June 26, 2008.

it does not include references to limitations on the patentability of medications, the possible use of compulsory licenses, or the issue of parallel importations.

C. Negotiating and Implementing FTAs

Another political opportunity arose in connection with the negotiation and implementation of free trade agreements (FTAs) between Chile and other countries. Establishing these agreements has been a priority for Chile's international economic relations. However, these agreements contain clauses related to intellectual property and medications that are very demanding.

The Chile–US Free Trade Agreement provides an example. In June 2003, after twelve years of negotiations, the United States and Chile signed a free trade agreement between the two countries. The Chilean government hoped that signing the FTA would bring more economic growth; more and better jobs; investment; and clear, transparent, and effective commercial conflict resolution. During the negotiations, Chile accepted almost all the United States' demands with respect to intellectual property in exchange for advantages in access to US markets (Escobar 2006: 55). Several modifications of local law were made to adapt to TRIPS, several other changes were made to address the new demands of the United States. Thus, the FTA established greater protection for pharmaceutical products, beyond the level established in TRIPS. These TRIPS-plus obligations included an increase in the period of pharmaceutical patent protection, leading to an effective exclusion of generics during the lifetime of the patent: first, the United States succeeded in obtaining several years of compensatory extension for patents when their approval is delayed; second, it negotiated for five years of protection for undisclosed information regarding the effectiveness and safety of new chemical combinations in medicines. Both provisions have a direct effect on the production and marketing of generic products.

On January 1, 2006 the two-year period established for internal implementation of the FTA obligations expired. After a delay, on January 26, 2007, Law No. 20.160 was published, modifying Law No. 19.039, and adapting it to both the FTA with the EU and the agreement with the United States. The goal of the law, with respect to medications, was compliance with Chilean obligations. There were, however, several disputed aspects. Some did not provoke major controversies. For example, the US FTA did not expressly determine a specific period for patent protection because the understanding was that the standard twenty years established by TRIPS would apply. As noted, however, the period can be extended and Law No. 19.996 provided for a three-year extension. But the FTA envisioned other and longer extensions, including extensions for both delays in granting patents and in authorizing products for marketing. Nevertheless, Law No. 20.160 recognized only the possibility of a discretionary extension as compensation for an unjustified reduction of the period of effective patent protection due to the marketing authorization process. Similarly, while the FTA limited the causes for revoking patents, the United States attempted to include another TRIPS-plus provision, which would have limited the use of compulsory licenses (Díaz 2006: 104).

The United States also wanted these licenses determined in a judicial, rather than an administrative, proceeding. However, the text of the FTA and Law No. 20.160 did not speak to either issue. The text of the FTA section regarding patents and medical products omitted several other topics of interest to the United States, such as procedural issues, the question of parallel importation, and the availability of second-use patents.

Other open issues led to considerable discussion. One decisive point regarding the adaptation of Chilean law to the FTA related to undisclosed information. The FTA established periods of protection for undisclosed information with respect to a "new chemical entity," but did not provide a definition for the term. This left both countries with considerable flexibility. Foreign companies as well as the United States attempted to increase information protection during the adaptation of Law No. 19.039 to TRIPS, while domestic groups, such as ASILFA and CIF, argued about whether to limit or expand such protection.

ASILFA rejected the opinion that FTA laws regarding undisclosed information were self-executing (National Library of Congress 2007: 82). It approved the government's efforts to avoid monopolies over molecules that were not patented or patentable by transnational companies in Chile, and thus to prevent the unjustified invocation of undisclosed information protection as a way to impede health and safety authorization (National Library of Congress 2007: 82). ASILFA also argued that the concepts of business secrets and undisclosed information should not be confused, as they have very different bases for protection. At the same time, however, CIF attempted to strengthen the protection of undisclosed information, including analytical methodologies, clinical studies, and stability studies, claiming that such information should be protected as business secrets.

Law No. 20.160 sided with ASILFA on certain aspects. For example, it provided that the party seeking information protection must file an application in Chile within twelve months of having obtained its first authorization to sell anywhere in the world. However, as required by the FTA, the law mandated five years' protection for undisclosed information relating to clinical trials on new chemical entities that were undertaken to demonstrate effectiveness and safety. Thus, even after a patent has expired, it is possible that generic medication businesses will be required to present their own studies to clear their products for the market.

To make the law fully operative, on November 28, 2005, the Ministry of Health published Supreme Decree No. 152, which specified concepts, clarified procedural mechanisms for the granting of protection, modified the ISP's role in the process, and established a system of opposition to the granting of health and safety authorization. It also imposed the obligation to safeguard undisclosed information presented when requesting health and safety authorization. This protection covers studies designed to guarantee effectiveness and security of the product (art. 4). The Decree's text did not, however, provide much clarity regarding whether protection of undisclosed information is only granted when expressly requested. Some laboratories were later disappointed by that ambiguity, as they believed they could receive protection by merely requesting health and safety authorization.

In 2008, the Decree was sent to the Comptroller General of the Republic in the Ministry of the Health, as it was thought that the aspects that restricted, clarified, or expanded legal concepts might exceed the regulatory powers of the executive. However, on December 1, 2010, Supreme Decree No. 107, a new Regulation to protect undisclosed information was approved. This emphatically established that in order for a firm to enjoy such protection, it must explicitly request it and submit a separate copy of the clinical trial data or other undisclosed information for which it seeks protection. The Decree allowed the person benefiting from such protection to divulge the information contained in the protected data, in part or in full, once the health and safety authorization has been granted (art. 9). The Decree also provided that protection would end in cases of compulsory licensing or to meet certain public needs related to public health, national emergency, or other circumstances of extreme urgency; for national security reasons; to permit non-commercial public use; or because the protection was requested more than twelve months after the first authorization to sell was granted abroad (art. 10). Decree No. 107 also exempted the ISP from determining whether the information had been divulged, instead putting that duty on those seeking protection. Currently there are around thirty pharmaceutical products that benefit from undisclosed information protection.

On the whole, the relevant players appear content with the level of protection granted to undisclosed information. Nonetheless, there is still a debate regarding when such protection begins. The United States supports an interpretation that starts the time period when the new chemical entity is registered in the country where protection is sought, regardless of whether the medication has already been registered elsewhere. Under this view, generic entry into domestic markets would be delayed, even when the information had been publicly disclosed in publications and to other public agencies. Because Chile regards the protection to be based on the undisclosed nature of the information, it contends that protection should be triggered by the first registration anywhere in the world. In any event, the United States and Chile continue to disagree about the solution offered under current law.

The other continuing bone of contention is the question of linking patent enforcement to health and safety authorization. The linkage mechanism is designed to prevent health authorities from granting authorization to generic drugs without first confirming that the active ingredient is not protected by a patent. Under this approach, so long as the patent is valid, authorization will be denied even if other requirements for marketing approval are met (Holguín 2008).

The new law is silent on the matter of linkage. However, from the middle of the 1990s, multinational companies have been seeking ways to enforce linkage within Chile and to require the ISP to consider patents in the approval process. Thus, these companies sought legal protection through constitutional challenges (art. 21 of the Constitution), arguing that health authorization for a generic pharmaceutical product while the original had patent protection constitutes a threat to their right to industrial property (Egaña 2010: 37). The ISP responded that the only action it could take was to advise that the generic drug's request is inappropriate, but that it could not resolve the dispute by denying authorization (Ordinario June 5, 1998, cited by Egaña 2010: 37). Later the ISP posted Circular No. 14 of Accreditation of Patents in Pharmaceutical Registries, which appeared to go further. However, the Circular was very difficult to apply as it did not specify what information was needed in order for an application to be denied. Nor did it say whether it would deny registration on account of patent applications (Egaña 2010: 37).

The situation for multinational pharmaceutical companies improved somewhat with the signing of the FTA with the United States. Chapter 17.10.2(c) of the Chile–US FTA provides that the parties shall "not grant marketing approval to any third party prior to the expiration of the patent term, unless by consent or acquiescence of the patent owner." However, it does not include a specific procedure akin to that found in US law (Roffe and Santa Cruz 2006).[22] Furthermore, according to the Comptroller General of the Republic, it is not a self-executing obligation.

In order to address the ambiguity produced by the FTA, on July 29, 2004, a few months after the FTA entered into force, the Ministry of Health published Decree No. 245-03, modifying Supreme Decree No. 1.876. This Decree eliminated references to the concept of "marketing" associated with the effects of a health and safety authorization, thus clarifying that the ISP would not, as the multinational pharmaceutical companies hoped, undertake a regulatory role regarding patent infringement. Thus, Juan Pablo Egaña has classified the government of Chile's attitude as "at least elusive" of its international obligations (Egaña 2010: 39). For Egaña,

> [t]he evident intention of this modification was to leave without support the application of norm 17.10 2. c) of the FTA that requires Chile to deny the marketing authorization of a pharmaceutical product. If no authority grants marketing permits of pharmaceutical products, in effect the law has no one to apply the FTA provision, and it will simply fall into disuse. In spite of the absurdity of this situation, given that it is undeniable that the health and safety authorization is required for a pharmaceutical product to be marketed in Chile, the discussions on this issue between the government and producers of brand-name and generic drugs has dragged on for years. (Egaña 2010: 39)

Even though the CIF and lawyers like Juan Pablo Egaña[23] view this modification as a trick or legal strategy to avoid compliance with international obligations, ASILFA and the government of Chile have defended this modification as a mere clarification derived from the Chilean constitutional regimen. In accordance with article 19.21

[22] In the United States, 21 U.S.C. § 355(j)(2)(B)) establishes that the applicant requesting health and safety authorization may present a certificate affirming that the patents declared in the request are null or will not be infringed by the generic product. The applicant is required to give notice to the patent owner in question within twenty days. In this notification, the applicant must indicate that he intends to manufacture, use, and commercialize the generic before the relevant patents expire, as well as indicate what arguments support patent nullity or non-infringement. The FDA can approve the abbreviated request unless the notified party presents a suit before the district court for patent infringement within forty-five days of notification. If the patent holder does present such a suit, approval is suspended for thirty months from notification (Cárdenas 2011: 11).

[23] Both Juan Pablo Egaña and José Manuel Cousiño (Director of the CIF) agreed on this in their interviews with the author.

of the Constitution, Chile guarantees the freedom to undertake all types of economic activities in the country, including the production and commercialization of pharmaceutical products. Thus, in Chile, a specific commercial authorization is not required for the sale of pharmaceutical products. Rather, only health authorization from the ISP is necessary, as established in the Regulations for the Management of Pharmaceutical Products of Supreme Decree No. 1876, published in 1995. The ISP grants health authorization to new medications. To do so it reviews studies and tests that support the application, but the authorization is for public health and not commercial purposes. Indeed, Supreme Decree No. 1.876 was modified to eliminate the requirement to cite information regarding previous patents, further emphasizing that health authorization and patents are completely distinct topics, and that the respective granting authorities must remain separate. Patents that claim a relationship between innovation and development are considered outside the competence of the ISP, as the law that establishes its functions indicates (National Library of Congress 2007: 91).

Based on this interpretation, the Directorate of International Economic Relations (Direcon) has insisted that Chile is complying with international standards of intellectual property rights, and has duly honored its international obligations. But the result may be unstable. The new, right-leaning government of Sebastián Piñera has a slightly different view on linkage and CIF has criticized the law for undermining patenting (National Library of Congress 2007: 50) and failing to comply with the FTA. On the other hand, ASILFA praised the definitive exclusion of linkage, a mechanism it considered equivalent to an "administrative patent" (National Library of Congress 2007: 82).

For its part, the USTR has been using the Special 301 procedure to pressure Chile to modify its legislation and appease transnational companies with respect to linkage. The Chilean government has resisted. As a result, in 2006, Chile was on the Watch List for its failure to address linkage issues. In 2007, it was included in the Priority Watch List. In 2008, Chile continued on the Priority Watch List for both linkage issues and insufficient protection of undisclosed information (USTR 2008: 35). The 2008 Report suggested that "further amendments to Chile's IPR legislation are needed to bring Chile's IPR regime into line with its multilateral and bilateral commitments" and in 2009 Chile made some changes. It created a specialized unit within the Chilean police to investigate intellectual property rights crimes. Additionally, it opened a National Institute of Industrial Property to control administrative actions related to industrial property, including patents and copyrights. Chile also accepted the Patent Cooperation Treaty, thus fulfilling an obligation in the US-Chile Free Trade Agreement framework. Some of these efforts were mentioned in the 2009 report (USTR 2009: 15, 22). Nonetheless, Chile remained on the Priority Watch List for "fall[ing] will below expectations of a U.S. free trade agreement partner" (USTR 2009: 22). Chile remained on the Priority Watch List of the USTR in 2010 and 2011, due to reports from multinational companies that Chile failed to adequately protect undisclosed information and for lack of linkage (USTR 2010: 25–6; USTR 2011: 34).

Each time Chile has appeared on the USTR Priority Watch List due to linkage or undisclosed information, it has caused controversy in the national press and debate among CIF, RECALCINE, and ASILFA. For ASILFA, the main reason that Chile continues to appear on the United States' "red list" of countries that do not offer sufficient intellectual property protection is because the USTR succumbed to pressure from the US pharmaceutical sector.[24] Regarding Chile's inclusion in the Watch List, the vice-president of ASILFA affirmed, "[i]t is time for the accusatory international pharmaceutical industry to present a complete list of the products and patents that they claim are infringed. It is unacceptable and reproachable that American pharmaceutical companies, with their powerful lobbies and unfounded public accusations, dirty the image of our companies, and, more importantly, our country."[25] With respect to this demand, neither the CIF nor the American embassy has presented a list of ongoing patent infringements, nor has it used the civil or criminal processes authorized by Law No. 19.039 for patent holders.

1. *The Role of Civil Society*

Negotiations of free trade agreements proceeded on a different path from the negotiation of TRIPS. This time, consultations offered an avenue for participation.

Concerning the FTA Chile–US, the presence and activities of the NGO Alliance for Just and Responsible Trade (ACJR) was especially important. Between December 1998 and 2002, this organization participated in public consultations and undertook other events and conferences related to the FTA. It was the only member of civil society that based public critiques of the adaptation of intellectual property norms in Chile on distributive justice arguments and on concerns about access to health.

ACJR began in the 1990s, with a small group of supporters of fair trade. As the movement for fair trade within Latin America expanded, eight other actors concerned with cultural and consumer rights in Chile joined. According to Smith and Korzeniewicz, "The Chilean Alliance for Just and Responsible Trade (ACJR in Spanish) was formed in post-Pinochet Chile by a variety of groups critical of their country's status as a 'model' for showcasing neoliberal economic restructuring. The ACJR's priority focus is on the negative social, economic, and environmental consequences of globalization via trade liberalization... Recently, the ACJR has taken the lead in lobbying the Chilean Foreign Ministry for a broader consultative role for Chilean civil society" (Korzeniewicz and Smith 2001: 35). It also began to connect fair trade topics to the problem of accessing medicines (Andrade 2009; Agloni and Ariztía 2012).

[24] Vice-president of ASILFA: "In the US the pharmaceutical lobby is brutal" (in Spanish, "En los Estados Unidos el lobby farmacéutico es brutal"), *El Diario Financiero*, April 26, 2010.

[25] María Angélica Sánchez, Letter to *La Tercera*, May 26, 2010, p. 2.

The organizational form of the ACJR corresponds more to that of a horizontal space where different organizations can converge.[26] Fair Trade, the Center for National Studies for Alternative Development, the Institute of Political Ecology, the National Council of Consumers and Users, the Inter-American Platform for Human Rights, the Group of Agricultural Studies, and Digital Rights, among others, participated in the common space ACJR created. There were, however, no longstanding, consolidated human rights organizations within the group. Human rights organizations remained focused on civil and political human rights; they did not concern themselves with the relationship between human rights and technological issues.

Despite ACJR's efforts (and its success in deliberations concerning the Free Trade Area of the Americas (FTAA)), civic participation was not very influential in the negotiation of the FTA. NGOs and other organizations were only periodically informed about the progress of the bilateral negotiations. According to Coral Pey, the delay in invitations, the mixed nature of the participants, and a unilateral structure where the negotiators informed the development NGO, and trade networks, prohibited any possibility for dialogue (Pey 2001).

With consultative participation, however, the ACJR had the opportunity to forge new alliances, including in a transnational context. It attempted to create a platform of alternative globalization, with the aims of resisting pressure from the United States and multinational pharmaceutical companies and elevating commitments to distributive justice above other interests with respect to the relationship between intellectual property and health. That objective was evident in a recommendation it made at the conclusion of the conferences of civil society regarding the FTAA: "[e]xclude the health issue from the international trade negotiations and, if applicable, grant it specific regulatory status other than the general services regime of the current agreement, which provides for the observance of international human rights law as regards the right to health" (FTAA.soc/civ/121 2004).

ACJR formed alliances with other civil society organizations, and together they disseminated information and held public debates regarding the right to health and access to medications. During these activities, ACJR advocated for a constitutional right to health, but neither public opinion nor the Chilean Congress paid much attention. Nonetheless, the capacity of AJCR to mobilize legal and economic experts who disagreed with the dominant opinion in global networks and public opinion was notable. It made strong arguments based on the continuous increase in the price of medications, which was more than double the overall increase in the cost of healthcare, and triple the increase of the Index of Consumer Prices (IPC) in the period between 1998 and 2005 (Silva 2004). With respect to the FTA with the United States, the ACJR targeted TRIPS-plus obligations, in particular the five-year exclusivity period, linkage, and the possibility of extending the period of protection for another four years. It was also concerned with the written aspects

[26] Pey, Coral, interview with Astiel Larrúa, "Today trade negotiations are a State Secret" (in Spanish, "Las negociaciones comerciales hoy en día son un Secreto de Estado"). Retrieved June 10, 2011 at: <http://www.nodo50.org/pretextos/Coral%20Pey.htm>.

of the treaty, principally the notable silence regarding parallel importations and the use of compulsory licenses (Silva 2004).

Unfortunately, the ACJR dissolved after five years and, during the period of study, was not replaced by other civil society organizations. It was thus the only actor that undertook consistent and relevant activity related to questioning the formation and implementation of intellectual property laws regarding medication from a public interest perspective. The lack of functional equivalents in other organizations and the reduction of the government to the role of mediator of the private interests of laboratory associations have meant that for this period, there was no one to articulate and defend the public interest.[27]

D. The Piñera Government and Continued Opposition in Implementation

When the cycle of central-leftist governments of the Coalition of Parties for the Democracy ended in 2010, the new government, ideologically center-right, needed to confront the same international and domestic pressures with which former governments had grappled. The unresolved topics—linkage, undisclosed information, and the like—were the same. Thus, there was a clear continuity between the opportunity structures of the current period and the prior ones. The commitment to an intellectual property system endured, as did the identity of actors who oppose the implementation of international obligations. The government of Sebastián Piñera, which has attempted to end the controversies, began with two policies in the health sector: the linkage law and the policy of bioequivalence of generics.[28]

[27] The debate over the TPP is, however, occurring in the midst of the mobilization of new social movements and cycles of protests. The protests have been largely aimed at promoting the environment, demanding public education, changing the structure of the economy, and enhancing democratic governance (Villalobos-Ruminott 2012; Garcés 2012; Garretón 2013). However, the changes in contention politics are also reflected in the health arena, where a movement called "Health, a Right" (Salud, un Derecho 2012) has formed. In addition, Chilean activists have coalesced with groups in Mexico and Peru to form TPPabierto.net to coordinate opposition to the TPP and with other conglomerates interested in medicine to form LAC-Global Alliance for the Access to Medicines to demand greater transparency in negotiations and to highlight the threats that the TPP poses to access. Significantly, in August 2013, the Senate accepted an agreement (Document No. 647/SEN/13) which asks the President to open a broader debate on the TPP.

[28] Since 2006, Chile has been involved in negotiations with Australia, Brunei Darussalam, Malaysia, New Zealand, Peru, Singapore, Vietnam, and the United States over the TPP. The details of the initiative have been confidential. However since this study was completed, information about the chapter on intellectual property has emerged. It has become clear that, if adopted, the TPP will impose many obligations with significant impact on the health arena, including rights to patent new uses of known products as well as diagnostic, therapeutic, and surgical methods; adjustments to the patent term to compensate for delays in awarding patents or marketing approval; extension of data exclusivity; and new measures protective of biological products. As noted in n. 27, the threat of the TPP has created new coalitions among international actors, including the formation of LAC-Global Alliance for Access to Medicine, which has highlighted the cost that Chile will incur if it joins the agreement (Public Citizen 2012).

1. Linkage: Proyecto de Ley del Linkage Judicial

As noted, Chile has been skeptical of the linkage mechanism on the ground that patent registration and health authorization are distinct issues, not only because their functions are different, but also because the information that needs to be considered in decision making is different. Patent registration is directed at determining whether molecules are new and have pharmaceutical potential, while health authorities consider studies that prove the safety and effectiveness of these medications. ASILFA also opposed linkage on different grounds. Thus, María Angélica Sánchez, Vice President of ASILFA, argues, "it is inappropriate to apply measures that will directly affect the poorest sectors of society, affecting the health of Chileans."[29]

Nonetheless, the CIF and the United States have continued to insist that linkage is necessary, that it must be administrated by the ISP, and that without linkage, Chile has not fulfilled its FTA obligations. Various interests groups agree. In debate with Sánchez, Gabriel Saliaznik, attorney for RECALCINE, describes administrative linkage as a "good strategy of 'administrative patenting' that consists in placing barriers to administrative and legal entry in order to frustrate or restrict the possibility that domestic laboratories commercialize low cost medications that lack a patent in Chile."[30] Groups in Chile that are close to the United States view non-compliance as an obstacle to the country's development and well-being. Thus, the president of AmCham has indicated that "without a doubt, Chile hopes to become a developed country, with opportunity, and without the poverty levels that currently plague us. Thus it is important, in particular in this specific case, that Chile respect the international agreements that it signs. We must always honor our obligations, and, in this case it is important to accept that in order to make our hopes reality, it is in our interest and benefit to support those who research, invent, and execute."[31]

To deal with the difference in views, the Piñera government proposed a type of linkage that did not affect the traditional obligations of the ISP. Thus, the government has proposed fulfilling the FTA obligation with so-called "judicial linkage." In this system, when the ISP receives the application for health authorization from a producer of generics, it would publish a detailed report of the information online. The ISP could grant the health authorization, but that would not automatically trigger the right to commercialize. Instead, the company that holds the patent would be notified about the application, given an opportunity to bring a legal action to defend its rights, and allowed to petition for provisionary measures which would suspend (up to a year) the grant of any marketing

[29] Pharmaceutical Patents (in Spanish, "Patentes Farmacéuticas"), Letter to *La Tercera*, January 26, 2011, p. 30.

[30] Gabriel Saliaznik, "Patents and Access to Medicines" (in Spanish, "Patentes y acceso a las medicinas"), *El Diario Financiero*, October 8, 2010, p.2.

[31] Oped by Javier Irarrázaval, President of AmCham, *La Tercera*, January 29, 2011. Retrieved on February 24, 2011 at: <http://blog.latercera.com/blog/murodenegocios/entry/chile_no_está_cumpliendo>.

registration that would threaten patent rights covering the active ingredients in the relevant medicines.

On January 20, 2012, this proposal was sent to Congress in the form of Bulletin 8183-3. It would create a public book, administrated by the ISP, in which all patent holders of active ingredients could include their patents. Only patents included in the book could be the subject of precautionary measures to suspend health authorization pending the determination of infringement.

Generic producers would be protected in several ways. Actions to suspend the ISP's grant of health registration would not suspend the Bolar exception included in the final section of article 49 of Law No. 19.039. Thus, the generic companies would be permitted to continue to utilize the patented invention in order to obtain information needed to acquire health authorization. To avoid abusive use of precautionary measures, the bill proposes fines for malicious use of the system. Finally, it limits the application of the system to active ingredients, leaving all other patents subject to the current regime.

Unfortunately, this proposal has not managed to reconcile the diverse interests involved. Some legislators opposed to the strict application of intellectual property rules requested that the Congressional process be withdrawn, and that the Constitutional Tribunal review the bill. The Constitutional Tribunal, in its decision of March 22, 2013, rejected the claim and upheld the constitutionality of the bill.

Nor has the United States government accepted the solution proposed by the bill. Thus, even if the proposal were to become law, the Piñera government may continue to see Chile on the USTR's Priority Watch List.[32] Despite the attempt at compromise, market rivals continue to assert non-negotiable positions in the implementation of international obligations in the pharmaceutical sphere.

2. *Bioequivalence: Consensus on the Need to Improve the Quality of Generic Drugs*

One issue that has become quite visible in recent years is the quality of generic medications. Although requiring bioequivalence is not a matter if international law, the difficulty in ensuring quality demonstrates how a clash among private interests can impede the adoption of socially important legislation even when the government takes a pro-active role and becomes more than a mediator of private interests.

In May 2011, the current Minister of Health, Jaime Mañalich, announced a proposal to create a new institution, the National Agency of Medicines (ANAMED) to oversee and control the quality, safety, and effectiveness of generic medications (approximately 340 drugs). The proposal, Bulletin 7805-11, would require the certification of the bioequivalence of generics. At the same time, the bill proposes a requirement that doctors prescribe medications with generic alternatives. This bill was later merged with a pending bill that authorizes direct sales of certain medicines in supermarkets (Bulletin 8133-03). Given the extremely low

[32] Furthermore, the bill would likely require revision if Chile accedes to the TPP in its current form, which purportedly includes a provision on linkage.

safety level with respect to the quality of generic medications, these are long-awaited measures. Despite polarization on other initiatives, these have the support of the principal players involved in the policy debates in the medicines arena.

Still, this approach faces significant obstacles. The quantity of active ingredients that must obtain certification is very large and aside from laboratories at the University of Chile, the Catholic University, and the University of Development, there are very few laboratories capable of undertaking bioequivalence studies. Even these labs are problematic, for many in the generics industry perceive them as taking a long time to make the demanding determinations of bioequivalence. Creating ANAMED is therefore an important first step to improving quality. The principal strategic areas ANAMED will focus on include the development of Good Manufacturing Practices, respecting bioequivalence requirements, increasing and reinforcing drug oversight, establishing a framework for clinical studies of medication, reinforcing relationships with other Latin American medical agencies, and reinforcing relationships with other public and private actors at the local and international level. For the current year, the objectives include accrediting good manufacturing standards for at least 50 percent of laboratories, achieving an average health authorization time of 152 days, founding three new centers for bioequivalence determination, and introducing bioequivalence as a requirement in national policies proposed by CENABAST.

The proposed legislation would affect the various sectors of the generic industry differently. As noted at the outset, the acceptability of generics has been largely based on relationships of trust. There are only a few certified generics on the market. These were voluntarily submitted to lab procedures at the University of Chile and the majority of the bioequivalence certificates obtained in the past (around 70) were requested in order to comply with health or commercialization authorization requirements in foreign—not local—markets. Domestically, legislation has been permissive. In accordance with Decree No. 1876, medication quality is the responsibility of the manufacturer, importer and distributor, but not the state. And while the ISP modified Supreme Decree No. 435 via Supreme Decree 1876/1995, Regulations of the National System of Control of Pharmaceutical Products, Foods for Medical Use, and Cosmetics to incorporate bioavailability as a requirement for authorization (article 4), the regulation was never followed (although the WTO has norms regarding Good Manufacturing Processes, they are not mandatory). According to the Ministry of Health, 9 of 34 laboratories in Chile have quality certification in their productive processes.[33]

Similarly, other attempts to ensure quality have affected only parts of the industry. In the National Policy of Medications in the Health Reform, established by Exempt Resolution No. 515 on April 2, 2004, the Ministry of Health indicated which existing generics were bioequivalent of brand-name drugs. On November 14, 2005, the ISP established a list of 43 active ingredients contained in pharmaceutical

[33] Arnaldo Guerra, "Generic Medicines Don't Work" (in Spanish, "Medicamentos genéricos no mejoran enfermos"), *Punto Final*, No. 714, July 23, 2010. Retrieved on April 20, 2011 at: <http://www.puntofinal.cl/714/genericos.php>.

products that must establish therapeutic equivalency through *in vivo* and *in vitro* studies via its Exempt Resolution No. 762. The Ministry of Health's Exempt Resolution No. 727 of 2005 established criteria to demonstrate therapeutic equivalency in pharmaceutical products in the country. However, it did not provide norms to accredit laboratories that undertake bioequivalence and bioavailability studies in the country. Later, it passed Exempt Resolution No. 4886 of 2008, which establishes technical guides for the realization of bioequivalence studies of pharmaceutical products and monodrugs on conditional release. Further, it has created forms for the presentation of required background information in order to undertake such studies. Also in 2008, Exempt Resolution No. 934 modified Exempt Resolution No. 726 to incorporate 36 additional molecules that must establish therapeutic equivalency through *in vivo* and *in vitro* studies.

The remaining similar generics, brand-name or not, that lack bioequivalence and bioavailability certification are in a limbo of uncertainty with respect to their quality, safety, and medical effectiveness. Laboratories continue to manufacture drugs without complying with minimum standards. One batch may not be manufactured the same as the following, and no one guarantees that any of the output is bioequivalent to a known pharmaceutical. Additionally, according to figures from ISP, 49 percent of medications sold in the country come from abroad. In many cases, the conditions under which they were manufactured cannot be known, nor can it be determined whether they have the therapeutic effect that their packages claim.

This situation is clearly creating serious problems. However the laboratories that produce generic drugs maintain that a drastic shift in policy in favor of bioequivalence could have a strong negative effect on the domestic pharmaceutical industry. Between 2004 and 2008, the Best Pharma Laboratory was sanctioned for irregularities 30 times. Laboratorio Chile received 8 fines, Sanderson had 7 sanctions, RECALCINE had 6, and Andrómaco, Biosan and Mintlab each had 4. Until its closing in 2008, Best Pharma had become the principal provider to the state, but a series of scandals closed the laboratory. In 2005, a 3.5 centimeter piece of glass was found in a vial. In 2006, an insect was found in an antibiotics strip. In 2007, a sewing thread appeared in a bottle of ampicillin. In 2008, a hair was found in a sealed bottle. Finally, in 2008, the ISP revoked Best Pharma's license, after a scandal in which the sale of a generic version of Tamoxifeno, a drug advertised to treat breast cancer, was found to produce no curative effect. Another medication, Midazolam, used as a sleep aid, was also found ineffective. The Cancer Institute undertook tests on the drug, and found that in more than 60 percent of patients it did not reach optimal effect. In total, Best Pharma accumulated 56 fines and investigations before it was closed.

Currently, there is no guarantee with respect to the quality of medications imported from foreign producers. This situation has been exacerbated by an explosive growth in Chinese and Indian imports. In 2008, in accordance with ISP estimates, 40 percent of medications imported to Chile are made in China. With respect to such drugs, the ISP does not strictly control their quality: it does not make visits to the laboratories in which they are produced to exercise control over their manufacturing conditions. Such conditions are only known to Chilean authorities via the reports provided by the companies themselves.

In 2011, the Ministry of Health changed the Regulation of Control of Medications, publishing Supreme Decree No. 3 on June 25, 2011. This Decree approves the Regulation of the National System of Control of Pharmaceutical Products for Human Use, which makes effective the bioequivalence requirement. Nonetheless, it still does not contemplate rules for Good Manufacturing Processes or accreditation for the standards of laboratories that produce generics. Through various resolutions (3225/08, 728/09, 2920/09, 244/11), around 400 generic drugs must certify their bioequivalence by the beginning of 2012, which will mean the end of similar drugs that do not manage to certify their bioequivalence before then.

As demonstrated by the data of ISP, laboratories have complied with deadlines for only 36 generic drugs.[34] Together with those, laboratories have voluntarily submitted to certification for an additional 18 bioequivalent generic medications. Only 54 drugs are WHO certified generics, out of a total of 12,564 registered medications—0.42 percent of all medications. To address this situation, the ISP has imposed more than 90 fines on non-compliant laboratories, but these labs have appealed these decisions to the Comptroller, which halted the bioequivalence process by determining that the ISP overstepped its role in imposing such sanctions.

In the meantime, laboratories that produce generic drugs have removed more than 100 products from the market and a study by consumer groups has raised fears that the strengthening of the process will likely raise the cost of generic drugs that obtain the bioequivalence certificate (SERNAC 2013). The bottom line is that despite the unusual consensus on improving drug quality, there is still considerable conflict between domestic and foreign laboratories. Chile is thus far from developing an effective, consensual policy of medications that resolves the problem of back door opposition. Neither the generics bioequivalence certification nor the judicial linkage policies undertaken by the current administration have managed to reduce tensions between the players of the pharmaceutical market with respect to implementation of intellectual property laws. Additionally, as noted in the margins, a confluence of social movements and Chile's participation in negotiations of the Transpacific Partnership Agreement has led to, a rejection of the private health model currently functioning in Chile, and within it, the policies that affect medicines.[35]

IV. Conclusions

In Chile, the collision between intellectual property rights—particularly patents and the protection of undisclosed information—can be characterized by two

[34] "Bioequivalence in Chile: Far from a Success" (in Spanish "Cumplimiento de bioequivalencia en Chile: muy lejos del éxito"), May 1, 2012. Retrieved June 20, 2012 at: <http://www.saludunderecho.cl/2012/03/cumplimiento-de-bioequivalencia-en-chile-muy-lejos-del-exito> and <http://www.politicasfarmaceuticas.cl/2012/03/01/cumplimiento-de-bioequivalencia-en-chile-muy-lejos-del-exito/>.

[35] See nn. 27–8.

phenomena. First, the basic tenets of Chilean foreign policy are oriented toward trade liberalization and voluntary subordination of national interests to the demands of private multinational companies. Second, public health policy related to medications is largely forged through debate among private interests—foreign and national laboratories. The government acts mainly as mediator between these interests. As a result, there is inadequate attention to the public interest.

On the whole, the result is a triumph for intellectual property rights, with gradual concessions to almost all of the demands of the United States and foreign pharmaceutical companies and an absence of public-regarding policies and laws safeguarding access interests. Nonetheless, one can find evidence of back door opposition. True, civil society was weak—the major exception was the Chilean Alliance for Just and Responsible Trade (ACJR), which is no longer active. Thus, civil society did not manage to furnish the expertise necessary to further local and public interests. Nor did NGOs prove capable of mobilizing resources to protect public goods. However, alliances between government officials and the domestic pharmaceutical industry, which were based on the desire to maintain a strong domestic pharmaceutical industry in the face of international competition, had an effect. Law concerning second-use patents, linkages between patents and safety and health registration, and rights over undisclosed information are marked by deliberate ambiguities in legal terminology and deliberate delays in implementation.

While not everyone is completely satisfied with what has been achieved, Chile has managed to address health problems with its current medications policy. Because it has maintained strong competition in the pharmaceutical market, it enjoys the lowest prices in the region. But this positive result may be one of the reasons that civil society activism has been lacking.

If the situation does not change and expert critics, a stronger civil society, and networking with social movements outside Chile do not emerge, then public interest problems regarding the effects of intellectual property laws on medications will continue to be inadequately unaddressed. But there is reason to be hopeful. Thanks to a cycle of social mobilizations in Chile that began in 2010, a social movement for the right to health is on the rise. Since this study was completed, there has been a growing opposition to policies that limit access to medicines, major knowledge resources are being mobilized, and there is increasing coordination and among national and international activists.

References

Agloni, Nurjk, and Tomás Ariztía. 2012. *Consumo ético en Chile: Una revisión de la investigación existente.* Report for the Project "Leveraging buying power for development: ethical consumption and sustainable procurement in Chile and Brazil" funded by ESRC-DFID. Santiago: Universidad Diego Portales.

Andrade, Fabián. 2009. "Comercio justo o economía solidaria." *Revista AFESE* 49: 103–18.

Brousseau, Eric, and Christian Bessy. 2006. "Public and Private Institutions in the Governance of Intellectual Property Rights." Pp. 243–77 in *Intellectual Property Rights:*

Innovation, Governance and the Institutional Environment, edited by Birgitte Andersen. Cheltenham: Edward Elgar Publishers.

Cardenas, José. 2011. "El uso de la información no divulgada y el linkage en el TLC con EE. UU. ¿A qué realmente se obligó el Estado de Chile y cómo ha cumplido?" *Revista de Derecho Económico Internacional* 1(2): 4–24.

CENABAST. 2011. "Política de Medicamentos, Rol de Cenabast." Presentation in the House of Representatives, May 2011. Viewed May 30, 2011: <http://www.camara.cl/pdf.aspx?prmid=2651&prmtipo=SOBRETABLA>.

Cid, Camilo, and Lorena Prieto. 2010. "Gasto de bolsillo en salud de los hogares y crisis." Presentation. Viewed June 28, 2011: <http://www.aislac.org/index.php?option=com_docman&task=doc_download&gid=614&Itemid=124>.

Contesse, Jorge, and Domingo Lovera. 2005. "Acceso a tratamiento médico para personas viviendo con VIH/SIDA: éxitos sin victoria en Chile." *Sur. Revista Internacional de Direitos Humanos* 5(8): 148–67.

Correa, Carlos. 2009. "Nota para discusión: jurisprudencia relevante sobre productos farmacéuticos en América Latina." Paper at Seminar for judges regarding recent trends in intellectual property law, with an emphasis on the pharmaceutical industry. Hotel "La Barcarolle," Prangins, Switzerland, October 26 and 27, 2009.

Couso, Javier, and Mauricio Reyes. 2009. "Notas acerca del origen y trayectoria del derecho constitucional a la protección a la salud en Chile." *Revista de Derecho, Universidad Católica del Norte* 16(2): 161–94.

Díaz, Alvaro. 2006. "TLC y Propiedad Intelectual: Desafíos de Política Pública – en 9 países de América Latina y el Caribe." LC/BRS/R.163. Brasilia. CEPAL

Diego Portales University. 2008. *Informe anual de Derecho Humanos, Hechos del 2007.* Human Rights Center. Santiago de Chile: Diego Portales University.

Egaña, Juan Pablo. 2010. "El linkage y el tratado de libre comercio con los Estados Unidos." Pp. 33–44 in *La propiedad intelectual en Chile y el tratado de libre comercio con los EE.UU.*, edited by AmCham, Series of Technical Studies, AmCham Chile, Document No. 2. Santiago de Chile: AmCham Chile.

Escobar, Natalia. 2006. "Intellectual Property Rights, The Big Controversy in the CHILE/UNITED STATES FTA and its Consequences for the Andes FTA Negotiation." Master's Thesis, Masters in Politics and Government, Universidad de Concepción-Flacso, Concepción.

Falkner, Gerda, Miriam Hartlapp, Simone Leiber, and Oliver Treib. 2004. "Non-compliance with EU Directives in the Member States: Opposition through the Backdoor?" *West European Politics* 27(3): 452–73.

FTAA Committee of government representatives on the participation of civil society. 2004. *Conclusions from Attendees on ALCA Services.* FTAA.soc/civ/121.

Garcés, Mario. 2012. *El "despertar" de la sociedad: Los movimientos sociales en América Latina y Chile.* Santiago: LOM.

Garretón, Manuel Antonio. 2013. "Progresismo y la refundación de la relación estado-sociedad." In *Los desafíos del Progresismo*, edited by Carlos Fortín, Augusto Varas, and Marcelo Mella. Santiago: RIL Editores.

Giacaman, Viviana, and Rocío Faundez. 2003. *Civic Participation in Foreign Relations: An Analysis of Participation in International Fora.* Santiago: Corporación Participa.

Godoy, Lucas. 2001. "Contención de costos en medicamentos la experiencia internacional y el caso chileno: estudio de Caso Nº 59." Magíster Workpaper, Gestión y Políticas Pública, Ingeniería Industrial, University of Chile, Santiago de Chile.

Goyenechea, Matías. 2013. "Medicamentos y el lucro en salud." *El Quinto Poder*, April 21. Viewed on August 28, 2013: <http://www.elquintopoder.cl/salud/medicamentos-y-el-lucro-en-salud>.

—— and Danae Sinclair. 2013. "La privatización de la salud en Chile." *Políticas Públicas* 6(1): 35–52.

Grande, Edgar. 2001. "The Erosion of State Capacity and the European Innovation Policy Dilemma: A Comparison of German and EU Information Technology Policies." *Research Policy* 30(6): 905–21.

Henríquez, Camila. 2010. "¿Activismo judicial en la obtención de cobertura adicional para enfermedades catastróficas? Análisis jurisprudencial 2006–2009." *Estudios Constitucionales* 8(1): 401–24.

Hill, Michael, and Peter Hupe. 2006. *Implementing Public Policy*. London: Sage Publication.

Holguín, Germán. 2008. *FTA, Health, and Medicine*. Círculo de Análisis Político, University of Los Andes.

Huenchuñir, Patricio, and Gastón Escudero. 2002. "Industrial Property of Medicine." *Administración y Economía UC* 46: 26–9.

Jordán, Tomás. 2013. "El cambio del eje referenciador del derecho a la protección de la salud a partir de la jurisprudencia constitucional sobre el sub-sistema privado de salud." *Estudios Constitucionales* 11(1): 333–80.

Korzeniewicz, Roberto, and William Smith. 2001. "Protest and Collaboration: Transnational Civil Society Networks and the Politics of Summitry and Free Trade in the Americas." Paper presented at the XXIII International Congress of the Latin American Studies Association, Washington, DC, September 6–8, 2001. Viewed June 30, 2011: <http://www.lasa.international.pitt.edu/Lasa2001/KorzeniewiczRobertoPatricio.pdf>.

Kottow, Miguel. 2009. "Trade and Healthcare: Politics, Treaties, and the Pharmaceutical Market." *Revista Medicina y Humanidades* 2: 1–9.

Latin Pharma. 2006. *Study of Supply and Demand in the Pharmaceutical Sector, Chile*. Santiago de Chile: ProChile.

León, Edgardo, and Amanda Martínez. 2011. *El mercado farmacéutico: Necesidades de políticas de medicamentos*. Chile 21, Colección Ideas, Year 12, No. 122, April 2011.

McLaughlin, Milbrey. 1987. "Learning from Experience: Lessons from Policy Implementation." *Educational Evaluation and Policy Analysis* 9(2): 171–8.

Mazmanian, David, and Paul Sabatier. 1983. *Implementation and Public Policy*. Glenview, IL: Scott, Foresman.

Meyer, Denis. 2004. "Protest and Political Opportunities." *Annual Review of Sociology* 30: 125–45.

—— and Debra Minkoff. 2004. "Conceptualizing Political Opportunity." *Social Forces* 82 (4): 1457–92.

MINSAL. 2007. *Primer estudio nacional sobre satisfacción y gasto en salud, informe de resultados: Módulos "F" y "G" gasto de bolsillo en salud*. Santiago: Ministry of Health.

National Library of Congress. 1991. *Historia de la Ley No.19.039*. Santiago de Chile: National Congress.

National Library of Congress. 2005. *Historia de la Ley No.19.996*. Santiago de Chile: National Congress.

National Library of Congress. 2007. *Historia de la Ley No.20.160*. Santiago de Chile: National Congress.

Pey, Coral. 2001. "Citizenship in the Globalization Age." *Le Monde Diplomatique*, Chile Edition, October. Viewed February 25, 2011: <http://www.insumisos.com/diplo/NODE/3518.HTM>.

PNUD. 2000. *Informe nacional sobre desarrollo humano Chile 2000: más sociedad para gobernar el futuro.* Cap 5: La confianza en la acción colectiva. Santiago de Chile: PNUD Chile.

Public Citizen. 2012. *Briefing Memo: Chile and the Trans-Pacific Partnership Agreement—Access to Medicines Risks & Continued Bullying from USTR.* Viewed on August 28, 2013: <http://www.citizen.org/documents/Chile-and-the-Trans-Pacific-Partnership-Agreement.pdf>.

Roffe, Pedro, and Maximiliano Santa Cruz. 2006. *Intellectual Property Rights in Free Trade Agreements Entered into by Latin American Countries with Developed Countries.* Santiago: CEPAL.

Rojas, Jorge. 2012. *Sociedad Bloqueada, Movimiento estudiantil, desigualdad y despertar de la sociedad chilena.* Santiago de Chile: Ril Editores.

Saavedra, Iván. 2010. "Estudios de Biodisponibilidad para establecer bioequivalencia de medicamentos." *Cuadernos Médico Sociales* 50(1): 11–23.

—— Adiela Saldaña, and Cristián Ruminot. 2006. "Medicamentos genéricos." *Cuadernos Médico Sociales* 46(3): 205–11.

Salud, un Derecho. 2012. *Manifiesto.* Viewed on August 25, 2013: <http://www.saludunderecho.cl/el-movimiento/manifiesto>.

Sell, Susan. 2003. *Private Power, Public Law: The Globalization of Intellectual Property Rights.* Cambridge: Cambridge University Press.

——. 2004. "The Quest for Global Governance in Intellectual Property and Public Health: Structural, Discursive, and Institutional Dimensions." *Temple Law Review* 77: 363–99.

SERNAC. 2013. *Estudio comparativo de precios de productos: Bioequivalentes v/s de Referencia, Área Metropolitana.* Santiago: SERNAC.

Silva, Consuelo. 2004. "Access to Medicine and ADPIC." Paper. Santiago de Chile: Chilean Alliance for Just and Responsible Trade.

Tansey, Geoff. 2006. "Introduction: Legal Fictions and Public Health." Pp. 1–5 in *Negotiating Health, Intellectual Property and Access to Medicines*, edited by Pedro Roffe, Geoff Tansey, and David Vivas. London, Sterling: Earthscan.

Thomson, Robert. 2010. "Opposition through the Back Door in the Transposition of EU Directives." *European Union Politics* 11(4): 577–96.

USTR. 2008. *2008 Special 301 Report.*

——. 2009. *2009 Special 301 Report.*

——. 2010. *2010 Special 301 Report.*

——. 2011. *2011 Special 301 Report*

Vassallo, Carlos. 2010. *El mercado de medicamentos en Chile: caracterización y recomendaciones para la regulación económica.* Consultation for DESAL, Ministry of Health, Government of Chile.

Villalobos-Ruminott, Sergio. 2012. "The Chilean Winter." *Radical Philosophy* 171: 11–15.

Zangl, Bernhard, and Michael Zürn. 2004. "Make Law, Not War: Internationale und transnationale Verrechtlichung als Baustein für Global Governance." Pp. 12–45 in *Verrechtlichung—Baustein für Global Governance?*, edited by Bernhard Zangl and Michael Zürn. Bonn: Verlag Dietz.

Zúniga, Alejandra. 2011. "El derecho a la vida y el derecho a la protección de la salud en la constitución: Una relación necesaria." *Estudios Constitucionales* 9(1): 37–64.

APPENDIX

Relevant Legal Decisions in Disputes Regarding Intellectual Property Rights over Medications

The majority of the debate surrounding the relationship between intellectual property and access to medications has taken place during the legislative process of adapting Chilean law to the norms imposed by international agreements. The judiciary has entertained few pharmaceutical patent cases. However, some litigation has taken place in the Comptroller General of the Republic, the courts, the Free Competition Court, and, recently, the Transparency Council. Decisions from these bodies have had a palpable impact on current controversies. Accordingly, the courts could be considered an additional locus of confrontation. But the cases show it to be a weak one. First, the confrontations are—once again—between the private interests of the large market players, foreign and domestic laboratories. As a result, judicial involvement has not produced judicial activism in the form of firmly establishing a right to health or articulating doctrine that promotes access medication. Second, as described above, the courts have mostly thrown the debate back into the legislative arena.

A. Pronouncements of the Comptroller General of the Republic

The internal body of administrative accounting and court of auditors of Chile, the Comptroller General of the Republic, entertained two important cases pitting several of the "usual suspects" against one another in arguments about the relationship between patent rights and health authorization. In the first case, Decision 51760 of December 17, 2002, CIF questioned ISP practices and ASILFA intervened. In the second, Decision No. 61817 of December 26, 2006, Bristol Myers Squibb Chile brought the challenge and the Department of International Economic Relations (DIRECON) participated. Both cases raised the familiar linkage question, on whether the ISP could register generic medications for marketing when some ingredients were protected by patents. The first challenge was based on rights under the patent statutes and the second also included claims based on the linkage requirement in Chile's FTA with the United States.

Rehearsing many of the same arguments made in the legislative debates, the Comptroller General decided the ISP could authorize sale of these products, and could even entertain successive requests for authorization from multiple generic companies. In the first case, the Comptroller reasoned that the ISP did not have the legal power to deny authorization. In the second, it stressed the conceptual distinction between determining safety and determining patentability. The second case also involved an argument that that authorization could not be granted because it required the ISP to rely on undisclosed information regarding quality, but the Comptroller rejected that as well. As to both the linkage and the data issue, it held that the FTA was not self-executing. Indeed, the Comptroller reasoned, that was why the legislature understood that it had to pass Law No. 19996 to implement the FTA.

B. The Courts

Chilean courts have shown themselves somewhat sympathetic to patent rights. For example, in a celebrated cases on patent infringement, Criminal Decision RIT 185-2007, *Sanofi-Aventis v. Royal Pharma*, the third chamber of the criminal court held a Royal Pharma manager guilty of criminal patent infringement for producing and distributing a medication whose active ingredient, Copidrogel, had been patented by the French laboratory Sanofi-Aventis. The case was an unusual one in that it involved two different crystalline forms of the same compound, both used to treat the same infirmity (arthritis); one argument in the case drew on work by noted lawyer and economist Carlos Correa, who argued that a patent on a new form of a known compound is invalid (Correa 2009). However, the court rejected the argument and fined the manager 100 UTM (approximately USD 4,000). Furthermore, the Constitutional Tribunal upheld the judgment against a constitutional challenge that the criminal law was being applied retroactively.

Sanofi-Aventis appears, however, to be exceptional. There have not been other significant cases finding patent violations, and certainly no criminal ones. Moreover, on issues related to implementing TRIPS and the US FTA, the courts have taken positions similar to the Comptroller General. In one 2003 case, Pfizer SA sued the ISP and RECALCINE, arguing that approval of a RECALCINE drug violated Pfizer's constitutional right to property because it permitted RECALCINE to engage in patent infringement.[36] The Supreme Court affirmed the decision of the Fifth Chamber of the Court of Appeals of Santiago, which rejected Pfizer's argument. A similar result was reached in the 2009 decision of Invalidity of Public Law, Rol No. 6313-2003, between Pfizer and RECALCINE. Here, the Court of Appeals of Santiago echoed a point the Comptroller made, holding that the ISP is not competent to consider patents when granting health authorization, and must only consider elements related to quality, safety, and effectiveness.

In another case, Appeal for Protection, Rol 2891-03, Eli Lilly tried a somewhat different argument, claiming that actions granting generic firms health authorization for patented inventions was illegal and arbitrary because the background information the ISP used included the patent. Lilly also asserted that the ISP threatened Lilly's legitimate exercise of the right to property, protected in article 19.24 of the Constitution. But once again, the ISP practice was upheld. The Court of Appeals of Santiago reasoned that the ISP's competence is limited to activities related to the quality control of medications, and thus it is barred from involving itself in the resolution of conflicts related to intellectual property. The Supreme Court's ratification of the decision helped convince foreign laboratories of the need to pressure the United States to continue to demand that Chile enact a strong linkage requirement.[37]

C. Cases of Free Competition (the Free Competition Court)

A review of actions of the Free Competition Court underscores the degree to which the judiciary in Chile has left confrontation to other spheres. In these cases, the generic industry tends to be the aggressor and to bring suits against foreign pharmaceutical firms for abusing patent law by pursing invalid claims. RECALCINE/Novartis Case, Decision No. 46, November 28, 2006 stemmed from a set of legal actions initiated by Novartis against the generic laboratory to enforce its patent on Glivac, which is used to combat myeloid

[36] Case *Laboratorios Recalcine SA v. Pfizer Chile SA* in Santiago Chile, March 26, 2003. Retrieved at: <http://www.gala-marketlaw.com/membersonly/pdfs/Amsterdam2003.pdf>.

[37] Ruling Rol No. 839-2007-INA.

leukemia. After the Court of Appeals found for RECALCINE, RECALCINE brought an action against Novartis, claiming that its attempt to enforce the patent violated Chilean competition laws.[38] The Free Competition Court rejected the petition and on July 30, 2007, the Supreme Court affirmed, holding that there was reasonable doubt regarding the issues in the case and that these doubts justified the suit.

A similar result was obtained in Tecnofarma/Sanofi-Aventis Case, Decision No. 52, of May 2, 2007. Like the Royal Pharma Case, it involved the two crystalline forms of Copidrogel. This time the generic laboratory sued Sanofi, claiming that Sanofi was abusing its patent by threatening infringement actions to stop use of a form and a process for manufacturing it that were not covered by its patents. The tribunal rejected Tecnofarma's petition, accepting that the use of such tactics is a legitimate defense of a patent holder's rights.

Both of these cases marked the beginning of judicial activity that became more frequent after 2010, as more suits for unfair competition based on the use of patent litigation to limit competition were filed. This judicial activity coincides with increasing questions regarding patent abuse. But since there are no clear regulations of this matter in Chile, these actions may open the door for more legislative confrontations.[39]

D. The National Transparency Council

The generic industry has also attempted to use judicial mechanisms in the fight over data protection. However, once again, the matter has been deflected to the legislature.

The Bago Case, Rol A103-09 began in April 2009, when Bago Laboratory requested access from the ISP to conduct research on registered components of Voltaren (patented by Novartis), Flexeril (Merk), Zytrex-D (GlaxoSmithKline), Ravotril (Roche), and Meticorten (Schering Plough). As these were documents that affected the intellectual property rights of third parties, the ISP consulted with these parties. After some of them protested, the ISP rejected the request. Bago then approached the Transparency Council to present a request for public information under the Transparency in Public Functions and Access to Information on the Administration of the State Law, Law No. 20.285 of 2008, a provision that establishes a procedure for obtaining public information.

In Bago's appeal before the Council, the Council affirmed that the opposition lacked a legal foundation and could impede the exercise of constitutional and legal rights. The Council also thought that withholding the information might thwart free competition.

However, given the complexity of the case, the Transparency Council contacted other institutions, including courts in the United States and the Information Commissioner's Office (ICO) in England, in the hope that their jurisprudence might help it make a final decision. Meanwhile, the foreign labs complained to media outlets that a tool designed to promote access to public information was being used to obtain professional secrets in search of private gain. On September 9, 2009, Bago withdrew its petition, and the Council closed the case—once again leaving a fight between private companies to legislative resolution.

[38] Significantly, the validity of this patent has been the subject of litigation elsewhere and found invalid, see *Novartis v. Union of India & Others* (2013), CIVIL APPEAL Nos. 2706–16 of 2013, available on site: <http://judis.nic.in/supremecourt/imgs1.aspx?filename=40212>.

[39] María Angélica Sánchez and Juan Pablo Egaña agreed on this in their interviews with the author.

Chapter 6

A Golden Straitjacket?

The Struggle over Patents and Access to Medicines in Colombia

César Rodríguez-Garavito

The norms that regulate economic globalization severely limit the range of policy options available to states that adopt them. In Latin America, such norms have spread from one country to another, as the institutional reforms derived from the "Washington Consensus," including reinforced intellectual property protection, were incorporated in national legal systems throughout the past two decades.[1] In this respect, global economic law acts as a straitjacket for nation-states. For the most enthusiastic defenders of economic globalization, it involves a virtuous constraint, a "golden straitjacket." As Thomas Friedman writes, "as your country puts on the Golden Straitjacket, two things tend to happen: your economy grows and your politics shrinks" (Friedman 2000).

Applying the metaphor to this book's topic, the global intellectual property laws of the TRIPS Agreement can be envisioned as a straitjacket that restricts the margin of maneuvering that states have to promote their citizens' access to medications. The straitjacket tightens, but does not necessarily suffocate. As explained in the introductory chapter to this volume, although TRIPS considerably tightened the straps of the jacket in favor of proprietary interests, it left open key concepts and provided flexibilities and exceptions. The relevant empirical question, then, is how tightly each country has put on the jacket through economic, political, and legal decisions subsequent to TRIPS.

The history of patent regulation in Colombia illustrates the reasons and effects of a country's decision to tie the straitjacket tightly and quickly. As we shall see throughout this chapter, since 2002, Colombia has adopted a clearly pro-patent legal position, which was perpetuated by the norms of the free trade agreements (FTAs) it signed with the United States (2005), the European Union (2010), and other countries. Contrary to what is suggested by Friedman's metaphor, however, the straitjacket does not necessarily create wealth for the country. Due to the effects

[1] On the Washington Consensus and the place of intellectual property reforms in the shift toward neoliberalism in Latin America, see the introductory chapter by Dreyfuss and Rodríguez-Garavito.

of patent laws and other failings of the health system, medicines are much more expensive in Colombia than in most of Latin America. Given that the Colombian Constitution, which recognizes a right to health, has been interpreted to require the government to pay for drugs, the high price of medicine has created a considerable burden on the national budget. Thus, more recent episodes in the story I analyze in this chapter include efforts by the Colombian government and courts to loosen the straitjacket during the implementation and application phases of TRIPS and FTAs. However, as we shall see, it is not easy to make a space for maneuvering. Despite the existence of an active civil society that has mobilized to defend the right of access to medicines in the last decade, the existing norms severely limit the range of options available.

By studying the Colombian case, I pursue two goals, one descriptive and one analytic. Descriptively, I track the trajectory of patent protection from its beginnings in the Andean Pact norms of 1991, to the changes introduced by the FTA with the United States between 2005 and 2012, and ending with the implementation phase of this treaty. To reconstruct this story, I make stops at critical junctures and document the actors, strategies, and arguments that marked the shift in patent regulation and its impact on the right to health.

From an analytic point of view, I highlight the central factors that help explain the Colombian trajectory. In line with the approach proposed in the analytical framework of this book, I argue that the changes in patent law embody the combined strengths of two sets of actors, governmental and nongovernmental, national and international, that defend distinct visions of property and the right to health. On the one hand, the dominant coalition in Colombia was formed by the United States Trade Representative (USTR), the association of multinational pharmaceutical companies, and the Ministry of Trade, which have defended the hardening of intellectual property rights. On the other hand, a coalition of national and international NGOs, the association of national pharmaceuticals, and the Ministry of Health has attempted to resist the advance of patent protection and advocated for the use of the flexibilities included in TRIPS.

To understand the evolution of this struggle, it is necessary to consider the interaction of national and international factors. To empirically ground this idea, I use the analytical framework of "political opportunity structures" that helps us understand windows of opportunity and restrictions that social movements face (in this case, the civic movement that promotes greater access to medications through the relaxing of patent laws).[2] Political opportunity structures are "consistent—but not necessarily formal or permanent—dimensions of the political environment that provide incentives [and constraints] for collective action by affecting people's expectations of success and failure" (Tarrow 1998: 77). When struggles over international treaties (such as TRIPS and FTAs) and domestic legislation are involved, relevant political dimensions operate both at the international and national scale. As Kathryn Sikkink's "dynamic multilevel governance" model demonstrates, opportunities are

[2] See the concluding chapter for a fuller account of this analytical framework and its application to the study of the struggle around patent protection and access to medicines in Latin America.

		International opportunity structure Closed	Open
Domestic opportunity structure	Closed	I. Diminished chance of activism 1995–2005	II. "Boomerang effect" 2005–2007
	Open	IV. Democratic deficit/defensive internationalism 2012–	III. Insider/outsider coalition model 2007–2012

Fig. 6.1 Sikkink's dynamic multilevel governance model
Source: Sikkink 2005: 156.

assessed in terms of "access to institutions, or how open or closed domestic and international institutions are to network or social movement pressure and participation"—in our case, networks and social movements advocating greater access to medicines (Sikkink 2005a: 155).

Figure 6.1 synthesizes possible scenarios through possible combinations of opportunities at the national and international scale.

In this chapter, I maintain that the evolution of opportunity structures that helps explain the Colombian trajectory has moved clockwise since the adoption of TRIPS. The situation represented in cell I (diminished chance of activism), in which national and international political contexts were relatively closed to pro-access mobilization, explains in large part the absence of contestation regarding TRIPS and relevant legislation prior to the FTA with the United States. While opening negotiations regarding the FTA gave the USTR a chance to argue for stronger patent protection, it also gave the social movement in favor of access to medications an opportunity to collaborate with allies in the United States to pressure the Colombian government (as well as the US government) to avoid adopting measures that went beyond TRIPS. In a classic "boomerang" effect, the controversies led to the renegotiation of the FTA clauses regarding intellectual property in 2007 in order to make them less detrimental to access to medications (cell II in Figure 6.1). Emboldened by this success, the pro-access coalition gained strength and participated in the mobilization that impeded ratification of the FTA in the US Congress until 2012 (cell III). With its entry into force that year, international opportunities have to a large extent closed, and the straitjacket has hardened, such that possibilities for contestation shifted to the spheres of treaty implementation and application at the local level (cell IV).

Against the backdrop of this analytical framework, in this chapter I defend four arguments. First, I maintain that a Colombian particularity helps explain the orthodox incorporation of international standards favorable to proprietary interests. Colombia is more exposed to regulatory pressures from the United States, as compared to other countries such as Argentina or Brazil and has traditionally benefited from preferential access to the US market in exchange for its collaboration in the "war on drugs." (Colombia is the largest recipient of military aid in the region, and one of the largest in the world.) Because of its stronger economic and political ties, USTR pressure is more effective and its national and international opportunity structures are more aligned with each other than in other countries. Additionally, I argue that the predominance of the Ministry of Trade and Treasury Department over the Ministry of Health has reinforced Colombian orthodoxy and tightening of the straitjacket. Given the pro-proprietary inclination of the economists of the Ministry of Trade and the Treasury Department, the dominant ideological position of government teams (and of the FTA negotiating delegations) has been favorable to patent protection.

Second, I posit that bilateral treaties have become a key site of the regulation and contestation of intellectual property. Once the FTA with the United States was signed, Colombia ushered in a wave of bilateral agreements with countries around the world, including Canada and the European Union. These have reinforced the standards of proprietary interest protection set in the FTA with the United States.

Third, I argue that, due to unfavorable opportunity structures that it must face, the pro-access coalition has been on the defensive since its inception. Thus, although its role has been essential to generating public debate over a technical issue that would otherwise have gone unnoticed, its impact has been limited. In effect, the coalition's impact has consisted in marginally moderating the advances in patent protection, by avoiding most TRIPS-plus standards and managing to keep the TRIPS standard on various issues.

Fourth, looking toward the future, I propose that evidence of exorbitant medicines costs and their impact on public finances may cause the pendulum to swing toward a more pro-access position during the implementation and application phase of the new trade agreements. In addition to obtaining a few governmental decisions in this direction, the pro-access coalition has brought its cause to the courts, which can offer more favorable political and legal opportunity structures than the executive and legislative branches.

To substantiate these arguments, I divide the chapter into five chronological sections. First, I track the origins of national intellectual property norms in the Andean legal system, which regulated intellectual property rights between 1978 and 2002. Second, I move from the regional to the national scale in order to examine the 2002 adoption of pro-patent domestic legislation—the laws that introduced TRIPS-plus standards even before the advent of the FTA era. Third, I pause to take a detailed look into the negotiation process of the FTA with the United States. In doing so, I examine the composition of the pro-access and the pro-patent camps, as well as the shifting political opportunity structures in which they operated. Fourth, I explore the implementation phase of the FTA and highlight the signs of growing resistance within the Colombian government against further extension of patent protection, as well as the gradual move of the pro-access coalition toward courts. Finally, I offer some conclusions.

Before proceeding with the analysis, a brief note on methodology is in order. The evidence presented in this chapter was collected through triangulation of qualitative methods, including interviews, archival research, and participant observation.[3] Field work included thirty-four semi-structured interviews with government officials in the ministries of trade and health (among them several that participated in the negotiations of the FTAs), as well as in the agency responsible for certifying drug safety and efficacy (Invima); staff members of NGOS and research centers that make up part of the pro-access movement; representatives of physicians' and patients' associations; and public health experts and academics. In addition to the interviews, data collection included systematic search and analysis of relevant news, decrees, laws, and court decisions in the period under examination. Finally, fieldwork encompassed participant observation in meetings of pro-access NGOs, academic conferences, Constitutional Court hearings, and Congressional debates related to the FTA and reforms to the healthcare system impinging upon access to medicines.

I. Regional Origins of Patent Protection: The Andean Regulations

Intellectual property protection was incorporated into the Colombian legal system through regional Andean regulations. Established in 1969, the Andean Pact (a free-trade bloc renamed the Andean Community of Nations in 1997) gave rise to the first regional intellectual property law, Decision 85 of 1978. Inspired by the import-substitution industrialization (ISI) model dominant throughout Latin America during that period, Decision 85 sought to incubate national pharmaceutical industries in the Andes by proscribing the grant of patents to transnational corporations (TNCs).

As explained in the introductory chapter, this approach was discredited as the so-called "debt crisis" hit Mexico in 1982 and spread throughout the region. Regional governments began to embrace neoliberalism through the adoption of reforms prescribed by the Washington Consensus (Williamson 1990). For our purposes, the key reform, aimed at facilitating export-oriented economic growth, was the transformation of civil and commercial laws and courts in order to strengthen the protection of property rights (including intellectual property).

This shift in emphasis became evident in regional intellectual property regulations with Decision 311 of 1991, which inaugurated the turn of Andean law toward stronger intellectual property rights. This transformation unfolded throughout the decade, as the Andean Commission issued Decision 313 of 1992, Decision 344 of 1993, and Decision 486 of 2000 (Helfer et al. 2009). The convergence of regional and global intellectual property regulations is particularly visible in Decision 344 of 1993, which was adopted as TRIPS was being negotiated and did away with the prohibition on pharmaceutical patents. The text of Decision 344 imported

[3] Data collection was conducted in collaboration with Diana Rodríguez-Franco and Luisa Ferreira Peralta.

wholesale the rules of the TRIPS Agreement then under discussion. For instance, it incorporated a twenty-year patent protection period starting from the date of the patent application.

The transformation of the regional intellectual property framework was completed by Decision 486 of 2000, which replaced Decision 344 of 1993. Prefiguring the level of patent protection that would be promoted in bilateral free trade agreements a few years later, Decision 486 allowed Andean countries to adopt TRIPS-plus standards. This is particularly visible with regards to exclusive test data protection, a provision I will use throughout the chapter to track the evolution of patent protection in Colombia.

Pharmaceutical test data can be defined as the information generated in the course of clinical trials of a drug. They are submitted to the national drug regulatory agency as part of the procedure to obtain the latter's market clearance authorization. The information is intended to provide evidence of the drug's safety and effectiveness. When other parties (in particular, producers of generics) gain access to such information has a direct impact on when cheaper generic versions of the drug become available.

TRIPS (art. 39.3) requires states to protect test data from *unfair* commercial use with regards to *undisclosed* test data originated from new chemical entities. This was the standard of protection that Decision 344 had adopted in 1993. Under this standard, the producer of the generic version of a given drug could invoke patent holders' test data as evidence of the drug's safety and effectiveness, without having to conduct new costly tests. However, the new standard adopted by Decision 486 of 2000 allowed states to grant an exclusive period of protection for *all* test data for *any* use, thus exceeding TRIPS requirements. That is, instead of protecting pharmaceutical companies from unfair competition, Decision 486 protects them from any type of competition, thus effectively granting them a monopoly over test data during the period of protection. As a result, generics manufacturers are required to carry out expensive clinical trials in order to introduce their generic versions into the market. By hindering the introduction of generics, data exclusivity leads to higher prices (Cortés et al. 2012).

What explains such a shift? In addition to the global convergence around TRIPS standards, the decisive pressure came from the United States government, through the USTR's use of Special 301 actions to conduct annual unilateral reviews and threaten sanctions as a way to prompt Andean countries to move in the direction of TRIPS and beyond (Sell 2003).[4] While this pressure is felt throughout the world, it is felt more acutely in those countries that are highly dependent on the United States for exports and aid, as were all of the Andean nations in the 1990s. Especially important to them was the privileged access to the US market granted by the 1991 Andean Trade Preferences Act, whereby certain products from Bolivia, Colombia, Ecuador, and Peru received duty-free treatment in the United States in exchange for the countries' cooperation in the "war on drugs." In the case of Colombia, the

[4] See the introductory chapter for a fuller discussion of Special 301 procedures.

USTR's influence was magnified. By 2000, the country had become the second largest recipient of US military aid in the world, through a multi-billion dollar, long-term military cooperation project (*Plan Colombia*) designed to crack down on drug traffickers and left-wing guerrilla groups (CIP 2004). As we will see, such a close alignment with the United States would be reproduced in the Colombian government's position on patent protection into the new century, even as other Andean countries (Bolivia, Ecuador, and Venezuela) drifted in the opposite direction.

USTR pressure on the Colombian and the Andean governments was evident in the annual reports published during the negotiation of Decision 486 of 2000. For instance, the 1998 Special 301 Review stated: "Colombia needs to take an active role in the Andean Community to bring Decision 344 (. . .) into conformity with TRIPS before the January 1, 2000 deadline. The lack of adequate pharmaceutical patent protection costs the U.S. industry substantial sums each year." Along the same lines, the 2000 report claimed: "on the patent side, Colombia and its Andean partners have not yet completed the revisions to Andean Decision 344 to bring it into conformity with the TRIPS Agreement. We will continue to consult informally with Andean Community governments in an effort to encourage them to resolve the outstanding TRIPS compliance concerns as soon as possible in the coming months." The adoption of Decision 486 of 2000 (with its TRIPs-plus provisions) shortly thereafter bears witness to the efficacy of this political and legal mechanism.

USTR pressure did not go uncontested. At the regional level, the General Secretariat of the Andean Community, inspired by the original orientation of the Andean Pact towards the ISI model, opposed TRIPs and TRIPs-plus standards, but was defeated by the national trade secretaries that made up the Andean Community's Commission (Rodríguez-Franco 2012). At the national level, domestic generics producers were virtually alone in criticizing the hardening of patent protection. For instance, the Association of Colombian Pharmaceutical Companies (Asinfar, for its Spanish initials) fought a lonely battle against relinquishing of TRIPS flexibilities (such as the ten-year transition period) and the incorporation of TRIPS and TRIPS-plus standards into Andean legislation. Although it failed to stem the tide, Asinfar succeeded in preventing the adoption of some TRIPS-plus standards, such as the recognition of second-use patents and a complete ban on compulsory licensing and parallel imports of drugs during national health emergencies.

To recap, the 1990s marked the transition from a regulatory approach focused on access to medicines and technology transfer, to one informed by TRIPS and centered on patent protection. By the end of the decade, Colombia and the rest of the Andean region, under pressure from the USTR, had gone so far as to incorporate some TRIPS-plus standards in key domains, such as data exclusivity. Although national producers' associations managed to counter proposals for further patent protection, civil society organizations were absent from those debates. Human rights NGOs and other civil society actors (for instance, physicians' associations) were largely unaware of the technicalities and potential impact of the Andean regulations and IP law at large.[5] Similarly, the level of public awareness on the consequences of IP rights on various fields remained low (Andia 2005).

Thus, at the turn of the century, political opportunity structures were closed at both the national and the international levels, as domestic regulations were dictated by the Andean decisions, which in turn aligned with TRIPS. It was a paradigmatic case of "diminished chance of activism," which explains the lack of contestation regarding patent regulation (see Figure 6.1).

As Andean regulations were superseded by national legislation in the new century, opportunity structures would gradually change. This is the period to which I now turn.

A. From Regional to National: The Dispute over Data Exclusivity

Interestingly, the route from the Andean to the national scale included two intermediate stops at the global level, through two developments that dramatically increased the visibility of the issue of pharmaceutical patents and jump-started pro-access activism in Colombia.

The first international influence stemmed from the reverberations of the 1998 legal suit brought by the transnational pharmaceutical industry, the United States, and the European Union against AIDS-ridden South Africa, for allegedly violating TRIPS through its legislation on patents over medicines. Coupled with threats of commercial sanctions by the United States and the European Union, the case was widely seen as an illustration of the overreach by pro-patent interests. The resulting uproar in South Africa resonated in countries throughout the global South, including Colombia.[6] In the face of this backlash, the plaintiffs eventually withdrew the lawsuit in 2001, and the USTR removed South Africa from its Watch List in 1999 (Klug 2005).

The second relevant international development was the WTO Ministerial Conference in Doha. The conference was the site of a new round of debates between actors advocating for stricter intellectual property laws (notably the United States and European countries, as well as multinational pharmaceutical companies) and advocates of the right to health and access to medicines (Southern countries led by the African Group and Brazil, the generics industry, the World Health Organization (WHO), as well as international NGOs and social movement organizations).

The result was the Doha Declaration, which initiated a swing of the political and legal pendulum away from TRIPS by emphasizing that the TRIPS Agreement "can and should be interpreted and implemented in a manner supportive of WTO members' rights to protect public health and, in particular, to promote access to medicines for all." Additionally, the Doha Declaration asserted states' power to make use of TRIPS' flexibilities and safeguards to protect public health.[7]

[5] Interview with Francisco Rossi, Ifarma Director, Bogotá, November 23, 2010.

[6] Interview with Germán Holguín, Misión Salud Director, Bogotá, August 27, 2012.

[7] See World Trade Organization, Ministerial Declaration of November 14, 2001, WT/MIN(01)/DEC/1, 41 I.L.M. 746 (2002); Declaration on the TRIPS agreement and public health, WT/MIN (01)/DEC/2 (November 14, 2001).

Ripples from Doha were immediately felt in Colombia. The South African case and the Doha Declaration emboldened pro-access advocates, who organized themselves into professional associations and NGOs that became visible, influential actors in public debates on new data exclusivity legislation. As explained, the Andean Community's Decision 486 of 2000 had created the possibility for member countries to pass legislation granting exclusive data protection to patent holders and thus delay the production of generic drugs. Following Decision 486, the USTR actively sought the adoption of legislation granting data exclusivity in countries of the region.

Local organizations on both sides of the debate rallied around the issue. In 2000, Afidro (the Colombian association representing transnational pharmaceutical companies) transformed itself from an occasional, relatively invisible player to an aggressive lobbyist for data exclusivity in particular, and patent protection in general. In fact, as several interviewees remarked, Afidro heavily lobbied the Colombian Ministry of Trade to ratchet up the protection of test data.[8] In reaction to Afidro's lobby, the Colombian coalition for access to medicines was formed, spearheaded by three actors: Misión Salud (Mission Health), an NGO connected to the Catholic Church; Ifarma, a think tank specifically founded to advocate greater citizen access to generic drugs; and Asinfar, the national association of generics producers. That two of these organizations (Misión Salud and Ifarma) were established largely in reaction to Afidro's lobby for data exclusivity demonstrates the centrality of this issue.[9] The debate on data exclusivity was also a turning point for the work of Asinfar.[10]

The local coalition quickly established transnational links. For instance, Ifarma networked with Health Action International (HAI) and several international NGOs, notably Médecins Sans Frontières (MSF) and Oxfam.[11] Another key international ally was the WHO, through its Program on Essential Drugs, which at the time was headed by Germán Velásquez, a prominent Colombian economist. Pro-access organizations also developed links with like-minded international experts, such as Argentine economist Carlos Correa, hired by Misión Salud in 2002 to write a report on the potential impact of data exclusivity.

The national and transnational coalition coalesced around a series of high-profile conferences organized in 2001 and 2002 for the purpose of "defending essential and generic medicines."[12] In addition to serving as a meeting point for the newly formed organizations, these events brought the issue of patents and access to medicines to the attention of the media and public opinion (Rodríguez-Franco

[8] Interview with Claudia Vacca, former advisor to the National Institute for Medicines and Food (Invima), Bogotá, May 31, 2008.

[9] Indeed, Misión Salud was established in 2000 and Ifarma was founded in 2002, precisely as the controversy over data exclusivity was at its highest point. Interview with Germán Holguín, Founding Director of Misión Salud Bogotá, August 27, 2012.

[10] Interview with Alberto Bravo, President of ASINFAR, Bogotá, February 21, 2007.

[11] Interview with Francisco Rossi, Ifarma Director, Bogotá, November 23, 2010.

[12] Invitation to the First Conference on the Defense of Essential and Generic Medicines, held at the National University of Colombia, Bogotá, June 2001.

2012). The coalition also gained the support of an influential ally: the Colombian Minister of Health, Juan Luis Londoño. He became the leader of a sector of the government that favored more expedient access to such information by generics producers, and pro-access regulation in general. After Londoño's tenure, the Ministry of Health tended to side with the right-to-health camp.

Ultimately, however, the pro-patent stance of the Minister of Trade, with the support of then President Uribe, carried the day. Partly out of conviction and partly out of fear of losing US trade preferences and military aid, the government introduced a new regulation (Decree 2085 of 2002) that granted data exclusivity to patent holders for a five-year period, as requested by the USTR. In so doing, the government went beyond the requirements of TRIPS.

Aside from the content of the new regulation, what is important for the purposes of this chapter is that the process of its passage led to the consolidation of the two contending influential coalitions regarding policy and legislation. Although still operating under unfavorable international and national opportunity structures, and thus losing the debate on data exclusivity, the pro-health coalition and the Ministry of Health managed to introduce several important exceptions into Decree 2085.[13] Thus, the struggle over data protection prefigured the issues and actors of the even more consequential, longer-term debate on patent clauses within bilateral free trade agreements. This is vividly illustrated by the negotiation of a FTA between Colombia and the United States.

II. Transforming Patent Protection through FTAs: The Colombia–United States Free Trade Agreement[14]

If the 1990s were the decade of the globalization of proprietary interests (as represented by the rise of TRIPS), the 2000s were a period of fragmentation and relocalization of struggles regarding patent protection and access to medicines.

In the Americas, this scalar shift stemmed from two sources. First, as in other regions of the world, the near collapse of multilateral free trade negotiations after the Doha round has increasingly closed off the global avenue to promoters of

[13] Decree 2085 of 2002 includes seven exceptions to mitigate the effect of data protection on access to medicines. According to the new regulation, protection does not apply to:

1. Test data that are already in the public domain or have not involved considerable effort from the patent applicant to produce.
2. Data on chemical entities that are already in the market. Thus, protection does not apply to minor changes to such data, e.g., those pertaining to new usages of a drug that has already been patented, new combinations of known chemical entities, new dosages, or different packaging.
3. Information on a new chemical entity that is similar to another one that has been commercialized in Colombia and whose protection period has expired.
4. Information whose disclosure is necessary to protect the public interest.
5. Data on a new chemical entity that is not commercialized within a year from the expedition of the marketing authorization.

[14] This section partially draws on Rodríguez-Garavito and Rodríguez-Franco 2010.

stronger, TRIPS-plus standards. Second, at the regional scale, negotiations of a Free Trade Agreement of the Americas stalled in 2003, partly over debates on patents and the right to health.

With the global and regional regulatory schemes increasingly impervious to further expansions of proprietary interests, actors in the pro-patent coalitions turned to bilateral trade agreements. The emerging importance of these negotiations is evident, for instance, in a statement of the USTR's Intellectual Functional Advisory Committee on Intellectual Property for Trade Policy Matters (IFAC-3):

> While [the Committee] recognizes that the negotiation of FTAs with individual countries and regions is labor-intensive, especially when compared with the negotiation of a multilateral agreement among the 146 Members of the WTO, FTA negotiations provide the most effective approach currently available to the United States for improving global intellectual property protection. (IFAC-3 2004: 5)

Thus, the strengthening of patent protection (and contestation around it) has taken place incrementally. In the case of Colombia, the FTA with the United States was the first one in a decade-long wave that have led to similar treaties with Canada, the European Union, South Korea, Israel, Japan, and Switzerland, as well as with Mexico, Guatemala, El Salvador, Honduras, the Caribbean Community, the Southern Cone Common Market (Mercosur), Peru, Chile, and Venezuela.

The stakes, actors, and outcomes of this transition are particularly visible in the negotiations of the United States–Colombia FTA, for two reasons. First, negotiations with Colombia were the most protracted among the bilateral free-trade treaties signed by the United States. Inaugurated in May 2004 and scheduled to finish by early 2005, negotiations dragged on for eight years, until the treaty finally entered into force in May 2012. The long duration of the discussions has allowed for detailed and public debates involving myriad national and transnational actors, among them the pro-patent and pro-access coalitions outlined in section I. Second, intellectual property rules have been at the core of this debate. Together with debates on labor rights and the liberalization of the agrarian sector, disagreements on provisions regarding intellectual property in general, and patents over medicines in particular, largely account for the unusually lengthy negotiations.

In order to reconstruct the protracted negotiations, in the following section, I briefly outline the process and highlight how disagreements over intellectual property help explain its many twists and turns. I then focus on three issues at the core of the debate: data exclusivity, compensation for delays in patent reviews, and administrative linkages between patent-granting and drug-safety agencies. In keeping with my analytical framework, I examine the evolution of national and international opportunity structures, and their impact on the struggle between pro-access and pro-patent coalitions.

A. The Negotiation Process and the Clash over Intellectual Property

Intellectual property clauses were an object of contention between Colombian and US representatives from the initiation of FTA talks in 2004. As told by the lawyer who led the Colombian government's IP delegation, disagreements on the details of intellectual property protection dragged on for over two years and fourteen rounds of negotiations, until the treaty was signed in November 2006.[15] Even then, as we will see, intellectual property clauses continued to generate debate both in the US and in Colombia, to the point that they were eventually modified by an additional protocol signed in 2007.

The duration and oscillations in dealings on the matter are partly attributable to the existence of solid political coalitions on both sides of the debate. Given that FTA negotiations were launched when the dust from the controversy regarding the regulation of data exclusivity had yet to settle, the pro-patent and pro-access organizations and coalitions that had been formed to address the exclusivity issue immediately leapt into the fray. Thus, although it entailed strong pressure to ratchet up patent protection, the FTA also opened an international opportunity for the pro-access movement. Transnational civil society organizations opposing the global diffusion of property interests through FTAs became important allies for the domestic movement. The onset of FTA negotiations, therefore, marked the transition to the "boomerang" effect situation, where local activists resort to international allies to press their cause at the local level (see Table 6.1).

The pro-access coalition was once again led by a combination of local NGOs and think tanks (notably Misión Salud and Ifarma), local generics producers (Asinfar), and international NGOs (notably MSF, Oxfam, and Caritas). The collaboration between local and international NGOs within this activist network was formalized in 2003, when they officially launched the Alliance of Organizations for the Defense of Health. Taking the Doha Declaration as its baseline, the coalition argued that TRIPS (as interpreted by Doha) offered an appropriate balance between IP and the right to health, and that additional expansions of TRIPS-plus protection in the FTA were both legally unnecessary and socially deleterious, inasmuch as they would further hamper Colombians' access to basic medications.

Spearheading the pro-patent camp were the USTR, the Colombian association of multinational pharmaceutical companies (Afidro), and the Pharmaceutical Research and Manufacturers of America (PhRMA), the US association of pharmaceutical and biotechnology firms. Starting from the gains established in Decree 2085 of 2002, the coalition advocated for the adoption of additional TRIPS-plus standards through the elimination of the exceptions established in Decree 2085, as well as through other changes to patent laws and procedures.

Both coalitions undertook multiple strategies to influence the negotiations. They commissioned studies to support their arguments for or against TRIPS-plus standards.[16] They were also present in the "side room" during each of the negotiation rounds (a meeting room located right next to the one where bilateral governmental

[15] Interview with Javier Gamboa, member of the Colombian government's delegation at the FTA negotiations, March 8, 2007.

[16] Prominent among these studies were, on the one hand, a 2004 report by Misión Salud making the case of the pro-access network (Holguín 2004) and, on the other, a publication by a prominent think tank (Fedesarrollo) providing economic ammunition to the pro-patent camp (Archila et al. 2005).

negotiations would take place, where government officials could interact with business and civil society representatives).[17]

Where did the Colombian and US governments stand on the issue? With which coalition did each of them tend to side? Interestingly, the position of both governments changed as the talks proceeded. On the Colombian side, the government's position oscillated between the pro-patent stance of the Ministry of Trade and the pro-access perspective of the Ministry of Health. The former was ready to accept TRIPS-plus standards in exchange for greater access to the US market, while the latter deemed such standards an unnecessary concession that would imperil access to medicines.[18] This internal rift, inherited from the struggle over data exclusivity regulations, helps explain why the government's offer with regard to patent protection changed over the course of fourteen rounds of negotiation. As in the case of the debate over data exclusivity, while the Ministry of Health initially had the upper hand, the tension was gradually resolved in favor of the pro-patent view of the Ministry of Trade, which, once again, received the backing of the Presidency and led to the signing of an FTA that included most of the TRIPS-plus rules proposed by the USTR.

On the US side, the government's position evolved for a different reason: electoral politics. The FTA had been negotiated by the Republican government of George W. Bush, backed by Republican majorities in the US Congress. However, just as the FTA was signed, Democrats took control of Congress. From the early days of the negotiations, prominent Democrats in Congress had been signing letters supporting the arguments of the pro-access coalition and criticizing USTR's insistence on protection of proprietary interests beyond TRIPS standards. Once their party won the majority of seats in Congress, they pressured the USTR to revise the intellectual property clauses in the FTA. In March 2007, twelve influential members of the US Congress, in a letter to USTR Susan Schwab, urged the "immediate reconsideration" of certain TRIPS-plus provisions in FTAs so as to ensure adherence to the Doha Declaration on TRIPS and Public Health. Such adherence, they said, "should be ensured both in FTAs already concluded with Colombia, Panama, and Peru and those being negotiated."[19]

With approval of the FTA in the US Congress still pending, the Democrats' pressure had an immediate impact on the US government and, in a classical "boomerang" effect, on the Colombian government as well. In June 2007, the United States and Colombia signed a Modifying Protocol that amended various sections of the FTA, including the intellectual property chapter. As we will see below, the Protocol brought patent protection back down to a level close to TRIPS standards.

The Colombian Congress and the Constitutional Court swiftly approved the FTA and the Modifying Protocol. Although Congressional ratification was expected, the fact that the highly activist and pro-human rights Constitutional

[17] Separate interviews with Luis Fernando Garcia and Luis Guillermo Restrepo, delegates of the Ministry of Health to the FTA negotiations, Bogotá, February 21, 2008.

[18] Interview with Miguel Cortés, Ifarma researcher, Bogotá, August 8, 2012. According to Cortés, "the FTA negotiations opened a window of opportunity for the Ministry of Health and civil society to weigh in; up until then, the only voice that was heard was that of the Ministry of Trade."

[19] See <http://www.twnside.org.sg/title2/wto.info/twninfo517.htm>.

Court upheld the intellectual property provisions took pro-access scholars and advocates by surprise, as there were constitutional grounds to question them (Rodríguez-Garavito and Rodríguez-Franco 2007).

In Washington, debate continued to rage in the US Congress over both Colombia's human rights and labor rights records. For our purposes, stagnation of the treaty process had an important effect: it opened the FTA to closer scrutiny and debate, thus creating opportunities for the pro-access coalition to use "boomerang" strategies. Intellectual property clauses were among those that critics of the treaty (notably Democrats in Congress and the pro-access coalition in Colombia) wanted to see revised before the treaty was finally signed. With Democrats taking over the US Presidency in 2009, this view grew even more influential and the struggle surrounding intellectual property rules was reignited.

B. The Renegotiation of the FTA Provisions

The new negotiations revolved around three main issues: data exclusivity, compensation for delays in granting a patent, and administrative coordination between patent-granting and public health agencies. We will look briefly at each of them in turn, and examine the ways in which the line between proprietary and access interests was drawn and redrawn during negotiations.

The above-mentioned discussion on data exclusivity was a hot button issue from the early rounds of talks. As explained, Decree 2085 of 2002 resolved the competing claims on access to test data by adopting a TRIPS-plus standard (a five-year period of data exclusivity for patent holders) and introducing some exceptions to mitigate its impact. As the new FTA negotiations began, both the pro-patent and pro-access coalitions sought to redraw the line: while the former advocated the elimination of exceptions to data exclusivity and the latter wanted data protection scaled down to the level established by TRIPS.

In light of the opportunity structures and the combination of forces within and between the governments during negotiations, the result of the negotiations was a clear victory for the pro-patent coalition. By removing virtually all of the exceptions established in Decree 2085, the intellectual property chapter established a strict system of secrecy and strong patent protection. The change was evident, for instance, in the extension of legal protection—which had previously covered only undisclosed information—to public data concerning the chemical entities of the drug under review. As a result, the only exception to data exclusivity that the FTA left standing was a generic category of situations that may affect public health, which was already included in TRIPS and Decree 2085. Importantly, the period of data exclusivity protection was also extended: while Decree 2085 had established a five-year term, the FTA set five years as the *minimum* period of protection. Government regulators were given power to extend it.

The fate of the FTA data exclusivity standards vividly illustrates how regulations fluctuated during the negotiations. Such standards were among the main targets of criticism by Democrats in the US Congress who, after winning a majority, demanded revisions similar to those proposed by the pro-access coalition. The result was the Modifying Protocol of 2007, which moved the line back to where Decree 2085 of 2000 had drawn it—that is, closer to TRIPS standards and further from the TRIPS-plus level of protection afforded by the original text of the FTA. Consequently, the revised intellectual property chapter includes the Decree 2085 exceptions and reestablishes five years as the "reasonable period" of data exclusivity protection.

A second issue that elicited considerable controversy was compensation for delays in obtaining market clearance. TRIPS sets a twenty-year period of patent protection. This period starts on the date of the application for a patent, but the term can be eroded by clinical studies to prove safety and efficacy and by administrative agency review of those studies. Market clearance can take between five and ten years, leaving an effective patent term of only ten to fifteen years.[20] After TRIPS went into force, pharmaceutical TNCs and other members of the pro-patent coalition made the case for an extension of the twenty-year term in order to compensate for administrative delay. The coalition prevailed in the negotiation of the original FTA. First, the treaty left no room for interpretation as to what "unreasonable delays" meant, setting a fixed five-year limit to any review of patent applications. Second, the FTA did not cap the potential extension of the effective duration of a patent. Through both rules, the FTA broadened the protection of patents well beyond TRIPS.

But as in the struggle over data exclusivity, the Modifying Protocol of 2007 softened the TRIPS-plus rules. With the protocol, compensation for delays moved from an obligation to a policy alternative to be considered during the process of implementing the FTA. Rather than setting fixed periods and caps, the Protocol emphasized governments' obligation to develop competent bureaucracies capable of efficiently reviewing patent applications.

Finally, debate raged during negotiations regarding a third TRIPS-plus mechanism: the so-called administrative "linkage" between patent-granting agencies and public health agencies. This type of linkage contrasts with the two-pronged administrative model that is predominant in Latin America and other parts of the world. In the latter system, patent applications are reviewed by the agency responsible for intellectual property protection, whereas studies of drugs' safety and effectiveness are carried out by a separate public health agency. Although under this two-pronged system, it behooves patent applicants and patent holders to supervise new applications so they can oppose those that might infringe upon their rights, no responsibility to protect patents falls on the health agency itself. In contrast, under a linkage system, state agencies must coordinate their actions and proactively warn patent holders of new applications.

Not surprisingly, pro-patent actors have tended to embrace and promote the linkage system as a mechanism to prevent and punish violations of patent rights. However, pro-access coalitions have generally opposed, arguing that it turns public health agencies into patent guarantors and passes on a private burden to already

[20] In practice, however, the term is shorter in countries such as Colombia, where public health agencies defer to previous tests run by their counterparts in the United States and Europe.

overwhelmed public agencies. The negotiations of the Colombia–US FTA were no exception to these trends. The US proposal included linkage regulations; they were adamantly opposed by Ifarma, Misión Salud and their international allies, together with the local generics industry.

The text of the original FTA confirmed the move toward proprietary interests. Indeed, the intellectual chapter included a wholesale adoption of the linkage system, thus deeply transforming the nature and obligations of the Colombian public health agency in charge of ensuring the safety and efficacy of medicines (Invima)—which, in fact, had been hitherto a vocal critic of TRIPS-plus standards in general.

The amendments introduced by the Protocol also confirm the pattern described in this section. By keeping the linkage system while introducing exceptions to mitigate its impact—notably by limiting the application of linkage to the few cases in which the Colombian public health agency runs its own tests rather than deferring to safety and efficacy tests conducted in the United States and other Northern countries—the Protocol reestablished the compromise between patents and access to medicines that had been achieved at the global scale (through TRIPS and the Doha Declaration) prior to the negotiation of the FTA.

III. The Struggle Surrounding the Implementation of the FTA

With the entry into force of the FTA in May 2012, international opportunity structures for pro-health mobilization effectively closed. Thus, the movement turned its attention to the national stage, where, rather surprisingly, political opportunities opened up with the rise to power of a pro-access technocracy within the administration of President Santos (2010–14). With this shift, political opportunity structures completed the clockwise turn that I have argued describes the evolution of contestation around patents in the last two decades in Colombia (see Figure 6.1).

After the treaty entered into force, an emboldened pro-access camp that included the Ministry of Health, as well as civil society organizations, managed to exploit some of the flexibilities in the text of the treaty, so as to bring the implementation laws closer to the lower end of patent protection allowed by the FTA, and thus closer to the initial regime set by TRIPS. As the Ministry of Health's legal counsel on intellectual property said in our interview, "the instruction coming from the President and the Ministry of Trade was not to go beyond what was strictly required by the FTA."[21]

This approach is embodied in two government decrees dealing with the issues of linkage and the Bolar exception. Resisting the USTR's pressure to introduce linkage provisions in the implementation decrees, the Colombian government opted for a regulatory framework that emphasizes publicity and transparency.

[21] Interview with Carolina Gómez, Advisor to the Minister of Health on intellectual property, Bogotá, August 2, 2012.

Instead of having Invima (the agency responsible for evaluating drug safety and efficacy) warn patent holders of applications that may impinge on their rights, Decree 733 of 2012 simply orders it to keep a public record of new applications.

Tellingly, the Colombian government also introduced a Bolar exception during the implementation phase. Decree 729 of 2012 allows generics producers to compare their drugs to the patented versions and prove bioequivalence before the expiration of the patent. Thus, their drugs may obtain approval from Invima to enter the market immediately after the patent expires.[22] This decree has had tangible effects, as it has put an end to a practice whereby patent holders, by challenging generic drug applications for market clearance before the expiration of the patent, can extend the duration of their monopoly by approximately six months, which is the length of time it usually takes Invima to review applications.

However, in light of the decidedly pro-patent straitjacket inherited from previous Colombian legislation and the original provisions of the FTA, even the flexibilities introduced by the 2007 Protocol to the FTA and the Santos government were not enough to bring national regulations closer to the standards of countries like Argentina or Brazil. This is particularly visible in the regulatory domain that has served as a benchmark throughout this chapter: data protection. As mentioned, data exclusivity legislation (Decree 2085 of 2002) predated the FTA by ten years. Thus, the TRIPS-plus standard of the FTA was a replica of Colombian legislation. Now elevated to the status of an international obligation, data exclusivity has become the most rigid and, according to virtually all of the public health experts interviewed for this study, presents the strongest obstacle to accessing reasonably priced medicines.

A study of the effects of the first decade of data exclusivity protection substantiates this view (Cortés et al. 2012). Between 2003 and 2011, the public health system spent approximately 1.3 million dollars on drugs protected with data exclusivity. When compared with the cost of the same drugs under competitive market conditions, it is estimated that data exclusivity cost the healthcare system nearly 400 million dollars during that period. This sum would have allowed the state to cover the annual health insurance costs of about 146,000 citizens.

The same study shows that, contrary to the argument that data exclusivity fosters innovation, only 1 percent of the chemical entities approved for commercialization during that period were new. When compared with the figures from countries that do not offer data exclusivity (e.g., Venezuela and Argentina), this finding suggests that such a heightened level of protection generates additional costs to the state and individuals, while failing to induce an increase in the number of new drugs entering the market. Significantly, the large majority (96 percent) of the new chemical entities received data exclusivity protection. This suggests that the Colombian regulatory agencies have, in practice, embraced a pro-patent interpretation of Decree 2085 and the FTA by lowering the bar on what it considers data obtained through "considerable effort" and thus subject to protection, and by making scant

[22] Interview with Juan Fernando García, intellectual property advisor to the Ministry of Trade and former member of the government's FTA negotiation team. Bogotá, September 3, 2012.

use of exceptions to data exclusivity on grounds such as the protection of the public interest.

In sum, even though the more moderate stance of the Santos administration managed to shift course on some fronts during the implementation phase, the legacy of over fifteen years of pro-patent legislation and international commitments continues to dominate the Colombian legal regime. The outcome is a regulatory framework that fits well within the TRIPS template, and even goes beyond it on issues such as data exclusivity. Moreover, successive governments have been reluctant to make use of many of the flexibilities that TRIPS allows, such as compulsory licensing. The straitjacket is tight indeed.

In light of the regulatory landscape, pressure for pro-access reform has come from civil society. With the executive and the legislature locked into pro-patent international regulations, public health experts and NGOs have taken their case to the courts, where opportunity structures have gradually opened. It is to this process of judicialization that I now turn.

IV. Back to the Local: Unaffordable Medicines and the Judicialization of Access

A. Judicial Activism and Legal Reform

By virtue of the 1991 Constitution, Colombian courts in general, and the Constitutional Court in particular, are highly independent and proactive in the protection of human rights. In the domain of access to medicines, courts have intervened through two routes. First, based on the strong right-to-health provision of the Constitution (art. 49),[23] they have granted hundreds of thousands of claims against public or private healthcare providers brought by patients denied a particular medication. Given the scale and costs associated with this type of litigation, judicial activism in the provision of medicines has created strong incentives for the government to regulate drug prices, albeit rarely through reforms of patent protection. Second, more recently, courts have begun to entertain cases specifically dealing with patent regulations, as illustrated by a pioneer case about compulsory licensing for Kaletra. Let us look at these two routes in turn.

In the first twenty years of the 1991 Constitution, Colombian courts handed down over one million constitutional rulings related to the right to health. The plaintiffs, patients asking the courts to order that their public or private healthcare

[23] According to Article 49 of the Colombian Constitution, "public health and environmental protection are public services for which the state is responsible. All individuals are guaranteed access to services that promote, protect, and rehabilitate public health. It is the responsibility of the state to organize, direct, and regulate the delivery of health services and of environmental protection to the population in accordance with the principles of efficiency, universality, and cooperation, and to establish policies for the provision of health services by private entities and to exercise supervision and control over them . . . " Unofficial translation by the University of Richmond Law School, available at <http://confinder.richmond.edu/admin/docs/colombia_const2.pdf>.

Table 6.1. *Tutela* actions regarding the right to health (1999–2012)

Year	*Tutela* actions on the right to health
1999	21,301
2000	24,843
2001	34,319
2002	42,734
2003	51,944
2004	72,033
2005	81,017
2006	96,226
2007	107,238
2008	142,957
2009	100,490
2010	94,502
2011	105,947

Source: National Ombudsman's Office.

provider supply them with a specific service or good (e.g., a specific medicine, treatment, doctor's appointment, or clinical test), have used the so-called *tutela* writs. These are judicial actions created by the 1991 Constitution to redress violations of human rights. The *tutela* mechanism is highly accessible (it can be filed by an individual without the intermediation of a lawyer), informal (the complaint can be presented orally), and expeditious (judges have up to ten days to hand down a ruling). Accordingly, they are very popular among Colombians, and have turned the courts into central actors in myriad policy domains that affect human rights. Table 6.1 gives a sense of the scale of this trend in the realm of the right to health during the period for which comparable data is available (1999–2012).

As the Table demonstrates, citizens have massively resorted to courts to demand *tutela* protection of their right to health. This "judicialization of health care" has led courts to adjudicate complex legal and economic issues, ranging from the benefits included in public and private insurers' healthcare plans, to funding of medicines or treatments that are not included in those plans, and the universalization of coverage (Rodríguez-Garavito 2013). Access to medicines has also been judicialized, as patients have sued private and public providers to demand drugs prescribed by their physicians. At the time of writing, litigation about medicines accounts for nearly 20 percent of *tutela* actions related to the right to health (i.e., approximately 20,000 cases per year) (El Tiempo 2012).

While *tutela* litigation has offered a valuable tool to patients who have been arbitrarily denied medicines or treatments, it has also led to abuse and corruption, as different actors, from regulators to pharmaceutical companies to healthcare providers, have found ways to game the system. Courts have routinely ruled for the plaintiffs and thus ordered providers to supply patients with the medicines prescribed by physicians, whether they are patented or generic, even when the drugs are not explicitly included in the patient's healthcare plan.

Although based on a progressive understanding of the right to health and offering the only effective institutional means to resolve patients' complaints, this jurisprudence has created incentives for commercial interests—including those of pharmaceutical companies—to exploit the judicialization of healthcare to their advantage. The incentives are particularly strong because the Colombian state, not the drug companies or the healthcare providers, ends up footing the hefty bill. This is so because private insurers are not legally mandated to pay for medicines that are not included in their coverage plans, they are entitled to recover the costs of those medicines from the state every time a court order instructs them to provide a patient with such a drug.

Instead of resisting this system, pharmaceutical companies and providers have found ways to profit from it by charging the state extraordinarily high prices for the drugs they give to patients. This strategy, with its associated corruption,[24] has bled the finances of the healthcare system, as charges ("recoveries") from providers to the Colombian state skyrocketed from 1.5 million dollars in 2001 to 550 million in 2008.[25] Importantly, medicines, especially patented ones, account for nearly 80 percent of those expenditures (Semana 2010). As the director of the national association of patients with Parkinson's disease said in our interview, "they usually want to give us generic medicines, so we end up going to court to demand patented versions, which we could not afford otherwise."[26] Given the financial support that manufacturers of patented drugs provide to some patients' associations, as well as manufacturers' active dissemination of dubious information about the allegedly inferior quality of generics, it comes as no surprise that such associations oftentimes lobby and litigate for access to patented medicines (Lamprea 2013)

At its core, however, the origin of the problem of unaffordable medicines lies in regulatory flaws, rather than in court interventions. And it extends to all medicines, rather than solely to those not included in coverage plans. Starting in 2006, the Uribe administration, which had agreed to the radical strengthening of patent protection in the original FTA, also yielded to pharmaceutical companies' pressures to deregulate drug prices. Based on a study funded by the association of transnational pharmaceutical corporations, the administration issued new rules that replaced the regulated market with a liberalized price system, despite the fact that, due to patents, the market for some of the drugs in highest demand was effectively a monopoly (Andia and Rodríguez-Garavito 2013). To increase demand for their products, the transnational industry also bankrolled medical associations,

[24] Corruption scandals regarding the healthcare system have raged since 2010. Ongoing investigations by the National Comptroller's Office and the Attorney General's Office involve public officials and private insurers' staff members who allegedly colluded to charge the government exorbitant prices for medical services and drugs, among other fraudulent activities (El Tiempo 2011).

[25] Figures submitted by the national government to the Colombian Constitutional Court during the procedures leading to ruling T-760 of 2008.

[26] Interview with Nuby Graciela Rodríguez, director of the National Association of Patients with Parkinson's Disease, August 28, 2012.

as well as patients' associations, law firms specializing in bringing *tutela* actions to the courts, and negative publicity campaigns regarding generic drugs.[27]

Because of the opacity of pharmaceuticals' price information, systematic comparative assessments of drug prices are hard to find. However, global and regional studies on specific drugs give an idea of high prices in Colombia. According to Health Action International (2009), Colombia had the highest price for a common antibiotic drug (ciprofloxacin) among the ninety-three countries surveyed. A more thorough assessment on the Andean region conducted in 2008 also showed Colombia at the top of the ranking of patented medicines prices (HAI 2008). More recently, the Minister of Health has acknowledged that "drug prices are higher than in many developing countries, even higher than in some developed countries... [For instance in] a sample of 59 frequently used medicines, 55 are more expensive than in Spain" (Gaviria 2013).

Given the prohibitive costs of the institutional status quo, both courts and the government changed course in recent years. First, the Constitutional Court shifted from a case-by-case approach to granting patients' petitions for medicines, to a structural approach that targets the regulatory and administrative failures that led to the massive *tutela* litigation. In decision T-760 of 2008, it handed down a structural injunction ordering the government to tackle the root causes of the inefficiencies and waste of public funds that were driving the public health industry into bankruptcy, including exorbitant drug prices of drugs. The Court has retained supervisory jurisdiction in the case and thus followed up on government's progress through new rulings and public hearings (Rodríguez-Garavito 2013).

Largely under pressure from the Court's orders, the Santos government introduced regulatory reforms aimed at rationalizing public expenditures on medicines. In 2010 (Decree 4474), it put a cap to the price at which the most sought-after medicines could be charged to the state. As an advisor to the Minister of Health stated in our interview, "the idea behind the new regulation was to apply a discount to the average prices of the most popular medicines, so as to bring some relief to the public budget, in the hope that the amount of medicines paid for by the state would be eventually capped too."[28] Prices, however, remained high; in 2013, the government strengthened the system of price controls, putting a cap on drug prices based on a comparison with those in seventeen countries with similar levels of economic development.

Although regulated prices have begun to stem the tide of skyrocketing public expenditures on medicines, it is telling that they are the government's legal instrument of choice. Indeed, the government has been unwilling to follow the course of other countries of the region (such as Brazil, Ecuador, and Argentina) that rely on TRIPS flexibilities to improve access. Thus, only recently have legal challenges to patent protection become part of the regulatory story in Colombia.

[27] Interview with Francisco Rossi, Ifarma Director, November 23, 2010.

[28] Interview with Rodrigo Moreira, advisor on Price Regulation to the Minister of Health, Bogotá, August 10, 2012.

In light of the government's reluctance, civil society and courts have once again taken the initiative, as the pioneering litigation around Kaletra bears witness.

B. Litigating Patent Protection: The Kaletra Case

The Colombian patent for Kaletra, a medication for the treatment of HIV/AIDS produced by Abbott Laboratories, is valid until the end of 2016. The protection of Kaletra through patents has been heavily criticized throughout the world, given that the medication consists of the combination of two already known active ingredients (lopinavir and ritonavir). In fact, in many countries, the patent has been denied for not meeting the "inventive step" requirement.[29]

In Colombia, the strategy was somewhat different. Facing a situation in which the price of Kaletra was three times higher than in neighboring countries (such as Brazil and Ecuador) despite the government's recommendation of a reference price, in early 2008, a coalition of NGOs decided to embark on an attempt to obtain a compulsory license. With the exception of an administrative norm that the Ministry of Health did not apply, the process for requesting compulsory licenses was not regulated in Colombia.[30] However, the TRIPS Agreement requires that the proposed user "make authorization from the right holder on reasonable commercial terms."[31] The coalition, which included some of the leading organizations of the pro-access movement, such as Ifarma and Misión Salud, as well as networks that specialized in AIDS activism, such as the Network of People Living with HIV and AIDS, the Roundtable of organizations that work with people living with HIV or AIDS, and the international NGO Public Citizen, therefore requested that Abbott grant a license voluntarily. The first time anywhere in the world that civil society organizations had initiated the process for obtaining a compulsory license,[32] the petition cited the high cost of the medication in Colombia, in comparison to other countries in the region.

As Abbott did not respond, in July 2008, the organizations took the next step. They petitioned the Ministry of Health requesting that the issue be declared a matter of public interest. They also sent another petition to the Superintendent of Industry and Commerce directly requesting the issuance of the compulsory license. In support of both petitions, the NGOs attached a technical document with pharmacological information, the number of patients, and the legal framework in which they were requesting the license.

The Ministry of Health responded by announcing the creation of a committee to decide whether the matter was an issue of public interest. During this process, the Superintendent of Industry and Commerce issued a regulation that defined the procedure to declare the existence of a public interest. Although the regulation clarified the procedure, issuing it prolonged the process of the Ministry of Health, which had to form an evaluation committee in accordance with the new guidelines.

[29] See <http://infojustice.org/archives/27851> and here: <http://www.citizen.org/Kaletra-campaign>.

[30] Interview with Luz Marina Umbasia, Ifarma's legal counsel, Bogotá, May 27, 2013.

[31] TRIPS Agreement, art. 31(b).

[32] TRIPS Agreement, art. 31(b).

In May 2009, the Ministry of Health responded, denying the declaration of a public interest, alleging that the Technical Committee for the declaration of matters of public interest found that problems of access to Kaletra had not been proven, in that it was included in the list of covered medications under public and private health plans.

As the medications advisor of the Ministry of Health recognized, however, presence in the formulary did not ensure access because healthcare providers imposed impossible demands for additional documentation and procedures.[33] A *tutela* action could have ensued and to forestall the usual result—an increase in price—in April 2009, the National Commission for Medication Prices issued a norm that fixed the price that the state would pay annually for Kaletra at 1,067 USD per patient.[34] This price was high in terms of international pricing, and in October 2009, the pro-access coalition decided to turn to the courts and present a class action requesting the compulsory license and a declaration of the violation of the collective right to public health.

The lawsuit was filed against Abbott, the Ministry of Health, the Superintendent of Industry and Commerce, and Invima. In February 2012, the trial judge ruled in favor of the petitioners, and declared that the price Abbott charged was higher than the reference value suggested by the national government, and was significantly higher than in neighboring countries, threatening and violating collective rights. The decision ruled against Abbott and the Ministry of Health and exonerated Invima. However, the court failed to order remedial relief and did not require the government to issue the compulsory license.

Abbott appealed, arguing that it always followed the price limits and other Colombian regulations, but noted that the reference price set by the government was in the form of a recommendation and was not mandatory. While the Ministry admitted responsibility for failing to control prices, it followed an erratic legal strategy: it filed an untimely appeal, then supported Abbott's appeal, and finally withdrew the appeal. The petitioners also appealed. In the words of Luz Marina Umbasia, the legal advisor to Ifarma, "what we were requesting was the compulsory license; it wasn't enough that the price of the medication had decreased a bit."[35]

In September 2012 the appeal court (the Cundinamarca Administrative Tribunal) confirmed the ruling against the Ministry of Health, but it too denied the compulsory license.[36] The Court recognized that the lack of state control affects patients' access to an infrastructure that guarantees public health. Nonetheless, it found that Abbott had not engaged in illegal activity, because the reference prices in the country were a recommendation that the patent holder could choose to follow

[33] Interview with Carolina Gómez, Advisor to the Minister of Health on intellectual property, Bogotá, August 2, 2012.

[34] See the Commission's Circular 02 of 2009.

[35] Interview with Luz Marina Umbasia, Ifarma's legal counsel, Bogotá, May 27, 2013.

[36] Cundinamarca Administrative Tribunal, ruling No. 2009-00269-01, September 27, 2012.

or not. Additionally, Abbott followed the maximum sale price established by the state in 2009.

Although the petitioners lost the case and failed in their attempt to obtain a compulsory license, the indirect effect of the litigation was that the price of Kaletra was reduced. In fact, the price of Kaletra in Colombia was reduced by 60 percent, in a large part due to the suits and negative publicity stemming from the litigation.[37] Additionally, the case opened the courts to disputes regarding patent regulation. In light of the progressive content of the Colombian Constitution and the pro-human-rights inclination of the courts, it is probable that this route offers an opportunity structure more open for those attempting to loosen the straitjacket of patents and facilitate access to medicines.

V. Conclusion

In this chapter, I have inquired into the evolution of patent regulations in Colombia and its intersection with the right to access to medicines. The case study has been informed by a conceptual perspective that places national and international opportunity structures at the foreground, as well as the political and legal struggles taking place within them.

Viewed from this analytical angle, the trajectories of the Andean intellectual property regime, and particularly the laws in Colombia, lay bare the power struggle between pro-patent and pro-access coalitions. While the 1970s and 1980s were characterized by the dominance of an inward-looking model privileging the development of local generic industries and citizens' access to inexpensive medicines, the 1990s and 2000s were the high-water mark of patent protection. Although the pro-patent trend continued to hold in the new wave of FTAs in the 2000s and 2010s, mounting public debate about exorbitant medicine prices, together with the increasing influence of a pro-access coalition in governmental, judicial, and civil society circles, suggests that the trend may swing back toward the compromise struck under TRIPS.

Further, evidence presented in the chapter shows that patent regulation has oscillated, from the ratcheting up of intellectual property norms and institutions (e.g., through the consolidation of a global regime around TRIPS in the 1990s), to the scaling down of the field through public resistance to the explosion of bilateral FTAs incorporating TRIPS-plus standards.

Finally, the unusually protracted process of negotiation and ratification of the FTA between Colombia and the United States has allowed us to see in detail the mechanisms, issues, and actors underpinning the rise of bilateral trade agreements as the key regulatory site where the boundaries between patent protection and access to medicines are redrawn. In the face of the collapse of multilateral talks within the WTO in the post-Doha world, FTAs have come to be the preferred

[37] Interview with Luz Marina Umbasia, Ifarma's legal counsel, Bogotá, May 27, 2013.

approach both for European and North American countries intent on strengthening patent protection in the Global South. Recent developments in Colombia offer an illustration of this trend. With the entry into force of the FTA with Canada in 2011, the signing of an FTA with the European Union in the same year, and the entry into force of the treaty with the United States in 2012, Colombia's intellectual property regime will be determined by its international commitments.

The impact of this change on Colombians' access to medicines will hinge on the interaction between the national and transnational forces highlighted in this chapter. At the national level, the balance between access and proprietary interests will depend on the details and correlation of forces around the laws that will implement the FTA provisions on patents and data exclusivity. As we see by comparing this case study to the others in the volume, these implementation laws can vary widely and have very different effects even among countries (like the CAFTA parties) bound by the same FTA. In addition, the balance will depend on emerging issues, such as the scope of patents over biotechnological innovations, as well as the manner in which the Colombian government uses non-patent regulatory instruments such as price controls (Andia 2011).

At the transnational level, the fate of the balance between intellectual property and the right to health in countries like Colombia will hinge on the evolution of the global movement advocating greater access to medicines, and its connections with other pro-access-to-knowledge coalitions. And it will crucially depend on the interstate struggle around the TRIPS regime, in which the role of emerging powers such as the BRICs countries (Brazil, Russia, India, and China) may prove decisive.

References

Andia, Tatiana. 2005. "Doctors, Patients, Pharmaceutical Industry and the State: Collective Action and Industrial Policy." MA thesis, Department of Economics, London School of Economics.

——. 2011. "The Invisible Threat: The Rise of Non-intellectual Property and Non-trade Pharmaceutical Regulations in Colombia." In *Intellectual Property, Pharmaceuticals and Public Health: Access to Drugs in Developing Countries*, edited by Kenneth C. Shadlen, Samira Guennif, Alenka Guzman, and Lalitha Narayanan. London: Edward Elgar Publishers.

—— and César Rodríguez-Garavito. 2013. "Colombia, ¿campeón mundial de medicamentos?" In *La Silla Vacía*, July 17. Available at <http://www.lasillavacia.com/elblogueo/blog/colombia-campeon-mundial-en-precios-de-medicamentos-45227>.

Archila, Emilio, Gabriel Carrasquilla, Marcela Meléndez, and Juan P. Uribe. 2005. "Estudio sobre la propiedad intelectual en el sector farmacéutico colombiano." Bogota: Fedesarrollo and Fundación Santa Fe.

Center for International Policy (CIP). 2004. "U.S. Military and Police Aid." Available at <http://www.ciponline.org/colombia> (retrieved July 6, 2005).

Cortés, Miguel Ernesto, Francisco Rossi, and Mayra Vásquez. 2012. *Impacto de 10 años de protección de datos en medicamentos en Colombia*. Bogotá: Ifarma.

El Tiempo (2011). "Contralora pide un replanteo del actual sistema y arremete contra las EPS." *El Tiempo*, November 12, 2011. Available at <http://www.eltiempo.com/justicia/ARTICULO-WEB-NEW_NOTA_INTERIOR-10756104.html>.

——. 2012. "Cada dos minutos se interpone una tutela de salud en Colombia." December 20, available at: <http://www.eltiempo.com/justicia/ARTICULO-WEB-NEW_NOTA_INTERIOR-12467503.html>.

Friedman, Thomas. 2000. *The Lexus and the Olive Tree: Understanding Globalization*. New York: Picador.

Gaviria, Alejandro. 2013. "Competenica hasta donde sea posible, regulación hasta donde sea necesaria." *El Tiempo*, July 20. Available at <http://www.eltiempo.com/vida-de-hoy/salud/ARTICULO-WEB-NEW_NOTA_INTERIOR-12939544.html>.

Health Action International (HAI). 2008. *Precios de medicamentos: Bolivia, Colombia, Ecuador, Nicaragua, Perú, Venezuela*. Bogota: HAI.

Helfer, Laurence, Karen Alter, and Maria Guerzovich. 2009. "Islands of Effective International Adjudication: Constructing an Intellectual Property Rule of Law in the Andean Community." *American Journal of International Law* 103: 1–47.

Holguín, Germán. 2004. *La bolsa y la vida: impacto de la agenda norteamericana para el TLC sobre el acceso a medicamentos y la salud pública*. Bogotá: H_20 Publicidad.

IFAC-3 (Intellectual Functional Advisory Committee on Intellectual Property for Trade Policy Matters). 2004. "The U.S.-Central American Free Trade Agreement (FTA): The Intellectual Property Provisions." Available at <http://www.ustr.gov/archive/assets/Trade_Agreements/Regional/CAFTA/CAFTA_Reports/asset_upload_file571_5945.pdf>.

Klug, Heinz. 2005. "Campaigning for Life: Building a New Transnational Solidarity in the Face of HIV/AIDS and TRIPS." In *Law and Globalization from Below: Toward a Cosmopolitan Legality*, edited by B. Santos and C. Rodriguez. Cambridge: Cambridge University Press.

Lamprea, Everaldo. 2013. *Health Care and Courts: The Colombian Case*. JSD Dissertation, Stanford Law School.

Rodríguez-Franco, Diana. 2012. "Globalising Intellectual Property Rights: The Politics of Law and Public Health." Pp. 139–69 in *Lawyers and the Construction of Transnational Justice*, edited by Yves Dezalay and Bryant Garth. London: Routledge.

Rodríguez-Garavito, César. 2013. "The Judicialization of Health Care: Symptoms, Diagnosis, and Prescriptions." In *Law and Development of Middle-Income Countries*, edited by Randall Peerenboom and Tom Ginsburg. Cambridge: Cambridge University Press.

—— and Diana Rodríguez-Franco. 2007. *¿Es constitucional el TLC?* Bogotá: Dejusticia.

————. 2010. "Constructing and Contesting the Global Intellectual Property Legal Field". Paper presented at the Law and Society Association Annual Meeting. Chicago, June.

Semana. 2010. "A precio de oro." November 6, available at <http://www.semana.com/nacion/articulo/precio-oro/124197-3>.

Sell, Susan K. 2003. *Private Power, Public Law: The Globalization of Intellectual Property Rights*. Cambridge: Cambridge University Press.

Sikkink, Kathryn. 2005. "Patterns of Dynamic Multilevel Governance and the Insider–Outsider Coalition." Pp. 151–74 in *Transnational Protest & Global Activism*, edited by D. Della Porta and S. Tarrow. New York: Rowman & Littlefield.

Tarrow, Sidney. 1998. *Power in Movement: Social Movements and Contentious Politics*. Cambridge: Cambridge University Press.

Williamson, John. 1990. "What Washington Means by Policy Reform." Pp. 7–38 in *Latin American Adjustment: How Much Has Happened?*, edited by J. Williamson. Washington, DC: Institute for International Economics.

Chapter 7

Pharmaceutical Intellectual Property Rights Protection and Access to Medicines in Ecuador

State Sovereignty and Transnational Advocacy Networks

Tatiana Andia

Introduction

Ecuador is a relatively small middle-income country with only 13 million inhabitants and a USD4.082 GDP per capita.[1] It has a pharmaceutical market worth USD720 million a year, only 17.5 percent of which is in the hands of domestic pharmaceutical companies (approximately 66 companies); foreign firms control the remaining 82.5 percent.[2] Despite the level of foreign control, Ecuador has a unique history of fighting attempts to increase intellectual property rights (IPRs) protection beyond the standards set by the World Trade Organization (WTO) in the Trade Related Aspects of Intellectual Property Rights (TRIPS) Agreement. Moreover, Ecuador has cleverly used the global intellectual property (IP) system to its own benefit.

Indeed, Ecuador entered the WTO in 1996, relatively soon after the completion of the Uruguay Round, in order to be part of a banana trade dispute pursued by the United States against the EU. In 2000, the country complied with the TRIPS Agreement through the Andean Community Decision 486. But in contrast to Brazil, the Andean countries refused to grant retroactive (pipeline) protection to inventions patented elsewhere. Furthermore, unlike Chile, Colombia, and Central America, Ecuador has not signed a free trade agreement with the United States or the EU, and has never agreed to protect test data submitted for marketing approval (so-called data exclusivity protection). Additionally, Ecuador was the first country to use the WTO dispute settlement in an innovative way: in 1999, it used noncompliance with intellectual property standards to cross-retaliate against the EU's excessive duties on banana imports. Similarly, ten years later in 2010, Ecuador formulated a compulsory license decree that allows the country to import or produce generic versions of patented drugs that are of public interest.

[1] Ecuador Central Bank, Economic Data, June 2011 (data in current USD).
[2] Intercontinental Marketing Services—IMS 2009 Report.

How has Ecuador been able to advance such an unorthodox IP agenda? This chapter will suggest that the unique Ecuadorian response to the expansion of the global intellectual property regime correlates with a persistent and strong conviction regarding state sovereignty and autonomy from foreign influences.[3] Various domestic groups have nurtured this sense of sovereignty throughout different historical moments. But somewhat paradoxically, some of those local actors have been linked to and nurtured by transnational advocacy networks (TAN) (Keck and Sikkink 1998).[4] More concretely, I argue that there have been two types of sovereignty discourses that have influenced IP policies: one tied to maintaining the country's productive capacity—and diversifying its economic base by protecting industry and promoting agricultural exports—and another tied to assuring access to medicines and access to health.

The first type of rhetoric was supported by the domestic pharmaceutical industry and by the domestic banana producers and was prevalent in the 1990s and early 2000s. That was when Ecuador entered the WTO to improve the conditions for the exportation of bananas; when it subscribed to a series of IP decisions of the Commission of the Andean Community that kept all flexibilities available; and when it used IP to cross-retaliate against the EU. Here, alliances with other international producers were key to the development of these strategies; more in the case of pharmaceuticals, where the local industry was weak, than in the case of bananas, where Ecuador produces 8 percent of the total banana supply in the world and has a 29 percent share of the world's banana exports.[5]

The second type of rhetoric—access to medicines and health—has been supported by human rights groups and indigenous movements and has been more prevalent since the mid-2000s. This was when Ecuador refused to sign bilateral trade agreements first with the United States and then with the EU, and when it issued its first compulsory license. Here, alliances with international human rights and access to health organizations were crucial, particularly to the issuing of the compulsory licenses regulation, less so to the FTA opposition, where indigenous mobilization proved to be the determining factor.

It is nevertheless worth noting that the productive capacity argument was not completely abandoned in the latter period and that the two discourses are considered complementary today. In fact, although the Ecuadorian pharmaceutical industry has not had the technological capacity to produce pharmo-chemicals and that they only compound active principles imported from India and China, almost simultaneously with the issuance of the compulsory licenses decree, Rafael Correa's government created the nationally owned pharmaceutical company ENFARMA. This company,

[3] I am referring here to what Stephen Krasner has called Westphalian sovereignty, "referring to the exclusion of external actors from domestic authority configurations" (Krasner 1999: 9).

[4] Following Keck and Sikkink's definition, a TAN includes those actors that work internationally on the same issue, linked by shared values, a common discourse, and dense exchanges of information and services.

[5] UNCTAD, Market information in the commodities area: <http://www.unctad.org/infocomm/anglais/banana/market.htm>. Also, the Ecuadorian Noboa Group is the fourth largest banana exporter after Chiquita International, Dole Fruit Co., and Del Monte Co. (Smith 2006).

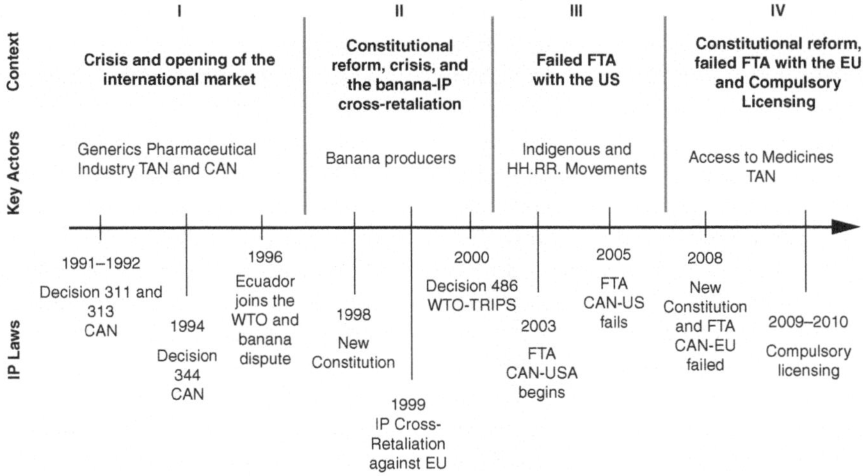

Fig. 7.1 Trajectory of Ecuadorean norms and actors on intellectual property

which was to begin production by the end of 2011, was openly presented by its CEO as "competing against the transnational pharmaceutical companies, to show that medicines are not a traditional commercial product but a health service that should reach every citizen."[6]

This chapter describes each sovereignty discourse and its main domestic supporters and transnational advocacy networks, while going through the episodes of IP regulation chronologically. This research was based on an archival and secondary literature review and approximately thirty interviews undertaken during April 2010 and June 2011 with government officials, representatives of nongovernmental organizations (NGOs), and industry representatives.[7] The questions were formulated so that they would allow me to go beyond the law on the books and identify the political dynamics and the interest groups behind every policy and normative shift. Although the questions largely coincide with the ones undertaken by the other authors in this volume, some of the inquiries were designed specifically for the Ecuadorian case.

As Figure 7.1 illustrates, the chapter is organized in four sections that correspond to four different stages of commercial integration and pharmaceutical regulation: (1) a first stage, in the first part of the 1990s, transitioning from an Import Substitution Industrialization model (ISI) to open competition, where the domestic

[6] Translated from a BBC World interview with Roberto Tadeo, January 2010. The original text says "El mercado con el que vamos a competir es el de las trasnacionales. La idea es que se vea a las medicinas no como una mercancía tradicional, sino como un servicio de salud que llegue a todos los ciudadanos," <http://www.bbc.co.uk/mundo/america_latina/2010/01/100119_0314_ecuador_farmaceutica_jrg.shtml>.

[7] The first set of interviews were undertaken thanks to a project on IP and access to medicines financed by the Pan American Health Organization. It allowed me to visit and research four Andean countries (Bolivia, Colombia, Ecuador, and Peru).

pharmaceutical industry played an important role; (2) a second stage, at the end of the 90s and the beginning of the 2000s, of failed attempts at deepening a commercial integration model, where the banana producers were the key to Ecuador's strategy at the WTO; (3) a third stage, in the mid-2000s, when indigenous mobilization was at the center of Ecuador's refusal to sign a bilateral FTA with the United States; and (4) a fourth stage, in the second half of the 2000s, of transition to a fully-fleshed national sovereignty model in which transnational access to health activists was crucial to the accomplishment of the Correa government goals.

The chapter concludes with a discussion section in which I consider the role of certain transnational advocacy networks. I develop the thesis that although Ecuador was a very unstable country, both politically and economically, during the 1990s and early 2000s, it has had a tradition of autonomy and sovereignty with regard to foreign trade policy and IP policy that is unusual for a small middle-income country. I nevertheless point out that the success of Ecuador's trade and IP policies and their positive effects on reducing the country's inequality depend on the nation's ability to make the most of the opportunities created in the international arena, particularly its capacity to distribute the benefits of globalization down to the most vulnerable population. The latter is not a given: in the late 1990s, a controversy over the low salaries and poor labor standards guaranteed by banana exporters suggested that the improvement in trade conditions that followed the "banana wars" did not benefit the poorest rural workers, but was instead appropriated by Grupo Noboa and other big exporting companies. Similarly, if the compulsory licensing policy introduced in 2009 is not supplemented by the massive purchase of cheaper compulsorily-licensed pharmaceuticals, it too will not have the positive effect on access to health that the government envisions.

I. The 1990s: Crisis and the Opening of the Global Market

The start of the 1990s in Ecuador was a period of economic recovery and institutional modernization. As with most Latin American countries, Ecuador had to deal with the consequences of the debt crisis of the eighties and implement structural adjustment reforms imposed by the International Monetary Fund (IMF).[8] The structural adjustment reforms were adopted chiefly during the administrations of Rodrigo Borja (1988–92) and Sixto Durán Ballén (1992–6) and consisted of orienting the Ecuadorian economy to foreign trade, stabilizing macroeconomic variables, and introducing fiscal reforms to limit public expenditure. At the time, oil made up more than 50 percent of the country's export; the increase in international oil prices in the first half of the 1990s, along with the economic measures Ecuador adopted, contributed to economic recovery. This was reflected in a slight increase in the gross domestic product and a decrease in inflation and in the

[8] This was in exchange for the restructuring of foreign debt, which in Ecuador's case reduced the debt load by more than 45 percent.

national deficit. However, the extremely high value of external debt barred a more complete economic recovery.

A. Intellectual Property Rights in the Andean Community of Nations

In precisely this period, Ecuador also began trade negotiations through the Andean Community of Nations (CAN): it relaxed tariffs with neighboring countries and began transitioning to an open international marketplace. With respect to intellectual property, in 1991 the Andean countries had signed CAN Decision 311, in which each country pledged to strengthen IPRs. In 1992, Decision 311 paved the way for Decision 213 on Industrial Property, and the immediate adoption of measures to protect IPRs, including the extension of patent protection to utility models and pharmaceutical products and increased trademark protection for brand names. In 1994, Andean member states signed a new agreement, replacing Decision 313 with Decision 344, which modified some policies, especially in reference to the patenting of plants. Decisions 313 and 344, however, also included ample flexibilities in regard to IPR protection. In particular, they permitted each country to grant compulsory licenses[9] and permitted the use of inventions before patent expiration for the manufacture of a competing generic (early-working). These Decisions did not provide for retroactive patents (pipeline patents) nor for patents on a new use for inventions that had been previously patented (second use patents).

These events all occurred before Ecuador joined the WTO on January 21, 1996, and thus before it signed the TRIPS Agreement. The accelerated pace with which Ecuador and its Andean partners pledged to protect IPR corresponds in large measure to the commercial pressures exercised by American businesses and by the United States government though the United States Trade Representative (USTR). Their involvement in Andean policy is illustrated, in part, by the fact that some countries from the region—Colombia in particular—were placed on the USTR Watch List starting in the 80s.[10] Indeed, despite Decision 313 in 1992 and Decision 344 in 1994, American business leaders continued to express concern over the weak protection of IPRs in the region (Stewart 1999).[11]

B. Resisting Pressures to Expand IPR Protection: Industrial Associations and CAN

In the middle of the economic vulnerability and political instability that characterized Ecuador during almost all of the 1990s, domestic resistance to pressures to expand IPR protection was relatively weak. What resistance there was, particularly

[9] Article 42 of Decision 313 and 46 of Decision 344 contemplated the grant of compulsory licenses for the public interest.

[10] For a description of the USTR's Watch List procedure, see Dreyfuss and Rodríguez-Garavito, Chapter 1 in this volume.

[11] "Intellectual Property in Andean Accord Worries US Industry, USTR Official Says." 10 Intl. Trade Rep. (BNA) No. 10, at 426 (March 10, 1993).

in the context of Andean community negotiations, was led by pharmaceutical manufacturing associations in each country, whose relative importance with respect to transnational companies was minimal. In effect, until 2000, more than 80 percent of the medicines consumed in Ecuador were imported and only eight transnational companies dominated more than 40 percent of the total pharmaceutical market (OPS 2000). Consequently, more important than the relative strength of the Ecuadorian manufacturing sector is the fact that domestic producers were organized into guilds, and these guilds were coordinated with those of other countries in a TAN. In fact, ALAFAR—the Ecuadorian Association of Pharmaceutical Laboratories—belonged to the Latin American Association of Pharmaceutical Industries, ALIFAR, together with Bolivian, Colombian, Peruvian, and Venezuelan associations.[12]

ALIFAR was created in November 1980 and comprised pharmaceutical business unions in Argentina, Brazil, Bolivia, Chile, Colombia, Costa Rica, Ecuador, El Salvador, Guatemala, Mexico, Paraguay, Peru, the Dominican Republic, Uruguay, and Venezuela. Its creation was a strategy by Latin American national pharmaceutical businesses to confront challenges posed by the globalization of the market and the sophisticated international organization of transnational manufacturers. In particular, ALIFAR's concern has always been the risk posed by the "particular triangular relationship amongst transnational corporations (herein TNCs), national governments, and international organizations" (White 1983). The position of the Andean pharmaceutical industry was defined and defended within and through this Latin American alliance.[13] The alliance highlighted the importance of strengthening national industrial capacity and maintaining each country's sovereignty. Its positions were expressed by domestic pharmaceutical producers to their respective governments. ALIFAR has remained active and consistent in its discourse; as ALIFAR's then-president Manuel Izaga put it to the organization's 2004 XXV Annual Assembly:

> The governments in the region have to support the pharmaceutical industry and ensure its competitive development. The industry only asks for clear, balanced and stable intellectual property norms. The pharmaceutical industry is a strategic productive activity that can lead to the economic and social development of Latin America. The industry fosters development more broadly because it mobilizes internal capital; it generates and maintains formal skilled and well paid jobs; and it offers medicines of excellent quality at cheaper prices, facilitating access to them.[14]

[12] The Bolivian Pharmaceutical Industry Chamber—CIFABOL in Spanish; Association of Colombian Pharmaceutical Industries—ASINFAR in Spanish; Peru's Association of National Pharmaceutical Industries—ADIFAN in Spanish; and the Venezuelan Pharmaceutical Industry Chamber—CIFAR in Spanish.

[13] Interview with Alberto Bravo, president of ASINFAR. August 3, 2010.

[14] ALIFAR XXV Annual Assembly, Recife—Brazil, May 18–21, 2004. Original text in Spanish: "Los Gobiernos de la Región deben apoyar a la industria y asegurar su desarrollo competitivo. La industria sólo solicita reglas de Propiedad Intelectual claras, equilibradas y estables en el tiempo. La Industria Farmacéutica es una actividad productiva estratégica en el desarrollo económico y social de Latinoamérica. La industria impulsa el desarrollo en general, pues moviliza los recursos internos disponibles, mantiene y genera fuentes de empleo especializado y adecuadamente remunerado y oferta

The results of ALIFAR's campaign in the Andean region were mixed: in effect, CAN began to award pharmaceutical patents much earlier than necessary, in 1991—in contrast, the deadline established by TRIPS was 2000—but it was able to preserve several flexibilities that other South American countries lost.[15]

Nevertheless, not too much later, Ecuador proved to be less able to resist US pressures to expand IPR protection than its Andean counterparts. Although CAN member states had agreed not to grant pipeline patents[16]—clarifying that for an invention to be patentable its priority date could not precede the date of the regional patent request,[17] Ecuador did not comply with the Andean pact on this matter. On October 15, 1993, Ecuador signed a bilateral trade agreement with the United States that committed it to the granting of retroactive patents. While the Ecuadorian Congress never ratified the agreement, President Durán Ballén signed a decree (Decree 1344-A of 1993) to implement the pact directly and the government proceeded to grant a total of twenty-three retroactive patents (Salazar Manrique 1998).

Ecuadorian local pharmaceutical companies reacted to this open violation of the Andean norm and brought suit with the Ecuadorian National Council, which in turn forwarded the case to the Court of Justice of the Andean Community. The Andean Court decided in favor of the plaintiffs but the Ecuadorian government did not adhere to the judgment and the Decree remained in force[18] (Helfer, Alter, and Guerzovich 2009). On October 30, 1996 a second suit was filed: the Secretary General of CAN brought an action against the Ecuadorian Ministry of Foreign Relations, Trade, and the Attorney General of the state for non-compliance with the Andean norm, and demanded that Decree 1344-A and its modifications be repealed.[19] The Andean Court decided in favor of the Secretary General, and this time the Ecuadorean government complied with the decision and repealed the decree. As a result, Ecuador denied 120 pipeline patents whose evaluation was already in progress (Helfer, Alter, and Guerzovich 2009). As expected, in 1997 Ecuador was included on the USTR Priority Watch List.[20] The USTR alleged that Ecuador had not complied with the TRIPS Agreement, and did not give national protection to the pharmaceuticals patented by American businesses. Significantly, this occurred in spite of the fact that the TRIPS compliance period for developing countries had yet to expire.

medicamentos de óptima calidad a menor precio, facilitando el acceso de los hospitales estatales y de la población, a los medicamentos" (<www.cifar.org.ve/boletines/2004/especial_alifar.htm>).

[15] For example, in contrast to the Andean countries, Brazil, Mexico, and Uruguay agreed to issue retroactive (pipeline) patents.

[16] As is clearly stated in the Decisions 311 of 1991, 313 of 1992, and 344 of 1994.

[17] This means that if the invention were prior to the Andean norm, it was not eligible for regional protection. The expectation was included in article 2 (on novelty) of Decision 344 in 1994 and similarly in prior Decisions: "For effects of novelty alone, within the state of technology, the content of a request for patenting in proceedings with the competent national body whose date of presentation or priority is prior to the date of request for patent examination shall be considered, whenever that content has been divulged" (Dec. 344 1994).

[18] Case 39-IP-98 (March 26, 1999). [19] Case 1-AI-96 (October 30, 1996).

[20] Press Release from April 30, 1997 (97-37), Office of the United States Trade Representative (Salazar Manrique 1998).

If not for CAN, Ecuador would probably not have been able to resist American pressures, especially in the context of the economic and political crisis in which it found itself in the first part of the 1990s. As we will see shortly, the importance of CAN and of the domestic pharmaceutical producers TAN changed considerably at the end of the 1990s.

II. The End of the 1990s and the Beginning of the 2000s: Constitutional Reform, Crisis, and the Banana Wars

The years following the first CAN IP agreements in Ecuador where characterized by great political and economic instability. In the span of only four years, between 1996 and 2000, the country suffered two presidential resignations (one from Abdalá Bucaram in 1997 and the other from Jamil Mahuad in 2000), in the middle of a profound economic crisis. Notably, the resignation of President Abdalá Bucaram was prompted by a massive indigenous protest led by the Confederation of Indigenous Nationalities of Ecuador, CONAIE in Spanish, an organization comprising 80 percent of the Ecuadorian indigenous population. In 1998, during the interim government of Fabián Alarcón, Ecuador undertook a constitutional reform for the purpose of stabilizing the country politically and economically, and to legitimate the state. The Constitution tried to reduce the risk of hyperinflation and stabilize the country macroeconomically by providing, among other measures, for the independence of the Central Bank from government interference. It also included several articles oriented toward Ecuador's economic integration with the rest of the world.

However, and in spite of external pressures from the Interamerican Development Bank (IDB) and the IMF to implement neoliberal reforms and limit the state's intervention in the economy, the Constitution preserved room for the implementation of welfare policies, including some in the health arena. Thus, the 1998 Constitution recognized the right to health and linked it to food security, the provision of drinking water, and basic sanitation, as well as to other environmental factors. Additionally, the Constitution guaranteed access to permanent uninterrupted healthcare services, in accordance with principles of equality, universality, solidarity, quality, and efficiency, provided at no cost by the state (arts. 42 and 43, 1998 Political Constitution of the Republic of Ecuador). The final text also reflects the influence of the Ecuadorian indigenous movement that participated actively in the Constitutional Assembly. Among the notable health reforms, and related to the IP provisions that would later be adopted by the 2008 Constitution, the State pledged to recognize, respect, and promote "the development of traditional and alternative medicines, whose use will be regulated by law and will foster scientific and technological advances in health care, under bio-ethical principles" (art. 44, Republic of Ecuador Policy of 1998).

It is during this period that the Ecuadorian indigenous movement was consolidated and legitimized as one of the main political powers in the country and as a front of resistance to the imposition of foreign neoliberal policies (Andolina 2003).

But the implementation embodied in the Constitution was cut short by Jamil Mahuad, elected president in 1998. While Ecuador was still paying its external debt to the IMF, and despite the fact that the debt had been recently refinanced, Mahuad faced the worst financial crisis in Ecuadorian history. Sixteen banks—out of a total of forty—went under. Their bankruptcy generated a general mistrust of the banking system as a foundation for the sucre, the national currency (Jácome 2004). Mahuad's response to the crisis consisted of freezing bank deposits, which successively brought on a social crisis of similar proportions to the Argentine crisis of 2001. In 2000, the per capita GDP fell 36 percent compared to 1997, reaching levels similar to those of 1977; public debt rose to 128.4 percent of the GDP, and inflation reached levels near 96 percent (Gerlach 2003). Confronted with the weakness of the Ecuadorian sucre and hyperinflation, by January 2000, Mahuad had opted for the dollarization of the economy.

Shortly thereafter, the indigenous masses, which were aligned with the military, marched in Quito and occupied the Supreme Court. Mahuad was deposed in the midst of a corruption scandal and replaced by an interim government headed by Colonel Lucio Gutierrez and the director of CONAIE, Antonio Vargas. However, after multiple consultations, the military government reestablished constitutional order and announced that Vice President Gustavo Noboa would become interim president (Zamosc 2007).

A. Healthcare and Access to Medicine in the Midst of the Crisis

Unsurprisingly, healthcare worsened during the economic crisis. Public health expenditure fell to 1.1 percent of GDP in 1995, and to 0.55 percent in 1999. In 2000 the prevalence of malnutrition in children below five years of age was greater than 40 percent, around 30 percent of the Ecuadorian population had no access to institutional health services, and three-fourths of the population did not have any social security protection (OPS 2000). However, despite the crisis Ecuador encouraged national practices to promote generic medicines. The fundamental policies focused on guaranteeing availability, access, quality, rational use, and lower pharmaceutical prices. Law 12 of 2000, "Production, Importation, Marketing, and Sale of Medicines for Human Use," established norms geared towards expanding the generics' market, promoting domestic pharmaceutical production and facilitating marketing approval through "standardized" procedures for imported products (OPS 2000).

Political instability led to an unfortunate delay of Law 12's implementation. Additionally, pharmaceutical regulatory policies in Ecuador have long struggled with the division of functions between the National Hygiene Institute (INH, in Spanish)—called Instituto Izquieta Perez and located in Guayaquil—in charge of granting marketing approval and quality control, and the Sanitary Control and Improvement Unit within the Ministry of Health in Quito, in charge of all other pharmaceutical regulatory policies.[21] The original division of labor was based on

[21] This sanitary unit has the following responsibilities: regulation (norms), technical evaluation, pharmacovigilance, counterfeiting controls, publicity regulation, and prices controls (Questionaire

geography. Although every government body is located in Quito, the majority of Ecuadorian industries are located in Guayaquil, the port city where imports and exports are made. For this reason, in addition to the regional disputes that have characterized the two cities, pharmaceutical marketing approval has been historically separated and administered with foreseeable inter-institutional coordination difficulties.[22]

Additionally, the INH was founded in the 1930s as a research institution for hygiene and tropical medicine with no other pharmaceutical regulatory capacity other than processing marketing approval applications. Since it continues to function only in this way even in 2010, the Institution still lacks the physical infrastructure necessary to accommodate files and records, and the human resources necessary for processing requests in reasonable timeframes. Nor has the post-registration process[23] been consolidated, meaning that quality control occurs solely at the moment of registration.[24]

B. Using Intellectual Property for Banana Exports

Despite the financial and institutional crisis that hit Ecuador at the turn of the century, toward the end of period, Ecuador was the protagonist in an unprecedented multilateral trade episode within the WTO. In November 8, 1999 Ecuador submitted the first request of "cross-retaliation"[25] in order to suspend its intellectual property obligations to the EU, which were valued at USD450 million. This episode was part of an extended dispute over banana trade—commonly known as the "banana wars"—that started in 1993, when the EU's regulation of banana imports gave preferential entry to bananas from overseas territories, and former colonies, of EU member countries. The regime strongly discriminated against Latin America and the United States. Accordingly, several countries, including Colombia, Costa Rica, Nicaragua, and Venezuela, opted to sign an agreement that would reduce in-quota tariffs (the tariffs the EU would levy on bananas produced in these countries) by about 10 percent.

The United States took a different tack. Once the WTO was in place, it initiated a complaint against the EU banana regime and sought the support of other Latin American banana exporters that had not signed the framework agreement with the EU. Ecuador entered the WTO in 1996 to be able to join these proceedings, which by then had the support of Guatemala, Honduras, and Mexico. However, as

answered by Lorena Ruiz Abril for the Organization of Iberoamerican Pharmaceutical Officials: <http://www.portaleami.org/directAutorid/home.htm>.

22 Interview with Victor Arauz, Medicine Advisor PAHO Ecuador, April 21, 2010.

23 Post-registration is the process by which random samples of the medication are taken from the market for quality control purposes.

24 Interview with Eduardo Sandoval, National Director of the INH, April 21, 2010.

25 The phrase "cross-retaliation" does not appear in the Dispute Settlement Understanding, but is shorthand to describe a situation where the complaining country retaliates (i.e. suspends concessions or other obligations) under a sector or an agreement which has not been violated by the defending country, see Dispute Settlement Understanding, art. 22.3(c).

described by James McCall Smith (2006), Ecuador negotiators were careful to maintain their independence. First, they did not rush to retaliate at the same time as the United States.[26] Instead, Ecuador decided to wait until the WTO panel ruled on the legality of the EU regulations. Then, when the EU and the United States reached an agreement in 2001, Ecuador rejected it and demanded important modifications.

The Ecuadorian negotiators[27] of this period entered a discourse that coincides with what Odell (2000) calls a "distributive strategy" which implies "a set of actions that promote the attainment of one party's goals when they are in conflict with those of the other party" (Odell 2000). In a press release issued by the Ecuadorian embassy in Brussels after the United States retaliated against the EU, then-Ambassador Roberto Betancourt, stated that:

> For Ecuador, a developing country that is highly dependent on banana exports and is a highly efficient producer of bananas, the [EU] regime is commercially harmful and completely inconsistent with the market-oriented philosophy of the WTO and other policies which the EU urges Ecuador and other developing countries to adopt in other contexts... The banana issue is too important to us to leave the solution in the hands of the USA and the EU; and we intend, as responsible WTO partners, to play a full part in developing a solution to this very difficult dispute. Both the US and EU need to recognize that other countries are heavily impacted by the prolonged bilateral "to-ing and fro-ing" that is taking place. While these two giants battle it out, Ecuador, whose industry really is at stake, is being caught in the middle.[28]

Right after Ecuador refused to join the United States in its retaliation against the EU, Ecuador initiated its own retaliation strategy by invoking the possibility of cross-retaliation. Ironically, the cross-retaliation mechanism had been included in the Uruguay Round agreements at the request of a coalition of developed countries, led by the United States. The mechanism was intended to allow these countries to exercise the power they wielded as importers of raw materials: for example, to execute commercial sanctions in response to violations of intellectual property or others norms, even if the matters were not directly related (Breuss, Griller, and Vranes 2003). Thus, the cross-retaliation request pioneered by Ecuador in 1999 was not in the original spirit of the norm. Rather, as it was creatively used in favor of a developing country.

Thus, in an innovative and unprecedented move, Ecuador threatened noncompliance with its IP obligations in order to guarantee that the EU would honor the General Agreement on Tariffs and Trade (GATT) (Odell 2006). The cross-retaliation

[26] The US imposed tariffs of 100 percent on $192 million worth of EU imports into the United States, see <http://www.ustr.gov/releases/1999/01/ban1-14.pdf>.

[27] Trade-related issues were in the hands of three main sets of government officials, the Ministry of External Relations, Heinz Moeller Freile; the Ecuadorian Embassy in Brussels that was in charge of the trade relations with the EU, first occupied by Roberto Betancourt and then by Alfredo Pinoargote Cevallos; and the Permanent Mission in Geneva that represents Ecuador at the WTO, first occupied by Roberto Betancourt and then by Mentor Villagomez.

[28] Ecuadorian Embassy in Brussels Press release, February 2, 1999, as quoted by Reuters and the Third World Network bulletin: <http://www.twnside.org.sg/title/eu-cn.htm>.

focused on industrial design patents, copyrights and related rights, and geographical indications.[29] Because Ecuador had not yet fully complied with TRIPS and its low technological capacity limited its ability to manufacture medicines, the retaliatory strategy did not include pharmaceuticals or other utility patents. Thus, it did nothing to improve the availability of important medicines (Basheer 2009: 163).[30] Commenting on the measure, Ecuador's ambassador Roberto Betancourt said:

> The EU has pushed Ecuador to the limit... It is now over two years since the WTO's Appellate Body ruled that the EU should comply with the WTO rulings... As Ecuador is a developing country, we must now take action both to protect ourselves and send a clear signal that the blatant non-compliance of the EU cannot be allowed to continue.[31]

The design of this strategy is in part explained by the prominence of the banana industry (it accounted for a third of total exports) and its control by domestic companies. But paradoxically, these measures at the WTO were undertaken during a period in which the relationship between the government and the largest producer and exporter of bananas in Ecuador—Alvaro Noboa, owner of Noboa group[32]—had been severely damaged by a political infighting over the domestic regulation of bananas and the role of the Noboa Group's founder, Luis Noboa Naranjo, in the government.

At one time, the relationship between the Noboa Group and the government was very close, particularly during the presidency of Febres Cordero in the late 1980s and until the mid-1990s. Nevertheless, the death of the Noboa Group's founder and leader Luis Noboa Naranjo in 1994 and a nine years long litigation in London, New York, and Guayaquil over his inheritance, gradually debilitated the relations between the government and the business group. Although Alvaro Noboa was a close ally of Abdalá Bucaram's and actively participated in his 1996 campaign, Bucaram's fast political decline motivated Noboa to become a presidential candidate. He tried three times: 1998, 2002, and 2006, losing all three times (the first time to Jamil Mahuad, the second to Lucio Gutierrez, and the third to Rafael Correa). From the end of Abdalá Bucaram's government the Grupo Noboa—110 companies constituting the largest domestic corporate conglomerate in Ecuador[33]—has been in opposition to the Ecuadorian official banana policy, especially policies aimed at guaranteeing that the benefits from international trade trickled down to the producers.[34]

[29] See TRIPS, Section 1 (copyright and related rights); art. 14 on the protection of performers, producers of phonograms, and broadcasting organizations), Section 3 (geographical indications), and Section 4 (industrial designs).

[30] Basheer explores the possibility of using cross-retaliation as a strategy for industrial policy but acknowledges that there is a tension regarding countries' "technology proficiency." He says: "The cross-retaliation tool may prove a stronger one in the hands of technologically proficient developing countries" (Basheer 2009: 176).

[31] Europolitics reported on Saturday November 20, 1999: <http://www.europolitics.info/eu-ecuador-wto-panel-set-up-on-euro-435-million-banana-claim-artr149569-44.html>.

[32] The Noboa Group is known for its Bonita brand, under which it markets other fruit products as well as bananas.

[33] The group is involved in agriculture, commodity trading, banking, mining, and sea transport, among other sectors.

[34] Both Jamil Mahuad (1999–2000) and Lucio Gutierrez (2003–5) nominated Salomón Larrea as the Ministry of Agriculture. Larrea is a banana producer himself who had previously worked as

However, despite the lack of support from the Noboa Group, the Ecuadorian independent trade strategy was supported by the National Banana Council (Conaban, in Spanish)—an association that represents domestic banana producers. Conaban backed the Ecuadorian negotiators' decision to reject the US strategy and opt instead to bargain independently. On February 1999, the president of Conaban, Enrique Gomez stated that: "the United States was not interested in Ecuador taking this matter to the WTO Dispute Settlement Board . . . but this issue should remain in the WTO arena."[35]

On May 18, 2000, the WTO Dispute Settlement Board (DSB) authorized Ecuador to suspend concessions to the EU, as it had requested. Later that year, the EU gave in to Ecuador's threat.[36] This action constituted Ecuador's first victory in the banana dispute and the first time that multilateral rules on intellectual property were used in a manner that favored a developing country. Fortified by its success, Ecuador pushed for better conditions and during the Doha Round of WTO negotiations, proposed the creation of a special ad hoc arbitration procedure for bananas (Smith 2006).

Although victory in the banana wars did not change the impact of the global system on access to medicine, the episode helped Ecuador understand international global trade and the intellectual property system, and made it see how these regimes could be used as tools for furthering national interests. This understanding informed its later behavior.

C. Complying with the TRIPS Agreement

Simultaneously with the banana dispute, Ecuador had, together with its Andean counterparts, embarked on the path toward multilateral economic integration with regard to intellectual property protection. In 2000, the Andean countries signed CAN Decision 486, which replaced the previous Decision 344 and conformed Andean norms to the TRIPS Agreement.

Among the modifications to Decision 344 made by Decision 486 in 2000, the ones on what is considered "non patentable material"[37] are especially significant (Table 7.1). While in 1994 "inventions relative to pharmaceutical products on the

manager of the Noboa Banana Exporting Company and as representative of Chiquita Brand. Despite the fact that Larrea was close to the Noboa Group, he introduced an internal banana pricing policy by which the government is allowed to establish a fixed price for the banana box that the exporter should pay to the producer; the policy also limited the hectares that can be cultivated so that overproduction does not jeopardize prices. In June 1999 the government defined a USD2.6 per box but the exporters never agreed on it and failed to comply with it. "Banano: hay precio pero no acuerdo." *El Comercio*, June 9, 1999.

[35] Banana dispute extended, February 4, 1999. *Hoy* journal. <http://www.hoy.com.ec/wphoy-imprimir.php?id=104858>.

[36] According to the CRS Report to Congress, December 2001, Ecuador got "additional market share through the 'newcomer category.' Rules for administering the newcomer category appear to give Ecuador a substantial share, especially of organic bananas, of that category" (Hanrahan 2001: 5).

[37] Art. 7 of Decision 344 and art. 20 of Decision 486.

Table 7.1 Comparison between intellectual property decisions "nonpatentable material"

Decision 344 in 1994 (CAN)	Decision 486 of 2000 (TRIPS)
a) Inventions against the public order, moral or proper traditions;	a) Inventions marketing of which in the member state territory must be prevented to protect public or moral order. *For these purposes, marketing of an invention will not be considered against public or moral order only because of a legal or administrative provision prohibiting its marketing*;
b) Inventions obviously against health or life of people or animals; preservation of plants; or preservation of the environment;	b) Inventions marketing of which in the member state territory must be prevented to protect the health or life of animals, or to preserve plans or the environment. *For these purposes, marketing of an invention will not be considered against the health or life of people, animals, or the preservation of plants or the environment only because of a legal or administrative provision prohibiting its marketing*;
c) Species, animal races, and essentially biological processes;	c) Plants, animals, and essentially biological processes for production of plants and animals, *that are not biological or microbiological*;
d) Inventions concerning components of the human body and genetic identity; and,	d) Therapeutic or surgical techniques for human or animal treatment, as well as diagnostic techniques applied to human beings or animals.[a]
e) Inventions relative to pharmaceutical products on the World Health Organization's list of essential medicines.	

[a] It is important to clarify that in Decision 344, surgical and therapeutic methods were not only unpatentable, but were, under Article 6, "not considered inventions."

Note: emphasis added in italics.

World Health Organization's essential medicines list" were excluded from patent protection, this exception completely disappeared in the 2000 Decision.

Although Decision 486 fully complied with TRIPS (and did not even allow for a "Bolar exception"[38]), it also used certain of flexibilities provided for by the Agreement. In effect, according to Oliveira et al., in 2004 only CAN member states, together with the Dominican Republic, Argentina, Honduras, and Panama, retained TRIPS flexibility with respect to parallel imports in Latin America. Additionally, the Andean community countries established the possibility of using unrestricted compulsory licensing in public interest cases; only Brazil and Argentina, however, asserted the right to compulsorily license when the patent owner failed to manufacture locally (Oliveira et al. 2004).

[38] The "Bolar" exception permits patented material to be used before the patent's expiration for the purpose of preparing for a generic's immediate market release upon the original's patent expiration.

III. The Mid-2000s: The FTA with the United States and Indigenous and Activist Protests over Healthcare

Gustavo Noboa's interim administration initiated a second round of discussions with the IMF to renegotiate its external debt. Noboa also stabilized the economy, and held elections in 2003, in which General Lucio Gutierrez, one of the protagonists of the rebellion against Mahuad, was popularly elected. Gutierrez's victory was a result of the coalition between CONAIE and the Movimiento de Unidad Plurinacional Pachakutik-Nuevo País-MUPP-NP party.

Upon assuming the presidency, and in spite of having portrayed himself as a populist candidate during the election, Gutierrez began to suggest austerity measures and the implementation of the reforms suggested by the IMF. This neoliberal shift in the administration offended the indigenous movement that had helped Gutierrez reach power. Six months after he assumed the presidency, CONAIE withdrew its support and indigenous party ministers renounced their cabinet positions. The indigenous movement attempted to organize protests against Gutierrez, but an internal division arose between indigenous peoples of the highlands and the Amazon (which supported the administration) and the protest was unsuccessful. However, in 2005 students and the Quito middle class initiated new protests. This time, Lucio Gutierrez was forced to step down (Zamosc 2007).

Free trade negotiations between the United States and CAN had, however, been initiated during Lucio Gutierrez's presidency. In November 2003 George Bush's administration notified the United States Congress of its intention to begin trade agreement negotiations with the Andean countries.[39] The first round of negotiations between the United States and the Andean bloc (Colombia, Ecuador, and Peru, with Bolivia as an observer) took place in Cartagena, Colombia, in May 2004. Twelve additional rounds were held afterwards,[40] but not without significant obstacles. On April 20, 2005, during the ninth round of negotiations, the Ecuadorian Congress dismissed President Lucio Gutierrez, replacing him with Vice President Alfredo Palacio; additionally, in what should have been the definitive round in Washington in November 2005, Ecuador and Colombia withdrew from negotiations because of problems with terms in the chapter on intellectual property and agricultural tariffs (Villarreal 2006).

From the beginning of the negotiations, the United States had been interested in strengthening intellectual property norms in the Andean region. It had six key demands: (1) five-year protection for testing data for pharmaceutical inventions; (2) linkage between the patents office and the ministry of health to prevent marketing

[39] USTR, "USTR Notifies Congress of Intent to Initiate Free Trade Talks with Andean Countries." Press Release. November 18, 2003.

[40] Cartagena (May 18–19, 2004); Atlanta (June 18, 2004); Lima, Peru (July 26–30, 2004); San Juan (September 13–17, 2004); Guayaquil, Ecuador (October 25–9, 2004); Tucson (November 20–December 4, 2004); Cartegena (February 7–11, 2005); Washington (March 14–18, 2005); Lima (April 18–22, 2005); Guayaquil (June 6–10, 2005); Miami (July 18–22, 2005); Cartagena (September 19–23, 2005); Washington (November 14–22, 2005).

approval for a generic product that violated patent law; (3) compensation, in the form of additional years of protection, for delays in the patent-granting process; (4) limitations on parallel imports; (5) protection of second use patents; and (6) patent recognition for genetic resources and certain vegetal varieties. In addition, the association of American pharmaceutical researchers and manufacturers, PhRMA, was concerned because Peru and Ecuador[41] had not developed norms for the protection of testing data (data exclusivity).[42] Accordingly, it was pressuring the US government to eliminate the tariff preferences it had provided to the Andean region in the Andean Trade Promotion and Drug Eradication Act (ATPDEA) (Villarreal 2006).

Confronted with the American demands, the Andean countries' negotiation team managed to draw some "red lines" around intellectual property, including limits concerning what could be negotiated. In general, they insisted that the terms of any agreement would not surpass internal Andean agreements or then current national norms. For example, in the Ecuadorian case, the red line consisted in not ceding to any of the American demands mentioned above. In November 2005, during the last round of negotiations in Washington DC, the US government unexpectedly replaced its negotiation team. The new negotiation chief attempted to ignore all previous negotations and restart the discussions on intellectual property from ground zero.[43] As a result, both Colombia and Ecuador decided to suspend negotiations until 2006. Peru, on the other hand, concluded negotiations and signed the agreement in December of 2005.

Colombia and Ecuador reinitiated negotiation at the beginning of 2006, and Colombia signed a definitive agreement in February 2006 (although as of the conclusion of the study (2011), it had yet to be ratified by the US Congress).[44] In Ecuador's case, the new discussions led to indigenous protests and blockades organized by CONAIE and supported by the Quito student movement. These grew to extraordinary proportions. Marchers occupied the Quito Cathedral and demanded that the FTA between Ecuador and the United States be submitted to popular vote; they also demanded annulment of a contract permitting excavations by an American oil company that had been contested in courts for several years. In a release to the Ecuadorian government CONAIE declared:

> We have anxiously observed how the transitional administration of Dr. Alfredo Palacio, in violation of the commitment made when assuming power in April of the past year, has continued the same policies of ex President Lucio Gutiérrez, handing over natural resources, especially water and oil, to transnational corporations... prejudicing national sovereignty and putting the country on a one-way path to a Free Trade Agreement with the United States.[45]

[41] Colombia had already ceded to the same pressures from the pharmaceutical industry in 2002 when it issued Decree 2085, which awarded protection of testing data for five years to new chemical entities registered with the National Institute of Medicine and Food Safety—INVIMA in Spanish.

[42] USTR, 2004 "National Trade Estimate Report on Foreign Trade Barriers" (p. 98).

[43] Interview with Luis Guillermo Restrepo, Colombian negotiator, February 8, 2010.

[44] For further information on Colombia, see César Rodríguez-Garavito's chapter in this volume.

[45] Delivered and signed in Quito, March 13, 2006, by Luis Macas, President of CONAIE.

COANIE's protests were joined by health experts concerned about the consequences that an eventual FTA with the United States would have for access to healthcare. In an open letter dated March 23, 2006, principal ex-ministers of health and representatives of human rights organizations, alleging weaknesses with the Ecuadorian negotiation team, demanded of President Alfredo Palacio:

> For no reason and under no pressure or context should you exceed, in an international negotiation the RED LINES in INTELLECTUAL PROPERTY previously established as a national commitment in several official documents which we fully support.[46]

Together with recommendations from Ecuadorian experts and human rights activists, international organizations in support of access to medicine—in particular, the Consumer Project on Technology (now Knowledge Ecology International, KEI), Médecins Sans Frontières, Health Action International, Oxfam, Treatment Action Campaign, Act Up Paris, and the Health Gap Coalition—issued releases criticizing the FTAs between the United States and Latin American countries. Some organizations based in the United States, including especially Public Citizen, sent similar statements directly to the American Congress (Castro and Westerhaus 2007).

Indigenous and civil society mobilization prevented the government from signing the agreement, and a state of emergency was declared in eight provinces in March 2006. Additionally, on May 15, 2006, the Minister of Energy, Ivan Rodriguez, announced that the oil exploration and excavation contract signed with the American company Occidental Petroleum, Oxy, would be cancelled. The minister stated that the decision was based on illegal operations undertaken by the company, including the unauthorized sale of 40 percent of the operation to the Canadian company, Encana.[47] In response, the Bush administration decided in turn to cancel trade negotiations. The USTR spokesperson, Neena Moorjani, stated that:

> for a country to attract investment, and certainly to be a prospective FTA partner of the United States, it must obey the rule of law with respect to foreign investors.[48]

As a result, Ecuador did not conclude the trade agreement with the United States and thus never acquiesced to any "TRIPS-plus" measure—that is, to any requirement surpassing those imposed by the TRIPS Agreement and implemented in CAN Decision 486 of 2000. However, the split among Peru, Colombia, Ecuador, and Bolivia that occurred during the Andean negotiations with the United States would bring consequences in subsequent dealings with the EU, and led to a general weakening of the Andean Community. Peru and Colombia had already assumed a different approach from that of Bolivia and Ecuador.

Given that Colombia and Peru had signed agreements with the United States that included data exclusivity clauses, a modification of the Andean norm was needed to accommodate this development. As described by Helfer et al. (2009),

46 "The FTA and Health." Open Letter to the President of the Republic, Quito, March 23, 2006: <http://www.cptech.org/ip/health/trade/andean/ecuadorletter03232006.html>.

47 WorldPress Article, June 4, 2006: <http://www.worldpress.org/Americas/2371.cfm>.

48 The Associated Press, Washington, May 18, 2006: <http://www.corpwatch.org/article.php?id=13586>.

several meetings were held to discuss this matter and all of them failed. However, there was a meeting scheduled for April 2006 in which neither Venezuela nor Bolivia could vote because they had not paid their dues. At that meeting, an agreement was reached among the remaining members and Decision 632—which provides that each member may choose the means to protect test data—was finally approved. The fact that this agreement was passed with the votes of only three members precipitated Venezuela's withdrawal from CAN and produced discomfort in the Bolivian government (Helfer et al. 2009: 18).

IV. The Rafael Correa Administration: Constitutional Reform, State Sovereignty, and Transnational Health Activism

On November 26, 2006, in a runoff election, Raphael Correa replaced Alfredo Palacio as president. The singular achievement of Correa's administration is without a doubt the National Constitutional Assembly and the approval of the new Constitution of the Republic of Ecuador in 2008. Despite the fact that his term was set to end in 2010, the new constitution called for new elections in 2009, in which President Correa was reelected popularly, prolonging his mandate until 2013.

A. Healthcare and Access to Medicine in the Constitution

Regarding healthcare, access to medicine, and intellectual property, the new Ecuadorian Constitution is one of the most specific in the Latin American region. In fact, art. 322 specifically mentions intellectual property rights, clarifying that they are prohibited when related to traditional knowledge and national biodiversity. Furthermore, art. 421 establishes that "the application of international commercial instruments will not impinge upon, directly or indirectly, the right to health care, access to medicine, supplies, services, or scientific and technological advances" (Constitution of the Republic of Ecuador 2008). Additionally, the Constitution makes specific reference to health as "a right guaranteed by the State, whose fulfillment is linked to the exercise of other rights, including the right to water, food, education, physical culture, work, social security, healthy environments, and other rights of a positive quality of life" (art. 32, Constitution of the Republic of Ecuador 2008).

The guarantee of the right to health is the responsibility of the state, though it is recognized that the promise can only be fulfilled progressively. However, within the new constitutional framework, the government was required to quickly begin a process of institutional reform and norm adaptation to the new constitutional mandates. This is an ongoing process, and it has been much slower than expected. For example, under the new Constitution, President Correa created seven coordinating ministries[49] and added five ministries to those that previously existed.[50]

[49] Ministry of Production, Social Development, Strategic Sectors, Politics, Economics, Cultural Patrimony, and Internal and External Security.

[50] Industry, Electricity, Sports, Culture, and Justice.

The coordinating ministries are conceived as entities that, as their name suggests, coordinate the activities of various bodies across intersecting issues. However, the proliferation of ministries has caused boundary problems as well as tensions amongst directors. In the healthcare sector, the coordinating ministry is that of Social Development.[51]

B. Inconclusive Negotiations between Ecuador and the European Union

The negotiation process of the Association Agreement between CAN and the EU began in 2007. The Europeans sought the same intellectual property concessions as the United States, but expanded on them with three additional points: (1) patenting of genetic resources and plants; (2) increase in data protection from five to ten years; and (3) strengthening commitments to enforce intellectual property rights.

Very quickly, the Andean governments disagreed on how far they wanted to go with the talks. Bolivia refused to cede to the Europeans on biodiversity and quickly withdrew from the negotiations; on the contrary, Colombia and Peru manifested their firm commitment to reach an agreement. Faced with these differences, President Correa, as temporary president of CAN, issued a press release on November 11, 2008, ratifying the division of the Andean bloc over the EU bilateral trade negotiations and expressing concern for the negative impact that this could have over the "strengthening of the Andean Community as a regional bloc of integration that has traditionally been an example and promoter of integration processes."[52]

In this same vein, on August 13, 2008, CAN Decision 689 was signed, specifying which provisions each member country could develop and deepen. The Decision once again gave Colombia and Peru sufficient freedom to implement their US FTAs and to negotiate bilaterally with the EU. Bolivia opposed the Decision but was outnumbered by the other three members; since then, it has filed several noncompliance suits with the Andean Court of Justice.

After these disagreements, the Ecuadorian negotiation process with the EU continued, but at a much slower pace than those of Colombia and Peru. And in July 2009, Ecuador interrupted negotiations with the EU over differences concerning the marketing of bananas. When the EU finally promised to reduce banana tariffs in May of 2010, the possibility of renewing negotiations arose. However, the Ecuadorian negotiator, Mentor Villagómez and President Correa have taken the position that negotiations will only be reinstituted if the EU compromises on various issues, including its demands regarding intellectual property.

[51] According to Executive Decree 242 of 2007, the Coordinating Minister of Social Development shall coordinate the policies and efforts of the following institutions: the Ministry of Finance, Ministry of Work and Employment, Ministry of Pubic Health, Ministry of Economic and Social Inclusion, Ministry of Education, Ministry of Urban and Housing Development, Minister of Agriculture, Livestock, Aquaculture and Fishing, the National Secretariat of Planning and Development, and the National Secretariat of Migration.

[52] Press Release #14, CAN. Quito, November 11, 2008.

C. Civil Society for Access to Medicine

In order to better respond to the challenges posed by FTAs negotiations with the EU in the Andean region, Health Action International and several Latin American civil society organizations joined together in 2008 and created the CAN-EU Alliance for Access to Medicines. The alliance was devoted to closely monitoring developments in IP and Public Health in the region, particularly with regards to FTA negotiations, in order to ensure that they did not incorporate measures that would limit access to medicines.

This Alliance has had a major influence on Colombian and Peruvian negotiations with the EU, preventing the considerable expansion of IPRs in both countries. In fact, at a rapid pace, and following the initiative partially implemented by participant organizations during the CAN negotiations with the United States, the Alliance positioned itself as a producer of technical impact studies of trade agreements.[53] Impact studies gave activists concrete, illustrative figures on risks associated with intellectual property and access to medicine.

The CAN-EU Alliance also paved the way for the LAC-EU Alliance, incorporating both Latin American and Caribbean countries, and finally, in 2010, for the LAC-Global Alliance, incorporating KEI, Public Citizen, Brazil-Médecins Sans Frontières, and the Brazilian Working Group on Intellectual Property, REBRIP. As we shall see, these groups furnished useful assistance in subsequent action by Ecuador to increase the supply of priority medicines.

D. Compulsory Licensing and Local Production Promotion

On October 23, 2009, President Correa signed Decree 118, making it possible for the first time in Ecuador and the Andean region to grant compulsory licenses for pharmaceutical patents.[54] According to Peter Maybarduk, Access to Medicines Program Director at Public Citizen, who participated in the process leading up to the issuance of the Decree:

> Since 2007 Ecuador had articulated the need for compulsory licenses. Besides, compulsory licenses are consistent with the National Development Plan and with the Ecuadorian Constitution.[55]

The 2009 Decree did not on its own issue compulsory licenses, but it established the procedures by which the government could subsequently decide, case by case, to use them to increase the supply of priority medicines. According to the Decree, the Ministry of Public Health must take account of public interests and determine

[53] The CAN-EU Alliance produced an impact study of the FTA between CAN and the EU on the medicine markets in Peru and Colombia, based on different possible scenarios of the evolution of negotiations. See AIS, Impact Study on Access to Medicine in the EU FTA.

[54] The Decree cites constitutional principles as well as provisions of the National Development Plan and international agreements, including the WTO TRIPS Agreement and the World Health Assembly Global Strategy and Plan of Action on Public Health, Innovation and Intellectual Property.

[55] Interview with Peter Maybarduk in July 1, 2011.

which medicines should be the object of compulsory licensing; the Intellectual Property Institute of Ecuador (IEPI) is responsible for establishing royalties and the other terms of the licenses.

As described in the English-version press release made on October 26, 2009, the Decree followed public pronouncements by President Correa that articulated a vision of intellectual property as "a mechanism for development for the people." Indeed, President Correa had previously given a speech on a government television program, *Citizen Connection* (*Enlace Ciudadano* in Spanish), in which he emphasized the relationship between right to health and sovereignty, saying:

> ... the subject of intellectual property is tremendously important. What is our vision? When something has been invented or discovered, the more people that use it, the better. For example, a medicine. We're talking about human rights. Do you think it's ethically sustainable that if a cure for cancer is invented, people could continue to die because they don't have the resources to pay? ... Intellectual property is a mechanism for development for the people. This is our vision of intellectual property. It's not a mechanism to enrich the pharmaceutical or agrochemical companies. It's a mechanism for development for the people.[56]

Later, on January 15, 2010, IEPI published an administrative guide on the compulsory licensing of the pharmaceutical patents.[57] This unprecedented step was taken in accordance with the Constitution, Andean intellectual property norms, and TRIPS, in order to "insure universal access to essential medicines and consolidate the authority and sovereignty of the State in the use of medicine and phytotherapeutic resources" (Decree 118 2009). A few months later, IEPI granted the first compulsory license for Kaletra, a product of by Abbott Laboratories, to the Indian pharmaceutical Cipla Ltd and its representative in Ecuador, Eskegroup SA.

Both the Decree and the actual license-granting process benefited from technical advice furnished by international civil society. The national and international activist community working to promote access to medicine considered them significant accomplishments of the Correa administration. On October 12, 2009 several civil society organizations, treatment advocates, development advocates, people living with HIV, and access to medicines movements signed a letter to president Correa to "congratulate Ecuador on its courageous plans to grant compulsory licenses for medical patents".[58] By the same token, after the issuing of the

[56] Partial translation of the clip made by Peter Maybarduk. The complete video is available at <http://www.youtube.com/watch?v=9cnsOctJ0wc>.

[57] It is worth mentioning that the then-director of IEPI, Andrés Ycaza, had been director of the Ecuadorean Association of Pharmaceutical Laboratories—ALFE in Spanish.

[58] The letter was signed by Eurasian Harm Reduction Network; GESTOS Brasil; Lawyers Collective HIV/AIDS Unit India; Health GAP (Global Access Project) USA; Mesa de Organizaciones con Trabajo en VIH/SIDA Colombia; International Treatment Preparedness Coalition Russia; Asia Pacific Network of People Living with HIV/AIDS (APN +); Third World Network; Health Action International Africa; Health Action International Europe; Health Action International Global; Positive Malaysian Treatment Access & Advocacy Group (MTAAG +); BUKO Pharma-Kampagne Germany; Foundation For Consumers (FFC) Thailand; Canadian HIV/AIDS Legal Network; Treatment Action Group USA; Health Care is Not for Commerce LAC; Center for Policy Analysis on Trade and Health (CPATH) USA; American Medical Student Association.

Lopinavir/Ritonavir compulsory license, the LAC-EU alliance issued a statement welcoming the Ecuadorian compulsory licensing policy, stating that:

> Various experts and civil society organisations that came together in a meeting of the Latin American and Caribe and European Alliance for Access to Medicines, positively evaluated the recent measures taken by the Ecuadorian government, through the application of a compulsory license on Kaletra®, (lopinavi/ritonavir) medicines of the treatment of HIV/AIDs.[59]

However, the regulation and compulsory license for Kaletra were not entirely well received by the Ministry of Public Health. To be sure, according to the Organic Health Law (Law 67 of 2006), the health authority must "adopt necessary measures to guarantee, in the event of a medical emergency, access and availability of necessary supplies and medicines for the purpose of confronting the emergency, making use of mechanisms provided in international agreements and treaties and current legislation." Further, the same law orders the Ministry to guarantee "to all persons living with HIV-AIDS specialized care, access and availability of antiretroviral and other medicines for opportunistic infections, with an emphasis on generic medicines." Nonetheless, the Ministry of Public Health was neither a protagonist nor facilitator of the compulsory licensing process managed by IEPI.[60]

Indeed, right after the compulsory license for Lopinavir/Ritonavir was granted, and even though the Eskegroup (Cipla) had competed in the public purchasing bid and offered a 20 to 30 percent discount over Abbott's price, the Ministry of Public Health obstructed the purchase of the medicines and endangering the legitimacy of the compulsory licensing process. Likewise, the transnational pharmaceutical industry association, IFI/Promesa, argued that the compulsory licensing process had been arbitrary, claiming that neither Eskegroup nor IEPI had attempted to obtain a voluntary license from Abbott before resorting to the compulsory license. Further, these transnational industries argued that the license was granted to a company that imported the product from India, defeating the rationale for compulsory licensing, which emphasized the goal of strengthening national production capacity, at least in the final manufacturing process.[61] Indeed, recently analyzed Wikileaks cables showed that some multinational pharmaceutical companies were sharing a strategy with US Embassy officials in Ecuador to limit Ecuador's use of compulsory licenses. The cables go so far as to suggest that US Embassy officials also met some of the companies' "well-placed contacts" in "potentially sympathetic ministries."[62]

Despite pressure against compulsory licenses in general and although by the end of 2012 the Ecuadorian Ministry of Health continued to buy Abbott's Kaletra

[59] Quito, April 21, 2010, <http://haieuropestaffblog.blogspot.com/2010/04/lac-eu-alliance-for-access-to-medicines.html>.

[60] In this respect the Ministry argues that the regulation concerning granting of compulsory licenses requires the Ministry of Health to declare a medical emergency prior to the granting of a compulsory license. Interview with Deyenira Camacho, Martha Cava, and José Manuel Martinez, IEPI, April 20, 2010.

[61] Interview with IFI/Promesa members, April 20, 2010.

[62] The cables are dated October 13 and 21 of 2009 and February 10 of 2010. <http://wikileaks.ch/cable/2009/10/09QUITO998.html> and <http://wikileaks.ch/cable/2009/10/09QUITO1068.html>.

instead of the generic version, on November 12, 2012, Ecuador authorized generic competition for yet another patented HIV/AIDS treatment. The IEPI granted a non-exclusive compulsory license for non-commercial public use to Acromax Laboratorio Quimico Farmaceutico SA for the import and production of abacavir + lamivudine for the remaining duration of the patent term until May 14, 2018. This time the Ministry of Health confirmed that abacavir + lamivudine was a priority medicine for the treatment of diseases that affect the Ecuadorean population.[63]

The compulsory licensing strategy has also been complemented with other policies to strengthen local production. For example, in December 2009, the state-owned pharmaceutical company, ENFARMA, was created (Decree 181 2009) for the purpose of researching and developing active ingredients of relevant and compulsorily licensed medicines. Additionally, in 2010, the purchasing policies used to supply the public health providers were modified to privilege national companies in the public bargaining process. Ecuadorian national pharmaceutical producers currently represent only 20 percent of the total national market, but they expect these efforts to encourage an increase in domestic production.[64] However, it is still too early to fully evaluate the implementation of these and other Correa administration initiatives.

V. Discussion: State Sovereignty and Transnational Advocacy Networks

Like other Latin American countries, throughout the past two decades Ecuador's economic and political development have been plagued by crises. However, the Ecuadorian case is distinctive particularly in the Andean region and in reference to Peru and Colombia. In contrast to these two countries, Ecuador has managed to resist transnational pressures to expand intellectual property protection beyond the TRIPS Agreement requirements. Moreover, its model of integration with the global market has not followed the trends of its neighbor nations in the Andean region or the developments in other small middle-income countries.

In effect, as we see in the four stages described in this chapter, Ecuador always appeared at odds with its Andean fellow member states and with global harmonization pressures. At the beginning of the 1990s, when CAN was still resisting foreign pressures with remnants of the ISI industrial model, Ecuador instead signed a premature trade agreement with the United States to protect pipeline patents (which was later invalidated). In the transition between the 1990s and the start of the 2000s, despite US pressures to retaliate against the EU, Ecuador decided to adopt an independent banana dispute strategy and later implemented an unprecedented cross-retaliation action against the EU, using IPRs to secure its rights in the

[63] IEPI Tramite No. 000006, November 12, 2012 (compulsory license for patent PI-08-1913).
[64] Interview with Jose Luis Troya, President of ALFE, April 21, 2010.

banana market. In the mid-2000s, when Peru and Colombia began integrating with the United States, Ecuador displayed extraordinary independence. Thanks to the indigenous and health activist movements, the nation halted negotiations with the United States over a free trade agreement. Finally, in the second half of the 2000s, when Colombia and Peru opted for consolidation of their integration with the global market through bilateral agreements with the EU, Ecuador again resisted and began to implement policies of national sovereignty more reminiscent of the ISI policies of the 1960s than the commercial integration and globalization movement of the 90s.

This chapter has argued that the unique Ecuadorian response to the expansion of intellectual property and to balancing IPRs against access to medicine concerns was possible mainly due to a strong sovereignty discourse combined with the presence of certain transnational advocacy networks (TAN). As illustrated in Figure 7.2, there have been periods in which the Ecuadorian state sovereignty discourse was complemented by the participation of TAN and other times when international cooperation was less needed. The work of transnational advocates was particularly important during two periods: the 1990s, when IPRs for pharmaceuticals were first introduced into Andean norms; and during the late 2000s, when a compulsory licensing policy was adopted. In contrast, in the period since the late 1990s until the mid-2000s local actors relied less on TAN for their national sovereignty campaigns. This was the case during the banana wars and the mobilization against the FTA with the United States.

Additionally, as is also illustrated in Figure 7.2, although sovereignty was always a key factor in the actions taken by the Ecuadorian government during the two decades, sovereignty considerations changed over time. From the 1990s until the early 2000s, the concern was mainly about domestic productive capacity, whereas after 2003, the main concern became access to health and consequently access to medicines.

Together, all these Ecuadorian developments regarding IP policy reflect a sense of sovereignty that contradicts much of the literature on globalization and global regulation. In fact, in Ecuador, sovereignty has not diminished its influence because of the new geography of power, as Saskia Sassen would suggest (Sassen 1996). In addition, and belying the traditional logic of bargaining power (Krasner 1976), Ecuador has enjoyed a high degree of self-determination even though it is a small middle-income country.[65] Even more interestingly, Ecuador has claimed its sovereignty in domestically weak productive sectors, such as the pharmaceutical industry. And when it insisted on its sovereignty with regard to a strong domestic sector, such as banana production, it did it with the support of small and dispersed producers rather than with the backing of the wealthy oligopolistic exporters. One possible explanation for the exceptional success of Ecuadorian claims to sovereignty is precisely the recurrent political and economic crises that the country suffered during the 1990s and early 2000s. The instability of its globalized economy, the burden of

[65] Proportional to size and or level of development.

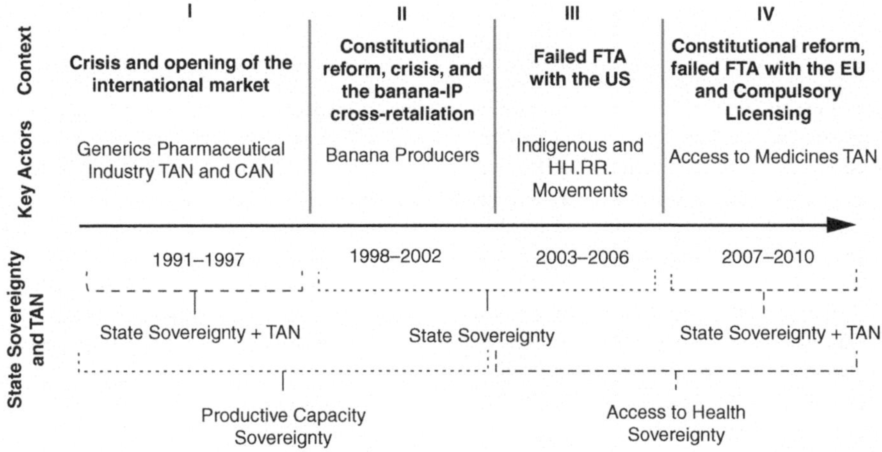

Fig. 7.2 TAN and types of sovereignty discourses

foreign debt, and the threat of mobilization by indigenous and other activist groups made Ecuador a country in which presidents are less inclined to favor the most powerful citizens.

But even if that is true, there is an implementation gap that separates unorthodox trade and IP policies at the international level from the domestic problem of distributing the benefits of self-determination to the most vulnerable citizens. For example, the gains of the "banana wars" have not fully trickled down to small producers and workers because of the lack of commitment on the part of exporters to guarantee a fixed price for the banana box to be paid to producers. The Ecuadorian government has sanctioned the Noboa Group on several occasions, for the meager wages it pays employees; the company repeatedly fights back—and wins.[66]

The compulsory licensing policy may suffer from the same implementation gap. Since the Lopinavir/Ritonavir license, it is not evident that the license granted to the Eskegroup (Cipla) to manufacture a generic version of Kaletra has led to massive purchases by the Ministry of Public Health. In fact, the government has not bought the generic version of Kaletra in public tenders, thus it is not clear that access to treatment has increased. It is still too soon to assess whether the compulsory license on abacavir + lamivudine will follow the same path or not. In conclusion, for the Ecuadorian international trade and IP strategies to succeed, the state sovereignty discourse must be made as effective locally as it has been globally.

[66] The group is still litigating the USD200,000 fine that the government imposed on it for non-payment of the government fixed box price in 2005. Also, the government closed two of Noboa's companies in May 2011 because of their uncompliance with the domestic price, but they were quickly reopened in June. In late July 2011 the government threatened imposing another USD500,000 fine on the Noboa group for the same reason.

References

Andolina, R. 2003. "The Sovereign and its Shadow: Constituent Assembly and Indigenous Movement in Ecuador." *Journal of Latin American Studies* 35(4): 721–50.

Basheer, S. 2009. "Turning TRIPS on its Head: An 'IP Cross Retaliation' Model." *ExpressO*. <http://works.bepress.com/shamnad_basheer/1>.

Breuss, F., S. Griller, and E. Vranes. 2003. *The Banana Dispute: An Economic and Legal Analysis*. Vienna: Springer Verlag.

Castro, A., and M. Westerhaus. 2007. "Access to Generic Antiretrovirals: Inequality, Intellectual Property Law, and International Trade Agreements" ("Acceso a antirretrovirales genéricos: desigualdad, derecho de propiedad intelectual y acuerdos"). *Cad. Saúde Pública* 23(Suppl. 1): S85–96.

Gerlach, A. 2003. *Indians, Oil, and Politics: A Recent History of Ecuador*. Wilmington, DE: Scholarly Resources Inc.

Hanrahan, Charles. 2001. *CRS Report to Congress—The US-EU Banana Dispute*. Accessed July 27, 2011: <http://www.google.com.co/search?q=CRS+Report+to+Congress+hanrahan+ecuador&ie=utf-8&oe=utf-8&aq=t&rls=org.mozilla:en-US:official&client=firefox-a>.

Helfer, L. R., K. J. Alter, and M. F. Guerzovich. 2009. "Islands of Effective International Adjudication: Constructing an Intellectual Property Rule of Law in the Andean Community." *American Journal of International Law* 103: 1–47.

Jácome, L. I. 2004. *The Late 1990s Financial Crisis in Ecuador: Institutional Weaknesses, Fiscal Rigidities, and Financial Dollarization at Work*. New York: International Monetary Fund.

Keck, M. E., and K. Sikkink. 1998. *Activists beyond Borders: Advocacy Networks in International Politics*. Ithaca, NY: Cornell University Press.

Krasner, S. D. 1976. "State Power and the Structure of International Trade." *World Politics: A Quarterly Journal of International Relations* 28: 317–47.

——. 1999. *Sovereignty: Organized Hypocrisy*. Princeton: Princeton University Press.

Odell, J. S. 2000. *Negotiating the World Economy*. Ithaca, NY: Cornell University Press.

——. 2006. *Negotiating Trade: Developing Countries in the WTO and NAFTA*. Cambridge: Cambridge University Press.

Oliveira, M. A., et al. 2004. "Has the Implementation of the TRIPS Agreement in Latin America and the Caribbean Produced Intellectual Property Legislation that Favours Public Health?" *Bulletin of the World Health Organization* 82(11): 815–21.

OPS. 2000. "Perfil del sistema de servicios de salud de Ecuador." <http://www.lachsr.org/documents/perfildelsistemadesaluddeecuador-ES.pdf>.

Salazar Manrique, Roberto. 1998. "The Andean Community's Intellectual Property Regime." In *The Andean Community and the United States: Trade and Investment Relations in the 1990s*. OAS—CAF.

Sassen, S. 1996. *Losing Control? Sovereignty in an Age of Globalization*. New York: Columbia University Press.

Smith, J. M. C. 2006. "Compliance Bargaining in the WTO: Ecuador and the Bananas Dispute." Pp. 257–88 in *Negotiating Trade: Developing Countries in the WTO and NAFTA*, edited by John S. Odell. Cambridge: Cambridge University Press.

Stewart, T. P. 1999. *The GATT Uruguay Round: A Negotiating History (1986–1994)*. Alphen aan den Rijn: Kluwer Law International.

Villarreal, M. Angeles. 2006. "Andean–U.S. Free-Trade Agreement Negotiations." CRS Report RL32770.

White, E. 1983. "Cooperation among National Drug Manufacturers: Asociacion Latino-americana de Industrias Farmaceuticas (ALIFAR)." *World Development* 11(3): 271–9.

Zamosc, L. 2007. "The Indian Movement and Political Democracy in Ecuador." *Latin American Politics and Society* 49(3): 1–34.

NORMS

Constitution of the Republic of Ecuador, 1998

Constitution of the Republic of Ecuador, 2008

Law 12 on "Production, importation, marketing, and sale of Human Use Medicines," 2000

Law 67 "Organic Health Law," 2006

Andean Community Decision 311 (Common Regime on Industrial Property), 1991

Andean Community Decision 486 (Common Intellectual Property Regime), 2000

Decree 1344-A, 1993

Decree 118, 2009

Decree 181, 2009

PART II

COMMENTARIES

Chapter 8

Special 301 and Global Administrative Law

Sean Flynn

As noted in other chapters of this book, one of the many sources of rules and enforcement mechanisms in the international intellectual property system is an annual unilateral adjudication of foreign intellectual property policies by the United States known as "Special 301." This chapter describes the legislative background and use of Special 301 and its relation to the international intellectual property system. It then examines efforts of US civil society advocates to impact policy within the program. The chapter concludes with comments in relation to Global Administrative Law themes reflected in this book.

I. Special 301 and the International Intellectual Property System

A. Special 301 Legislative Background

The Special 301 program takes its name from and builds upon the administrative structure of Section 301 of the Trade Act of 1974 (Flynn 2010a). Section 301 was a central instrument of the "aggressive unilateralism" in trade policy adopted by the United States in the 1970s and 80s (Bhagwati and Patrick 1991). The program was established in response to the weaknesses in the enforcement regime in the General Agreement on Tariffs and Trade (GATT), which required that all dispute panel decisions had to be unanimously approved by the GATT Council—including the disputing parties. An uncooperative party could, and often did, block trade adjudication by withholding consent to the formation or decision of a dispute panel. Section 301 authorized the US government to undertake a unilateral "investigation" of industry trade complaints and impose sanctions regardless of the outcome or initiation of international adjudication. Indeed, the law did not require that the foreign conduct be subject to an international agreement, broadly authorizing economic sanction for foreign practices if they are "unreasonable" or "discriminatory" and "burden or restrict United States commerce." Sanctions under Section 301 could include suspension of "benefits of trade agreement concessions," "duties or other import restrictions," or the suspension of the General System of Preferences (GSP) benefits extended to developing countries (Glick 2008).[1]

Section 301 became the focus of pharmaceutical industry efforts to shape the international intellectual property system in the early 1980s. At a time when there were no international agreements requiring countries to have a patent law (Correa 2007; Balasubramaniam 1987), the pharmaceutical industry lobbied the Reagan Administration to use Section 301 to sanction foreign countries that lacked patents on pharmaceutical products. After these initial requests were rebuffed, the pharmaceutical industry joined a broad industry campaign, including the media and software industries, to convince the US Congress to explicitly authorize Section 301 in intellectual property matters (Drahos and Braithwaite 2003). Congress responded with a 1984 amendment to Section 301 defining lack of "adequate and effective protection of intellectual property rights" as an example of "unreasonable" conduct that could be subject to 301 sanction.

Following the 1984 amendment, the Reagan Administration used the program's sanctions and threats to convince two major industrializing countries—Korea and Brazil—to expand their patent laws to cover pharmaceutical products. Brazil initially countered the threat of 301 sanctions with a GATT suit, but the United States blocked the formation of a dispute settlement panel and Brazil ultimately changed its law to the satisfaction of the United States (Bayard and Elliott 1994). The Korea case ended with a bilateral agreement with the United States on intellectual property, which a US negotiator later described as a "blueprint" for the intellectual property chapter of the North American Free Trade Agreement (Drahos and Braithwaite 2003: 103).

In 1988, while the Korea and Brazil 301 cases were ongoing, the 301 program was amended to require what has become known as Special 301. Under this new step in the process, the administration, through the Office of the United States Trade Representative (USTR),[2] was required to publish annually a list of countries that deny "adequate and effective protection of intellectual property" or "deny fair and equitable market access for U.S. firms that rely on intellectual property." The statute requires designation of a country with "the most onerous or egregious acts, policies, or practices" as a "Priority Foreign Country." Designation as a Priority Foreign Country triggers a thirty-day countdown during which targeted countries must "[enter] into good faith negotiations" or "[make] significant progress in bilateral or multilateral negotiations" or face a Section 301 investigation and possible sanction.[3]

[1] 19 U.S.C. § 2411. GSP benefits are additional trade preferences granted unilaterally by developed countries to aid developing countries. As described further below, they are authorized by an exception to the most favored nation duty in the WTO to avoid discrimination in tariff preferences among member countries.

[2] The United States Trade Representative in common parlance is both an agency and a person. This chapter uses the acronym "USTR," with no "the" preceding it, to refer to the agency—the Office of the United States Trade Representative. When it is important to signify the particular individual occupying the presidentially appointed position of United States Trade Representative, the chapter uses "the US Trade Representative" or "the United States Trade Representative."

[3] 19 U.S.C. 2242.

The "Special 301 Report" is a contrivance of USTR to meet its statutory obligations. Initially, USTR met the statutory requirement by publishing an eight-page "Fact Sheet," including a "Legal Determination" that every country in the world lacked adequate and effective intellectual property protection. The Fact Sheet equated the meaning of "adequate and effective intellectual property" in Special 301 to the terms of the US proposal for an intellectual property agreement in the Uruguay round negotiations. Following this interpretation, it reported: "USTR has determined that all countries are eligible for potential priority designation" under Special 301 because none met all of the terms of the US proposal and therefore "all countries 'deny adequate and effective protection of intellectual property rights' within the meaning of the [301] statute."[4] Having effectively named every country in the world on the statutorily mandated list, rendering mention in the list without much significance, USTR announced two new lists not required by statute—"a Watch List and a Priority Watch List of trading partners identified for further attention or scrutiny and action." The first announcement thus changed the terms of what it meant to be listed. Rather than being a finding of which countries lack "adequate and effective intellectual property"—which it defined as including all countries in the world—it listed only countries identified for further "scrutiny and action," an entirely subjective standard. USTR began calling the annual announcement a "Special 301 Report" in later years. The bulk of each Report continues to be identification of countries on the Watch List and Priority Watch List not required by statute.

The current process for compiling the Report begins with a request for written comments published in the US Federal Register of official notices. After the comments are received, USTR staff members summarize the comments in an internal document shared with members of the Interagency Trade Policy Group, the Patent and Trademark Office, and the Copyright Office.[5] As noted in the 1989 Fact Sheet, the latter agencies "advise" USTR throughout the process, but USTR remains responsible for its findings.[6]

B. Special 301 and the World Trade Organization

The Special 301 program has a complex and contested relationship with the World Trade Organization (WTO). In its early years, Special 301 threats and sanctions were used liberally to pressure countries to accept an intellectual property chapter in the WTO. The United States placed many of the leading countries opposing TRIPS in the first Special 301 Report in 1989, including Brazil, India, Argentina, and Egypt. Two years later, India, China, and Thailand became the first countries

[4] USTR Fact Sheet (May 25, 1989), available at <http://keionline.org/sites/default/files/ustr_special301_1989.pdf>.

[5] The existence of this summary document was reported in confidential interviews with government officials.

[6] Further information is available at the USTR website, see Interagency Role, available at <http://www.ustr.gov/about-us/interagency-role> and Executive Branch Agencies on the Trade Policy Staff Committee and the Trade Policy Review Group, <http://www.ustr.gov/about-us/executive-branch-agencies-trade-policy-staff-committee-and-trade-policy-review-group>.

to grace the Priority Foreign Countries list. Brazil was sanctioned with a loss of GSP benefits in 1988; Thailand in 1989; and India in 1992—all on matters related to pharmaceutical patents.

After the WTO accords went into effect,[7] Special 301 became part of a new regulatory hierarchy. The WTO agreements included a binding Dispute Settlement Understanding (DSU) providing that "Members shall not make a determination to the effect that a violation has occurred . . . except through recourse to . . . this understanding."[8] But in its WTO implementing legislation, the US Congress kept Section 301 on the books and amended Special 301 to specify that "[a] foreign country may be determined to deny adequate and effective protection of intellectual property rights, notwithstanding . . . compliance with the specific obligations of the World Trade Organization agreement on Trade Related Aspects of Intellectual Property Rights" (TRIPS).[9]

The European Community filed a facial WTO challenge to the US failure to repeal Section 301. The WTO panel in that case found that the continuation of the statute created a "presumptive violation" of the WTO agreements, but upheld Section 301 because of the existence of a "Statement of Administrative Action" in which the United States pledged to use the DSU to determine any alleged WTO violation.[10] The WTO decision did not address Special 301 listings. But its reasoning cast doubt on the continued validity of Special 301, especially in its admonishment that a "threat of unilateral action, especially when it emanates from an economically powerful Member," may "disrupt the very stability and equilibrium which multilateral dispute resolution was meant to foster."[11]

The continued use of the Special 301 Report to threaten GSP benefit reductions, including for failure to adhere to TRIPS-plus demands of the United States, has not been adjudicated in the WTO and largely continues. This practice appears vulnerable to challenge under the WTO's GSP enabling clause. This clause is an exception to the agreement's most favored nation (MFN) clause, which requires that tariff treatment provided to one member of the WTO be provided to all. The major exceptions to this rule are for issues adjudicated to violate the WTO, for preferences negotiated through a free trade area agreement and, through the

[7] Marrakesh Agreement Establishing the World Trade Organization, April 15, 1994, 33 I.L.M. 81 (1994).

[8] Dispute Settlement Understanding, art. 23.2.

[9] 19 U.S.C. § 2242(d)(4).

[10] Panel Report, United States—Sections 301–10 of the Trade Act of 1974, WT/DS152/R (December 22, 1999). The Statement of Administrative Action states in relevant part that in cases involving alleged WTO violations the Trade Representative will:

- invoke DSU dispute settlement procedures, as required under current law;
- base any section 301 determination that there has been a violation or denial of US rights under the relevant agreement on the panel or Appellate Body findings adopted by the DSB;
- following adoption of a favourable panel or Appellate Body report, allow the defending party a reasonable period of time to implement the report's recommendations; and
- if the matter cannot be resolved during that period, seek authority from the DSB to retaliate.

[11] Panel Report, United States—Sections 301–10: para. 7.89.

GSP enabling clause, for trade preferences based on criteria that are "generalized, non-reciprocal and non discriminatory" and "addressed to a particular development, financial or trade need" of developing countries.[12]

The WTO Appellate Body—the highest court in the WTO system—ruled in a case successfully challenging a European Community GSP program that the developed countries are not free to define GSP program criteria to promote their own economic interests. The Appellate Body stressed that GSP criteria must be tailored to the needs of developing countries, and held that such needs may not be "based merely on an assertion to that effect by . . . a preference-granting country." Rather, the basis for GSP criteria must be an "objective . . . [b]road-based recognition of a particular need," such as those "set out in the WTO Agreement or in multilateral instruments adopted by international organizations."[13]

This decision, read in conjunction with the Dispute Settlement Understanding's ban on unilateral adjudication, puts any continued threats of sanctions under 301 for issues not litigated in the WTO in a potential legal catch 22. TRIPS-plus demands for GSP receipt can be challenged as being insufficiently "objective" and "broad-based," therefore in derogation of the GSP enabling clause. Reducing GSP benefits for alleged, but non-litigated, TRIPS violations may be challenged as unilateral adjudication prohibited by the DSU (Flynn 2013).

In practice, USTR altered its use of Special 301 to limit its most explicit threats of sanctions. It has dramatically decreased its listing of WTO members on the Priority Foreign country list, listing only two—Paraguay and Ukraine—since the WTO's inception. But it has not eliminated the threat of WTO litigation. The 2013 Priority Foreign Country listing of Ukraine alleged a series of digital copyright issues not expressly covered by TRIPS and threatened GSP benefit reductions without any DSU litigation as a potential sanction. This puts all Watch List and Priority Watch List members on notice that they may be subject to similar GSP criteria. The reasoning in the 1999 WTO case that threats of unilateral action are as harmful to the international fabric as actual sanctions may give standing to any Watch List or Priority Watch List member to challenge the 301 listings in the WTO.

Rather than challenge the program in the WTO, many countries dismiss the program as a paper tiger with no real bite and not worthy of their attention. Most of the countries listed in Special 301 each year refuse to submit comments in its process. Some countries, such as Chile, openly challenged the program's legitimacy in the world trading system on the occasion of its publication (Masnik 2013). But other countries, especially those most dependent on US foreign policy or aid, still pay close attention to the program and make great efforts to alter their policies and laws to comply with its demands.

12 General Agreement on Tariffs and Trade, October 30, 1947, art. 1, T.I.A.S. 1700, 55 U.N.T. S. 194 and associated appendices; WTO, Differential and More Favourable Treatment Reciprocity and Fuller Participation of Developing Countries, L/4903 (November 28, 1979).

13 Appellate Body Report, European Communities—Conditions for the Granting of Tariff Preferences to Developing Countries, WT/DS246/AB/R, para. 163 (April 20, 2004).

For intellectual property-intensive industries, the reduction of the sanctioning power of the program has not reduced its importance. Each year, the two main pharmaceutical industry organizations—Pharmaceutical Research and Manufacturers Association (PhRMA) and Biotechnology Industry Organization (BIO)—submit extensive comments to USTR with specific listing decisions recommended for dozens of countries. They make significant investments in following up the complaints with visits from high-level officials and lobbyists to multiple agency offices.

The large annual investments by private industry in advocacy to construct the annual 301 Report are made in part because statements in it, endorsed by the presidentially appointed US Trade Representative and mandated by Congress, have the imprint of official policy. This makes the Report a useful tool to increase influence in a variety of ways. Wikileaks cables show that 301 findings regularly become the subject of pressure from US Embassy personnel toward foreign governments (Knowledge Ecology International Undated b). Industry lobbyists report that 301 condemnations can open doors of foreign government offices that may otherwise have no interest in meeting with such businesses.[14]

II. Special 301 and Access to Medicine Advocacy

Despite the continued central role of Special 301 for intellectual property-intensive industries, public interest nongovernmental organizations (NGOs) have been largely absent from the process until recently. But 301 has long been a focus of NGO advocacy on the outside of the program, including through a successful campaign to end its use on pharmaceutical issues in Sub-Saharan Africa in 1999–2000. This section explores 301-related advocacy by NGOs in more detail, including how changes in presidential administrations and in the procedural rules governing the program have impacted NGO willingness to participate in it.

A. Special 301 and the Origins of the Access to Medicine Movement

The beginning of a distinct "access to medicine" civil society movement can be traced to resistance to policies expressed, in part, in the Special 301 program. After the passage of the TRIPS Agreement, the United States used Special 301 and other threats to pressure South Africa to amend a statute authorizing parallel importation of lower priced patented medicines from other countries. It also used Special 301 and a WTO suit to pressure Brazil to restrict the grounds for which it authorized compulsory licenses to make generic copies of branded medicines. Health advocates in the United States, South Africa, and Brazil took to the streets in protest. In the United States, AIDS and human rights advocates, organized

[14] Interview with an anonymous lawyer who works for intellectual property-intensive industries on foreign law reform campaigns.

under a new umbrella organization named HealthGAP, began "bird-dogging" presidential candidate Al Gore at campaign events—shouting, raising signs, and otherwise drawing attention to an administration policy they considered shameful ('t Hoen 2009; Sell 2002; Weissman 1996). The tactic worked—in response to the protests, the Clinton Administration called off its pressure on South Africa, settled the Brazil dispute and announced a new executive order banning the use of "sections 301–310 of the Trade Act of 1974 [to seek] the revocation or revision of any [TRIPS-compliant] intellectual property law or policy [in sub-Saharan Africa] that regulates HIV/AIDS pharmaceuticals or medical technologies."[15] The 2000 Special 301 Report explained this policy in somewhat broader terms, pronouncing that if a country was to "avail itself of the flexibility the WTO TRIPS agreement provides to address a health care crisis, the United States will raise no objection."[16]

By 2001, the focal point of the access to medicines movement had shifted to the international level, producing the Doha Declaration on the TRIPS Agreement and Public Health. The Doha Declaration, which was heavily influenced by NGO advocacy and technical assistance ('t Hoen 2009; Sell 2002; Weissman 1996), was mindful of past uses of Special 301 when it affirmed "the right of WTO Members to use, to the full," the "flexibility" in TRIPS to "promote access to medicines for all" (Correa 2002).[17]

Back in the US, the policy momentum was shifting the other way. President George W. Bush's USTR vigorously pursued trade agreements and used threats through Special 301 to promote a wide range of "TRIPS-plus" policies criticized as threatening access to medicine in developing countries.[18] Countries were pressed to limit grounds for compulsory licenses, restrict freedom to define the scope of patentability, prohibit parallel importation, extend patents beyond twenty years, implement "linkage" between drug registration and assertions of patent protection, and adopt "data exclusivity" rules providing nonpatent-based market exclusivity for newly introduced products. The administration justified these pressures in spite of its international commitments in the Doha Declaration with the assertion that "IP rights ultimately enhance public health . . . and that therefore this approach is consistent with the Doha Declaration."[19]

[15] Exec. Order No. 13,155, 65 Fed. Reg. 30,521 (May 12, 2000).

[16] USTR Special 301 Report (2000).

[17] The Declaration on the TRIPS Agreement and Public Health, World Trade Organization, Ministerial Declaration of November 20, 2001, para. 17, WT/MIN(01)/DEC/1, 41 I.L.M. 746 (2002); World Trade Organization, Declaration on the TRIPS Agreement and Public Health, WT/MIN(01)/DEC/2, November 20, 2001, 41 I.L.M. 755 (2002).

[18] United States House of Representatives, Committee on Government Reform—Minority Staff, Special Investigations Division, Trade Agreements and Access to Medications under the Bush Administration, Prepared for Rep. Henry A. Waxman (June 2005), available at <http://oversight-archive.waxman.house.gov/documents/20050609094902-11945.pdf>.

[19] US Government Accountability Office. 2007. Report to Congressional Requesters: US Trade Policy Guidance on WTO Declaration on Access to Medicines May Need Clarification, Publication No. GAO-07-1198 (2007), available at <http://www.gao.gov/new.items/d071198.pdf>.

B. Special 301 and the Access to Medicine Movement 2008–2013

1. *HealthGAP*[20]

During the 2008 presidential campaign, HealthGAP and two allied student organizations—Universities Allied for Access to Essential Medicines (UAEM) and the Student Global AIDS Campaign—appeared at campaign events of the Democratic Party nominee, Barack Obama, and raised signs, asked questions, and otherwise drew the candidate's and the public's attention to access to medicine issues. The activists had links to individuals working on the Obama campaign through current Yale Law Professor Amy Kapczynski, a founder of UAEM, and through other UAEM members. As the direct action at campaign events worked the "outside" to create pressure on the campaign to generate a response, the "insiders" worked with their contacts in the campaign to draft language for the platform. The campaign platform ultimately pledged that Obama's presidency would "break the stranglehold that a few big drug... companies have on these life-saving drugs," and would support "the rights of sovereign nations to access quality-assured, low-cost generic medication to meet their pressing public health needs under the WTO's Declaration on Trade Related Aspects of Intellectual Property Rights (TRIPS)."[21] The activists were satisfied—"It was real. It was a major accomplishment."

After the election, HealthGAP organized a meeting with transition team officials that addressed the campaign promises. There was a major march of 5,000 or so treatment activists in Washington DC on domestic and international AIDS policies. The march went to the transition team offices where a meeting was held between select representatives from the march and the transition team, including the lead for global health, Karen Richardson. The meeting went well from the perception of the activists. "[The transition representatives] acknowledged the campaign platform and said they want to make it happen. We were optimistic." But the optimism faded, and attention shifted, when influential figures in the new administration began calling for reductions in spending on AIDS treatment programs abroad.

> We never got to the stage where we were helping to draft an executive order or something to implement the policy. Early [in the new administration,] there was an anti-AIDS treatment push. There was a pull back from treatment. Zeke Emanuel, Rahm's brother, was pushing an anti-treatment agenda. The term "treatment mortgage" was being used by people in the Administration. The AIDS world responded mostly on budget. Protecting treatment programs became the biggest and most important priority. The activist attention shifted away from the IP promises.

Changes in the substance and process of Special 301 were implemented by the Obama Administration beginning in 2009. Procedurally, the 2009 Special 301

[20] Unless otherwise noted, the information and quotations in this section derive from an interview with Matt Kavanagh, HealthGAP Senior Policy Analyst, August 5, 2013.

[21] Office of the President-elect, The Obama-Biden Plan to Combat Global HIV/AIDS (2008), available at <http://change.gov/pages/the_obama_biden_plan_to_combat_global_hiv_aids>.

notice and comment process granted an additional two weeks for countries to submit comments after other "interested persons," such as the Pharmaceutical Research and Manufactures' Association (PhRMA), had submitted their comments. Prior to 2009, industry and country comments were due on the same day—effectively prohibiting any response to industry allegations. On substance, for the first time in 2009, the Report explicitly mentioned support for use of compulsory licenses, stating: "the United States respects our trading partners' rights to grant compulsory licenses in a manner consistent with the provisions of the TRIPS Agreement."[22] Language in the Report supporting the Doha Declaration was also broadened somewhat.[23] But the number of countries listed and the description of the grounds for their listing remained substantially unchanged between 2008 and 2009.

In 2010, USTR introduced a second procedural change. It added an open public hearing as part of the notice and comment process.[24] Previously, the Report was constructed after a written notice and comment only, with no opportunity to make oral statements.

The addition of a public hearing was followed by a significant increase in NGO participation. A major impetus for the increase was the organization of treatment activists who used the procedural change as an opportunity to re-engage the administration on its campaign commitments. "The community kind of woke up to the fact that it got nothing on IP [from the campaign promises] and we decided to try to push it." The 2010 Special 301 Report and "the new openness in the process became the focal point for that new effort."

HealthGAP worked to organize access to medicine groups to submit comments in the 301 process and to appear at the open hearing. A joint submission by HealthGAP and other groups urged the Administration to ban the use of Special 301 to seek "the revocation or revision of any [TRIPS compliant] intellectual property or pharmaceutical price or competition regulation of any developing country that promotes access to affordable pharmaceuticals or medical technologies" (Flynn 2010b). The submission and HealthGAP's oral testimony specifically challenged USTR's TRIPS-plus pressure on pharmaceuticals as being contrary to the interests of the President's Emergency Plan for AIDS Relief (PEPFAR), which purchases drugs overseas for developing country treatment.

The 301 submissions helped open communication channels with some allies in the administration.

> We got questions back from the hearing. "Heard you testified, etc." "Could you give us more information on your concerns." We had follow up responses where the Department of

[22] USTR Special 301 Report (2009).

[23] Early 301 Reports described the Doha Declaration as affirming the use of TRIPS flexibilities to "address a major health crisis," USTR Special 301 Report (2003). The 2008 Report had somewhat broader language, recognizing the application of the Doha Declaration to "serious public health problems." The 2009 Report eliminated the qualification "serious," explaining: the "United States respects a country's right to protect public health, in particular, to promote access to medicines for all."

[24] For an example, see Transcript of Special 301 Review Public Hearing (February 20, 2013), available at <http://www.ustr.gov/trade-topics/intellectual-property>.

State, especially, stated that they would like to know more about our complaints with Special 301. What we were saying got back to people who implement programs because we specifically called out PEPFAR as being disadvantaged by USTR's policy of pressing for higher prices and more IP rights abroad. We have long standing relationships in the State Department through PEPFAR. It seemed like folks [on the 301 committee] went back and reported to other offices and it got back to allies in the State Department who then called us.

Our hope was that it would lead to policy change. But State Department folks got slapped back by USTR. As far as I can tell, concerns were raised by State asking whether our concerns were valid. That inquiry received a forceful response that this was out of bounds by State.

On some important issues, there were changes between the 2009 and 2010 Report. For example, the number of countries cited in the Report for a lack of adequate data protection for pharmaceuticals decreased from twenty-one in 2009 to fifteen in 2010. The language used to describe the complaint shifted from, in 2003, explicitly requesting "a period of exclusivity during which second-comers may not rely on the data that the innovative company has created to obtain approval for their copies of the product"[25] to 2010's much more general complaint urging countries to "provide an effective system for protecting against unfair commercial use, as well as unauthorized disclosure, of undisclosed test or other data."[26] On the issue of patent-registration "linkage," the number of countries cited decreased from twelve in 2009 to eight in 2010. And the language on this issue changed from 2009's demand to "implement an effective system to prevent the issuance of marketing approvals for unauthorized copies of patented pharmaceutical products"[27] to 2010's request for "an effective system to address patent issues expeditiously in connection with applications to market pharmaceutical products."[28]

HealthGAP saw the changes in the 2010 Report on medicine issues as "mostly just a sham." The perception is that "there has been an increase in the number of times that the Special 301 Report supports the Doha Declaration" and that the Report has decreased the explicitness of pressure on other countries for using TRIPS flexibilities.

The major impact of NGO representation on the Report itself seems to be to make the allegations more vague. The language got less sharp. But the coded language is still largely there. We have no sense that the vague complaints are any less threatening. Countries are no more clear on what it means.

The 301 list has always been a different thing in the WTO era. It is not a direct threat of sanctions. It is an implied and secondary threat of sanctions and other pressures. It is a signal that the U.S. will mobilize what tools it has. India, Thailand and handful of other places—they receive vague threats, but diplomats still fly to those countries and lobby hard and reward and withhold preferences that they can. It is just more closed-door. They know they cannot sanction officially and openly. So they use less obvious sanctioning mechanisms that are nonetheless effective. When USTR says we are concerned about transparent decision

[25] USTR Special 301 Report (2003).
[26] USTR Special 301 Report (2010).
[27] USTR Special 301 Report (2009).
[28] USTR Special 301 Report (2010).

making about compulsory licenses in the future, everyone knows it means don't issue licenses—instead negotiate with companies.

After the 2010 Special 301 Report was released, a coalition led by HealthGAP filed a complaint with Anand Grover, Special Rapporteur for the Right to Health, challenging the Special 301 program as a human rights violation (Flynn and Kavanagh 2010). The human rights complaint led to more outreach from the administration, but ultimately another forceful response that this was an area where policy was not going to change.

After we filed [the complaint with the Special Rapporteur], we forwarded the complaint to officials in the Administration. We got responses. We briefed PEPFAR, the White House. The response was—this is for USTR. We did not seek a meeting with USTR. We did not think USTR would be responsive. It was literally the same staff from the Bush Administration making the same decisions. So we did not ask for a meeting with them.

We thought it might lead to more. There were initially people at State that were willing to take the issue up the chain. But they were told that it was a USTR issue and not for State to be taking a lead on.

One of the things that happened is that the Obama administration decided what its battle with PhRMA would be—and it was health care reform. There was no room to undercut promises made to the pharmaceutical industry to get support for Affordable Care Act.

Despite seeing futility in its broader policy agenda of ending TRIPS-plus pressure on medicine issues after its 2010 experience, HealthGAP continued to participate in the 301 hearing and comment process. HealthGAP's participation had two main objectives: mobilizing potential allies in the administration who might support more access-friendly policies, and "shaming the folks who should be ashamed."

There is a combination inside/outside strategy. Mobilize allies to push back on the inside. Create a political cost through shaming and media on the outside.

In these goals, the open hearing has been "somewhat important."

You can't shame someone by writing technical papers. More importantly, we have used it for finding opportunities for potential supporters and allies who exist in the administration but are unlikely to be mobilized by a technical submission but in the process of being shamed in public may become useful in this and other forums. The public forum matters because different people are there—literally at the table.

HealthGAP is now considering whether additional investments in participating in the Special 301 process are worth the effort. The organization's advocacy resources "are still sucked up by the budget campaigns." And participating in the 301 process is seen as "of diminishing value unless a much more public effort is made to make the participation matter."

In the first iteration [of the open hearings]—it was new and public and on the record. The hearings have gotten smaller and less focused and not novel. Unless we can use the public piece to get media—we are in a situation of diminishing returns.

2. *Knowledge Ecology International*[29]

Knowledge Ecology International (KEI), previously known as the Consumer Project on Technology (CPTech), is a small DC-based think tank and advocacy organization with a long history of work on intellectual property and access to medicine issues. It has the longest experience among NGOs of participating in the 301 notice and comment process, dating back to filings by James Love with Ralph Nader in 1995 (Knowledge Ecology International Undated a).

KEI has regularly submitted comments on 301 "in part because it is important to say that we are participating" in any available public process. "USTR will say we gave everyone the opportunity. KEI will engage in any process they give to us." KEI staff recognize that the "perception among NGOs that have dropped out of the process may be that you go and say what you say and it makes no difference." But KEI has achieved successes in modifying language and policies in the Report, and such policy victories provide a sufficient incentive for their continued participation.

> Any impact we can make is minimal. It is not none, but it is minimal. The impact is not as big as we like. You can't stop showing up. It is not zero. 301 is not taken that seriously. But you can't give it up. There is some impact.

The most effective way of "actually winning an issue" in the 301 process is "to spend considerable time meeting with members of the 301 committee in the period during which the 301 Report is being drafted."

> To succeed on an issue, it takes phone calls and emails and a lot analysis tracking back and showing change in position. You need to outreach to as many officials as possible.

Often KEI incorporates discussions of its concerns with Special 301 in more general meetings with government officials.

> We might not have meetings specifically on Special 301. We often don't. But we have regular meetings with offices about international IP policy—with State, USTR, Commerce. Rarely are the meetings 301 specific. But we raise 301 issues there if we have them.
>
> We probably have six or more meetings with USTR a year on IP issues. A similar number with the US PTO. They are the two offices that have been the most open and receptive to meeting. USTR always responds to our requests and takes phone calls and meetings. PTO has also been getting more open and responsive. Some other offices are harder to get a response from. Some won't meet with us at all. Others we see at meetings, often at a public meeting arranged by KEI, and we get the chance to talk with them there.

In their efforts to influence the Report, KEI describes the introduction of a hearing in 2010 as "positive," but "not the most important part of influencing the process."

> One important fact is that it takes place after the written submissions, allowing NGOs to respond to the accusations of industry. Some of the most influential industries, including

[29] Unless otherwise noted, the information and quotations in this section come from interviews with James Love, Executive Director, and Krista Cox, Staff Attorney, Knowledge Ecology International, August 6, 2013.

PhRMA and BIO don't even present at the hearing any more. They submit extensive written comments. Hundreds of pages. But they don't do the oral hearing. They set up private meetings instead.

There is a general feeling that industry groups have an inside track. Some come and have meetings with Commerce, State, etc. and do not testify—do not need to. They come and watch the open hearing. But they give their opinions in one-on-one meetings. That appears more effective, otherwise they would testify. The fact that they fly people here and do all that and not testify suggests that time is better spent lobbying than appearing at the hearing.

KEI had a recent victory in advocating for changes to language in the 2011 Special 301 Report on least developing countries (LDCs). As it was preparing for its submission, KEI staff "looked back at past Special 301 Reports and saw a shift in the 2011 Report on language about TRIPS implementation by Least Developed Countries (LDCs)." In previous Reports, there was a section several paragraphs in length that mentioned various groups of countries working to implement TRIPS. In 2011, the section was restructured into one paragraph that only mentioned LDCs and ended with a threat that if "additional progress [toward implementation] is not achieved, the United States will consider alternative means of encouraging implementation, including the possibility of recourse to WTO dispute settlement."[30]

The change in the language referring to LDCs was seen by KEI as particularly threatening to the world's poorest countries, which put the United States into a bad light. The LDC language was also read by KEI as having broader policy significance. The language appeared at the same time that there were efforts being made in the TRIPS Council to extend the general (non-patent and data) deadline for LDC implementation of TRIPS, which was scheduled to be triggered in 2013.

The language could be read as an argument the administration was not supporting an extension of the waiver for LDCs. Our opinion was that change in language was important. We believed that USTR was pushing back on the extension of the transition for LDCs in the TRIPS Council. There really was a shift in policy toward the 2013 deadline (for the TRIPS LDC extension).

KEI raised its concerns with the LDC language at the 2012 oral hearing. But the hearing was just one component of its advocacy effort.

We did a lot of other work on the issue. The open hearing is helpful. It gets the issue on the public record. Press are there. All the agency representatives are there—including folks you

[30] The 2011 Special 301 Report stated:

> LDC members have until 2016 to implement their TRIPS Agreement obligations for patent and data protection for pharmaceutical products, as proposed by the United States at the Doha Ministerial Conference of the WTO. The United States looks forward to the successful completion of this transition. The United States will continue to work with WTO members and expects further progress in the near term towards completing their TRIPS Agreement implementation process. However, in those instances in which additional progress is not achieved, the United States will consider alternative means of encouraging implementation, including the possibility of recourse to WTO dispute settlement.

might not otherwise know or meet. We did a paper analyzing the language and circulated it widely—to the Department of Commerce, State. We did meetings. We sent a letter to Kirk. Then we had a back and forth with [Assistant USTR] Stan [McCoy]. We sent him an analysis of the language mentioning LDCs and the issue of TRIPS implementation.

KEI received a letter back from USTR Kirk stating that KEI's submission "points to an opportunity to clarify further the relevant language in future Reports," and "I have therefore instructed my staff to update and clarify the 2012 Special 301 Report to reduce the chances that readers might misunderstand underlying US positions" (Love 2011). KEI subsequently sent proposed language for the 2012 Report to Kirk and his staff. The 2012 Report language was changed to express support for the TRIPS Council discussion on extending the LDC transition period, stating:

In December 2011, WTO Ministers decided to invite the TRIPS Council to give full consideration to a duly motivated request from LDC members for an extension of the TRIPS Agreement transition period. The U.S. supports this decision and looks forward to continuing to work with LDCs and other WTO members in this regard.[31]

KEI "thought the new language was a much more positive signal." The success in shifting the language was also seen as having ramifications on the position the US ultimately took on the issue in the TRIPS Council.

Achieving the language change embarrassed USTR into taking affirmative action to change the language in the 301 Report. KEI believed that USTR at the time was preparing to push an administration position to oppose the LDC extension in the TRIPS council. The 301 submissions made people in the administration and in USTR more sensitive to the issue. The 301 process affected the TRIPS council process by providing a forum for the USTR position to go more public and ultimately be rolled back. That made it harder for the USTR to resist the extension in the TRIPS Council.

The campaign to change the language on LDCs was emblematic of KEI's preferred approach to 301 participation: "craft letters on specific issues you can drill down deep into. Use a rifle shot." KEI continues to use such a "rifle shot" approach to changing specific issues in 301 despite its overall position that Special 301 "should be abolished" and that countries should challenge its legitimacy.

The U.S. cannot unilaterally define the global standards. It is embarrassing for countries that come and testify—sitting before USTR as if USTR is sole arbiter of IP policy. But despite the perceived illegitimacy of the program, the problem is that countries do take it seriously and may not understand why.

Getting rid of Special 301 would have a huge impact. Countries would spend less time worrying about doing things completely allowed by international law. Other governments would be more willing to use TRIPS flexibilities and would spend less time responding to USTR demands. Some countries spend weeks of time responding to 301. But there is not a real strategy to get rid of 301 now. We spend most of our time invested in other issues. 301 comes up once a year.

[31] USTR Special 301 Report (2012).

3. *Public Citizen*[32]

Public Citizen's Global Access to Medicines Program, formerly organized as part of Essential Action, provides technical assistance to civil society organizations and public agencies in other countries on the use of compulsory licensing to increase access to affordable medications. The Program started regularly participating in the 301 process in 2010. Since then, it has used the Special 301 process and Report for three major purposes: to defend policies on compulsory licensing in specific countries, to study and publicize policy evolution, and to contribute to public criticisms of the program and its processes.

A core motivation for Public Citizen's participation has been to defend specific instances of compulsory licensing on medicine patents, especially in countries where it has provided technical assistance. Public Citizen's submissions in Special 301 defending Ecuador's compulsory licenses on medicines provide a case in point.

Public Citizen has worked for many years providing technical assistance to the Ecuador government on how to issue TRIPS-compliant compulsory licenses to promote access to medicine. The government's policy in this regard was announced in 2009. In 2010, Public Citizen filed 301 comments about Ecuador's policies. Ecuador at the time was facing a broad-based attack for a perceived decline in the "rule of law," which Senator Orin Hatch and others were using as arguments for suspending GSP benefits.

> The issues named were always the Chevron case,[33] its pull out of a Bilateral Investment Treaty with the U.S. and the compulsory license. These three issues were used as evidence of a decline in the rule of law in Ecuador. Three is often a magic number. It was portrayed as a pattern.
>
> The [301] list is available for these kind of political objectives and uses. It becomes evidence. If an issue is not there, then there is no evidence that whatever policy is a problem.

The link between the 301 complaints and GSP benefit determinations led Ecuadorian officials to consider responding to the 301 complaints.

> Ecuador gets $18 million or so in benefits. So it is some people's job in Ecuador to worry about it. They were looking for help understanding compulsory licenses in the context of those larger attacks on Ecuador. 301 was seen as significant.

The people designated to "worry about" loss of GSP benefits and similar repercussions from US foreign policy are often staff at the local embassy. The relative inexperience of such staff in compulsory licensing policies motivated Public Citizen to intervene.

> We felt a need to represent those policies here in the U.S. We are often better able to represent those policies than the people in the Embassy assigned to that task. We know the

[32] Unless otherwise noted, the information and quotations in this section are from an interview with Peter Maybarduk, Public Citizen's Global Access to Medicines Program Director, August 7, 2013.

[33] The "Chevron case" refers to a decision in Ecuador's courts holding the company liable for billions of dollars in pollution clean-up expenses (Baker 2013).

policies and the interests they serve and the international law. People assigned to respond to Special 301 complaints are often generalists who have not worked on the policy and do not fully understand it. The people in charge of defending licenses are not always the people most invested in or knowledgeable about the policy.

Public Citizen's work to defend Ecuador within the 301 process operated on multiple levels.

We did a fair amount of work to get agencies comfortable with the Ecuador compulsory license action. We went to a meeting at USTR with 10 or so people, chaired by Tim Reif, General Counsel of USTR. It was tense. It was the first time the compulsory license was discussed. We prepared detailed documents. We met with the Ecuador Embassy. We worked with Oxfam on congressional pressure. We sat down at USTR again.

We also responded to third party information. There was an Emergency Committee for American Trade document that was highly misleading. We called someone at USTR or State to talk to them about it. We prepared an analysis of it and submitted it.

The work by Public Citizen defending Ecuador's compulsory license was part of an effort to affirmatively use the program "as the location where the discussion should happen."

We tried to get in front of the story. We put out analysis up front, before there was any listing. We wanted the agencies to get their information from us.

Part of the decision to use the 301 process affirmatively to discuss the Ecuador compulsory license was its relative transparency. "We know who is responsible and we can talk to them."

In the 2010 Report, the issue of compulsory licensing was mentioned in the listing of Ecuador on the 301 Watch List. But the language of the listing was guarded, stating: "The United States will continue to monitor recent developments concerning compulsory licensing of pharmaceutical and agricultural chemical products in Ecuador, bearing in mind the discussion of the Doha Declaration on TRIPS and Public Health in Section I of this Report."[34] Ecuador was not elevated from the Watch List, where it had been listed in 2009. Public Citizen saw these as successes from its advocacy.

The Ecuador work was effective. We spent considerable time on it. The first Special 301 comment on the license was that the USTR would "monitor" it. We felt that was a win. We would have preferred no mention of the license. Any mention in the Report is a "soft sanction." But the language was very vague. With all the time we put in Ecuador, the time spent in the Special 301 process to defend the compulsory license was worth it. It made a difference. It was helpful.

Another dimension of Public Citizen's work in relation to Special 301 has been documenting US policy changes over time.

We are trying to look at evolutions and patterns to facilitate what other countries are doing. The fact that it is published allows us to study the document and find patterns that reflect

[34] USTR Special 301 Report (2010).

evolution of policy. We can see evidence that there will not be reprisals for certain kinds of actions. It allows us to take that evidence to other countries and say "see, they were not listed—you will not get beaten up over this."

We have used it as the indicator for the pressure. If you can get something off 301 then it is OK. 301 provides a means for measuring the pressure. If the issue is not listed, then no one can make a big deal about it. The Report provides one of the few areas in Washington where you can measure that kind of change. It represents the low bar. If you can change it there—keep it from being listed—then where will it be complained about? If it is not in 301, then it is not a real complaint anymore.

The need to document such changes is compelled by Public Citizen's experience that "[e]ven without any threats of hard sanctions, 301 has been effective at slowing down compulsory licenses abroad."

The sense that the US does not like them slows down the process. That is what 301 is really about—it is to signal that if you go down certain roads you are picking a fight with the United States Government

The monitoring of the Special 301 Report has been used to exploit new language beginning in the 2009 Special 301 Report declaring: "the United States respects our trading partners' rights to grant compulsory licenses in a manner consistent with the provisions of the TRIPS Agreement."[35] After that language appeared, Public Citizen began "putting a challenge to USTR" to adhere to the declared policy and stop listing TRIPS-compliant compulsory licenses in the Report. The advocacy to not list Ecuador's compulsory license was part of the challenge. Public Citizen also produced an analysis of the treatment of compulsory licenses in the Report over time.

We did a review—outside of the Canada-Rwanda compulsory license, every compulsory license to promote access to affordable medicine around the world between 2003 and 2012 had been listed in the Report, either expressly or implicitly. Sometimes the listing has been implicit, like the language about Thailand.[36] But everyone knew what it was about. It makes the US government look mean.

This blend of advocacy for delisting of countries for compulsory licensing and monitoring of changes in the Report enabled Public Citizen to claim a recent policy change.

[35] USTR Special 301 Report (2009).

[36] In 2007, Thailand was elevated to the Priority Watch List (PWL) in large part for its announcement of compulsory licenses for excessively priced medicines needed to treat AIDS and heart disease. In 2009, Thailand was kept on the PWL, noting concerns about "the uncertainty created by the previous Government's policies concerning the issuance of compulsory licenses on patented pharmaceutical products." Many NGO submissions in 2010 addressed the compulsory licenses in Thailand directly, and asked USTR to cease pressuring Thailand on their uses of licenses that NGOs argued were fully in compliance with TRIPS requirements. Thailand remained on the 2010 Priority Watch List. But references to its compulsory licensing were eliminated from the entry. The Report more vaguely called for Thailand "to engage in a meaningful and transparent manner with all relevant stakeholders, including owners of intellectual property rights, as it considers ways to address Thailand's public health challenges."

At least on HIV, we think we may have a credible argument that the U.S. has shifted its policy—it won't beat up countries for issuing compulsory licenses for that purpose.

In 2013, there was some progress. The Ecuador compulsory licenses were not listed. A renewal of a compulsory license in Brazil was not listed or referenced in any way. The 2013 Report was more focused on India.[37] But the lack of mention of other licenses that were issued puts us in a position to say that USTR is not focused on pressing countries on all HIV drug compulsory licenses. If countries can do a compulsory license on an HIV medicine and have no mention of it in Special 301—then it is a good sign of policy evolution.

A final goal of Public Citizen's participation in Special 301 has been to support and magnify criticisms of Special 301's legitimacy.

It has been helpful to have that criticism as part of the public record so other countries and researchers can see it. Mass criticism of the process is important. Internationally what it does in the literature is provide a rich body of criticism of 301's legitimacy, which can help countries resist it. This is not a formal hearing. But it is constructed as if the policies are on trial. But they are perfectly legitimate policies. The criteria used by Special 301 to criticize is not transparent. The process is really a sham. It feels like a tribunal set up to challenge policies that do not need defense. When did [USTR staff] get the authority to sit as a judge on foreign policies?

Special 301 is described by Public Citizen as an administrative process hopelessly captured by industry interests.

The synergy between PhRMA's 301 list and USTR is too great. They turn in comments in the form of a draft Report, and they pretty much get what they ask for. The 301 list cavalierly legitimizes industry complaints. The big question is how to challenge 301 institutionally. We don't have clear strategies there.

Like HealthGAP, Public Citizen is considering whether it should continue participating in the 301 process given the administration's rejection of more wholesale policy changes. Whether Public Citizen can continue to promote and chart

[37] India had recently approved a compulsory license for the cancer medication branded and sold by Bayer as Nexavar. The drug was sold in India at nearly fifty times the average annual income of an Indian citizen. But the compulsory license was sought not only because of its high price but also because the drug was not manufactured in India. The latter ground raised the contentious and unresolved issue on the meaning of the TRIPS ban on "discrimination" based on "whether products are imported or locally produced." The 2013 301 Report entry on India appears to take great efforts to criticize the license while adhering to the policy expressed elsewhere in the Report to not condemn the use of TRIPS-compliant compulsory licenses, stating:

> The United States will also continue to monitor closely developments concerning compulsory licensing of patents in India, particularly following the broad interpretation of Indian law in a recent decision by the Indian Intellectual Property Appellate Board (IPAB), while also bearing in mind the Doha Declaration on TRIPS and Public Health, discussed in the Intellectual Property and Health Policy section of this Report. In particular, India's decision in this case to restrict patent rights of an innovator based, in part, on the innovator's decision to import its products, rather than manufacture them in India, establishes a troubling precedent. Unless overturned, the decision could potentially compel innovators outside India—including those in sectors well beyond pharmaceuticals, such as green technology and information and communications technology—to manufacture in India in order to avoid being forced to license an invention to third parties.

progress in protecting compulsory licensing policies from criticism is a key metric for deciding whether it will continue participating in the program.

> At first the hearings were an opportunity to make robust interventions. We had some big policy asks. But they were ignored. Now, you can play that and continue to ask for the big stuff or you can go in and defend specific things that should not need defense. I get sore that each year we have to go to it again before all these same agencies where they attack the compulsory license and ask questions about something that countries have every right to do. We don't have a lot of time and resources. The law is clear on this. Why do we have to keep going and explaining it?
>
> The countervailing tension is that if things are not changing enough should we participate less? If we can continue to shift policy—reduce listings for compulsory licenses—then it is worth it to continue.

III. Conclusions

For nearly a quarter century, Special 301 has been an important and contested source of rules and enforcement practices in the transnational regulatory framework governing intellectual property. Its annual call for comments and the process for the drafting of the Report has been a prime forum for some actors in the field—primarily transnational corporations and USTR, more recently including NGOs—to express their interests and struggle to define the system's norms and practices. As such, it provides a rich subject for Global Administrative Law analysis.

The history of Special 301 and its changes over time provides a useful study of how different levels of the global system interact with and shape each other, sometimes in unpredictable ways. After the WTO accords went into effect, its bans on unilateral trade adjudication and "reciprocal" or "discriminatory" trade preference programs became available to regulate the operation of Special 301. The threat of intervention at the international level affected the operation of Special 301, but did not eliminate it. The annual Report is now more vague and its threats less direct. But whether this change has reduced the influence of the program is less clear. Many countries still pay attention to the Report and strive to change policies to keep outside of its watchful gaze. The program remains a focal point of advocacy for intellectual property intensive industries.

Changes in 301 over time provide a means for the study of how procedure and opportunity structures motivate and capacitate activism. With the coming of the Obama Administration and the opportunity for policy change it represented, US health advocates ramped up advocacy over trade policy and achieved an early, but short-term, victory. The derailing of focus on winning the issue in the early administration displays how assessing policy opportunities for activism is often one of opportunity cost. What motivated HealthGAP to suspend its work pressing for intellectual property demands early in the Obama Administration was not an analysis of whether it could win that issue, but rather an analysis whether the cost of winning in terms of its dedication of advocacy resources would jeopardize its ability to fend off budget changes it perceived as posing more net harm to treatment objectives.

The rise and fall of participation before and after the 2010 procedural change can also be analyzed in Global Administrative Law terms. The procedural change in 2010 became a new focus of advocacy for many NGOs in part because of a hope that its novelty would draw more public and administration attention and become a forum for the adoption of broad policy changes. When more significant NGO demands were rebuffed, sometimes forcefully, many NGOs eliminated their participation and refocused on other, often international, forums for impacting the global system. This may be seen as a reflection of Sikkink's (2005) hypothesis, examined in the concluding chapter of this book, that there will be a diminished chance of activism in a domestic institution that is seen as closed to network or social movement pressure, especially where other international forums are perceived as more receptive. HealthGAP's shift of its complaints toward the international Special Rapporteur for the Right to Health after the 2010 Report may be seen as a pursuit of such a more responsive international forum. But the history of Special 301 also displays how the evaluation of the cost and benefits of activism will not be the same for all organizations. Even with recognition after 2010 that NGO influence in Special 301 in the Obama Administration will be limited, and the process perceived as still captured by corporate lobbyists with an inside track, KEI and Public Citizen appear prepared to continue participating in the program's processes to achieve small changes in 301 wording and policy. This may help demonstrate that what is a closed system may vary between organizations and their capacities as well as with the stakes at issue. For these two organizations, their repeat player status with administrative officials may increase their capacity for influence (reducing the cost side). At the same time, the importance of US policy pressure in shaping the international system may be seen as making small changes in its demands worth while (increasing the perceived benefit side).

In the end, the kind of change that NGOs most desire from the program—ending it—may be more likely to come from without than within. With the United States still using the program to threaten reduction of GSP benefits without initiating WTO dispute settlement, including for TRIPS-plus demands not required by any objective and broad-based multilateral agreement, the program remains vulnerable in the rules of the international system. However, bringing such a challenge would require a different kind and scale of advocacy. Only countries can bring WTO complaints and the countries most likely to be willing to challenge US policy (e.g. Brazil) are the same nations that dismiss the program's relevance. It should also be noted that eliminating Special 301 might not be a universally positive occurrence as it would also get rid of one of the few avenues to observe and formally participate in the construction of US foreign policy on intellectual property. Without the Special 301 procedure, pressure on countries at the behest of the intellectual property intensive industries would likely still take place, but it would be shrouded in additional secrecy.

References

Baker, David. 2013. "How Chevron Turned the Tables in Ecuador." Available at <http://blog.sfgate.com/energy/2013/06/28/how-chevron-turned-the-tables-in-ecuador/>.

Balasubramaniam, Kumariah. 1987. "Pharmaceutical Patents in Developing Countries: Policy Options." 22 *Econ. & Political Weekly* 22: 103–20.

Bayard, Thomas O., and Kimberly Ann Elliott. 1994. *Reciprocity and Retaliation in U.S. Trade Policy*. Washington, DC: Institute for International Economics.

Bhagwati, Jagdish, and Hugh T. Patrick. 1991. *Aggressive Unilateralism: America's 301 Trade Policy and the World Trading System*. Ann Arbor: University of Michigan Press.

Correa, Carlos. 2002. "Implications of the Doha Declaration on the Trips Agreement and Public Health." World Health Organization. Available at <http://apps.who.int/medicinedocs/en/d/Js2301e/>.

——. 2007. *Guidelines for the Examination of Pharmaceutical Patents, Developing a Public Health Perspective: A Working Paper*. Geneva: International Centre for Trade and Sustainable Development, available at Guidelines for the Examination of Pharmaceutical Patents, Developing a Public Health Perspective.

Drahos, Peter, and John Braithwaite. 2003. *Information Feudalism: Who Owns the Knowledge Economy?* New York: The New Press.

Flynn, Sean. 2010a. "Special 301 of the Trade Act of 1974 and Global Access to Medicine." *Journal of Generic Medicines* 7(4): 309–33.

——. 2010b. "Submission on Behalf of Global Health Organizations in re 2010 Special 301 Report." Available at <http://www.wcl.american.edu/pijip/go/301>.

——. 2013. "How Listing Ukraine as a Priority Foreign Country in Special 301 Violates the World Trade Organization Agreements." Infojustice.org. Available at <http://infojustice.org/archives/29556>.

——— and Matt Kavanagh. 2010. Press Release, "Human Rights Groups Challenge USTR Special 301." <http://www.wcl.american.edu/pijip/go/blog07202010>.

Glick, Leslie Alan. 2008. *Guide to United States Customs and Trade Laws after the Customs Modernization Act* 150 (3rd edn.). Austin, TX: Wolters Kluwer Law & Business.

Knowledge Ecology International. Undated a. "Cables Mentioning 'Special 301'—Details of US Trade Pressure on IPR." Available at <http://keionline.org/node/1244>.

——. Undated b. The USTR Special 301 Reports, 1989 to 2012, available at <http://keionline.org/ustr/special301>.

Love, James. 2011. "USTR to 'Clarify' its Position on Extension of LDC Transition Period for TRIPS." Knowledge Ecology International. Available at <http://keionline.org/node/1339>.

Masnik, Mike. 2013. "Chile Says It Does Not Recognize the Legitimacy of the USTR's Special 301 Report." Available at <http://www.techdirt.com/articles/20130505/23161522956/chile-says-it-does-not-recognize-legitimacy-ustrs-special-301-report.shtml/>.

Office of the United States Trade Representative, Special 301 Reports (2007–13) are available at the USTR website, <http://www.ustr.gov/about-us/press-office/reports-and-publications/2013/2013-special-301-report>. Earlier reports are available at <http://keionline.org/ustr/special301>.

Sell, Susan. 2002. "TRIPS and the Access to Medicines Campaign." *Wisconsin International Law Journal* 20: 481.

Sikkink, Kathryn. 2005. "Patterns of Dynamic Multilevel Governance and the Insider–Outsider Coalition." Pp. 151–74 in *Transnational Protest & Global Activism*, edited by D. Della Porta and S. Tarrow. New York: Rowman & Littlefield.

't Hoen, Ellen. 2009. *The Global Politics of Pharmaceutical Monopoly Power: Drug Patents, Access, Innovation and the Application of the WTO Doha Declaration on TRIPS and Public Health*. Amsterdam: AMB.

Weissman, Robert. 1996. "A Long, Strange TRIPS: The Pharmaceutical Industry Drive to Harmonize Global Intellectual Property Rules, and the Remaining WTO Legal Alternatives Available to Third World Countries." *University of Pennsylvania Journal of International Economic Law* 17: 1069.

Chapter 9

The Influence of the Andean Intellectual Property Regime on Access to Medicines in Latin America

Laurence R. Helfer and Karen J. Alter

The Andean Community, a regional integration pact among a small group of developing countries on the mountainous western edge of South America, entered its fifth decade riven by political and economic schisms. Divisions among the member states have waxed and waned over the years, but in general they have prevented the Community from living up to its potential as the continent's second largest trading bloc. In addition, the Andean Community's supranational institutions—which include a Commission of national executives, a General Secretariat of regional administrators, and a Tribunal of Justice (the ATJ or the Andean Tribunal)[1]—have had only mixed results in promoting robust economic or political integration. Not surprisingly, many judges, lawyers, civil society groups, and commentators have either ignored the Andean Community or dismissed it as a failure.

Yet the Andean integration project has had remarkable success within one area of its legal system—the rules governing the protection of intellectual property (IP). Those rules are found in extensive and detailed supranational laws—officially known as "Decisions"—that regulate patents, trademarks, copyrights, and other IP subjects. Andean IP Decisions have direct effect and serve as the national IP legislation in each of the member states, occasionally supplemented by domestic IP decrees promulgated by national executives. Once adopted, Andean IP Decisions and domestic IP decrees are interpreted and applied by the ATJ, by national courts, and by IP administrative agencies in each of the member states. The result, as we have explained elsewhere, is an effective rule of law island for IP, an island in which Andean legal rules—rather than power, political influence, or bribery—regulate the behavior and decision making of government officials and private firms (Helfer, Alter, and Guerzovich 2009).[2]

[1] These supranational institutions were modeled on those of the highly successful European Community (Alter, Helfer, and Saldías 2012).

[2] Our published studies of the Andean legal system, summarized in part in this chapter, are based on a systematic coding and in-depth analysis of the decisions of the Andean Tribunal of Justice (ATJ)

Two aspects of this rule of law island are especially noteworthy. The first is the overwhelming dominance of IP cases on the docket of the Andean Tribunal. Of the 1,338 preliminary references that national judges sent to the ATJ through the end of 2007, 1,303 concern IP.[3] The domestic origin of these rulings is also remarkably uniform: 1,285 cases began as challenges to an administrative agency's decision to grant or deny an application to register a trademark, patent, or other IP right. This striking statistic reveals that IP agency registration decisions are responsible for nearly 96 percent of all ATJ preliminary rulings (Helfer and Alter 2009).

The second important feature of this system is the balance that Andean Decisions strike between the interests of IP owners and those of consumers. As we explain, the Andean Tribunal and domestic administrative agencies have rebuffed multiple efforts to expand IP protection of pharmaceuticals to include pipeline patents, second use patents, and data protection. As the case studies in this volume reveal, these actions have enabled Andean countries to maintain a balanced legal regime that limits the rights of private IP owners and expands the public's access to medicines.

Section I of this chapter explains how the repeated interactions between the IP administrative agencies and the ATJ helped to build an effective IP rule of law in the Andean Community and to solidify pro-consumer interpretations of regional patent and trademark rules. Section II documents how ATJ judges and agency officials enabled Andean governments to resist pressure from the United States and its pharmaceutical industry to expand patent rights in violation of express limits on IP protection required by Andean IP rules. Section III evaluates the Andean Community's relative success in balancing the interests of IP owners and consumers. Section III also considers the broader implications for access to medicines in Latin America, drawing on examples from the national case studies in this volume.

I. Constructing a Balanced IP Rule of Law in the Andean Community: The Relationship between the Andean Tribunal of Justice and Domestic IP Agencies

Over the last two decades, a powerful symbiotic relationship developed between the ATJ and the domestic IP agencies in the Andean member states.[4] Beginning in the early 1990s, the agencies received a growing number of applications to register

and interviews with more than forty judges, government officials, attorneys, and interest groups in Colombia, Ecuador, and Peru.

[3] Of these 1,338 rulings, 1,165 (87 percent) interpret Andean trademark laws; 103 (8 percent) involve Andean patent; 11 (1 percent) concern copyrights; and 24 (2 percent) concern other IP rights. Only 35 cases (3 percent) concern other legal issues.

[4] This relationship was strongest in Peru and Colombia and somewhat less developed in Ecuador and Venezuela. It was weakest in Bolivia, the least economically developed Andean Community member, which also has weaker judicial and administrative systems and limited IP-related foreign investment (Helfer, Alter, and Guerzovich 2009: 22, 35–6).

trademarks and patents. In reviewing those applications, officials identified gaps and ambiguities in Andean IP rules, and they actively sought the ATJ's guidance to address them. The agencies have helped to frame the legal questions that national courts later referred to the ATJ, they have participated in litigation before the Andean Tribunal, and they have provided information to ATJ judges to defend their registration decisions and substantive policy positions. ATJ jurisprudence, in turn, has been influenced by national IP agencies' broad subject matter competences—which include consumer protection, competition, and bankruptcy as well as IP—and a culture in which officials viewed themselves as engaged in highly skilled and technical activities.

When referrals reached the ATJ, its judges responded by issuing decisions that bolstered the agencies' independence, transparency, and fidelity to the rule of law. The Andean Tribunal recognized that agencies were not immune from political interference. In response, it stressed the need for "administrative and economic autonomy to free officials from any kind of pressures or influences that derogate from" determining the interests of "the [IP] owner as well as the public or consumer."[5]

The ATJ also clarified and augmented the procedures that the agencies were to follow when reviewing patent and trademark applications. For example, the ATJ emphasized that officials had a responsibility to exercise particular care when IP applications are contested, including an obligation to articulate reasons for rejecting an opposition and to provide sufficient facts and legal analysis to enable the parties to challenge registration decisions in court. Taken together, these procedures helped to foster a hospitable climate for fair and even-handed adjudication of IP registration disputes.[6]

As the agencies revised their procedures in response to ATJ rulings, their officials also influenced the Andean Tribunal's jurisprudence to reflect the officials' desire for IP rules that balance the interests of consumers and those of IP owners. In Peru, for example, the National Institute for Defense of Competition and Protection of Intellectual Property, better known by its Spanish acronym INDECOPI, included a division devoted to enforcing consumer protection laws and educating Peruvians about unlawful market practices. The agency developed an internal culture that held consumer rights in high regard. This culture also influenced the work of INDECOPI's administrative tribunal, whose decisions reviewing patent and trademark registrations and denials were later appealed to national courts and then referred to the ATJ. Over time, the agency's pro-consumer orientation influenced ATJ judges, preserving the public interest aspects of Andean IP rules (Helfer and Alter 2009: 915–18).

The foregoing discussion reveals how the registration decisions of domestic IP administrative agencies, appeals to national courts, and preliminary references to

[5] Case 27–IP–95, at 15 (October 25, 1996).

[6] See, e.g., Case 5–IP–99, at 6–8 (October 25, 2000); Case 16–IP–2003, at 7 (March 12, 2003); Case 44–IP–2006, at 10 (May 3, 2006); see also Case 35–IP–98 (October 30, 1998) (instructing the national judge to determine whether the administrative agency had appropriately justified its decision).

the ATJ generated a positive feedback mechanism that helped build an effective IP rule of law in the Andean Community. Early ATJ rulings improved the agencies' procedures, promoted reasoned decision making, clarified ambiguities in Andean IP rules, and helped to insulate officials from domestic political pressure. The resulting climate of predictability and legal certainty encouraged firms to file an increasing number of applications for IP protection, notwithstanding the agencies' pro-consumer orientation. Many of these firms appealed the agencies' registration decisions to national courts. The judges on those courts, in turn, referred a growing number of cases to the ATJ, which further clarified Andean IP Decisions and administrative procedures. The cycle was completed when the Andean Tribunal's case law was applied by the same agencies whose registration decisions had spawned the first wave of ATJ referrals.

II. Enforcing Andean IP Rules in Response to National Violations and Resisting Pressures for Stronger IP Protection of Pharmaceuticals

The symbiotic relationship that developed between the ATJ judges and agency officials played a key role in three high-profile cases challenging domestic IP decrees as contrary to Andean law. The cases concerned Andean rules that restricted IP rights—specifically, pipeline patents, second-use patents, and five years of exclusive protection for pharmaceutical test data—to achieve public interest and public health goals. The TRIPS Agreement does not require states to protect these rights. As a result, commentators generally describe a government that denies such protections as exercising the "flexibilities" that TRIPS provides to tailor domestic IP laws to other policy goals.[7] In the Andean Community, in contrast, these restrictions on IP rights were mandatory. When adopting Andean IP Decisions, member states made a collective decision to capitalize on TRIPS's flexibilities as a way to promote public health. After these Decisions were adopted, however, the United States and US pharmaceutical firms increasingly pressured individual countries to adopt stronger IP protection in violation of Andean law. The ATJ provided a forum for opponents of these efforts to push back.

In the pipeline patent case, decided in 1996, the ATJ invalidated a decree based on a bilateral IP agreement between Ecuador and the United States that extended the patent rights of foreign drug manufacturers. In the second-use patent case of 2001, the ATJ overturned a Peruvian decree—adopted in response to pressure by the US pharmaceutical giant Pfizer—that authorized domestic IP agencies to grant second-use patents—including the lucrative patent for Viagra—in contravention of Andean law. And in the data protection case, decided in 2005, the ATJ found fault

[7] E.g. Musungu and Oh 2005; Pires de Carvalho 2010: 62 ("The term 'flexibilities' means the alternative ways through which TRIPS obligations can be transposed into national law so that national interests are accommodated and yet TRIPS provisions and principles are complied with").

with a Colombian decree—adopted under pressure from the United States—that protects test data that pharmaceutical firms submit to the national health ministry when seeking approval to market new medicines. In each case, the ATJ and the domestic IP agencies provided a bulwark against pressure from the United States and its pharmaceutical industry to provide stronger IP protection of pharmaceuticals than Andean IP Decisions allowed.

A. Enforcing the Ban on Pipeline Patents

In the early 1990s, as part of an effort to conform regional IP rules to the soon-to-be-adopted TRIPS Agreement, Andean governments for the first time recognized the patentability of pharmaceutical products. Aware that such protection would raise the price of medicines, the governments phased in protection incrementally. They recognized patents for new drugs developed after a major overhaul of Andean IP rules in 1992. But they refused to protect medicines patented in other countries during the years when it was impossible to apply for a pharmaceutical patent in any of the Andean countries. Although many of these foreign drugs were in the production "pipeline" before the change in Andean law, the member states nevertheless refused to recognize them in reliance on a theory of "absolute novelty."[8]

The United States, adopting the legal position of pharmaceutical firms, pressured the Andean countries to protect preexisting patented drugs. Most Andean states resisted this pressure. In 1993, however, Ecuador and the United States signed a bilateral treaty that mandated pipeline protection. Ecuador's legislature never ratified the treaty, but the country's president adopted a decree to implement it domestically. Relying on this decree, over the next two years the Ecuadoran IP agency awarded twenty-three pipeline patents to foreign pharmaceutical manufacturers such as Pfizer and Novartis.

In response, domestic generic drug producers successfully lobbied lawyers at the Andean General Secretariat to file a noncompliance suit against Ecuador alleging that the pipeline decree violated the absolute novelty requirement Andean Decision 344, which regulated patents and trademarks. Ecuador defended the domestic decree as consistent with a provision of the Decision authorizing members to adopt domestic legislation or international agreements that "strengthen the industrial property rights" (Andean Decision 344, art. 143 (1993)). The General Secretariat countered that the decree contradicted an unambiguous restriction in Andean patent rules and created an incentive for foreign firms to seek pharmaceutical patents in Ecuador but not in other member states. In a judgment issued in 1996, the ATJ sided with the Secretariat. The Tribunal interpreted the word "strengthen" in a teleological fashion, reasoning that national laws and treaties must complement the regional IP system, not contradict it. Ecuador had thus violated Andean IP law "by establishing an exceptional regime . . . granting advantages to

[8] The doctrine of absolute novelty "implies that for an invention to be new and not to be included in the state of the art [and thus eligible for patent protection], it must . . . be known neither within the country where the patent is being sought, nor in any other country" (Manrique 1998).

patenting in its own country, in a manner that was unfair under the common regime applied in the other Andean countries" (Manrique 1998: 217). The ATJ also categorically rejected Ecuador's claim that "an international commitment [could] be invoked as a reason to validate noncompliance with a prior Community obligation" (Case 1–AI–96, at 30 (October 30, 1996)).

Within weeks of the ruling, the President of Ecuador adopted a decree revoking the prior law. Relying on the new decree, the domestic IP agency rejected at least 120 pending applications from foreign firms seeking to register pipeline patents (Helfer, Alter, and Guerzovich 2009: 27). When the firms challenged the agency's denials, national courts referred the cases to the ATJ. The Andean Tribunal supported the agencies, reaffirmed its prior ruling, and stated categorically that "[a]ny patent requested on the basis of the pipeline principle must be denied or, if granted, nullified" (Case 25–IP–2002, at 18 (May 8, 2002)). Since the ATJ's 1996 judgment, the Ecuadoran IP agency has not granted any additional pipeline patents, and nor have the IP agencies in the other four member countries. The agencies thus played a key role in enforcing an important flexibility provision in Andean IP law.

B. Enforcing the Ban on Second-Use Patents

Andean IP Decisions contain a second flexibility provision relating to access to medicines—a prohibition on second-use patents.[9] This ban was contested by the American pharmaceutical company Pfizer, which filed second-use patent applications in all Andean countries after discovering, in the mid-1990s, that its heart medication pyrazolpyrimidinones (Viagra) had the side effect of treating male impotence. In Peru, INDECOPI applied Andean IP law and rejected the company's application. A few months later, President Alberto Fujimori issued a decree recognizing second-use patents in direct contravention of Andean law. Pfizer then asked INDECOPI to reexamine its patent applications. Relying on the new decree, the agency granted the applications. Pfizer then threatened to sue Peruvian firms that were manufacturing or selling generic versions of Viagra.

With domestic litigation looming, the Association of Pharmaceutical Industries of National Origin (ADIFAN), a trade association of generic drug firms, filed a complaint with the Andean General Secretariat. The Secretariat upheld the complaint and submitted the case to the ATJ. In a 2001 judgment, the Tribunal agreed with the generics companies that Fujimori's decree violated the ban on second-use patents in Andean law, and it directed Peru "to leave without effect the patent granted to" Pfizer (Case 89–AI–2000, at 40). ADIFAN then petitioned INDECOPI to revoke the patent for Viagra, and the agency did so several months later. Peru never repealed the domestic decree, but neither did it pressure INDECOPI to

[9] Andean IP law categorically rejects second-use patents: "Products or processes already patented and included in the state of the art... may not be the subject of new patents on the sole ground [that the product was] put to a use different from that originally contemplated by the initial patent." Decision 486, art. 21; Decision 344, art. 16.

enforce it. This suggests that the government was willing to circumvent Andean law but unwilling to challenge agency officials or the ATJ on behalf of Pfizer—actions that would have involved a more serious challenge to the Andean legal system. Since the Viagra case, INDECOPI has not granted any second-use patents.

Litigation in Venezuela and Ecuador followed a similar pattern. The IP agency in each country registered a second-use patent for Viagra prior to the ATJ ruling against Peru, and national associations of generic drug companies turned to the Andean legal system to challenge the registrations. When the General Secretariat and the ATJ reaffirmed their prior rulings, the agencies reversed their positions and invalidated the patents.[10] In Colombia, the IP agency was bolder—it rejected Pfizer's application. The company then appealed to a national court, which referred the case to the ATJ for a preliminary ruling. The Tribunal reiterated the ban on second-use patents and the court implemented the ATJ's decision (El Tiempo 2009).

As a result of this wave of litigation, all of the domestic IP agencies in the Andean Community denied or annulled patents for Viagra. This region-wide refusal to recognize second-use patents remains a major irritant to the US pharmaceutical firms. The industry's 2008 Special 301 Report to the Office of the US Trade Representative places the blame squarely on the ATJ. The report criticized the Tribunal for "issu[ing] several legal opinions... forcing Andean Community members to refuse recognition of patents for second uses[.] The [ATJ] position is dispositive on the issue and no further domestic appeals/remedies are possible" (PhRMA 2008: 236).

C. The Politics of Data Protection and the Reversal of an ATJ Ruling

The third Andean IP noncompliance dispute concerns the test data that drug companies submit to domestic health ministries when seeking approval to market new medicines. The pharmaceutical industry favors laws that give patent owners the exclusive right to control such data. Absent such protection, the industry claims, competitors can unfairly rely on the drug companies' data without conducting their own safety tests.

Disputes over data protection in the Andean Community have a long history. Decision 344, adopted in 1993, prohibited the disclosure of unpublished test data—a form of legal protection mandated by TRIPS.[11] But the Decision also made this protection exclusive for five years; in contrast, TRIPS did not mandate a specific term of protection, requiring only that the data should not be put to "unfair

[10] Case 01–AI–2001, at 39 (June 27, 2002) (judgment against Venezuela); Case 34–AI–2001, at 51–2 (August 21, 2002) (judgment against Ecuador); see also Pacheco and Nebrada 2006.

[11] Andean Decision 344, arts. 78 and 79. Art. 79 provides:

> No one other than the person who has supplied the data referred to in [Article 78] may, without the latter's authorization, invoke that data in support of an application for the approval of a product during a period of not less than five years following the date on which the Member Country granted approval for the marketing of the product to the person who produced the data.

commercial use."[12] Some Andean governments interpreted this language as permitting a shorter period of protection. During negotiations to revise Decision 344, the issue sharply divided the member states. The region was home to a large generics industry, which would benefit from less stringent protection of test data. But the United States and US pharmaceutical firms were pressuring Andean countries to maintain the five-year period of data exclusivity and include it in a draft US-Andean trade agreement. In the end, the new Andean legislation—Decision 486, adopted in 2000—removed the reference to a five-year term of exclusivity and instead simply required protection of test data "against any unfair commercial use." The key provision of Decision 486 also added an ambiguous final sentence allowing member states to "take the necessary action to guarantee the protection provided for in this article."[13]

Relying on this provision, in 2002 Colombia enacted a domestic decree that granted up to five years of exclusive protection for test data. The Association of Colombian Pharmaceutical Industries (ASINFAR) promptly challenged the decree, but the General Secretariat upheld the law as permitted under the above-quoted sentence. ASINFAR appealed to the ATJ, which rejected the Secretariat's interpretation—a first in IP litigation before the Andean Tribunal—and held that the Colombian decree violated Decision 486. The judges reasoned that data protection must be interpreted in light of the Andean Community's interest in promoting public health, interests that precluded Colombia from enacting data protection rules that deviated from the regional standard.[14]

The ATJ's ruling had immediate consequences for the ongoing free trade talks with the United States. Andean governments made clear to their American counterparts that a five-year period of exclusivity was now "off the table." In an effort to save the decree and the negotiations, the Colombian Ministry of Foreign Trade asked the other member states to clarify that the country's 2002 decree was consistent with Andean Decision 486. All prior Decisions had been approved by consensus, but on this issue the governments were deadlocked. After several attempts to reach agreement failed, the Andean Commission (a body comprising executive branch officials from each member country) scheduled a meeting for April 2006. Bolivia and Venezuela were unable to vote at that meeting because they had not paid their membership dues. In their absence, the remaining three states adopted Andean Decision 632 by consensus. The Decision "clarifies the intent of the legislators . . . that each Member Country shall have the authority to choose the means for protecting test data, including the possibility of establishing time periods" of exclusive protection—a retroactive validation of the Colombian decree (Decision 632, 2006, preamble).

This resolution of the data protection dispute exacerbated an already tense political climate in the Andes. Regional trade negotiations broke down in late

[12] TRIPS, art. 39.3. [13] Andean Decision 486, art. 266.

[14] Case 114–AI–2004, at 41 (December 8, 2005) ("[T]he Community interest that must regulate the marketing of pharmaceutical products . . . is directed to the protection of public health and the improvement of the standard of living of the inhabitants of the subregion").

2005 when Peru and Colombia agreed to negotiate bilateral trade agreements with the United States that require five years of test data exclusivity. In contrast, Bolivia, Ecuador, and Venezuela do not provide for such protection, nor have they entered into bilateral trade agreements with the United States. These divisions triggered Venezuela's withdrawal from the Andean Community two weeks after the adoption of Decision 632. "President Chavez stated publicly that the reason for the withdrawal was the entry of other member countries into free trade agreements with the United States..." (USTR 2007: 621). Officials in Colombia's foreign trade ministry concurred, but characterized Decision 632 as the "last straw" in precipitating Venezuela's break with the regional integration pact.[15]

Two common threads tie together the pipeline patent, second-use patent, and data protection cases. First, rulings by the ATJ made it more difficult for individual member countries to defect from Andean Community IP policies in response to demands for stronger IP protection of pharmaceuticals by the United States and US firms. In the pipeline and second-use cases, national judges and agency officials initially followed domestic decrees that benefited US drug companies but violated Andean IP Decisions. These actors changed course, however, after the ATJ invalidated the decrees and ordered the agencies to overturn patents registered based on the decrees. National governments acquiesced in these reversals, even though the conflicting degrees nominally remained on the books. The outcome of the third case—data protection—was more equivocal. Colombia argued that the ATJ had erroneously interpreted an ambiguity in Andean IP law. Rather than openly defy the Andean Tribunal's ruling, however, Colombia orchestrated the adoption of a new Decision (one that permits but does not require data exclusivity) using a procedure in Andean law for states to interpret regional legislation.

Second, domestic IP agencies were important behind-the-scenes actors in all three cases. The agencies had a stake in Andean IP laws, a stake that the Andean General Secretariat nurtured in the late 1990s during the drafting of Decision 486. The General Secretariat consulted agency officials to ensure that the new IP legislation rectified concerns and closed lacunae in the prior regional IP law—Decision 344, adopted in 1994 (Helfer, Alter, and Guerzovich 2009: 12–13). Having contributed to the content of Andean IP Decisions, the agencies had an interest in upholding them. When governments tried to circumvent the Decisions, agencies were put in a difficult position. They could not ignore legally valid domestic decrees. But they also recognized that Andean IP law—"their" law—was being sidestepped in ways that could undercut low-cost access to medicines. The ATJ may have been willing to push back against the decrees because it knew that agency officials would support its rulings. The symbiotic relationship between the ATJ and the agencies can be summed up as follows: domestic IP agencies are committed to following Andean IP Decisions as interpreted by the Andean

[15] Interviews at the Colombia Ministry of Trade, Industry and Tourism, Bogotá (September 14, 2007).

Tribunal. This commitment, in turn, has enabled the ATJ to hold governments to regional IP standards.

The cooperative relationship between Andean judges and administrative agencies helped the ATJ to enforce pro-consumer Andean IP rules in the three cases discussed in this section. Nevertheless, the United States and its pharmaceutical industry have continued to pressure governments in Latin America to provide stronger IP protection for new medicines. Such pressure is unrelenting, and over time the United States has won important concessions, principally through the negotiation of bilateral trade treaties containing TRIPS-plus standards. The bilateral free trade agreements with Colombia and Peru are notable examples.[16] For these three issues, however, Andean countries have been more successful than their neighbors in maintaining key elements of a more balanced approach to IP, one that seeks to reconcile the social and economic needs of developing countries with the interests of private rights holders.

III. Lessons of the Andean Experience for Access to Medicines in Latin America

The experience of the Andean Community, summarized above, offers four insights for understanding the relationship of IP and access to medicines in Latin America. First, it highlights the importance of examining how international IP norms are incorporated into national legal systems. Second, the Andean experience foregrounds the role of administrative agencies in shaping whether patents and data protection are barriers to access to medicines. The third lesson relates to whether local generics industries can effectively advance broader public interest goals pertaining to the human right to health. The final insight highlights the wider administrative and regulatory contexts in which Andean IP rules are embedded.

A. Domesticating International IP Norms

Most studies of the relationship between IP protection and access to medicines focus on international instruments such as the TRIPS Agreement, TRIPS-plus treaties, the Doha Declaration on TRIPS and Public Health, and emerging treaties, such as the Anti-Counterfeiting Trade Agreement (Ho 2011; Pogge, Rimmer, and Rubenstein 2010; Yamane 2011). These studies closely analyze these international instruments to identify the flexibilities they contain and the policy discretion they afford to governments. The studies give less attention, however, to how international IP instruments are incorporated into national legal systems. They mainly

[16] Bilateral treaties are also driving IP lawmaking in the Andean Community. The most recent Andean IP legislation, Decision 689, adopted in August 2008, gives individual member states greater leeway to strengthen domestic IP protection rules. Colombia and Peru lobbied for the Decision to enable them to comply with their respective bilateral treaties with the United States (Barreda 2008; Kelechava 2008).

focus on high-profile issues, such as compulsory licenses, or on economically important developing nations, most notably Brazil (Bird and Cahoy 2008), India (Kapczynski 2009), South Africa (Forman 2008; Klug 2008), and Thailand (Ho 2009).[17]

Our studies of the Andean legal system add to this literature in two important respects. First, unlike the countries listed above, the national IP legislation of Bolivia, Colombia, Ecuador, Peru, and (until 2006) Venezuela is *Andean* law—law that is negotiated at the supranational level and has direct domestic effect. Domestic IP administrative agencies across the region apply these supranational rules to determine whether to register patents and trademarks, the agencies exchange best practices when they confront unclear aspects of the law, and governments ask for the agencies' views when revising supranational IP rules. These features give agency officials a stake in ensuring that Andean IP Decisions are respected.

Second, Andean governments decided to incorporate TRIPS flexibilities as obligatory features of Andean law to promote public health goals and encourage local generics industries. This approach differs from other Latin American countries, which view the flexibilities as helpful—but not mandatory—instruments of state policy. As a result, these countries have often succumbed to US pressure to recognize pipeline and second-use patents and to provide a multi-year term of protection for pharmaceutical test data (Helfer, Alter, and Guerzovich 2009: 28, 30, 34). For example, Brazil is among the most aggressive countries in Latin America in threatening and invoking TRIPS flexibilities such as local working requirements and compulsory licenses. Yet Brazil also recognizes pipeline patents for pharmaceuticals, even though it has not ratified any TRIPS-plus treaties that require such protection and notwithstanding trenchant critiques of pipeline protection by commentators (Guise Rosina et al. 2010).

In the Andes, the existence of a supranational venue for IP lawmaking helped to ensure that TRIPS flexibilities were given effect. Generic drug companies worked with the General Secretariat to protect their interests, and the Secretariat ensures that Andean IP rules took into account consumer interests. We are uncertain why the actors discussed in the other chapters in this volume—such as national judges and civil society groups—have had less influence in shaping the balance between IP protection and access to medicines in other countries. We suggest that one answer may be the absence of a supranational legal system whose competence includes IP issues. All of the actors we interviewed in the Andes—agency administrators, lawyers, generic drug producers, and Andean officials—indicated that national judges were generally uninformed about IP law. They also expressed a preference for balancing patent protection, consumer rights, and access to medicine at the supranational rather than the national level—a possibility that does not exist elsewhere in South America.

[17] Far fewer studies (e.g., Bernieri 2006; Kunisawa 2009; Shadlen 2011; Shadlen 2009) have addressed the relationship between IP and access to medicines in Latin America.

B. The Underappreciated Role of Domestic Administrative Agencies

Scholars of IP and human rights have long recognized the importance of national courts in interpreting and applying international law (Benvenisti 2008; Dinwoodie 2000; Helfer and Slaughter 1997). Courts can construe domestic laws in harmony with treaty obligations, they can adapt international norms to national values, and they can serve as compliance partners for the rulings of international tribunals. Only recently, however, have commentators given equal attention to the analogous functions performed by domestic administrative agencies. Peter Drahos's comprehensive comparison of national patent offices is a prominent recent example, as are analyses of national human rights institutions (Drahos 2010; Mertus 2009; Murray 2007).

Our research reveals that administrative agencies are more important compliance partners than national courts in ensuring implementation of Andean IP rules and in balancing IP against other priorities. One reason is that the IP agencies in Colombia and Peru are also charged with protecting consumers and policing markets. Another is the history of Andean IP policy, which had long required only minimal patent protection for pharmaceuticals as a strategy to promote public health and nurture local generics industries. Governments changed course in the 1990s when they adopted TRIPS-compatible IP rules for new drugs. But the memory of IP as a tool of social policy lived on and was carried forward by administrative agency officials as they implemented Andean rules governing IP, consumer protection, and competition law.

The contributions to this volume highlight other ways in which administrative agencies are important to IP implementation politics. The first example concerns the authority of Brazil's National Health Surveillance Agency (ANVISA) to review applications for pharmaceutical patents previously considered by the country's National Institute of Industrial Property (INPI). This dual review mechanism promotes the rigorous examination of patent applications and prevents the granting of drug patents that have adverse public health consequences.[18] But this shared competence has also engendered competition between the agencies, court challenges, and uncertainty over the scope of the agency's review powers.[19] The second example relates to the patent "linkage" mechanism that prevents national health ministries from approving generic medicines for distribution without first confirming that active ingredients are not protected by a patent.[20] As a result of the linkage requirement, "drug regulatory offices are mandated to ensure that products they license are in full compliance with IP law," a task they "are neither trained nor funded to do."[21]

[18] Mônica Steffen Guise and Adelina de Oliveira Novaes in this volume.

[19] For a comprehensive analysis and a proposal for legislative reform, see Brazilian House of Representatives and Center for Strategic Studies and Debate 2013: ch. 8.

[20] Salvador Millaleo in this volume.

[21] The United States has included linkage requirements in TRIPS-plus treaties adopted by several countries in Latin America. Angelina Snodgrass Godoy in this volume.

C. Generics Industries and the Public Interest

Another theme that connects the case studies to our analysis of the Andean Community is the prominent role of generic drug companies and industry associations. In the Andean context, these companies and associations had powerful financial incentives to oppose domestic IP decrees that make it more difficult to distribute cheaper copies of patented medicines. In lawsuits challenging these decrees, representatives of the generics industry raised a variety of legal arguments, including not only the violation of Andean IP Decisions but also the contravention of consumer protection principles and the human right to health.

So long as the generics industry focused its opposition on TRIPS-plus patents, its private interests more or less aligned with the broader public interest. As the contributions to this volume reveal, however, such an alignment cannot be taken for granted. Generics companies have not shied away from asserting IP rights to gain or preserve market share or otherwise advance their commercial interests. The prevalence of branded generics in Argentina, with prices that exceed those of their proprietary cognates, is a prominent illustration.[22] Public interest civil society groups have recognized that the generics industry does not always act as proxy for efforts to expand access to medicines. As result, these organizations have, with considerable success, challenged the lack of access as a violation of the rights to life and health guaranteed in national constitutions[23] and in the American Convention on Human Rights.[24]

D. Situating the Andean Experience in a Wider Context

Our research reveals how the Andean Tribunal, domestic administrative agencies, and generic drug companies contributed to building an IP rule of law in the Andean Community that helped balance IP rights against public health goals. Our interviews with these actors also suggest a somewhat less hopeful prediction for future efforts to expand access to medicines in Latin America.

First, it is worth recalling that prior to the early 1990s, Andean IP law, like that of most developing countries, did not provide any patent protection for pharmaceutical products. Seen from this vantage point, "absolute novelty"—the legal doctrine that underpins Andean law's ban on pipeline and second-use patents—was a major concession by proponents of access to medicines. For domestic IP

[22] See Paola Bergallo and Agustina Ramón Michel in this volume.

[23] For example, many high courts in Latin America, including in Argentina, Colombia, Costa Rica, Peru, and Venezuela have recognized a right of patients with HIV/AIDS to medical treatment, including antiretroviral medications, under their national constitutions (Oquendo 2008; Yamin and Parra-Vera 2009).

[24] In *Jorge Odir Miranda Cortez et al. v. El Salvador*, Case 12.249, Report No. 29/01, OEA/Ser.L/V/II.111 Doc. 20 rev. at 284 (2000), for example, the Inter-American Commission on Human Rights found admissible a claim that El Salvador had violated the right to life, health, and well-being of HIV/AIDS patients by failing to provide them with triple therapy medication. While the claim was pending the government approved provision of antiretroviral therapy for persons with HIV or AIDS, and the case ended in a friendly settlement.

agencies, however, this concession was uncontroversial. Governments created the agencies in the 1990s when they they revised Andean IP rules. They staffed the agencies with pro-reform economists, lawyers, and administrators, many of whom had foreign training or work experience. These officials accepted a global IP regime as a given. But they also prioritized the development of balanced rules that would help local actors—both businesses and consumers—to capture the benefits of IP protection.[25] Although opinions differed over where to strike the balance, all of the participants we interviewed recognized the advantages of developing Andean-wide IP legislation. For access to medicines advocates, such legislation helped national actors resist foreign pressures to circumvent legal doctrines such as absolute novelty. For businesses seeking to market products in multiple countries, common regional standards were preferable to disparate national standards.

Second, our focus on the substantive content of Andean IP Decisions omits other factors—such as changes in industry regulations—that may also affect access to medicines. One anecdote from our interviews is illustrative. According to the President of the Colombian generics manufacturers association ASINFAR, the number of laboratories producing medicines in that country declined from more than 275 in 1995 to just over 100 at the end of 2000. The President identified two causes of this decline. First, new production standards required investments that were too onerous for many local producers to meet, and these producers simply went out of business. Second, for multinational drug companies, the new standards—together with liberalized access to the Colombian market—made drug production in other countries economically attractive. ASINFAR's President estimated that, by 2007, 90 percent of all pharmaceuticals distributed in Colombia were produced elsewhere.[26] These changes highlight the importance of considering how the broader regulatory environment intersects with substantive IP rules to influence the scope of access to medicines.

IV. Conclusion

IP protection and access to medicines are in an uneasy and often contested relationship in Latin America. In the Andean Community, an alliance between domestic IP administrative agencies and the Andean Tribunal enabled governments to resist pressures from the United States and foreign pharmaceutical firms to circumvent Andean IP rules that facilitated access to medicines. This alliance was at its zenith from the mid-1990s to the mid-2000s, a decade during which generic drug companies repeatedly and successfully challenged domestic degrees

[25] The IP agencies also helped local firms and entrepreneurs secure trademark protection for their goods and services. The agencies worked hard to make the trademark registration process affordable and relatively simple for small businesses without the need for legal assistance. The result has been a rapid rise in local demand for trademarks and an increase in trademark oppositions (Helfer, Alter, and Guerzovich 2009: 18–19).

[26] Interview with the President of the Associación de Industrias Farmacéuticas Colombianas (ASINFAR), September 14, 2007.

that expanded IP protection of pharmaceuticals. More recently, political and economic fractures among Andean Community member states have hampered regional cooperation efforts and enabled the United States to negotiate TRIPS-plus agreements with Colombia and Peru. Even so, Andean IP law retains restrictions on IP—such as a ban on pipeline and second-use patents—that many other Latin American nations abrogated in response to foreign pressures. The Andean Community's experience thus provides important insights for governments, civil society groups, and individuals seeking to expand access to medicines throughout the region.

References

Alter, Karen J., Laurence R. Helfer, and Osvaldo Saldias. 2012. "Transplanting the European Court of Justice: The Experience of the Andean Tribunal of Justice." *American Journal of Comparative Law* 60: 709–44.

Barreda, José. 2008. Summary of Andean Decision 689, <http://iptango.blogspot.com/2008/08/new-andean-decision-689.html>.

Benvenisti, Eyal. 2008. "Reclaiming Democracy: The Strategic Uses of Foreign and International Law by National Courts." *American Journal of International Law* 102: 241–74.

Bernieri, Rosa Castro. 2006. "Intellectual Property Rights in Bilateral Investment Treaties and Access to Medicines: The Case of Latin America." *Journal of World Intellectual Property* 9: 548–72.

Bird, Robert, and Daniel R. Cahoy. 2008. "The Impact of Compulsory Licensing on Foreign Direct Investment: A Collective Bargaining Approach." *American Business Law Journal* 45: 283–330.

Brazilian House of Representatives and Center for Strategic Studies and Debate. 2013. *Brazil's Patent Reform: Innovation Towards National Competitiveness*. Brasília-DF.

Dinwoodie, Graeme B. 2000. "A New Copyright Order: Why National Courts Should Create Global Norms." *University of Pennsylvania Law Review* 149: 469–622.

Drahos, Peter. 2010. *The Global Governance of Knowledge: Patent Offices and their Clients*. Cambridge: Cambridge University Press.

Eltiempo.com. 2009. "Multinacional Pfizer no puede patentar principio activo del potenciador sexual Viagra en Colombia." January 6.

Forman, Lisa. 2008. "'Rights' and Wrongs: What Utility for the Right to Health in Reforming Trade Rules on Medicines?" *Health and Human Rights* 10: 37–52.

Guise Rosina, Monica Steffen, Daniel Wei Liang Wang, and Thana Cristina de Campos. 2010. "Access to Medicines: Pharmaceutical Patents and the Right to Health." Pp. 103–34 in *Access to Knowledge in Brazil: New Research on Intellectual Property, Innovation and Development*, edited by Lea Shaver. New York: Bloomsbury Academic.

Helfer, Laurence R., and Karen J. Alter. 2009. "The Andean Tribunal of Justice and Its Interlocutors: Understanding Preliminary Reference Patterns in the Andean Community." *New York University Journal of International Law and Politics* 41: 871–930.

——and M. Florencia Guerzovich. 2009. "Islands of Effective International Adjudication: Constructing an Intellectual Property Rule of Law in the Andean Community." *American Journal of International Law* 103: 1–47.

—— and Anne-Marie Slaughter. 1997. "Toward a Theory of Effective Supranational Adjudication." *Yale Law Journal* 107: 273–392.

Ho, Cynthia M. 2009. "Patent Breaking or Balancing? Separating Strands of Fact from Fiction under TRIPS." *North Carolina Journal of International Law and Commercial Regulation* 34: 371–469.

—— 2011. *Access to Medicine in the Global Economy: International Agreements on Patent and Related Rights*. New York: Oxford University Press.

Kapczynski, Amy. 2009. "Harmonization and its Discontents: A Case Study of TRIPS Implementation in India's Pharmaceutical Sector." *California Law Review* 97: 1571–650.

Kelechava, Erin. 2008. "Andean IP Changes Allow Peru to Sign US FTA." *Managing Intellectual Property*, August 28.

Klug, Heinz. 2008. "Law, Politics and Access to Essential Medicines in Developing Countries." *Politics and Society* 36: 207–45.

Kunisawa, Viviane. 2009. "Patenting Pharmaceutical Inventions on Second Medical Uses in Brazil." *Journal of World Intellectual Property* 12: 297–316.

Manrique, Roberto Salazar. 1998. "The Andean Community's Intellectual Property Regime." Pp. 212–18 in *The Andean Community and the United States: Trade and Investment Relations in the 1990s*, edited by Miguel Rodriguez et al. Washington, DC: Inter-American Dialogue.

Mertus, Julie. 2009. *Human Rights Matters: Local Politics and National Human Rights Institutions*. Palo Alto, CA: Stanford University Press.

Murray, Rachel. 2007. *The Role of National Human Rights Institutions at the International and Regional Levels*. Leiden: Martinus Nijhoff Publishers.

Musungu, Sisule F., and Cecilia Oh. 2005. "The Use of Flexibilities in TRIPS by Developing Countries: Can They Promote Access to Medicines?" Geneva: Commission on Intellectual Property Rights, Innovation and Public Health.

Oquendo, Angel R. 2008. "The Solitude of Latin America: The Struggle for Rights South of the Border." *Texas International Law Journal* 43: 185–203.

Pacheco, Carlos, and María Milagros Nebrada. 2006. "Venezuela: How to Protect Inventions of Use." *Managing Intellectual Property*. October 1.

Pharmaceutical Research and Manufacturers of America (PhRMA). 2008. Special 301 Submission.

Pires de Carvalho, Nuno. 2010. *The TRIPS Regime of Patent Rights*. Alphen aan den Rijn: Kluwer Law International.

Pogge, Thomas, Matthew Rimmer, and Kim Rubenstein, eds. 2010. *Incentives for Global Public Health: Patent Law and Access to Essential Medicines*. Cambridge: Cambridge University Press.

Shadlen, Kenneth C. 2009. "The Politics of Patents and Drugs in Brazil and Mexico: The Industrial Bases of Health Policies." *Comparative Politics* 42: 41–58.

——. 2011. "The Political Contradictions of Incremental Innovation: Lessons from Pharmaceutical Patent Examination in Brazil." *Politics and Society* 39: 143–74.

United States Trade Representative. 2007. National Trade Estimate Report on Foreign Trade Barriers.

Yamane, Hiroko. 2011. *Interpreting TRIPS: Globalisation of Intellectual Property Rights and Access to Medicines*. Oxford: Hart Publishing.

Yamin, Alicia Ely, and Oscar Parra-Vera. 2009. "How Do Courts Set Health Policy? The Case of the Colombian Constitutional Court." *Public Library of Science Medicine* 6: 147–50.

Chapter 10

Going Local in the Era of TRIPS Implementation

Amy Kapczynski

Intellectual property (IP) law is today the subject of a great deal of controversy and contestation. It has also been "internationalized" to an unusual degree. Multilateral treaties establish high minimum levels of IP protection, and sanctions can be levied against countries that are found to violate their legal obligations. The international IP regime therefore offers us a key locus for exploring the dynamics of international legality.

There is nowhere better to consider the workings of this regime than the domain of access to medicines. It is here that it has received the most attention, and is arguably the most consequential. The vast majority of countries in the world are signatories to the Trade-Related Aspects of Intellectual Property (TRIPS) Agreement, which requires members to offer product patents on medicines. Many developing countries prohibited such patents before TRIPS, because patents tend to raise the price of medicines, often substantially. Even small increases in medicine prices can put them out of the reach of many people in developing countries, where public health systems are often underfunded, average incomes are low, and individuals frequently must pay for their own drug costs out of pocket.

TRIPS requires that developing countries restructure a critically important area of domestic law, to adopt a regime that increases the price of resources that are essential to life itself. It is unsurprising, then, that intense conflict over the agreement has emerged. Developing countries and medicines campaigners have criticized the agreement itself, and have become deeply engaged in arguments over its meaning. They have worked to develop a menu of "TRIPS flexibilities," legal provisions that countries can use to implement the Agreement in accordance with local priorities, while conforming to their international obligations. A great deal is also at stake for the companies and wealthy governments that promoted the TRIPS Agreement. The industries that conceived of the Agreement—a coalition that included Hollywood, multinational publishers, agribusiness, and the multinational pharmaceutical industry—see restrictive IP laws around the world as critical to their own future. They convinced developed country governments, in particular the United States and the EU, that strong international IP norms were critical to their national interest (Drahos and Braithwaite 2002). These governments demanded that TRIPS become a requirement of entry into the World Trade Organization (WTO).

Much of the academic literature on the dynamics of the international IP regime focuses on activities in the international realm—offering interpretations of international norms, or analyzing the workings of international IP institutions and negotiations. This is with good reason. New and very consequential norms have rapidly proliferated. The negotiation of TRIPS was also followed by an "explosion of interest in IP issues in a broad array of international fora" (Helfer 2004: 5). For example, developing countries and medicines activists have raised concerns about the impact of TRIPS upon access to medicines not only in the WTO, but also in the World Health Organization and within United Nations human rights bodies. These institutions in turn questioned the implications of TRIPS for health and human rights, and urged countries to make use of TRIPS flexibilities that would help constrain the treaty's impact on access to medicines (Helfer 2004).

This diffusion of IP issues throughout a wide variety of international institutions has been described as "forum shifting," a practice where states and other actors switch between international fora to "challeng[e] established legal prescriptions and generat[e] new principles, norms, and rules of intellectual property protection for states and private parties to follow" (Helfer 2004: 6). Developing country governments and medicines campaigners regime shift, on Helfer's account, but so do multinational companies and the developed country governments that support them. The United States and EU demanded that the TRIPS Agreement be negotiated in the WTO framework, because the shift away from the usual regime for negotiating such treaties (the World Intellectual Property Organization) offered them benefits. As opposition to stronger IP norms within the WTO gained strength, the US and EU have shifted regimes again. Today, the WTO plays host to very few negotiations or disputes about international IP. Instead, international law is now largely made in bilateral agreements, or in new plurilateral agreements that are negotiated entirely outside of existing institutions (such as the recently completed Anti-Counterfeiting Trade Agreement, or the pending Trans-Pacific Partnership). Because TRIPS is the anchor of the international IP regime, I will, however, focus my comments on its provisions.

Helfer's conception of regime shifting has gained wide currency in the field of international IP, and deservedly so. But today, international norm-making endeavors have slowed (although by no means ended), and we have entered an "era of implementation" (Kapczynski 2009). Developing countries' TRIPS obligations have come due, and many have made significant changes to their local law to implement TRIPS. But they have done so in substantially different ways, and with importantly different effects.

It is for that reason that this volume, with its focus on the complex dynamics of local implementation of international IP obligations, is such a welcome addition to the field. It reflects the fact that the conflict over IP norms and access to medicines has, to a very significant degree, gone local. Companies and activists alike are engaging *local* institutions and courts in the struggle over IP and access to medicines. Because these fights occur within national borders, it might be tempting to see them as "simply" domestic in nature. And yet as these pages amply show, much of what happens when international IP law "goes local" is influenced by, and comes to influence, the international regime itself.

In that sense, it is becoming increasingly difficult to distinguish the international and the local in this domain. This is not only for the obvious reason that international law establishes the parameters of IP law at the local level. It is also because transnational actors today frequently move back and forth between international and local institutions, in attempts to influence the meaning and implementation of the international IP regime. As I shall discuss, transnational actors sometimes raise arguments about the meaning of TRIPS directly in local courts. In some countries courts give the Agreement direct effect, and in many more, courts may interpret ambiguous local laws to render them consistent with international legal commitments.

Transnational actors also make less formal attempts to influence the international regime by engaging the local. Transnational pharmaceutical companies, transnational social movements, and multilateral agencies such as the UN Development Program (UNDP) act as key conduits for what has become a highly transnationalized policy and legal debate about the meaning and appropriate implementation of international IP commitments. For example, transnational activists have used local conflicts over IP and access to medicines to develop arguments and campaigns that have altered the terrain of international law. Pharmaceutical companies, in response, have tried to create new international norms that respond to local attempts to maximize countries' flexibilities under the TRIPS Agreement. As fights over IP and medicines have gone local, increasingly dense and immediate connections between the transnational and local have developed. In this context, the local, far from being a distinct sphere of authority and action, has become another front in transnational struggles over the meaning and implementation of international law.[1] As a result, the case studies offered here are worthy of examination not only for all that they can tell us about movement dynamics and local struggles, but also for what they can tell us about the complex interrelationship between the local and transnational in international IP.

I. TRIPS Flexibilities in Law and Practice

To understand the significance of the localization of fights over IP and access to medicines for the international IP regime, it helps to begin with some background on that regime.

Intellectual property has long been the subject of very significant international legal commitments. The foundations of the current regime were laid back in the 1880s, with the conclusion of the Paris and Berne Conventions. Those treaties

[1] I use the term transnational here to refer to dynamics across national borders, and the term international to refer to international institutions and laws.

established certain basic norms, such as nondiscrimination against foreigners, and required states to provide certain minimum levels of IP protection, particularly in the area of copyright. Paris and Berne were amended many times over the years, and gained a broad range of signatories. Around them grew up the World Intellectual Property Organization (WIPO), which facilitated the negotiation of several important IP treaties over the years, such as the Patent Cooperation Treaty.

The terrain of international IP law was radically remade in the 1990s, with the conclusion of TRIPS. TRIPS serves as the core of the international IP system, and went beyond existing agreements in three critical ways: first, it brought international IP into the WTO, thus making IP commitments subject to the WTO's dispute settlement body. That body can hear disputes brought by members, and levy trade sanctions against the losers. Second, accession to TRIPS was the price of admission to the WTO, bringing new parties to the table who were otherwise unwilling to sign on to new IP commitments. Third, TRIPS introduced important new substantive requirements for member states, including the obligation to offer patents on medicines.

While TRIPS entails very significant commitments for members, it also leaves an enormous amount up for grabs. Consider a few examples from the pharmaceutical context. With this terse formulation, TRIPS is understood to oblige all members to offer patents on pharmaceutical products: "patents shall be available for any inventions, whether products or processes, in all fields of technology. . . . " (TRIPS art. 27). (Many developing countries did not permit such patents at the time the Agreement was concluded, in part because they drive up medicine prices.) But TRIPS also permits governments to override patents, by issuing so-called "compulsory licenses." Such licenses are not limited to emergencies, but can be granted at the state's discretion, as long as certain procedural requirements are met. For example, prior to a compulsory license, patent holders usually must be approached for permission to use the patent on "reasonable commercial terms and conditions," and any compulsory license issued must provide "adequate remuneration" (TRIPS art. 31). Neither of these terms is defined by the Agreement, leaving significant uncertainty about precisely what countries' obligations are when taking advantage of this flexibility.

Additionally, member countries are not required by TRIPS to use injunctions as the exclusive remedy for patent infringement. They are only bound to give judges "the authority" to issue injunctions, leaving unclear how and when such authority should be exercised (TRIPS art. 44). TRIPS seems thus to permit judges adjudicating claims of patent infringement to allow generic production of medicines in certain cases. If interpreted broadly, this would permit a form of judicial compulsory licensing that could allow significant scope for generic medicines even after product patents on medicines are introduced.

Another typical TRIPS provision states: "Members may require, as a condition of the acquisition or maintenance of the intellectual property rights . . . compliance with reasonable procedures and formalities." This requirement indicates that *some* conditions a state might put on a patent seeker are unreasonable, and forbidden. But which ones? Again, the Agreement does not specify.

Such provisions, of course, could be the subject of elaboration in a dispute settlement process. In such a dispute, a panel would rely on the conventional tools of treaty interpretation, but in many cases these will provide little guidance. The Vienna Convention on the Law of Treaties, for example, instructs decision-makers to consider the "ordinary meaning" and "object and purpose" of an Agreement, themselves capacious concepts (Vienna Convention art. 31). Treaty preparatory work and "subsequent practice in the application of the treaty which establishes the agreement of the parties" regarding the meaning of international agreements may also serve as guides (Vienna Convention arts. 31 and 32), but such material is commonly scarce or ambiguous in the realm of international IP. Moreover, there have been very few TRIPS cases brought to a WTO panel to date, and the trend is toward fewer rather than more.[2] There thus remain significant provisions in the Agreement—including innumerable questions of importance to access to medicines issues—that remain uninterpreted.

The abstractness of TRIPS commitments, along with the Agreement's commitment to national discretion in implementation and the fact that countries are subject only to prospective sanctions (retrospective damages are not allowed), mean that while TRIPS introduces important new obligations, it also leaves countries very substantial legal flexibility. As I showed in a recent case-study of India's implementation of TRIPS, countries can adopt a series of flexibilities broad enough to maintain very substantial scope for the generic pharmaceutical sector, and still plausibly claim to be adhering to TRIPS (Kapczynski 2009).

Importantly, though, most developing countries do not make consistent use of the full range of TRIPS flexibilities (Deere 2008). The meaning of TRIPS is therefore not simply established by its textual obligations and implicit flexibilities, but also by the variety of constraints that influence countries' interpretation and implementation of the Agreement. As the Introduction to this volume nicely shows, countries implement TRIPS in different ways. The differences in the Latin American context are substantial, and cannot plausibly be explained through a rubric of national interest. Rather, they must be understood through more contextual analysis that attends to differences in other dimensions, such as access to expertise and the existence of local political opportunities and advocacy groups (Dreyfuss and Rodríguez-Garavito in this volume).

TRIPS flexibilities also can be adopted in law yet be difficult to deploy. India, for example, has adopted a very wide range of TRIPS flexibilities to protect generic medicines. But it also faced obstacles in effectively deploying these flexibilities. Limited resources make it difficult for local patent offices to work against the grain of an international system that funnels huge numbers of patents to them, along with preliminary recommendations on patentability derived from the more lax standards of developed country patent systems. A high-protectionist transnational

[2] For a list of TRIPS disputes to date, see <http://www.wto.org/english/tratop_e/dispu_e/dispu_agreements_index_e.htm?id=A26#selected_agreement>. Only 33 disputes have been initiated in the 17 years of the Agreement. Most of these were settled or terminated, or are still pending. For a trend analysis, see Pauwelyn 2010.

legal culture works against the use of flexibilities, for example, when local patent examiners are trained by WIPO or the European Patent Office, and when courts or agencies look to the readily available norms in high-protectionist jurisdictions to understand the meaning of legal terms of art, such as "obviousness" in the context of patent law. Extra-legal pressure is also brought to bear on countries seeking to use TRIPS flexibilities, through mechanisms such as the US Special 301 watchlist. Bilateral pressure is repeatedly brought to bear on countries contemplating compulsory licenses, for example, and has made developing countries reluctant to engage in the practice despite its very clear legality under TRIPS (Kapczynski 2009; Guise and de Oliveira Novaes in this volume).

With so much underdetermined by international legal commitments, transnational and local actors alike are reverting to local institutions to gain traction in the struggle over the meaning of the international IP regime. A few examples will help to illustrate.

II. Going Local in the Era of TRIPS Implementation

Going local in fights over the implementation of international IP law is not a new practice, particularly for transnational firms. For example, in 1998, the Pharmaceutical Manufacturers Association of South Africa (PMA), a group of thirty-nine multinational drug companies, brought suit against the South African government in a local court, seeking to invalidate a local law, the Medicines and Related Substances Control Act. In particular, the companies took aim at provisions in that law that sought to make it easier to import affordable medicines. The key IP provision at stake was one that authorized parallel importation, a practice in which drugs already lawfully sold abroad may be imported without the permission of a patent holder (Fisher and Rigamonti 2005). The firms argued that the statute violated constitutional rights to property and also the TRIPS Agreement itself (relevant because the South African Constitution requires consideration of international law in cases interpreting domestic constitutional rights) (Foreman 2008; South African Constitution art. 39(1)). They also made due process arguments, arguing that the discretion given to government officials would produce arbitrary and unfair results (Fisher and Rigamonti 2005).

Along the way, activists from the Treatment Action Campaign sought to join the case to dispute these claims, and to urge the court to consider not only TRIPS, but also other international agreements—most prominently, human rights agreements that they argued gave the South African government a positive duty to ensure access to medicines through TRIPS flexibilities like those challenged in the case (Treatment Action Campaign 2001). The case was settled before judgment was reached, in part because of an extraordinary level of public mobilization against the drug company position. Supported by transnational activist and humanitarian groups like Médecins Sans Frontières, campaigners mobilized demonstrations in thirty cities around the world and a petition with over 250,000 signatures urging the companies to drop the case (Foreman 2008).

The PMA case offers a good place to begin to understand what is at stake when fights over access to medicines and IP go local. Most obviously, local law may be shaped through such conflicts. Precisely because there are so many possible ways to implement TRIPS, the meaning of TRIPS commitments can be importantly influenced by engaging local, and not just transnational, institutions. Because TRIPS itself is so capacious, local practice in turn becomes a key focal point in transnational context. The accretion of many local decisions to adopt a certain flexibility can generate legitimacy for that flexibility that in turn may diminish the influence of extra-legal pressure, transnational legal culture, and resource limitations. As I have shown in my work on India, countries can seek safety in numbers by harmonizing their codification and deployment of TRIPS flexibilities (Kapczynski 2009). Developments at the local level can thus help to fuel a dynamic of counter-harmonization that has significant practical implications for how countries implement the Agreement.

The kind of local engagement evidenced in the PMA case also can produce arguments that have transnational and international effects. The plaintiffs and amici in the PMA case sought to use South African courts to elaborate new legal claims about the proper interpretation of TRIPS, and the relationship between IP provisions and other legal norms such as due process rights and health rights. Had the South African Constitutional Court concluded in the PMA case, for example, that certain strategies countries adopt to lower medicine prices violated TRIPS, the precedent would have reverberated around the world in subsequent conflicts over IP and access to medicines. Other courts would have considered the opinion in related cases. Before a WTO panel, a party might have argued that such a precedent constituted "subsequent practice" that establishes what the parties understand TRIPS to mean. A judgment that articulated due process problems, takings problems, or human rights problems with particular IP provisions would also have likely had influence elsewhere. Many countries make domestic commitments to such rights, and a well-articulated judgment that concluded that human rights required the use of a particular TRIPS flexibility would surely be invoked in a related dispute at the WTO.[3]

Such a precedent would also have helped shape the normative and political field in which legal decisions are made. A decision that a particular IP provision violated property rights or, to the contrary, was required by a commitment to human rights, would surely be cited widely outside of courts too, in the competition over the proper framing of IP law—for example, whether deviations from US-style IP practice are seen as theft, or whether patents are instead viewed as dangerous to health. A WTO panel might reject any formal link between the human rights system and the trade system, but nonetheless be loathe to interpret TRIPS in a way that generated a conflict between the Agreement and national constitutional commitments.

[3] Textual arguments exist that would permit a panel to give human rights law some effect in the context of a WTO dispute, although scholars disagree over their persuasiveness (Hestermeyer 2007).

What's more, the PMA case clearly *had* an effect on the transnational legal domain, though it was settled before it made any law. The case helped bring the conflict between access to medicines and international IP law into public view, by providing a focal point for international press and for intensive campaigning by transnational activists. It is, unsurprisingly, treated by many as a watershed moment in the access to medicines campaign, and as a factor that helped generate critical momentum toward the 2001 Doha Declaration on TRIPS and Public Health ('t Hoen 2009). That Declaration resulted in the only amendment to a core WTO Agreement that has occurred to date.[4] Local conflicts over IP and access to medicines can thus provide focal points for campaigning and meaning-making that come to influence the international legal regime in a variety of different ways.

It should now be clear why "going local" can affect international and transnational, and not merely domestic, IP laws and norms. And as the pages of this book show, the practice of going local that was exemplified in the PMA case has in fact become ubiquitous. A close read of the case studies turns up many other examples that have received little or no attention in the literature.

For example, the Chilean chapter shows that multinational pharmaceutical companies have availed themselves of local courts in other countries too, in cases similar to the PMA case. Pfizer and Eli Lilly both went to the Chilean Supreme Court when the Instituto de Salud Publica (Public Health Institute) registered generic forms of their drug, arguing that this move violated the constitutional right to property (Millaleo in this volume).

These cases are similar to several better-known Indian cases, where multinational companies have sought to use courts to interpret local law to their advantage. Novartis has litigated fiercely over the patents to Gleevec in India, for example arguing (unsuccessfully) that the patent office's interpretation of India's novel patentability standard was incorrect as a matter of Indian law, and also in violation of TRIPS (Kapczynski 2009).

Such local contests have also been brought back into the international domain by drug companies seeking to route around their defeats at the local level. For example, multinational companies convinced the US to seek to negotiate a provision disallowing the Indian patentability standard in the multilateral Trans-Pacific Partnership negotiations (Médecins Sans Frontières 2013).

Similarly, companies sometimes seek to achieve at the local level provisions that have been denied to them at the international level. In 2009, for example, the multinational drug company Bayer appealed to a local Indian court arguing that Indian patent law itself prohibited drug regulators from approving a generic form of a drug if the drug violated a local patent (SpicyIP 2010). This was, in effect, an unsuccessful attempt to create at the domestic level the equivalent of linkage requirements that have been the subject of much contention in free trade agreement negotiations. Notably, the local court cited international negotiations as evidence that the Indian legislature was aware of attempts to create linkage

[4] For a discussion of Doha, see Kapczynski 2008.

requirements, and was unlikely to have created them by implication in local law.[5] Clearly, then, a repertoire of common moves and arguments is being developed by transnational companies, and also in courts, in complex patterns of iteration and reiteration between the domestic and international domains.

The case studies in the book also reveal interconnections between local conflicts over access to medicines and IP in the Latin American context, and local conflicts elsewhere. For example, activists in India have been working to shape the contours of the Patent Law introduced there in 2005 to comply with TRIPS. One important strategy that they have relied upon has been the use of pre-grant oppositions. Indian activists have gone to local patent offices to argue that particular patent applications accepted elsewhere do not meet local Indian requirements, and advocating for access-friendly interpretations of the new law in the process (Kapczynski 2009). As the Brazil case study shows, this strategy has also been adopted by Brazilian activists, who have recently lodged oppositions to patents covering two important AIDS drugs (Guise and de Oliveira Novaes in this volume). The overlap between activist strategies should not be a surprise, given what these pages also show us about the globalized nature of the access to medicines campaign. Angelina Snodgrass Godoy's case study in this volume offers particularly striking evidence of the network of connections between global and local activists (and some of the conflicts that have emerged at that interface).

The Guise and Novaes chapter on Brazil in this volume describes another notable example of the emergence of parallel strategies emerging in different local conflicts. When Brazil brought its law into conformity with TRIPS, it created a transitional provision that permitted a patent to be retrospectively granted on a showing that it had been granted in another country. Activists challenged these patents in court, arguing that they are unconstitutional because they were not subject to the usual examination procedure for patents, and because they are against the public interest (Guise and de Oliveira Novaes in this volume; Médecins Sans Frontières). Medicines campaigners argue that retrospective patent protection raises medicine prices, but does not at the same time promote innovation (since one cannot retrospectively incentivize inventors). As such, they contend that these patents undermine the purpose of patent law, because it generates harm (higher prices), without offsetting gains. Those familiar with the recent US Supreme Court copyright docket will recognize this move, which echoes one made by copyright activists in the recent cases of *Eldred v. Ashcroft* and *Golan v. Holder*. Again, this should not be surprising—the discourse around IP and social justice is one that is emerging in dialogic fashion, with connections being made not just between campaigners working on the same issue areas, but also between campaigners working on different aspects of IP law (Kapczynski 2008). Although the Brazilian constitutional case is still pending, transnational activists have already called attention to it, seeking to legitimate the claims of local organizations, and perhaps suggest the litigation as a model for other countries (Médecins Sans Frontières n.d.). Moreover,

[5] *Bayer v. Union of India*, Delhi High Court (2009), available at <http://www.i-mak.org/pharma-patent-decisions/>.

the case has already gained traction: a lower court recently relied on the argument that pipeline patents are unconstitutional as a basis to invalidate a patent in an infringement suit (GTPI Press Release 2012).

Two other cases that have arisen outside of the Latin American help to show the dynamic way that local decisions or arguments in one place can come to be reiterated in other local contexts, through a chain of legal references. This time, the conduit was the South African AIDS activist organization, the Treatment Action Campaign (TAC). The issue in question in the case *Cipla Medpro v. Aventis Pharma* was whether an injunction was an appropriate preliminary remedy in a patent infringement suit. In a friend of the court brief, TAC argued that the local patent law, and the constitutional right to health, require that before any such injunction issue, a patent holder must show that the injunction would not harm patients (Treatment Action Campaign 2012). The brief cited as a reference an Indian case called *Roche v. Cipla*. There, a court denied an injunction in a patent dispute because it would have led to significantly higher drug prices, and thus would have undermined the public interest, and created tension with the constitutional right to life itself (Kapczynski 2009). *Roche*, in turn, cited a recent US Supreme Court case, *eBay v. MercExchange*, which concluded that permanent injunctions should not be issued automatically in patent cases, but rather only after a consideration of factors that include the public interest. TAC also cited a just-decided case from Kenya, *Ochieng v. Attorney General*, in which a court used the constitutional right to health to invalidate a local "anti-counterfeiting" law that restricted the distribution of generic medicines. While the South African court in *Aventis* declined to follow TAC's constitutional reasoning, it accepted its argument that injunctions must satisfy the public interest, prominently citing *eBay* and related US cases.

III. Discussion

When conflicts over access to medicines and IP go local, they may or may not directly address the meaning of TRIPS. But there are many other ways that such local conflicts can have implications for debates about the meaning of TRIPS in other countries, or in international institutions.

The arguments made in *Aventis* and related cases offer one example: there is much room for debate over how to understand the TRIPS requirement that judges "have the authority" to issue injunctions.[6] The emergence of cases such as *Roche* and *Aventis* have begun to assert a norm that local courts need not broadly grant injunctions where life-saving medicines are concerned. Such interpretations could have significant influence in other countries, in part because transnational

[6] A recent WTO dispute settlement on the issue sheds little light on the proper interpretation of the clause. See China—Measures Affecting the Protection and Enforcement of Intellectual Property Right, DS362, January 2009, available at <http://www.wto.org/english/tratop_e/dispu_e/cases_e/ds362_e.htm>.

organizations and multilateral institutions are likely to take them up and disseminate them widely as examples of good practice.

For example, a recent United Nations Development Program (UNDP) publication, *Good Practice Guide: Improving Access to Treatment with Flexibilities in TRIPS*, cites limits on remedies of the sort promoted in *Aventis* and *Roche v. Cipla* as an example for other countries to follow (UNDP 2011). It also uses other local examples discussed here, such as limits on patentability and pre-grant oppositions in the Indian style, to expand the menu of flexibilities normally recommended by international agencies.

Going local by engaging patent offices, by launching patent oppositions and seeking to influence the interpretation and application of patent laws can also have effects on the implementation of TRIPS. Contests between activists and companies in India have already profoundly shaped the application of the scope of patentability in Indian law. Oppositions lodged in one place (India) have reverberated in other jurisdictions (Brazil). Very recently, Médecins Sans Frontières launched a website, <http://patentoppositions.org/>, to instruct activists around the world in how to bring oppositions in their own country, and to provide a clearinghouse for opposition materials from which activists and generic companies can borrow. If this triggers a wave of new opposition work, and activists succeed in making use of local patent oppositions, and creating legislation that permits them where they are disallowed, this in turn could have a significant impact not only on what is patentable in different countries, but also on what countries understand to be acceptable and common practice in the adaptation to TRIPS. Multinational drug companies who opposed these developments have drawn on these local events as a template for new international legal commitments, such as the draft provision in the TPP negotiations allegedly promoted by the US that would bar pre-grant patent oppositions (Médecins Sans Frontières 2013).

Local developments even have the potential to destabilize the international regime itself. Consider, finally, the recent report by a high-level Global Commission on HIV/AIDS and the Law (Global Commission on HIV/AIDS and the Law 2012). That Commission, which was convened by UNDP, engaged in national consultations and reviewed national evidence about the implementation of TRIPS. It concluded that "[i]n spite of their potential benefits, TRIPS flexibilities have proved insufficient in obviating the shortages of affordable medicines that TRIPS itself has contributed to creating" (Global Commission on HIV/AIDS and the Law 2012: 81). The Commissioners—who included former Presidents of Brazil and Botswana, and Congresswoman Barbara Lee from the United States—concluded by urging the UN Secretary General to convene a high-level body to recommend a new international IP regime for pharmaceutical products, and urging that pending this review, WTO members should "suspend TRIPS as it relates to essential pharmaceutical products for low- and middle-income countries" (Global Commission on HIV/AIDS and the Law 2012: 86). The Commission's recommendations—to make ample use of TRIPS flexibilities developed in local contexts *and* to revise the international IP regime to undo the conflicts the Commission perceived between that regime and access to medicines—both rely heavily on local experience with TRIPS implementation that occurred in the previous decade. By going local, activists generated evidence of the difficulties of using TRIPS flexibilities that the Commission has deployed to challenge the normative foundation of the TRIPS Agreement itself. This is a final example of the complex and dense interconnections between the local and the international that have come to characterize the international IP regime, and that are so richly illustrated in this book.

References

Deere, Carolyn. 2008. *The Implementation Game: The TRIPS Agreement and the Global Politics of Intellectual Property Reform in Developing Countries.* Oxford: Oxford University Press.

Drahos, Peter, and John Braithwaite. 2002. *Information Feudalism: Who Owns the Knowledge Economy.* New York: New Press.

Fisher III, William, and Cyril P. Rigamonti. 2005. "The South Africa AIDS Controversy: A Case Study in Patent Law and Policy." At <http://cyber.law.harvard.edu/people/tfisher/South%20Africa.pdf>.

Foreman, Lisa. 2008. "'Rights' and Wrongs: What Utility for the Right to Health in Reforming Trade Rules on Medicines?" *Health and Human Rights* 10(2): 37–52.

Global Commission on HIV/AIDS and the Law. 2012. *Risks, Rights and Health.* New York: UNDP.

GTPI Press Release. 2012. "GTPI Supports Judicial Decision Annulling the Patent for a HIV/AIDS Medicine." Available at <http://www.patentes.org.br/media/file/Notas%20GTPI/GTPI_ABIA_statment.pdf>.

Helfer, Laurence R., 2004. "Regime Shifting: The TRIPs Agreement and New Dynamics of International Intellectual Property Lawmaking." *Yale Journal of International Law* 29(1): 1–83.

Hestermeyer, Holger. 2007. *Human Rights and the WTO: The Case of Patents and Access to Medicines.* Oxford: Oxford University Press.

Kapczynski, Amy. 2008. "The Access to Knowledge Mobilization and the New Politics of Intellectual Property." *Yale LJ* 17: 804–85.

——. 2009. "Harmonization and its Discontents: A Case Study of TRIPS Implementation in India's Pharmaceutical Sector." *Calif. L. Rev.* 97(6): 1571–650.

Médecins Sans Frontières. n.d. "Are Brazilian Pipeline Patents Constitutional?" At <http://www.msfaccess.org/our-work/hiv-aids/article/1307>.

——. 2013. Briefing Note, Trading Away Health: The Trans-Pacific Partnership Agreement.

Pauwelyn, Joost. 2010. "The Dog that Barked But Didn't Bite: 15 Years of Intellectual Property Disputes at the WTO." Available at <http://papers.ssrn.com/sol3/papers.cfm?abstract_id=1708026>.

SpicyIP. 2010. "Nay Patent Linkages: Bayer v. UOI upheld by the Division Bench of Delhi HC." Blog, February 10.

't Hoen, Ellen. 2009. *The Global Politics of Pharmaceutical Monopoly Power.* Amsterdam: AMB Publishers.

UNDP. 2011. *Good Practice Guide: Improving Access to Treatment with Flexibilities in TRIPS.*

BRIEFS CITED

Treatment Action Campaign, Heads of Argument, *Aventis v. Cipla* Case No. 138/12 (2012), in the Supreme Court of South Africa (on file with author).

Treatment Action Campaign, Heads of Argument on Behalf of the Treatment Action Campaign, submitted in *Pharmaceutical Manufacturers' Association of South Africa v. Mandela*, No. 4183/98 (April 17, 2001), available at <http://www.tac.org.za/Documents/MedicineActCourtCase/pharmace.txt>.

Chapter 11

Human Rights Frames in IP Contests

Molly Land

Introduction

One of the most dramatic developments in the area of intellectual property in the last two decades has been the shift in regulation from the domestic to the international. Although treaties such as the Berne and Paris Conventions have long set international intellectual property standards, the conclusion of the Agreement on Trade Related Aspects of Intellectual Property (TRIPS Agreement) in 1994 ushered in a new era of globalization. Since that time, we have seen a plethora of new international instruments articulating global intellectual property norms, ranging from the Development Agenda of the World Intellectual Property Organization (WIPO) and the Declaration on the TRIPS Agreement and Public Health to bilateral free trade and investment agreements containing "TRIPS-plus" norms.

Recent years, however, have seen a renewed emphasis on the importance of domestic implementation and enforcement of global prescriptions. The ways in which states conform their domestic law to international standards and whether, and if so how, they enforce them play a crucial role in the effect these standards have on the ground. The chapters in this book are an important part of this reorientation toward the domestic. Spanning an impressive range of countries in South America (Argentina, Brazil, Chile, Colombia, Ecuador) and Central America (Costa Rica, El Salvador, and Guatemala), these studies examine the actors, institutions, and discourses employed in domestic contestations over intellectual property standards and their effect on public health. As such, this volume provides a valuable contribution to our understanding of the domestication of international intellectual property norms.

This Comment adds to this discussion by examining the role of norms and framing—specifically, human rights norms and framing—in the processes of domestic change described in these case studies. More precisely, it seeks to understand the general absence of human rights norms and frames in many of these stories. Despite considerable attention to the human rights impact of intellectual property rules by international human rights institutions and the prominence human rights norms and language have had in domestic battles over intellectual property in South Africa and Brazil, human rights has played far less of a role in shaping the discourse around innovation and medicines in other places. By comparing those cases with the experience of activism around medicines in South Africa and Brazil, the Comment draws some preliminary conclusions about the legal, societal, and cultural conditions that may lend themselves to the use of human rights frames in activism around intellectual property issues.

The Comment also begins tracing the trajectory of human rights framing in debates about the effect of intellectual property on health. This tracing reveals that in the area of human rights and intellectual property, the path of norm diffusion appears to have been turned on its head. Although discussions about norm diffusion often assume a general downward directionality from the international to the domestic, the normative framing of intellectual property as a human rights issue was a bottom-up enterprise. Human rights norms were first used to frame intellectual property issues on the national level. These frames were then "uploaded" to the international level, provoking a series of international pronouncements on the relationship between human rights and intellectual property. Over time, however, these frames gave way to the language of "access to knowledge" or A2K. The Comment concludes by considering the reasons for this and arguing that a complete strategy for challenging the effect of intellectual property rights on access to medicines requires the use of both human rights and A2K frames.

I. Frame Determinants

One of the most surprising aspects of many of the volume's case studies is the relatively limited reference to human rights. In these case studies, intellectual property contestations were framed more frequently in terms of consumer's rights, dignity, free competition, the environment, and the rights of the poor. The narratives use the phrase "human rights" throughout, but they do so most often in a general sense, as a placeholder for the public interest, rather than as a distinctly *legal* entitlement guaranteeing to each individual the right to a particular standard of treatment simply by virtue of being human.

That human rights law did not play a larger role in many of the case studies is all the more unexpected in light of the high-profile experiences of South Africa and Brazil, where human rights played a central role in organizing opposition to intellectual property reform. In South Africa, the human right to health was a key organizing element in the work of the Treatment Action Campaign (TAC), a community-based organization that took the lead in the South African effort to promote access to treatment in the context of HIV/AIDS (Kapczynski and Berger 2009). TAC's litigation over access to medicines explicitly invoked the right to health under the South African Constitution, which was modeled on and drew inspiration from international instruments protecting the human right to health. In Brazil, human rights norms, which had played an important role in Brazil's transition from authoritarianism, provided a powerful and readily available frame for activism around medicines in the context of the HIV/AIDS epidemic (Galvão 2005). The efforts of Brazilian activists galvanized the government and led to the establishment of a healthcare system based on a principle of universal access (de Mello e Souza 2005). Although the struggles in South Africa and Brazil helped catalyze the debate about access to medicines and intellectual property in other countries, these later debates were not typically framed in human rights terms. Thus, this Comment began as a way to better understand this shift, asking why human rights was employed as a frame in some cases and not others. Comparing these cases reveals two primary factors that correlate with the use of human rights law as a framing device in intellectual property contexts: the extent to which human rights norms are embedded in domestic law, and the involvement of organizations with human rights expertise in the debate about access to medicines and intellectual property.

First, international human rights norms appear to be more commonly used to frame intellectual property discussions when they are also embedded in domestic constitutional law. Legal embeddedness can imbue a claim with a legitimacy it might not otherwise be perceived to have, and reliance on a legal right offers at least the possibility of enforcing desired objectives with the police power of the state. Legal embeddedness was a crucial factor in the framing of access to medicines as a human right in both South Africa and Brazil. In South Africa, human rights norms are explicitly part of national constitutional law. The existence of this right on the books was a galvanizing element in the South African campaign for access to medicines and a critical factor in TAC's adoption of a human rights frame in challenging the role of intellectual property in making medicines unaffordable. By framing high drug prices as a human rights violation under the South African Constitution, TAC was demanding a *legal* remedy (Heywood 2009). As Rosina and Novaes discuss in their chapter on Brazil in this volume, access to healthcare is also a constitutional right in Brazil, protected in Article 196 of the 1988 Brazilian Constitution. Implementing this right, Brazilian law establishes a Unified System of Healthcare (Sistema Único de Saúde or SUS), which provides for universal public healthcare open to all regardless of means. Access to medicines is also explicitly embedded in Brazilian legislation. For example, Law 9.313 requires the government to provide those with HIV/AIDS the medication needed for their treatment. This embeddedness of the right to health in Brazilian law played an important role in driving healthcare policy on access to medicines and to treatment (Flaer and Younis 2009).

Second, human rights frames also require the involvement of organizations that use human rights norms and institutions in their advocacy work. The work of intermediaries plays a crucial role in the process of translation, as international norms are appropriated and translated into local cultural narratives (Merry 2006). When intermediaries with experience in human rights were among the first to respond to increased drug prices resulting from the enforcement of intellectual property rights, the problem was much more likely to be defined in human rights terms. In South Africa, for example, TAC first championed the right to access treatment for HIV/AIDS and challenged the price increases that resulted from the introduction of patents on pharmaceuticals. Human rights had been a central component of TAC's work from the very start (Heywood 2009). In large part, this orientation was a function of TAC's leadership. The chairman of TAC, Zackie Achmat, had been active in the United Democratic Front, which had used a human rights approach to challenge apartheid. TAC also formed alliances with lawyers and other organizations (such as the Law and Treatment Access Unit of the AIDS Law Project) that used human rights law in their work (Matthews 2001).

In Brazil, human rights was also deeply embedded in the practices of the organizations that first worked for access to medicines. Early advocacy around the HIV/AIDS epidemic included widespread civic mobilization within the gay community in São Paulo working in conjunction with the *movimento sanitária*, a democratization and human rights movement that had come of age challenging the country's military dictatorship and advocating for universal access to healthcare (Galvão 2005; Gómez 2011). In the 2000s, the human rights organization Conectas joined the effort to increase access to medicines, becoming involved in the Working Group on Intellectual Property of the Brazilian Network for People's Integration; as part of that group, Conectas has been involved in the legal challenge to pipeline patents and patent oppositions before the National Industrial Property Institute (INPI) (Vieira and de Almeida 2011; Conectas 2011; Conectas 2009). As Rosina and Novaes note in their chapter in this volume, Conextas was one of three non-governmental organizations that the individuals they interviewed identified as most active in responding to the effect of intellectual property laws on the right to health.

Other than in the case of Brazil, the cases studied in this volume generally possessed the first but not the second of these framing determinants. Although they protected human rights in their national laws and constitutions, the actors leading the campaigns against intellectual property tended not to be organizations with human rights expertise or a history of using human rights norms in their work. This was particularly evident where resistance to higher intellectual property standards was driven by the local pharmaceutical industry. In Chile, for example, the national generic pharmaceutical industry took the lead in lobbying against intellectual property reform. Similarly, in Argentina, the initial contestations over intellectual property reforms took place within the government, with the executive in favor of incorporating standards urged by the United States and the parliament engaged in acts of resistance. The resistance of the legislature was supported by legal professionals, scientists, and other academics, accompanied by only a small group of actors from within civil society. Even those civil society actors involved in this movement were industry oriented, such as medical and pharmaceutical associations. In Colombia, the situation was slightly different. To be sure, debates about data exclusivity were led primarily by the organization ASINFAR, a national association of generic pharmaceutical producers, but public health was also part of the discussion. However, even here, those involved were organizations focused on public health, not human rights.

It is perhaps most surprising that parliamentary actors in Argentina did not rely on human rights arguments to advocate for greater policy space to develop local innovation policies. Human rights discourse, because it involves a claim that the state *must* act in a particular way to comply with its international obligations, can be used strategically by political actors seeking to increase their bargaining power domestically (de Mello e Souza 2005; Ferreira 2002). Human rights frames might have presented the parliamentary actors resisting reforms with political resources in opposing the executive. It is possible, however, that human rights frames are adopted more easily by those branches of government directly involved in foreign relations and thus most familiar with the law and institutions of human rights.

II. The Trajectory of Human Rights Framing

Comparing the case studies in this collection with the examples of South Africa and Brazil also allows us to begin to chart the trajectory of human rights norms in intellectual property contestations. The access to medicines story is an example of normative frame diffusion—the dissemination of a particular way of legitimizing the demands of activism and identifying desired outcomes. The normative framing of intellectual property policies as a human rights issue followed a unique path. Intellectual property was first considered a matter of human rights domestically and then that conceptualization was uploaded to international and other national arenas. After that, narratives of human rights were joined by an emerging frame of "access to knowledge" or A2K.

Although advocacy around global intellectual property norms and access to medicines dates back to the early 1990s, these issues were not initially thought of in human rights terms. Resistance to the expansion of intellectual property law and concern about its effects on the public interest began in the early 1990s with protests by farmers over the TRIPS Agreement in India and mobilization around databases in the European Union (Kapczynski 2008). The transnational network that eventually emerged around access to HIV/AIDS drugs was originally a US-based movement led by Ralph Nader and James Love of the Consumer Project on Technology (CPTech, now Knowledge Ecology International, or KEI). These activists began with a focus on drug prices in the United States but then turned their attention to concerns about international equity after the conclusion of the TRIPS Agreement (de Mello e Souza 2005). Several other international organizations eventually joined in the access to medicines campaign, including Health Action International, Essential Action, Médecins Sans Frontières/Doctors Without Borders, Oxfam, Act Up Paris, Health Gap Coalition, Third World Network, and the International Centre for Trade and Sustainable Development (Barnard 2002). These NGOs were consumers' rights groups, public health advocates, and humanitarian aid organizations; they did not self-identify as human rights organizations nor did they explicitly use human rights norms or institutions in their work.

Conversely, human rights circles initially paid little attention to intellectual property. Although the HIV/AIDS epidemic was being increasingly viewed as a human rights issue, there was no consideration of the role of intellectual property, even in discussions on the affordability of medicines. For example, the United Nations High Commissioner for Human Rights and the Joint United Nations Programme on HIV/AIDS jointly organized the United Nations Second Annual Consultation on HIV/AIDS and Human Rights in 1996. That effort produced the first version of the Guidelines on HIV/AIDS and Human Rights two years later, in 1998—the same year that TAC was formed in South Africa. The guidelines discussed medicines, noting that states "should enact legislation to provide for the regulation of HIV-related goods, services and information, so as to ensure widespread availability of . . . safe and effective medication at an affordable price," but no mention was made of intellectual property law's role in the availability or affordability of medicines (Guidelines 1998).

It was only after the initial framing of intellectual property as a human rights issue in South Africa and the media attention generated by this movement in the late 1990s and early 2000s that human rights institutions became involved. Indeed, the year 2001 saw international human rights organizations and institutions engaged in a veritable flurry of activism and lawmaking activity in the area of intellectual property. In one of the earliest invocations of a human rights framework on issues of intellectual property, the South African lawsuit led Oxfam to write to Mary Robinson, then the United Nations High Commissioner for Human Rights, that the lawsuit was preventing the South African government from complying with its international human rights obligations (Oxfam 2001). This was also the year of, among other things, a report on the impact of the TRIPS Agreement on human rights by the United Nations High Commissioner for Human Rights, a resolution on intellectual property and human rights by the United Nations Sub-Commission on the Promotion and Protection of Human Rights, a report on intellectual property and human rights by the United Nations Secretary General, and a resolution from the Commission on Human Rights calling on states to pursue policies that promote access to medicines as a part of the right to health (Helfer and Austin 2011).

In short, the framing of intellectual property as a human rights issue was a bottom-up enterprise. Intellectual property was *first* framed as a human rights issue in South Africa and *then* shifted up to international arenas. The bottom-up framing of intellectual property in human rights terms demonstrates the complexity of the relationship between the domestic and international arenas in both norm diffusion and framing. Although theories of norm diffusion tend to assume a general downward directionality, with norms being articulated internationally and then diffusing downward and resulting in domestic political change, the reality is much more complex (Finnemore and Sikkink 1998). Frames shift and flow both vertically and horizontally as they are taken up by actors with the resources and opportunity to exploit them. The use of human rights law to challenge intellectual property policies in South Africa was itself a product of norms domesticated in other, earlier contests. It was a continuation of a human rights story that had deep roots in the struggle against apartheid, which was influenced in important ways by transnational norms and activism (Black 1998). Human rights norms—which were transformed and domesticated in the process—were institutionalized in the post-apartheid legal structure. The socialization of activists and the embeddedness of human rights in law contributed significantly to the later choice of human rights as a frame for struggles around access to medicines and intellectual property.

III. A2K and Human Rights

Although there were important benefits associated with the use of human rights language and norms in early battles over access to medicines in South Africa, Brazil, and elsewhere, human rights law did not seem to provide a strong basis for tackling the powerful economic and innovation-based arguments deployed on behalf of intellectual property rights. A new frame, one organized around "access to knowledge" or A2K, soon emerged to provide that basis. Over time, this shift led to less reliance on human rights norms in framing issues of intellectual property. This section charts some of the reasons for this shift and then returns to the case studies to consider what they illustrate about synergies between human rights and A2K framings in debates about intellectual property and access to medicines.

There were several benefits associated with the use of human rights norms and language in initial contests around the impact of intellectual property on individual health and welfare. First, the human rights frame offered a clear alternative to the economic narrative of intellectual property expansion and thereby reoriented debates on the effect of intellectual property policies on individual people. Discussions about the global regulation of intellectual property were often cast in economic terms, focused on the extent to which intellectual property regulation fostered innovation or promoted economic growth and development. Human rights provided an "alternative moral framework," one that emphasized the right to life and health rather than piracy and counterfeiting (Matthews 2011: 103). Human rights also offered the advantage of clarity. The complexity of intellectual property issues allowed industry initially to frame the debate in terms advantageous to itself (de Mello e Souza 2005). Human rights, with its focus on the individual, allowed activists to tell a much simpler and far more compelling story that placed the consequences of intellectual property policies for individuals on the same level as the effect of these policies on innovation and development (Klug 2005; Forman 2008).

Second, human rights also provided an established set of norms, language, and networks for thinking about the problems associated with intellectual property reforms that South African and then transnational and local activists could access immediately. Going into conversations about intellectual property and human health, industry coalitions had an advantage because they had helped set the multilateral agenda. Being able to tap into an existing framework allowed access to medicines activists to "jump start" a discussion of the issue in terms favorable to their agenda and provided activists with important preexisting networks, resources, and audiences (de Mello e Souza 2005). The use of this established framework linked domestic struggles around access to medicines to other international and domestic advocacy networks and provided legitimacy for the demands of activists.

After considerable activity by international human rights organizations and institutions on intellectual property issues in the early 2000s, the pace slowed considerably. Human rights institutions continued to consider the intersection of human rights and intellectual property, including through a 2006 interpretive comment of the Committee on Economic, Social and Cultural Rights on creators' rights. Overall, however, there has been far less activity since then. For example, a 2009 interpretive comment on the right to take part in cultural life makes no mention of intellectual property rights, despite the importance of copyright for the ability to create and enjoy cultural works.

The A2K frame, in contrast, has played an increasingly important role in organizing debates about intellectual property. The Development Agenda, for example, originally proposed by Brazil and Argentina in 2004 to reorient the work of WIPO on the innovation and knowledge needs of developing countries, is now administered by WIPO's Committee on Development and Intellectual Property. The Committee is charged with developing plans of action for implementing each of the original forty-five recommendations in the Development Agenda. Among other things, working groups under the auspices of the Committee are creating databases of experts who can provide technical assistance, fostering the development of local capacity on intellectual property issues through assistance in establishing national intellectual property institutions and systems, and providing information and technical support for local efforts to use copyright and its flexibilities to increase access to knowledge (WIPO Program Activities).

In part, it may have been the very strengths of the human rights frame that also led to its declining use in discussions about the impact of innovation and intellectual property policies. Human rights provides a clear orientation on the minimum standards of health and welfare to which each individual is entitled. It does not, however, provide a good basis for critiquing the means chosen by states for meeting these minimum standards. As long as the state has the appropriate structures, processes, and outcomes (Chapman 2007), human rights law is relatively agnostic about how the state chooses to achieve those goals. As a result, human rights law provides a poor basis for responding to rights owners' arguments that strong intellectual property rights would in fact foster innovation and human rights. What advocates needed was an analytical frame they could use to engage in a detailed critique of particular innovation policies and to develop alternatives that might result in more protection for human rights.

That frame emerged around "access to knowledge" or A2K. Activists from a variety of fields, ranging from healthcare to agriculture to open source software, questioned the assumption that exclusive rights are necessary to encourage innovation and argued that overprotection can be as harmful for innovation as underprotection. This international activism on intellectual property and the public interest began to coalesce around a frame of "access to knowledge," which allowed new groups of activists to collaborate on intellectual property issues and their impact on public welfare (Kapczynski 2008). A2K framings, with their emphasis on law and expertise in both intellectual property and economic structures, were ideally suited for critiquing the content of innovation policies.

Although there continued to be important collaborations between the human rights and A2K advocacy communities, the A2K frame began exercising a "gravitational pull" (Kapczynski 2008: 860) and crowding out human rights language in debates about intellectual property and medicines. This was for several reasons. First, the deepening engagement with intellectual property rationales posed expertise barriers for human rights organizations. Although NGOs had driven the initial domestic framing of intellectual property as a human rights issue in South Africa and Brazil, activity on the international level had been concentrated within the human rights institutions of the United Nations. For the framing of intellectual property as a human rights issue to take hold elsewhere, it would have to be taken up by domestic and international NGOs. The level of engagement needed to refute the market-based rationales driving higher drug prices, however, made it difficult for international and domestic organizations without expertise in intellectual property issues to enter into this discussion.

Second, A2K advocates grew increasingly concerned that human rights law could be used to support claims to intellectual property rights themselves. International human rights law does protect some of the attributes associated with ownership of intellectual property rights—namely, an author's moral and material interests in his or her work. Regional human rights law has also been interpreted as protecting intellectual property rights directly (Helfer 2007). A2K advocates grew increasingly skeptical of human rights frames, fearing their use would only strengthen the position of rights holders (Helfer 2007) and "further entrench some dangerous ideas about property: in particular, that property rights as human rights ought to be inviolable and ought to receive extremely solicitous attention from the international community" (Raustiala 2007: 1032).

Third, the technical nature and complexity of intellectual property and its interface with human health and welfare made it much more difficult to fit intellectual property stories into human rights frames. Medicine is a relatively easy case; in South Africa and elsewhere, it was possible to directly connect the introduction of patents to increases in the cost of antiretrovirals. In other areas, however, intellectual property affects individual rights in a much more indirect way. For example, mapping the relationship between copyright and the right to education requires a sophisticated understanding of copyright law, the market for educational materials, and economics. On the surface, copyright does not seem to be a significant barrier to the distribution of textbooks; copyright protects only expression and not ideas, so if one textbook were too expensive the state would be free to commission other textbooks that conveyed the same information. However, if the state did not have the actual capacity to develop new books—because there were no individuals to produce or manufacture them, for example—then copyright does contribute to an access problem (Chon 2007; Helfer and Austin 2011). This, however, is a very complicated story, and human rights campaigns are most successful when they can tell a clear causal story and identify those responsible for the harm in a direct and concise manner (Keck and Sikkink 1998).

Although the use of human rights to frame intellectual property issues has diminished with time, there are important reasons for employing both human rights and A2K frames in challenging the effect of intellectual property rights on access to medicines. The language of A2K provides a powerful tool for understanding and responding to some of the market distortions that can be caused by intellectual property. At the same time, the way in which A2K understands the nature of the problem and the solutions it proposes can lack resonance in some contexts. The Central American case study in this book illustrates why it can be helpful to pair human rights and A2K frames in advocacy around access to medicines.

Although A2K was an excellent frame for the debate about solutions to problems with innovation systems, it sometimes did not translate well. In the case study of Central America, advocacy around the intellectual property provisions of the

Central American Free Trade Agreement was largely driven by transnational groups focused on the public interest effects of intellectual property. As Godoy explains in her chapter in this volume, these groups encountered difficulty in getting local civil society groups engaged with the issue of intellectual property because health issues had historically been understood in terms of the dysfunctionality of state institutions in charge of purchasing and administering drugs, not in terms of international market forces on price. The A2K mobilization, to the extent it was focused on the effects of intellectual property, may not have been viewed as responding to local needs in places where intellectual property was only one, and perhaps not even the most important, factor affecting realization of the right to health.

Human rights, in contrast, might be a more effective frame for mapping intellectual property issues onto local concerns in such contexts. A human rights approach is rights-driven—that is, it is oriented toward and organized around individual rights. This focus on rights encourages consideration of the broad range of activities that can affect those rights, rather than just the effect of particular laws. For example, in the context of HIV/AIDS, a human rights framework emphasizes the variety of factors that can affect the rights of individuals with HIV/AIDS, including but not limited to stigmatization, discrimination, and violence (Galvão 2005). For this reason, the human rights frame may have more resonance when intellectual property is only one of many barriers to access to knowledge. In such situations, adopting a rights-driven framework may provide a more effective strategy for advocates seeking to address distributional inequities in the area of access to knowledge.

Human rights and A2K also provide complementary frames for identifying the actors who bear responsibility for ensuring affordable medicines. As I have discussed in more detail elsewhere (Beutz Land 2009), a human rights frame generally tends to propose solutions oriented toward the state and failures of public authority. A2K, in contrast, with its deep engagement with the market-based rationale of intellectual property, focuses more often on the role played by corporations, markets, and the global economic order. The South African example suggests that both approaches are needed. Although the South African government had initially seemed supportive of the claims of the access to medicines movement, economic pressure and AIDS denialism eventually led the government to resist reforms (Klug 2005; Nolan 2007; Heywood 2003). The government's about-face forced TAC to examine not only the responsibility of pharmaceutical companies but also the obligations of the state more broadly to control prices and create innovation policies that promote access to medicines (Heywood 2009). The Central American case study similarly reflects the importance of developing strategies that focus on both public and private actors. As Godoy's chapter in this volume observes, local advocates resisted the intellectual property agenda in part because of a lack of trust in the quality of generic production and a concern that generic producers would charge high prices. Although generic production could have made important contributions to making medicines more affordable, it was not an acceptable solution in the absence of regulatory measures designed to ensure the generics would be both safe and affordable.

IV. Conclusion

Human rights framing played an important role in catalyzing activism around intellectual property and access to medicines. Particularly in places where human rights law was embedded in both law and public discourse, human rights provided a bottom-up framing of intellectual property as much more than a means for incentivizing creation, but rather as a set of policy choices that can have profound effects on human lives. The trajectory of that framing also reveals important synergies between the frames of human rights and A2K. The analytical approach of A2K allowed activists to challenge the economic incentive rationales underlying claims of expanded protection. Although the discourse of A2K came to partly displace human rights language in debates about intellectual property, both frames play an important role in successful organizing around access to medicines. Human rights frames provide an orientation toward failures of state authority and a broader context for understanding the harms of intellectual property that may be particularly important in low-resource settings. A2K frames, in turn, offer a powerful response to the innovation rationales of intellectual property. The case studies in this book not only aid our understanding of how international norms on intellectual property have been domesticated, but also the importance of employing both human rights and A2K frames in the process.

References

Barnard, D. 2002. "In the High Court of South Africa, Case no. 4138/98: The Global Politics of Access to Low-Cost AIDS Drugs in Poor Countries." *Kennedy Institute of Ethics Journal* 12(2): 159–74.

Beutz Land, M. 2009. "Protecting Rights Online." *Yale Journal of International Law* 32: 1–46.

Black, D. 1998. "The Long and Winding Road: International Norms and Domestic Political Change in South Africa." Pp. 78–108 in *The Power of Human Rights: International Norms and Domestic Change*, edited by T. Risse et al. Cambridge: Cambridge University Press.

Chapman, A. R. 2007. "Development of Indicators for Economic, Social and Cultural Rights: The Rights to Education, Participation in Cultural Life and Access to the Benefits of Science." Pp. 111–52 in *Human Rights in Education, Science and Culture: Legal Developments and Challenges*, edited by Y. Donders and V. Volodin. Aldershot: Ashgate Publishing, Ltd.

Chon, M. 2007. "Distributive Justice and Intellectual Property: Intellectual Property 'from Below': Copyright and Capability for Education." *U.C. Davis Law Review* 40: 803–54.

Conectas. 2009. "In Support of the Unconstitutionality of the Patents Pipeline" [Press Release]. Retrieved from <http://www.conectas.org/en/artigo-1/in-support-of-the-unconstitutionality-of-the-patents-pipeline>.

——. 2011. "Civil Society Group Challenges Extension of Patent that Hinders Access to Essential AIDS Drugs" [Press Release]. Retrieved from <http://www.conectas.org/en/

artigo-1/civil-society-group-challenges-extension-of-patent-that-hinders-access-to-essen tial-aids-drugs>.

de Mello e Souza, A. 2005. "The Power of the Weak: Advocacy Networks, Ideational Change and the Global Politics of Pharmaceutical Patent Rights." Thesis, Stanford University.

Ferreira, L. 2002. "Access to Affordable HIV/AIDS Drugs: The Human Rights Obligations of Multinational Pharmaceutical Corporations." *Fordham Law Review* 71: 1133–79.

Finnemore, M., and K. Sikkink. 1998. "International Norm Dynamics and Political Change." *International Organization* 52(autumn): 887–917.

Flaer, P. J., and M. Z. Younis. 2009. "The Brazilian Experiment: HIV Drugs for All." *Journal of Health Care Finance* 36(2): 90–6.

Forman, L. 2008. "'Rights' and Wrongs: What Utility for the Right to Health in Reforming Trade Rules on Medicines?" *Health & Human Rights: An International Journal* 10(2): 37–52.

Galvão, J. 2005. "Brazil and Access to HIV/AIDS Drugs: A Question of Human Rights and Public Health." *American Journal Public Health* 95(7): 1110–16.

Gómez, E. J. 2011. "How Brazil Outpaced the United States when it Came to AIDS: The Politics of Civic Infiltration, Reputation, and Strategic Internalization." *Journal of Health Politics, Policy and Law* 36(2): 317–52.

Helfer, L. R. 2007. "International Rights Approaches to Intellectual Property: Toward a Human Rights Framework for Intellectual Property." *UC Davis Law Review* 40: 971–1020.

—— and G. W. Austin. 2011. *Human Rights and Intellectual Property: Mapping the Global Interface.* New York: Cambridge University Press.

Heywood, M. 2003. Preventing Mother-to-Child HIV Transmission in South Africa: Background, Strategies and Outcomes of the Treatment Action Campaign Case against the Minister of Health." *South African Journal of Human Rights* 19: 278–315.

——. 2009. "South Africa's Treatment Action Campaign: Combining Law and Social Mobilization to Realize the Right to Health." *Journal of Human Rights Practice* 1(1): 14–36.

Kapczynski, A. 2008. "The Access to Knowledge Mobilization and the New Politics of Intellectual Property." *Yale Law Journal* 117: 804–85.

—— and J. M. Berger. 2009. "The Story of the TAC Case: The Potential and Limits of Socio-economic Rights Litigation in South Africa." Pp. 43–80 in *Human Rights Advocacy Stories*, edited by D. Hurwitz et al. New York: Thomson Reuters/Foundation Press.

Keck, M. E., and K. Sikkink. 1998. *Activists beyond Borders: Advocacy Networks in International Politics.* Ithaca, NY: Cornell University Press.

Klug, H. 2005. "Campaigning for Life: Building a New Transitional Solidarity in the Face of HIV/AIDs and TRIPS." Pp. 118–39 in *Law and Globalization from Below: Toward a Cosmopolitan Legality*, edited by B. de Sousa Santos and César A. Rodríguez-Garavito. Cambridge: Cambridge University Press.

Matthews, D. 2001. "When Framing Meets Law: Using Human Rights as a Practical Instrument to Facilitate Access to Medicines in Developing Countries." Queen Mary University of London School of Law, Legal Studies Research Paper No. 92/20011.

——. 2011. *Intellectual Property, Human Rights and Development: The Role of NGOs and Social Movements.* Cheltenham: Edward Elgar Publishing Limited.

Merry, S. 2006. *Human Rights & Gender Violence: Translating International Law into Local Justice.* Chicago: University of Chicago Press.

Nolan, S. 2007. *28 Stories of AIDS in Africa.* New York: Walker and Company.

Office of the High Commissioner for Human Rights & Joint United Nations Programme on HIV/AIDS. 1998. HIV/AIDS and Human Rights International Guidelines, HR/PUB/98/1.

Oxfam. 2001. "Drug Giant Set to Cause Violation of Human Rights." Press Release. April 12.

Raustiala, K. 2007. "International Rights Approaches to Intellectual Property: Commentary: Density and Conflict in International Intellectual Property Law." *UC Davis Law Review* 40: 1021–38.

Vieira, O. V., and E. M. de Almeida. 2011. "Strategic Advocacy in Human Rights: Conectas' Experience." *International Journal on Human Rights* 8(15): 181–205.

WIPO Program Activities, Projects for Implementation of Development Agenda Recommendations, <http://www.wipo.int/ip-development/en/agenda/projects.html>.

Chapter 12

The Rights-Based Approach to Intellectual Property and Access to Medicine

Parameters and Pitfalls

Smita Narula

Introduction

Access to essential medicines is a fundamental component of the human right to adequate health. In the face of global pandemics, rising drug costs continue to attract a great deal of attention and have opened up a space for the broader conversation around the interaction of states' human rights obligations with their international financial commitments, particularly in the realm of trade and intellectual property.

The relationship between human rights and intellectual property is a troubled one and is epitomized by the contentious issue of access to patented medicines (Helfer and Austin 2011: 90). Patent protection can interfere with access to medicine in two key ways: by granting exclusive rights in pharmaceutical production, raising the cost of medicines to often unaffordable prices; and by providing a profit mechanism that incentivizes research of diseases primarily affecting countries with lucrative markets over diseases prevalent in developing countries (Helfer and Austin 2011: 140, 42).[1] The result is a "global drug gap" wherein novel drugs are often inaccessible to most of the world's population (Helfer and Austin 2011: 140).

Helfer and Austin (2011) suggest that the human right to health offers a valuable framework for addressing this gap by: "refram[ing] existing legal discourses that privilege legal rules protecting intellectual property over those protecting individual rights and social values"; "provid[ing] a mechanism to hold governments accountable for providing at least minimal levels of health care"; and "emphasiz[ing] the need to restructure incentives for medical research and innovation toward the treatment of neglected diseases and the health needs of the world's poor" (Helfer and Austin 2011: 144).

[1] The authors add that a number of other obstacles, such as poverty and limited government funding of healthcare, also interfere with access to medicine in developing countries.

This chapter provides an overview of the rights-based approach to access to medicines and focuses on the work of international human rights bodies, mechanisms, and procedures on the question of balancing intellectual property and human rights. A plethora of human rights committees, actors, and institutions have developed out of the canon of human rights law to monitor the implementation of various treaties and to breathe normative content into various rights, including the right to health.

Section I of this chapter outlines both the broad and specific parameters of the rights-based approach to intellectual property and access to medicine, while section II addresses the impediments and obstacles to implementing such an approach in practice. These obstacles arise in connection to key interrelated deficits in international human rights law around the issues of legitimacy, accountability, and domestic capacity.

The chapter concludes that the full and equitable realization of the right to adequate health depends greatly on the capacity and political inclination of domestic actors to enforce international norms. Conclusions regarding the extent to which human rights primacy can be realized in the realm of access to medicines are therefore highly country and context specific.

I. The Rights-Based Approach to Intellectual Property and Access to Medicine

The human right to health, protected under various international, regional, and domestic constitutional instruments, has served as the starting point for the human rights community's interactions with access to medicine and the intellectual property regime. A number of human rights institutions and actors have played a critical role in the development of these norms.[2] These include treaty bodies such as the UN Committee on Economic, Social and Cultural Rights;[3] intergovernmental bodies such as the UN Human Rights Council (formerly the Commission on Human

[2] For a comprehensive compilation of relevant texts from international actors see Helfer and Austin (2011: 53–6).

[3] See, e.g., Committee on Economic, Social & Cultural Rights, *General Comment No. 17: The Right of Everyone to Benefit from the Protection of the Moral and Material Interests Resulting from Any Scientific, Literary or Artistic Production of Which He Is the Author*, art. 15(1)(c), UN Doc. E/C.12/GC/17 (January 12, 2006) [hereinafter General Comment No. 17] (asserting that states parties must "ensure that intellectual property regimes contribute, in a practical and substantive way, to the full realization of all the Covenant rights"); ECOSOC, Committee on Economic, Social & Cultural Rights, *Substantive Issues Arising in the Implementation of the International Covenant on Economic, Social and Cultural Rights*, UN Doc. E/C12/2001/15 (December 14, 2001) [hereinafter CESCR 2001] ("national and international intellectual property regimes must be consistent with" economic, social, and cultural rights obligations). See also Committee on the Rights of the Child, *General Comment No. 3: HIV/AIDS and the Rights of the Child*, para. 28, UN Doc. CRC/GC/2003/3 (March 17, 2003) ("The obligations of States parties under the Convention extend to ensuring that children have sustained and equal access to comprehensive treatment and care, including necessary HIV-related drugs").

Rights);[4] and special procedures and individual office holders such as the UN High Commissioner for Human Rights,[5] and the UN Special Rapporteurs on the rights to health and food.[6]

Regional and domestic actors are also increasingly involved in the development and implementation of human rights norms as they relate to the issue of access to medicine. At the regional level, these include the Inter-American Commission on Human Rights[7] and the African Commission on Human and Peoples' Rights.[8] Domestically, a number of courts have played a critical role in translating these norms into tangible rights and benefits.[9]

[4] See, e.g., Commission on Human Rights, Res. 2001/33, UN Doc. E/CN.4/RES/2001/33 (April 23, 2001) [hereinafter Commission on Human Rights 2001] (states must "adopt legislation or other measures, in accordance with applicable international law" to "safeguard access" to such medications "from any limitations by third parties"); Commission on Human Rights, *Access to Medication in the Context of Pandemics such as HIV/AIDS*, UN Doc. E/CN.4/RES/2002/32 (April 22, 2002) [hereinafter Commission on Human Rights 2002]; Human Rights Council, *Access to Medicine in the Context of the Right of Everyone to the Enjoyment of the Highest Attainable Standard of Physical and Mental Health*, Res. 12/24, UN Doc. A/HRC/RES/12/24 (October 2, 2009).

[5] See, e.g., Commission on Human Rights, *Report of the High Commissioner on the Impact of the Agreement on Trade-Related Aspects of Intellectual Property Rights on Human Rights*, UN Doc. E/CN.4/Sub.2/2001/13 (June 27, 2001) [hereinafter Report of the High Commissioner 2001] (analyzing the Agreement on Trade-Related Aspects of Intellectual Property Rights (TRIPS) and criticizing TRIPS implementation from a human rights perspective).

[6] See, e.g., UN Special Rapporteur on the right of everyone to the enjoyment of the highest attainable standard of physical and mental health, *Report of the Special Rapporteur on the Right of Everyone to the Enjoyment of the Highest Attainable Standard of Physical and Mental Health*, 61st Sess., UN Doc. A/61/338 (2006) [hereinafter Special Rapporteur on the Right to Health 2006]; UN Special Rapporteur on the Right of Everyone to the Enjoyment of the Highest Attainable Standard of Physical and Mental Health, *Human Rights Guidelines for Pharmaceutical Companies in Relation to Access to Medicines*, UN Doc. A/63/263 (August 11, 2008) (prepared by Paul Hunt) [hereinafter Special Rapporteur on the Right to Health 2008] (addressing the human rights obligations of pharmaceutical companies); UN Special Rapporteur on the Right to Food, Report to UN General Assembly, UN Doc. A/64/170 (July 23, 2009) (prepared by Olivier De Schutter) (addressing the interaction between human rights and intellectual property); UN Special Rapporteur of the Commission on Human Rights on the Right to Food, *Report to Commission on Human Rights*, UN Doc. E/CN.4/2004/10, para. 39 (February 9, 2004) (prepared by Jean Ziegler) (addressing the interaction between human rights and intellectual property).

[7] See, e.g., *Jorge Odir Miranda Cortez et al. v. El Salvador*, Case 12.249, Report No. 29/01, OEA/Ser.L/V/II.111 Doc. 20 rev. at 284 (2000) (a claim by HIV-infected individuals that the El Salvador government had violated, *inter alia*, the rights to life and health by failing to provide antiretroviral drugs; the Inter-American Commission issued a precautionary measures order and declared the complaint admissible, but the case ended in a friendly settlement after the El Salvadorian Supreme Court ordered that drugs be provided in a similar case).

[8] See, e.g., African Commission on Human and Peoples' Rights, *Resolution on Access to Health and needed Medicines in Africa*, ACHPR/Res.141 (XXXXIIII)08 (November 24, 2008) (urging states to "guarantee the full scope of access to needed medicines" and calling on states to fulfill their duties by promoting, protecting, and fulfilling access to medicines).

[9] See, e.g., *South Africa—Minister of Health v. Treatment Action Campaign (TAC)*, 5 SA 721 (CC 2002) (holding that the South African government's restrictions on the distribution of antiretroviral drugs to pregnant women amounts to a violation of the constitutional right to health); *López, Glenda y otros v. Instituto Venezolano de los Seguros Sociales (IVSS)* s/acción de amparo. Expediente 00-1343. Sentencia No. 487; *Cruz del Valle Bermúdez y otros vs. MSAS s/amparo*, Expediente No. 15.789, Sentencia No. 196 (Venezuelan Constitutional Court 1999) (ordering the Venezuelan government to provide antiretrovirals on a regular and reliable basis to a group of individuals living with HIV/AIDS); *Viceconte, Mariela v. Estado Nacional (Ministerio de Salud y Ministerio de Economía de la Nación) s/ Acción de Amparo*, Causa No. 31.777/96 (Argentinian Federal Administrative Court of Appeals 1998)

This section summarizes some of the most salient points of the human rights approach as it has emerged over the past decade, and outlines domestic and international responsibilities for both states and third parties.

A. The Right to Health and Access to Medicines under International Human Rights Law

1. Right to Health and Access to Medicines: The Framework

The right to health is primarily codified under Article 12 of the International Covenant on Economic, Social and Cultural Rights (ICESCR), which asserts that states must recognize "the right of everyone to the enjoyment of the highest attainable standard of physical and mental health."[10] The UN Committee on Economic, Social and Cultural Rights has interpreted the right to health to include "underlying determinants of health, such as access to safe and potable water and adequate sanitation, an adequate supply of safe food, nutrition and housing, healthy occupational and environmental conditions, and access to health-related education and information."[11] Additionally, it requires the availability and accessibility of "[f]unctioning public health and health-care facilities, goods and services, as well as programmes."[12] Access to essential medicine is conceptualized as a subcomponent of the broader right to adequate health.[13]

(finding a violation of the right to health under art. 12 of the ICESCR and ordering the Argentinian government to produce and distribute a vaccine).

[10] International Covenant on Economic, Social, and Cultural Rights, art. 12, December 16, 1966, 993 U.N.T.S. 3 [hereinafter ICESCR], available at <http://www2.ohchr.org/english/law/pdf/cescr.pdf>. The right to health is also contained in other international as well as regional instruments. See, e.g., Convention on the Elimination of All Forms of Discrimination against Women [CEDAW], art. 12, December 18, 1979, 1249 U.N.T.S. 13, available at <http://www.un.org/womenwatch/daw/cedaw/text/econvention.htm>; Convention on the Rights of the Child [CRC], art. 24(2)(b), November 20, 1989, 1577 U.N.T.S. 3, available at <http://www2.ohchr.org/english/law/pdf/crc.pdf>; African [Banjul] Charter on Human and Peoples' Rights, art. 16, June 27, 1981, OAU Doc. CAB/LEG/67/3 rev. 5, 21 I.L.M. 58, available at <http://www1.umn.edu/humanrts/instree/z1afchar.htm>; American Declaration of the Rights and Duties of Man, art. 11, EA/Ser.L.V/II.82 doc. 6 rev.1 (1948), available at <http://www1.umn.edu/humanrts/oasinstr/zoas2dec.htm>; and the Additional Protocol to the American Convention on Human Rights in the Area of Economic, Social and Cultural Rights, "Protocol of San Salvador," art. 10, November 14, 1988, O.A.S.T.S. No. 69, 28 I.L.M. 156 (1989), available at <http://www.oas.org/juridico/english/treaties/a-52.html>; European Social Charter, art. 11, October 18, 1961, 529 U.N.T.S. 89 available at <http://conventions.coe.int/Treaty/en/Treaties/Html/035.htm>.

[11] ECOSOC, Comm. on Econ., Soc. & Cultural Rights, *General Comment No. 14: The Right to the Highest Attainable Standard of Health (Art. 12)*, para. 4, UN Doc. E/C.12/2000/4 (August 11, 2000), available at <http://www.unhcr.org/refworld/pdfid/4538838d0.pdf> [hereinafter "General Comment No. 14"]. Although the status of General Comments under international law is unclear, and potentially contestable, they still constitute carefully considered and systematic analyses emanating from a body uniquely placed to offer an interpretation of the norms contained in the ICESCR.

[12] (n. 11) para. 12(a).

[13] See, e.g., UN Special Rapporteur on the Right of Everyone to the Highest Attainable Standard of Physical and Mental Health, *Addendum: Mission to the World Trade Organization*, para. 18, UN Doc. E/CM.4/2004/49/Add.1 (March 1, 2004) (prepared by Paul Hunt) (asserting that the right to health encompasses "access to essential medicines").

The rights-based framework for access to medicines rests on four pillars: availability; accessibility; cultural acceptability; and quality.[14] Specifically, states must ensure *availability* of medicines. This could include, for example, making use of compulsory license flexibilities in the Agreement on Trade-Related Aspects of Intellectual Property Rights (TRIPS) to ensure sufficient quantities of medicines within their countries, and supporting research and development of drugs to address diseases that place a particular burden on developing countries.[15]

On the issue of *accessibility* of medicines, states must ensure access in geographic, physical, and economic terms and without discrimination. Geographic or physical accessibility means that health services must be physically accessible to all individuals in all parts of the country, while economic accessibility concerns the issue of affordability of medicines, which in turn has implications for how medicines are priced.[16] States must also ensure accessibility of information on the basis of which individuals can, *inter alia*, make informed decisions about the medicines that they are taking.[17] The World Health Organization has also highlighted that essential medicines must be available in appropriate dosage forms, which may for example require adaptation to local limitations on refrigeration or distribution.[18] Calls for both availability and accessibility have been especially pronounced in the face of various global pandemics such as HIV/AIDS, malaria, and tuberculosis.[19]

Cultural acceptability, the third pillar of the access to medicine framework, calls on states to: support the proper use of traditional medicines and the integration of those medicines into national programs; and ensure compliance with medical ethics so that clinical trials are carried out with informed consent.[20] Finally, states must ensure that medicines are of good *quality*.[21]

[14] General Comment No. 14, (n. 11), para. 12; Special Rapporteur on the Right to Health 2006 (n. 6), paras. 47–51; African Commission on Human and Peoples' Rights, *Resolution on Access to Health and needed Medicines in Africa*, ACHPR/Res.141 (XXXXIIII)08 (November 24, 2008).

[15] Special Rapporteur on the Right to Health 2006, (n. 6), para. 47 (stating that countries "might have to make use of the Agreement on Trade-Related Aspects of Intellectual Property Rights (TRIPS) flexibilities by passing and using compulsory licence legislation, thereby ensuring that medicines reach their jurisdictions in adequate quantities").

[16] General Comment No. 14 (n. 11), para. 12(b); Special Rapporteur on the Right to Health 2006 (n. 6), para. 49.

[17] General Comment No. 14 (n. 11), para. 12(b); Special Rapporteur on the Right to Health 2006 (n. 6), para. 49.

[18] World Health Organization, "Essential Medicines Lists," available at <http://www.who.int/medicines/services/essmedicines_def/en/index.html>.

[19] See, e.g., Commission on Human Rights 2002 (n. 4) (calling upon states to promote: "availability... of pharmaceuticals... to treat pandemics such as HIV/AIDS"; "accessibility to all without discrimination, including the most vulnerable sectors of the population"; and "assurance that pharmaceuticals... are scientifically and medically appropriate and of good quality).

[20] General Comment No. 14 (n. 11), para. 12(c); Special Rapporteur on the Right to Health 2006 (n. 6), para. 50.

[21] General Comment No. 14 (n. 11), para. 12(d); Special Rapporteur on the Right to Health 2006 (n. 6), para. 51.

2. Right to Health and Access to Medicines: The Duty-Bearers

a. States

States are the primary duty-bearers under international human rights law and must *respect*, *protect*, and *fulfill* rights[22] in line with the guidance outlined above. The duty to respect is essentially a duty of non-interference with existing access to rights.[23] Under the duty to protect, states must exercise *due diligence* to ensure that non-state actors—such as corporations—are not interfering with individual rights.[24] This includes a duty to investigate all instances in which a private individual or corporation may be interfering with human rights,[25] and to take steps to remedy violations that have taken place.[26] As noted, this may also include regulating the price, availability, and accessibility of medicine. The duty to fulfill includes the duty to *facilitate* and in some cases *provide* human rights.[27] Inherent in these obligations is the duty to provide an effective remedy when human rights violations have taken place.[28]

While the ICESCR allows for "progressive realization" of the rights contained therein,[29] states parties have an immediate obligation to: ensure non-discrimination in the provision of economic, social, and cultural rights; and take immediate steps toward the realization of these rights.[30] Economic, social, and cultural rights also

[22] See Office of the High Commissioner for Human Rights, International Human Rights Law, <http://www.ohchr.org/EN/ProfessionalInterest/Pages/InternationalLaw.aspx> (last visited July 27, 2011).

[23] Office of the High Commissioner for Human Rights (n. 22).

[24] See, e.g., General Comment No. 14 (n. 11), para. 33 ("The obligation to *protect* requires States to take measures that prevent third parties from interfering with article 12 guarantees."). See also I/A Court H.R., *Velásquez Rodriguez v. Honduras*, Judgment of July 29, 1989, Series C, No. 4, paras. 172, 176, available at <http://www1.umn.edu/humanrts/iachr/b_11_12d.htm>.

[25] See, e.g., *Velásquez Rodriguez* (n. 24, para. 176 ("The State is obligated to investigate every situation involving a violation of the rights protected by the Convention.").

[26] *Velásquez Rodriguez* para. 172.

[27] See, e.g., General Comment No. 14 (n. 11), para. 13 ("The obligation to *fulfil (facilitate)* requires States *inter alia* to take positive measures that enable and assist individuals and communities to enjoy the right to health. States parties are also obliged to *fulfil (provide)* a specific right contained in the Covenant when individuals or a group are unable, for reasons beyond their control, to realize that right themselves by the means at their disposal").

[28] International Covenant on Civil and Political Rights, art. 2(3), December 16, 1966, 999 U.N.T.S. 171 [hereinafter ICCPR], available at <http://www2.ohchr.org/english/law/pdf/ccpr.pdf>.

[29] ICESCR, (n. 10), art. 2(1). For an interpretation of the legal obligations of art. 2(1), see generally ECOSOC, Comm. on Econ., Soc. & Cultural Rights, *General Comment No. 3: The Nature of States Parties Obligations (Art. 2,* para. *1 of the Covenant)*, UN Doc. E/1991/23 (December 14, 1990), available at <http://www.unhchr.ch/tbs/doc.nsf/(Symbol)/94bdbaf59b43a424c12563ed0052b664?Opendocument> [hereinafter General Comment No. 3].

[30] ICESCR (n. 10), paras. 1–2; ECOSOC, Comm. on Econ., Soc. & Cultural Rights, *General Comment No. 20: Non-discrimination in Economic, Social and Cultural Rights (art. 2, ¶2, of the International Covenant on Economic, Social and Cultural Rights)*, para. 7, UN Doc. E/C.12/GC/20 (July 2, 2009), available at <http://www2.ohchr.org/english/bodies/cescr/docs/E.C.12.GC.20.doc> [hereinafter General Comment No. 20]; ICESCR (n. 13), at art. 2(2); Comm. on the Elimination of Racial Discrimination, *General Recommendation No. 14: Definition of Discrimination (Art., par. 1)*, para. 2, UN Doc A/48/18 (March 22, 1993), available at <http://www.unhchr.ch/tbs/doc.nsf/%28Symbol%29/d7bd5d2bf71258aac12563ee004b639e?Opendocument>; Human Rights Comm., *General Comment No. 18: Non-Discrimination*, para. 7, UN Doc. HRI\GEN\1\Rev.1 (November 10, 1989), available at <http://www.unhcr.org/refworld/docid/453883fa8.html>.

include a "minimum core" of attendant obligations that states must realize as soon as possible.[31] Additionally, states may not engage in conduct that causes this realization of human rights to regress.[32]

The principle of non-discrimination is a central tenet of international human rights law. States must ensure both non-discrimination and substantive equality in the enjoyment of human rights.[33] Vulnerable groups, in particular, must not be left out of the purview of rights protections and states may need to take special measures to ensure their substantive equality.[34] Specific covenants protect those members of the population that might suffer from discrimination, and commentary on the right to health emphasizes the obligation to provide health services to socially disadvantaged groups.[35] A rights-based approach additionally emphasizes principles of participation, inclusion, and accountability.[36] Finally, international human rights law recognizes that no one state can act alone to fulfill the rights at stake. Under the obligation of "international cooperation" states must cooperate in ensuring the fulfillment of economic and social rights globally.[37]

The principles outlined above are aimed primarily at states but increasingly human rights bodies are also addressing the responsibilities of multi-state actors such as intergovernmental organizations, and non-state actors such as corporations. These actors, who were on the sidelines of the conversation as recently as a decade ago, are now very much at its center.

b. International Organizations

Human rights bodies have called upon both states and international organizations, such as the World Trade Organization (WTO) and the World Intellectual Property Organization (WIPO), to take account of states' human rights obligations when negotiating, signing, and implementing international agreements. States are urged to integrate human rights policies into domestic legislation that implements

[31] General Comment No. 3 (n. 29), para. 10. For an interpretation of the core obligations of the right to health, see General Comment No. 14 (n. 11), paras. 43–5.

[32] See General Comment No. 3 (n. 29), para. 9 ("any deliberately retrogressive measures in that regard [in contrast to progressive realization] would require the most careful consideration and would need to be fully justified by reference to the totality of the rights provided for in the Covenant and in the context of the full use of the maximum available resources").

[33] General Comment No. 14 (n. 11), para. 12(b); General Comment No. 20 (n. 30), para. 8.

[34] General Comment No. 20 (n. 30), para. 27; Special Rapporteur on the Right to Health 2006 (n. 6), paras. 52, 54; General Comment No. 14 (n. 11), para. 35.

[35] General Comment No. 14 (n. 11), paras. 12, 19.

[36] See The Human Rights Based Approach to Development Cooperation: Towards a Common Understanding among the UN Agencies (May 2003), available at <http://www.crin.org/docs/resources/publications/hrbap/HR_common_understanding.doc>.

[37] ICESCR (n. 10), art. 2(1) ("Each State Party to the present Covenant undertakes to take steps, individually *and through international assistance and co-operation*, especially economic and technical, to the maximum of its available resources, with a view to achieving progressively the full realization of the rights recognized in the present Covenant . . . "); UN Charter art. 1 (purpose of the United Nations is achieving international cooperation to solve economic, social, cultural and humanitarian problems and promoting human rights for all without distinction).

international obligations,[38] as well as to take into account their obligations when negotiating and signing new international agreements.[39] States do not leave their human rights obligations at the door when entering into international agreements such as TRIPS. Foreign states must also respect the ability of other states to implement their human rights obligations. In other words, powerful states must refrain from exerting their influence in a manner that undermines the ability of weaker states to fulfill their economic, social, and cultural rights obligations.[40] Finally, states have a duty to facilitate, wherever possible, access to essential medications in other countries.[41]

While much of the above commentary is directed at states, human rights bodies have also addressed the obligations directly owed by intergovernmental organizations in general, and the WTO specifically, requesting that they "integrate into their policies, practices and operations," provisions that "protect the social function of intellectual property" in accordance with international human rights law.[42]

[38] See, e.g., ECOSOC, Sub-Commission on the Promotion & Protection Of Human Rights, *Intellectual Property Rights and Human Rights*, Res. 2000/7, UN Doc. E/CN.4/Sub.2/RES/2000/7 (August 17, 2000) [hereinafter Sub-Commission 2000] (urging members to implement the minimum standards of the TRIPS Agreement bearing in mind both their human rights obligations as well as the flexibility inherent in the TRIPS Agreement, and recognizing that "human rights are the first responsibility of Governments"); Commission on Human Rights, *Access to Medication in the Context of Pandemics such as HIV/AIDS, Tuberculosis and Malaria*, Resn 2004/26 (April 16, 2004) para. 10(b) [hereinafter Commission on Human Rights 2004] (calling on states "[t]o ensure . . . the application of international agreements is supportive of public health policies that promote broad access to safe, effective and affordable preventive, curative or palliative pharmaceutical products and medical technologies).

[39] See, e.g., ECOSOC, Sub-Commission on the Promotion and Protection of Human Rights, *Intellectual Property and Human Rights*, Res. 2001/21, UN Doc. E/CN.4/Sub.2/RES/2001/21 (August 16, 2001) [hereinafter Sub-Commission 2001], para. 6 (urging "all Governments to take fully into account existing State obligations under international human rights instruments in the formulation of proposals for the ongoing review of the TRIPS Agreement"); Commission on Human Rights 2004 (n. 38), para. 10(b) (calling on states "To ensure that their actions as members of international organizations take due account of the right of everyone to the enjoyment of the highest attainable standard of physical and mental Health . . . "; OHCHR and UNAIDS, *HIV/AIDS and Human Rights: Guideline 6*, HR/PUB/2002/1 (2002), para. z ("States should, in light of their human rights obligations, ensure that bilateral, regional and international agreements, such as those dealing with intellectual property, do not impede access to HIV/AIDS prevention, treatment, care and support, including access to antiretroviral and other medicines, diagnostics and related technologies").

[40] Special Rapporteur on the Right to Health 2006 (n. 6), para. 64 (asserting that "no rich State should encourage a developing country to accept intellectual property standards that do not take into account the safeguards and flexibilities included under the TRIPS Agreement").

[41] Commission on Human Rights 2001,(n. 4), para. 4(a) (calling on states to "facilitate, wherever possible, access in other countries to essential preventive, curative or palliative pharmaceuticals or medical technologies . . . as well as to extend the necessary cooperation, wherever possible, especially in times of emergency;"); Commission on Human Rights 2002 (n. 4), para. 6(a); Commission on Human Rights 2004 (n. 41), para. 10(a).

[42] Sub-Commission 2000 (n. 38), para. 6, 8; CESCR 2001 (n. 3) (noting that realms of trade, finance and investment are in no way exempt from human rights principles and that "international organizations with specific responsibilities in those areas should play a positive and constructive role in relation to human rights").

c. The Private Sector

The private sector is also increasingly being addressed by human rights actors. In 2008, the Special Rapporteur on the right to health issued human rights guidelines addressed directly to pharmaceutical companies calling on them, *inter alia*, to: respect the right of countries to use to the fullest extent possible the flexibility afforded by TRIPS; make and respect a public commitment not to lobby for more demanding intellectual property protections than those required by TRIPS;[43] and respect the Doha Declaration on the TRIPS Agreement and Public Health (2001).[44]

Although TNCs have not traditionally been viewed as directly bound by international human rights law, the idea that businesses should at the very least respect human rights is gaining traction at the UN. Support has recently emerged for the "Protect, Respect, Remedy" framework, a set of obligations which, if fully embraced, would impose some international human rights responsibilities directly on businesses. Originally proposed by the UN Special Representative of the Secretary General on the issue of human rights and transnational corporations and other business enterprises, John Ruggie—and approved by the Human Rights Council in 2008[45]—the Framework states that corporations and other business enterprises must, as a baseline expectation, *respect* human rights.[46] This responsibility to respect means that businesses should "avoid infringing on the human rights of others and should address adverse human rights impacts with which they are involved."[47] Businesses should also "[s]eek to prevent or mitigate adverse human rights impacts that are directly linked to their operations, products or services by their business relationships, even if they have not contributed to those impacts."[48] To meet these requirements, businesses must exercise due diligence to "become aware of, prevent and address adverse human rights impacts."[49]

[43] Special Rapporteur on the Right to Health 2008 (n. 6), para. 26.

[44] Special Rapporteur on the Right to Health 2008 (n. 6), para. 27. The Declaration recognizes states' "right to protect public health and, in particular, to promote access to medicines for all." World Trade Organization, Ministerial Decision of November 14, 2001, WT/MIN(01)/DEC/1.41 I.L.M. 746 (2002), para. 4 [hereinafter Doha Declaration].

[45] UNHRC, 8th Session, Report of the Special Representative of the Secretary-General on the issue of human rights and transnational corporations and other business enterprises, John Ruggie, "Protect, Respect and Remedy: A Framework for Business and Human Rights" (April 7, 2008) A/HRC/8/5, available at <http://www.reports-and-materials.org/Ruggie-report-7-Apr-2008.pdf> [hereinafter "Protect, Respect and Remedy"].

[46] See "Protect, Respect and Remedy" (n. 45), paras. 9, 54–5.

[47] UNHRC, 17th Session, Report of the Special Representative of the Secretary-General on the issue of human rights and transnational corporations and other business enterprises, John Ruggie, "Guiding Principles on Business and Human Rights: Implementing the United Nations 'Protect, Respect and Remedy,'" (March 21, 2011) UN Doc. A/HRC/17/31 [hereinafter "Guiding Principles"], available at <http://www.businesshumanrights.org/media/documents/ruggie/ruggie-guiding-principles-21-mar-2011.pdf>, para. 6, Annex para. 11.

[48] "Guiding Principles," Annex para. 13.

[49] "Protect, Respect and Remedy" (n. 45), para. 56. Furthermore, "[f]or the substantive content of the due diligence process, companies should look, at a minimum, to the international bill of human rights [i.e. the Universal Declaration of Human Rights, as well as the International Covenant on Civil and Political Rights and the International Covenant on Economic, Social and Cultural Rights] and the

In 2011, the UN Human Rights Council unanimously approved a set of Guiding Principles that offer a set of practical recommendations for operationalizing the "Protect, Respect and Remedy" framework.[50] Advocates are now beginning to consider how to hold pharmaceutical companies directly accountable for their impact on human rights, and are starting to make use of the Ruggie standards to evaluate corporate conduct (Gruskin and Read 2010; Hunt and Khosla 2010).[51]

Attempts to lasso the big private actor into the human rights conversation must of course contend with the significant power dynamics that are at play. These and other obstacles to implementing a rights-based approach to access to medicine are described in section II.

B. Reconciling the Right to Health with Intellectual Property Rights

There are multiple ways of addressing the interaction between international human rights law and international and domestic intellectual property regimes. Several trends emerge among the human rights bodies that have addressed access to medicines from a right to health perspective.

First, human rights bodies must address the apparent protection for intellectual property within human rights instruments. Both the Universal Declaration of Human Rights (UDHR) and the ICESCR guarantee the right of everyone to "enjoy the benefits of scientific progress and its applications"[52] and the right to benefit from "the protection of the moral and material interests resulting from any scientific, literary or artistic production of which he is the author."[53] Such protections can also be found in regional instruments.[54] Human rights bodies such as the Committee on Economic, Social and Cultural Rights and the Sub-Commission on

core conventions of the ILO, because the principles they embody comprise the benchmarks against which other social actors judge the human rights impacts of companies." "Protect, Respect and Remedy," para. 58. Businesses' obligations extend both to the effects of direct activities as well as, sometimes, to the conduct of actors over whom the business has leverage. "Protect, Respect and Remedy," paras. 68, 72. Additionally, corporations cannot act in complicity with third parties, whether state or non-state actors, who are committing human rights violations. "Protect, Respect and Remedy," para. 73.

[50] See generally "Guiding Principles" (n. 47).

[51] See, e.g., Gruskin and Read 2010 (suggesting three approaches to concretely assessing drug companies' compliance with human rights responsibilities); Hunt and Khosla 2010 (suggesting that pharmaceutical companies are not living up to their human rights responsibilities, and suggesting the contours and participants of an international institution to serve as an "effective right-to-health accountability mechanism[]" to confirm whether or not allegations of failure are well founded, and to make sensible practical recommendations for all parties).

[52] ICESCR (n. 10), at art. 15(b). The corollary to this right in the UDHR is framed as the right to "share in scientific advancement and its benefits." Universal Declaration of Human Rights [hereinafter UDHR], art. 27(1), GA res. 217A (III), UN Doc A/810 at 71 (1948).

[53] ICESCR (n. 10), at art. 15(c); UDHR (n. 52), art. 27(2).

[54] See, e.g., Charter of Fundamental Rights of the European Union, 2000 O.J. (C 364) 1, art. 17 ("Everyone has the right to own, use, dispose of and bequeath his or her lawfully acquired possessions.... Intellectual property shall be protected."). American Declaration of the Rights and Duties of Man, OEA/Ser.L./V.II.23, doc. 21, rev. 6 (1948), art. 13 (giving every person the "the right to the protection of his moral and material interests as regards his inventions or any literary, scientific or artistic works of which he is the author.").

the Promotion and Protection of Human Rights have sought to distinguish the protection of intellectual property as a human right from intellectual property regimes that protect broader commercial interests. They argue that, as framed in human rights law, this right concerns the relationship of individuals to their creation and is not one that corporations can avail themselves of to protect corporate interests.[55] The "social function" of intellectual property, they add, must be protected.[56]

Having outlined this distinction, human rights bodies go on to assert the primacy of human rights over economic policies and agreements.[57] The "first responsibility" of states, it is argued, is to attend to human rights.[58] As the argument goes, human rights take precedence over economic policies and agreements. They are of a higher order.

Such an approach may suggest a conflict between human rights and intellectual property regimes. But according to key commentators (Helfer and Austin 2011: 65–7)[59] and human rights actors, the issue is not so simple; there exist other approaches as well. The "coexistence" approach, for example, sees "human rights law and intellectual property law as essentially compatible but as in tension over where to strike the balance between incentives [to innovate] on the one hand and access [to the public] on the other" (Helfer and Austin 2011: 73).[60]

[55] General Comment No. 17 (n. 3), para. 2, 7. Specifically, the right protects the "moral interest" of authors to be "recognized as the creators" of their work, and to "object to any distortion, mutilation or other modification of, or other derogatory action in relation to, such productions, which would be prejudicial to their honour and reputation." General Comment No. 17, 13. The right also protects the author's "material interests," which can be linked to other human rights, such as the rights to own property, to adequate remuneration, and to an adequate standard of living. General Comment No. 17, 15.

[56] CESCR 2001 (n. 3), para. 4 ("Ultimately, intellectual property is a social product and has a social function. The end which intellectual property protection should serve is the objective of human well-being, to which international human rights instruments give legal expression").

[57] See, e.g., Sub-Commission 2000 (n. 38) (criticizing the implementation of the TRIPS agreement and "remind[ing] all Governments of the primacy of human rights obligations over economic policies and agreements").

[58] Report of the High Commissioner 2001 (n. 5), para. 60: "Out of the 141 members of WTO that have undertaken to implement the minimum standards of IP protection in the TRIPS Agreement, 111 have ratified ICESCR. Members should therefore implement the minimum standards of the TRIPS Agreement bearing in mind both their human rights obligations as well as the flexibility inherent in the TRIPS Agreement, and recognizing that 'human rights are the first responsibility of Governments'."

[59] Arguing that "although the conflicts approach appears conceptually straightforward, in fact it masks a number of embedded assumptions and ambiguities. Among the most important of these are (1) identifying the nature of the conflict that must exist before a state's human rights obligations supersede its intellectual property commitments, and (2) analyzing the legal justification for giving primacy to human rights over other international rules."

[60] For alternative visions of interaction between the two fields see: Yu 2007 (suggesting that two different approaches are needed to resolve distinct areas of conflicts between human rights and intellectual property: "external conflicts (conflicts at the intersection of the human rights and intellectual property regimes) and internal conflicts (conflicts between rights within the human rights regime)"); Helfer 2007 (emphasizing the need for a more comprehensive human rights approach to intellectual property, and mapping three potential directions which the interface between the two fields could follow which include the possibility of using intellectual property to achieve human rights goals); and Okediji 2007 (arguing that "human rights should be viewed as a means of preserving the objectives of intellectual property using existing intellectual property tools" and that "[a]t the very least, human rights justify the objectives of intellectual property and could be used to impose an internal constraint

No matter the theoretical approach adopted by human rights bodies, there exist significant obstacles to implementing a rights-based approach in practice. Implementation difficulties arise not only in the context of transnational corporations and IFIs, as mentioned, but also in the operationalization of more settled legal frameworks such as states' international and even national duties towards their own populations, as described in section II.

II. Obstacles to Implementing a Rights-Based Approach

The field of international human rights law, and its ability to influence developments in parallel legal realms, has developed significantly over the past several decades. Despite these developments, a number of obstacles remain to implementing a rights-based approach to access to medicine and to effectively asserting the primacy of human rights in the context of international financial agreements. These obstacles arise in connection to key interrelated deficits in international human rights law around the issues of legitimacy, accountability, and domestic capacity.

A. The Legitimacy Deficit

Human rights norms enjoy varied levels of credibility and institutional backing, which in turn influence their domestic implementation. Despite significant developments in the field of economic, social, and cultural rights (of which the right to health is one), this subset of human rights is still playing catch-up to civil and political rights. Though economic, social, and cultural rights formed a core part of the post-World War II body of human rights doctrine, they were soon unlinked from civil and political rights. The drafters of the UDHR had intended it to be the precursor of a single Human Rights Covenant that would make the principles of the Declaration binding on ratifying states.[61] But Cold War politics resulted in the creation of two Covenants instead of one (Lyon 2002: 539–41): the ICESCR and the International Covenant on Civil and Political Rights (ICCPR).[62] In so doing, economic, social, and cultural rights were essentially subordinated to their civil and political counterparts (Steiner, Alston, and Goodman 2008: 271),[63] despite the obvious interdependence and indivisibility of the two sets of rights.[64]

within the intellectual property system so that those objectives remain critical to the legitimacy of the system").

61 UN GAOR, *Annotations on the text of the draft International Covenants on Human Rights*, 10th Sess., pt. 2, UN Doc. A/2929 (1955), at 7.

62 ICCPR (n. 28), at 171.

63 Attempts to include economic, social, and cultural rights in the UDHR also faced strong opposition. See Steiner, Alston, and Goodman 2008: 271.

64 See generally Scott 1989; see also CHR Res. 2001/30, *Question of the Realization in all Countries of the Economic, Social and Cultural Rights Contained in the Universal Declaration of Human Rights and in the International Covenant on Economic, Social and Cultural Rights, and Study of Special Problems which the Developing Countries Face in their Efforts to Achieve these Human Rights*, para. 4(d), UN Doc. E/CN.4/RES2001/30 (April 20, 2001) (Comm'n on Hum. Rts. reaffirming "the universality,

Much has changed in the decades since the promulgation of the ICCPR and ICESCR to push economic, social, and cultural rights to the front of the human rights agenda, and navigate their salience in the context of economic globalization (Narula 2006). But economic, social, and cultural rights still lack the normative pull and moral cachet that is enjoyed by civil and political rights. Advocates seeking to ensure that states are held accountable to these obligations therefore face this additional hurdle on top of navigating an already complex field.

B. The Accountability Deficit

International human rights law embodies a set of hard obligations that states must live up to as states parties to various human rights treaties. But what does it mean to have hard obligations without accompanying mechanisms to ensure enforcement? International human rights law suffers from a case of primacy without enforceability leading to a significant accountability deficit. While the normative content of right to health and access to medicines may enjoy greater clarity, the ability to enforce these rights or effectively reconcile them with international financial obligations remains relatively weak.

This is especially so in the context of intellectual property law, which embodies a highly developed transnational regulatory framework. The TRIPS Agreement "contains detailed, comprehensive substantive rules and is linked to the WTO's comparatively hard-edged dispute settlement system in which treaty bargains are enforced through mandatory adjudication backed up by the threat of retaliatory sanctions" (Helfer 2006: 2). Where human rights obligations come into conflict with WTO obligations, the pressure to adhere to WTO rules is far stronger than is the pressure to uphold human rights; countries may be punished for failing to follow WTO rules but not for ignoring the recommendations of UN human rights treaty bodies. Violating human rights may lead to swift condemnation by civil society groups, but these protests do not generate the same level of pressure as is imposed by the market and domestic financial actors to stay the course with economic policy rules.

States are also not the only actors at play. Both intergovernmental organizations and non-state actors such as big pharmaceutical companies play a significant role in shaping and determining access to medicine globally. Yet despite significant efforts to broaden the scope of human rights duty-bearers to include other actors, as briefly described in section I, international human rights law remains a very state-centric enterprise. The majority of human rights adjudicative decisions limit states' obligations to respecting, protecting, and fulfilling the rights of individuals in their territory or under their jurisdiction, and the foundational human rights documents do not adequately address the obligations of transnational corporations and international financial institutions (Narula 2012). Powerful foreign states are increasingly urged to

indivisibility, interdependence and interrelatedness of all human rights and fundamental freedoms... promoting and protecting one category of rights should therefore never exempt or excuse States from the promotion and protection of other rights").

take cognizance of their extra-territorial obligations. While the idea is gaining force, it is still a relative newcomer to the scene (Langford et al. 2012).

There remains of course the problem of a lack of political will on the part of states. In many cases, the issue is not that international financial institutions and corporations are not accountable to international human rights law; it is that states are not accountable to their citizens, allowing them to selectively implement only those obligations that favor members of the domestic elite.

Given the difficulties outlined here, how and whether these obligations and norms translate in-country can depend greatly on the capacity and political inclination of domestic actors, as well as the extent to which domestic agendas align with the goals of transnational networks.

C. The Capacity Deficit

In the absence of an effective international regulatory framework for human rights, domestic actors and mechanisms act as the enforcers of human rights obligations.[65] The extent to which international pronouncements and norms find coherence domestically and effectively overcome both legitimacy and accountability deficits therefore depends on a number of factors: Does civil society have the capacity and inclination to play an active role? Is there legislative and judicial support to translate and implement human rights obligations? How robust is the support and pressure exerted by other global actors, including transnational advocacy networks?

A number of domestic actors can potentially play a role in successfully giving domestic traction to international norms and agreements. Yet these actors may lack the capacity to effectively take on this critical role. For one, if both the state's and civil society's engagement with human rights have largely been framed in civil and political rights terms, as is the case for a number of countries that are the subject of this volume, then the capacity or even political inclination of domestic actors to engage with economic and social rights—which engage broad-based macro-economic and public health frames—may be severely limited.

These actors also do not benefit from sufficient guidance from human rights treaty bodies set up to monitor states' implementation of their human rights obligations. A number of countries that are the subject of case studies in this volume have appeared before treaty bodies as part of a periodic review of their human rights performance. Guidance offered to these states and domestic actors therein comes in the form of concluding observations and recommendations but is not laid out in great detail.[66] The reason, in part, is the significant leeway and

[65] Indeed, as part of their duty to fulfill and facilitate human rights, states must undertake legislative, administrative, budgetary, and judicial action in order to create a general framework in which these rights may be realized. General Comment No. 14 (n. 11), para. 33.

[66] See, e.g., CESCR, *Concluding Observations of the Committee on Economic, Social and Cultural Rights: Chile*, para. 60, UN Doc. E/C.12/1/Add/105 (November 26, 2004) (concluding that "[t]he Committee encourages the State party to provide greater access to generic medicine making use of the flexibility clauses permitted in the World Trade Organization on Trade-related Aspects of Intellectual Property Rights (the TRIPS Agreement)").

deference given to states to tailor their approaches as they see fit taking into consideration the contextual specificity of conditions in-country.

Litigation has played a key role in the enforcement of rights (see also Forman 2009).[67] A great deal of advocacy is, for example, occurring in national courts in Central and South America (Helfer and Austin 2011: 152).[68] But litigation has its limits. In Brazil, for example, even though the constitutional recognition of the right to health has been broadly interpreted to mean an individual right to the best treatment—leading to a large tide of access to medicines litigation—the benefits of litigation have not been equally distributed across the population and seem to have been captured by those who can afford to adjudicate their claims (Ferrz 2009: 34). The ability of these cases to affect broader systemic reform has also come into question (Ferrz 2009: 34).

Difficulties also arise in the very act of adjudicating the right to access to medicine. States and corporations could effectively argue that intellectual property laws fulfill these rights obligations in the long term by fostering innovation, even if they hamper access in the short term. Unless legislatures take on the role of providing strong direction regarding the primacy of human rights, judicial pronouncements will likely be weak.

Even when domestic actors succeed in incorporating human rights elements into agreements, domestic implementation may fall far short of expectations due to structural impediments and institutional problems. India's experience is a case in point. When India signed the TRIPS Agreement in 1995, the country's large generic drug manufacturing sector and active civil society were already alert to the possible implications for the right to health and access to essential medicines (Kapczynski 2009). Despite intense domestic and international advocacy, and a relatively successful campaign to incorporate public health flexibilities into national implementing legislation, research has shown that it has been difficult to make use of the existing legal flexibilities. Limits on administrative resources restrict patent offices' abilities to rigorously impose existing standards and impede the ability to find out about, and therefore contest, problematic patent claims (Kapczynski 2009: 1617–18).[69] The transnational legal expertise that often accompanies intellectual property advice and litigation tends to gloss over unique elements in the Indian law, exerting a harmonizing effect with more restrictive standards from other jurisdictions (Kapczynski 2009: 1622). Finally, there is always the threat that jurisdictions offering a high amount of patent protection will unilaterally retaliate if flexibilities are too liberally implemented (Kapczynski 2009: 1627).

[67] See, e.g., cases cited in n. 9. See also, Forman 2009 (arguing that "the AIDS medicine experience and the seminal corporate litigation in South Africa in 2001, in particular, point to the transformative potential of the right to health to raise the priority of public health needs in trade-related intellectual property rights, and to advance access to critical health interventions in resource-poor settings").

[68] Citing Yam and Parra-Vera 2009 (stating that Central and South America are "characterized by rights-rich constitutions, high social exclusions, and systemic failures of representation by the political branches of government").

[69] Sudip Chaudhuri, Chan Park, and K. M. Gopakumar, *Five Years into the Product Patent Regime: India's Response* (United Nations Development Programme 2010) at 16.

The extent to which domestic agendas are able to link up with global advocacy priorities also seems to be a critical factor for other countries. In South Africa, for example, the domestic generic pharmaceutical industry played a key role in bringing forward a lawsuit that eventually authorized the use of key public health flexibilities in TRIPS. The first round of litigation brought by the domestic industry representatives focused on the provisions of the TRIPS Agreement itself and South Africa's constitutional protections for property (Forman 2009: 42). It was not until the appellate stages of litigation that civil society organizations became involved, using a right to health framework that drew from international and domestic law and which allowed them to argue that the right to health should have primacy over corporate property rights (Forman 2009: 42). South African human rights groups were also able to coordinate with a large international advocacy community, creating an international day of action spanning thirty cities on the day the case was heard, and obtaining statements of support from the European Union, Holland, Germany, France, and the World Health Organization (Forman 2009: 42).

As this makes clear, there are significant obstacles to implementing the rights-based approach to intellectual property and access to medicines. These obstacles emerge in the context of both horizontal and vertical fragmentation in the realm of international law. Horizontally, states' human rights obligations may not cohere with their financial commitments, despite calls for such coherence by numerous human rights actors. Vertically, international norms may not translate into domestic implementation. As briefly described in section III, such fragmentation has already rolled back some hard fought civil society gains.

III. Concluding Observations

The past decade has witnessed immense developments in international human rights law on the issue of intellectual property and access to medicines. The significant and enduring involvement of a number of human rights and civil society actors has led to the development of principles and guidelines that have kept pace with the globalization of international trade rules and have sought to respond to the urgency of ensuring access to medicines in the context of global pandemics (Kapczynski 2009: 1584–5).[70] Advocacy by international human rights and global health advocates has also secured important TRIPS-related flexibilities and has raised awareness of these issues within the WTO. Health activists' engagement with the WTO was most extensive in 2001, when NGOs and developing countries worked in tandem to push through the Doha Declaration on TRIPS and Public Health (Kapczynski 2009: 1585–6).[71]

[70] Noting that the HIV/AIDS crisis provided a focal point for access to medicines campaigners, who articulated TRIPS as a key barrier to affordable generic AIDS medicines in developing countries.

[71] "The Declaration extended the transition period afforded to least-developed countries with regard to pharmaceuticals, addressed certain limitations on the export of generic medicines under

More recent negotiations in the WTO have stalled, however, perhaps leading to an increased focus on human rights bodies on the one hand, and bilateral or multilateral regional trade agreements on the other (Helfer 2006: 973–5). Hard-won TRIPS flexibilities are turning out to be quite cumbersome, making people rethink the "win" (Helfer and Austin 2011: 124).[72] Countries have also been pressured to sign TRIPS-plus regional or bilateral treaties, with patent protection rules that go well beyond TRIPS (Abbott and Reichman 2007).

Although it may be that "in this maelstrom of reaction, resistance, and regime shifting, international human rights law is poised to become an increasingly central subject of contestation" (Helfer 2006: 975), it is not clear how effective the pronouncements of human rights bodies are or will be. Ongoing problems remain with implementation of the hard-won TRIPS flexibilities and of recommendations made by UN human rights bodies and Special Rapporteurs. Even the most robust articulations of human rights domestically or the most significant victories internationally do not necessarily translate into a bottom-up realization of rights.

Ultimately the full and equitable realization of the right to adequate health depends greatly on the capacity and political inclination of domestic actors to ensure that international norms enjoy local traction. Conclusions regarding the extent to which human rights primacy can be realized in the realm of access to medicines are therefore highly country and context specific. A key contribution of the case studies in this volume will be to provide the specificity needed to draw such conclusions and press critical rights claims.

References

Abbott, Frederick, and Jerome Reichman. 2007. "Doha Round's Public Health Legacy: Strategies for the Production and Diffusion of Patented Medicines under the Amended TRIPS Provisions." *J. Int'l Econ. L.* 10: 921–87.

Ferrz, Octavio Luiz Motta. 2009. "The Right to Health in the Courts of Brazil: Worsening Health Inequities?" *Health & Hum. Rts.* 11: 33–45.

Forman, Lisa. 2009. "'Rights' and Wrongs: What Utility for the Right to Health in Reforming Trade Rules on Medicines?" *Health & Hum. Rts.* 10: 37–52.

Greenbaum, Jessica. 2008. "TRIPS and Public Health: Solutions for Ensuring Global Access to Essential AIDS Medication in the Wake of the Paragraph 5 Waiver." *J. Contemp. Health L. & Pol'y* 25: 142–65.

compulsory license, and affirmed unequivocally that TRIPS "can and should be interpreted and implemented in a manner supportive of WTO members' right to protect public health and, in particular, to promote access to medicines for all."

[72] Citing Abbott and Reichman 2007 (the TRIPS waiver and amendment are "saddled with unnecessary administrative hurdles" that make the export of generic versions of patented drugs neither "simple [n]or expeditious") and Greenbaum 2008 (commenting that there are numerous practical obstacles outside the intricacies of the formal legal system that stand in the way of effectively utilizing the flexibilities. *See also* Helfer and Austin 2011 at 127–43, detailing individual countries' difficulties in implementing compulsory license flexibilities.

Gruskin, Sofia, and Zyde Read. 2010. "Are Drug Companies Living up to their Human Rights Responsibilities? Moving toward Assessment." *PLoS Medicine* 7: 1–3.

Helfer, Laurence. 2006. "Regime Shifting: The TRIPS Agreement and New Dynamics of International Intellectual Property Lawmaking." *Yale J. Int'l L.* 29: 1–83.

——. 2007. "Toward a Human Rights Framework for Intellectual Property." *UC Davis L. Rev.* 40: 971–1020.

——— and Graeme Austin. 2011. *Human Rights and Intellectual Property Mapping the Global Interface.* New York: Cambridge University Press.

Hunt, Paul, and Rajat Khosla. 2010. "Are Drug Companies Living up to their Human Rights Responsibilities? The Perspective of the Former United Nations Special Rapporteur (2002–2008)." *PLoS Medicine* 7: 1–3.

Kapczynski, Amy. 2009. "Harmonization and its Discontents: A Case Study of TRIPS Implementation in India's Pharmaceutical Sector." *Cal. L. Rev.* 97: 1571–649.

Langford, Malcolm, Martin Scheinin, Wouter Vandenhole, and Willem van Genugten (eds.). 2012. *Global Justice, State Duties: The Extra-Territorial Scope of Economic, Social and Cultural Rights in International Law.* New York: Cambridge University Press.

Lyon, Beth. 2002. "Discourse in Development: A Post-Colonial 'Agenda' for the United Nations Committee on Economic, Social and Cultural Rights." *Am. U. J. Gender Soc. Pol'y & L.* 10: 535–77.

Narula, Smita. 2006. "The Right to Food: Holding Global Actors Accountable under International Law." *Colum. J. Transnat'l L.* 44: 691–799.

——. 2012. "International Financial Institutions, Transnational Corporations and the Duties of States." Pp. 114–51 in *Global Justice, State Duties: The Extra-Territorial Scope of Economic, Social and Cultural Rights in International Law,* edited by M. Langford, M. Scheinin, W. Vandenhole, and W. van Genugten. New York: Cambridge University Press.

Okediji, Ruth. 2007. "Securing Intellectual Property Objectives: New Approaches to Human Rights Considerations." P. 211 in *Casting the Net Wider: Human Rights, Development and New Duty-Bearers,* edited by Margot E. Salomon et al. Cambridge: Intersentia.

Scott, Craig. 1989. "The Interdependence and Permeability of Human Right Norms: Towards a Partial Fusion of the International Covenants on Human Rights." *Osgoode Hall LJ* 27: 769.

Steiner, Henry, Philip Alston, and Ryan Goodman. 2008. "Economic and Social Rights." Pp. 263–374 in *International Human Rights in Context: Law, Politics, Morals.* 3rd edn. New York: Oxford University Press.

Yam, Alicia Ely, and Oscar Parra-Vera. 2009. "How Do Courts Set Health Policy? The Case of the Colombian Constitutional Court." *Pub. Libr. Sci. Med.* 6: 147–50.

Yu, Peter. 2007. "Reconceptualizing Intellectual Property Interests in a Human Rights Framework." *UC Davis L. Rev.* 40: 1039–149.

Chapter 13

The Role of WIPO in Access to Medicines

Ruth L. Okediji

Introduction

The World Intellectual Property Organization (WIPO) is at the forefront of some of the most significant challenges facing the global economy today, not the least of which is access to medicines. This is not necessarily because WIPO should, or wants to be, the focus of globalization's most vexing problems. But WIPO predictably has a role because intellectual property (IP) protection, as the orthodox narrative recounts, is a critical component of public and private responses to these shared global concerns.

Public health matters are particularly fundamental to the development aspirations and economic growth of developing and least-developed countries (World Bank 2013; Bubela et al. 2011; IMF 2004). Even in the developed economies, there is an indisputable link between healthcare availability, the cost of pharmaceutical products, and economic growth (Ney 2012; Chernew 2010). Yet, access to medicines remains a point of significant tension and, at times, intense discord among state and non-state actors over the role and impact of the patent system on public health. In the minds of many observers and commentators, the considerable challenge of making drugs accessible to the world's most vulnerable citizens has transformed the patent system—and pharmaceutical patents in particular—into the poster child of all that is wrong with IP harmonization under the Agreement on Trade-Related Aspects of Intellectual Property Rights (TRIPS Agreement) (Van Puymbroeck 2010; Sun 2004; Attaran 2003).

The global debate over access to medicines spans two related public international law frames, namely humanitarianism and human rights (Gold 2013; Barnett 2005). The complementary ends of these two regimes overlay, and at times supplant, the economic imperatives of the private rights that are at the heart of the global patent system,[1] as evidenced by the Doha Declaration on TRIPS and

[1] The TRIPS Agreement recognizes that intellectual property rights are private rights. TRIPS Agreement, pmbl. *P.A.O. & 2 Others v. Attorney Gen.* (High Court of Kenya, 2012), <http://kenyalaw.org/Downloads_FreeCases/85611.pdf>. ("Should the Act be implemented as it is, the danger that it poses to the right of the petitioners to access essential medicine which they require on a daily basis in order to sustain life is far greater and more critical than the protection of the intellectual

Public Health.[2] Of the many international institutions that deal with access to medicines and global health governance, WIPO arguably is the least involved with the structures and processes that directly shape *national* obligations to supply public goods such as healthcare, or that determine appropriate responses to public health crises. Government health agencies, humanitarian departments, human rights, foreign and defense ministries, and powerful international humanitarian organizations such as the International Red Cross or Médecins Sans Frontières (MSF) all are a far cry from the IP agencies, trade, investment, or commerce ministries with which WIPO has traditionally been associated.

Moreover, the diverse legal and policy mandates of national actors in the field of public health involve constitutional and governance issues unique to the specific local environment in which they operate, interwoven with humanitarian aid efforts and any related conditions imposed when and as cases of specific threats to health and human well-being arise. Put simply, the complex legal, normative, and institutional landscape within which solutions to access to medicines must emerge as part of the legal and humanitarian responses to disease is not a terrain in which WIPO has historically had much experience or credibility. Yet, because patent rights are a major underpinning for pharmaceutical innovation, WIPO recently has assumed a visible role in addressing access to medicines and global public health (ICTSD 2011; WIPO 2011). The extent and impact of its involvement remain difficult to measure.

In this chapter, I briefly consider the nature of WIPO's functions and suggest possible ways in which the Organization could positively exercise its tremendous technical assistance capacity consistent with facilitating access to medicines. I begin by reflecting on WIPO's mandate in an international environment in which competing visions of the IP system continue to engender challenges to the norms WIPO is tasked to supply and defend.

I. WIPO and Institutional Identity

A. The WIPO Mandate in the Context of Public Health

From its obscure beginnings in the late nineteenth century as an administrative headquarters providing managerial functions for member states of the principal IP conventions,[3] WIPO's mandate "to promote the protection of intellectual property throughout the world through cooperation among States"[4] has placed the

property rights that the Act seeks to protect. The right to life, dignity and health of the petitioners must take precedence over the intellectual property rights of patent holders.")

[2] Declaration on the TRIPS Agreement and Public Health, November 14, 2001, WT/MIN(01)/DEC/2.

[3] Paris Convention for the Protection of Industrial Property, as last revised at the Stockholm Revision Conference, July 14, 1967, 21 U.S.T. 1583, 828 U.N.T.S. 303; Berne Convention for the Protection of Literary and Artistic Works, September 9, 1886, as revised at Paris on July 24, 1971 and amended in 1979, S. Treaty Doc. No. 99-27 (1986).

[4] WIPO Convention art. 3, 2186 U.N.T.S. 121.

Organization at the epicenter of debates about a number of global issues such as climate change, food security, and public health. In recent years, WIPO has undertaken numerous initiatives and partnerships with other international organizations to exercise influence in the global discourse on these issues and to be part of evolving solutions.[5] But given that WIPO's principal charge is norm-setting activities to protect, strengthen, and harmonize IP rules,[6] its role in relation to problems, the solutions to which require consideration of ways to constrain the impact of IP on social welfare, potentially raises questions of constitutional magnitude for the Organization. These questions are particularly weighty with respect to public health and access to medicines and there are strong reasons why one might urge reticence on WIPO's part.

Pharmaceutical patents have historically been a sensitive area of norm-setting in global patent law (Sangsuvan 2013). As is well known, the uneven scope and availability of protection for pharmaceutical patents across countries in large part fueled the resolve of the developed countries to conclude the World Trade Organization (WTO) TRIPS Agreement (Weissman 1996). While formal agreement on core standards in TRIPS created improved opportunities for norm convergence in patent law, domestic application of these norms continues to reveal unabated interest in major developing countries, and in the international community, to apply global patent rules in ways that best serve national interests, notwithstanding domestic patent legislation that mirrors those of the developed countries, or is at times even stronger. This emphasis on national interest is of course no different from what occurs in the developed countries as well (Stein 2005; Murashige 1994). National patent policy invariably must respond to domestic political and economic pressures or face countervailing skepticism that erodes public confidence in the regime more broadly (Okediji 2013).

B. WIPO, Domestic Institutions, and Public Health

The TRIPS Agreement safeguards the unilateral exercise of domestic authority by assuring in article 1 that "Members shall be free to determine the appropriate method of implementing the provisions of this Agreement within their own legal system and practice."[7] So long as the implementation of TRIPS norms is filtered through legitimate national institutions and processes, the outcomes are far less likely to be successfully challenged as non-compliant,[8] even when those outcomes

[5] WIPO, *Climate Change*, <http://www.wipo.int/globalchallenges/en/climate> (last visited August 9, 2013); WIPO, *Food Security*, <http://www.wipo.int/globalchallenges/en/food> (last visited August 9, 2013); WIPO, *Public Health*, <http://www.wipo.int/globalchallenges/en/health> (last visited August 9, 2013).

[6] WIPO, *About WIPO*, <http://www.wipo.int/about-wipo/en> (last visited August 12, 2013).

[7] See Agreement on Trade-Related Aspects of Intellectual Property Rights art. 1(2) April 15, 1994, Marrakesh Agreement Establishing the World Trade Organization, Annex 1C, 1869 U.N.T.S. 299.

[8] In the seminal TRIPS dispute between the US and India, a WTO Appellate Body agreed that India's purported implementation of the mailbox and pipeline provisions in TRIPS articles 70(8)(a) and 70(9) was non-compliant with India's obligations. However, this was due in no small part to a lack of evidence that India's chosen mode of implementation, so-called administrative instructions, was

diverge from what prevails in other member states. The Indian Supreme Court's decision in *Novartis Ag v: Union of India et al.*,[9] which rejected Norvatis's application for its cancer fighting drug Glivec despite its protection in many other countries, is illustrative. There, India's Patent Act[10] embodied the standards required by the TRIPS Agreement, yet the Court applied those standards with a particular view of the patent system and its role in protecting inventions in the context of unique policy trade-offs and national interests.[11]

Other examples might include recent legislative amendments in China and Brazil requiring mandatory disclosure of the source of genetic material associated with an invention, the violation of which carries severe sanctions up to forfeiture of the patent.[12] In short, national patent systems often reflect policy biases that tilt the practical operation of global norms in preferred directions without violating the letter of the treaty.[13] This suggests that credible, if contestable, forms of implementation consistent with national public interests and determined through appropriate institutional processes likely will be more insulated from threats of WTO sanctions even if trade partners are otherwise displeased.[14] WIPO is far less positioned to intervene in such cases on grounds that particular interpretations of patent norms are consistent or otherwise with the global patent *acquis*.[15] Not only does WIPO lack any institutional facility or authority to issue such analysis, the well-acknowledged political tenor of unresolved debates within the WTO over the social bargain embedded in the TRIPS Agreement cannot be justifiably mediated by the one-size-fits-all approach, which historically has been WIPO's chief undertaking.

Until very recently, WIPO was conspicuously absent from global public policy debates about public health and, some may argue, it was curious if at all only for reasons of institutional self-interest. But as the chief custodian of the globalized IP norms that influence policy responses to technology deficits, WIPO's involvement

consistent with India's normal lawmaking process, making the alleged instructions of dubious legal character. See Appellate Body Report, *India–Patent Protection for Pharmaceutical and Agricultural Chemical Products*, WT/DS50/AB/R (December 19, 1997).

9 *Novartis Ag v. Union of India, et. al.*, Nos. 2706-2716 of 2013 (SLP(C) Nos. 20539-20549 of 2009) (2013) available at <http://supremecourtofindia.nic.in/outtoday/patent.pdf>.

10 Patent Amendment Act, No. 15 of 2005 [India].

11 *Novartis Ag. v. Union of India* (n. 9) at para. 66.

12 Provisional Act No. 2.186-16, August 23, 2001 (Genetic Heritage & Traditional Knowledge) [Brazil], <http://www.wipo.int/wipolex/en/details.jsp?id=5897>; Patent Law of the People's Republic of China art. 26 (promulgated by the Standing Comm. Nat'l People's Cong., March 12, 1984, amended December 27, 2008, effective October 1, 2009).

13 Article 1 of TRIPS does not subject this discretion over implementation to the limiting catchphrase "provided that such measures are consistent with the provisions of this Agreement." This proviso attaches to the first sentence in article 1 and other TRIPS provisions, such as article 8, recognizing that countries may act to protect certain public interest objectives. See also TRIPS art. 40(2).

14 The US Trade Representative has critiqued the India Supreme Court's Novartis decision. U.S. Trade Rep., 2013 Special 301 Report 38 (2013), <http://www.ustr.gov/sites/default/files/05012013%202013%20Special%20301%20Report.pdf>.

15 Indeed, in those few instances where WIPO's opinion has been invited by a WTO dispute panel, the response has been merely factual (Dinwoodie and Dreyfuss 2009).

is understandably viewed by other international organizations as an important component of global responses to these problems. For example, WIPO is identified as a stakeholder by the World Health Organization (WHO) in the implementation of the latter's Global Strategy and Plan of Action on Public Health, Innovation and Intellectual Property (2011). A recent, joint, high-level study by the "triumvirate" of organizations formally tasked with various aspects of global public health issues—the WHO, WIPO, and the World Trade Organization—also reflects a meaningful shift in WIPO's effort to participate in the public health dialogue (2012).

II. WIPO's Role in TRIPS Implementation

A. WIPO or the WTO in Influencing Domestic Patent Flexibility?

WIPO's technical assistance activities, directed primarily at developing and least-developed countries, have profoundly shaped domestic understanding of the appropriate implementation of patent norms in those jurisdictions (Flynn, et al. 2013; Pager 2012; Yu 2012; Sell 2011; Deere 2008),[16] including the perception of how much wiggle room is afforded under TRIPS standards to address barriers to access to medicines. From producing model patent laws,[17] to training programs for IP offices and officials (New 2012; New 2001), and other forms of "technical assistance" projects,[18] WIPO designs, deploys, and oversees a pervasive network of activities that directly and indirectly infuse domestic laws of developing and least-developed countries with strong normative predispositions, consistent with the interests of maximalist patent standards and, typically, minimalist public interest limitations (Kostecki 2006). So while overtly intervening with the administration of the TRIPS Agreement may be implausible for WIPO, it is WIPO, not the WTO, that has been most powerful in influencing, establishing, and nurturing the domestic normative context in which TRIPS norms are implemented.

The core obligations of the TRIPS Agreement build upon the substantive norms of the classic WIPO treaties, namely the Paris Convention and the Berne Convention.[19] Both of these instruments have an enduring legacy in defining the expectations of countries about the scope of international protection available, the rights granted to foreigners, and the economic impact of global IP protection (Okediji 2013). WIPO has long been at the forefront of expanding the reach of these treaties globally, and in developing a narrative about the role of IP in economic development. Given how significantly WIPO has been involved in defining the domestic

[16] See also World Intell. Prop. Org. Secretariat, An External Review of WIPO Technical Assistance in the Area of Cooperation for Development, Doc. CDIP/8/INF/1 (September 1, 2011) (by Carolyn Deere Birkbeck and Santiago Roca).

[17] WIPO, Model Law for Developing Countries on Inventions (1979), <ftp://ftp.wipo.int/pub/library/ebooks/ModelLaws/840e_vol_1.pdf>.

[18] Geneva Declaration on the Future of the World Intellectual Property Organization (October 4, 2004), available at <http://www.cptech.org/ip/wipo/futureofwipodeclaration.pdf> (urging reform of WIPO technical assistance programs to promote development rather than strong IP protection).

[19] See TRIPS Agreement, art. 2.

landscape of IP laws in many developing and least-developed countries, there is no question that the difficulty in persuading local officials of the degree and right to exercise national discretion in TRIPS implementation strategies is likely strongly linked to the precedential effect of WIPO's activities in those countries since their independence (Okediji 2008; Okediji 2003).

B. The Political Economy of Public Health

In both developed and developing/least-developed countries, providing access to medicines is a quintessentially political undertaking with which governments at all levels are deeply involved (Liberman 2012; Oriola 2007). Price regulation of drugs (Lexchin 2006), outright subsidies to consumers (Sichelman 2010), compulsory licensing of patents (Reichman and Hazhenzal 2003), and regulatory incentives (Thomas 2013) are all examples of tools deployed in developed countries to facilitate and safeguard the government's capacity to provide essential health services to the public. In short, rarely is the public's access to drugs in any country left solely to the vicissitudes of the proprietary interests of pharmaceutical patent owners regardless of the level of economic maturity. As scholars have already established, compulsory licenses for pharmaceutical goods have been more widely used in the developed countries than is commonly acknowledged (Reichman 2009), despite the often harsh reactions to similar attempts by developing and least-developed countries (Abdel Latif 2011). The fact is that government procurement of drugs imposes significant externalities on fiscal budgets (Sichelman 2010; Gallego 2006), causing governments to maneuver between regulatory measures to directly contain costs, or tamper with the robustness of patentability criteria such as non-obviousness to curb patents over pharmaceutical products (Devlin 2010).

III. WIPO and the TRIPS Agreement in Relation to Public Health

A. A Human Right to Health in the TRIPS Framework?

The right of countries to adopt measures to protect public health is one of the grounds explicitly mentioned as part of the principles of the TRIPS Agreement,[20] and the Doha Declaration subsequently established elements of this right, including the residual power of countries to unilaterally determine the conditions in which public health needs can override patent privileges.[21] Access to medicines is

[20] See TRIPS Agreement, art. 8.

[21] TRIPS Agreement, art. 8; see World Intellectual Property Organization [WIPO], Committee on Development and Intellectual Property, *Patent-Related Flexibility in the Multilateral Legal Framework and their Legislative Implementation at the National and Regional Levels—Part II*, at 5, WIPO Doc. CDIP/7/3 (March 18, 2011) (describing provisions from TRIPS and the Doha Declaration that provide least-developed countries with IP enforcement flexibilities based on their "economic, financial and administrative constraints, and their need for flexibility to create a viable technological base," and to "address . . . public health problems" in the pharmaceutical field).

an integral part of the human right to health in many countries (Lee and Hunt 2012). WIPO, however, has been far less embracing of human rights approaches to IP as a basis for access to medicines despite robust scholarly examination and affirmation of a positive effect of the IP-human rights link on access to medicines (Land, this volume; Land and Pakenham-Walsh 2012; Helfer and Austin 2011). To the extent patent grants circumscribe the terms of access, human rights norms provide countervailing arguments of equal or, arguably, greater moral force. These normative strategies of resistance to maximalist patent rights have had a measurable impact on access to medicines campaigns across Brazil, Latin America, South Africa, and East Africa. At a minimum, human rights arguments, because they so easily galvanize global public concern, can exert significant bottom-up pressure that eventually affects the scope and direction of the exercise of IP rights.[22] Even when formally marginalized within politically agile organizations such as WIPO or the WTO, human rights arguments constitute a centripetal force compelling normative reconsideration of global patent norms. This overlapping regime complex, which frames the access to medicine challenge, requires shared competence across international organizations in addressing public health and access to medicines.

The most obvious institutional partnership for IP-related barriers to access to medicines is between WIPO and the WHO (ICTSD 2011; Sell 2004). The WTO's jurisdiction over the TRIPS Agreement also gives it direct authority to act on related public health concerns both independent of, and in coordination with, other international agencies. Among these three leading international organizations—WIPO, WTO, and the WHO—WIPO has the weakest link to the issue of access to medicines both in terms of its mandate and its accountability to the global public demand for effective solutions. The disjuncture between WIPO's well-defined role in producing harmonized patent norms, including supplying information about the patent system to international actors, and its relatively weak links to the global governance of public health issues, is problematic on at least two fronts. First, this disjuncture facilitates an *à la carte* involvement with initiatives to address access to medicines, which really requires systemic and coordinated efforts across related institutions, especially those efforts that may involve limits to the exercise of patent rights. Second, this disjuncture makes it hard to determine and maintain the appropriate allocation of competency over access to medicines issues. In an institutional setting where the mandate for global public health and the mandate for global patent norms are distinctly managed with uncertain mechanisms to compel measurable outcomes, it is easier for the organizations and actors involved to be less transparent and more complicit in avoiding the tough task of dealing with the role of patent law as a barrier to access to medicines. In light of a strong human rights

[22] This point is amply demonstrated by recalling the strong dissatisfaction of the developing and least-developed countries with WIPO's approach to patents and public health following the Doha Declaration. It became one of the lead factors in the bold demand by these countries for a reorientation of WIPO's activities, and ultimately produced the WIPO Development Agenda.

basis to address access to medicines within the TRIPS Agreement (Helfer 2007),[23] WIPO's role should be more purposefully constructed to align with the explicit objectives and patent-related measures expressed in the Doha Declaration. WIPO's exclusive mandate over IP neither privileges nor prioritizes its view on the normative tension between the human rights, humanitarian, and IP regimes. But a more consistent relationship between WIPO's norm-producing authority and the Organization's recent unambiguous visibility in partnering with other organizations working for solutions to access to medicines is necessary and should be pursued.

B. Rethinking WIPO's Role

It is clear from the range of WIPO's involvement in the global public health debate that it is unwilling to have the issue of access to medicines branded solely by the work of other international organizations. And as noted earlier, there has been a positive evolution of WIPO's acknowledgement and careful embrace of its role. Certainly, refusal to engage in the intense multilateral discussion about public health issues and access to medicines issues would have entailed a grave risk for WIPO's continued leadership in matters concerning global IP governance, particularly in the wake of the establishment of the WTO (Dinwoodie 2002). As indicated above, however, WIPO is far from peripheral to the implementation and expansion of the patent norms established by TRIPS. WIPO's institutional redesign (Dinwoodie 2002)[24] and expansive portfolio of initiatives, programs, and activities (McGarry 2008) since the conclusion of the TRIPS Agreement were more than just astute acts of self-preservation. These efforts have reinvigorated and provided a self-selected organizational basis for an expanded global platform for WIPO, giving the Organization legitimacy and authority to speak on these pressing global issues of our time. Today, WIPO is one of the most complex, politically nimble, and well-resourced international organizations, certainly as compared to other specialized United Nations (UN) agencies. It maintains a vast network of relations among states, private organizations, non-governmental organizations, and other international bodies. Far from becoming less relevant in global matters, WIPO's role in shaping national and international responses to global challenges is unprecedented (Trujillo 2009; Borges Barbosa et al. 2007).

There is already evidence that developed countries are likely to oppose meaningful normative outcomes directly facilitated by WIPO on access to medicines. The protracted stalemate in establishing a work program for the Standing

[23] UN Human Rights Council, Res. 23/14, Access to Medicines in the Context of the Right of Everyone to the Enjoyment of the Highest Attainable Standard of Physical and Mental Health, UN Doc. A/HRC/23/L.10/Rev.1 (2013).

[24] See, e.g., WIPO, Global Challenges Division, *Global Challenges and Intellectual Property*, <http://www.wipo.int/globalchallenges/en> (last visited August 12, 2013) (dealing with climate change, public health, and food security). For a description of a more recent restructuring, see WIPO, *Strategic Realignment: Stream Three—Restructuring*, <http://www.wipo.int/aboutwipo/en/strategic_realignment/organigram.html> (last visited August 12, 2013).

Committee on Patents (SCP), despite recent positive movement (Hermann 2013), is just one example among many dispersed points of tension between member states at WIPO. Nonetheless, WIPO, like other international organizations, has an institutional pathology that reveals its capacity to act independently of member states (Barnett and Finnemore 1999; Alvarez 2005; Okediji 2008). At a minimum, WIPO could leverage its tremendous institutionalized experience and relationships with IP offices in developing and least-developed countries to encourage these countries to undertake measures to ensure access to medicines, rather than just focusing on or reinforcing adoption of the strongest IP norms.

There are significant possibilities for a more definitive and productive role for WIPO in the area of access to medicines beyond its politically constrained room for maneuver. Here, I highlight five possible overarching principles of a suggested WIPO "enhanced action plan":

1. *National Responses to Access to Medicines:* To the extent countries resort to unilateral IP policy tools to address health challenges specific to their citizens, WIPO's influence is less visibly exercised but potentially more difficult to orient toward constructive ends to support access to medicines. As such, there is virtue in the public nature of WIPO's recent engagement with the WHO and WTO in regard to access to medicines (2013); it facilitates greater accountability and transparency than is otherwise usually available in the Organization's traditional norm-setting activities (Lerner 2008). If WIPO is inextricably connected with the implementation of global patent norms, then it must also play a positive role in shaping any national reform efforts consistent with facilitating access to medicines. Certainly, since 2009 with the election of a new Director General, WIPO has made important tactical shifts from "isolation" to "engagement" of issues affecting the supply of global public goods and this is a positive first step for the Organization (Abdel Latif 2011; Smith 2009). But it cannot be the last one. There are suggestions in the case studies in this volume that WIPO's activities fill domestic policy space with untested normative claims about IP that ultimately constrain the scope and possibility of policy experimentation. Such experimentation is vital to a sustainable evolution of IP laws that meaningfully account for the supply of public goods, including public health. WIPO arguably has an ethical obligation to provide technical assistance that is consistent with the public health flexibilities recognized in the TRIPS Agreement and confirmed by relevant WTO dispute panels.[25] Moreover, this would be an important application of the Development Agenda Recommendation 14 to "make available advice to developing countries and LDCs, on the implementation and operation of the rights and obligations and the understanding and use of flexibilities contained in the TRIPS Agreement."[26]

2. *Co-Existence with Human Rights Organizations to Address Public Health Ends:* While WIPO could play an important role in assisting in efforts to implement

[25] *Canada–Patent Protection of Pharmaceutical Products*, WT/DS114/R March 17, 2000.

[26] WIPO, *The 45 Adopted Recommendations under the WIPO Development Agenda* (2007), available at <http://www.wipo.int/ip-development/en/agenda/recommendations.html>.

normative flexibility in national and regional laws for access to medicines, sometimes the most important role it can assume is to allow organizations with greater credibility in human rights and humanitarian efforts to help shape local policies regarding access to medicines. Instead of model laws and technical assistance focused on compliance with the "rights" side of the patent system, WIPO could produce materials to help inform and supplement the work of human rights agencies on the limitations used in the developed countries that might positively assist the developing and least-developed countries in their efforts to straddle the IP and human rights divide. In short, WIPO cannot logically escape the human rights approaches that have become a vital part of the political and policy environments in which countries are addressing access to medicine. This is especially true with respect to the powerful role of human rights nongovernmental organizations (NGOs) whose strategic partnerships with governments (Barnett 2005) have already produced unprecedented contributions in facilitating access to medicines. Moreover, regional courts have emerged as powerful actors in the IP/human rights and trade/human rights interfaces (Gathii 2013; Helfer, Alter, and Guerzovich 2009). As judicial lawmaking and enforcement activities continue in these courts, WIPO could lose opportunities to inform and influence the important discourse on IP and human rights. Consequently, WIPO's role in access to medicines issues may also be of lesser consequence in the countries subject to the courts' jurisdiction. Finally, if WIPO remains coldly distant from human rights frames, it risks strengthening global popular perception that the challenge of access to medicines is solely about the improvidence of the IP system, and that IP rights cannot be part of the global solution. This in turn will create a cycle of pressure on the Organization and its member states with respect to future IP harmonization efforts.

3. *The WTO-WIPO Agreement:* Under this Agreement, WIPO assists the WTO in particular exercises and functions.[27] Indeed, part of WIPO's technical assistance to developing and least developed countries involves a longstanding workshop it co-sponsors with the WTO, offering training to IP officials from developing and least-developed countries.[28] Within the context of such joint activities, WIPO should assume equal accountability with the WTO for its TRIPS implementation training activities. By actively leveraging its partnership with the WTO to engage public health issues, WIPO can more aggressively experiment with legal options available within the TRIPS Agreement (and even beyond it) for policy choices advanced to developing and least-developed countries. In this manner, WIPO could lessen the gap between its role as a source of global patent norms and its lack of a formal mandate to deal with public health concerns. Importantly, training activities should not simply "dump" information on mid-level bureaucrats, but ideally integrate interdisciplinary approaches to the IP and public health relationship. The objectives of these and other similar training activities should be clear: to empower officials to

[27] Agreement between WIPO and WTO of December 22, 1995, 35 I.L.M 754 (1996).

[28] WIPO and WTO have conducted joint workshops on technical assistance since 1996. World Intell. Prop. Org., Cooperation with the World Trade Organization, Annex, Doc. WO/GA/24/5 Rev. 5 (August 4, 1999).

better appreciate, understand, and consider the various competing views and range of possible responses to access to medicines, including the costs of alternative strategies. Put differently, the WTO-WIPO Agreement offers an opportunity for WIPO to work explicitly within trade policy frameworks as part of its array of tools to address the role of IP in public health.

4. *Developing Expertise in Competition-Related Constraints:* WIPO has done some work in competition law-related matters,[29] but surprisingly this area appears to be the least advanced of its IP-related activities. As seen from the example of South Africa, where competition law was successfully used to address access to medicines (Klug 2012), this is an area of promise for developing countries and least-developed countries (Rosenberg 2012), and one that is explicitly integrated in the TRIPS Agreement as a limitation to the exercise of patent rights.[30] WIPO's technical assistance activities could focus on assisting developing country governments with appropriate tools and principles to manage the patent law/competition interface. So far, this policy space does not appear to have been occupied by any international organization, despite the important role competition law could play in access to medicines.

5. *Patent Law and Innovation for Public Health:* Facilitating access to existing medicines is only one part of the public health equation. Pharmaceutical innovation to address diseases such as malaria, tuberculosis, and other tropical diseases remains a vital public need for the developing world (WHO 2007). In this regard, WIPO's Re:Search initiative[31] is a notable first step. Some of the most difficult questions regarding access to medicines have to do with access to medicines that have not yet been developed. The effect of patent rights on downstream research and other socially productive uses is just as important as ongoing efforts to mitigate the costs of access to existing drugs, including through promoting equitable licensing and research partnerships. In the long run, neither access to medicines nor ongoing research for diseases can be treated as an expendable item on WIPO's public welfare agenda. WIPO should consider how to respond to criticism of its Re: Search initiative, particularly with respect to the need to expand its scope beyond least-developed countries. The judicious approach WIPO has traditionally used to embark on innovative ideas such as Re:Search may not serve it well going forward, particularly as public insistence on result-driven outcomes continues to exert pressure on norm-setting activities. Patent rights are a predictably omnipresent tool in the innovation cycle, but rights must continue to be circumscribed by effective limits, including those designed to maximize the teaching, communicating, and research functions of the patent system (Seymore 2010).

[29] See, e.g., WIPO, *Competition and Patents*, <http://www.wipo.int/patent-law/en/developments/competition.html> (last visited August 12, 2013).

[30] Article 40.

[31] See WIPO, *About WIPO*, <http://www.wipo.int/research/en/about> (last visited August 20, 2013).

C. WIPO, Residual Sovereignty, Path Dependency, and the Role of the Patent System

It is well established that the TRIPS Agreement did not resolve many important differences in the underlying national patent policies of member states. As a result, the leading patent law jurisdictions remain at odds on numerous issues and employ a variety of approaches to preserve domestic public interest priorities. Scholars have urged developing countries to adopt these same strategies (Cheng 2012; Van Puymbroeck 2008). The case studies in this volume suggest that this is not enough. Further, as valid as these arguments may be, they confine developing and least-developed countries to particular exercises of sovereign discretion, based not on an inherent flexibility in patent law (Sullivan 2008; Duong 2007; UNCTAD 2011), but on power in international relations. The emphasis on recycling policy measures of the developed countries suggests that only what is tried by the powerful can count as legitimate end runs of the patent monopoly. Such copycat policy mechanisms only replace one form of path dependency—unbalanced patent protection as a sole solution to technology deficits—with another.

Patent law and the institutions responsible for developing and administering patent policy have an important role not only for access to medicines for today's global health challenges but also for those in the future. The efficacy of the international patent framework to deliver on the public welfare promise of the patent system is linked to having the appropriate policy levers more meaningfully integrated into national patent laws. In this regard, WIPO's role as the principal purveyor of technical assistance on IP issues is of considerable importance for access to medicines. With increasing competitive pressure from international trade, *all* countries will want to exercise their residual sovereignty under TRIPS to fashion domestic patent policies that are suited to address important, long-term national economic interests. WIPO's role in access to medicines should reflect this changing landscape of rival approaches to public welfare, and should afford new opportunities to facilitate policy experimentation, international institutional coordination, and an alignment of human rights and IP norms in a far more transparent, coherent, and credible manner within the public international law framework. If WIPO does not take on this richer role, undoubtedly the moral, ethical, and humanitarian demands of various public health crises will force other institutional actors to fill this gap.

IV. Conclusion

Sustainable access to medicines is viewed most passionately in humanitarian terms as an international challenge encompassing issues of poverty, innovation, human rights, and economic development. Large-scale humanitarian efforts, such as those witnessed at the height of the HIV epidemic in Sub-Saharan Africa, will always have a role to play in addressing access to medicines. But access to medicines cannot, and should not, be addressed on humanitarian grounds alone. To do so would unfairly erode the right and the responsibility of developing and least-developed countries to develop national patent, competition, and other legal regimes necessary to secure public welfare goals. It would make them perpetual recipients of charity instead of masters of their own public good. And it would eliminate pressure to hold the international patent system accountable for the ends for which it is justified and on which WIPO's very existence is premised.

References

Abdel Latif, Ahmed. 2011. "Change and Continuity in the International Intellectual Property System: A Turbulent Decade in Perspective." *WIPO Journal* 3: 37–42.

Alvarez, José E. 2005. *International Organizations as Law-Makers*. New York: Oxford University Press.

Attaran, Amir. 2003. "Assessing and Answering Paragraph 6 of the Doha Declaration on the TRIPS Agreement and Public Health: The Case for Greater Flexibility and a Non-Justiciability Solution." *Emory International Law Review* 17: 743.

Barnett, Michael N. 2005. "Humanitarianism Transformed." *Perspectives on Politics* 3: 723.

—— and Martha Finnemore. 1999. "The Politics, Power, and Pathologies of International Organizations." *International Organization* 53: 705–09.

Borges Barbosa, Denis, et al. 2007. "Slouching towards Development in International Intellectual Property." *Michigan State Law Review* 2007: 86.

Bubela, Tania, et al. 2011. "Wicked Issues for Canada at the Intersection of Intellectual Property and Public Health: Mechanisms for Policy Coherence." *McGill Journal of Law and Health* 4: 40–1.

Cheng, Thomas K. 2012. "A Developmental Approach to the Patent-Antitrust Interface." *Northwest Journal of International Law and Business* 33: 65–72.

Chernew, Michael. 2010. "Health Care Spending Growth: Can We Avoid Fiscal Armageddon?" *Inquiry* 47: 285.

Deere, Carolyn. 2008. *The Implementation Game: The TRIPS Agreement and the Global Politics of Intellectual Property Reform in Developing Countries*. New York: Oxford University Press.

Devlin, Alan. 2010. "Patent Law's Parsimony Principle." *Berkeley Technology Law Journal* 25: 1722.

Dinwoodie, Graeme B. 2002. "The Architecture of the International Intellectual Property System." *Chicago-Kent Law Review* 77: 1005.

—— and Rochelle C. Dreyfuss. 2009. "Designing a Global Intellectual Property System Responsive to Change: The WTO, WIPO, and Beyond." *Houston Law Review* 46: 1231.

Drahos, Peter. 2008. "'Trust Me': Patent Offices in Developing Countries." *American Journal of Law and Medicine* 34: 151.

Duong, Wendy N. 2007. "Following the Path of Oil: The Law of the Sea or Realpolitik—What Good Does Law Do in the South China Sea Territorial Conflicts?" *Fordham International Law Journal* 30: 1101–2.

Flynn, Sean M., et al. 2012. "The U.S. Proposal for an Intellectual Property Chapter in the Trans-Pacific Partnership Agreement." *American University International Law Review* 28: 105.

Gallego, G. 2006. *The Australian Health Care System and High Cost Medications (HCMs)* 27. Sydney: University of Sydney. Available at <http://ses.library.usyd.edu.au/bitstream/2123/1008/2/02whole.pdf>.

Gathii, James Thuo. 2013 (forthcoming). "Mission Creep or a Search for Relevance: The East African Court of Justice's Human Rights Strategy." *Duke International and Comparative Journal* 24. Available at <http://papers.ssrn.com/sol3/papers.cfm?abstract_id=2178756>.

Gold, E. Richard. 2013. "Patents and Human Rights: A Heterodox Analysis." *Journal of Law, Medicine, and Ethics* 41: 185.

Helfer, Laurence R. 2007. "Toward a Human Rights Framework for Intellectual Property." *UC Davis Law Review* 40: 971.

——, Karen J. Alter, and M. Florencia Guerzovich. 2009. "Islands of Effective International Adjudication: Constructing an Intellectual Property Rule of Law in the Andean Community." *American Journal of International Law* 103: 1–46. Available at <http://scholarship.law.duke.edu/faculty_scholarship/2072>.

—— and Graeme W. Austin. 2011. *Human Rights and Intellectual Property: Mapping the Global Interface*. New York: Cambridge University Press.

Hermann, Rachel Marusak. 2013. "WIPO Patent Law Committee Cinches Agreement on Future Work." Retrieved August 21, 2013 at <http://www.ip-watch.org/2013/03/01/wipo-patent-law-committee-cinches-agreement-on-future-work>.

International Centre for Trade and Sustainable Development (ICTSD). 2011. "WTO, WIPO and WHO Examine Role of Patent Information in Access to Medicines." *Bridges Weekly Trade News Digest* 15(7). Available at <http://ictsd.org/i/news/bridgesweekly/101767>.

International Monetary Fund (IMF). 2004. "Health and Development: Why Investing in Health Is Critical for Achieving Economic Development Goals." Available at <http://www.imf.org/external/pubs/ft/health/eng/hdwi/hdwi.pdf>.

Klug, Heinz. 2012. "Access to Medicines and the Transformation of the South African State: Exploring the Interactions of Legal and Policy Changes in Health, Intellectual Property, Trade, and Competition Law in the Context of South Africa's HIV/AIDS Pandemic." *Law and Social Inquiry* 37: 297.

Kostecki, Michel. 2006. "Issue Paper No. 12: Intellectual Property and Economic Development: What Technical Assistance to Redress the Balance in Favour of Developing Nations?" *Programme on IPRs and Sustainable Development*. International Center for Trade and Sustainable Development (ICTSD).

—— and Neil Pakenham-Walsh. 2012. "Access to Health Information Under International Human Rights Law." Institute for Information Law and Policy, White Paper Series 11/12 #01. Available at <http://www.nyls.edu/user_files/1/2/23/144/1345/Access%20to%20Health%20Information%20White%20Paper.pdf>.

Lee, Joo-Young, and Paul Hunt. 2012. "Human Rights Responsibilities of Pharmaceutical Companies in Relation to Access to Medicines." *Journal of Law, Medicine, and Ethics* 40: 220.

Lerner, Jack. 2008. "Intellectual Property and Development at WHO and WIPO." *American Journal of Law and Medicine* 34: 273.

Lexchin, Joel. 2006. "The Pharmaceutical Industry and the Pursuit of Profit" Pp. 11, 15 in *The Power of Pills: Social, Ethical and Legal Issues in Drug Development, Marketing, and Pricing*, edited by Jillian Claire Cohen, Patricia Illingworth, and Udo Schuklenk. Ann Arbor: Pluto Press.

Liberman, Jonathan. 2012. "Combating Counterfeit Medicines and Illicit Trade in Tobacco Products: Minefields in Global Health Governance." *Journal of Law, Medicine, and Ethics* 40: 326.

McGarry, Kevin. 2008. "Comment: U.S. Patent Reform and International Public Health: Issues of Law and Policy." *Intercultural Human Rights Law Review* 3: 299.

Murashige, Kate H. 1994. "Harmonization of Patent Laws." *Houston Journal of International Law* 16: 591.

New, William. 2012. "US, WIPO Training Programme on IP Rights in Africa Comes under Fire." *Intellectual Property Watch*. Retrieved February 12, 2012 at <http://www.ip-watch.org/2012/02/12/us-wipo-training-programme-on-ip-rights-in-africa-comes-under-fire>.

——. 2001. "WIPO Defends Involvement in IP Enforcement Meeting in the Philippines." *Intellectual Property Watch*. Retrieved October 24, 2001 at <http://www.ip-watch.org/2011/10/24/wipo-defends-involvement-in-ip-enforcement-meeting-in-the-philippines>.

Ney, Steven. 2012. "Making Sense of the Global Health Crisis: Policy Narratives, Conflict, and Global Health Governance." *Journal of Health Politics, Policy, and Law* 37: 275.

Okediji, Ruth L. 2003. "The International Relations of Intellectual Property: Narratives of Developing Country Participation in the Global Intellectual Property System." *Singapore Journal of International and Comparative Law* 7: 315.

——. 2008. "WIPO-WTO Relations and the Future of Global Intellectual Property Norms." *Netherlands Yearbook of International Law* 39: 69.

——. 2014. "Towards a Global Patent Law Canon." In *Patent Law in Global Perspective*, edited by Ruth L. Okediji and Margo Bagley. New York: Oxford University Press (forthcoming).

Oriola, Taiwo A. 2007. "Against the Plague: Exemption of Pharmaceutical Patent Rights as a Biosecurity Strategy." *University of Illinois Journal of Law, Technology, and Policy* 2007: 309.

Pager, Sean A. 2012. "Accentuating the Positive: Building Capacity for Creative Industries into the Development Agenda for Global Intellectual Property Law." *American University International Law Review* 28: 292–93.

Reichman, Jerome H. 2009. "Comment: Compulsory Licensing of Patented Pharmaceutical Inventions: Evaluating the Options." *Journal of Law, Medicine, and Ethics* 37: 247.

—— and Catherine Hazhenzal. 2003. "Non-Voluntary Licensing of Patented Inventions: Historical Perspective, Legal Framework under TRIPS, and an Overview of the Practice in Canada and the United States of America" (ICTSD Issue Paper 5). Available at <http://ictsd.org/i/publications/11764/?view=document>.

Rosenberg, Barbara. 2012. "Antitrust Assessment of IP-Related Matters in Brazil: Recent Developments." *Competition Law International* August: 28, 30.

Sangsuvan, Kitsuron. 2013. "Separation of Powers in Intellectual Property Rights: Balancing Global Intellectual Property Rights or Monopoly Power in the Twenty-First Century by Competition Law." *New York International Law Review* 26: 16.

Sell, Susan K. 2004. "The Quest for Global Governance in Intellectual Property and Public Health: Structural, Discursive, and Institutional Dimensions." *Temple Law Review* 77: 365.

——. 2011. "TRIPS Was Never Enough: Vertical Forum Shifting, FTAS, ACTA, and TPP." *Journal of Intellectual Property Law* 18: 476.

Seymore, Sean B. 2010. "The Teaching Function of Patents." *Notre Dame Law Review* 85: 621.

Sichelman, Ted. 2010. "Commercializing Patents." *Stanford Law Review* 62: 386.

Smith, Adam. 2009. "Gurry Evaluates Historic WIPO Reform Project." *World Trademark Review*. Retrieved August 20, 2013 at <http://www.worldtrademarkreview.com/daily/detail.aspx?g=73312b61-f7f5-410e-88dd-1389c01429f8>.

Stein, Haley. 2005. "Intellectual Property and Genetically Modified Seeds: The United States, Trade, and the Developing World." *Northwest Journal of Technology and Intellectual Property* 3: 160, para. 41.

Sullivan, Scott M. 2008. "Rethinking Treaty Interpretation." *Texas Law Review* 86: 796.

Sun, Haochen. 2004. "The Road to Doha and Beyond: Some Reflections on the TRIPS Agreement and Public Health." *European Journal of International Law* 15: 123.

Thomas, Jay R. 2014. "Toward a Theory of Regulatory Exclusivity." In *Patent Law in Global Perspective*, edited by Ruth L. Okediji and Margo Bagley. New York: Oxford University Press (forthcoming).

Trujillo, Elizabeth. 2009. "From Here to Beijing: Public/Private Overlaps in Trade and their Effects on U.S. Law." *Loyola University Chicago Law Journal* 40: 705.

United Nations Conference on Trade and Development (UNCTAD). 2011. *Using IPRs to Stimulate Pharmaceutical Production in Developing Countries: A Reference Guide* (UNCTAD/DIAE/PCB/2009/19).

Van Puymbroeck, Rudolf V. 2008. "Beyond Sex: Legal Reform for HIV/AIDS and Poverty Reduction." *Georgetown Journal on Poverty Law and Policy* 15: 781 (recommending various policies).

——. 2010. "Basic Survival Needs and Access to Medicines—Coming to Grips with TRIPS: Conversion + Calculation." *Journal of Law, Medicine, and Ethics* 38: 520.

Weissman, Robert. 1996. "A Long Strange TRIPS: The Pharmaceutical Industry Drive to Harmonize Global Intellectual Property Rules, and the Remaining WTO Legal Alternatives Available to Third World Countries." *University of Pennsylvania Journal of International Economic Law* 17: 1076–77, 1082–85.

World Bank, 2013. "Health Overview." Retrieved August 9, 2013 at <http://www.worldbank.org/en/topic/health/overview>.

World Health Organization (WHO). 2007. "Fact Sheet: The Top Ten Causes of Death." Retrieved August 19, 2013 at <http://www.who.int/mediacentre/factsheets/fs310.pdf>.

——. 2011. *Global Strategy and Plan of Action on Public Health, Innovation and Intellectual Property* 23–31. Available at <http://www.who.int/phi/publications/Global_Strategy_Plan_Action.pdf>.

——, World Intellectual Property Organization (WIPO), and World Trade Organization (WTO). 2012. *Promoting Access to Medical Technologies and Innovation: Intersections Between Public Health, Intellectual Property, and Trade*. Available at <http://www.wto.org/english/res_e/booksp_e/pamtiwhowipowtoweb13_e.pdf>.

World Intellectual Property Organization (WIPO). 2011. "Access to Medicines: Patent Information and Freedom to Operate: A Joint Technical Symposium by WHO, WIPO and WTO." Available at <http://www.wipo.int/meetings/en/2011/who_wipo_wto_ip_med_ge_11/program.html>.

Yu, Peter K. 2012. "Intellectual Property Training and Education for Development." *American University International Law Review* 28: 311.

Chapter 14

Conclusion: Balancing Wealth and Health in a Transnational Regulatory Framework

Rochelle Cooper Dreyfuss and César Rodríguez-Garavito

Balancing patent and health policy is a daunting task, requiring a delicate weighing of domestic and international interests. Joining the World Trade Organization (WTO) and adopting the Trade-Related Aspects of Intellectual Property (TRIPS) Agreement required the countries in our study to increase their levels of intellectual property protection. Partly, they increased protection—and adopted patent law protective of pharmaceutical products—as the quid pro quo for gaining access to world markets for their output (principally raw materials). Eager to attract foreign investments, they also raised standards to signal their determination to improve business conditions. Most obviously, they hoped that a strong intellectual property regime would, as it does in the North, increase incentives to innovate and to produce products (such as medicines) that raise living standards and improve the quality of life.

Obtaining these benefits was not, however, without cost, particularly in the health sector. Complying with TRIPS can raise the price of medicine and jeopardize access to life-enhancing treatments. Rights over scientific information can also impede research, reduce domestic training opportunities, and delay each country's ability to reach the technology frontier and innovate at world levels (Reichman and Dreyfuss 2007). As experience with TRIPS has accumulated, it has also become evident that the promise of TRIPS has been largely illusory. Foreign investment has not been forthcoming (Braga and Fink 1998). Because commodity goods can never be priced far above cost, access to world markets has not tended to generate enough profits to offset the supracompetitive prices commanded by protected information products. Not only do the incentive effects produced by these rights have little purchase in countries, such as those in Latin America, that lack an innovative pharmaceutical sector, their dependence on a market mechanism means that patents do not even encourage foreign innovators to conduct research on diseases, such as dengue fever and river blindness, which mainly afflict the poor (Wong and Dutfield 2011).

Of course countries can adopt strong proprietary protection and safeguard health through other means, such as with price controls, government subsidies, rational selection processes (for example, reliance on approved formularies), and improved infrastructure (Kuanpoth 2010: 163). Indeed, Colombia adopted that approach. But as the case study of Colombia demonstrates, exclusive rights nonetheless heavily influence access to adequate healthcare. Even the most cost-conscious formulary is likely to contain some patented products; the higher the price the government must pay to provide medicine to its population, the less it has available to meet other needs. In both Colombia and Argentina, government support for pharmaceutical purchases also opened opportunities for corruption and created a class of people interested in maintaining high prices.

It is no surprise then, that all of the countries in our case studies sought to utilize the flexibilities in TRIPS to keep as much material as possible free of claims to ownership and to withstand bilateral and unilateral attempts, including through the use of free trade agreements (FTAs) or Special 301 actions, to impose TRIPS-plus obligations. Some did better at this than others. Ecuador resisted the pressure to raise intellectual property levels above those required by TRIPS. It even turned the tables and suspended obligations under the TRIPS Agreements to force the European Union to open its banana market. To a somewhat lesser extent, Argentina resisted as well. Chile took a highly technical approach to tailoring its intellectual property law. Using TRIPS flexibilities, it enabled its pharmaceutical industry to prosper. Although it otherwise adopted strong standards, competition kept the prices in Chile down to accessible levels.

Other countries were less successful in furthering access concerns. The Central American nations ultimately succumbed to the demands of the United States: the standards of the Central American Free Trade Agreement (CAFTA) are among the strictest in all the FTAs between developing and developed nations. Colombia, despite a long negotiation process with the United States, ultimately signed an FTA that requires only somewhat less protection than does CAFTA. Brazil's approach has been termed schizophrenic. It rushed to implement TRIPS before it was required to do so, leading to a premature rise in the price of medicines. At the international stage, however, it actively promotes access interests and locally, it has developed an institution (ANVISA) to insure that the TRIPS flexibilities that were implemented into local law are applied accurately.

The chapters thus present a fascinating picture. From both an intellectual property and procedural perspective, the countries studied in this volume all began in approximately the same place. Prior to TRIPS, they all denied patents to pharmaceutical products. All are democracies and protect due process. All are civil law countries. In addition, all experienced political upheavals. These provided contestation opportunities that permitted the body politic to reexamine first principles. So what explains the differences in outcome? The Colombian study illustrates that the level of dependence on foreign assistance matters a great deal. However, the other countries in the study were not as deeply within the United States' sphere of influence as Colombia, and yet there were significant differences among them. Because TRIPS and FTAs embed negotiations over intellectual property in a broad array of trade issues, it is also possible that each country simply made an individualized calculation of the appropriate trade-off between recognizing strong intellectual property rights and acquiring access to foreign markets for local products. But given the disparity between the benefits these countries could rationally expect from intellectual property protection and the costs associated with these rights, that explanation can account for only a small part of the divergence in outcomes.

To be sure, market size may play an important role. Ecuador's market, for example, is so small that countries in the global North may not consider it worthwhile to expend political capital on demanding high levels of protection. Market differentials cannot, however, explain the differing outcomes in Argentina and Brazil or among the countries of Central America. Possibly, the history of these countries' engagement with intellectual property is also important: countries that were more involved in drafting TRIPS may have succeeded in inserting provisions that helped them craft law responsive to their needs. However, Brazil and Argentina have been leaders in intellectual property negotiations, yet they did not do significantly better than Chile, which has had a lower international profile.

At least part of the explanation would seem, then, to reside in the efficacy of contestation. The case studies, in short, allow us to assess, if not the validity of the Global Administrative Law (GAL) thesis, then the conditions necessary for the effectuation of its goals. The studies offer detailed evidence on the ways in which procedural and substantive issues are intertwined and they demonstrate how far adherence to administrative values can go in producing substantive results that are accepted as legitimate. The studies also reveal the nodes, links, and internal mechanisms of transnational networks of experts, activists, and decision makers. And they open a window into the political and legal struggles through which the regulatory line between intellectual property and access has been drawn in different countries.

In fact, the differing outcomes documented in these studies of similarly situated countries suggest that procedural opportunities are inadequate, in and of themselves, to resist foreign pressure to enact law that is illegitimate (or inappropriate) from a local perspective. Fields become subject to transnational regulation when powerful nations find that an international approach suits their interests. But once such nations are involved, others operate at a disadvantage. Transparency, opportunities to be heard, rights to review, are simply not enough to successfully contest foreign demands that arise in an international sphere characterized by significant power and resource differentials. If global administrative norms are to be effective substitutes for democracy or sources of legitimacy, and if they are to promote local accountability, then more than mere opportunity or adherence to administrative values is required: the needs of some populations are simply too easy for international administrators to disregard (Stewart forthcoming).

The chapters shed light on the factors that permit effective resistance in an asymmetric contestation environment. Our discussion focuses on five variables that appear to have influenced the outcomes in these cases: expertise, the structure of civil society, institutional competence, normative commitments, and political opportunity structures.

I. Expertise

As the foregoing suggests, balancing proprietary and access interests in the health realm requires a grasp of pharmacology, the economics of the global pharmaceutical sector, and the potentialities of the domestic drug industry, as well as a nuanced command of the arcane fields of patent, trade secrecy, and data exclusivity law. It is necessary to know what actions are needed to secure the benefits of conforming to foreign demand and where lines must be drawn to safeguard vital local interests. It is also necessary to understand what is legally possible: as the Central American study shows, terms like "data exclusivity" can have many different meanings, so too can "new" and "inventive step." For this reason, expertise stands out as a key explanatory variable. Susan Sell (2003) has documented the extensive efforts made by the creative industries to prepare US negotiators in the run-up to the Uruguay Round and many of the studies in this volume similarly describe the expertise that the proprietary drug sector furnished to pro-intellectual property forces during debates over FTAs and implementation. For contestation over access to be fair or legitimating, equivalent capacity is needed on the other side.

The experience of Chile is illustrative. Chile, both before and after the Augusto Pinochet regime, was interested in joining the global economy and the emerging global regulatory system. Thus, it was willing to accept levels of intellectual property protection more appropriate to those of developed countries. Strong protection could, however, have endangered Chile's vibrant generic drug sector, which thrived on copying proprietary pharmaceuticals and selling cheaper versions, both inside and outside Chile. Although the vitality of this sector may have been the reason that the United States made Chile one of its first targets of attention in Latin America, the industry was also the source of Chile's negotiation strength. When FTA negotiations began, the national laboratories organized. With the help of the University of Chile's School of Economics and its Center of Applied Research for Business (as well as advice from the University of Minnesota), it assembled studies to show that, contrary to the contentions of the proprietary industry, prices would rise with the advent of strong patent protection. Even more important, the generic industry identified points of inflection within the proposed international regime.

The result was an extraordinarily technical debate. The parties argued about many of the issues discussed in other countries—whether protection should extend to second uses of known substances, the extent to which delays in granting patents or health authorization justified extending the patent term, and whether linkage between patent enforcement and health regulation was possible or desirable. But they also negotiated details that other countries appear to have largely missed: the allocation of the burden of proof on various issues; the problem of evergreening; what constituted a novel molecular composition for purposes of linkage or the protection of undisclosed information; and when the clock on data protection should begin to tick, when data is first revealed anywhere in the world, or when it is submitted to Chilean authorities. While many concessions were made to US demands, Chile stood firm on enough issues to keep the generic industry strong, the price of pharmaceuticals low (and its name on Special 301 watch lists). Similar observations apply to Ecuador. Its drug industry is small, but a coalition of regional laboratories supplemented its expertise in ways that improved the bargaining position of those interested in a pro-health agenda.

Relying on the generic drug industry to furnish expertise can be effective, but the studies also show that it is not a complete answer. Not all countries have strong generic drug industries. As the introductory chapter noted, prior to TRIPS all the countries in our study had adopted an import substitution industrialization (ISI) model of development and most denied patent protection to pharmaceuticals in order to promote local industry. However, not all the countries in the study were equally successful at creating a strong pharmaceutical sector. Indeed, that is why the Doha Declaration was so important: it changed the proviso in TRIPS that had limited resort to compulsory licenses to predominantly local use so that countries without generic producers would be able to use the procedure. The Central American case study demonstrates how difficult it can be to counter pressure in the absence of a vibrant generic sector.

Even when there is a generic sector, its interests may not be aligned—or perceived to be aligned—with those of the public. In Argentina, for example, the ISI policy fostered a "similars" industry which produced medicaments that were not of high quality; it became a matter of speculation as to whether the arguments and the data these firms offered were any less faulty. In both Argentina and Colombia, the ISI policy also created a "branded" sector which produced high-quality products. But the firms in this sector rely heavily on trademarks to differentiate themselves from the companies producing similars. Thus, they may have had little interest in mounting arguments about the effect of intellectual property protection on price and access. In Argentina, the alignment was possibly even more imperfect: the branded sector had strong business relations with foreign proprietary companies and it began to see itself as innovative, export oriented—and patent dependent. Even in Chile, where the generic industry was better regarded, its effect was somewhat limited. The fight over the FTA was seen as a debate among *private* interests and it did not lead to the articulation of public-regarding policies. Thus, no matter how effectively Chile contested the imposition of patent law, the outcome may not have come across to the public as legitimating the ultimate regulatory regime.

Finally, there is the possibility of corruption. In Argentina, where healthcare is subsidized, those who were responsible for purchasing pharmaceuticals were in a strong position to receive kickbacks from branded or proprietary companies. Colombia benefited greatly from Asinfar, its national association of generic producers, but the endurance of high prices there is suggestive of a similar situation. Kickbacks calculated as a percentage of sale prices diminish the incentives of recipients to lend their expertise to the fight to avoid high standards for intellectual property protection.

Other sources of expertise are therefore critical. The Chilean and Argentine studies highlight the importance of academia in supplying empirical evidence and other research on the relationship between price and access. Indeed, Argentina was particularly fortunate in that Carlos Correa, an economist and lawyer who writes extensively about the impact of TRIPS and FTAs on healthcare, teaches at the University of Buenos Aires. Colombia and some of the countries in Central America also availed themselves of Correa's expertise. In addition, Colombia enjoyed the benefit of organizations in the pro-health camp, such as Ifarma, a think tank founded to advocate for greater citizen access to generic drugs, and prominent experts who could provide links to international organizations and epistemic networks. Most notable was Germán Velásquez, a Colombian expert, who at the time of major contestations was the head of the Program on Essential Drugs at the World Health Organization (WHO). In some countries, public entities also played a role. In the Brazilian study, for example, the work of FIOCRUZ, a public health research institute that develops vaccines, was particularly important.

Some countries may, however, lack both an industry to serve as a proxy for the public interest and also academic and other scholarly oriented resources. In those circumstances, global administrative norms may not be effective at promoting legitimacy unless external efforts are made to insure that all sides can make equivalent use of procedural opportunities. In fact, the TRIPS Agreement can be read as embodying such a commitment. As we saw in Chapter 1, it obligates the WTO to provide technical assistance to developing countries; a commitment the WTO executed, in part, through an agreement with WIPO. While the assistance does not directly extend to negotiating bilateral or plurilateral agreements on TRIPS-plus standards, the TRIPS provision expressly covers matters—drafting laws and regulations, enforcing rights, controlling abuse, establishing domestic offices and training personnel—which could certainly provide much of the information necessary to negotiate strategically. Notably, however, not one of the country studies mentioned WIPO advisors. Indeed, as the Brazilian study recounts, WIPO is often perceived negatively. Its mission, to "promote the protection of intellectual property around the world,"[1] suggests why that might be: its technical assistance appears designed to furnish accountability to the creative industries of the North rather than to the citizens of the South. Other international organizations, such as WHO and the UN Conference on Trade and Development (UNCTAD), also furnish information that is access oriented. But significantly, their activities did not feature heavily in the case studies either. As the Argentine chapter suggests, the efforts of the IMF and the World Bank, which largely support the interests of the developed economies, appear to have been more influential.

The question, then, is why the influence of these organizations varies so widely. One answer is surely that the IMF and World Bank can offer benefits (in the form of grants and loans) which the other organizations cannot. They have also been at the forefront of restructuring efforts in these countries regarding a host of other matters, and have explicitly conditioned funding on governments' commitment to institutional reforms along the lines of the Washington Consensus, which includes better protection of intellectual property. However, there are also recurring anecdotes that the United States (along with the European Union) pressures countries to ignore the advice of access-oriented organizations.[2] If that is so, then GAL norms

[1] Convention Establishing the World Intellectual Property Organisation, Preamble & Articles 3–4 (14 July 1967) 21 U.S.T. 1749 and 848 U.N.T.S. 3.

[2] A telling example was the veto that the US government imposed on Carlos Correa, the Argentinian expert and well-known access advocate who had been hired by the Colombian government to provide it with advice on how to negotiate intellectual property clauses in the FTA with the United States. When, in 2004, Correa sat with Colombian representatives at the negotiating table, the US representatives refused to continue the talks until Correa was removed, arguing that he was a foreign

will be ineffective unless supplemented with a commitment by all relevant parties to refrain from interfering with advice-giving.

More affirmatively, the GAL agenda might be expanded to recognize a right to the "assistance of counsel"—that is, to regard as legitimate only those obligations undertaken with equivalent expertise on all sides of the negotiation (or dispute-resolution) table. A norm drawing attention to the symmetry of bargaining conditions would create an impetus to furnish poorer countries with the assistance they need to evaluate their options accurately. In addition, it would be helpful for organizations that provide pro-access advice to do considerably more to publicize the availability of their resources. Further, they should consider including in the advice they give more information relevant to the TRIPS-plus obligations demanded by FTAs and plurilateral agreements. As important, they should provide the kind of information that Chile used so well. That would include granular details about where international obligations leave space for protecting the public interest and individualized assessments of the effects of patents on price (or, even better, on healthcare) within each nation's territory and in light of its circumstances.

II. Local Civil Society and Transnational Advocacy Networks

The studies suggest that civil society also plays an important role in making effective use of procedural opportunities. In the Central American study, the absence of effective resistance to CAFTA was viewed as partly caused by the paucity of civil society input in many of the countries. Similarly, in Chile, where resistance was perceived as largely a matter of accommodating private concerns, civil society was largely absent from the debates on patent rights. In other places, however, civil society appeared to play a significant role. In Brazil, Central America, and Ecuador for example, coalitions were forged among groups interested in cognate issues, such as human rights, social justice, or indigenous rights. In Colombia, access groups connected with Misión Salud, a faith-based organization interested in healthcare and in El Salvador, the groups concerned with access to medicine allied themselves with activists protesting the elevation of copyright standards. In part, the involvement of civil society can make up for shortfalls in local expertise, but NGOs can also do much more: they can mobilize resistance; create connections with other, perhaps more powerful, constituencies; and bring the potential effects of international regulation to the attention of the public. Furthermore, they may compensate, at least partially, for other capacity problems noted in Chapter 1, such as the difficulty of negotiating in far-flung forums or building international alliances among like-minded countries.

In some low-income and middle-income countries, domestic civil society is, however, somewhat handicapped. In terms of expertise, they may have no greater

advisor rather than a member of the Colombian government. Although the Colombian negotiating team suspended the talks on intellectual property in protest, they bowed to the US veto in the subsequent round. See Moral (2004).

resources at their disposal than does the local healthcare sector. If there are few academics versed in intellectual property matters or doing research into the impact of protection on access to medicines, it is not likely that local NGOs can compensate for their absence. Furthermore, there is no guarantee that local groups will coordinate their activities. In Central America, for example, intellectual property was a "newcomer:" the debate over CAFTA was largely dominated by the concerns of more established civil society groups, such as those interested in labor rights, agricultural sustainability, and the environment. In Ecuador, one of activist groups was mainly interested in control over oil resources, and only later joined in the debate over healthcare. In the post-Peron era, Argentinian NGOs focused more on civil liberties than on the price of medicine. Even among healthcare activists, there can be differences in emphasis. Central America's "white marches" were dominated by doctors mainly interested in other healthcare matters. In Chile, the concern was about whether pharmaceuticals should be sold in supermarkets. In some places, advocacy for access was initially framed around HIV/AIDs medications. For example, in Brazil, a strong and successful civil society coalition was formed to advocate for access to antiretrovirals. Centered around the Brazilian Interdisciplinary Association for AIDS (ABIA), the coalition expanded to pro-access advocacy in general. It mounted highly visible campaigns and was perceived as an important defender of access to medicines. But the success of AIDs activism may not be easily generalized; indeed, focusing debate on this issue may have an adverse impact in very conservative societies.

Transnational NGOs, operating in groups or through linkage to local civil society, may be able to considerably amplify local voices.[3] Organizations such as Doctors Without Borders, Oxfam, KEI (Knowledge Ecology International, formerly CPTech), and Third World Network (TWN) have substantial experience with international intellectual property negotiations, with the flexibilities available within TRIPS, and with the demands made in FTAs worldwide. Indeed, in a study that included Brazil, Duncan Matthews (2007) showed that transnational NGOs have provided information and strategic advice to country delegates, presented information on their behalf in the course of negotiations, raised public awareness, and furnished technical expertise and links to outside experts. They can also link epistemic communities. For example, the efforts of Carlos Correa, who played an important role in Argentina, Colombia, and some of the Central American countries, were broadly shared through his work for TWN (Correa 2001). The Ecuador study demonstrates that these groups can make a considerable contribution, both in terms of strengthening local resistance and modulating the demands of the United States.

Matthews mainly addressed the aid that transnational civil society provides in negotiations over multinational instruments. The success of transnational civil society in that setting does not, however, necessarily translate into success in local debates on bilateral agreements or implementation decisions. In multinational negotiations, the expertise that is needed is general knowledge about intellectual

[3] In her comment in Chapter 10 in this volume, Amy Kapczynski provides a further discussion of the complex relationship between local and transnational advocacy groups.

property law and its policy implications, rather than information about local industry, the needs of the domestic population, and the potential impact of specific regulations. Moreover, the attraction these organizations have for work on behalf of a principle, or a particular region, or a large developing country, may not extend to helping smaller developing nations and least developed countries (Matthews 2007: 1378). In multilateral settings this might not matter as the work often inures to the benefit of all countries interested in a similar outcome. But that will be less true of negotiating FTAs or making decisions on implementation, which can require more individuated consideration.

There is also a matter of trust. In international settings, transnational NGOs work with delegates who see themselves as internationalists; "in [national] capitals" (as Matthews puts it), the wisdom of foreign representatives of transnational organizations may be received with skepticism (Matthews 2007: 1383). Transnational activists may also misapprehend the local situation, fail to "vernacularize" international scripts, and displace local actors (Merry 2006). The Central American study demonstrates the result. Outside health activists advised civil society to work with generic producers. While such alliances had been helpful elsewhere, they were ineffective in countries where the poor quality of "similar" drugs engendered local hostility. Furthermore, human rights activists failed to frame their positions in a manner conducive to influencing the local intellectual property debate. Most unfortunately, the foreign activists left too soon, and without training locals to fill their shoes. Thus, another lesson from these studies is that if transnational civil society is to have an impact on the availability of medicine, it must look beyond the opportunities provided in multilateral settings. Access equally depends on the results of bilateral negotiations and on implementation decisions. For contestation to be effective in those settings, NGOs must furnish advice tailored to the circumstances of each country. Civil society must also recognize that the *demandeurs* of strong protection are persistent and will simply shift to a different regime when they lose in a particular forum. Transnational NGOs may therefore be better off devoting their resources to building local capacity and stable transnational advocacy networks than engaging directly in single episodes in a recursive fight that is sure to take place partly in their absence.

III. Institutional Competence

It need hardly be said that the efficacy of administrative values is heavily dependent on the strength of the institutions in which contestation takes place. These institutions must offer due process. Moreover, they must be unbiased, independent, thorough, and thoughtful. For example, the courts, the legislature—even the plebiscite—largely failed in the CAFTA debate to promote access to health in the countries of Central America. In contrast, the success enjoyed by Argentina can largely be attributed to the strength of its institutions. During the period of study, Argentine politics offered more opportunities for contestation than perhaps any other nation covered in this volume. The government radically changed direction;

during portions of that period, its legislature was unusually deliberative, holding multiple hearings on issues related to intellectual property policy. Its National Ministries of Finance and Health both took active roles in the debates and were heavily involved in crafting policy. The economic crisis created an opening to safeguard access interests through a national medicines policy which subsidized pharmaceutical purchases and may, incidentally, have accentuated the government's interest in the effects of patenting on price (if it did not instill corruption).

The Argentina study also shows the critical importance of a strong patent office and good courts. Once it became clear to the Argentine ministries that stronger intellectual property policy would be enacted, the government was quick to ensure that its patent office, the INPI, had the authority and capacity to review applications with care. INPI was hospitable to patent challenges and took a hard line on patent holders' demands. It refused to countenance *patentes de reválida*, which would have recognized local patents based on foreign awards. Furthermore, it refused to grant product protection based on prior process protection or to grant twenty-year patents during Argentina's transition period. For its part, the court system—in particular, the Supreme Court—provided an important backstop. Whereas lower courts took the proprietary industry's side on these issues, the Supreme Court reinstated the INPI's decisions. The upshot for Argentina was a détente on patent policy. The law was clarified through legislation, regulation, and litigation. The industry then reorganized in a manner that preserved access interests while meeting Argentina's international obligations.

To be sure, not all countries enjoy a similarly effective institutional infrastructure. For example, studies of India suggest that even though the country has a legislature capable of enacting patent law responsive to healthcare concerns, its patent office is so understaffed and overwhelmed, it cannot apply the carefully drawn statutory criteria accurately (Kapczynski 2009; Sampat and Amin 2013). Of course, in some cases, weak institutions may actually work in favor of access interests. If patent offices are slow. a patent on an important product will fail to issue during the period when demand is at its zenith. More important, if the court system is weak, it may be impossible to stop infringement. While the TRIPS Agreement includes obligations to enforce intellectual property rights, it does not "create any obligation to put in place a judicial system for the enforcement of intellectual property rights distinct from that for the enforcement of law in general [or] any obligation with respect to the distribution of resources as between enforcement of intellectual property rights and the enforcement of law in general."[4] Thus, a country with a weak judicial system could, in effect, foster access by failing to efficiently recognize or enforce intellectual property rights.

On balance, however, strong institutions are preferable to weak ones and there are several ways to compensate for deficiencies. As noted earlier, WIPO provides expert assistance to countries that need help implementing their laws. Analogously, the European Patent Office (EPO) and US patent office offer training to new

[4] TRIPS, art. 41.5.

examiners. But since the substantive law taught in these settings is the law of the countries that provide the training, the institutional competence acquired can make it even less likely that the law implemented by the governments of the South will be applied accurately (Drahos 2008; Drahos 2010). The EPO, for example, is likely to teach an examiner to allow a claim covering a second use of a known product, even if her local law would prohibit it, because European law recognizes second-use patents.

Better, then, is to take an approach that preserves resources for the important cases—for example, for challenges to patents on particularly crucial pharmaceuticals. The Brazilian case study demonstrates this strategy. Like Argentina, Brazil had ministries interested in health issues and as we saw, sources of academic and other specialized expertise. It crafted a variation on the linkage requirement demanded by several FTAs. However, instead of tying marketing clearance to patent *enforcement*, Brazil tied clearance to patent *examination.* Under its 2001 Prior Approval mechanism, Brazil's patent office (INPI) would send the pharmaceutical patents it has granted to the National Health Surveillance Agency (ANVISA in Portuguese) for approval. ANVISA would review them and sometimes reverse INPI's decision. The procedure thus ensured accessibility to medicines that should not be patented under Brazilian law, encouraged INPI to engage in rigorous examination, compensates for any capacity problems INPI experiences, and deters it from granting patents based on foreign issuances. In short, the ample contestation opportunities available in Brazil did more than enable pro-access interests to resist TRIPS-plus obligations, they also produced a new institution.

While the constitutionality of the Brazilian procedure is, as of this writing, under review, Brazil has indicated that it plans to make ANVISA a permanent feature of its system.[5] Other countries that lack fully staffed patent offices might consider this strategy as well. Variations are also possible. Thus, Kapczynski (2009) describes India's solution to the institutional capacity deficit: it allows any interested party to challenge an issued patent in a post grant review procedure. As in the Brazilian case, this has the advantage of putting someone (in the Indian case, challengers; in Brazil, the health authority) in a position to identify the products that are important enough to expend precious examination resources. Kapczynski further suggests that developing countries adopt an inverse of a strategy the United States has demanded. Instead of *issuing patentes de reválida* based on patent allowances in the global North, these countries could *invalidate* patents based on invalidations and denials in other developing countries. In that way, institutions like ANVISA and India's post grant review procedures could be leveraged to protect access interests over a broader geographic area (Kapczynski 2009: 1640–1).

Another, complementary, approach focuses on courts. Judicial review and the incorporation of international human rights standards through a new wave of constitutions and constitutional courts have increased the salience and independence of the judiciary in many Latin American countries. In Argentina, Brazil, and

[5] See ANVISA Resolution RDC No. 21/2013.

Colombia it is very likely that the laws that will implement FTA obligations will be challenged in these newly activist courts. Furthermore, both the Colombian and Chilean studies included a series of legal cases involving more granular claims, including challenges to the validity of patents, their scope, their anticompetitive effects, and asserting the need for compulsory licensing and government support. Under the conditions of Latin American neoconstitutionalism, strong courts thus appear likely to play an increasingly central role in the struggle to strike a balance between intellectual property protection and the right to health.

Regionalization and alliances among transnational regulators provide another option. For example, the European Patent Organization performs examinations on behalf of many of the countries in Europe (including those in the European Union), issuing national patents based on patentability requirements of the European Patent Convention. Africa is somewhat similarly organized into two patent-granting institutions, the African Regional Industrial Property Organization (ARIPO) and the African Organization of Intellectual Property (OAPI), and is in the process of developing a regional system, the Pan African Intellectual Property Organization (PAIPO).[6] Along similar lines, representatives of the European, US, and Japanese patent offices meet regularly to talk though differences and improve examination across the trilateral system. Depending on the nature of the alliance, a strong facility can be created without imposing excessive costs on any one country (Pager 2007). Unfortunately, however, a regional patent system (or an alliance among systems) works best when all of the member states have adopted the same law. But as the case studies show, successive unilateral and bilateral actions by the United States (as well as other developed countries) have imposed different obligations on the countries of Latin America and these have led to different patent laws. This "divide and conquer" strategy has therefore done more than eliminate the possibility of a united opposition; it also means that it would be difficult to create an effective regional patent office. Admittedly, under the Patent Cooperation Treaty (PCT),[7] which most of these countries have joined, one patent office can provide others with a preliminary examination which can then be customized. However, the offices that provide these examinations are generally in the North. Without a strong local institution to engage in further examination under local law, the PCT cannot be expected to safeguard access interests. By the same token, countries creating regional systems must insure that the capacity building that the global North makes available is not used to undermine the public interest imperatives of the region (Ncube and Laltaika 2013).

Countries in the global South could, however, also provide for better contestation opportunities through regional courts. Thus, in a contribution to this volume and in separate work, Larry Helfer and his coauthors (Helfer, Alter, and Guerzovich 2009) demonstrate the key role that the Andean Tribunal of Justice (ATJ) has played in shaping the intellectual property law of the Andean Community (Bolivia,

[6] African Union, Final Draft Statute of the Pan-African Intellectual Property Organization (PAIPO), AU/STRC/522.

[7] Patent Cooperation Treaty, June 19, 1970, 28 U.S.T. 7645.

Colombia, Ecuador, Peru, and Venezuela), bolstering the efforts of domestic patent offices, and promoting global administrative values. When Ecuador initially granted pipeline patents pursuant to a bilateral agreement with the United States, the Court invalidated the provision on the ground that Andean law required absolute novelty. The domestic agency then rejected over 100 applications. Similarly, the ATJ held the line on second-use patents, rejecting the arguments that the TRIPS Agreement required them and that TRIPS trumped Andean law. In contrast, the studies show that several non-Andean countries have both pipeline and second-use patents.[8]

As with regional patent offices, however, this tactic does not work well when countries must negotiate transnational agreements on an individual basis. Unlike Ecuador, Colombia did not resist the pressure to enact an FTA. Its agreement with the United States requires protection for undisclosed data, which was also disapproved by the ATJ on the basis of Andean law and policy. Colombia, however, managed to convince the Community that its actions were compliant with its obligations. That decision then led Venezuela to withdraw from the Community. The episode points to a larger lesson: that no amount of procedural protection will make transnational regulation legitimate if it is conducted in a manner that gives short shrift to the institutional structures of the countries upon which it will impact. The observation echoes a common critique of TRIPS. It is regarded as coercive partly because high protectionist countries managed to isolate developing countries (like Argentina and India) that were strong advocates for access rights, from their natural allies through the same set of actions (FTAs and Special 301 watch lists) used in Latin America to demand TRIPS-plus concessions (Sell 2003; Drahos 1995).[9]

IV. Normative Commitments: Human Rights, Indigenous Rights, Sovereignty, Consumer Rights

The Andean experience suggests something else as well: substantive law can be a critical component of successful resistance. For example, according to Helfer and his coauthors, Ecuador's resistance to pipeline patents and protection for second uses was, in part, predicated on a Community law requiring absolute novelty. Outside the context of binding regional intellectual property law, constitutive values and international norms (such as human rights and *ius cogens*) provide the legal hooks for effective contestation. The United States furnishes an illustration. As recent Supreme Court cases illustrate, it has a deep commitment to free speech.[10] TRIPS, however, includes very limited exceptions to copyright protection. For

[8] A similar outcome may result from the increasing involvement of the Inter-American Human Rights institutions—the Commission and the Court—in the protection of socio-economic rights, including the right to health.

[9] Sean Flynn's contribution to this volume discusses transnational activism to soften the impact of Special 301 actions, see Chapter 8.

[10] See, e.g., *Brown v. Entertainment Merchants Association*, 131 S.Ct. 2729 (2011); *Citizens United v. Federal Election Commission*, 558 U.S. 310 (2010).

example, the general exceptions provision is derived from a provision of the Berne Convention, which was negotiated before the United States joined.[11] Thus, with respect to that provision, the United States is in the same position as many of the countries in our study regarding access to medicines—its international commitments clash with its domestic values. But although the WTO's Dispute Settlement Body (DSB) has construed the TRIPS exceptions provision as extremely narrow,[12] it is inconceivable that the United States would abandon its open-ended "fair use" exception,[13] which it considers an important safeguard of free-speech values (Okediji 2000). Indeed, it has yet to comply with the DSB decision, which invalidated a significantly more limited provision of US law.[14]

The effect of strong substantive law can be discerned in the case studies. Thus, the right to health was certainly an important part of the Brazil's efforts to foster a domestic generic drug industry and to protect access to medicines. The right, which is enshrined in the Brazilian constitution, undergirded much of the discussion of implementing TRIPS requirements and has played a key role in court cases. In Colombia, similarly strong constitutional protection of the right to health has played an important role in backing the demands of pro-access organizations, as well as the increasingly activist role of the Constitutional Court in litigation stemming from the structural flaws of the healthcare system. And in some of the countries, other substantive guarantees also created traction. In Ecuador, access to medicine claims were folded, with access-enhancing results, into concerns about the rights of indigenous people; in Argentina, rights over pharmaceuticals were seen as a consumer protection issue. However, none of the countries succeeded in using constitutive values and other norms to protect access to medicines as effectively as free speech is protected in the United States. Even in Argentina, the outcome left much to be desired: Argentina protected access by underwriting the cost of medication, but if health activists had won more on the intellectual property issues, the same government funds could have been channeled to other national priorities, such as training doctors or building hospitals. And as previously noted, the commitment to health might, ironically, have opened the door to corruption.

It may be too early to pass judgment on these efforts; it is possible that pro-access strategies centered on human rights will eventually level the playing field. After all, barely two decades have passed since the new constitutions were enacted and new institutions were put in place. And the explosion of litigation and judicial decisions adopting an expansive understanding of the right to health offer strong legal tools that activists can utilize in future court cases and in other forums. Indeed, the normative debates on the scope of patents in Latin America has already begun and the Colombian cases suggest they may succeed, if not at the implementation level, than at the time of application. But it may well be that world-over, the norms surrounding patents are weak (much weaker than norms related to copyright). For example, it has been argued that there is a norm favoring the right to freely engage

[11] TRIPS, art. 13; Berne Convention, art. 9.2.

[12] United States—Section 110(5) of the US Copyright Act, WT/DS/160/R (June 15, 2000).

[13] 17 U.S.C. § 107. [14] 17 U.S.C. § 110(5)(B).

in research (Zimmerman 1993). Such a norm would support rights to experimentation defenses and, perhaps, a Bolar exception. However, a claim like this has never succeeded, even in the United States. Furthermore, as Smita Narula argues in her comment in this volume, because human rights is a two-edged sword, protecting both creators and consumers of knowledge products, a human-rights based approach to access issues is difficult to implement. The case studies demonstrate that it is only recently that courts have begun to interpret how the balance between these norms applies on the ground.

Moreover, because the "knowledge economy" is so new, there is no *ius cogens* of knowledge governance or a significant international articulation of access norms. The Berne and Paris Conventions were written against a backdrop of free copying; they were mainly aimed at creating norms of intellectual property ownership, not norms of free access. TRIPS simply adapted these earlier conventions. Thus, in the language of global administrative law theorists, existing substantive norms strengthen accountability, but only to the interests of certain actors in the North, not to the South or to others interested in access issues. To be sure, the Doha Declaration did acknowledge the other side of the intellectual property coin, and it played an important role in the debate in Colombia and in Brazil, but Doha is itself very new.

Thus, while the case studies are suggestive of the need to supplement global administrative values with substantive commitments, much more needs to be done to strengthen the norms that would be needed if contestation is to promote legitimacy. Scholars, activists, and policymakers are, however, beginning to turn their attention to the issue. One objective of WIPO's Development Agenda is a more detailed articulation of exceptions to intellectual property rights, including patent rights.[15] Maggie Chon (2006) has developed a distributive justice approach to copyright regulation. Similarly, Bernt Hugenholtz and Ruth Okediji (2008) have proposed a soft law instrument delineating exceptions and limitations on the rights of copyright owners. APEG-IPEG has, under the leadership of Luis Villarroel Villalon of Chile, conducted a survey of exceptions and limitations for Asia-Pacific countries (Asia-Pacific Economic Cooperation 2010). All of these copyright-based approaches may be generalizable to patents. Furthermore, Annette Kur and her coauthors have suggested a formal proposal for amending the TRIPS Agreement and transforming it into a more balanced instrument (Kur and Levin 2011). More recently, Graeme Dinwoodie and Rochelle Dreyfuss (2012) have called for the creation of an international acquis composed of access norms implicit in existing international instruments (and in some cases, expressly denoted). Among other things, the acquis would include the proposition that intellectual property laws cannot remove information from the public domain. If such a commitment were recognized, it would be clear that no country could grant *patentes de reválida* on material already in local use. Further, there would be substantial reason to question second-use patents and data protection for material that had been made public anywhere in the world. Should

[15] See, e.g., WIPO Standing Committee on Patents, Experts' Study on Exclusions from Patentable Subject Matter and Exceptions and Limitations to the Rights, SCP/15/3 (October 2010) (prepared by Lionel Bently, et al.).

new norms develop for patent law, the next cycle in the intellectual property debate might look very different. As Molly Land suggests in her comment in this volume, it will be interesting to see how a new substantive commitment to access to knowledge will interact with existing human rights norms.

V. Political Opportunities for Contestation

Even if all the factors discussed in this chapter are favorably disposed for a Southern country, the case studies suggest that in the final analysis, the success of contestation depends heavily on politics, political history, and political clout—that is, on the political environment and strategies that we seek to capture through the lens of political opportunity structure theory. In line with our multilevel approach to political opportunities, the case studies suggest that openings from contestation result from the interaction between national and international institutions, on the one hand, and the relations among transnational institutions, on the other.

Katherine Sikkink's "dynamic multilevel governance model" is helpful for distilling the interaction between national and international opportunities for contestation as they arise from the case studies. In her model, opportunities are assessed on the basis of "access to institutions, or how open or closed domestic and international institutions are to network or social movement pressure and participation" (Sikkink 2005: 155). The distinction between open and closed institutions at the domestic and international scales gives rise to four combinations constituting different patterns of political opportunity for contestation, as shown in Figure 14.1.

Clockwise, category I ("diminished chance of activism") corresponds to situations where both national and international institutions are relatively impervious to pressure from local and transnational advocacy networks. Category II represents the situation in which activists confronted with a national state indifferent or inimical

		International opportunity structure	
		Closed	Open
Domestic opportunity structure	Closed	I. Diminished chance of activism	II. "Boomerang effect"
	Open	IV. Democratic deficit/defensive internationalism	III. Insider/outsider coalition model

Figure 14.1 Sikkink's dynamic multilevel governance model

Source: Sikkink (2005: 156)

to their arguments call upon supranational actors (for instance, sympathetic international institutions or foreign governments) to put pressure on state institutions in their country of origin—thus seeking to produce a "boomerang effect" that opens up opportunities at the local level (Keck and Sikkink 1998). Category III corresponds to those situations in which both national and international opportunity structures are accessible and susceptible to movement pressure. Under these particularly favorable conditions, coalitions of insiders and outsiders are likely to arise and constitute feedback loops of domestic and international pressure. The final category (IV) corresponds to cases where national institutions are open while international ones are closed. This is notably the case of transnational institutional frameworks that suffer from a "democratic deficit" relative to national ones, of which the European Union is the clearest example.

A. International-National Opportunity Structures

All of the chapters document the crucial influence of Northern countries in shaping spaces for contention in Latin America. For instance, they document in detail attempts by the United States and the European Union to use trade pressure to force the countries in the study to accept levels of intellectual property protection that satisfy Northern interests. Given Latin American dependence on trade with these countries, such attempts heavily constrain the political room that governments and civil society organizations have to maneuver and decide how to strike the balance between intellectual property and access to medicines. Importantly, however, the studies also show that they can create additional opportunities for transnational solidarity, as Latin American pro-health advocates and state agencies forge alliances with counterparts in the global North.

As the case studies show, the national-international interplay created different structures of opportunities in the countries analyzed. In terms of the typology of Figure 14.1, the CAFTA countries offer the clearest illustration of the classical type of diminished chance of activism (category I in Figure 14.1). Indeed, the combination of small states with a history of dependence on the United States and little geopolitical clout, and civil societies with weak transnational connections in the field of intellectual property activism, resulted in a "steam-rolling" process of wholesale adoption of TRIPS-plus standards through CAFTA. With the notable exception of Costa Rica—where an anti-CAFTA mobilization (partly based on the defense of the public healthcare system) nearly won the vote on the treaty's ratification in Congress—the existence and effectiveness of contestation was minimal in comparative perspective.

Colombia provides the paradigmatic illustration of the "boomerang effect" situation in the typology (category II in Figure 14.1), where relatively closed national institutions were offset by opportunities at the international and transnational levels. Colombia was dependent on the United States not only for trade aid, but also for military aid associated with the so-called "war on drugs." It began negotiations during a period when pressure from and dependence on the United States was particularly intense, as the country became the second-largest recipient of US military aid in the world through an anti-drug and anti-insurgency multi-year plan (*Plan Colombia*).

To the extent it resisted, two international political factors loomed in importance. Foremost among them: the politics in the United States changed during the three years in which the Colombia–US FTA was negotiated. The Democratic majority that took control of the US Congress in late 2006 had more sympathy for access values than the Republican majority that dominated it when the negotiations began in 2004. Under pressure from Democratic members of Congress, the US government agreed to amend the intellectual property chapter of the FTA in 2007 to tone down the TRIPS-plus standards of the original agreement. Second, Colombia benefited from the political history of the healthcare debate. During the period of negotiations, CAFTA raised sensitivities to the access-to-medicines issue (a point also made in the Central American case study). The Doha Declaration, and with it, the commitment by all WTO members to consider the impact of patents on developing countries, made it more difficult for the *demandeurs* to argue for protection that might interfere with the delivery of adequate health products and services. Perhaps as important, during the negotiation period, both South Africa and Brazil resisted the most extravagant demands of the United States. The momentum provided by these events helped Colombian pro-access coalitions realize that resistance is possible.

Clearly, the "outsider/insider coalition" situation offers the best chance for effective contestation, as it combines openings at the national and the international and transnational level (category III in Figure 14.1). The Brazil and Argentina stories come closest to this type, as both have national institutions that are relatively permeable to pro-health demands (although Argentina to a greater extent than Brazil), while also using their stronger geopolitical muscle to create openings at the international and transnational levels. As the prior discussion indicates, both countries have had enough presence internationally to insert nodes for resistance into the key international instruments. For example, the compulsory licensing provision in TRIPS allows countries to declare national emergencies and issue compulsory licenses if demand for pharmaceuticals is not met at reasonable prices. Because Brazil and Argentina had generic drug industries, they could make such threats credible (in contrast, none of the countries in Central America could do the same). And although the United States initially challenged the Brazilian policy in the DSU, Brazil also had enough power, expertise, and resources to defend its position. In the end, the specter of compulsory licensing (and the loss of substantial potential revenue entailed) led the United States to back down on its more extreme demands. As important, both countries have markets large enough to be of interest to traders within the United States; it is thus no wonder then that neither has an FTA with the United States forcing the adoption of TRIPS-plus standards. The absence of an FTA has, in turn, prevented the further closure of political opportunities experienced by Central American countries, Chile, and Colombia.

Finally, Ecuador is alone in illustrating the situation envisaged in category IV in Figure 14.1. Given its unique trajectory in the 2000s—as a small country with a resolutely pro-access government willing to withstand international pressures—it offers a good example of the possibilities, and the risks, of a nationalist state and civil society strategy to contest the global strengthening of intellectual property protection through domestic public health policies.

B. Relations among Transnational Institutions

To fully understand the impact of political power, it is also necessary to look beyond the relationships among Westphalian states, for the success of contestation is significantly affected by the relative power of the international organizations operating in the intellectual property arena. As we noted earlier, international lawmaking has been characterized by successive rounds of regime shifting—WIPO to the WTO (and possibly back); WTO to bilaterals; bilaterals to regionals such as the Anti-Counterfeiting Trade Act (ACTA) and the Trans-Pacific Partnership Agreement (TPP).[16] Lawmaking has also been affected by the work of other institutions, such as the IMF, World Bank, WHO, and UNCTAD. These organizations take differing approaches to such issues as the balance between health and access. Some (IMF, WTO) are clearly more pro-intellectual property, while others (WHO) are more geared to protecting access interests. As significantly, the relative strength and influence of these organizations also vary. Organizations such as WHO have little more than moral authority; the IMF and World Bank enjoy greater influence because they are in a position to bestow important financial benefits. But as many observers have noted, an organization with a dispute resolution system and an internal compliance mechanism can exert near-dispositive authority (Guzman 2001; McGinnis and Movsesian 2004).

Of course, international organizations could make greater attempts to work together. For example, in her contribution to this volume, Ruth Okediji suggests several ways in which WIPO could provide greater focus to the efforts of all the organizations interested in the intersection of health and intellectual property. But absent voluntary cooperation, the regime-shifting phenomenon presents a real threat to the GAL approach to legitimation. While the case studies demonstrate that regulatory competition can have salutary effects in the form of input from institutions possessing a variety of expertise and experience, the strong sense of the studies is that from the perspective of the South, the overall impact of overlapping authority is negative. The North has made it very clear that if one organization refuses to meet its demands, it will use its superior power to shop for a place where it can get what it wants. These continual moves not only take advantage of the differing authority of these institutions, they also increase the burden on countries less able to undertake the expensive business of negotiating at the international level. Thus, they create a perception—if not the reality—of illegitimacy quite apart from the other concerns articulated by global administrative law theorists. As one of us has previously suggested, if the GAL initiative is to succeed, it is imperative to develop a set of norms to deal with the problem (Dreyfuss 2009). Within TRIPS, this might include a robust understanding of the clause that permits additional protection only so long as "such protection does not contravene the provisions of

[16] See Anti-Counterfeiting Trade Agreement (Draft of 3 December 2010), available at <http://www.dfat.gov.au/trade/acta/Final-ACTA-text-following-legal-verification.pdf>; TPP Parties Wrap Up Seventh Round of Talks: New Proposals Advanced in IP, Transparency, 82 Patent, Trademark & Copyright Journal 297 (July 1, 2011).

this Agreement."[17] Were the Agreement understood as providing countries of the global South a guarantee of market access whenever they meet the minimum obligations of TRIPS, much of the current regime shifting might abate.[18]

Outside TRIPS, there is a need for an international principle of res judicata or a doctrine of primary jurisdiction. Under these approaches, a minimum standards agreement (such as TRIPS), if duly negotiated in a setting that fully recognized procedural protection for all players, would be regarded as final. Any attempt to negotiate over the same issues in another forum would be considered illegitimate and the effects would not be cognizable under international law. A country that insisted on compliance with the second agreement would be considered in violation of the first. Instead, a country that wished to alter the international regime would be required to resort to the first (primary) forum. In that way, investments made by weaker countries in developing the expertise and alliances needed to negotiate effectively would not be lost in a regime shift. Nor would it be possible for countries to cherry pick "coalitions of the willing" to negotiate new instruments, and then follow up with bilaterals that bootstrap its requirements into global law (Cornish 1997).

Less drastically, the polarizing nature of regime shifting and the dominance of organizations with dispute resolution systems might be reduced through interpretive mechanisms. For example, Martti Koskenniemi, writing on behalf of the International Law Commission, has suggested several ways in which the Vienna Convention on the Law of Treaties could be used to minimize international fragmentation.[19] Under this approach, an organization—such as the WTO—with an international tribunal could avoid trumping the values recognized by other institutions by infusing values promulgated elsewhere—such as in the WHO—into its decision making. As Robert Howse (2007: 40) has suggested, "[w]eak norms and soft law . . . can appear less polyannish when one considers that, through interpretation, they can have important normative effects on international economic relations." And if nations understood that the political power of a particular institution will not necessarily affect outcomes, they might be less eager to shop for a forum that will do their bidding. By the same token, if organizations like the WTO refused to consider agreements that had been negotiated in secret and without adequate process, there would be more incentive for organizations to adopt and follow administrative norms (Dinwoodie and Dreyfuss 2012).

VI. Conclusion

The case studies on the debate over the effect of proprietary rights on access to medicines demonstrate that contestation opportunities are not alone enough to

[17] TRIPS, art. 2.1.

[18] Cf. United States Sections 301–10 of the Trade Act of 1974, WT/DS152/R (December 22, 1999).

[19] Vienna Convention on the Law of Treaties, UN Doc. A/Conf. 39/27, 8 I.L.M. 679 (1969) (January 27, 1980); Int'l L. Comm'n, Fragmentation of International Law: Difficulties Arising from the Diversification and Expansion of International Law: Report of the Study Group on the Fragmentation of International Law, Finalized by Martti Koskenniemi UN Doc. A/CN.4/L.682 (April 13, 2006).

legitimate a global regulatory regime in which players are at vastly different places in terms of resources, capacity, institutional infrastructure, legal traditions, and political clout. Exogenous variables can make a difference. Transnational activists can supply expertise and mobilize domestic actors. However, there are transnational players on both sides of the debate and pro-intellectual property transnational corporations may have more resources and staying power than pro-health activists. Regional compacts can increase political clout, but those in favor of strong intellectual property protection have developed strategies to break up effective alliances. In other areas, international norms can go a long way toward mitigating demands. Nonetheless, transnational intellectual property law largely concerns itself with proprietary interests; there is no *ius cogens* and little customary law promoting access. Human rights law is, however, emerging as a powerful countervailing influence. Thus, several of the studies detail the rising role of courts in the enforcement of international and national obligations on socio-economic rights in general, and the right to health in particular.

This study examined access to medicine, which is but one component of the larger question of protecting health and welfare. Other factors include access to treatment, the quality of health-related infrastructure (such as physicians, nurses, and hospitals), the availability of prophylactic measures (including vaccination programs), as well as clean water and food security. Furthermore, there are access-to-medicines issues that are not related to patents, such as price controls, quality assurance, and the rational selection of drugs included in formularies. Thus, our conclusions on access to medicines do not necessarily track health outcomes. Indeed, as the Appendix demonstrates, Ecuador, Brazil, and Colombia score rather low on the health-related components of the UN human development index, even though all three had some success in resisting TRIPS-plus norms. While pharmaceutical companies sometimes cite these statistics to suggest that their demands are not the cause of health problems, it is undeniable that the two countries that came out best in the patent debate—Argentina and Chile—also have the best statistics in the region. And the Central American countries, which were required to enact the rather onerous requirements of CAFTA, did the worst.

To be sure, drawing correlations between the effect of patents on health is fraught with difficulty: there are path dependence issues (as demonstrated by the Chilean generic drug industry's superior ability to negotiate for law that could be adapted to its needs) and the direction of causality is impossible to discern (thus Argentina's ability to protect the health of its citizens may have contributed to its capacity to withstand demands for stronger intellectual property protection). Moreover, none of the studies considered the possibility that patents were encouraging research into health issues of relevance to the South. More work is therefore needed on the role that intellectual property plays in safeguarding health.

As Latin America becomes more familiar with intellectual property protection and more adept at utilizing the openings for contestation and the tools available in global administrative space, it will be interesting to see how the balance between wealth and health in the Southern Hemisphere is struck in future rounds of debate. Some of the countries we studied (particularly Argentina and Brazil) have become leaders in international negotiations; as their role becomes more pronounced, and if their reliance on the tools of global administrative law grows, their actions may improve both the accommodation between proprietary and access interests and the legitimacy of transnational administration.

References

Asia-Pacific Economic Cooperation. 2010. *APEC-IPEG Survey on Copyright Limitations & Exceptions Report on Copyright L&E in APEC Economies.* Retrieved October 31, 2013 at <http://publications.apec.org/publication-detail.php?pub_id=971>.

Braga, Carlos, and Carsten Fink. 1998. "The Relationship between Intellectual Property Rights and Foreign Direct Investment." *Duke J. Comp. & Int'l L.* 9: 163–87.

Chon, Margaret. 2006. "Intellectual Property and the Development Divide." *Cardozo L. Rev.* 27: 2821–912.

Cornish, William. 1997. "Genevan Bootstraps." *Eur. Intell. Prop. Rev.* 19: 336–8.

Correa, Carlos. 2001. "Review of the TRIPS Agreement: Fostering the Transfer of Technology to Developing Countries." *TWN Trade & Development Series 13.* Retrieved October 31, 2013 at <http://www.twnside.org.sg/title2/t&d/tnd13.pdf>.

Dinwoodie, Graeme, and Rochelle Dreyfuss. 2012. *A Neofederalist Vision of TRIPS: Building a Resilient International Intellectual Property System.* New York: Oxford University Press.

Drahos, Peter. 1995. "Global Rights in Information: The Story of TRIPS at the GATT." *Prometheus* 13: 6–19.

——. 2008. "Trust Me: Patent Offices in Developing Countries." *Am. J. L. & Med.* 34: 151–74.

——. 2010. *The Global Governance of Knowledge: Patent Offices and their Clients.* New York: Cambridge University Press.

Dreyfuss, Rochelle. 2009. "Fostering Dynamic Innovation, Development and Trade: Intellectual Property as a Case Study in Global Administrative Law." *Acta Juridica* 2009: 237–82.

Guzman, Andrew. 2001. "Global Governance and the WTO." *Harv. Int'l LJ* 45: 303–51.

Helfer, Laurence, Karen Alter, and Florencia Guerzovich. 2009. "Islands of Effective International Adjudication: Constructing an Intellectual Property Rule of Law in the Andean Community." *Am. J. Int'l L.* 103: 1–47.

Howse, Robert. 2007. "The Use and Abuse of Other 'Relevant Rules of International Law' in Treaty Interpretation: Insights from Trade/Environment Litigation." Working Paper No. 1, Institute for International Law and Justice, New York. Retrieved October 31, 2013 at <http://iilj.org/publications/documents/2007-1.Howse.web.pdf>.

Hugenholtz, Bernt, and Ruth Okediji. 2008. "Conceiving an International Instrument on Limitations and Exceptions to Copyright." Commissioned Monograph, Open Society Institute, Baltimore. Retrieved October 31, 2013 at <www.ivir.nl/publicaties/hugenholtz/finalreport2008.pdf>.

Kapczynski, Amy. 2009. "Harmonization and its Discontents: A Case Study of TRIPS Implementation in India's Pharmaceutical Sector." *Calif. L. Rev.* 97: 1571–649.

Keck, Margaret, and Kathryn Sikkink. 1998. *Activists beyond Borders: Advocacy Networks in International Politics.* Ithaca, NY: Cornell University Press.

Kuanpoth, Jakkrit. 2010. *Patent Rights in Pharmaceuticals in Developing Countries: Major Challenges for the Future*. Cheltenham: Edward Elgar Publishing.

Kur, Annette, and Marianne Levin (eds.). 2011. *Intellectual Property in a Fair World Trade System: Proposals for Reforming the TRIPS Agreement*. Cheltenham: Edward Elgar Publishing.

McGinnis, John, and Mark Movsesian. 2004. "Against Global Governance in the WTO." *Harv. Int'l LJ* 45: 353–65.

Matthews, Duncan. 2007. "The Role of International NGOs in the Intellectual Property Policy-Making and Norm-Setting Activities of Multilateral Institutions." *Chi.-Kent L. Rev.* 82: 1369–87.

Merry, Sally. 2006. *Human Rights and Gender Violence: Translating International Law into Local Justice*. Chicago: University of Chicago Press.

Moral, María 2004. "EEUU, Colombia, Perú y Ecuador presentaron sus propuestas para el TLC." *America Economica.com*. Retrieved October 31, 2103 at <http://www.americaeconomica.com/numeros4/276/reportajes/maria276.htm>.

Ncube, Caroline B., and Eliamani Laltaika. 2013. "A New Intellectual Property Organization for Africa?" *J. Intell. Prop. L. & Prac.* 8: 114–17.

Okediji, Ruth. 2000. "Toward an International Fair Use Doctrine." *Colum. J. Transnat'l L.* 39: 75–175.

Pager, Sean. 2007. "Patents on a Shoestring: Making Patent Protection Work for Developing Countries." *Ga. St. UL Rev.* 23: 755–808.

Reichman, Jerome, and Rochelle Dreyfuss. 2007. "Harmonization without Consensus: Critical Reflections on Drafting a Substantive Patent Law Treaty." *Duke LJ* 57: 85–130.

Sampat, Bhaven, and Tahir Amin. 2013. "How Do Public Health Safeguards in Indian Patent Law Affect Pharmaceutical Patenting in Practice?" *J. Health Pol. Pol'y. & L.* 38: 735–55.

Sell, Susan K. 2003. *Private Power, Public Law: The Globalization of Intellectual Property Rights*. Cambridge: Cambridge University Press.

Sikkink, Kathryn. 2005. "Patterns of Dynamic Multilevel Governance and the Insider–Outsider Coalition." Pp. 151–74 in *Transnational Protest & Global Activism*, edited by D. Della Porta and S. Tarrow. New York: Rowman & Littlefield.

Stewart, Richard. Forthcoming. "Solving the Problems of Disregard in Global Administrative Governance: Accountability, Participation and Responsiveness."

Wong, Tzen, and Graham Dutfield (eds.). 2011. *Intellectual Property and Human Development: Current Trends and Future Scenarios*. Cambridge: Cambridge University Press.

Zimmerman, Diane. 1993. "Scientific Speech in the 1990s." *NYU Envtl. LJ* 2: 254–78.

APPENDIX

Health Indicators in Selected Latin American Countries

HDI rank		RESOURCES			RISK FACTORS					MORTALITY				
					Infants lacking immunization against		HIV prevalence							
		Expenditure on Health	Physician	Hospital Beds	DPT	Measles	Youth (% ages 15–24)		Adult (% ages 15–49)	Infant	Under-five	Adult (per 1,000 people)		Age-standardized death rates from non-communicable diseases
		Per capita (PPP $) 2007	(per 10,000 people) 2000–2009[a]		(% of one-year olds) 2008		Female 2007	Male	Total	(per 1,000 live births) 2008	2008	Female 2008	Male 2008	(per 100,000 people) 2004
45	Chile	863	11	23	4	8	0.2	0.3	0.3	7	9	60	116	458
46	Argentina	1,322	32[b]	41	4	1	0.3	0.6	0.5	15	16	86	160	515
62	Costa Rica	899	13	13	10	9	0.2	0.4	0.4	10	11	68	124	439
73	Brazil	837	17	24	3	1	0.6	1.0	0.6	18	22	106	210	625
77	Ecuador	434	15	6[a]	25	34	0.2	0.4	0.3	21	25	121	207	484
79	Colombia	516	14	10	8	8	0.3	0.7	0.6	16	20	75	162	483
88	Dom. Republic	411	19	10	23	21	0.6	0.3	1.1	27	33	127	188	794
90	El Salvador	402	12	8[c]	6	5	0.5	0.9	0.8	16	18	136	301	518
106	Honduras	235	6	7[c]	7	5	0.4	0.7	0.7	26	31	129	227	761
115	Nicaragua	232	4	9[c]	4	1	0.1	0.3	0.2	23	27	123	209	705
116	Guatemala	334	—	6[c]	15	4	1.5	—	0.8	29	35	159	302	515

[a] Data refer to the most recent year available during period specified.
[b] Refers to an earlier year than that specified.
[c] Public sector only.

Source: UN Human Development Report 2010. *The Real Wealth of Nations*. New York: UNDP

Index

The manufacturer's authorised representative in the EU for product safety is Oxford University Press España S.A. of El Parque Empresarial San Fernando de Henares, Avenida de Castilla, 2 - 28830 Madrid (www.oup.es/en or product.safety@oup.com). OUP España S.A. also acts as importer into Spain of products made by the manufacturer.
Printed and bound by CPI Group (UK) Ltd, Croydon, CR0 4YY
14/09/2026
02216304-0011